THE

Narrative

READER

EDITED BY

MARTIN McQUILLAN

LONDON AND NEW YORK

First published 2000
by Routledge
11 New Fetter Lane, London EC4P 4EE

Simultaneously published in the USA and Canada
by Routledge
29 West 35th Street, New York, NY 10001

Routledge is an imprint of the Taylor & Francis Group

© 2000 Martin McQuillan

Typeset in Sabon and Frutiger by Keystroke, Jacaranda Lodge, Wolverhampton
Printed and bound in Great Britain by TJ International Ltd, Padstow, Cornwall

*British Library Cataloguing in Publication
Data*
A catalogue record for this book is available
from the British Library

*Library of Congress Cataloging in
Publication Data*
McQuillan, Martin.
The narrative reader / Martin McQuillan.
p. cm.
Includes bibliographical references and index.
1. Narration (Rhetoric) I. Title.
PN212 .M39 2000
808–dc21   00–032308

ISBN 0–415–20533–6 (pbk)
ISBN 0–415–20532–8 (hbk)

THE

Narrative

EADER

...e Narrative Reader provides a comprehensive survey of theories of narrative from
Mar.ito to post-structuralism. The selection of texts is bold and broad, demonstrating the
Tel: tent to which narrative permeates the entire field of literature and culture. It shows
....e ways in which narrative crosses disciplines, continents and theoretical perspectives,
...d is a long overdue and welcome addition to the field. *The Narrative Reader* will
...cinate students and researchers alike, providing a much needed point of entry to the
....reasingly complex field of narrative theory.

Canonical texts are combined with texts which are difficult to get hold of elsewhere,
...nd new translations and introductory material. The texts cover many crucial issues
and topics including:

- formalism
- structuralism
- responses to narratology
- narrative and sexual difference
- psychoanalysis
- race
- phenomenology
- history
- deconstruction

Part III is designed to guide the student reader through the texts, including a helpful
chronology of narrative theory, a glossary of narrative terms and a checklist of narrative
theories.

S...ected authors include: Plato, Aristotle, E. M. Forster, Walter Benjamin, Mikhail
Ba...itin, John Berger, Claude Lévi-Strauss, Jonathan Culler, Roland Barthes, Umberto
...co, ...an-François Lyotard, Laura Mulvey, Barbara Hernstein Smith, Jacques Derrida,
...aul Ricoeur, Fredric Jameson, Edward Said, Shoshana Felman, Henry Louis Gates, Jr,
...omi K. Bhabha.

...artin McQuillan is lecturer in cultural theory and analysis at the University of Leeds.
His other books include *Deconstructing Disney* (1999) with Eleanor Byrne, and the
co-edited collection *Post-Theory: New Directions in Criticism* (1999).

Contents

Acknowledgements   ix
How to use this book   xi

Introduction: Aporias of Writing: Narrative and Subjectivity   1

PART I: openings   **35**

    1 Form and Discourse   **37**

i. Classical Analysis   **37**
Plato, *The Republic*, Chapter XXV, 'The Allegory of the Cave'   37
Aristotle, from *The Poetics*, 'Plot'   39

ii. Twentieth-century Analysis   **44**
E.M. Forster, 'The Story' and 'The Plot'   44
Walter Benjamin, 'The Storyteller: Reflections on the Works of Nicolai Leskov'   46
Mikhail Bakhtin, from *The Dialogic Imagination*   53
Vladimir Propp, 'Oedipus in the Light of Folklore'   58
Victor Shlovsky, 'Sterne's *Tristram Shandy*: Stylistic Commentary'   63
Boris Tomashevsky, 'Thematics'   67
Wayne Booth, from *The Rhetoric of Fiction*   69

    2 Structuralism   **75**

i. Definitions   **75**
Claude Lévi-Strauss, 'The Structural Study of Myth'   75
Mieke Bal, from *Narratology*   81
Christain Metz, 'Notes Toward a Phenomenology of the Narrative'   86

ii. Theories   **91**
Gérard Genette, 'Order in Narrative'   91
Seymour Chatman, 'Point of View'   96
Gerald Prince, 'Introduction to the Study of the Narratee'   99
Jonathan Culler, 'Story and Discourse in the Analysis of Narrative'   104

iii. Readings   **109**
Roland Barthes, 'Introduction to the Structural Analysis of Narratives'   109
Umberto Eco, 'Narrative Structure in Ian Fleming'   115
Tsvetan Todorov, 'The Typology of Detective Fiction'   120

3 Post-narratology   128

i. Reflections   128
Gérard Genette, from *Narrative Discourse Revisited*   128
Gerald Prince, 'On Narratology (Past, Present, Future)'   129
Roland Barthes, 'Textual Analysis: Poe's "Valdemar"'   130

ii. Responses   138
Barbara Hernstein Smith, 'Narrative Versions, Narrative Theories'   138
Peter Brooks, from *Reading for the Plot*   145
Andrew Gibson, from *Towards a Postmodern Theory of Narrative*   152

iii. Beyond   157
Jean-François Lyotard, from *The Postmodern Condition*   157
Donald N. McCloskey, 'Storytelling in Economics'   161
Bernard S. Jackson, 'Narrative Theories and Legal Discourse'   163
Rom Harré, 'Some Narrative Conventions of Scientific Discourse'   165
Susan McClary, 'The Impromptu That Trod on a Loaf: or How Music
     Tells Stories'   166
John Berger, 'Stories'   170

PART II: diaspora   175

4 Psychoanalysis   177
Laura Mulvey, 'Visual Pleasure and Narrative Cinema'   177
Laura Mulvey, 'Afterthoughts on "Visual Pleasure and Narrative
     Cinema" Inspired by *Duel in the Sun*'   182
Stephen Heath, 'Narrative Space'   184
Elizabeth Bronfen, 'Spectral Stories'   192

5 Sexual Difference   198
Susan S. Lanser, 'Toward a Feminist Narratology'   198
Nilli Diengott, 'Narratology and Feminism'   201
Teresa de Lauretis, 'Desire in Narrative'   204
Judith Roof, from *Come As You Are: Sexuality and Narrative*   212

6 Deconstruction   220
Jacques Derrida, 'The Law of Genre'   220
Paul de Man, 'Reading (Proust)'   227
J. Hillis Miller, 'Line'   231
Barbara Johnson, 'The Critical Difference: BartheS/BalZac'   238

7 Phenomenology   244
Wolfgang Iser, 'A Conversation with Wayne Booth'   244
Dorrit Cohn, from *Transparent Minds: Narrative Modes for Presenting
     Consciousness in Fiction*   250
Paul Ricoeur, 'Narrative Time'   255

8 History   262

Shoshana Felman, from *Testimony: Crises of Witnessing in Literature,*
  Psychoanalyis and History   262
Fredric Jameson, from *The Political Unconscious: Narrative as a*
  Socially Symbolic Act   266
Samuel Weber, 'Capitalizing History: Thoughts on *The Political*
  Unconscious'   269
Hans Kellner, 'Narrativity in History: Post-structuralism and Since'   275

9 Race   284

Edward Said, from *Culture and Imperialism*   284
Henry Louis Gates, Jr., 'Thirteen Ways of Looking at a Black Man'   288
Homi K. Bhabha, 'DissemiNation: Time, Narrative and the Margins of
  the Modern Nation'   292
Trin Minh-Ha, 'Grandma's Story'   297

PART III: taxonomies   309

A chronology of narrative theory in the twentieth century   311
A glossary of narrative terms   314
A checklist of narrative theories   330

Index   347

Acknowledgements

This volume has a convoluted narrative of its own and I would like to thank all those who at some stage, knowingly or not, have been instrumental in its construction. So, in (I believe) chronological order I would like to thank Sandra Kemp, Drummond Bone, Patrick Reilly, Vassiliki Kolokotroni, Eleanor Byrne, Gun Orgun, Robin Purves, Graeme Macdonald, Stephen Thomson, Claire Brennan, Ellen Jackson, Damien Walsh, Mary Reilly, John Boyle, Shona Allan, Janet Stewart, Jane Cavani, Willy Maley, Bob Maslen, Julian Wolfreys, John Coyle, Robert Eaglestone, Andrew Gibson, Jim Phelan, Sophie Gibson, Rosie Waters, Liz Brown, Talia Rogers, Stephen Heath, John Berger, and my colleagues and friends at Staffordshire University (past and present).

For permission to reproduce material, I would like to thank the following copyright holders: Plato, from *The Republic*, trans. F. Cornford, reprinted by permission of Oxford University Press. Aristotle, from *The Poetics*, trans. T. S. Dorsch, reprinted by permission of Penguin Books. E. M. Forster, *Aspects of the Novel*, reprinted by permission of the Provost and Scholars of Kings' College, Cambridge. Walter Benjamin, 'The Storyteller', trans. H. Zohn, reprinted by permission of Harcourt, Brace & World Inc. Mikhail Bakhtin, from *The Dialogic Imagination*, reprinted by permission of the University of Texas Press. Victor Shlovsky, 'Sterne's *Tristram Shandy*: Stylistic Commentary' and Boris Tomashevsky, 'Thematics', reprinted by permission of the University of Nebraska Press. Wayne Booth, from *The Rhetoric of Fiction*, reprinted by permission of Penguin Books. Claude Lévi-Strauss, 'The Structural Study of Myth', reprinted by permission of Penguin Books. Mieke Bal, from *Narratology*, reprinted by permission of the author and the University of Toronto Press. Christain Metz, 'Notes Toward a Phenomenology of the Narrative', reprinted by permission of Oxford University Press, New York. Gerard Genette, from *Narrative Discourse*, reprinted by permission of Basil Blackwell Ltd. Seymour Chatman, from *Coming to Terms*, reprinted by permission of Cornell University Press. Gerald Prince, 'Introduction to the Study of the Narratee', reprinted by permission of the author. Jonathan Culler, 'Story and Discourse in the Analysis of Narrative', reprinted by permission of Routledge. Roland Barthes, 'Introduction to the Structural Analysis of Narrative', reprinted by permission of Stephen Heath. Umberto Eco, 'Narrative Structure in Ian Fleming', reprinted by permission of Indiana University Press. Tsvetan Todorov, 'A Topology of Detective Fiction', reprinted by permission of Cornell University Press. Roland Barthes, 'Analysis of Poe's Valdemer', reprinted by permission of Routledge. Barbara Hernstein Smith, 'Narrative Versions, Narrative Theories', reprinted by permission of the author and the University of Chicago Press. Peter Brooks, from *Reading for the Plot*, reprinted by permission of Harvard University Press. Andrew Gibson, from *Towards a Postmodern Theory of Narrative*, reprinted by permission of Edinburgh University Press. Jean-François Lyotard, from *The Postmodern Condition*, reprinted by permission of Manchester University Press. Extracts from Christopher Nash (ed.) *Narrative in Culture*, reprinted by permission of Routledge. Susan McLary, 'How

Music Tells Stories', reprinted by permission of Ohio State University Press. John Berger, from *Another Way of Telling*, reprinted by permission of the author. Laura Mulvey, 'Narrative Cinema and Visual Pleasure' and 'Afterthoughts on "Narrative Cinema and Visual Pleasure" Inspired by *Duel in the Sun*' reprinted by permission of *Screen* and the author. Stephen Heath, 'Narrative Space', reprinted by permission of *Screen* and the author. Elizabeth Bronfen, from *Over Her Dead Body: Death, Feminity, and the Aesthetic*, reprinted by permission of Manchester University Press. Susan Lanser, 'Towards a Feminist Narratology', and Nilli Diengott, 'Narratology and Feminism', reprinted by permission of *Style*. Teresa de Lauretis, from *Alice Doesn't: Feminism, Cinema, Semiotics*, reprinted by permission of the author and Indiana University Press. Judith Roof, from *Come As You Are: Sexuality and Narrative*, reprinted by permission of Columbia University Press. Jacques Derrida, 'The Law of Genre', reprinted by permission of the author and *Glyph*. Paul de Man, from *Allegories of Reading*, and J Hillis Miller, from *Ariadne's Thread*, reprinted by permission of Yale University Press. Barbara Johnson, 'The Critical Difference: BartheS/BalZac', reprinted by permission of Johns Hopkins University Press. Wolfgang Iser, 'A Conversation with Wayne Booth', reprinted by permission of Johns Hopkins University Press. Dorrit Cohn, from *Transparent Minds: Narrative Modes for Presenting Consciousness in Fiction*, reprinted by permission of Princeton University Press. Paul Ricoeur, 'Narrative Time', reprinted by permission of the author and Chicago University Press. Shoshana Felman, from *Testimony: Crises of Witnessing in Literature, Psychoanalyis and History*, reprinted by permission of Routledge. Fredric Jameson, from *The Political Unconscious: Narrative as a Socially Symbolic Act*, reprinted by permission of Routledge. Samuel Weber, 'Capitalizing History: Thoughts on *The Political Unconscious*', reprinted by permission of *Diacritics*. Hans Kellner, 'Narrativity in History: Post-structuralism and Since', reprinted by permission of *History and Theory*. Edward Said, from *Culture and Imperialism*, reprinted by permission of Chatto and Windus. Henry Louis Gates Jr., 'Thirteen Ways of Looking at a Black Man', reprinted by permission of the author and Random House. Copyright 1997 by Henry Louis Gates. Originally published in *The New Yorker*. Homi K Bhabha, 'Dissemination', reprinted by permission of Routledge. Trin Minh-Ha, from *Woman, Native, Other*, reprinted by permission of Indiana University Press.

The editor and publishers would like to thank the above who have kindly given permission for the use of copyright material. Every effort has been made to contact copyright holders; at this stage it has not proved possible to contact the estate of Vladimir Propp. Any queries should be addressed to Routledge, London.

How to use this book

The Narrative Reader follows the classical structure of narrative. It has a beginning (or at least several attempts at a beginning), a middle, and an end. Histories of narrative theory tend to follow a familiar pattern, and there are enough of them around for me not to repeat their work here. The story goes: In the beginning there was Aristotle who theorised 'plot', then there came the novelists who theorised their own plots, then after some false starts (Propp, Benjamin, Bakhtin) narrative theory really took off with narratology (the structuralist-led 'science of narrative'). However, like the dinosaurs, narratologists died out and were replaced by more mobile, covert forms of narrative theory within a 'post-structuralist' diaspora. Narrative theory now lives on, embedded in the work and tropes of post-structuralism. The selection of material for this volume would not like to disappoint this somewhat over-familiar history. In certain respects the order in which the essays appear (and what those essays have to say) in this collection tells a story of its own regarding the history of narrative theory. However, I might quibble regarding the idea of narrative which this genetic history proposes. *The Narrative Reader* begins with Aristotle but also with Plato, offering the allegory of the cave as a text of narrative theory. Plato's allegory, in so far as it is an allegory, is also a narrative because it constantly refers to something other than itself, but it is also a text about representation and the 'misrecognition' of the real in the virtual. As such it is a text about narrative. Therefore (despite the historical leap between classical Greece and twentieth-century Europe made in the selection of contents here) one might argue that the problem of narrative is a problem of conceptualisation, which runs through the entire western tradition. At stake in such a question would be issues such as origins, knowledge, desire, representation, voice, writing, death, myth, perception, progress, history, power, identity, difference, and so on. In short, the entirety of the philosophical and non-philosophical fields. For example, one might read Paul Ricoeur's three levels of mimesis in *Time and Narrative* as an inscription of the dialectic and as part of the work of mourning for western metaphysics, and so trace this figure of narrative through the phenomenological tradition and beyond. Thus narrative (if it is a concept) has a history, of which structuralism and post-structuralism (whose very name signals the impossibility of a clean break with structuralism) are only the most recent and briefest of incursions. *The Narrative Reader*, with the exception of a number of contextualising texts, provides a selection of material only from this latest stage in the genealogy of narrative *qua* concept. Such is the limitation and benefit of a 'Reader', which must be both accessible to students new to narrative theory and a source of reference to more advanced readers.

Part I of the Reader, 'Openings', presents a selection covering key texts in the history of narrative theory, structuralist narratology and what I have called here 'post-narratology'. The linearity of this history is not assured since the texts by, say, Benjamin and Bakhtin seem to have more in common with post-structuralist narrative theory than with narratology. While texts by Propp and Shlovsky seem to presage the insights of structuralism in ways which are not always necessarily transparent or straightforward,

E. M. Forster's text on plot seems to defy the neat categorisations of this section entirely. Part I of the Reader revolves around the selection of texts in Section 2, 'Structuralism', giving definitions of 'narratology', examples of narrative theorisation and narratological readings. In so far as Aristotle's *Poetics* is a formalist reading of certain tragic plays, there is nothing aberrant about narratology as a formal approach to literary narrative. In so far as post-structuralism continues to operate with structuralist models of narrative then narratology cannot be said to have come to an end. Narratology is of particular interest, not because of its claims to scientific rigour (other approaches to reading have claimed more pernicious things than this), but because the heterogeneous texts gathered under this name represent a sustained concentration of thinking about the problems of narrative, the effects of which we are only now beginning to recognise and analyse (for example, see Judith Roof's brilliant 'rereadings' of Barthes and Todorov in *Come As You Are: Sexuality and Narrative*). In this context, 'post-narratology' perhaps means a breathing space, a period of reflection, within the ongoing task of narrative theory.

Part II, 'Diaspora', examines the role played by the narrative question in post-structuralism. Much of what we think of today as 'contemporary literary/critical theory' (post-structuralism) is really only a continuation of the structuralist project, which accedes to the Anglo-American academy via narratology. Such a speculation would require several volumes of detailed argument to substantiate. However, in brief, each of the sections here (on psychoanalysis, sexual difference, deconstruction, phenomenology, history, race) demonstrates a double logic in which, say, psychoanalytic theory illuminates a new direction in the study of narrative, while the question of narrative installs itself as a problem which goes to the roots of psychoanalysis. It is not just a case of so-called 'theory' reading narrative (narrative remaining a fixed object of study with different theoretical tools being taken from the medicine chest to illustrate its various aspects). Rather, narrative proves to be an indispensable concept which each theoretical gesture finds it impossible to ignore because each theoretical turn discovers that its own work is predicated on an idea of narrative which must be thought through. For example, how can history be separated from narrative? How can sexual/racial/psychoanalytic identity or subjectivity be distinct from an idea of construction through narrative? What would a metaphysics of closure, or the metaphysic of time, be without narrative? This section represents work in progress and its partial selection can only give some insights into the continued importance and centrality of narrative as the experience of a question of difficulty within each of these ways of thinking.

Part III, 'Taxonomies', provides maps for student and scholar alike. The 'Glossary of narrative terms' provides a dictionary of terminology used by essays in this collection. It is not exhaustive but should be used for purposes of orientation within some of the more opaque passages of Parts I and II. The 'Checklist of Narrative Theories' is again partial but will provide the reader with suggestions for further reading and also contextualise the work extracted for this volume. The extracts, for reasons of space and accessibility, have been edited and cannot act as a substitute for reading the primary texts from which they are derived. The purpose of a Reader is to encourage reading and so enable the student to turn to the texts in the checklist, having consulted the Reader as the first port of call. To this end, overt editorial commentary on each extract has been avoided (the temptation to substitute one for the other is always overwhelming), so allowing for longer extracts to speak for themselves and their juxtaposition to tell their own story.

As an introduction, 'Aporias of Writing: Narrative and Subjectivity' is ambitious. It is an opening onto the selection of the volume and the problems of narrative, as well as an opening within the field of narrative theory. It begins with the speculation 'What if there were no more stories?' and goes on to draw upon each of the sections of this Reader to think through this question as a fundamental problem for our current understanding of narrative. An argument follows (not necessarily an original one) that the model of narrative presently in use is not the innate or natural form of 'narrative' but a stage in the conceptualisation of narrative. As such it remains absolutely necessary to thinking about narrative and structurally insufficient to that task. This introduction takes on Barbara Hernstein Smith's exordium to think through the problems of narrative with all that we currently know about language and culture. Here it leans upon the work represented by Part II, while facing the task of analysis posed by Part I. Perhaps, in small measure, it will add to the continuing work of narrative theory, or encourage others to do so in response. Finally, it might suggest that the question of narrative is the impossible space in which philosophy and literature meet one another.

Introduction
Aporias of Writing: Narrative and Subjectivity

[Narrative] is simply there, like life itself.
                                    Barthes

Un recit? Non, pas de recit, plus jamais.
[A story? No. No stories, never again.]
                                    Maurice Blanchot

THE LIMITS OF NARRATIVE THEORY

What if there were no more stories? What if stories, contrary to narrative theory's fundamental article of faith (that narrative, like love, is all around us), were coming, or had already come, to an end? How would we know? What would we do? How would we identify or constitute the 'we' of these questions? If stories (or Story, the idea of Story) had already come to an end it would not be that simple a task to declare it so. The world (our? world) is replete with stories (the second fundamental tenant of narrative theory). Given the multitude of stories which surround us every day in all their generic and trans-media guises, how would we know that the production, or invention, of new stories had stopped? We (or one person or group of persons on our behalf) would have to sample all stories, while simultaneously knowing what it means to talk of 'Story', in order to say for definite that stories had indeed come to an end. And there would have to be an unshakeable certainty, which could account for the absolute unknowability of the future, for us to declare that there would be no more stories, ever. One can imagine teams of top readers in elite research institutions working round the clock, poring through innumerable volumes, films, television programmes and oral accounts. Dividing this Herculean task between them; meeting at conferences to compare results and discuss a newly identified strain of story discovered by social anthropologists in urban Los Angeles or by literary critics on a fact-finding mission to the Outer Hebrides. Having declared that this was indeed a new story and not just a variant of an already known one, the task would begin again: a new story would be needed to disprove the hypothesis that story was at an end. After years of exhaustive research, and a decent period having elapsed since a team of German economists brought back rare examples of story-telling structures from a meeting of industrialists in Berlin, the International Centre for Narrative Research would present to the heads of the world's leading nations the conclusion that stories had indeed come to an end. The news would be rushed around the globe by telephone, the internet and satellite. Newspaper vendors would stand in the centres of cities shouting 'Read all about it: No more stories!' Ashen-faced newscasters would look severely into the camera and pronounce the words on the autocue with deliberation: 'Tonight's news: stories, and the idea of Story as we understand it, are officially over.'

This scenario, we might even say story, would certainly present a challenge to Roland Barthes' famous assertion in 1966, which by now is taken for granted by most students of narrative, that:

> The narratives of the world are numberless. Narrative is first and foremost a prodigious variety of genres, themselves distributed amongst different substances – as though any material were fit to receive man's stories. Able to be carried by articulated language, spoken or written, fixed or moving images, gestures, and the ordered mixture of all these substances; narrative is present in myth, legend, fable, tale, novella, epic, history, tragedy, drama, comedy, mime, painting (think of Carpaccio's *Saint Ursula*), stained-glass windows, cinema, comics, news items, conversation. Moreover, under this almost infinite diversity of forms, narrative is present in every age, in every place, in every society; it begins with the very history of mankind and there nowhere is nor has been a group of people without narrative. All classes, all human groups, have their narratives, enjoyment of which is very often shared by men with different even opposing, cultural backgrounds. Caring nothing for the division between good and bad literature, narrative is international, transhistorical, transcultural: it is simply there, like life itself.[1]

For a reader as sensitive to the singular vagaries of specific texts as Barthes, this is a bold claim to make. Even if the idea of a 'science of narrative' [*narratologie*] has faded from the cultural landscape along with other ephemera of the 1960s, like English footballing excellence and French involvement in colonial North Africa, the supposed universality of narrative remains a conspicuously strong idea within the collection of discourses known as critical and cultural theory. So much so that Jean-François Lyotard follows Barthes in his report on the state of knowledge in contemporary society, *The Postmodern Condition*, to declare that because narratives are the communal method by which knowledge is stored and exchanged 'they thus define what has the right to be said and done in the culture in question, and since they are part of that culture, they are legitimated by the simple fact that they do what they do'.[2] Here, Lyotard is working with the etymological root of narrative: 'gnarus', the Greek verb meaning 'to know'. Thus a narrative is, etymologically speaking, a form of knowledge, and a 'narrator' is 'one who knows', and so on.

Lyotard's logic that narratives 'are legitimated by the simple fact that they do what they do' bears a familiar proximity to Barthes' view that narrative exists in all cultures, all histories and all languages as a primal method of communication and the expression of experience, the universality of 'man's stories' in Barthes being analogous to the immanence of Lyotard's epistemological story-telling. Even sophisticated analysts of the most contemporary literary theories, like Andrew Bennett and Nicholas Royle, seem to be in agreement with Barthes. They offer five propositions around which they orientate their discussion of narrative:

1   Stories are everywhere.

2   Not only do we tell stories, but stories tell us: if stories are everywhere, we are also in stories.

3   The telling of a story is always bound up with power, property and domination.

4   Stories are multiple: there is always more than one story.

5   Stories always have something to tell us about stories themselves: they always involve self-reflexive and metafictional dimensions.[3]

The first two propositions here, upon which the next three depend, boldly align themselves to Barthes' initial hypothesis that, bluntly put, 'stories are everywhere'. Even those scholars of narrative who, in the light of Bennett and Royle's third proposition, identify the ways in which narratives are used to disadvantage specific 'human groups' seem to agree on the universality of narrative (for example, see the feminist critic and film-maker Teresa de Lauretis, or the queer theorist Judith Roof, this volume). De Lauretis suggests that because narrative is universal there is no escaping it, and therefore groups oppressed by certain uses of narrative should work within narrative to turn its figures and operations against narrative determinations. 'The most exciting work in cinema and in feminism today,' she notes, 'is not anti-narrative . . . quite the opposite. It is narrative . . . with a vengeance, for it seeks to stress the duplicity of that scenario and the specific contradiction of the female subject in it, the contradiction by which historical women must work with and against [narrative].'[4]

However, what if all this were wrong? What if stories, despite their international and transhistorical multiplicity, had come to an end? After all, every story must come to an end sooner or later, so why not the idea of Story as well? The story with which this introduction opened imagines just such a scenario. However, as a story it undoes the very proposition on which it depends. The end of stories, if such a thing were possible, is itself a story which would have to be told – as it is above by the newscaster who reports as news (a news story) the end of stories. Similarly, the telling of the end of story is itself another story which would have to be reported: the story being that the reporting of the end of stories has been reported. In theory, this reporting could stretch itself to infinite regress in which the reporting of the reporting of the end of stories has been reported and so on. As long as there is a future there will always be new stories, even if they are of the order of these Russian dolls. Perhaps more accurately, as long as human beings retain an idea of time which presupposes a past, present and future there will always be stories because stories report the past in terms of the present for a future audience. There will always be time for stories might be a minimal synopsis of Paul Ricoeur's argument in volume one of *Time and Narrative*.[5] The story of the end of story is the supplementary story which the 'end of story' story cannot accommodate. There will always be one extra story which eludes any attempt to put a limit on the idea of Story, and that will be the story of story itself.

However, it is necessary to address the discrepancy introduced above, deliberately so, between 'story' and 'narrative'. In everyday speech we seldom distinguish between the two, one acting as a synonym for the other. Yet much ink has been spilled within narrative theory attempting to provide a rigorous definition of 'narrative' while reserving the term 'story' for a quite separate concept. Perhaps the key activity of narrative theory is precisely this differentiation between stories ('novella, epic, history, tragedy, drama, comedy', to list just some of Barthes' examples of the kind of thing we think we know we are referring to when we say 'stories') and narratives (as a process of grammatical structuration within language and an object of rigorous, even 'scientific', analysis). What follows in this introduction might be thought of as a sustained meditation on precisely this speculation: if all stories are narratives, are all narratives stories, and would the end of stories mean the end of narrative and vice versa? The very name 'narrative theory', whatever this might be, seems to suppose a difference between narrative and story: after all this book is not called *The Story Reader*. Since 'narrative theory' is keen to retain 'narrative' and 'story' as separate terms (their separateness implying their non-reducibility, one to the other), it will be necessary to pursue the question of 'what is a narrative' through the history of narrative theory as represented by the texts gathered together in this volume. In so doing this introduction will seek to think through the nature of narrative in relation to the principles of narratology and a number of the issues raised by the post-structuralist narrative diaspora. Such a strategy will be inadequate because it is forced to leave, for the moment, the question of story to one side as an unformulated concept. This provisional approach will, by necessity, retain a certain understanding of the sort of thing we think we know we are referring to when we use the term 'story', or ask 'What if there were no more stories?', just as its work on the question of narrative will demonstrate that we might not know what we mean. Furthermore, pushing the question 'What is a narrative?' may lead to a crisis for the very idea of a 'narrative theory': a set of rules, predictions and formulae which will hold good for every instance of 'narrative', if such a thing exists.

WHAT IS A NARRATIVE?

> One should first of all take into account that the mode of existence of narrative structures is a virtual mode of existence. Narrative structures do not exist *per se* but are a mere moment in the generation of signification.
>
> A J Greimas[6]

In classic narratology, as in Russian formalism, a distinction is made between the events reported by a 'narrative' and the way in which they are told. In formalism this notional separation is identified by the terms '*fabula*' and '*sjuzhet*', in structuralism by either '*histoire*' and '*discours*' in the French tradition, or '*story*' and '*discourse*' in the Anglo-American academy. Tuning our ears to this sensitive difference ('story', 'histoire', 'fabula' (fable) as the events of a story, 'discourse', 'discours', 'sjuzhet' (confusingly, the Russian word for 'story') as the way those events are told in a narrative) will provide a starting point for speculation on the question 'What is a narrative?' In so far as this 'model' of narrative represents a pervasive way of thinking within narrative theory, it is necessary to interrogate it as a dualistic approach to its object of study. The sway held by this duality is evident not only in structuralist and formalist texts but also in, for example, the threefold mimesis of Paul Ricoeur's *Time and Narrative* (which proposes a textual refiguration of narrative in a nascent prefigured form, as a complication of a dualistic model while retaining the assumption of duality), the deep and surface structure of Chomsky's transformational generative grammar, and the neo-narratology of Peter

Brooks or Seymour Chatman. An examination of the narratological imagination, as a precondition of responding to the question 'What is a narrative?', necessarily involves a consideration of what is at stake in this pervasive dualism. Barbara Herrnstein Smith offers a commentary on this methodological doubling in her essay 'Narrative Versions, Narrative Theories'.[7] Smith quotes the narratologist Claude Bremond as representative of seemingly 'dualist' accounts of narrative, and specifically his assertion that every narrative contains:

> A layer of autonomous significance, endowed with a structure that can be isolated from the whole of the message . . . [this basic and autonomous structure] may be transposed from one to another medium without losing its essential properties.[8]

She then proceeds to challenge this position as containing a 'lingering strain of naive platonism'(p.209) and as being:

> Not only empirically questionable and logically frail but also methodologically distracting, preventing us from formulating the problems of narrative theory in ways that would permit us to explore them more fruitfully in connection with whatever else we know about language, behaviour and culture.
>
> (p.227)

Smith's complaint is that dualistic models are 'confined to the examination of decontextualised structures' and are 'deficient in descriptive subtlety and explanatory force' (p.231). Furthermore, their distinction between two levels within narrative (between what is told – *histoire*, *fabula*, 'story' – and how it is told – *récit*, *sjuzhet*, discourse) is misguided and indefensible.

A reader's ability to construct a summary of the 'story' from a text does not, according to Smith, demonstrate an essential 'narrative' component within the text. Rather, it shows a readerly competence which will differ from reader to reader and culture to culture. Seymour Chatman suggests that 'there is in every story, regardless of its medium of representation, a portion which is *purely* narrative in structure, independent of that medium, that portion having its own structure.'[9] Smith views this as an attempt to identify an unidentifiable 'plot-summary' (or 'pure' story), which various readers would construct differently depending upon their summarising technique and area of interest. Smith concludes that there is:

> No single *basically* basic story . . . but rather, an unlimited number of other narratives that can be *constructed in response* to it or *perceived as related* to it. . . . None of these retellings, however, is more absolutely basic than any of the others.
>
> (p.217; italics in original)

Smith likens this search for 'pure' story to the dream of the Platonic ideal. She notes that any précis of a given narrative is merely another textual inscription and subject to précis itself. The consequence of this is that any attempt to extract a narrative grammar or structure from a given text will merely create a new text and a new narrative. This new narrative is related to, but not the same as, the first text. Therefore, implies Smith, the textual inscription of the narrative *is* the narrative itself (i.e. 'story' and 'narrative' are one and the same). While there may be 'versions' of the narrative, every version is unique and no version can be completely substituted for any other.[10] Smith uses versions of *Cinderella* to demonstrate her point but examples could be multiplied. This leads Smith to an interesting conclusion. She is compelled to re-examine structuralist and formalist definitions of narrative as they appear in the narratological heritage of recent narrative theory. She suggests that while this model may represent a generic distinction within literature, it fails to account for 'the relation of narrative discourse to other forms of discourse and, thereby, to verbal, symbolic, and social behaviour generally' (p.228). She suggests that:

> In the narrow linguistic sense, narrative discourse may be composed of quite brief, bare, and banal utterances as well as such extensive and extraordinary tellings as might occupy 1,001 nights or pages . . . almost all verbal utterance will be laced with more or less minimal narratives. . . . Indeed, narrative discourse is, at one extreme, hardly distinguishable from description or simply assertion. That is, 'telling someone that something happened' can, under certain circumstances, be so close to 'saying that something is (or was) the case' that it is questionable if we can draw any logically rigorous distinction between them or, more generally, if any absolute distinction can be drawn between narrative discourse and any other form of verbal behaviour.

In short, when one begins to push at the established distinction between 'story' and 'narrative' the whole question of what a narrative might be begins to unravel, to the extent that so-called narrative discourse might not be distinguishable from any other linguistic act. It would seem that the working, or presumed understanding within narrative theory of what a narrative is (as a recognisable and discreet entity) depends upon this false opposition between 'story' and 'narrative'.

Smith's undoing of this binary logic has met resistance from 'neo-structuralists' (a term used with due caution given that the very structure of the word 'post-structuralism' signifies the impossibility of a break with structuralism). Seymour Chatman wrote in reply to Smith's essay that structuralism's dualistic proposal:

> Seems so modest, so little more demanding than the constructs that pass effortlessly through pages of literary history and criticism . . . that it is hard to believe it is being challenged . . . Smith's narrative theory is totally language orientated . . . words . . . are not the ultimate components of narratives; those ultimate elements are, rather, events and existents in a chain of temporal causality or at least contingency.

> (p.262)

One feels that the tension which arises here between Smith and Chatman has more to do with the institutional context of narrative theory than it does with epistemological difference. 'Narrative theory' has never stopped being structuralist. It cannot be otherwise; its two eponymous terms depend upon the structuralist project for their definition. Furthermore, it is doubtful whether structuralist narratology was ever vulgarly 'structuralist' in the sense that this term now connotes. The work of what I call the 'post-structuralist narrative diaspora' shows the ways in which the operations of structuralism haunt post-structuralist practice, and indicates how both terms are neither epochs nor self-contained 'methods' but mere labels of homogeneous convenience bestowed by scholars to conceptualise heterogeneity, the sorts of 'imaginary resolution of real contradictions' which 'pass effortlessly through pages of literary history and criticism': Romanticism, Modernism, Postmodernism, Structuralism, Post-Structuralism. Smith's critique does not undo narratology; rather, by stating that words are 'the ultimate components of narratives' she provides a 'properly' structuralist account of the ways in which the human subject is caught up in signifying practices – not that there may be an 'ultimate' or determining component of narrative. Following Smith, I will insist that it is through language that the subject constructs meaningful realities and cognitive processes, while 'events and existents' are not anterior to or knowable outside of language, nor are they unaffected by the fundamentally constitutive function of language.[11]

Let us define a narrative as any minimal linguistic (written or verbal) act. Wittgenstein observed, in relation to linguistic events, 'fundamental assumptions are not arbitrary, but are connected with reality.'[12] Barthes may claim that narrative is universal, 'international, transhistorical, transcultural: it is simply there, like life itself.' However, the generic works of literature analysed by Barthes, or the historiography which Ricoeur analyses, for example, are certainly not present in every age and culture. Rather, it is language which is common to both literature and historiography and which has been common to every society and constitutive of the inter-subjective experience of history. Narratives are linguistic constructs but (in light of Smith's trenchant commentary) it is necessary to ask at what minimal stage it is possible to identify a narrative as a narrative. Should we stop after one sentence, after two sentences, after one word, after two words? Indeed, it might also be asked whether this is the correct question to ask at all. In contrast to the seeming 'dualism' at work in his own theory of emplotment, Peter Brooks views narrative as:

> Not a matter of typology or of fixed structures, but rather a structuring operation peculiar to those messages that are developed through temporal succession, the instrumental logic of a specific mode of human understanding.[13]

According to this argument, narrative is both necessarily metaphysical – narrative has a necessary connection to time – and a cognitive process by which the subject constructs meaningful realities. Teresa de Lauretis is also in tune with the post-narratological turn from a concern with structure as such to a concern with 'structuration', and like Brooks and Ricoeur analyses narrativity rather than narrative. She wishes to describe 'not so much the structure of narrative (its component units and their relations) as its work and effects' (p.105). She seeks to understand 'the nature of the structuring and destructuring, even destructive, process at work in textual and semiotic production' (p.105). She comments:

> Many of the current formulations of narrative process fail to see that subjectivity is engaged in the cogs of narrative and indeed constituted in the relation of narrative,

meaning, and desire; so that the very work of narrativity is the engagement of the subject in certain positionalities of meaning and desire.

(p.106)

These revisionist accounts of narrative suggest that narrativity is involved in the construction of the subject and the conditions of inter-subjective experience. Alan Singer proposes that, at every moment, narrative both 'determines a position for the Subject to inhabit' and 'submits to the contingencies of that determination'.[14] The consensus of narrative theory after structuralism has implied that the subject, when 'born into language', is also born into the narrative-forming processes existent within the communal use of language (one might think of Bennett and Royle's five points). The use of language, and the construction of the subject through language, is a matter of learned narrative competence. In an echo of Ricoeur's 'homo fabulan', Fredric Jameson calls narrative 'the central function or *instance* of the human mind'.[15] In accounting for the question 'What is a narrative?' it will be necessary to investigate the connection, suggested by certain post-structuralist narratologies, between language and narrative.

Any speech act, and therefore any production of meaning, can never be merely paradigmatic.[16] Whether or not the speech act is identifiably metonymic in a syntagmatic representation, any utterance depends upon a syntagmatic context to frame meaning. That is to say, there can be no possibility of meaning outside of an inter-subjective use of language. This is an *a priori* of post-Saussurean linguistics. However, the tradition of language theory instigated by Wittgenstein would also argue that 'language is an institutionalised being-able-to because it is from the beginning the element of a communal form of life, [and] there is no private language'.[17] There can be no use of language which is anterior to grammar. The paradigmatic and the syntagmatic function together to produce meaning. Following Jakobson's provocative description, one might say that the choice or selection of signification is paradigmatic while the utterance is syntagmatic. Grammar is a description of the use of a word – Wittgenstein notes that 'the location of the word in the grammar is its meaning' – and meaning is dependent upon use.[18] Use is a matter of inter-subjective practice between communicating subjects. The context in which the speech act is made allows for its intelligibility and thus communication. It is this context which is the 'story' (a term I will use only provisionally) told in the narrative utterance of any minimal linguistic or verbal act.

For example, both 'Could you pass the salt?' and 'Help!' might be thought of as narratives. The first states, depending upon the inter-subjective context, not merely a request but perhaps also that 'this food is tasteless' or 'I'm about to conduct a chemical experiment'. Under the appropriate conditions it can act as flirtation, rebuke, instruction (examples could be multiplied) to tell a number of different 'stories'. It may be useful then to define the action of a narrative as the representation of an instance, no matter how small, of inter-subjective experience: 'events and existents in a chain of temporal causality or at least contingency' to borrow Chatman's terms. To produce a narrative is to make a moment of inter-subjective experience knowable, or discernible as such, through communication. Walter Benjamin describes the action of the story-teller as taking 'what he tells from experience – his own or reported by others. And he in turn makes it the experience of those listening to his tale.'[19] Similarly, the minimal narrative utterance makes the experience which it relates, the experience of the listener by making it knowable or discernible through linguistic communication. The second of these examples, the one word 'Help', is thus also a narrative. As Jakobson's example of Stanislavaskij's player demonstrates, the same signifier can produce a range of different meanings depending upon the context in which it is used. Thus different experiences are made knowable.[20] The point of a narrative so defined is that by the production of narrative, communication is made possible. It follows that narratives are the inevitable form which communication between subjects takes (one might think back to the claims of narrative universalism with which this introduction began).

This definition of narrative – as any minimal linguistic act – is, in a certain sense, a departure from 'structuralist', 'formalist' or 'hermeneutic' models which, while developing a narrative grammar from the contiguation of minimal parts, concentrate upon the effects produced by the whole textual unit, such as the novel or film. Indeed, the narrative grammar produced by such models, and the effects they discuss, is based upon a more or less untroubled conceptualisation of the novel as paradigmatic of all narrative action (literary or otherwise). However, the novel is merely one form of narrative representation among others. While the novel may display exemplary characteristics of the processes of narrativity, these aspects of narrative are merely a description of a limited production within the entire field of linguistic communication. In terms of describing the form and process of narrative production, structuralism, and other novel-based models of narrative, are restrained by the cultural specificity of its object of study.[21] Indeed the history of narrative analysis depends upon the categorisation of culturally specific literary narratives. Minimal indices include the introductions of Henry James, Bakhtin's reading of Dostoevsky, Barthes' analysis of Balzac, Todorov's typology of detective fiction, Peter Brooks' reading of Conrad, Paul Ricoeur's commentary on Proust, Barbara Herrnstein Smith's examination of Cinderella, and Derrida's reading of Blanchot. Alain Robbe-Grillet observes of the institutional performance of theories of narrative:

> The narrative, as our academic critics conceive it – and many readers after them – represents an order. This order, which we may in effect qualify as natural, is linked to an entire rationalistic system, whose flowering corresponds to the assumption of power by the middle class.[22]

The mediation of the novel as paradigmatic of all narrative production both calls attention to, and inevitably bypasses, the ideological function involved in the selection of narrative forms within this limited field of linguistic production. The reliance of narrative models upon the form of the novel is a consequence of the discipline of narrative theory's beginnings within departments of literature in the French, and later the Anglo-American, academy. The episteme of narrative has a wider relevance outside of this context, but the model of narrative determined by this context has changed little.

However, a questioning of the ideological content of the imagination, which informs narrative theory, will necessarily involve a discussion of the implications of the literary. In Derrida's words it will be necessary 'to discern exactly the historically determined phenomenon of social conventions and the institutions which give rise, give its place, to literature.'[23] This would be a lengthy undertaking, which would complicate any understanding of narrative and its theorisation. It will suffice for the moment to consider the cultural specificity of the model of narrative, to which the hegemony of literary studies, within the discipline of narrative theory, gives rise (in so far as the sociopolitical space of literary production does not just surround texts but affects them structurally). If the powerfully inertial effects of the institutional practice of literature are to be, in some way, circumvented (and Barthes' claim for the universality of narrative is to be substantiated, for nothing I am saying here necessarily contradicts Barthes or his interlocuters), then the question of what a narrative might be needs to be thought in relation to a consideration of the ideological effects of that institutional practice. From all that has gone before, and all that will necessarily follow, clearly it would be impossible to separate the theorisation of narrative from literary practice, assuming that one could identify such a thing in a rigorous way. However, a so-called *Narrative Reader* (particularly one with the presumption to invoke the definite article) which attempts to draw together and push forward current theories of narrative must be alert to the institutional practice from which it emerges. The first step in such a precarious strategy has been a re-examination of the existing definitions of narrative.

CONTEXT AND ITERATION

The definition of a narrative as any minimal linguistic act (or mark) depends upon the clarification of two related concepts: context and iteration. Any linguistic act such as a conversation, a restaurant bill, graffiti, a television programme or a novel is linguistic because the production of meaning by such acts is a signifying practice dependent upon the producing subject's implication within language. Thinking of these marks as textually inscribed will allow the relation between these acts, or any other minimal narrative mark, and context to be conceptualised more thoroughly. By 'textual', or textually inscribed, I mean that these marks are constituted by the figurative dimension of language and inhabited by the interference, one with the other, of the performative and referential functions of language. If deconstruction's much misunderstood assertion that 'there is no-outside-text' means anything it means that 'one never accedes to a text without some relation to its contextual opening'.[24] That is to say that the linguistic production of the text cannot be made meaningful except through the text's existence in a syntagmatic frame of reference, namely, in a context: inter-subjective, historical, political, etc. The paradigmatic mark of the text is only knowable, and can only be produced within, the syntagmatic frame of the context. This sort of 'overrun', which spoils the divisions and boundaries of text and world, forcing an extension of what is considered textual, greatly complicates – or, depending upon your point of view, simplifies – any definition of what a narrative might be. This is not necessarily a matter of Jakobson's notion of the text produced by the syntagmatic axis selecting from the paradigmatic axis with the syntagmatic chain retaining its privileged position of a logically formed linearity.[25] Rather, the questioning of the boundaries of a 'well-defined' text suggests that the textual process not only extends into, but is dependent upon, the contextualising referential apparatus which contains and makes possible that textual unit. In other words, the production of a meaningful reality by the subject-within-language means that the understanding of that reality is textually inscribed and therefore all subjective knowledge is textual in form. There is no extra-text, there is no frame. If a single word, a single letter, a sign or a single mark can qualify as a narrative (that is, can represent, under the appropriate contextual conditions, some instance of inter-subjective experience) then a narrative mark can no longer be thought of as an identifiably well-defined set of borders generically separate from other forms of verbal or written discourse. Rather, the term 'narrative' would signify any unit of meaning made knowable by the textually inscribed context of inter-subjectivity and the signifying chain. 'Narrativity' is the process which constitutes that textual inscription of the inter-subjective context and the signifying chain. When the boundaries of structuralist, formalist or hermeneutic definition have been removed from well-defined 'narrative texts' through their contextual accession, what remains is a narrativised and narrativising context, 'a differential network, a fabric of traces referring endlessly to something other than itself, to other differential traces'.[26] If the process of narrative is momentarily considered outside of the restraints of novelistic, filmic or historiographic form, it is possible to discern that the general structures of textuality are also the general structures of narrative production. Narrative is both the minimal unit of meaning and the cognitive process which makes meaning possible.[27]

The unknown handmaid in Margaret Atwood's novel comments that 'context is all' (p.154). 'Pass me the salt' is a narrative not because it can be decontextualised and named as such (as in, say, 'dualist' models of narrative). Instead, it is a narrative because, like the flaw Smith detects in Chomsky's deep and surface structure, 'Pass me the salt' cannot be separated from the context in which it appears and retain the same meaning. This is not to say that the mark is either valid or invalid outside of a context but, on the contrary, as Derrida notes, 'there are only contexts without centre or absolute anchoring'.[28] This narrative-mark 'Pass me the salt' *relates* or *tells* the signification, which is both determined by and determining of the context. The relationship between the utterance and the context is not one in which either component is privileged. The context provides the utterance with meaning, while the utterance constitutes the context. In other words, meaning is made possible through the context and the context is only possible through meaning. This is a reformulation of Smith's critique of methodological dualism. There can be no separation of the paradigmatic narrative-mark from the syntagmatic narrativised and narrativising context, which results in the production of identical narratives. The paradigmatic narrative-mark has no fixed constitutional boundaries (large or small) because there is no position exterior to the syntagmatic narrativised and narrativising context. In so far as iteration is a necessary condition of meaning, the narrative-mark is inevitably iterable.[29]

In order for the mark to be meaningful within its narrative-context, it must also be possible for this narrative-mark to carry different significances when used as part of a different narrative-context.[30] A narrative-mark must be able to tell different 'stories', or present different instances of inter-subjective experience. It must mean something different and therefore be a different narrative. For a narrative-mark to be able 'to tell' anything at all it must be able to tell different, or even contradictory, 'stories' when it is part of another context. The possibility of the narrative-mark to signify in the first context depends upon the possibility of its existence in the other context. The immediate consequence of this is that it allows for a definition of the narrative-context. The iterability of the narrative-mark both establishes the meaning of the mark as specific to one context and immediately opens up that never saturable context on to the possibility of recontextualisation. The iteration of the narrative-mark makes the context meaningful while at the same time making the bordering of that context impossible. Hence, the 'telling' of the narrative – the instance of inter-subjective experience made readable or, put another way, the intelligibility of the narrative-context – by the paradigmatic narrative-mark, is continually open to the possibility of renarrativisation. The context is not fixed but part of a larger differential narrative matrix, which is endlessly telling something other than itself. While Smith is correct to identify the irreducibility of the narrative-mark, the iterability of the narrative-mark means that the metonymic power of the syntagmatic signifying chain will always come to inscribe any narrative in a 'relation without relation' with its renarrativisations. That is to say that when a mark signifies anything, the possible iterative meanings of that mark are contained within the citational structure of that signification. It is the context which determines performative meaning but which depends upon a general metonymic economy of iteration (one for the other, one part for the whole) to do so.

In this way, all narrative-marks are differentially *related*, as are the narrative contexts they constitute. I shall call this field without limit in which this economy takes place 'the communal narrative-matrix' (not a matrix from which all narratives can be programmed but one which extends without limit to generate and reclaim all narratives, folding back on itself as a double-loop, a narrative of narratives). To distinguish between 'narrative-mark' and 'narrative-context' is not to reappropriate a dualistic model of narrative. Rather, it is to insist upon the aporetic relation between the two and to demonstrate how one 'installs the haunting of the one in the other'.[31] It is not possible to separate the narrative-mark from its narrative-context; both are constitutive of each other. It is only possible to make related statements about both narrative-mark and narrative-context through the iteration of the mark and the recontextualization of the context. Thus, if the non-saturable narrative-context is open to the influence of endless recontextualisation (renarrativisation) simply as a condition of being able to tell anything at all, it must also be made clear that the boundary of the narrative-mark is similarly without limit. Therefore, a narrative – which I have defined as a mark, which makes knowable an instance of inter-subjective experience – is any minimal linguistic or verbal act. The form of generic 'literary narratives' is an entirely different matter.

This is an enlarged definition of narrative, which takes up Smith's invitation to think narrative in connection with recent knowledge concerning language, behaviour and culture. For example, it builds upon Ricoeur's phenomenological appreciation of narrative as a constant refiguration of a network of narratively structured signification. It differs from Ricoeur in the suggestion that the processes of narrativity are not merely a refiguration – a term which implies a fixed set of identifiable rules and tropological patterns. I do not propose the extension into 'the extra-textual realm' of the reassuringly familiar structures of the textual narrative unit – thus transforming the world into one big narrative by the dissolution of boundaries (to paraphrase Derrida's defence of his definition of textuality in 'Living On: Border Lines'). Rather, it attempts to work out the theoretical and practical system of narratological margins and borders once more, from the ground up. What then are the consequences of this minimalist definition of narrative? Narrative without boundaries is narrative without the definition of a limit. A limit is the point at which the other begins its prescencing; as soon as the limit is drawn, what lies beyond that limit begins its existence as an exclusion. While a limit is necessary to define the inside of a system, such as a narrative, the definition of a limit will inevitably work to identify what lies outside the system. In this way, the definition of what lies inside the limit depends as much upon what lies outside as on its own quiddity. Hence the limit, as such, merely defines a relation of interdependence between inside and outside, between system and other. The other speaks before, in and through the system, defining the system in advance. The limit then does not divide and separate but is permeable and always already in decomposition as outside-inside define one another. The moment a limit is set, its own dismantling, as a limit, begins. The narratological limits of narrative text (novel, short story, biography, folk-tale) define the coherence of the text but are always open to the entire narrative-matrix beyond the text (and which speaks in the text, defining it as a narrative syntagm and contextualising its narrative competence). Conversely, the decomposition of that limit folds the text back upon itself, the arbitrary nature of the limit (one point in a syntagm in preference to any other), calling attention to the text as a contingent contiguity, any part of which could impose its own random limit and retain the shape and character of a narrative. Why stop at thirty-two chapters? Why not thirty, why not two, why not four sentences, why not two words? All verbal and linguistic acts become narratives as articulations of the inter-subjective, which hide their narrative character as part of an all-inclusive narrative-matrix. This excludes the possibility of placing a limit on their formal status as narratives.

This narrative-matrix is similarly a matrix without limits that folds itself back along a path, which it produces but which has always already begun. The narrative-matrix provides the simulation of narrative through its inexhaustible writing, generating limits just as those limits collapse back into the matrix. The narrative-matrix produces a 'narrative' (contiguous and within limits) as simulacra of itself, disguising its own recounting which effaces the act of telling, speaking in a way that problematises recounting as an adequate description. The narrative-matrix makes the entire field of human cognition possible. Language and inter-subjectivity are held in a relationship without privileged terms with this matrix and as part of this matrix. In this way a threefold relationship between language, inter-subjectivity and narrativity both instigates and is dependent upon meaning. The matrix is itself structured like a narrative. It is constituted by narrative and is only acceded to by the narrative-mark. Furthermore, it is only knowable as a narrative. To use Judith Roof's formulation, the logic of narrative is that which cannot be stated but can only be narrated. This might also be the law of the textual event and the law of the aporia in general: that which cannot be thought but which can only perform its thinking in a text. It is the paradox of narrative that the inseparability of the narrative-mark from the narrative-context, and the possibility of narrative without limit or boundary, depend upon a narratological notion of narrative as well defined and with fixed limits. This is because a definition which places a limit upon the narrative-mark makes possible the analysis of the narrative-mark, as an object of study, independent of its context. Thus it allows individual narratives to be identified and the concept of 'narrative' to be thought through.

However, the moment a boundary is introduced to limit the narrative-mark, 'degenerescence', to use Derrida's word, of the boundary occurs. This is because the text of the narrative-mark (defined within narratological margins) is acceded to only through the narrative-context. In so doing, these margins, which make possible the definition of the narrative-mark, can be seen to be differential traces within the syntagmation of the narrative-matrix. The limits of the well-defined narrative-mark are constantly referring to instances within the narrative-matrix other than themselves. When, through the metonymic power of a necessary general economy of iterability these margins are broached, the end of the limit has begun. Thus the definition of the limits of the narrative-mark make the retention of those limits impossible. Every devolution of the limits of the narrative-mark, from the narrative-context, is a retention of the narrative-mark within the narrative-context and an affirmation of the ubiquity of the narrative-matrix. The narrative-matrix is a narrative of narrative without edges. It is boundless and relates all narrative-marks one to the other, and denies the possibility of limit to the narrative-mark. All possible marks within the matrix are narrative, and so any minimal linguistic act is a narrative. This definition of degenerescence is only possible through the existence within the narrative-matrix of legible if arbitrary boundaries of narrative definition.

ECONOMICS AND EXCHANGE

If, as an *a priori*, I continue to insist that both language and the individual subject are meaningless outside of inter-subjectivity it is because I think that the notion of subjectivity has been sufficiently altered by the work of Lacan and Derrida, and others, to be able to insist upon this (most of the narrative theory collected in the diaspora section of this volume works on this assumption). In light of the aporetic relation, which constitutes the field of the narrative-matrix, it follows that inter-subjective communication is a communal exchange of narratives. It is this exchange of narratives within the narrative-matrix which constitutes subjectivity, and subjectivity itself is structured like a narrative. The use of language is a consequence of the subject's conditions of existence within the narrative-matrix and any use of language inevitably takes the form of a narrative. Just as a post-Saussurean linguistics defines the aporetic relation between the subject and language, a post-structuralist narratology must similarly define the aporetic relation between the linguistically constituted subject and the production of narrative. It is now perhaps appropriate to define narrativity as the narrative-forming processes characteristic of the use of language. As the examples of 'Pass the salt' and 'Help' show, narrativity is above all a grammatical function. It places the paradigmatic mark in a dependent syntagmatic signifying chain: for no naming process can ever be simply a naming. Narrativity, language and inter-subjectivity are inextricably linked within the citational structure of the narrative-matrix, which is constituted by the economy of the communal exchange of narratives. This communal exchange of narratives is at once the form of the narrative-matrix itself and a production of the structure of the matrix. The matrix is constituted by the exchange of narrative and makes possible the exchange of narrative.

The introduction of these terms 'economy' and 'exchange' must be accounted for. Derrida notes, 'the gift will be linked to the – internal – necessity of a certain narrative [*récit*] or of a certain poetics of narrative.'[32] The gift as such is impossible. The moment the gift is recognised it is no longer a gift but a marker of obligation and debt, placing the recipient and giver in an economy of exchange. The giver is seen to give, thus placing the recipient in a position of gratitude, hence the gift is not 'free' but produces debt. The return of the gift creates a cycle of debt by which the gesture towards the gift is always caught in a system of exchange predicated upon the mutual implication of giver and receiver in a relation of debt. Derrida, after Mauss, describes this logic as 'a logic of madness but also of narration, the condition of possibility and impossibility of narration' (p.55). The gift is connected to narrative because both give, demand or take time. The gift (that which is given by the gift), like a narrative (that which is told by a narrative), initiates a set of temporal relations: existing in time but also constructing the experience of time. Following Ricoeur's mediation of the aporias of phenomenological temporality through narrative, one might say that narrative is necessarily metaphysical. Narrative has a necessary relation to the representation and understanding of temporality, and therefore narrative provides, for the Heideggerian Derrida and Ricoeur, a means by which the question of being can be thought of as a question of presence. Narrative depends upon an idea of the past-present ('this happened') in contrast to a point-like present (now) and a future-present ('this will happen'). However, narrative is one of the primary means whereby the impossibility of a present-now (which is both always already past and always already still to happen) is transposed into a mode of consciousness as the operation of time. In order for us to imagine that the past action of a narrative took place we must be prepared to imagine the referential illusion of a point-like presence. This is the gift which narrative gives, just as the operation of narrative constantly collapses this present into a future and a past which was never actually present or potentially present but which can never be fully reactivated, even potentially, or thought of as a past-present now dormant. Exchange, one thing for another, is temporal and narrative because it is metonymic. The consequence of temporal exchange (the illusion of a present for a narrative past) is that time begins to appear as that which undoes this distinction between taking and giving, and so between receiving and giving, or narrating and listening. Therefore, an economy of exchange in which the means of exchange is the graphemetically structured narrative-matrix, and the thing which is exchanged is the narrative-mark, makes that economy what Derrida calls 'aneconomic. Not that it remains foreign to the circle, but it must keep a relation of familiar foreignness. It is perhaps in this sense that the gift is impossible' (p.7). It might be argued that it is in this sense that narrative exchange is strictly impossible.

If narrative is to be characterised as a metaphysical necessity (both in terms of its essential relation to the conceptualisation of temporality and its aporetic relation to the construction of the subject within language) then, as far as the horizon of the question of narrative possibility can be posed as a question of presence, it must be stated clearly that narrative (*stricto sensu*) is impossible. If narrative exists in the form of exchange then this 'aneconomy' of exchange defines the conditions of possibility for the impossible narrative. As Derrida writes:

> As for the economy of the narrative and the narrative of the economy, we have glimpsed the reason for which the gift, if there is any, requires and at the same time excludes the possibility of narrative. The gift is on condition of the narrative, but simultaneously on the condition of possibility and impossibility of the narrative.
>
> (p.103)

Because there can never be a completed exchange between linguistically constituted subjects, the process of narrative can never be completed. This is problematic but not a problem *per se*: narrative loses nothing from this claim that it is impossible. The exchange of narrative is the process of linguistic communication because all linguistic acts take place within the narrative-matrix. Communication, as Lacan shows, is the incomplete response of the other to the subject's appeal to the Other in language.[33] The desire which motivates narrative is therefore the desire for the Other. The impossibility of satisfaction of this desire compels the interminability of narrative exchange. This will need to be addressed.

DESIRE AND INTERMINABILITY

'A story,' says Teresa de Lauretis, 'is always a question of desire.'[34] However true this assertion may be, Peter Brooks fears that desire itself is 'a concept too broad, too fundamental, almost too banal to be defined'.[35] Following all that has been said so far regarding the construction of subjectivity within the narrative-matrix, I would like to define the process of narrativity within inter-subjectivity as both the subject's appeal to the Other in speech and the inadequate response of the other to that call. Lacan comments, 'What I seek in speech is the response of the Other. What constitutes me as a Subject is my question.'[36] There is no originary narrative; every narrative is a differential mark within a de-centred narrative-matrix. Therefore, and as a consequence of the citational structure of the narrative-matrix, every narrative is simultaneously a possible response to the subject's appeal to the Other already active within the narrative-matrix. This is because the matrix does not exist anterior to inter-subjectivity. Furthermore, every narrative-mark is also an appeal in itself. Every mark initiates future responses in the syntagmatic construction of the matrix. Lacan notes, 'there is no speech without a reply, even if it is only met with silence' (p.40). As Margaret Atwood's abandoned handmaid reminds her reader, 'You don't tell a story only to yourself. There is always someone else. Even when there is no one' (p.49).

The field of the narrative-matrix thus acts as a syntagmatic chain of narrative-marks. Each mark is simultaneously an appeal to the Other and a response from the other. While this aporetic exchange privileges neither the response of the other nor the appeal to the Other, it may be easier to begin a theorisation of these conditions of exchange with a study of the appeal. Lacan suggests, 'the first object of desire is to be recognised by the other' (p.58). In such a psychoanalytic reading it follows that the relation of desire to narrative is primarily that of the mediation of the subject's appeal for recognition by the other. The production of a narrative-mark is an appeal to the other. Each narrative-mark – each determination of an instant of inter-subjective experience – seeks the Other in a demand for recognition. Recognition by the Other would be a form of affirmation of the existence of that experience. The subject thus constitutes itself through the act of narrative exchange. For Lacan:

> The Other is, therefore, the locus in which is constituted the I who speaks to him who hears, that which is said by the one being already the reply, the other deciding to hear it whether the one has or has not spoken.[37]

The production of narrative always involves an activity of exchange in which the other provides an incomplete response to the subject's appeal to the Other, and thus implies an audience. This relationship of exchange is quite different from the relationship between narrator and narratee (or reader) as defined by narratology, which is essentially a transparent relation of untroubled consciousness. The act of narrative production determines the location of the Other – the Other being the locus of linguistic possibility within the inter-subjective narrative-matrix. Furthermore, the response of the Other is always already contained within the act of narrative production itself. However, as Lacan proposes, the Other is only ever acceded to by the other:

> In order to be recognised by the other, I utter what was only in view of what will be. In order to find him, I call him by a name that he must refuse in order to reply to me.[38]

The virtual position of the Other can only be appealed to through the positioned subject of the other. The recognition of the Other can never be the same as recognition by the other; it is always inadequate, always unable to satisfy. The desire to produce narrative can never be satisfied by the reception of the narrative-mark, and the desire to determine an instant of inter-subjective experience can never be satisfied by the social acknowledgement of that instant. Iteration (the necessary condition which makes the act of narrative production, and therefore the narrative-matrix, meaningful and possible) ensures that the reception of the narrative-mark by the socially positioned other is always a relationship of incomplete receivership.

Thus the exchange of narrative-marks within inter-subjective communication is always disrupted by the figurative nature of the graphematically structured narrative-mark. Furthermore, the narrative-mark is only acceded to by the differential network of the narrative-matrix. In this way, the act of narrative production – because it involves a reception of the mark by an other – is always incomplete. If one agrees with Lacan, the recognition of the subject by the other is always in part a misrecognition. It is always an incomplete response to the subject's appeal to the Other and the desire which initiates the production of narrative cannot be entirely satisfied. Wittgenstein warned – in the context of the 'language-game' of narration – not to 'regard it too much as a matter of course that one can tell anything to anyone'.[39] The act of narrative production takes place and an instance of inter-subjective experience is determined. However, the reception of that instance by the other within inter-subjective communication is open to the iteration of the mark, which determines it and so opens it on to its own indeterminacy.

It is not only the necessary misrecognition of the appeal to the Other, in the socially positioned response of the other, which blocks the satisfaction of the desire to produce narrative. The act of narrative production always contains the possibility of a response within its own structure. The position of reception-of-the-mark-by-the-other is merely an inverted form of the narrative-mark's own production by the subject. In other words, to quote Lacan, 'speech [one might say narrative] always subjectively includes its own reply.'[40] In so far as the narrative-mark is acceded to by the narrative-matrix (which constitutes its act of production) and is a link in the syntagm of narrative exchange (which constitutes the narrative-matrix), it follows that the narrative-mark always already contains within its own rigorously undecidable parameters the unsatisfactory response of the other. That is to say that the desire to produce narrative is – from the beginning – a desire which can never be satisfied.[41]

A desire, which can never be satisfied, compels the interminability of the production of narrative and ensures the progression of the syntagmation of the chain of narrative exchange. Thus the continuation of the linguistic exchange characteristic of human communication, or inter-subjective experience, is ensured by the very structure of narrative production. The desire to produce narrative is never satisfied and the desire to receive a narrative-mark, which is contained within and presupposed by the desire to produce a narrative-mark, is also never satisfied. Therefore, the syntagm of narrative exchange never concludes. Communication goes on and the inter-subjective persists. In other words, narrative exchange is interminable. An adequate identification of/by the Other within an exchange would result in a satisfaction of desire and an end to the process of exchange. The termination of the syntagm of exchange in a state of plenitude would lead to silence. Silence is the cessation of the use of language. It would arise because the narrative exchange characteristic of inter-subjective communication, and therefore of linguistic production, would have ended. An experience of plenitude would mean that there is nothing left to say because there is no incident of inter-subjective experience to determine.

Thus the work of narrativity, in de Lauretis' words, 'is the engagement of the subject in certain positionalities of meaning and desire' (p.106). The subject is constantly seeking the Other through the production of narrative, only to be endlessly deferred, and so compelled along the syntagmation of narrative exchange within the narrative-matrix. However, this description of the desire to tell as the insatiable pursuit of a perpetually lost object should not be read as a re-inscription of the Oedipal desire. Clearly the Oedipal desire and the desire to produce narrative have certain affinities. However, this is only a matter of sharing the same mechanics of desire, which are the common experience of the linguistically constituted subject. The Oedipus narrative, with its interest in the search for the perpetually deferred object, is certainly part of the narrative-matrix and may simply be, as de Lauretis says, 'paradigmatic of all narratives' (p.112). However, the desire to produce narrative is structured like Freud's formulation of the desire of the hysteric, 'the desire for an unsatisfied desire'.[42] It is the insatiability of the desire to produce the narrative-mark which constitutes the act of narrative production. The possibility of satisfaction of this desire would halt narrative syntagmation and establish a boundary to the chain of narrative exchange. The consequence of this would be the determination of a limit to, and the positioning of a centre for, the differential relations within the narrative-matrix. Such a teleological determination of signification would not be possible if one were to accept all that has been said previously regarding the exemplary economy of iteration which structures the narrative-matrix. It is a necessary condition of the production of narrative, and the interminable syntagmation of narrative exchange, that the desire to produce/receive the narrative-mark is an insatiable desire.

The desire to produce/receive the narrative-mark and the narrative-matrix, which constructs the mark and is constituted by it, is, to use Althusser's phrase, 'a structure immanent in its effects'.[43] The narrative-matrix is aporetically related to the desire to produce/receive. The effects of one are not outside of the structure which contains the other, rather, 'the whole existence of the structure consists of its effects' (p.25). Ursula K. Le Guin recognises this. Using the allegory of a rattle-snake's struggle to ensure survival, Le Guin suggests there is no alternative to the use of narrative.[44] The syntagmation of narrative exchange is a necessary condition of inter-subjective experience. The subject produces narrative, according to de Lauretis, 'just in order to exist, or to sustain desire even as we die from it' (p.157). We die from it because this desire compels us towards the end of the necessarily discrete textual unit of narrative. The impossible conditions of possibility of this unit allow for the possibility of the impossible narrative-matrix. Le Guin writes:

When a hoop snake wants to get somewhere – whether because the hoop snake is after something, or because something is after the hoop snake – it takes its tail (which may or may not have rattles on it) into its mouth, thus forming itself into a hoop, and rolls. Jehovah enjoined snakes to crawl on their belly in the dust, but Jehovah was an easterner. Rolling along, bowling along, is a lot quicker and more satisfying than crawling. But, for the hoop snakes with rattles, there is a drawback. They are venomous snakes, and when they bite their own tail they die, in awful agony, of snakebite. All progress has these hitches. I don't know what the moral is. It may be in the end safest to lie perfectly still without crawling. Indeed it's certain that we shall all do so in the end, which has nothing else after it. But then no tracks are left in the dust, no lines drawn; the dark and stormy nights are all one with the sweet bright days, this moment of June – and you might as well never have lived at all. And the moral of that is, you have to form a circle to escape from the circle. Draw in a little closer around the campfire. If we could truly form a circle, joining the beginning and the end, we would, as another Greek remarked, not die. But never fear. We can't manage it no matter how hard we try. But still, very few things come nearer the real Hoop Trick than a good story.

(pp.189–90)

Here, Le Guin uses allegory to negotiate the problematic logic of narrative. Through the use of a narrative she gives an account of the structure of narrative which defers a definition of what might characterise that structure while depending upon the very principle it defers. There is something in narrative which is disturbing and elusive, and Le Guin's metafiction successfully describes this interminable deferral through an employment of that very desire. Her narrative of the snake suggests that the narrative-matrix is constructed by a network of figuratively structured marks and consists of ideologically contested sites of linguistic use. Le Guin identifies the complex linguistic phenomenon of the narrative-matrix as the process by which the subject is aporetically implicated within inter-subjectivity by a set of imaginary relations (what she calls 'the Hoop Trick'). As a consequence of the inevitable expression of language in the form of a narrative, the inter-subjective is compelled into the prolongation of the exchange of narrative as the only alternative to silence and termination. Misrecognition and insatiability predicate inter-subjective experience and produce interminability.

Such a speculation returns us to the narrative of the 'death' of narrative with which this introduction began. At this point it is possible to suggest that the production of meaning in an inter-subjective exchange is related to conditions of silence. The structure of signification is determined by the manner in which silence demands the subject's utterance. If this is so, a response to our opening account of the possibility of the 'death' of narrative might suggest that narrative exchange constructs subjectivity, but paradoxically it is silence and the 'threat' of the death of narrative which structures that exchange and so subjectivity. What is meant by 'death' when it is discussed within the context of narrative theory? I have used the term 'death' to mean the atrophy of language, that moment when language ceases to signify and, as a consequence 'being', is negated. In this context I would like to define 'being' as the existence of the subject within an inter-subjectivity. This may occur when the empirical frame through which language comes to exist (the mortal body) is no longer able to physically sustain the effort of language when the body reaches the end of its life. It may also occur at some unimaginable point (and as a consequence the iterable nature of language, impossible point) of plenitude when the call to Otherness within the process of narrative production is completely satisfied. The reproduction of the body of the inter-subjective, and the insatiability of the desire to produce narrative, ensure that the death of narrative, or the death of language, is impossible. Only a cessation of reproduction or the violent mortality of the body of the inter-subjective will result in the death of narrative. That is, when there is no one left to produce or receive the narrative-mark. Certainly, Benjamin is correct when he aphoristically notes that 'death is the sanction of all that is possible for the storyteller',[45] but only the conditions of impossibility of death make such a sanction possible.

TELEOLOGY AND TOTALISATION

The interminable exchange of narrative is predicated by the narrating subject's insatiable appeal to the Other. Paradoxically this exchange both depends upon narrative as its necessary form of expression and is also resistant to that narrative form. The exchange can only be made through narrative marks, but the interminability of the exchange excludes the possibility of the move towards totalisation characteristic of the contiguity of narrative form; what Jameson calls 'the expressive causality [of] . . . its intolerable closure'.[46] Here I would like to define totalisation as the formal project of narrative syntagmation to encapsulate completely its descriptive object, i.e., to achieve a state of plenitude in relation to the narrating subject's appeal to the Other. The interminable exchange of narrative and the consequent prolongation of inter-subjective experience within the boundless field of the narrative-matrix negates the possibility of closure within narrative syntagmation. The imaginary nature of, in Derrida's words, 'the unfigurable figure of clusion' has been the object of extensive study by post-structuralist narratologies. However, it is a less radical insight than it may appear. Rather, the imaginary nature of closure is a necessary condition of existence for the production of narrative. If a narrative syntagmation were able to achieve closure, this would result in the termination of narrative exchange which depends upon the boundless and differential nature of syntagmation. The move towards closure in the formal characteristics of longer textual narrative units is merely an image or a 'figure', to quote De Lauretis (p.144). This figure is formally determined for the purposes of conceptualisation and by chronological necessity; namely, narrative is necessarily the means by which the subject represents and understands the metaphysical implications of temporality.

As such, narrative must provide a means by which the subject can construct a present as a distinct ontological region of reality. This is achieved by placing an imaginary limit on the boundless and differential syntagm of narrative exchange. Once an imaginary horizon has been set within the narrative-matrix, the subject is then able to position itself within a teleologically determined past, present and future. In this way, the imaginary figure of closure, as a trope within the production of narrative, is a consequence of the aporetic relation between narrative and temporality. By using the figure of closure, the act of narrative production disguises an illusion of presence as a metaphysical necessity. Closure is only one tropological possibility within the production of narrative syntagmation and has no absolute authority in relation to the interminable narrative exchange. On the contrary, closure provides that necessary limit to the narrative-mark which makes possible the 'degenerescence' of the boundaries of the narrative-mark and so determines the success of the narrative-mark as a differential trace within the narrative-matrix. The placing of a limit of closure upon a narrative syntagm makes the retention of that limit impossible. When the boundaries of the narrative-mark are broached by the chain of appeal to the Other and response by the other, which determines narrative exchange, the end of the limit of closure begins and narrative is possible. Le Guin's 'Hoop Trick' is a reminder that we 'have to form a circle to escape from the circle' and closure is an impossible condition of the boundless.

As a consequence of these impossible conditions of closure, narrative syntagmation enjoys the property of never being able to complete its formal project of totalisation. This formal aim of narrative, to encapsulate completely its descriptive object, is never fulfilled and consequently narratives are inhabited by the condition of *ateleology*. This atelicism is a resistance of language to its necessary expression as social communication in the totalising form of a narrative. The narrative syntagm attempts to encapsulate its object of description. However, the linguistic construction of the syntagm within a wider differentially structured linguistic community, and its signification through chronological contiguity, means that the narrative syntagm is ultimately unable to reproduce its object. When the act of narrative production reveals a moment of inter-subjective experience it also produces a narrative-mark which, as a result of chronological contiguity, also becomes a moment of inter-subjective experience. This mark then adds to the amount of material held within the field of the narrative-matrix. If this material is to be knowable, it must necessarily be expressed in narrative form. It follows from this that even if a narrative-mark were able to totalise a response to the narrative-mark which preceded it in the syntagm, the attempt to include within itself a description of its own narrative act – in order to achieve full totalisation – would compel the narrative-mark towards an indefinite limit. Tristram Shandy, who attempted to offer a complete encapsulation of his experiences, discovered that 'the more I write the more I shall have to write'.[47]

Any understanding of the object of description of a narrative-mark, in so far as that object is not knowable outside or anterior to language, is itself a meaningful mark. Similarly, it is constituted in the form of a narrative. Knowledge of the object exists within, and is made meaningful by, the linguistic frame of the narrative-matrix. Thus any narrative is necessarily a renarrativisation of another narrative. Perhaps this is what Ricoeur has in mind when he suggests his threefold mimetic. The figuration of narratively expressed inter-subjective experience into another narrative-mark, which seeks to describe it, can be identified as the very process of narrative syntagmation. Accordingly, it is possible to suggest that narrative syntagmation involves an attempt at dialectical synthesis of existing narrative utterances. Each new point in the syntagm, which attempts to respond to the appeal to the Other, which the previous syntagmation represents, both carries over and cancels out narrative material from the previous syntagmation. It is at this point in the study of the production of narrative that narratologically defined form becomes important (precis, prolepsis, analepsis, etc.) as techniques for tropologically, or finitely, expressing boundless material.

The process of producing a narrative-mark to respond to the rest of the exchange cannot accommodate the entire existing narrative material of the syntagm in a single moment of presence. By necessity it must exclude, or edit out, elements of the previously existing narrative syntagm. There are practical reasons for this; Margaret Atwood's handmaid notes that every narrative is a 'reconstruction'. She reminds the reader:

> It's impossible to say a thing exactly the way it was, because what you say can
> never be exact, you always have to leave something out, there are too many parts,
> sides, crosscurrents, nuances; too many gestures, which could mean this or that,
> too many shapes which can never be fully described, too many flavours, in the air
> or on the tongue, half-colours too many.
>
> (p.144)

This remaining and unarticulated material (these 'half-colours') form other narratives
within the differential network of the narrative-matrix and take up a contrapuntal
position in relation to the formalised closure attempted by the editing out of narrative
material. I would like provisionally to term this movement towards an imaginary closure
within narrative syntagmation, by constructing an 'adequate' response through editing
out narrative material, as the 'dominant' narrative strand. This will have to be accounted
for. The inability of any individual narrative-mark to totalise the entire syntagm as a
truly adequate response to the appeal to the Other leads to the interminability of narrative
syntagmation. The iterable structure of the narrative-matrix ensures that each strand
of narrative installs the haunting of the one in the other. The communal exchange of
narrative and the process of narrative syntagmation are therefore marked by the continual
contestation of narrative voice, in which the dominant strand(s) are inhabited by resistant
form(s). This is the moment when the production of narrative – to use Blanchot's words
concerning literature – places 'itself in the affirmation of all the opposing moments'.
The existence of these contrapuntal strands relies on the ability of narrative production
to 'change both its meaning and its sign' depending upon which strand the narrative
syntagmation follows towards closure.[48] This is a property of narrative but it is also
merely an effect of power.[49] This contestation over what is to be narrated makes the
narrative-mark what De Lauretis terms 'structurally insoluble because undecidable'
(p.156). This needs to be explained.

CONTRAPUNTAL READING, CONTRAPUNTAL WRITING

Henry Louis Gates suggests that:

> People arrive at an understanding of themselves and the world through narratives
> – narratives purveyed by school teachers, newscasters, 'authorities', and all the
> other authors of our common sense. Counternarratives are, in turn, the means by
> which groups contest that dominant reality and the fretwork of assumptions that
> supports it. Sometimes delusion lies that way; sometimes not. There's a sense in
> which much of black history is simply counternarrative that has been documented
> and legitimatized, by slow, hard-won scholarship.[50]

To leave the problems of documenting a minority history to one side (even if they are
at the forefront our concerns here), this analysis of a site of contest within the North
American academy provides both an example and a working definition of the processes
of narrativity within the communal narrative-matrix. The inability of a narrative to
complete the totalising ambition of its teleologically determined form, and the necessity
of narrative syntagmation to continue in a chain of exchange, leads to the constant

production – within the differential network of narrative-marks – of a systematics of narrative and counternarrative. This contest between narrative-marks for the representation of the 'truth' of experience, and to present themselves as both a full appeal to and an adequate response of the Other within the chain of narrative statement and request which constitutes inter-subjective experience, is at once never resolvable and necessarily incomplete. The privileging of one narrative-mark over another is not possible because every narrative-mark is only defined by its differential relation to all other marks. Thus no mark can represent an adequate response to/of the Other because the Other always already speaks in every mark. Furthermore, the contest between narrative and counternarrative is in fact the very action which structures the narrative-matrix. As a consequence of the differential relation between narrative-marks there is no point of exteriority in relation to the narrative-matrix for the narrative-mark. In fact the position of any narrative-mark within the matrix is determined and conditioned by the counternarratives, which contest this position. These counternarratives are immanent to the processes, which produce the narrative-mark they contest. Indeed, when considered in isolation a counternarrative can be seen to be a single narrative-mark itself, which is similarly contested by other counternarratives. Therefore, every narrative is also a counternarrative. This is not to say that neither a narrative nor a counternarrative is in itself representative of truth. Rather, as a condition of its production a narrative will always initiate a counternarrative. Truth is the stake in the contest between these narratives.

The condition of the counternarrative arises because the form of the narrative syntagm cannot express a totality of experience, although it attempts to disguise this necessary 'failing' in the imaginary figure of closure. Counternarratives are a necessary part of the production of the communal narrative-matrix and are therefore necessary to the prolongation of inter-subjective experience. As this reading of Gates suggests, this condition of contrapuntality is continually present in the social space of the inter-subjective. A narrative syntagmation, inasmuch as its form represents the contiguous relation of several narrative-marks, is a site of contestation by a number of different counternarratives. It is also dependent upon these counternarratives for its constitution. Any theory of narrative, which follows the impossible logic of aporetic conditions, must be alert to the possibilities of counternarratives. They offer both a contrapuntal experience to that presented by the singular narrative-mark and constitute the irreducible representation of experience in that initial narrative-mark.

While this present theorisation of the conditions of contrapuntality is related to what is an already well-established reading practice in post-colonial discourse, it is not quite the same thing. Walter Benjamin notes that 'There is no document of civilisation which is not at the same time a document of barbarism.'[51] If Benjamin is correct, the production of any literary or artistic text depends upon a system of sociopolitico-economic hierarchical production, the residue of which is excluded from the text. This, however, is merely to recognise that the atelicism of narrative syntagmation means that a totalisation of experience by a narrative-mark is impossible, and this impossibility is disguised in the process of editing and selection which creates the imaginary figure of closure. Edward Said builds upon Benjamin's insight to propose his own notion of 'contrapuntal reading'. He recognises that 'all literary texts . . . are not bounded by their formal historical beginnings and endings.'[52] This is to recognise that the narrative-mark is made meaningful by its position within the syntagmation of the inter-subjective narrative-matrix. The matrix both precedes and follows on from the position of the mark within the syntagmatic chain and has a constitutive and differential relation to the narrative-mark. In other words, Said recognises that the production of a narrative-mark depends upon the experience of the communal narrative-matrix out of which it arises, and has a relation of difference to the other marks within that matrix. This relation of difference means that for the subject to be more fully informed of the experience represented by the narrative-mark, it must also read the counternarratives which both contest and constitute the narrative-mark:

> The point is that contrapuntal reading must take account of both processes, that of imperialism and that of resistance to it, which can be done by extending our reading of the texts to include what was once forcibly excluded.
>
> (p.79)[53]

Reading the counternarrative entails, for Said, identifying the material which the editing and selection process of the singular narrative-mark has eschewed. The identification and piecing together of this material constitutes, on the part of the readerly subject, the production of a narrative syntagmation which holds together several narrative-marks in a chain of contiguity. In this context, the 'readerly subject' can refer to either the other in the chain of exchange or to the narrating subject which receives its own response: the positions of the production and reception install the haunting of one inside another. In this way the reading subject enacts its own immanence within the communal narrative-matrix and the narratively inscribed experience of inter-subjectivity. The reading subject produces a singular narrative syntagm open to, and constituted by, counternarrative. By this act, the reading subject demonstrates the existence of counternarratives in relation to the initial singular narrative-mark and shows that this mark only exists as an activity of production on the part of a readerly subject. Said's identification of a relation of difference between narrative and counternarrative leads him to conclude that, in terms of the experience represented in literary-narratives: 'The striking consequence has been to disguise the power situation and to conceal how much the experience of the stronger party overlaps with and, strangely, depends on the weaker' (p.231). In other words, both narrative and counternarrative are immanent within a shared system of production. This shared system is the process of narrative production in the communal narrative-matrix. The conditions of contrapuntality are therefore necessary conditions of narrativity which are the processes of narrative production within the communal narrative-matrix.

However, this is not necessarily a conclusion drawn by Said, who is content to re-establish the illusion of legitimacy by privileging a relation of priority between counternarrative and narrative, rather than insisting upon a differential relation between two singular narrative-marks. The political pertinence of Said's project determines this gesture and so reproduces the act of contest and disguise rather than embracing the undecidability of the subject's relation to the narrative-mark. This would not invalidate Said's writing of counternarrative but rather would make clear the conditions under which it is possible. Lacan comments, 'this play of the signifiers is not, in effect, an inert one, since it is animated in each particular part by the whole history of the ancestry of real others that the denomination of signifying Others involves in the contemporaneity of the subject.' In this sense it is the very production of signification by 'real others', within the communal narrative-matrix, which conveys a political pertinence upon the narrative-mark and not its differential relation to other narratives.[54] The understanding of contrapuntality that I am suggesting here depends upon making the differential relation between narrative and counternarrative 'transparent' (as far as this is possible) within a general systematics of writing. Contest between narrative and counternarrative is merely a symptom of the linguistic predicament of all narrative production. As a linguistic product, and as the means of linguistic production, narrative is inevitably both a cause and effect of the 'will-to-power' which determines the subject's position within inter-subjectivity. As Barthes comments, 'No help for it: language is always on the side of power; to speak is to exercise a will to power: in the space of speech, no innocence, no safety.'[55]

Just as the use of language places the subject within a position of immanence in relation to the uses and effects of power, then so too narrative (as an aporetic construct, both linguistic product and producer of language) must find itself in an immanent relation to the systematics of power, which are at work within the communal narrative-matrix of inter-subjectivity.[56] It follows from this that the condition of power relation is also the condition of narrative production. This is true in terms of the contest between narrative and counternarrative, and in the process of editing and selection which produces the singular narrative syntagm or mark. Michel Foucault provides a cogent analysis of the immanence of power relations when he writes:

> There is no binary division to be made between what one says and what one does not say; we must try to determine the different ways of not saying such things, how those who can and those who cannot speak of them are distributed, which type of discourse is authorised, or which form of discretion is required in either case. There is not one but many silences, and they are an integral part of the strategies that underlie and permeate discourses.[57]

Foucault is suggesting that the task for the reading subject is not necessarily, as Said would have it, to offer a narrative configuration of what is 'forcibly excluded' from the text. Rather, it is to recognise that all material excluded in the process of narrative editing and selection installs itself hauntologically within the material which the narrative presents. The relation between narrative and counternarrative is not binary but aporetic. The differential relation between narrative-marks calls for 'discernment' on the part of the reading subject, rather than the replacement of one illusion of authorisation with another. It is necessary to recognise that all narrative-marks are a way of not saying things. No singular narrative syntagm is exterior to this condition. There is not just one counternarrative but many, and these are structurally integral to the production of any narrative-mark. The narrator of Salman Rushdie's novel *Shame* notes, 'now I must stop saying what I am not writing about, because there is nothing so special in that; every story one chooses to tell is a kind of censorship, it prevents the telling of other tales.'[58]

This has several consequences for the production of narrative. First, to paraphrase Wittgenstein, there is no escaping narrative by means of narrative. Foucault notes:

> By constantly referring to positive technologies of power, you are playing a double game . . . there is no escaping from power, that it is always-already present, constituting that very thing which one attempts to counter it with.
>
> (p.82)

The production of a counternarrative – what I termed previously a 'resisting narrative strand' and which may be thought of as a positive technology of power – does not transcend the problematics of power, which constitute the necessary conditions of narrative production. This counternarrative also edits and selects and is itself a singular narrative-mark in relation to other counternarratives. Second, the narrative syntagmation which produces the interminable exchange between narrative appeal and response is constituted by the power relations immanent to the processes of narrative production. Interminability is a consequence of the relentless performance of power struggles. As Foucault says of any power relation:

> It is defined in a strangely restrictive way, in that, to begin with, this power is poor in resources, sparing of its methods, monotonous in the tactics it utilises, incapable of invention, and seemingly doomed always to repeat itself.
>
> (p.85)

On the one hand, it is a power struggle which determines the interminability of the chain of narrative syntagmation; on the other hand (and aporetically so), power should not be thought of as exterior to narrative but as a product of the necessary expression of language in the form of a narrative. Foucault writes:

> It seems to me that power must be understood in the first instance as the multiplicity of force relations immanent in the sphere in which they operate and which constitute their own organisation; as the process which, through ceaseless struggles and confrontations, transforms, strengthens, or reverses them; as the support which these force relations find in one another, thus forming a chain or a system, or on the contrary, the disjunctions and contradictions which isolate them from one another; and lastly, as the strategies in which they take effect, whose general design or institutional crystallisation is embodied in the state apparatus, in the formulation of the law, in the various social hegemonies.
>
> (pp.92–3)

In other words, the power relations which determine the production of narrative both in the process of editing and selection, and in the contest between narrative and counternarrative, can be understood as a 'multiplicity of force relations immanent in the sphere in which they operate and which constitute their own organisation'.

It is these force relations which hold the communal narrative-matrix together just as they threaten to tear it apart. The interdependence of these force relations, and the production of the 'various social hegemonies' within the experience of inter-subjectivity, are masked by the very thing which constitutes them, namely, the structure of narrative. One force relation is not innately superior to any other. Each depends differentially on any other. However, power is exercised when the differential equality between two force relations is disguised by the imposition of an imaginary limit of closure, which is constructed by the process of editing and selecting enacted by 'real others'. A resisting narrative strand is not necessarily in opposition to a dominant narrative strand, only the illusion of the figure of closure makes it appear so.[59] The semantic value-judgement implied in the relation of 'resistance' and 'power' is not necessarily a condition of the virtual means of narrative production, although the process of dominant and excluded force relations certainly is. It is only when the production of narrative is enacted by real others that the ethically determined weight of this vocabulary is applicable. Of course, this means that it is applicable to every instance of narrative production, because such production can never be exterior to the real others of an inter-subjective life-praxis.

Once again we are presented with impossible conditions as the conditions of possibility. Immanent narrative force relations are both independent of the politico-ethical determination of power struggles between real others and always already implicated within them. The conditions of contrapuntality are the necessary conditions for the production of any narrative-mark, and the production of any irreducibly singular narrative-mark, or syntagm, necessarily depends upon the production of counter-narratives. Foucault's commentary on hegemonic discourse is equally applicable to the singular narrative-mark or syntagm:

> Their existence depends on a multiplicity of points of resistance: these play the role of adversary, target, support, or handle in power relations. These points of resistance are present everywhere in the power network. Hence there is no single locus of great refusal, no soul of revolt, source of all rebellions, or pure law of the revolutionary. Instead there is a plurality of resistances, each of them a special case.
>
> (pp.95–6)

This 'plurality of resistances' merely represents the network of differential relations, which place the singular narrative-mark within the non-saturable communal narrative-matrix. Contrapuntality is not an option: rather it is a necessary and aporetic condition of narrativity.

THE APORIA OF LITERATURE

The property of interminability sets up an exchange which both establishes the social process for the construction of subjectivity and ensures that the communal use of language does not atrophy into 'languageless' silence. Silence is the impossibility of meaning and the possibility of the termination of inter-subjective contiguity. It is these impossible conditions of the possibility of silence which compel the syntagmation of narrative exchange. 'Silence=Death', as the Act-Up slogan ran in the 1980s. However, this silence is not the end of the story; on the contrary it is the beginning. Silence is a necessary condition of the act of narrative production, it is – to paraphrase Maurice Blanchot – 'an opening onto a complexity yet to come'.[60] Benjamin observes that 'death is the sanction of everything the storyteller can tell', and it is the impossibility of the possibility of silence (the need to delay it and the figure of closure which moves towards it) that enables narrative production. Death is the aporia characteristic of narrative production. An aporia, according to Jameson, 'cannot be unknotted by the operation of pure thought, and which must therefore generate a whole more properly narrative apparatus – the text itself' (pp.82–3). An understanding of the operation of the aporias of writing would therefore seem to necessitate a return to narrative texts. It may seem a further paradox that after pushing, extending and undoing the definitions and methodologies of the discipline of narrative theory, I am now proposing a return to literary narratives. An explanation is in order.

Any linguistic act necessarily takes the form of a narrative-mark. However, what is identified through an institutional practice as 'literary narrative' represents a special object of study. The emergence of a 'truth-claim' within the inter-subjective use of language disguises the formal characteristics of narrative, as linguistic action, in the majority of social-praxis.[61] The ethical determination of 'truth' sets the limits of an imaginary figure of closure and so masks the narrative construction of ideologically motivated social discourse. It is in the cultural products of a linguistic community that narrative forms can be seen most clearly. The self-consciously 'fictional' status of literary narratives allows a display of the 'Fictional' process of the construction of subjectivity, which is disguised elsewhere. By 'Fictional' I mean that these processes are textually inscribed within the linguistic use of the communal narrative-matrix and are structured like a narrative. The use of a capitalised 'F' is an explicit attempt not to efface the difference between fictional and historical narratives, although as Ricoeur demonstrates, the two are aporetically linked. The suspended relation of reference which characterises literary narrative is not an aberrant event within inter-subjectivity but rather provides a blueprint for the process of narrative production, which constitutes the experience of inter-subjectivity itself. At this moment it may also be advisable to bear in mind Saussure's suggestion in the *Cours General* regarding the study of linguistic phenomena:

> Would matters be simplified if one considered the ontogenesis of linguistic phenomena, beginning with a study of children's language, for example? No. It is quite illusory to believe that where language is concerned the problem of origins is any different from the problem of permanent conditions. There is no way out of the circle.
>
> (p.9)

In other words, a theorisation of the aporetic conditions of narrative production would not necessarily be advanced by taking the previously defined minimally linguistic narrative-mark as its object of analysis. The conditions of narrative production, which could be identified by an examination of such marks, will also be discernible in 'literary-fictions'.[62] The use of the minimal definition of narrative has been the way in which it has directed my enquiry into an analysis of these necessary conditions.

If, as my argument implies, one can read any linguistic act as narrative, I would suggest that some textual events lend themselves to this better than others. These texts, one might say, have a greater narrative potential because their narrative performativity and formal narrative characteristics appear more obvious in the smallest possible space. These texts are of interest because they have much to say about their own status as narratives and therefore about their own conditions of production. However, any evaluation of these texts is only an evaluation inscribed in a context 'to positioned readings which are themselves formalising and performative', as Derrida says of literature.[63] In other words, the narrative potential of these texts is not hidden within them as an intrinsic property any more so than other textual events, but rather the choice of literary-fictions as an object of analysis is a condition of one's own position in the institutional practice of literary-narrative theory, which has a certain history and vocabulary of analysis. There are two points to be made here. First, literary-fictions are always in a relation of festival to their own processes. Indeed, it is a condition of the suspended relation to meaning and reference characteristic of literary narratives that these processes are thematised within the production of these texts. Therefore, literary-fictions are, to quote Derrida, 'a privileged guiding thread for access to the general structure of textuality' (p.71). Second, this privileging of literary-fictions is a result of an institutional practice which, in the first instance, identified the object of analysis 'narrative' as a socio-philosophical-linguistic concept (something more fundamental and atavistic than literature). This is not a criticism, it is an aporia.

NOTES

1   Roland Barthes, 'Introduction to the Structural Analysis of Narrative', trans. Stephen Heath, in *A Roland Barthes Reader*, ed. Susan Sontag (London: Vintage, 1994), pp.251–2. 'Introduction a l'analyse structurale des récits', in *Communiçations*, 8 (1966). See Section 2, this volume.

2   Jean-François Lyotard, *The Postmodern Condition: A Report on Knowledge*, trans. Geoffrey Bennington and Brian Massumi (Manchester: Manchester University Press, 1984), p. 23. See Section 3, this volume.

3   Andrew Bennett and Nicholas Royle, *An Introduction to Literature, Criticism and Theory: Key Critical Concepts* (London: Prentice Hall, 1995), p. 41. I recommend this chapter on narrative as a supplement to everything this volume has to say.

4   Teresa de Lauretis, 'Desire in Narrative', in *Alice Doesn't: Feminism, Semiotics, Cinema* (London: Macmillan, 1984), p.157. See Section 5, this volume.

5   Paul Ricoeur, *Time and Narrative* (vols. 1, 2, 3), trans. K. McLaughlin and D. Pellauer (London: University of Chicago Press, 1984, 1985, 1988). See Section 7, this volume.

6   A. J. Greimas, 'Debate with Paul Ricoeur', in Mario J. Valdés (ed.) *Reflection and Imagination: A Ricoeur Reader* (London: Harvester Wheatsheaf, 1991), p. 293.

7   Barbara Herrnstein Smith, 'Narrative Versions, Narrative Theories', in W. J. T. Mitchell (ed.) *On Narrative* (Chicago, IL: Chicago University Press, 1981). See Section 3, this volume.

8   Claude Bremond, quoted in Smith, 'Narrative Versions', p. 210.

9   Seymour Chatman, 'Reply to Barbara Herrnstein Smith', in W. J. T. Mitchell (ed.) *On Narrative*, p. 260.

10 As the narrator in Margaret Atwood's *The Handmaid's Tale* explains, 'one and one and one and one doesn't equal four. . . . Just one and one and one and one'. Each 'one' remains unique, there is no substitutive or combinative relation which does not efface the irreducibility of the object. She notes, 'they cannot be exchanged, one for the other. They cannot replace each other. Nick for Luke or Luke for Nick. *Should* does not apply.' Each version of lover or narrative is its own unique inscription. Margaret Atwood, *The Handmaid's Tale* (Virago: London, 1987), pp. 201–2.

11 Saussure warned in 1916, 'to think that there is an incorporeal syntax outside material units distributed in space would be a mistake.' Ferdinand de Saussure, *Course in General*

Linguistics, ed. Charles Balley *et al.*, trans. Wade Baskin (London: Fontana, 1974), p. 139. Just as this notion applies to the interrelation of the grammar of *langue* and the praxis of *parole*, so too 'narrative grammar' should not be thought of as existing prior to its textual inscription in a narrative praxis.

12 Ludwig Wittgenstein, *Philosophical Grammar* (Part III), in *The Essential Wittgenstien*, ed. Gerd Brand, trans. Richard Innis (Oxford: Blackwell, 1979), p. 3.

13 Peter Brooks, *Reading for the Plot: Design and Intention in Narrative* (New York: Knopf, 1984).p. 10. See Section 3, this volume.

14 Alan Singer, 'The Methods of Form: On Narrativity and Social Consciousness', *Substance*, 41 (1983), p. 72.

15 Fredric Jameson, *The Political Unconscious: Narrative as a Socially Symbolic Act* (Ithaca, NY: Cornell University Press, 1981), p. 13. See Section 8, this volume.

16 I am using Jakobson's terms 'paradigmatic' and 'syntagmatic'. 'Paradigmatic' refers to the naming function of differential reference within language, 'syntagmatic' corresponds to the syntactic function of contiguous meaning. For a full discussion of this terminology see Roman Jakobson, 'Closing Statement: Linguistics and Poetics', in Thomas Sebeok (ed.) *Style in Language* (Cambridge, MA: MIT Press, 1960).

17 Ludwig Wittgenstein, *Philosophical Investigations*, trans. G. E. M Anscombe (Oxford: Blackwell, 1968), p. 243.

18 Ludwig Wittgenstein, *Philosophical Grammar*, quoted in *The Essential Wittgenstein*, ed. Gerd Brand, p. 23.

19 Walter Benjamin, 'The Storyteller: Reflections on the Life of Nikolai Leskow', in *Illuminations*, ed. Hannah Arendt, trans. Harry Zohn (London: HarperCollins, 1992), p. 87. See Section 1, this volume.

20 Jakobson outlines this paradigm in 'The Emotive Element of Speech', in L.R Waugh *et al.* (eds) *Jakobson on Language* (London: Harvard University Press, 1990). Actors who auditioned for Stanislavskij's Moscow theatre were asked to perform the same signifier, '*segodnja vecrom*' [good evening], so that it had fifty different meanings.

21 Attempts to formulate a theory of narrative exterior to the novel include: William Labov and Joshua Waletzky, 'Narrative Analysis: Oral Versions of Personal Experience', in *Essays on the Verbal and Visual Arts* (Seattle: University of Washington Press, 1967); Vladimir Propp, *Morphology of the Folktale* (Austin: University of Texas Press, 1968); Erving Goffman, *Frame Analysis: An Essay on the Organization of Experience* (New York: Harper, 1974). However, all such attempts follow the categorisations associated with the analysis of literary narrative, consciously or otherwise, and certainly presuppose the prominence of literature *qua* model.

22 Alain Robbe-Grillet, *For a New Novel: Essays on Fiction*, trans. R. Howard (Illinois: Northwestern University Press, 1989), p.32.

23 Jacques Derrida, '"This Strange Institution Called Literature": An Interview with Jacques Derrida', in Derek Attridge (ed.) *Acts of Literature* (London: Routledge, 1992), p.71.

24 Jacques Derrida, 'Biodegradables: Seven Diary Fragments', trans. Peggy Kamuf. *Critical Inquiry*, 15(4), (1989), p. 841. See also Jacques Derrida, 'The End of the Book and the Beginning of Writing', in *Of Grammatology*, trans. Gayatri Chakravorty Spivak (Chicago, IL: Chicago University Press, 1976), p.158.

25 'The poetic function projects the principle of equivalence from the axis of selection into the axis of combination'. Roman Jakobson, 'Closing Statement', p.358.

26 Derrida, 'Living On: Border Lines', p.84.

27 Bakhtin and Medvedev suggest a similar reading of the relation between text and context in their 1928 book, *The Formal Method in Literary Scholarship*. They write:

> Every concrete utterance is a social act. At the same time that it is an individual material complex, a phonetic, articulatory, visual complex, the utterance is also a part of social reality. It organizes communication oriented toward reciprocal action, and itself reacts; it is also inseparably enmeshed in the communication event . . . Not only the meaning of the utterance but also the very fact of its performance is of historical and social significance.

(M.M Bakhtin and P.N Medvedev, *The Formal Method in Literary Scholarship: a Critical Introduction to Sociological Poetics*, trans. Albert J Wehrle (London: Johns Hopkins University Press, 1978), p.25.) Bakhtin suggests that the singularity of the text depends upon its performance within a historical and social context. It is the 'reciprocal action' of communication within such a context which determines signification for the text.

28 Jacques Derrida, 'Limited Inc', *Glyph* 2 (1977), p. 220.

29 If, as Derrida says, 'all meaningful marks are iterable', then as a consequence of iteration all marks are meaningful. Iteration is its own consequence and a necessary condition of meaning.

30 From now on I will use the terms 'narrative-context' to denote 'syntagmatic narrativised and narrativising context' and 'narrative-mark' will be used to denote 'paradigmatic constituted and constitutive narrative-mark'.

31 Jacques Derrida, *Aporias*, trans. T. Dutoit (Stanford, CA: Stanford University Press, 1993), p.20.

32 Jacques Derrida, *Given Time: 1. Counterfeit Money*, trans. Peggy Kamuf (London: University of Chicago Press, 1992), p.41.

33 Throughout my argument I will use the terms 'other' and 'Other' as translations of Lacan's '*objet petit a*' and '*grand Autre*'. Similarly, both terms should act as algebraic signs within a simulacra of exchange which simultaneously differentiates and relates the terms. However, when it becomes necessary to do so I will later identify the 'other' as a position within inter-subjectivity which the subject cannot occupy and subsequently with real people. The Other will remain as an understanding of Lacan's usage as an impossible position of signification, the locus of which is presupposed in any utterance and the relation to which is not a satisfaction of a need but a response to an appeal as a token of love.

34 Teresa de Lauretis, 'Desire in Narrative', p.112.

35 Peter Brooks, *Reading for the Plot*, p. 37.

36 Jacques Lacan, 'The Function and Field of Speech and Language in Psychoanalysis', in *Ecrits: a Selection*, trans. A. Sheridan (London: Routledge, 1995), p.86.

37 Jacques Lacan, 'The Freudian Thing' in *Ecrits*, p.141.

38 Jacques Lacan, 'Function and Field of Speech and Language', in *Ecrits*, p.86.

39 L. Wittgenstein, *Philosophical Investigations*, p.363.

40 Jacques Lacan, 'Function and Field', in *Ecrits*, p.85.

41 As Henri the diarist in Jeanette Winterson's novel, *The Passion* (London: Penguin, 1988), notes, 'I go on writing so that I will always have something to read' (p.159).

42 Jacques Lacan, 'The Direction of the Treatment and the Principles of its Power', in *Ecrits*,

p.257. Lacan is following Freud in 'A Case of Hysteria'. To liken the desire to produce narrative to the desire of the hysteric is perhaps to tempt a series of unwanted comparisons between this study of narrative and the substantial amount of work carried out in relation to hysteria. However, I use Lacan's formulation to suggest a related mechanics of desire.

43   Louis Althusser quoted in Fredric Jameson, *The Political Unconscious*, p.24.

44   Ursula K. Le Guin, 'It was a Dark and Stormy Night; or, Why are we Huddling about the Campfire', in W. J. T. Mitchell (ed.) *On Narrative*, p.188. See Section 3, this volume.

45   Walter Benjamin, 'The Storyteller', p.99.

46   Fredric Jameson, *The Political Unconscious*, pp. 26, 83.

47   Lawrence Sterne, *The Life and Opinions of Tristram Shandy, gentleman* (New York: Signet, 1960), p.230.

48   Maurice Blanchot, 'Literature and the Right to Death', in *The Work of Fire*, trans. Charlotte Mandell (Stanford, CA: Stanford University Press, 1995), p.342.

49   Atwood's narrator, whose story is itself a resistance to the dominant strand of a narration – 'We were the people who were not in the papers. We lived in the blank spaces at the edges of print. . . . We lived in the gaps between stories'(p.67) – believes that resistance is always present: 'there can be no light without shadow; or rather no shadow unless there is also light. . . . Whatever is silenced will clamour to be heard, though silently' (p.115).

50   Henry Louis Gates, 'Thirteen Ways of Looking at a Black Man', *New Yorker*, 23 October 1995, p.57. See Section 9, this volume.

51   Walter Benjamin, 'Thesis on the Philosophy of History', in Hannah Arendt (ed.), *Illuminations*, p. 248.

52   Edward Said, *Culture and Imperialism* (London: Chattos and Windus, 1993), p.78. See Section 9, this volume.

53   Lyotard hints at the necessary condition of the production of counternarrative through exclusion by tracing the etymology of 'what in Low Latin were called *narratiunculae*. That is what writing – including musical writing – is looking for: what is not inscribed.' J-F. Lyotard, 'God and the Puppet', in *The Inhuman: Reflections on Time*, trans. G. Bennington and R. Bowlby (Cambridge: Polity Press, 1991), p.158.

54   Lacan, 'The Agency of the Letter in the Unconscious', in *Ecrits*, p.196.

55   Roland Barthes, *The Rustle of Language*, trans. Richard Howard (London: Blackwell, 1986), p.311.

56   Fredric Jameson seems to concur in *The Political Unconscious* when he suggests: 'the *normal form* of the dialogical is essentially an antagonistic one, and that the dialogue of class struggle is one in which two opposing discourses fight it out *within the general unity of a shared code*, (p.84, my italics).

57   Michel Foucault, *The History of Sexuality: Volume 1, An Introduction* (London: Penguin, 1990), p.27. All page references to this monograph are hereafter contained in the text of this chapter.

58   Salman Rushdie, *Shame* (London: Pan, 1984), p.71.

59   Foucault suggests, 'Where there is power, there is resistance, and yet, or rather consequently, this resistance is never in a position of exteriority in relation to power.' *The History of Sexuality: Volume 1*, p.95.

60   Maurice Blanchot, 'The Language of Fiction', in *The Work of Fire*, p.75.

61   Lacan suggests that 'it is with the appearance of language the dimension of truth emerges.' 'The Agency of the Letter in the Unconscious', in *Ecrits*, p.172.

62   I am only too aware of the inadequacy of 'literary fiction' as a term to describe the texts

under consideration. Literature is an institutional practice with its own arbitrary criteria of definition: not all fictions are literary and not all literature is fictional. However, I will persist with this terminology (hereby signified by the hyphenated construction 'literary-fiction') as a way of stressing both the suspended relation of reference characteristic of such texts (fiction) and their implication within an institutional practice (literary). The same institutional practice gave rise to the discipline of narrative theory.

63   Jacques Derrida, 'That Strange Institution Called Literature', p.47.

I
openings

This arsenal like any other, will inevitably be out of date before many years have passed, and all the more quickly the more seriously it is taken, that is, debated, tested, and revised with time.

(Gérard Genette)

1
Form and Discourse

i CLASSICAL ANALYSIS

Plato, *The Republic*, Chapter XXV, 'The Allegory of the Cave'[*]

See also
Aristotle (1.i)
Benjamin (1.iii)
Smith (3.ii)
Gibson (3.ii)
Derrida (6)
Ricoeur (7)

Next, said I, here is a parable to illustrate the degrees in which our nature may be enlightened or unenlightened. Imagine the condition of men living in a sort of cavernous chamber underground, with an entrance open to the light and a long passage all down the cave. Here they have been from childhood, chained by the leg and also by the neck, so that they cannot move and can see only what is in front of them, because the chains will not let them turn their heads. At some distance higher up is the light of a fire burning behind them; and between the prisoners and the fire is a track with a parapet built along it, like the screen at a puppet-show, which hides the performers while they show their puppets over the top.

I see, said he.

Now behind this parapet imagine persons carrying along various artificial objects, including figures of men and animals in wood or stone or other materials, which project above the parapet. Naturally, some of these persons will be talking, others silent.

It is a strange picture, he said, and a strange sort of prisoners.

Like ourselves, I replied; for in the first place prisoners so confined would have seen nothing of themselves or of one another, except the shadows thrown by the fire-light on the wall of the Cave facing them, would they?

Not if all their lives they had been prevented from moving their heads.

And they would have seen as little of the objects carried past.

Of course.

Now, if they could talk to one another, would they not suppose that their words referred only to those passing shadows which they saw?

Necessarily.

[*] Oxford: Oxford University Press, 1941, trans. F. Cornford, pp. 222–6

And suppose their prison had an echo from the wall facing them? When one of the people crossing behind them spoke, they could only suppose that the sound came from the shadow passing before their eyes.

No doubt.

In every way, then, such prisoners would recognize as reality nothing but the shadows of those artificial objects.

Inevitably.

Now consider what would happen if their release from the chains and the healing of their unwisdom should come about in this way. Suppose one of them set free and forced suddenly to stand up, turn his head, and walk with eyes lifted to the light; all these movements would be painful, and he would be too dazzled to make out the objects whose shadows he had been used to see. What do you think he would say, if someone told him that what he had formerly seen was meaningless illusion, but now, being somewhat nearer to reality and turned towards more real objects, he was getting a truer view? Suppose further that he were shown the various objects being carried by and were made to say, in reply to questions, what each of them was. Would he not be perplexed and believe the objects now shown him to be not so real as what he formerly saw?

Yes, not nearly so real.

And if he were forced to look at the fire-light itself, would not his eyes ache, so that he would try to escape and turn back to the things which he could see distinctly, convinced that they really were clearer than these other objects now being shown to him?

Yes.

And suppose someone were to drag him away forcibly up the steep and rugged ascent and not let him go until he had hauled him out into the sunlight, would he not suffer pain and vexation at such treatment, and, when he had come out into the light, find his eyes so full of its radiance that he could not see a single one of the things that he was now told were real?

Certainly he would not see them all at once.

He would need, then, to grow accustomed before he could see things in that upper world. At first it would be easiest to make out shadows, and then the images of men and things reflected in water, and later on the things themselves. After that, it would be easier to watch the heavenly bodies and the sky itself by night, looking at the light of the moon and stars rather than the Sun and the Sun's light in the day-time.

Yes, surely.

Last of all, he would be able to look at the Sun and contemplate its nature, not as it appears when reflected in water or any alien medium, but as it is in itself in its own domain.

No doubt.

And now he would begin to draw the conclusion that it is the Sun that produces the seasons and the course of the year and controls everything in the visible world, and moreover is in a way the cause of all that he and his companions used to see.

Clearly he would come at last to that conclusion.

Then if he called to mind his fellow prisoners and what passed for wisdom in his former dwelling-place, he would surely think himself happy in the change and be sorry for them. They may have had a practice of honouring and commending one another, with prizes for the man who had the keenest eye for the passing shadows and the best memory for the order in which they followed or accompanied one another, so that he could make a good guess as to which was going to come next. Would our released prisoner be likely to covet those prizes or to envy the men exalted to honour and power in the Cave? Would he not feel like Homer's Achilles, that he would far sooner 'be on earth as a hired servant in the house of a landless man' or endure anything rather than go back to his old beliefs and live in the old way?

Yes, he would prefer any fate to such a life.

Now imagine what would happen if he went down again to take his former seat in the Cave. Coming suddenly out of the sunlight, his eyes would be filled with darkness. He might be required once more to deliver his opinion on those shadows, in competition with the prisoners who had never been released, while his eyesight was still dim and unsteady; and it might take some time to become used to the darkness. They would laugh at him and say that he had gone up only to come back with his sight ruined; it was worth no one's while even to attempt the ascent. If they could lay hands on the man who was trying to set them free and lead them up, they would kill him.

Yes, they would.

Every feature in this parable, my dear Glaucon, is meant to fit our earlier analysis. The prison dwelling corresponds to the region revealed to us through the sense of sight, and the firelight within it to the power of the Sun. The ascent to see the things in the upper world you may take as standing for the upward journey of the soul into the region of the intelligible; then you will be in possession of what I surmise, since that is what you wish to be told. Heaven knows whether it is true; but this, at any rate, is how it appears to me. In the world of knowledge, the last thing to be perceived and only with great difficulty is the essential Form of Goodness. Once it is perceived, the conclusion must follow that, for all things, this is the cause of whatever is right and good; in the visible world it gives birth to light and to the lord of light, while it is itself sovereign in the intelligible world and the parent of intelligence and truth. Without having had a vision of this Form no one can act with wisdom, either in his own life or in matters of state.

Aristotle, from *The Poetics*, 'Plot'*

See also:
Plato (1.i)
Genette (2.ii)
Culler (2.ii)
Barthes (2.iii)
Brooks (3.ii)
Derrida (6)
Miller (6)

* See T. S Dorsch (ed. and trans.), *Classical Literary Criticism: Aristotle, Horace, Longinus* (Harmondsworth: Penguin, 1965), pp. 38–45

A DESCRIPTION OF TRAGEDY

. . . . For the moment I propose to discuss tragedy, first drawing together the definition
of its essential character from what has already been said.

Tragedy, then, is a representation of an action that is worth serious attention,
complete in itself, and of some amplitude; in language enriched by a variety of artistic
devices appropriate to the several parts of the play; presented in the form of action, not
narration; by means of pity and fear bringing about the purgation of such emotions. By
language that is enriched I refer to language possessing rhythm, and music or song; and
by artistic devices appropriate to the several parts I mean that some are produced by the
medium of verse alone, and others again with the help of song.

Now since the representation is carried out by men performing the actions, it
follows, in the first place, that spectacle is an essential part of tragedy, and secondly
that there must be song and diction, these being the medium of representation. By diction
I mean here the arrangement of the verses; song is a term whose sense is obvious to
everyone.

In tragedy it is action that is imitated, and this action is brought about by agents
who necessarily display certain distinctive qualities both of character and of thought,
according to which we also define the nature of the actions. Thought and character are,
then, the two natural causes of actions, and it is on them that all men depend for success
or failure. The representation of the action is the plot of the tragedy; for the ordered
arrangement of the incidents is what I mean by plot. Character, on the other hand, is
that which enables us to define the nature of the participants, and thought comes out in
what they say when they are proving a point or expressing an opinion.

Necessarily, then, every tragedy has six constituents, which will determine its
quality. They are plot, character, diction, thought, spectacle, and song. Of these, two
represent the media in which the action is represented, one involves the manner of
representation, and three are connected with the objects of the representation; beyond
them nothing further is required. These, it may be said, are the dramatic elements that
have been used by practically all playwrights; for all plays alike possess spectacle,
character, plot, diction, song, and thought.

Of these elements the most important is the plot, the ordering of the incidents; for
tragedy is a representation, not of men, but of action and life, of happiness and
unhappiness – and happiness and unhappiness are bound up with action. The purpose
of living is an end which is a kind of activity, not a quality; it is their characters, indeed,
that make men what they are, but it is by reason of their actions that they are happy or
the reverse. Tragedies, are not performed, therefore, in order to represent character,
although character is involved for the sake of the action. Thus the incidents and the plot
are the end aimed at in tragedy, and as always, the end is everything. Furthermore,
there could not be a tragedy without action, but there could be without character; indeed
the tragedies of most of our recent playwrights fail to present character, and the same
might be said of many playwrights of other periods. A similar contrast could be drawn
between Zeuxis and Polygnotus as painters, for Polygnotus represents character well,
whereas Zeuxis is not concerned with it in his painting. Again, if someone writes a
series of speeches expressive of character, and well composed as far as thought and diction
are concerned, he will still not achieve the proper effect of tragedy; this will be done

much better by a tragedy which is less successful in its use of these elements, but which has a plot giving an ordered combination of incidents. Another point to note is that the two most important means by which tragedy plays on our feelings, that is, 'reversals' and 'recognitions', are both constituents of the plot. A further proof is that beginners can achieve accuracy in diction and the portrayal of character before they can construct a plot out of the incidents, and this could be said of almost all the earliest dramatic poets.

The plot, then, is the first essential of tragedy, its life-blood, so to speak, and character takes the second place. It is much the same in painting; for if an artist were to daub his canvas with the most beautiful colours laid on at random, he would not give the same pleasure as he would by drawing a recognizable portrait in black and white. Tragedy is the representation of an action, and it is chiefly on account of the action that it is also a representation of persons.

The third property of tragedy is thought. This is the ability to say what is possible and appropriate in any given circumstances; it is what, in the speeches in the play, is related to the arts of politics and rhetoric. The older dramatic poets made their characters talk like statesmen, whereas those of today make them talk like rhetoricians. Character is that which reveals personal choice, the kinds of thing a man chooses or rejects when that is not obvious. Thus there is no revelation of character in speeches in which the speaker shows no preferences or aversions whatever. Thought, on the other hand, is present in speeches where something is being shown to be true or untrue, or where some general opinion is being expressed.

Fourth comes the diction of the speeches. By diction I mean, as I have already explained, the expressive use of words, and this has the same force in verse and in prose.

Of the remaining elements, the music is the most important of the pleasurable additions to the play. Spectacle, or stage-effect, is an attraction, of course, but it has the least to do with the playwright's craft or with the art of poetry. For the power of tragedy is independent both of performance and of actors, and besides, the production of spectacular effects is more the province of the property-man than of the playwright.

THE SCOPE OF THE PLOT

Now that these definitions have been established, I must go on to discuss the arrangement of the incidents, for this is of the first importance in tragedy. I have already laid down that tragedy is the representation of an action that is complete and whole and of a certain amplitude – for a thing may be whole and yet lack amplitude. Now a whole is that which has a beginning, a middle, and an end. A beginning is that which does not necessarily come after something else, although something else exists or comes about after it. An end, on the contrary, is that which naturally follows something else either as a necessary or as a usual consequence, and is not itself followed by anything. A middle is that which follows something else, and is itself followed by something. Thus well-constructed plots must neither begin nor end in a haphazard way, but must conform to the pattern I have been describing.

Furthermore, whatever is beautiful, whether it be a living creature or an object made up of various parts, must necessarily not only have its parts properly ordered, but also be of an appropriate size, for beauty is bound up with size and order. A minutely small creature, therefore, would not be beautiful, for it would take almost no time to see it and our perception of it would be blurred; nor would an extremely large one, for it could not be taken in all at once, and its unity and wholeness would be lost to the view of the beholder – if, for example, there were a creature a thousand miles long.

Now in just the same way as living creatures and organisms compounded of many parts must be of a reasonable size, so that they can be easily taken in by the eye, so too plots must be of a reasonable length, so that they may be easily held in the memory. The limits in length to be observed, in as far as they concern performance on the stage, have nothing to do with dramatic art; for if a hundred tragedies had to be performed in the dramatic contests, they would be regulated in length by the water-clock, as indeed it is said they were at one time.[1] With regard to the limit set by the nature of the action, the longer the story is the more beautiful it will be, provided that it is quite clear. To give a simple definition, a length which, as a matter either of probability or of necessity, allows of a change from misery to happiness or from happiness to misery is the proper limit of length to be observed.

UNITY OF PLOT

A plot does not possess unity, as some people suppose, merely because it is about one man. Many things, countless things indeed, may happen to one man, and some of them will not contribute to any kind of unity; and similarly he may carry out many actions from which no single unified action will emerge. It seems, therefore, that all those poets have been on the wrong track who have written a *Heracleid*, or a *Theseid*, or some other poem of this kind, in the belief that, Heracles being a single person, his story must necessarily possess unity. Homer, exceptional in this as in all other respects, seems, whether by art or by instinct, to have been well aware of what was required. In writing his *Odyssey* he did not put in everything that happened to Odysseus, that he was wounded on Mount Parnassus, for example, or that he feigned madness at the time of the call to arms, for it was not a matter of necessity or probability that either of these incidents should have led to the other; on the contrary, he constructed the *Odyssey* round a single action of the kind I have spoken of, and he did this with the *Iliad* too. Thus, just as in the other imitative arts each individual representation is the representation of a single object, so too the plot of a play, being the representation of an action, must present it as a unified whole; and its various incidents must be so arranged that if any one of them is differently placed or taken away the effect of wholeness will be seriously disrupted. For if the presence or absence of something makes no apparent difference, it is no real part of the whole.

POETIC TRUTH AND HISTORICAL TRUTH

It will be clear from what I have said that it is not the poet's function to describe what has actually happened, but the kinds of thing that might happen, that is, that could happen because they are, in the circumstances, either probable or necessary. The difference between the historian and the poet is not that the one writes in prose and the other in verse; the work of Herodotus might be put into verse, and in this metrical form it would be no less a kind of history than it is without metre. The difference is that the one tells of what has happened, the other of the kinds of things that might happen. For this reason poetry is something more philosophical and more worthy of serious attention than history; for while poetry is concerned with universal truths, history treats of particular facts.

By universal truths are to be understood the kinds of thing a certain type of person will probably or necessarily say or do in a given situation; and this is the aim of poetry, although it gives individual names to its characters. The particular facts of the historian are what, say, Alcibiades did, or what happened to him. By now this distinction has become clear where comedy is concerned, for comic poets build up their plots out of probable occurrences, and then add any names that occur to them; they do not, like the iambic poets, write about actual people.[2] In tragedy, on the other hand, the authors keep to the names of real people, the reason being that what is possible is credible. Whereas we cannot be certain of the possibility of something that has not happened, what has happened is obviously possible, for it would not have happened if this had not been so. Nevertheless, even in some tragedies only one or two of the names are well known, and the rest are fictitious; and indeed there are some in which nothing is familiar, Agathon's *Antheus*, for example, in which both the incidents and the names are fictitious, and the play is none the less well liked for that. It is not necessary, therefore, to keep entirely to the traditional stories which form the subjects of our tragedies. Indeed it would be absurd to do so, since even the familiar stories are familiar only to a few, and yet they please everybody.

What I have said makes it obvious that the poet must be a maker of plots rather than of verses, since he is a poet by virtue of his representation, and what he represents is actions. And even if he writes about things that have actually happened, that does not make him any the less a poet, for there is nothing to prevent some of the things that have happened from being in accordance with the laws of possibility and probability, and thus he will be a poet in writing about them.

Of simple plots and actions those that are episodic are the worst. By an episodic plot I mean one in which the sequence of the episodes is neither probable nor necessary. Plays of this kind are written by bad poets because they cannot help it, and by good poets because of the actors; writing for the dramatic competitions, they often strain a plot beyond the bounds of possibility, and are thus obliged to dislocate the continuity of events.

However, tragedy is the representation not only of a complete action, but also of incidents that awaken fear and pity, and effects of this kind are heightened when things happen unexpectedly as well as logically, for then they will be more remarkable than if they seem merely mechanical or accidental. Indeed, even chance occurrences seem most remarkable when they have the appearance of having been brought about by design – when, for example, the statue of Mitys at Argos killed the man who had caused Mitys's death by falling down on him at a public entertainment. Things like this do not seem mere chance occurrences. Thus plots of this type are necessarily better than others.

SIMPLE AND COMPLEX PLOTS

Some plots are simple, and some complex, for the obvious reason that the actions of which they are representations are of one or other of these kinds. By a simple action

I refer to one which is single and continuous in the sense of my earlier definition, and in which the change of fortune comes about without a reversal or a discovery. A complex action is one in which the change is accompanied by a discovery or a reversal, or both. These should develop out of the very structure of the plot, so that they are the inevitable or probable consequence of what has gone before, for there is a big difference between what happens as a result of something else and what merely happens after it.

NOTES

1   There is no evidence elsewhere that this was ever done, and it seems an improbable proceeding. One is almost tempted to accept Schmidt's emendation (ειωθασιν for φασιν) and translate, 'as is regularly done at certain other times', i.e., with pleas in the law-courts.
2   The old iambic or lampooning poets, of whom the earliest and greatest was Archilochus (seventh century BC), wrote about real people, as did the poets of the Old Comedy, such as Aristophanes. In the New Comedy, of which Menander is the greatest representative, the names were stock names which, though they might sometimes by association or etymology have a certain appropriateness, were not those of real people.

ii TWENTIETH-CENTURY ANALYSIS

E. M. Forster, 'The Story' and 'The Plot'*

See also:
Aristotle (1.i)
Eco (2.iii)
Culler (2.ii)
Berger (3.iii)

We shall all agree that the fundamental aspect of the novel is its story-telling aspect, but we shall voice our assent in different tones, and it is on the precise tone of voice we employ now that our subsequent conclusions will depend.

Let us listen to three voices. If you ask one type of man, 'What does a novel do?' he will reply placidly: 'Well – I don't know – it seems a funny sort of question to ask – a novel's a novel – well, I don't know – I suppose it kind of tells a story, so to speak.' He is quite good-tempered and vague, and probably driving a motor-bus at the same time and paying no more attention to literature than it merits. Another man, whom I visualize as on a golf-course, will be aggressive and brisk. He will reply: 'What does a novel do? Why, tell a story of course, and I've no use for it if it didn't. I like a story. Very bad taste on my part, no doubt, but I like a story. You can take your art, you can take your literature, you can take your music, but give me a good story. And I like a story to be a story, mind, and my wife's the same.' And a third man, he says in a sort

---

* From *Aspects of the Novel* (Harmondsworth: Penguin, 1963), pp. 40–2 and 87.

of drooping regretful voice: 'Yes – oh dear yes – the novel tells a story.' I respect and admire the first speaker. I detest and fear the second. And the third is myself. Yes – oh dear yes – the novel tells a story. That is the fundamental aspect without which it could not exist. That is the highest factor common to all novels, and I wish that it was not so, that it could be something different – melody, or perception of the truth, not this low atavistic form.

For, the more we look at the story (the story that is a story, mind), the more we disentangle it from the finer growths that it supports, the less shall we find to admire. It runs like a backbone – or may I say a tapeworm, for its beginning and end are arbitrary. It is immensely old – goes back to neolithic times, perhaps to palaeolithic. Neanderthal man listened to stories, if one may judge by the shape of his skull. The primitive audience was an audience of shock-heads, gaping round the camp-fire, fatigued with contending against the mammoth or the woolly rhinoceros, and only kept awake by suspense. What would happen next? The novelist droned on, and as soon as the audience guessed what happened next they either fell asleep or killed him. We can estimate the dangers incurred when we think of the career of Scheherazade in somewhat later times. Scheherazade avoided her fate because she knew how to wield the weapon of suspense – the only literary tool that has any effect upon tyrants and savages. Great novelist though she was – exquisite in her descriptions, tolerant in her judgements, ingenious in her incidents, advanced in her morality, vivid in her delineations of character, expert in her knowledge of three oriental capitals – it was yet on none of these gifts that she relied when trying to save her life from her intolerable husband. They were but incidental. She only survived because she managed to keep the king wondering what would happen next. Each time she saw the sun rising she stopped in the middle of a sentence, and left him gaping. 'At this moment Scheherazade saw the morning appearing and, discreet, was silent.' This uninteresting little phrase is the backbone of the *One Thousand and One Nights*, the tapeworm by which they are tied together and the life of a most accomplished princess was preserved.

We are all like Scheherazade's husband, in that we want to know what happens next. That is universal and that is why the backbone of a novel has to be a story. Some of us want to know nothing else – there is nothing in us but primeval curiosity, and consequently our other literary judgements are ludicrous. And now the story can be defined. It is a narrative of events arranged in their time-sequence – dinner coming after breakfast, Tuesday after Monday, decay after death, and so on. Qua story, it can only have one merit: that of making the audience want to know what happens next. And conversely it can only have one fault: that of making the audience not want to know what happens next. These are the only two criticisms that can be made on the story that is a story. It is the lowest and simplest of literary organisms. Yet it is the highest factor common to all the very complicated organisms known as novels.

. . .

Let us define a plot. We have defined a story as a narrative of events arranged in their time-sequence. A plot is also a narrative of events, the emphasis falling on causality. 'The king died and then the queen died' is a story. 'The king died, and then the queen died of grief' is a plot. The time-sequence is preserved, but the sense of causality overshadows it. Or again: 'The queen died, no one knew why, until it was discovered that it was through grief at the death of the king.' This is a plot with a mystery in it, a form capable of high development. It suspends the time-sequence, it moves as far away from the story as its limitations will allow. Consider the death of the queen. If it is in a story we say: 'And then?' If it is in a plot we ask: 'Why?' That is the fundamental difference between these two aspects of the novel. A plot cannot be told to a gaping audience of cave-men or to a tyrannical sultan or to their modern descendant the movie-public. They can only be kept awake by 'And then – and then –' they can only supply curiosity. But a plot demands intelligence and memory also.

Walter Benjamin 'The Storyteller: Reflections on the works of Nikolai Leskov'*

See also:
Bronfen (4)
de Lauretis (5)
Jameson (8)
Kellner (8)
Minh-Ha (9)

I

. . . . The art of storytelling is coming to an end. Less and less frequently do we encounter people with the ability to tell a tale properly. More and more often there is embarrassment all around when the wish to hear a story is expressed. It is as if something that seemed inalienable to us, the securest among our possessions, were taken from us: the ability to exchange experiences.

One reason for this phenomenon is obvious: experience has fallen in value. And it looks as if it is continuing to fall into bottomlessness. Every glance at a newspaper demonstrates that it has reached a new low, that our picture, not only of the external world but of the moral world as well, overnight has undergone changes which were never thought possible. With the [First] World War a process began to become apparent which has not halted since then. Was it not noticeable at the end of the war that men returned from the battlefield grown silent – not richer, but poorer in communicable experience? What ten years later was poured out in the flood of war books was anything but experience that goes from mouth to mouth. And there was nothing remarkable about that. For never has experience been contradicted more thoroughly than strategic experience by tactical warfare, economic experience by inflation, bodily experience by mechanical warfare, moral experience by those in power. A generation that had gone to school on a horse-drawn streetcar now stood under the open sky in a countryside in which nothing remained unchanged but the clouds, and beneath these clouds, in a field of force of destructive torrents and explosions, was the tiny, fragile human body.

. . .

---

* From *Illuminations*, ed. H. Arendt, trans. H. Zohn (London: HarperCollins, 1992), pp. 83–107.

IV

An orientation toward practical interests is characteristic of many born storytellers. More pronouncedly than in Leskov this trait can be recognized, for example, in Gotthelf, who gave his peasants agricultural advice; it is found in Nodier, who concerned himself with the perils of gas light; and Hebel, who slipped bits of scientific instruction for his readers into his *Schatzkästlein*, is in this line as well. All this points to the nature of every real story. It contains, openly or covertly, something useful. The usefulness may, in one case, consist in a moral; in another, in some practical advice; in a third, in a proverb or maxim. In every case the storyteller is a man who has counsel for his readers. But if today 'having counsel' is beginning to have an old-fashioned ring, this is because the communicability of experience is decreasing. In consequence we have no counsel either for ourselves or for others. After all, counsel is less an answer to a question than a proposal concerning the continuation of a story which is just unfolding. To seek this counsel one would first have to be able to tell the story. (Quite apart from the fact that a man is receptive to counsel only to the extent that he allows his situation to speak.) Counsel woven into the fabric of real life is wisdom. The art of storytelling is reaching its end because the epic side of truth, wisdom, is dying out. This, however, is a process that has been going on for a long time. And nothing would be more fatuous than to want to see in it merely a 'symptom of decay,' let alone a 'modern' symptom. It is, rather, only a concomitant symptom of the secular productive forces of history, a concomitant that has quite gradually removed narrative from the realm of living speech and at the same time is making it possible to see a new beauty in what is vanishing.

V

The earliest symptom of a process whose end is the decline of storytelling is the rise of the novel at the beginning of modern times. What distinguishes the novel from the story (and from the epic in the narrower sense) is its essential dependence on the book. The dissemination of the novel became possible only with the invention of printing. What can be handed on orally, the wealth of the epic, is of a different kind from what constitutes the stock in trade of the novel. What differentiates the novel from all other forms of prose literature – the fairy tale, the legend, even the novella – is that it neither comes from oral tradition nor goes into it. This distinguishes it from storytelling in particular. The storyteller takes what he tells from experience – his own or that reported by others. And he in turn makes it the experience of those who are listening to his tale. The novelist has isolated himself. The birthplace of the novel is the solitary individual, who is no longer able to express himself by giving examples of his most important concerns, is himself uncounselled, and cannot counsel others. To write a novel means to carry the incommensurable to extremes in the representation of human life. In the midst of life's fullness, and through the representation of this fullness, the novel gives evidence of the profound perplexity of the living. Even the first great book of the genre, *Don Quixote*, teaches how the spiritual greatness, the boldness, the helpfulness of one of the noblest of men, Don Quixote, are completely devoid of counsel and do not contain the slightest scintilla of wisdom. If now and then, in the course of the centuries, efforts have been made – most effectively, perhaps, in *Wilhelm Meisters Wanderjahre* – to implant instruction in the novel, these attempts have always amounted to a modification of the novel form. The *Bildungsroman*, on the other hand, does not deviate in any way from the basic structure of the novel. By integrating the social process with the development of a person, it bestows the most frangible justification on the order determining it. The legitimacy it provides stands in direct opposition to reality. Particularly in the *Bildungsroman*, it is this inadequacy that is actualized.

VI

One must imagine the transformation of epic forms occurring in rhythms comparable to those of the change that has come over the earth's surface in the course of thousands of centuries. Hardly any other forms of human communication have taken shape more slowly, been lost more slowly. It took the novel, whose beginnings go back to antiquity, hundreds of years before it encountered in the evolving middle class those elements which were favourable to its flowering. With the appearance of these elements, storytelling began quite slowly to recede into the archaic; in many ways, it is true, it took hold of the new material, but it was not really determined by it. On the other hand, we recognize that with the full control of the middle class, which has the press as one of its most important instruments in fully developed capitalism, there emerges a form of communication which, no matter how far back its origin may lie, never before influenced the epic form in a decisive way. But now it does exert such an influence. And it turns out that it confronts storytelling as no less of a stranger than did the novel, but in a more menacing way, and that it also brings about a crisis in the novel. This new form of communication in information.

Villemessant, the founder of *Le Figaro*, characterized the nature of information in a famous formulation. 'To my readers,' he used to say, 'an attic fire in the Latin Quarter is more important than a revolution in Madrid.' This makes strikingly clear that it is no longer intelligence coming from afar, but the information which supplies a handle for what is nearest that gets the readiest hearing. The intelligence that came from afar – whether the spatial kind from foreign countries or the temporal kind of tradition – possessed an authority which gave it validity, even when it was not subject to verification. Information, however, lays claim to prompt verifiability. The prime requirement is that it appear 'understandable in itself.' Often it is no more exact than the intelligence of earlier centuries was. But while the latter was inclined to borrow from the miraculous, it is indispensable for information to sound plausible. Because of this it proves incompatible with the spirit of storytelling. If the art of storytelling has become rare, the dissemination of information has had a decisive share in this state of affairs.

Every morning brings us the news of the globe, and yet we are poor in noteworthy stories. This is because no event any longer comes to us without already being shot through with explanation. In other words, by now almost nothing that happens benefits storytelling; almost everything benefits information. Actually, it is half the art of storytelling to keep a story free from explanation as one reproduces it. Leskov is a master at this (compare pieces like 'The Deception' and 'The White Eagle'). The most extraordinary things, marvellous things, are related with the greatest accuracy, but the psychological connection of the events is not forced on the reader. It is left up to him to interpret things the way he understands them, and thus the narrative achieves an amplitude that information lacks.

. . .

VIII

There is nothing that commends a story to memory more effectively than that chaste compactness which precludes psychological analysis. And the more natural the process by which the storyteller forgoes psychological shading, the greater becomes the story's claim to a place in the memory of the listener, the more completely is it integrated into his own experience, the greater will be his inclination to repeat it to someone else someday, sooner or later. This process of assimilation, which takes place in depth, requires a state of relaxation which is becoming rarer and rarer. If sleep is the apogee of physical relaxation, boredom is the apogee of mental relaxation. Boredom is the dream bird that hatches the egg of experience. A rustling in the leaves drives him away. His nesting places – the activities that are intimately associated with boredom – are already extinct in the cities and are declining in the country as well. With this the gift for listening is lost and the community of listeners disappears. For storytelling is always the art of repeating stories, and this art is lost when the stories are no longer retained. It is lost because there is no more weaving and spinning to go on while they are being listened to. The more self-forgetful the listener is, the more deeply is what he listens to impressed upon his memory. When the rhythm of work has seized him, he listens to the tales in such a way that the gift of retelling them comes to him all by itself. This, then, is the nature of the web in which the gift of storytelling is cradled. This is how today it is becoming unravelled at all its ends after being woven thousands of years ago in the ambience of the oldest forms of craftsmanship.

. . .

XI

Death is the sanction of everything that the storyteller can tell. He has borrowed his authority from death. In other words, it is natural history to which his stories refer back. This is expressed in exemplary form in one of the most beautiful stories we have by the incomparable Johann Peter Hebel. It is found in the *Schatzkästlein des rheinischen Hausfreundes*, is entitled 'Unexpected Reunion,' and begins with the betrothal of a young lad who works in the mines of Falun. On the eve of his wedding he dies a miner's death at the bottom of his tunnel. His bride keeps faith with him after his death, and she lives long enough to become a wizened old woman; one day a body is brought up from the abandoned tunnel which, saturated with iron vitriol, has escaped decay, and she recognizes her betrothed. After this reunion she too is called away by death. When Hebel, in the course of this story, was confronted with the necessity of making this long period of years graphic, he did so in the following sentences: 'In the meantime the city of Lisbon was destroyed by an earthquake, and the Seven Years' War came and went, and Emperor Francis I died, and the Jesuit Order was abolished, and Poland was partitioned, and Empress Maria. Theresa died, and Struensee was executed. America became independent, and the united French and Spanish forces were unable to capture Gibraltar. The Turks locked up General Stein in the Veteraner Cave in Hungary, and Emperor Joseph died also. King Gustavus of Sweden conquered Russian Finland, and the French Revolution and the long war began, and Emperor Leopold II went to his grave too. Napoleon captured Prussia, and the English bombarded Copenhagen, and the peasants sowed and harvested. The millers ground, the smiths hammered, and the miners dug for veins of ore in their underground workshops. But when in 1809 the miners at Falun . . .'

Never has a storyteller embedded his report deeper in natural history than Hebel manages to do in this chronology. Read it carefully. Death appears in it with the same regularity as the Reaper does in the processions that pass around the cathedral clock at noon.

. . .

XIII

It has seldom been realized that the listener's naïve relationship to the storyteller is controlled by his interest in retaining what he is told. The cardinal point for the unaffected listener is to assure himself of the possibility of reproducing the story. Memory is the epic faculty *par excellence*. Only by virtue of a comprehensive memory can epic writing absorb the course of events on the one hand and, with the passing of these, make its peace with the power of death on the other. It is not surprising that to a simple man of the people, such as Leskov once invented, the Czar, the head of the sphere in which his stories take place, has the most encyclopedic memory at his command. 'Our Emperor,' he says, 'and his entire family have indeed a most astonishing memory.'

Mnemosyne, the rememberer, was the Muse of the epic art among the Greeks. This name takes the observer back to a parting of the ways in world history. For if the record kept by memory – historiography – constitutes the creative matrix of the various epic forms (as great prose is the creative matrix of the various metrical forms), its oldest form, the epic, by virtue of being a kind of common denominator includes the story and the novel. When in the course of centuries the novel began to emerge from the womb of the epic, it turned out that in the novel the element of the epic mind that is derived from the Muse – that is, memory – manifests itself in a form quite different from the way it manifests itself in the story.

Memory creates the chain of tradition which passes a happening on from generation to generation. It is the Muse-derived element of the epic art in a broader sense and encompasses its varieties. In the first place among these is the one practised by the storyteller. It starts the web which all stories together form in the end. One ties on to the next, as the great storytellers, particularly the Oriental ones, have always readily shown. In each of them there is a Scheherazade who thinks of a fresh story whenever her tale comes to a stop. This is epic remembrance and the Muse-inspired element of the narrative. But this should be set against another principle, also a Muse-derived element in a narrower sense, which as an element of the novel in its earliest form – that is, in the epic – lies concealed, still undifferentiated from the similarly derived element of the story. It can, at any rate, occasionally be divined in the epics, particularly at moments of solemnity in the Homeric epics, as in the invocations to the Muse at their beginning. What announces itself in these passages is the perpetuating remembrance of the novelist as contrasted with the short-lived reminiscences of the storyteller. The first is dedicated to *one* hero, *one* odyssey, *one* battle; the second, to *many* diffuse occurrences. It is, in other words, *remembrance* which, as the Muse-derived element of the novel, is added to reminiscence, the corresponding element of the story, the unity of their origin in memory having disappeared with the decline of the epic.

. . .

XV

A man listening to a story is in the company of the storyteller; even a man reading one shares this companionship. The reader of a novel, however, is isolated, more so than any other reader. (For even the reader of a poem is ready to utter the words, for the benefit of the listener.) In this solitude of his, the reader of a novel seizes upon his material more jealously than anyone else. He is ready to make it completely his own, to devour it, as it were. Indeed, he destroys, he swallows up the material as the fire devours logs in the fireplace. The suspense which permeates the novel is very much like the draft which stimulates the flame in the fireplace and enlivens its play.

It is a dry material on which the burning interest of the reader feeds. 'A man who dies at the age of thirty-five,' said Morits Heimann once, 'is at every point of his life a man who dies at the age of thirty-five.' Nothing is more dubious than this sentence – but for the sole reason that the tense is wrong. A man – so says the truth that was meant here – who died at thirty-five will appear to *remembrance* at every point in his life as a man who dies at the age of thirty-five. In other words, the statement that makes no sense for real life becomes indisputable for remembered life. The nature of the character in a novel cannot be presented any better than is done in this statement, which says that the 'meaning' of his life is revealed only in his death. But the reader of a novel actually does look for human beings from whom he derives the 'meaning of life.' Therefore he must, no matter what, know in advance that he will share their experience of death: if need be their figurative death – the end of the novel – but preferably their actual one. How do the characters make him understand that death is already waiting for them – a very definite death and at a very definite place? That is the question which feeds the reader's consuming interest in the events of the novel.

The novel is significant, therefore, not because it presents someone else's fate to us, perhaps didactically, but because this stranger's fate by virtue of the flame which consumes it yields us the warmth which we never draw from our own fate. What draws the reader to the novel is the hope of warming his shivering life with a death he reads about.

XVI

'Leskov,' writes Gorky, 'is the writer most deeply rooted in the people and is completely untouched by any foreign influences. A great storyteller will always be rooted in the people, primarily in a milieu of craftsmen. But just as this includes the rural, the maritime, and the urban elements in the many stages of their economic and technical development, there are many gradations in the concepts in which their store of experience comes down to us. (To say nothing of the by no means insignificant share which traders had in the art of storytelling; their task was less to increase its didactic content than to refine the tricks with which the attention of the listener was captured. They have left deep traces in the narrative cycle of *The Arabian Nights*.) In short, despite the primary role which storytelling plays in the household of humanity, the concepts through which the yield of the stories may be garnered are manifold. What may most readily be put in religious terms in Leskov seems almost automatically to fall into place in the pedagogical perspectives of the Enlightenment in Hebel, appears as hermetic tradition in Poe, finds a last refuge in Kipling in the life of British seamen and colonial soldiers. All great storytellers have in common the freedom with which they move up and down the rungs of their experience as on a ladder. A ladder extending downward to the interior of the earth and disappearing into the clouds is the image for a collective experience to which even the deepest shock of every individual experience, death, constitutes no impediment or barrier.

'And they lived happily ever after,' says the fairy tale. The fairy tale, which to this day is the first tutor of children because it was once the first tutor of mankind, secretly lives on in the story. The first true storyteller is, and will continue to be, the teller of fairy tales. Whenever good counsel was at a premium, the fairy tale had it, and where the need was greatest, its aid was nearest. This need was the need created by the myth. The fairy tale tells us of the earliest arrangements that mankind made to shake off the nightmare which the myth had placed upon its chest. In the figure of the fool it shows us how mankind 'acts dumb' toward the myth; in the figure of the youngest brother it shows us how one's chances increase as the mythical primitive times are left behind; in the figure of the man who sets out to learn what fear is it shows us that the things we are afraid of can be seen through; in the figure of the wiseacre it shows us that the questions posed by the myth are simple-minded, like the riddle of the Sphinx; in the shape of the animals which come to the aid of the child in the fairy tale it shows that nature not only is subservient to the myth, but much prefers to be aligned with man. The wisest thing – so the fairy tale taught mankind in olden times, and teaches children to this day – is to meet the forces of the mythical world with cunning and with high spirits. (This is how the fairy tale polarizes *Mut*, courage, dividing it dialectically into *Untermut*, that is, cunning, and *Übermut*, high spirits.) The liberating magic which the fairy tale has at its disposal does not bring nature into play in a mythical way, but points to its complicity with liberated man. A mature man feels this complicity only occasionally, that is, when he is happy; but the child first meets it in fairy tales, and it makes him happy.

. . .

In fact, one can go on and ask oneself whether the relationship of the storyteller to his material, human life, is not in itself a craftsman's relationship, whether it is not his very task to fashion the raw material of experience, his own and that of others, in a solid, useful, and unique way. It is a kind of procedure which may perhaps most adequately be exemplified by the proverb if one thinks of it as an ideogram of a story. A proverb, one might say, is a ruin which stands on the site of an old story and in which a moral twines about a happening like ivy around a wall.

Seen in this way, the storyteller joins the ranks of the teachers and sages. He has counsel – not for a few situations, as the proverb does, but for many, like the sage. For it is granted to him to reach back to a whole lifetime (a life, incidentally, that comprises not only his own experience but no little of the experience of others; what the storyteller knows from hearsay is added to his own). His gift is the ability to relate his life; his distinctions to be able to tell his entire life. The storyteller: he is the man who could let the wick of his life be consumed completely by the gentle flame of his story. This is the basis of the incomparable aura about the storyteller, in Leskov as in Hauff, in Poe as in Stevenson. The storyteller is the figure in which the righteous man encounters himself.

Mikhail Bakhtin, from *The Dialogic Imagination**

Forms of Time and of the Chronotope in the Novel
Notes toward a Historical Poetics

See also:
Propp (1.iii)
Shlovsky (1.iii)
Tomashevsky (1.iii)
Lévi-Strauss (2.i)
Heath (4)
Miller (6)
Ricoeur (7)
Jameson (8)
Said (9)

The process of assimilating real historical time and space in literature has a complicated and erratic history, as does the articulation of actual historical persons in such a time and space. Isolated aspects of time and space, however – those available in a given historical stage of human development – have been assimilated and corresponding generic techniques have been devised for reflecting and artistically processing such appropriated aspects of reality.

We will give the name *chronotope* (literally, 'time space') to the intrinsic connectedness of temporal and spatial relationships that are artistically expressed in literature. This term [space-time] is employed in mathematics, and was introduced as part of Einstein's Theory of Relativity. The special meaning it has in relativity theory is not important for our purposes; we are borrowing it for literary criticism almost as a metaphor (almost, but not entirely). What counts for us is the fact that it expresses the inseparability of space and time (time as the fourth dimension of space). We understand the chronotope as a formally constitutive category of literature; we will not deal with the chronotope in other areas of culture.[1]

In the literary artistic chronotope, spatial and temporal indicators are fused into one carefully thought-out, concrete whole. Time, as it were, thickens, takes on flesh, becomes artistically visible; likewise, space becomes charged and responsive to the movements of time, plot and history. This intersection of axes and fusion of indicators characterizes the artistic chronotope.

The chronotope in literature has an intrinsic *generic* significance. It can even be said that it is precisely the chronotope that defines genre and generic distinctions, for in literature the primary category in the chronotope is time. The chronotope as a formally

* *The Dialogic Imagination: Four Essays by M. M. Bakhtin*, trans. Caryl Emerson and Michael Holquist (Austin: University of Texas Press, 1994), pp. 84–5, 243–7, 250.

constitutive category determines to a significant degree the image of man in literature as well. The image of man is always intrinsically chronotopic.[2]

As we have said, the process of assimilating an actual historical chronotope in literature has been complicated and erratic; certain isolated aspects of the chronotope, available in given historical conditions, have been worked out, although only certain specific forms of an actual chronotope were reflected in art. These generic forms, at first productive, were then reinforced by tradition; in their subsequent development they continued stubbornly to exist, up to and beyond the point at which they had lost any meaning that was productive in actuality or adequate to later historical situations. This explains the simultaneous existence in literature of phenomena taken from widely separate periods of time, which greatly complicates the historico-literary process.

. . .

CONCLUDING REMARKS

A literary work's artistic unity in relationship to an actual reality is defined by its chronotope. Therefore the chronotope in a work always contains within it an evaluating aspect that can be isolated from the whole artistic chronotope only in abstract analysis. In literature and art itself, temporal and spatial determinations are inseparable from one another, and always colored by emotions and values. Abstract thought can, of course, think time and space as separate entities and conceive them as things apart from the emotions and values that attach to them. But *living* artistic perception (which also of course involves thought, but not abstract thought) makes no such divisions and permits no such segmentation. It seizes on the chronotope in all its wholeness and fullness. Art and literature are shot through with *chronotopic values* of varying degree and scope. Each motif, each separate aspect of artistic work bears value.

In these chapters we have analyzed only the major chronotopes that endure as types and that determine the most important generic variations on the novel in the early stages of its development. As we draw our essay to a close we will simply list, and merely touch upon, certain other chronotopic values having different degree and scope.

In the first chapter we mentioned the chronotope of encounter; in such a chronotope the temporal element predominates, and it is marked by a higher degree of intensity in emotions and values. The chronotope of the *road* associated with encounter is characterized by a broader scope, but by a somewhat lesser degree of emotional and evaluative intensity. Encounters in a novel usually take place 'on the road.' The road is a particularly good place for random encounters. On the road ('the high road'), the spatial and temporal paths of the most varied people – representatives of all social classes, estates, religions, nationalities, ages – intersect at one spatial and temporal point. People who are normally kept separate by social and spatial distance can accidentally meet; any contrast may crop up, the most various fates may collide and interweave with one another. On the road the spatial and temporal series defining human fates and lives combine with one another in distinctive ways, even as they become more complex and more concrete by the collapse of *social distances*. The chronotope of the road is both a point of new departures and a place for events to find their denouement. Time, as it were, fuses together with space and flows in it (forming the road); this is the source of the rich metaphorical expansion on the image of the road as a course: 'the course of a life,' 'to set out on a new course,' 'the course of history' and so on; varied and multi-leveled are the ways in which road is turned into a metaphor, but its fundamental pivot is the flow of time.

The road is especially (but not exclusively) appropriate for portraying events governed by chance. This explains the important narrative role of the road in the history of the novel. A road passes through the ancient everyday novel of wandering, through Petronius' *Satyricon* and Apuleius' *Golden Ass*. Heroes of medieval chivalric romances set out on the road, and it often happens that all the events of a novel either take place on the road or are concentrated along the road (distributed on both sides of it).

And in such a novel as Wolfram von Eschenbach's *Parzival*, the hero's real-life course or path to Montsalvat passes imperceptibly into a metaphor of the road, life's course, the course of the soul that now approaches God, now moves away from Him (depending on the mistakes and failings of the hero and on the events that he encounters in the course of his real life). The road is what determined the plots of the Spanish picaresque novel of the sixteenth century (*Lazarillo* and *Guzman de Alfarache*). On the boundary line between the sixteenth and seventeenth centuries, Don Quixote sets out on the road in order that he might encounter all of Spain on that road – from galley-slaves to dukes. By this time the road had been profoundly, intensely etched by the flow of historical time, by the traces and signs of time's passage, by markers of the era. In the seventeenth century, Simplicissimus sets out on a road rutted by the events of the Thirty Years War. This road stretches onward, always maintaining its significance as major artery, through such critical works in the history of the novel as Sorel's *Francion* and Lesage's *Gil Blas*. The importance of the road is retained (although weakened) in Defoe's (picaresque) novels, and in Fielding. The road and encounters on the road remain important in both Wilhelm Meister's *Lehrejahre* and *Wanderjahre* (although here their ideological sense is substantially changed, since the concepts of 'chance' and 'fate' have been radically reinterpreted). Novalis' Heinrich von Ofterdingen and other heroes of the Romantic novel set out on a road that is half-real, half-metaphorical. Finally, the road and encounters on it are important in the historical novel. Zagoskin's *Yury Miloslavsky*,[3] for example, is structured around the road and road encounters. Grinev's meeting Pugachev on the road in a snowstorm determines the plot in *The Captain's Daughter*. We recall as well the role of the road in Gogol's *Dead Souls* and Nekrasov's 'Who Lives Well in Russia.'

Without touching here upon the question of the changing functions of the 'road' and 'encounter' in the history of the novel, we will mention but one crucial feature of the 'road' common to all the various types of novels we have covered: the road is always one that passes through *familiar territory*, and not through some exotic *alien world* (Gil Blas' 'Spain' is artificial, and Simplicissimus' temporary stay in France is also artificial, since the foreignness of this foreign country is illusory, there is not a trace of the exotic); it is the *sociohistorical heterogeneity* of one's own country that is revealed and depicted (and for this reason, if one may speak at all about the exotic here, then it can only be the 'social exotic' – 'slums,' 'dregs,' the world of thieves). This function of the 'road' was exploited outside the novel as well, in such nonnarrative genres as journalistic accounts of travel in the eighteenth century (the classic example is Radishchev's *Journey from Petersburg to Moscow*), and in the journalistic travel notes of the first half of the nineteenth century (for example, Heine's). The peculiarity of the 'road' serves to distinguish these novels from that other line of development present in the novel of travel, represented by such novelistic types as the ancient novel of wandering, the Greek Sophist novel (to whose analysis we have devoted the first part of this essay) and the Baroque novel of the seventeenth century. In these novels, a function analogous to the road is played by an 'alien world' separated from one's own narrative land by sea and distance.

Toward the end of the seventeenth century in England, a new territory for novelistic events is constituted and reinforced in the so-called 'Gothic' or 'black' novel – the *castle* (first used in this meaning by Horace Walpole in *The Castle of Otranto*, and later in Radcliffe, Monk Lewis and others). The castle is saturated through and through with a time that is historical in the narrow sense of the word, that is, the time of the historical past. The castle is the place where the lords of the feudal era lived (and consequently also the place of historical figures of the past); the traces of centuries and generations are arranged in it in visible form as various parts of its architecture, in furnishings, weapons, the ancestral portrait gallery, the family archives and in the particular human relationships involving dynastic primacy and the transfer of hereditary rights. And finally legends and traditions animate every corner of the castle and its environs through their constant reminders of past events. It is this quality that gives rise to the specific kind of narrative inherent in castles and that is then worked out in Gothic novels.

The historicity of castle time has permitted it to play a rather important role in the development of the historical novel. The castle had its origins in the distant past; its orientation is toward the past. Admittedly the traces of time in the castle do bear a somewhat antiguated, museum-like character. Walter Scott succeeded in overcoming the danger of excessive antiquarianism by relying heavily on the legend of the castle, on the link between the castle and its historically conceived, comprehensible setting. The organic cohesion of spatial and temporal aspects and categories in the castle (and its environs), the historical intensity of this chronotope, is what had determined its productivity as a source for images at different stages in the development of the historical novel.

In the novels of Stendhal and Balzac a fundamentally new space appears in which novelistic events may unfold – the space of parlors and salons (in the broad sense of the word). Of course this is not the first appearance of such space, but only in these texts does it achieve its full significance as the place where the major spatial and temporal sequences of the novel intersect. From a narrative and compositional point of view, this is the place where encounters occur (no longer emphasizing their specifically random nature as did meetings 'on the road' or 'in an alien world'). In salons and parlors the webs of intrigue are spun, denouements occur and finally – this is where *dialogues* happen, something that acquires extraordinary importance in the novel, revealing the character, 'ideas' and 'passions' of the heroes.

The narrative and compositional importance of this is easy to understand. In the parlors and salons of the Restoration and July Monarchy is found the barometer of political and business life; political business, social, literary reputations are made and destroyed, careers are begun and wrecked, here are decided the fates of high politics and high finance as well as the success or failure of a proposed bill, a book, a play, a minister, a courtesan-singer; here in their full array (that is, brought together in one place at one time) are all the gradations of the new social hierarchy; and here, finally, there unfold forms that are concrete and visible, the supreme power of life's new king – money.

Most important in all this is the weaving of historical and socio-public events together with the personal and even deeply private side of life, with the secrets of the boudoir; the interweaving of petty, private intrigues with political and financial intrigues, the interpenetration of state with boudoir secrets, of historical sequences with the everyday and biographical sequences. Here the graphically visible markers of historical time as well as of biographical and everyday time are concentrated and condensed; at the same time they are intertwined with each other in the tightest possible fashion, fused into unitary markers of the epoch. The epoch becomes not only graphically visible [space], but narratively visible [time].

. . .

What is the significance of all these chronotopes? What is most obvious is their meaning for *narrative*. They are the organizing centers for the fundamental narrative events of the novel. The chronotope is the place where the knots of narrative are tied and untied. It can be said without qualification that to them belongs the meaning that shapes narrative.

We cannot help but be strongly impressed by the *representational* importance of the chronotope. Time becomes, in effect, palpable and visible; the chronotope makes narrative events concrete, makes them take on flesh, causes blood to flow in their veins. An event can be communicated, it becomes information, one can give precise data on the place and time of its occurrence. But the event does not become a figure [*obraz*]. It is precisely the chronotope that provides the ground essential for the showing-forth, the representability of events. And this is so thanks precisely to the special increase in density and concreteness of time markers – the time of human life, of historical time – that occurs within well-delineated spatial areas. It is this that makes it possible to structure a representation of events in the chronotope (around the chronotope). It serves as the primary point from which 'scenes' in a novel unfold, while at the same time other 'binding' events, located far from the chronotope, appear as mere dry information and communicated facts (in Stendhal, for instance, informing and communicating carry great weight; representation is concentrated and condensed in a few scenes and these scenes cast a light that makes even the 'informing' parts of the novel seem more concrete – cf., for example, the structure of *Armance*). Thus the chronotope, functioning as the primary means for materializing time in space, emerges as a center for concretizing representation, as a force giving body to the entire novel. All the novel's abstract elements – philosophical and social generalizations, ideas, analyses of cause and effect – gravitate toward the chronotope and through it take on flesh and blood, permitting the imaging power of art to do its work. Such is the representational significance of the chronotope.

NOTES

1   In the summer of 1925, the author of these lines attended a lecture by A. A. Uxtomskij on the chronotype in biology; in the lecture questions of aesthetics were also touched upon.

2   In his 'Transcendental Aesthetics' (one of the main sections of his *Critique of Pure Reason*) Kant defines space and time as indispensable forms of any cognition, beginning with elementary perceptions and representations. Here we employ the Kantian evaluation of the importance of these forms in the cognitive process, but differ from Kant in taking them not as 'transcendental' but as forms of the most immediate reality. We shall attempt to show

the role these forms play in the process of concrete artistic cognition (artistic visualization) under conditions obtaining in the genre of the novel.

3   *Yury Miloslavsky* (1829) is a historical novel about the Polish occupation of Moscow in 1612. Its author, M. N. Zagoskin (1789–1852), while far from being in the same class as his idol Walter Scott, did help to create a vogue for historical romance.

Vladimir Propp, 'Oedipus in the Light of Folklore'*

See also:
Bakhtin (1.iii)
Shlovsky (1.iii)
Tomashevsky (1.iii)
Levi-Strauss (2.i)
Barthes (2.iii)
Eco (2.iii)
Mulvey (4)
de Lauretis (5)

1   METHODOLOGICAL PRECONDITIONS

One of the most important tasks of 'folklorology' is to compare folklore with historical reality. The task, however, is not just to reveal some correspondence between particular elements of folklore and events of our historical past; it is to find the reasons which bring the folklore itself (and its particular plots) to life. This is comparatively easy if a plot directly reflects this past. For example, a comparison of the heroes' match-making with forms of marriage, which existed in the past, is relatively simple. In many cases it is possible to show that the forms of match-making in folklore correspond to the forms of marriage, which existed historically, but which later fell out of use. Our task is complicated when we come across folklore motifs and plots, which are not directly related to any historical reality: winged horses, magic pipes, colliding mountains, one-eyed giants, and so on. The past here is either obscured and deformed, or, the motif is based on some thought process, which has not been studied and understood sufficiently.

The extensive study of the historical development of folklore shows that in cases where history produces new forms of life, new economic achievements, new forms of social relations (and these changes penetrate folklore), older forms do not always die off or become replaced by new ones. The old continues to coexist with the new, either simultaneously or by creating different hybrid combinations (impossible in nature or in history) with it. Giving the impression of pure fiction, they nevertheless appear independently from each other, wherever the historic transformations, which call them into being, take place. For example, the winged horse is the combination of a bird and a horse, which appears at a time when the horse had been domesticated and the cult role of the bird was transferred from bird to horse. Any similar observation must be proven by extensive analysis of factual, historical and folklore sources. Let us consider another example: a popular tale tells of a hero who sees a house in the wood. There is

---

* 'Edip v svete fol'klora', *Serija filogiceskich nauk*, 9 (72) (1944), pp. 138–75.

no door and it is impossible to enter the house, but he sees 'a little door, hardly noticeable, in a small pillar'[1] and enters the house through it. What has happened here? Buildings constructed on piles and pillars existed at this time, such buildings can be traced effectively in popular tales.[2] Historically, these raised buildings were later replaced by ordinary ones with ground-level entrances. Their replacement leads to this combination in the imagination (the transfer of the new to the old). The door is transferred on to the pillar, with the resultant image of the door in the pillar. Indeed, the same process is constantly reflected in art, everyday life, and in language.[3]

As Marr shows, the deer, as the earliest riding animal, gave way to the horse. This material replacement results in the combination of the two in human consciousness, the deer meets the horse and forms a hybrid figure of deer and horse. Although such a combination is impossible in nature, the hybrid mental image of deer and horse is so 'realistic' and powerful that it is transferred to reality and is created artificially. Marr did not yet know that deer antlers were in fact put on horses, and such horses, adorned with deers antlers, were ridden. A statue of a horse with such decorations is on display in the Hermitage in St Petersburg. When researching phenomena like this, it is necessary to determine what collides with what, and which figures are produced. Such hybridity not only underpins separate words or visual images in everyday speech or folklore, it can also explain motifs, plot situations and entire plots. In particular, a similar hybrid figure forms the basis of the plot about a hero, who kills his father and marries his mother.

2 THE CHARACTER OF OEDIPUS IN FOLKLORE

The scope of this study does not embrace all of the problems connected with Oedipus. This would require extensive research, the proposition here is more modest: to trace the collisions of historic contradictions reflected in the Oedipal plot. There is a vast literature on Oedipus. However, these works cannot satisfy us. So far, no summary of all the existing material is available and present research is currently being done on limited, rather than comparative, folklore material. Secondly, this work cannot satisfy us in terms of its research method or by the problems broached in it. If we leave aside Freudian works and work undertaken in the spirit of the mythological school, then the main question widely discussed in science is whether this plot is borrowed from antiquity or not. But this question does not resolve the fundamental issue. Even if the borrowing (or its absence) can be finally established, this does not solve the problem of the origin of this plot.

In order to answer this question, sources from one or two cultures will not be enough; all of the existing material will have to be used. In folklore the Oedipal plot is available in the form of a popular tales, legends, epic songs, lyrical songs and popular books. Apart from this, in the literature which has a 'quasi-folklore' character, it takes the form of tragedy, drama, poetry, and short stories. It is known by all European peoples and also in Africa (Zulu) and Mongolia. The list of sources is so vast that it can hardly be accounted for in a small article such as this: a survey of the material could become the subject of a special historical and literary inquiry. The indices of the fairy-tale stories provide two types (931 and 933) of plot. In fact, four plot-types can be identified, into which all European material fits. These types are as follows.

Versions of the legend of Andrew of Crete always start with a prophecy. The hero is set adrift at sea and brought up in a monastery or by ship-wrights or fisherman, etc. He learns that he is a foundling and leaves his educator. He applies for a job guarding the orchard of his parents' household; kills his father, who comes to check up on him, and subsequently marries his widow. Discovering the truth, he takes or imposes a penance on himself: he finds redemption underground (burying himself in a well, etc.). When he is remembered about, he is already dead, but he has become a saint or he dies a saint, completing his famous canon – the canon of Andrew of Crete. This is the most complete version of the plot and the closest one to Oedipus, with one exception: the hero does not ascend the throne. This version is told only in Russia, the Ukraine, Byelorussia and, in a somewhat abridged and different form, among Serbs.

The story of Judas develops initially in the same way to that of Andrew of Crete. When living with his teacher, he kills his stepbrother and runs away. Unlike Andrew of Crete, he is sometimes raised in a royal environment, having been found by a queen. In his native land, he applies to the governor of his home town, usually Pilate, for a job. In order to please him, he steals apples from the orchard of his father. Caught at the scene of his crime, he kills his father. He marries his father's widow, and on discovering the truth he joins Jesus Christ as his apostle. This version is very close to that of Andrew of Crete and differs from it only by its details, its end, and the interpretation of the hero as a villain.

The story of St Gregory begins with an incestuous marriage between a brother and a sister. A child is born and sent away, the child's father then goes to Jerusalem to pray for forgiveness and dies there. The place of the hero's upbringing is subject to significant variations. Having learned about his origins, he seeks his parents. As a rule, Gregory marries a queen, whom he frequently liberates from her oppressors. His father's death, which occurred in the past, eliminates patricide from the plot. Gregory ascends the throne (though a bourgeois telling of the plot exists as well). On discovering the truth, he (unlike Andrew of Crete) does not bury himself, but becomes a hermit in a cave on an island. He is later found and elected Pope. The glory of his holiness spreads all over the world and reaches his mother. She comes to him to confess and they recognise each other. This version is typical of the Catholic West and Poland. It is also told among Czechs and among Russians in the manuscript tradition.

Stories of St Alban begin with the incestuous marriage between a king and his daughter. The boy is taken to a foreign land and is left by the roadside. The beggars who find him bring him to the king of this country. He is brought up and remains here. The king takes him for his son and marries him to the daughter of a neighbouring king and then dies. This king's daughter is none other than the boy's mother. But because he is born from the incestuous marriage between a father and a daughter, his wife is simultaneously his mother and his sister, while his father is simultaneously his grandfather and the father of his mother. When the truth is discovered, his wife summons her father, and all three flee into the desert. However, the devil once more tempts the old father and again he sins with his daughter. The young son catches and kills both of his parents, and runs into the desert. He later becomes a saint and his dead body is said to work miracles. This version is somewhat rare and only prevails in Latin manuscripts, not the folklore tradition. However, it also echoes the One Thousand and One Nights.

Even this brief account of the subject is enough to come to the conclusion that the European tradition of folklore combines not only *Oedipus Rex* but also *Oedipus at Colonus*. The hero flees to a cave, under the ground, to the grave, or becomes a saint. While *Oedipus Rex* gives rise to an extensive literature, the connection between European folk sources and *Oedipus at Colonus* has gone completely unnoticed. We will examine the whole plot, motif after motif, using the method established above. The plot does not appear to be a direct reflection of a social structure, it emerges from collision, from the contradiction of structures which displace one another. Our main task is to trace those contradictions, to trace what collides with what historically, and to analyse how this collision produces the plot. To respond to this problem we will make use of all the known sources related to this plot, and also of the idea of the fairy-tale as such, since 'Oedipus', in terms of composition, is a typical fairy-tale.

[Propp presents ten further sections each treating a structurally necessary component of the tale. Section 11 and part of Section 12 are translated below.]

3   Prophecy
4   Parents' marriage
5   The sending away of a baby
6   Raising a baby
7   Exile
8   Sphinx
9   Patricide and marriage
10   The first apotheosis of Oedipus

11   DISCLOSURE

Disclosure begins: the last act of Oedipus' poetic biography and the first act of the tragedy. The folklore-epic tradition demonstrates the primordial form of disclosure. In the fairy-tale, disclosure takes place in a simple way and is limited to two or three lines. The 'incester' on his nuptial bed is recognised by: scars on his stomach and neck, by the brand on his foot, by an icon, or by the Gospel put in his basket, or even by the basket itself, which he always carries with him (like Pelius and Neleus in Sophocles' lost tragedy *Tiro*). Zelinsky remarks that Pelius, 'by some reasons unknown to us', brings with him a trough in which he, together with his brother, was found by his adoptive father. In such circumstances it is necessary to speak, not of reasons, but of poetic purposes: the recognition is prepared by this somewhat naive method. The duration of the marriage differs, from one night to several years, and in some (very rare) cases children are born in this marriage.

If Sophocles had acted in accordance with modern tradition (in which the disclosure takes place instantly) then no tragedy, as an artistic whole, would have been possible. The material evidence (the hero's pierced feet), which plays a decisive role in folklore, plays a secondary role in Sophocles. In the folk-tale the mother-wife who discovers the scar in the nuptial bed immediately realises the truth and reveals it to the hero and to the listener. There is no need to talk here about the high artistic value with which Sophocles arranged the disclosure. Starting with the plague, which from the beginning suggests the future disclosure of some obscure and mysterious misfortune, the truth emerges by succession. Tiresias reveals the truth to the audience. Jocasta, when relating the killing of Laius, reveals the truth about patricide to Oedipus, but she herself does not understand. The shepherd reveals the incest to Jocasta (but not to Oedipus) and then the incest is revealed to Oedipus, thus confirming the patricide, as well.

Thus the whole tragedy is built on the unfolding of one aspect of the epic tradition – disclosure. This is precisely the tragedy, it lies in the discovery of truth. All other features are relegated to the background, they are necessary for the construction of the plot but they are mentioned only briefly and in retrospect. They are needed only in so far as they lead the action to this last, terrible moment: they serve as steps to this moment.

12   THE SECOND APOTHEOSIS OF OEDIPUS

Oedipus and the legends of St Gregory and Andrew of Crete develop in similar ways. In the Oedipus story the hero becomes the hero by the force of the earth; in the Andrew legend, he becomes a saint but the saint of an order not recognised by the Church. The Church did not accept the life of Andrew as the legend relates it. The hero of the legend, who becomes the Pope, does not present Catholic ideals and the Church did not and could not canonise him. Behind the description of Gregory or Andrew the researcher sees the monumental image of the antique Oedipus, whose remains also work miracles. Not in religious terms, rather they guard the town from its enemies.

What was the attraction of the plot after it lost its original sacred character? Its attraction lay primarily in the hero's suffering. Such suffering was generally alien to Greece. A Greek was first and foremost a public person and yet in Greece, already in its golden age when the first signs of decline began to make themselves felt, the suffering in Oedipus has a personal character. Oedipus (the embodiment and focus of the town, of its valour and prosperity) is suddenly rejected by this society and is abandoned. He loses his crown, which he never abused for selfish ends but used to serve his people. He loses the person who was his wife and his mother, who was the pulse and blood of life for him. It is not coincidental that he thrusts her hairpin into his eyes: darkness is the sign and expression of his estrangement from the world. He must also lose his children. A Greek wants a son – again, this is the expression of a profound social and state instinct. Oedipus has a son and a daughter and it is through the tenderness of his daughter that later he, partly, returns to the world. The scene of valediction, perhaps the most striking in the whole tragedy, is the moment when humanity is born within him, the moment when humanity emerges in European history.

It is here that we find a key to the adoption of the plot by Christianity as Christian legend. The plot acquires a new historical sacredness, and had acquired it already in Greece. Hence the second apotheosis of Oedipus. The first apotheosis is the overthrowing of the sphinx and the accession to the throne. The second apotheosis is the devouring of the sufferer by the earth and his idolisation. But typically of old healthy Greece, he, as a deity, is not a patron of suffering; rather, he becomes a defender of the town from military danger. The side which possesses his dead body will be victorious. The medieval legend did not adopt this first apotheosis and reinterpreted the second one, but here one cannot limit oneself to the analysis of just the plot itself. It must be examined against the background of its whole history: how this plot was affected by the life of Zulu cattle-breeders, of nomadic Berbers, mountaineers of the Caucusus, and Greeks, how it was affected by the struggle between Catholicism and human aspirations of the Renaissance and Humanism, by the gloomy eighteenth century and the unconscious ideals of peasantry – all this can only be shown by extensive cultural and historical research.

(*Translated by Natalia Ratcheiskova and Martin McQuillan*)

NOTES

1   *Jivaw Starina*, XXI, 1912, str. 346.
2   V. W. Propp, *Mujskoy dom v russkoy skazke*. 'Uc. zapiski LGU', N 20, Ser. filol. nauk, v/p. 1, 1939.
3   N. W. Marr, Sredstva peredvijeniw, orudiw samoza\it/ i proizvodstva v doistorii. Izbr. rab., t. III, 1934, str. 123–51.

Victor Shlovsky, 'Sterne's *Tristram Shandy:* Stylistic Commentary'*

See also:
Bakthin (1.iii)
Propp (1.iii)
Culler (2.ii)
Brooks (3.ii)
Gibson (3.ii)

. . .

In this essay I do not propose to analyze Laurence Sterne's novel, but rather to illustrate general laws of plot. Formalistically, Sterne was an extreme revolutionary; it was characteristic of him to 'lay bare' his technique. The artistic form is presented simply as such, without any kind of motivation. The difference between a novel by Sterne and the ordinary kind of novel is exactly that between ordinary poetry with its phonetic instrumentation and the poetry of the Futurists, written in obscure language.[1] Yet nothing much is written about Sterne any more; or, if it is, it consists only of a few banalities.

The first impression upon taking up Sterne's *Tristram Shandy* and beginning to read it is one of chaos. The action is continually interrupted; the author repeatedly goes backward or leaps forward; whole ten-page passages are filled with whimsical discussions about fortifications or about the influence of a person's nose or name on his character. Such digressions are unrelated to the basic narrative.

Although the beginning of the book has the tone of an autobiography, it drifts into a description of the hero's ancestors. In fact, the heroes birth is long delayed by the irrelevant material squeezed into the novel. The description of a single day takes up much of the book; I quote Sterne himself:

* From L. T. Lemon and R. J. Rees (eds), *Russian Formalist Criticism: Four Essays* (Lincoln: University of Nebraska Press, 1965), pp. 27–9 and 55–7.

I will not finish that sentence till I have made an observation upon the strange state of affairs between the reader and myself, just as things stand at present – an observation never applicable before to any one biographical writer since the creation of the world, but to myself – and I believe will never hold good to any other, until its final destruction – and therefore, for the very novelty of it alone, it must be worth your worships attending to.

I am this month one whole year older than I was this time twelve-month; and having got, as you perceive, almost into the middle of my fourth volume – and no farther than to my first day's life – 'tis demonstrative that I have three hundred and sixty-four days more life to write just now, than when I first set out; so that instead of advancing, as a common writer, in my work with what I have been doing at it – on the contrary, I am just thrown so many volumes back.

(pp.285–6)[2]

But when you begin to examine the structure of the book, you see first of all that the disorder is intentional and, in this case, poetic. It is strictly regulated, like a picture by Picasso. Everything in the book is displaced; everything is transposed. The dedication occurs on page 15, contrary to the three basic requirements of content, form, and place. Nor is the Preface in its usual position. It takes up approximately a quire, not at the beginning of the book but rather in Volume III, Chapter 20, pages 192 through 203. Sterne justifies the Preface in this way: 'All my heroes are off my hands; – 'tis the first time I have had a moment to spare, – and I'll make use of it, and write my preface' (p. 192). The Preface contains, of course, as many entanglements as ingenuity permits. But the most radical of the displacements is the transposition of entire chapters (Chapters 18 and 19 of Volume IX are placed after Chapter 25). Sterne justifies the transposition so: 'All I wish is, that it may be a lesson to the world, *"to let people tell their stories their own way"*' (p. 633).

But this transposition of chapters reveals another of Sterne's basic techniques – that of impeding the flow of the action. In the beginning, Sterne introduces an anecdote about an act of sexual intercourse interrupted by a woman's question (p. 5). Here is how the anecdote is brought in. Tristram Shandy's mother sleeps with his father only on the first Sunday of each month and on 'precisely that evening Mr Shandy winds the clock in order to get both of these domestic duties 'out of the way at one time, and be no more plagued and pester'd with them the rest of the month' (p. 8). As a result, an unavoidable association has formed in his wife's mind, so that she 'could never hear the said clock wound up, – but the thoughts of some other things unavoidably popp'd into her head, – & *vice versa*' (p. 9). Here is the exact question with which Tristram's mother interrupted the activity of his father: '*Pray, my dear, . . . have you not forgot to wind up the clock?*' (p. 5).

This anecdote is introduced into the work first by a general comment upon the inattentiveness of the parents (pp. 4–5), then by the mother's question, the context of which we do not yet know. At first we think she had merely interrupted the father's conversation. Sterne plays with our error:

Good G —! cried my father, making an exclamation, but taking care to moderate his voice at the same time, – *Did ever woman, since the creation of the world, interrupt a man with such a silly question?* Pray, what was your father saying? – Nothing.

(p. 5)

Then his remarks about the homunculus (fetus) are spiced with anecdotal references to its right to legal defense (pp. 5–6). Only on pages 8 through 9 do we get an explanation of this whole passage and a description of the odd punctiliousness of the father in his family affairs.

Thus, from the very beginning, we find displacement of time in *Tristram Shandy*. The causes follow the consequences, and the author himself prepares the groundwork for erroneous assumptions. This is one of Sterne's characteristic techniques. The quibbling about the coitus motif itself, related to a definite day and referring back to what has already happened in the novel, reappears from time to time and ties together the various sections of this masterfully constructed and unusually complicated work.

If we visualize the digressions schematically, they will appear as cones representing an event, with the apex representing the causes. In an ordinary novel such a cone is joined to the main story line at its apex; in *Tristram Shandy* the base of the cone is joined to the main story line, so that all at once we fall into a swarm of allusions.

. . .

I have not even the slightest wish to follow Sterne's novel to the end because that is not what interests me; I am interested, rather, in the theory of the plot. I shall now remark on the abundance of quotations. It certainly would have been possible to have made fuller use of the material introduced in each quotation because almost no technique is represented anywhere in its pure form; but such an approach would have transformed my work into something like an interlinear translation with grammatical remarks. I would have forgotten the material and so exhausted it that I would have deprived the reader of the possibility of understanding it.

In order to follow the course of the novel in my analysis, I have had to show the whole of its 'inconsistency.' The unusualness of the general plan and the order of the novel, even of the frequently extraordinary handling of the most ordinary elements, is what is characteristic here.

By way of a conclusion and as a demonstration of Sterne's awareness of his work and his exaggerated violations of the usual plot structure, I introduce his very own graphs of the flow of the story of *Tristram Shandy*:

I am now beginning to get fairly into my work; and by the help of a vegitable diet, with a few of the cold seeds, I make no doubt but I shall be able to go on with my uncle *Toby*'s story, and my own, in a tolerable straight line. Now,

(p. 473)[3]

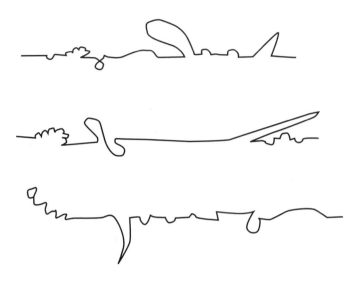

(p. 474)

These were the four lines I moved in through my first, second, third, and fourth volumes. – In the fifth volume I have been very good, – the precise line I have described in it being this:

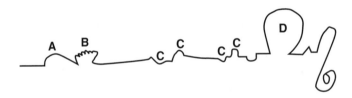

By which it appears, that except at the curve, marked A. where I took a trip to *Navarre*, – and the indented curve B. which is the short airing when I was there with the Lady *Baussiere* and her page, – I have not taken the least frisk of a digression, till *John de la Casse*'s devils led me the round you see marked D. – for as for *c c c c* they are nothing but parentheses, and the common *ins* and *outs* incident to the lives of the greatest ministers of state; and when compared with what men have done, – or with my own transgressions at the letters A B D – they vanish into nothing.

(pp. 473–4)

Sterne's diagrams are approximately accurate, but they do not call attention to the crosscurrent of motifs.

The idea of *plot* is too often confused with the description of events – with what I propose provisionally to call the *story*. The story is, in fact, only material for plot formulation. The plot of *Evgeny Onegin* is, therefore, not the romance of the hero with Tatyana, but the fashioning of the subject of this story as produced by the introduction of interrupting digressions. One sharp-witted artist (Vladimir Miklashevsky) proposed to illustrate *Evgeny Onegin* mainly through the digressions (the 'small feet,' for example); considering it as a composition of motifs, such a treatment would be proper.

The forms of art are explainable by the laws of art; they are not justified by their realism. Slowing the action of a novel is not accomplished by introducing rivals, for example, but by simply *transposing* parts. In so doing the artist makes us aware of the aesthetic laws which underlie both the transposition and the slowing down of the action.

The assertion that *Tristram Shandy* is not a novel is common; for persons who make that statement, opera alone is music – a symphony is chaos.

Tristram Shandy is the most typical novel in world literature.

Victor Shklovsky, Tristram Shandy *Sterna: Stilistichesky kommentary* (Petrograd, 1921).

NOTES

1   That is, in ordinary poetry the 'phonetic instrumentation' – rhyme, meter, alliteration, etc. – is often said to accompany a 'meaning,' to which it is subordinate; Futurist poetry called attention to, or 'laid bare,' the devices of instrumentation. *Tristram Shandy* is like Futurist poetry in that it also calls attention to technical devices that are usually subordinated.

2   Shklovksy read the Russian version of *Tristram Shandy* published in the journal *Panteon Literatury* [*Pantheon of Literature*] in 1892. Our quotations are taken from *The Life and Opinions of Tristram Shandy, Gentleman*, ed. James Aiken Work (New York: Odyssey Press, 1940); all page and chapter references are to this edition. *Ed. note.*

3   These four diagrams are inverted in the Russian text. We have set them aright.

Boris Tomashevsky 'Thematics'*

STORY AND PLOT

A theme has a certain unity and composed of small thematic elements arranged in a definite order.

We may distinguish two major kinds of arrangement of these thematic elements: (1) that in which causal-temporal relationships exist between the thematic elements, and (2) that in which the thematic elements are contemporaneous, or in which there is some shift of theme without internal exposition of the causal connections. The former are *stories* (tales, novels, epics); the latter have no 'story,' they are 'descriptive' (e.g., descriptive and didactic poems, lyrics, and travel books such as Karamzin's *Letters of a Russian Traveller* or Goncharov's *The Frigate Pallas*).

We must emphasize that a story requires not only indications of time, but also indications of cause. Time indicators may occur in telling about a journey, but if the

* From L. T. Lemon and R. J. Rees (eds), *Russian Formalist Criticism: Four Essays* (Lincoln: University of Nebraska Press, 1965), pp. 66–8.

account is only about the sights and not about the personal adventures of the travelers, we have exposition without story. The weaker the causal connection, the stronger the purely chronological connection. As the story line becomes weaker, we move from the novel to the chronicle, to a simple statement of the sequence of events (*The Childhood Years of Bagrov's Grandson*[1]).

Let us take up the notion of the story, the aggregate of mutually related events reported in the work. No matter how the events were originally arranged in the work and despite their original order of introduction, in practice the story may be told in the actual chronological and causal order of events.

Plot is distinct from story. Both include the same events, but in the plot the events *are arranged* and connected according to the orderly sequence in which they were presented in the work.[2]

The idea expressed by the theme is the idea that *summarizes* and unifies the verbal material in the work. The work as a whole may have a theme, and at the same time each part of a work may have its own theme. The development of a work is a process of diversification unified by a single theme. Thus Pushkin's 'The Shot' develops the story of the narrator's meetings with Silvio and the Count, and the story of the conflict between the two men. The story of life in the regiment and the country is developed, followed by the first part of the duel between Silvio and the Count, and the story of their final encounter.

After reducing a work to its thematic elements, we come to parts that are irreducible, the smallest particles of thematic material: 'evening comes,' 'Raskolnikov kills the old woman,' 'the hero dies,' 'the letter is received,' and so on. The theme of an irreducible part of a work is called the *motif*; each sentence, in fact, has its own motif.

It should be noted that the meaning of 'motif,' as used in historical poetics – in comparative studies of migratory plots (for example, in the study of the *skaz* [or yarn][3] – differs radically from its meaning here, although they are usually considered identical. In comparative studies a motif is a thematic unit which occurs in various works (for example, 'the abduction of the bride,' 'the helpful beast' – that is, the animal that helps the hero solve his problem – etc.). These motifs move in their entirety from one plot to another. In comparative poetics, reduction to the smaller elements is not important; what is important is only that within the limits of the given genre these 'motifs' are always found in their complete forms. Consequently, in comparative studies one must speak of motifs that have remained intact historically, that have preserved their unity in passing from work to work, rather than of 'irreducible' motifs. Nevertheless, many motifs of comparative poetics remain significant precisely because they are also motifs in our theoretical sense.

Mutually related motifs form the thematic bonds of the work. From this point of view, the story is the aggregate of motifs in their logical, causal-chronological order; the plot is the aggregate of those same motifs but having the relevance and the order which they had in the original work. The place in the work in which the reader learns of an event, whether the information is given by the author, or by a character, or by a series of indirect hints – all this is irrelevant to the story. But the aesthetic function of the plot is precisely this bringing of an arrangement of motifs to the attention of the reader. Real incidents, not fictionalized by an author, may make a story. A plot is wholly an artistic creation.

NOTES

1   A volume of reminiscences by Sergey Aksakov, published in 1858.
2   In brief, the story is 'the action itself,' the plot, 'how the reader learns of the action.'
3   Possibly the nearest equivalent of *skaz* is 'yarn.' Technically, a *skaz* is a story in which the manner of telling (the normal speech patterns of the narrator – dialect, pronunciation, grammatical peculiarities, pitch patterns, etc.) is as important to the effect as the story itself. For a description of the American equivalent of the *skaz*, see Samuel Clemens' widely reprinted 'How to Tell a Story.'

Wayne Booth, from *The Rhetoric of Fiction**

See also:
Benjamin (1.iii)
Chatman (2.ii)
Prince (2.ii)
de Man (6)
Iser (7)

TYPES OF NARRATION

We have seen that the author cannot choose to avoid rhetoric; he can choose only the kind of rhetoric he will employ. He cannot choose whether or not to affect his readers' evaluations by his choice of narrative manner; he can only choose whether to do it well or poorly. As dramatists have always known, even the purest of dramas is not purely dramatic in the sense of being entirely presented, entirely shown as taking place in the moment. There are always what Dryden called 'relations' to be taken care of, and try as the author may to ignore the troublesome fact, 'some parts of the action are more fit to be represented, some to be related.'[1] But related by whom? The dramatist must decide, and the novelist's case is different only in that the choices open to him are more numerous.

If we think through the many narrative devices in the fiction we know, we soon come to a sense of the embarrassing inadequacy of our traditional classification of 'point of view' into three or four kinds, variables only of the 'person' and the degree of omniscience. If we name over three or four of the great narrators – say Cervantes' Cid Hamete Benengeli, Tristram Shandy, the 'I' of *Middlemarch*, and Strether, through whose vision most of *The Ambassadors* comes to us, we realize that to describe any of them with terms like 'first-person' and 'omniscient' tells us little about how they differ from each other, or why they succeed while others described in the same terms fail.[2] It should be worth our while, then, to attempt a richer tabulation of the forms the author's voice can take.

Person

Perhaps the most overworked distinction is that of person. To say that a story is told in the first or the third person[3] will tell us nothing of importance unless we become more

---

* 2nd edn (Chicago, IL: University of Chicago Press, 1974), pp. 149–58.

precise and describe how the particular qualities of the narrators relate to specific effects. It is true that choice of the first person is sometimes unduly limiting; if the 'I' has inadequate access to necessary information, the author may be led into improbabilities. And there are other effects that may dictate a choice in some cases. But we can hardly expect to find useful criteria in a distinction that throws all fiction into two, or at most three, heaps. In this pile we see *Henry Esmond*, 'A Cask of Amontillado,' *Gulliver's Travels*, and *Tristram Shandy*. In that, we have *Vanity Fair*, *Tom Jones*, *The Ambassadors*, and *Brave New World*. But in *Vanity Fair* and *Tom Jones* the commentary is in the first person, often resembling more the intimate effect of *Tristram Shandy* than that of many third-person works. And again, the effect of *The Ambassadors* is much closer to that of the great first-person novels, since Strether in large part 'narrates' his own story, even though he is always referred to in the third person.

Further evidence that this distinction is less important than has often been claimed is seen in fact that all of the following functional distinctions apply to both first- and third-person narration alike.

Dramatized and undramatized narrators

Perhaps the most important differences in narrative effect depend on whether the narrator is dramatized in his own right and on whether his beliefs and characteristics are shared by the author.

The implied author (the author's 'second self'). – Even the novel in which no narrator is dramatized creates an implicit picture of an author who stands behind the scenes, whether as stage manager, as puppeteer, or as an indifferent God, silently paring his fingernails. This implied author is always distinct from the 'real man' – whatever we may take him to be – who creates a superior version of himself, a 'second self,' as he creates his work.[4]

In so far as a novel does not refer directly to this author, there will be no distinction between him and the implied, undramatized narrator; in Hemingway's 'The Killers,' for example, there is no narrator other than the implicit second self that Hemingway creates as he writes.

Undramatized narrators. – Stories are usually not so rigorously impersonal as 'The Killers'; most tales are presented as passing through the consciousness of a teller, whether an 'I' or a 'he.' Even in drama much of what we are given is narrated by someone, and we are often as much interested in the effect on the narrator's own mind and heart as we are in learning what else the author has to tell us. When Horatio tells of his first encounter with the ghost in *Hamlet*, his own character, though never mentioned, is important to us as we listen. In fiction, as soon as we encounter an 'I,' we are conscious of an experiencing mind whose views of the experience will come between us and the event. When there is no such 'I,' as in 'The Killers,' the inexperienced reader may make the mistake of thinking that the story comes to him unmediated. But no such mistake can be made from the moment that the author explicitly places a narrator into the tale, even if he is given no personal characteristics whatever.

Dramatized narrators. – In a sense even the most reticent narrator has been dramatized as soon as he refers to himself as 'I,' or, like Flaubert, tells us that 'we' were in the classroom when Charles Bovary entered. But many novels dramatize their narrators with great fulness, making them into characters who are as vivid as those they tell us about (*Tristram Shandy, Remembrance of Things Past, Heart of Darkness, Dr. Faustus*). In such works the narrator is often radically different from the implied author who creates him. The range of human types that have been dramatized as narrators is almost as great as the range of other fictional characters – one must say 'almost' because there are some characters who are not fully qualified to narrate or 'reflect' a story (Faulkner can use the idiot for part of his novel only because the other three parts exist to set off and clarify the idiot's jumble).

We should remind ourselves that many dramatized narrators are never explicitly labeled as narrators at all. In a sense, every speech, every gesture, narrates; most works contain disguised narrators who are used to tell the audience what it needs to know, while seeming merely to act out their roles.

Though disguised narrators of this kind are seldom labeled so explicitly as God in Job, they often speak with an authority as sure as God's. Messengers returning to tell what the oracle said, wives trying to convince their husbands that the business deal is unethical, old family retainers expostulating with wayward scions – these often have more effect on us than on their official auditors; the king goes ahead with his obstinate search, the husband carries out his deal, the hell-bound youth goes on toward hell as if nothing had been said, but we know what we know – and as surely as if the author himself or his official narrator had told us. 'She's laughing at you to your face, brother,' Cleante says to Orgon in *Tartuffe*, 'and frankly, without meaning to anger you, I must say she's quite right. Has there ever been the like of such a whim? . . . You must be mad, brother, I swear.'[5] And in tragedy there is usually a chorus, a friend, or even a forthright villain, to speak truth in contrast to the tragic mistakes of the hero.

The most important unacknowledged narrators in modern fiction are the third-person 'centers of consciousness' through whom authors have filtered their narratives. Whether such 'reflectors,' as James sometimes called them, are highly polished mirrors reflecting complex mental experience, or the rather turbid, sense-bound 'camera eyes' of much fiction since James, they fill precisely the function of avowed narrators – though they can add intensities of their own.

> Gabriel had not gone to the door with the others. He was in a dark part of the hall gazing up the staircase. A woman was standing near the top of the first flight, in the shadow also. He could not see her face but he could see the terracotta and salmon-pink panels of her skirt which the shadow made appear black and white. It was his wife. She was leaning on the banisters, listening to something. . . . He asked himself what is a woman standing on the stairs in the shadow, listening to distant music, a symbol of [Joyce's 'The Dead'].

The very real advantages of this method, for some purposes, have provided a dominant theme in modern criticism. Indeed, so long as our attention is on such qualities as naturalness and vividness, the advantages seem overwhelming. Only as we break out of the fashionable assumption that all good fiction tries for the same kind of vivid illusion in the same way are we forced to recognize disadvantages. The third-person reflector is only one mode among many, suitable for some effects but cumbersome and even harmful when other effects are desired.

Observers and narrator-agents

Among dramatized narrators there are mere observers (the 'I' of *Tom Jones, The Egoist, Troilus and Criseyde*), and there are narrator-agents, who produce some measurable effect on the course of events (ranging from the minor involvement of Nick in *The Great Gatsby*, through the extensive give-and-take of Marlow in *Heart of Darkness*,[6] to the central role of Tristram Shandy, Moll Flanders, Huckleberry Finn, and – in the third person – Paul Morel in *Sons and Lovers*). Clearly, any rules we might discover about observers may not apply to narrator-agents, yet the distinction is seldom made in talk about point of view.

Scene and summary

All narrators and observers, whether first or third person, can relay their tales to us primarily as scene ('The Killers,' *The Awkward Age*, the works of Ivy Compton-Burnett and Henry Green), primarily as summary or what Lubbock called 'picture'! (Addison's almost completely non-scenic tales in *The Spectator*), or, most commonly, as a combination of the two.

    Like Aristotle's distinction between dramatic and narrative manners, the somewhat different modern distinction between showing and telling does cover the ground. But the trouble is that it pays for broad coverage with gross imprecision. Narrators of all shapes and shades must either report dialogue alone or support it with 'stage directions' and description of setting. But when we think of the radically different effect of a scene reported by Huck Finn and a scene reported by Poe's Montresor, we see that the quality of being 'scenic' suggests very little about literary effect. And compare the delightful summary of twelve years given in two pages of *Tom Jones* (Book III, chap. i) with the tedious showing of even ten minutes of uncurtailed conversation in the hands of a Sartre when he allows his passion for 'durational realism' to dictate a scene when summary is called for. . . . the contrast between scene and summary, between showing and telling, is likely to be of little use until we specify the kind of narrator who is providing the scene or the summary.

Commentary

Narrators who allow themselves to tell as well as show vary greatly depending on the amount and kind of commentary allowed in addition to a direct relating of events in scene and summary. Such commentary can, of course, range over any aspect of human experience, and it can be related to the main business in innumerable ways and degrees. To treat it as a single device is to ignore important differences between commentary that is merely ornamental, commentary that serves a rhetorical purpose but is not part of the dramatic structure, and commentary that is integral to the dramatic structure, as in *Tristram Shandy*.

Self-conscious narrators

Cutting across the distinction between observers and narrator-agents of all these kinds is the distinction between *self-conscious narrators*, aware of themselves as writers (*Tom Jones, Tristram Shandy, Barchester Towers, The Catcher in the Rye, Remembrance of*

Things Past, Dr. Faustus), and narrators or observers who rarely if ever discuss their writing chores (*Huckleberry Finn*) or who seem unaware that they are writing, thinking, speaking, or 'reflecting' a literary work (Camus's *The Stranger*, Lardner's 'Haircut,' Bellow's *The Victim*).

Variations of distance

Whether or not they are involved in the action as agents or as sufferers, narrators and third-person reflectors differ markedly according to the degree and kind of distance that separates them from the author, the reader, and the other characters of the story. In any reading experience there is an implied dialogue among author, narrator, the other characters, and the reader. Each of the four can range, in relation to each of the others, from identification to complete opposition, on any axis of value, moral, intellectual, aesthetic, and even physical. (Does the reader who stammers react to the stammering of H. C. Earwicker as I do? Surely not.) The elements usually discussed under 'aesthetic distance' enter in of course; distance in time and space, differences of social class or conventions of speech or dress – these and many others serve to control our sense that we are dealing with an aesthetic object, just as the paper moons and other unrealistic stage effects of some modern drama have had an 'alienation' effect. But we must not confuse these with the equally important effects of personal beliefs and qualities, in author, reader, narrator, and all others in the cast of characters.

NOTES

1   *An Essay of Dramatic Poesy* (1668). Though this quotation comes from Lisideius, in his defense of French drama, and not from Neander, who seems to speak more nearly for Dryden, the position is taken for granted in Neander's reply; the only dispute is over which parts are more fit to be represented.

2   There is no point in listing any of the conventional classifications here in order to reject them. They range from the simplest and least useful, in a clever popular essay by C. E. Montague ('"Sez 'e' or "Thinks 'e,"' *A Writer's Notes on His Trade* (London, 1930; Pelican edn, 1952), pp. 34–5) to the valuable study by Norman Friedman ('Point of View,' *PMLA*, LXX (December 1955), 1160–84).

3   Efforts to use the second person have never been very successful, but it is astonishing how little real difference even this choice makes. When I am told, at the beginning of a book, 'You have put your left foot . . . You slide through the narrow opening. . . . Your eyes are only half open . . . ,' the radical unnaturalness is, it is true, distracting for a time. But in reading Michel Butor's *La Modification* (Paris, 1957), from which this opening comes, it is surprising how quickly one is absorbed into the illusory 'present' of the story, identifying one's vision with the 'vous' almost as fully as with the 'I' and 'he' in other stories.

4   A fine account of the subtleties that underlie the seemingly simple relations between real authors and the selves they create as they write can be found in 'Makers and Persons,' by Patrick Cruttwell, *Hudson Review*, XII (Winter, 1959–60), 487–507.

5   From an unpublished translation by Marcel Gutwirth.

6   For a careful interpretation of the development and functions of Marlow in Conrad's works, see W. Y. Tindall, 'Apology for Marlow,' in *From Jane Austen to Joseph Conrad*, ed. Robert

C. Rathurn and Martin Steinmann, Jr. (Minneapolis, MI., 1958), pp. 274–85. Though Marlow is often himself a victim of Conrad's ironies, he is generally a reliable reflector of the clarities and ambiguities of the implied author. A much fuller treatment, and a remarkable work for an undergraduate, is James L. Guetti, Jr., *The Rhetoric of Joseph Conrad* ('Amherst College Honors Thesis,' No. 2 (Amherst, MA., 1960).

2
Structuralism

i DEFINITIONS

Claude Lévi-Strauss, 'The Structural Study of Myth'[*]

See also:
Propp (1.iii)
Barthes (2.iii)
Eco (2.iii)
Lyotard (3.iii)
Mulvey (4)
de Lauretis (5)
Derrida (6)
Jameson (8)
Said (9)

. . .

Now for a concrete example of the method we propose. We shall use the Oedipus myth, which is well known to everyone. I am well aware that the Oedipus myth has only reached us under late forms and through literary transmutations concerned more with esthetic and moral preoccupations than with religious or ritual ones, whatever these may have been. But we shall not interpret the Oedipus myth in literal terms, much less offer an explanation acceptable to the specialist. We simply wish to illustrate – and without reaching any conclusions with respect to it – a certain technique, whose use is probably not legitimate in this particular instance, owing to the problematic elements indicated above. The 'demonstration' should therefore be conceived, not in terms of what the scientist means by this term, but at best in terms of what is meant by the street peddler, whose aim is not to achieve a concrete result, but to explain, as succinctly as possible, the functioning of the mechanical toy which he is trying to sell to the onlookers.

The myth will be treated as an orchestra score would be if it were unwittingly considered as a unilinear series; our task is to re-establish the correct arrangement. Say, for instance, we were confronted with a sequence of the type: 1,2,4,7,8,2,3,4,6, 8,1,4,5,7,8,1,2,5,7,3,4,5,6,8 . . ., the assignment being to put all the 1s together, all the 2s, the 3s, etc.; the result is a chart:

[*] *Structural Anthropology*, trans. C. Jacobson and B. G. Schoepf (London: Allen Lane, 1967), pp. 213–19, 229–30.

1	2		4			7	8
	2	3	4		6		8
1			4	5		7	8
1	2			5		7	
		3	4	5	6		8

We shall attempt to perform the same kind of operation on the Oedipus myth, trying out several arrangements of the mythemes until we find one which is in harmony with the principles enumerated above. Let us suppose, for the sake of argument, that the best arrangement is the following (although it might certainly be improved with the help of a specialist in Greek mythology):

Cadmos seeks his
sister Europa,
ravished by Zeus

Cadmos kills
the dragon

The Spartoi kill
one another

Labdacos (Laios'
father) = *lame* (?)

Oedipus kills his
father, Laios

Laios (Oedipus'
father) – *left-sided*
(?)

Oedipus kills
the Sphinx

Oedipus =
swollen-foot (?)

Oedipus marries
his mother, Jocasta

Eteocles kills his
brother, Polynices

Antigone buries her
brother, Polynices,
despite prohibition

We thus find ourselves confronted with four vertical columns, each of which includes several relations belonging to the same bundle. Were we to *tell* the myth, we would disregard the columns and read the rows from left to right and from top to bottom. But if we want to *understand* the myth, then we will have to disregard one half of the diachronic dimension (top to bottom) and read from left to right, column after column, each one being considered as a unit.

All the relations belonging to the same column exhibit one common feature which it is our task to discover. For instance, all the events grouped in the first column on the left have something to do with blood relations which are overemphasized, that is, are more intimate than they should be. Let us say, then, that the first column has its common feature the *overrating of blood relations*. It is obvious that the second column expresses the same thing, but inverted: *underrating of blood relations*. The third column refers to monsters being slain. As to the fourth, a few words of clarification are needed. The remarkable connotation of the surnames in Oedipus' father-line has often been noticed. However, linguists usually disregard it, since to them the only way to define the meaning of a term is to investigate all the contexts in which it appears, and personal names, precisely because they are used as such, are not accompanied by any context. With the method we propose to follow the objection disappears, since the myth itself provides its own context. The significance is no longer to be sought in the eventual meaning of each name, but in the fact that all the names have a common feature: all the hypothetical meanings (which may well remain hypothetical) refer to *difficulties in walking straight and standing upright*.

What then is the relationship between the two columns on the right? Column three refers to monsters. The dragon is a chthonian being which has to be killed in order that mankind be born from the Earth; the Sphinx is a monster unwilling to permit men to live. The last unit reproduces the first one, which has to do with the *autochthonous origin* of mankind. Since the monsters are overcome by men, we may thus say that the common feature of the third column is *denial of the autochthonous origin of man*.[1]

This immediately helps us to understand the meaning of the fourth column. In mythology it is a universal characteristic of men born from the Earth that at the moment they emerge from the depth they either cannot walk or they walk clumsily. This is the case of the chthonian beings in the mythology of the Pueblo: Muyingwu, who leads the emergence, and the chthonian Shumaikoli are lame ('bleeding-foot,' 'sore-foot'). The same happens to the Koskimo of the Kwakiutl after they have been swallowed by the chthonian monster, Tsiakish: When they returned to the surface of the earth 'they limped forward or tripped side ways.' Thus the common feature of the fourth column is *the persistence of the autochthonous origin of man*. It follows that column four is to column three as column one is to column two. The inability to connect two kinds of relationships is overcome (or rather replaced) by the assertion that contradictory relationships are identical inasmuch as they are both self-contradictory in a similar way. Although this is still a provisional formulation of the structure of mythical thought, it is sufficient at this stage.

Turning back to the Oedipus myth, we may now see what it means. The myth has to do with the inability, for a culture which holds the belief that mankind is autochthonous (see, for instance, Pausanias, VIII, xxix, 4: plants provide a *model* for humans), to find a satisfactory transition between this theory and the knowledge that human beings are actually born from the union of man and woman. Although the problem obviously cannot be solved, the Oedipus myth provides a kind of logical tool which relates the original problem – born from one or born from two? – to the derivative problem: born from different or born from same? By a correlation of this type, the overrating of blood relations is to the underrating of blood relations as the attempt to escape autochthony is to the impossibility to succeed in it. Although experience contradicts theory, social life validates cosmology by its similarity of structure. Hence cosmology is true.

Two remarks should be made at this stage.

In order to interpret the myth, we left aside a point which has worried the specialists until now, namely, that in the earlier (Homeric) versions of the Oedipus myth, some basic elements are lacking, such as Jocasta killing herself and Oedipus piercing his own eyes. These events do not alter the substance of the myth although they can easily be integrated, the first one as a new case of auto-destruction (column three) and the second as another case of crippledness (column four). At the same time there is something significant in these additions, since the shift from foot to head is to be correlated with the shift from autochthonous origin to self-destruction.

Our method thus eliminates a problem which has, so far, been one of the main obstacles to the progress of mythological studies, namely, the quest for the *true* version, or the *earlier* one. On the contrary, we define the myth as consisting of all its versions; or to put it otherwise, a myth remains the same as long as it is felt as such. A striking example is offered by the fact that our interpretation may take into account the Freudian use of the Oedipus myth and is certainly applicable to it. Although the Freudian problem has ceased to be that of autochthony *versus* bisexual reproduction, it is still the problem of understanding how *one* can be born from *two*: How is it that we do not have only one procreator, but a mother plus a father? Therefore, not only Sophocles, but Freud himself, should be included among the recorded versions of the Oedipus myth on a par with earlier or seemingly more 'authentic' versions.

An important consequence follows. If a myth is made up of all its variants, structural analysis should take all of them into account. After analyzing all the known variants of the Theban version, we should thus treat the others in the same way: first, the tales about Labdacos' collateral line including Agave, Pentheus, and Jocasta herself; the Theban variant about Lycos with Amphion and Zetos as the city founders; more remote variants concerning Dionysus (Oedipus' matrilateral cousin); and Athenian legends where Cecrops takes the place of Cadmos, etc. For each of them a similar chart should be drawn and then compared and reorganized according to the findings: Cecrops killing the serpent with the parallel episode of Cadmos; abandonment of Dionysus with abandonment of Oedipus; 'Swollen Foot' with Dionysus' *loxias* that is, walking obliquely; Europa's quest with Antiope's; the founding of Thebes by the Spartoi or by the brothers Amphion and Zetos; Zeus kidnapping Europa and Antiope and the same with Semele; the Theban Oedipus and the Argian Perseus, etc. We shall then have several two-dimensional charts, each dealing with a variant, to be organized in a three-dimensional order, as shown in Figure 1, so that three different readings become possible: left to right, top to bottom, front to back (or vice versa). All of these charts cannot be expected to be identical; but experience shows that any difference to be observed may be correlated with other differences, so that a logical treatment of the whole will allow simplifications, the final outcome being the structural law of the myth.

At this point the objection may be raised that the task is impossible to perform, since we can only work with known versions. Is it not possible that a new version might alter the picture? This is true enough if only one or two versions are available, but the objection becomes theoretical as soon as a reasonably large number have been recorded. Let us make this point clear by a comparison. If the furniture of a room and its arrangement were known to us only through its reflection in two mirrors placed on opposite walls, we should theoretically dispose of an almost infinite number of mirror images which would provide us with a complete knowledge. However, should the two mirrors be obliquely set, the number of mirror images would become very small; nevertheless, four or five such images would very likely give us, if not complete information, at least a sufficient coverage so that we would feel sure that no large piece of furniture is missing in our description.

On the other hand, it cannot be too strongly emphasized that all available variants should be taken into account. If Freudian comments on the Oedipus complex are a part of the Oedipus myth, then questions such as whether Cushing's version of the Zuni origin myth should be retained or discarded become irrelevant. There is no single 'true' version of which all the others are but copies or distortions. Every version belongs to the myth.

The reason for the discouraging results in works on general mythology can finally be understood. They stem from two causes. First, comparative mythologists have selected preferred versions instead of using them all. Second, we have seen that the structural analysis of *one* variant of *one* myth belonging to *one* tribe (in some cases, even *one* village) already requires two dimensions. When we use several variants of the same myth for the same tribe or village, the frame of reference becomes three-dimensional, and as soon as we try to enlarge the comparison, the number of dimensions required increases until it appears quite impossible to handle them intuitively. The confusions and platitudes which are the outcome of comparative mythology can be explained by the fact that multi-dimensional frames of reference are often ignored or are naïvely replaced by two- or three-dimensional ones: Indeed, progress in comparative mythology depends largely on the cooperation of mathematicians who would undertake to express in symbols multi-dimensional relations which cannot be handled otherwise.

. . .

Three final remarks may serve as conclusion.

First, the question has often been raised why myths, and more generally oral literature, are so much addicted to duplication, triplication, or quadruplication of the same sequence. If our hypotheses are accepted, the answer is obvious: The function of repetition is to render the structure of the myth apparent. For we have seen that the synchronic-diachronic structure of the myth permits us to organize it into diachronic sequences (the rows in our tables) which should be read synchronically (the columns). Thus, a myth exhibits a 'slated' structure, which comes to the surface, so to speak, through the process of repetition.

However, the slates are not absolutely identical. And since the purpose of myth is to provide a logical model capable of overcoming a contradiction (an impossible achievement if, as it happens, the contradiction is real), a theoretically infinite number of slates will be generated, each one slightly different from the others. Thus, myth grows spiral-wise until the intellectual impulse which has produced it is exhausted. Its *growth* is a continuous process, whereas its *structure* remains discontinuous. If this is the case, we should assume that it closely corresponds, in the realm of the spoken word, to a crystalin the realm of physical matter. This analogy may help us to better understand the relationship of myth to both *langue* on the one hand and *parole* on the other. Myth is an intermediary entity between a statistical aggregate of molecules and the molecular structure itself.

Prevalent attempts to explain alleged differences between the so-called primitive mind and scientific thought have resorted to qualitative differences between the working processes of the mind in both cases, while assuming that the entities which they were studying remained very much the same. If our interpretation is correct, we are led toward a completely different view – namely, that the kind of logic in mythical thought is as rigorous as that of modern science, and that the difference lies, not in the quality of the intellectual process, but in the nature of the things to which it is applied. This is well in agreement with the situation known to prevail in the field of technology: what makes a steel ax superior to a stone ax is not that the first one is better made than the second. They are equally well made, but steel is quite different from stone. In the same way we may be able to show that the same logical processes operate in myth as in science, and that man has always been thinking equally well; the improvement lies, not in an alleged progress of man's mind, but in the discovery of new areas to which it may apply its unchanged and unchanging powers.

NOTE

1   We are not trying to become involved with specialists in an argument; this would be presumptuous and even meaningless on our part. Since the Oedipus myth is taken here merely as an example treated in arbitrary fashion, the chthonian nature ascribed to the Sphinx might seem surprising; we shall refer to the testimony of Marie Delcourt: 'In the archaic legends, [she is] certainly born of the Earth itself' (*Oedipe ou la légende du conquérant* (Liège: 1944), p. 108). No matter how remote from Delcourt's our method may be (and our conclusions would be, no doubt, if we were competent to deal with the problem in depth), it seems to us that she has convincingly established the nature of the Sphinx in the archaic tradition, namely, that of a female monster who attacks and rapes young men; in other words, the personification of a female being with an inversion of the sign. This explains why, in the handsome iconography compiled by Delcourt at the end of her work, men and women are always found in an inverted 'sky/earth' relationship.

As we shall point out below, we selected the Oedipus myth as our first example because of the striking analogies that seem to exist between certain aspects of archaic Greek thought and that of the Pueblo Indians, from whom we have borrowed the examples that follow. In this respect it should be noted that the figure of the Sphinx, as reconstructed by Delcourt, coincides with two figures of North American mythology (who probably merge into one). We are referring, on the one hand, to 'the old hag,' a repulsive witch whose physical appearance presents a 'problem' to the young hero. If he 'solves' this problem – that is, if he responds to the advances of the abject creature – he will find in his bed, upon awakening, a beautiful young woman who will confer power upon him (this is also a Celtic theme). The Sphinx, on the other hand, recalls even more 'the child-protruding woman' of the Hopi Indians, that is, a phallic mother *par excellence*. This young woman was abandoned by her group in the course of a difficult migration, just as she was about to give birth. Henceforth she wanders in the desert as the 'Mother of Animals,' which she withholds from hunters. He who meets her in her bloody clothes 'is so frightened that he has an erection,' of which she takes advantage to rape him, after which she rewards him with unfailing success in hunting. See H. R. Voth, 'The Oraibi Summer Snake Ceremony,' *Field Columbian Museum*, Publication No. 83, Anthropological Series, Vol. III, No. 4 (Chicago: 1903), pp. 352–3 and p. 353, n. 1.

Mieke Bal, from *Narratology**

See also:
Metz (2.i)
Barthes (2.iii)
Smith (3.ii)
Brooks (3.ii)
Gibson (3.ii)
Lanser (5)
Diengott (5)
Roof (5)
Derrida (6)

INTRODUCTION

Narratology is the theory of narrative texts. A theory is a systematic set of generalized statements about a particular segment of reality. That segment of reality, the corpus, about which narratology attempts to make its pronouncements consists of narrative texts. One should actually be able to say that the corpus consists of all narrative texts and only those texts which are narrative. One of the first problems in advancing such a theory is the formulation of characteristics with which we can delimit that corpus. Although everyone has a general idea of what narrative texts are, it is certainly not always easy to decide whether or not a given text should be considered narrative.

If the necessary characteristics can successfully be defined, these same characteristics can then serve as the point of departure for the next phase: a description of the way in which *each* narrative text is constructed. Once this is accomplished, we have a description of a *narrative system*. On the basis of this description, we can then examine the variations

* *Narratology: Introduction to the Theory of Narrative*, trans. C. van Boheemen (London: University of Toronto Press, 1985), pp. 3–9.

that are possible when the narrative system is concretized into narrative texts. This last step presupposes that an infinite number of narrative texts can be described using the finite number of concepts contained within the narrative system. This book presents an exposition of a coherent, systematic narratology and of the concepts pertaining to it. Readers are offered an instrument with which they can describe narrative texts. This does not imply that the theory is some kind of machine into which one inserts a text at one end and expects an adequate description to roll out at the other. The concepts that are presented here must be regarded as tools. These tools are useful in that they enable us to formulate a textual description in such a way that it is accessible to others. Furthermore, discovering the characteristics of a text can also be facilitated by insight into the abstract narrative system.

The textual description obtained with the aid of this theory can by no means be regarded as the only correct description possible. Another individual may perhaps use the same concepts differently, emphasize other aspects of the text, and, consequently, produce a different textual description. If the description of a text is understood as a proposal that can be presented to others, the fact that the description is formulated within the framework of a systematic theory carries with it one important advantage: it facilitates any discussion of the proposed description. With this in mind, we can return to the question of the corpus of narrative texts. What does this corpus consist of? At first glance, the answer seems obvious: novels, novellas, short stories, fairy tales, newspaper articles, and so forth. But, with or without motivation, we are establishing boundaries, boundaries with which not everyone would agree. Some people, for example, argue that comic strips belong to the corpus of narrative texts, but others disagree. If these people hope to reach an agreement, they must first be able to explain how they have arrived at their decisions. In this case, the explanation is very simple. Those individuals who consider comic strips to be narrative texts broadly interpret the concept *text*. In their view, a text does not have to be a *language* text. In comic strips another, non-linguistic, sign system is employed, namely the *picture*. Other individuals, sharing a more restricted interpretation of what constitutes a text, reserve this term for *language* texts only.

As this simple example demonstrates, it is important that we precisely define the concepts which we use. A definition should be formulated so clearly that everyone who works with the concept shares the same understanding of the notion as it was originally defined. This ideal situation is sometimes difficult to realize as, for example, when the concept in question has been used so often that it has begun to lead a life of its own and is understood somewhat differently by every user. Such is the case with very common and seemingly obvious notions such as *literature, text, narrative*, and *poem*. If, when working with such a notion, one does not feel capable of decisively resolving the problem of definition, it is, of course, possible to use a definition that is valid only for the particular study (lesson, discussion, thesis, article, etc.) with which one is engaged. The readers must then decide whether or not they will adopt the definition for use in other contexts; at any rate, the concepts under discussion have been clarified. A disagreement about the status of comic strips would quickly be settled if the definition of a text were first agreed on.

As suggested above, presenting a theory about narrative texts entails defining a number of central concepts. Within the scope of this Introduction, then, a *text* is a finite, structured whole composed of language signs. A *narrative text* is a text in which an agent relates a narrative. A *story* is a fabula that is presented in a certain manner. A *fabula* is a series of logically and chronologically related events that are caused or experienced by actors. An *event* is the transition from one state to another state. *Actors* are agents that perform actions. They are not necessarily human. *To act* is defined here as to cause or to experience an event. The assertion that a narrative text is one in which a story is related implies that the text *is* not the story. If two terms clearly have the same meaning, it is preferable to discard one. What is meant by these two terms can be clearly illustrated by the following example. Everyone in Europe is familiar with the story of Tom Thumb. However, not everyone has read that story in the same text. There are different versions; in other words, there are different texts in which that same story is related. There are noticeable differences among the various texts. Some texts are considered to be literary while others are not; some can be read aloud to children, others are too difficult. Evidently, narrative texts differ from one another even if the related story is the same. It is therefore useful to examine the text separate from the story.

The example of 'Tom Thumb' can again be used to illustrate the next distinction, that between story and fabula. This distinction is based upon the difference between the sequence of events and the *way in which* these events are presented. That difference lies not only in the language used. Despite their having read different texts, readers of 'Tom Thumb' usually agree with one another as to which of the characters deserves sympathy. They applaud the clever boy and they rejoice at the giant's misfortunes. In order that Tom might triumph over his enemy readers are quite prepared to watch unabashedly as Tom exchanges crowns so that the giant unwittingly eats his own children. Readers are, in fact, delighted by this trick. Evidently this rather cruel fabula is presented in such a way in all of the texts that the readers are willing to sacrifice one group of children for another. When 'Tom Thumb' is 'related' in another sign system – in a film, for example – the same reactions are evoked. This phenomenon demonstrates that something happens with the fabula which is not exclusively language-related.

These definitions suggest that a three-layer distinction – text, story, fabula – is a reasonable basis for a further study of narrative texts. This distinction is the point of departure for the theory of narrative texts that is presented here. Such a distinction carries with it the assumption that it is possible to analyse the three layers separately. That does not mean that these layers exist independently of one another. The only material which we have for our investigation is the text before us. And even this statement is not correctly put; the readers have only the book, paper and ink, and they must use this material to establish the structure of the text. That a text can be divided into three layers is a theoretical supposition based upon a process of reasoning. Only the text layer, embodied in the sign system of language, is directly accessible. The researcher distinguishes different layers of a text in order to account for particular effects which the text has upon its readers. Naturally, the reader, at least the 'average reader' – not the researcher – does not make such a distinction. In this Introduction, intended as an instrument for examining texts, the theory is based upon the notion of distinct layers, a distinction that is necessary for text analysis. It is, therefore, inevitable that that which is in effect inseparable should temporarily be disjoined.

* * *

Within this framework, the following topics will be discussed. The fabula, understood as material that is worked into a story, has been defined as a series of events. This series is constructed according to certain rules. We call this the *logic of events*. Structuralists often work from the assumption that the series of events that is presented in a story must answer to the same rules as those controlling human behaviour, since a narrative text would otherwise be impossible to understand. If human behaviour is taken as the criterion for describing events, then the question immediately arises of the function of the instruments of action, the actors. Greimas' suggestion that the actors be described in relation to the events provides one possible answer to this question. However, neither Bremond nor Greimas takes into account two other elements in a fabula that are logically describable. An event, no matter how insignificant, always takes up *time* in reality. This time has a hypothetical status: in a fabula the events have not 'actually' occurred. Nevertheless, the time is often important for the continuation of the fabula and must, consequently, be made describable. If Tom Thumb had not had seven-mile boots at his disposal, he would never have been able to flee from the giant in time. The difference between the time that Tom Thumb needs to escape from the giant's grasp and the time that the giant needs to wake up is, in this case, decisive for the close of the fabula. Furthermore, events always occur *somewhere*, be it a place that actually exists (Amsterdam) or an imaginary place (C.S. Lewis' Narnia). Events, actors, time, and location together constitute the material of a fabula. In order to differentiate the components of this layer from other aspects, I shall henceforth refer to them as *elements*. These elements are organized in a certain way into a story. Their arrangement in relation to one another is such that they can produce the effect desired, be this convincing, moving, disgusting, or aesthetic. Several processes are involved in ordering the various elements into a story. These processes are not to be confused with the author's activity – it is both impossible and useless to generalize about the latter. The principles of ordering which are described here have a hypothetical status only and their purpose is to make possible a description of highly refined material in the story.

1   The events are arranged in a sequence which can differ from the chronological sequence.
2   The amount of time which is allotted in the story to the various elements of the fabula is determined with respect to the amount of time which these elements take up in the fabula.
3   The actors are provided with distinct traits. In this manner, they are individualized and transformed into characters.
4   The locations where events occur are also given distinct characteristics and are thus transformed into specific places.
5   In addition to the necessary relationships among actors, events, locations, and time, all of which were already describable in the layer of the fabula, other relationships (symbolic, allusive, etc.) may exist among the various elements.
6   A choice is made from among the various 'points of view' from which the elements can be presented.

The results of these several processes is a specific story which is distinct from other stories. I shall refer to the traits which are specific to a given story as *aspects*.

A fabula that has been ordered into a story is still not a text. A narrative text is a story that is told in language; that is, it is converted into language signs. As was evident from the definition of a narrative text, these signs are produced by an agent who relates. This agent cannot be identified with the writer. Rather, the writer withdraws and calls upon a fictitious spokesman, an agent technically known as the *narrator*. But the narrator does not relate continually: Whenever direct speech occurs in the text, it is as if the narrator temporarily transfers this function to one of the actors. When describing the text layer, it is thus important to ascertain *who* is doing the narration.

A text does not consist solely of narration in the specific sense. In every narrative text, one can point to passages that concern something other than events: an opinion about something, for example, or a disclosure on the part of the narrator which is not directly connected with the events, a description of a face or of a location, and so forth. It is thus possible to examine *what* is said in a text, and to classify it as narrative, descriptive, or argumentative. The one question that still remains is *how* all of this is narrated. There is often a noticeable difference between the narrator's style and that of the actors. As a result of this strict division into three parts, a division based upon the three distinct layers previously discussed, some topics that traditionally constitute a unified whole will be treated separately in different stages of this study.

On the basis of what has been said above, it should now be possible to formulate more precisely those characteristics that can be instrumental in specifying the corpus of narrative texts, the corpus for which this theory should be valid. However, this presents problems. Ideally, the charactertistics of narrative texts should be as follows:

1   Two types of spokesmen are to be found in a narrative text; one does not play
     a role in the fabula whereas the other does (NB: this difference exists even when
     the narrator and the actor are one and the same person as, for example, in
     a narrative related in the first person. The narrator is the same person, but at
     another moment and in another situation than when s/he originally experienced
     the events).
2   It is possible to distinguish three layers in a narrative text: the text, the story, and
     the fabula. Each of these layers is describable.
3   That with which the narrative text is concerned, the 'contents,' is a series of
     connected events caused or experienced by actors.

Together, these characteristics should produce a definition: a narrative text is a text in which the above three characteristics may be found. The third characteristic also applies, for example, to dramatic texts. The problem, however, remains that there are texts which display all three characteristics, but which nevertheless, on the basis of either tradition or intuition, are not regarded as narrative texts. This is true of many poems. *The Waste Land* by T.S. Eliot is one of the numerous examples. A poem such as this may be termed a narrative poem, and its narrative characteristics may also be narratologically described. That this does not often occur can be attributed to the fact that the poem displays other, more salient characteristics, namely poetic characteristics; Eliot's poem remains first a poem, and its narrative characteristics are of but secondary importance. Evidently, the characteristics mentioned above do not lead to an absolute, watertight specification of the corpus. This in turn implies that a narrative theory makes describable only the narrative aspects of a text and not all the characteristics of a narrative text. It is, therefore, impossible to specify a fixed corpus; we can only specify a corpus of texts in which the narrative characteristics are so dominant that their description may be considered relevant. Another possibility is to use the theory to describe segments of non-narrative texts as well as the narrative aspects of any given text, such as, for example, the above-mentioned poem by Eliot. The problem of specifying a corpus is then solved in the sense that the relativity of such a specification is clearly established.

Christain Metz, 'Notes Toward a Phenomenology of the Narrative'*

See also:
Lévi-Strauss (2.i)
Barthes (2.iii)
Berger (3.iii)
Mulvey (4)
Heath (4)
Iser (7)
Ricoeur (7)

. . .

According to Algirdas Julien Greimas (*Semantique structurale*), the minimum structure any signification requires is the presence of two terms and the relationship linking them; thus, he notes, signification presupposes perception (of the terms and of their relation). Similarly, it might be said that the main interest of structural analysis is only in being able to find what was already there, of accounting with more precision for what a naïve consciousness had 'picked up' without analysis. Let us also remember what Claude Lévi-Strauss wrote about myths in his *Structural Anthropology*: that a myth is always recognized as being such by those to whom it is recited, even when it has been translated from one idiom into another, even when its exact formulation has been somewhat modified.

Let us say, therefore – perhaps a little cavalierly – that structural analysis always assumes, by virtue of an implicit or explicit prior stage, something like a phenomenology of its subject, or, again, that *signification* (which is constructed and discontinuous) renders explicit what had first been experienced only as a perception (which is continuous and spontaneous). It is from this point of view that I would like to explore some answers to the question: How is a narrative recognized, prior to any analysis?

I

A narrative has *a beginning and an ending*, a fact that simultaneously distinguishes it from the rest of the world and opposes it to the 'real' world. It is true that certain types of narrative, culturally highly elaborated, have the peculiarity of *cheating on the ending*

* *Film Language* (London: Oxford University Press, 1974), pp. 16–24.

(conclusions that are withheld or are evasive, 'mirror' constructions in which the end of the recited event establishes and explains the conditions that produced the instance of recitation, denouements in an endless spiral, etc.), but these are only secondary elaborations, which enrich the narrative without destroying it, and which are neither intended nor able to remove it from its basic requirement of *enclosure*. It is the reader's imagination, and not the substance of the narrative sequence, that these trick endings project into infinity. In a literary narrative that trails off in points of suspension (whether real or implied), the effect of being suspended does not apply to the narrative object, which, for its part, retains a perfectly clear ending – indicated, precisely, by the three dots. The British film *Dead of Night* concludes in a spiral,[1] but, as a suite of images, it has a definite ending – the last image of the film.

Children are not fooled when being told stories. For them, the question of knowing whether the story has ended is always relevant, even when they have the maturity to glimpse possible extensions of the *semantic substance* of the story (but not of the story itself). They ask, 'Is that the end? But *afterward* what does the prince do?'

II

A beginning and an ending – that is to say, the narrative is a *temporal sequence*. A doubly temporal sequence, one must hasten to specify: there is the time of the thing told and the time of the telling (the time of the significate and the time of the signifier). This duality not only renders possible all the temporal distortions that are commonplace in narratives (three years of the hero's life summed up in two sentences of a novel or in a few shots of a 'frequentative' montage in film, etc.). More basically, it invites us to consider that one of the functions of narrative is to invent one time scheme in terms of another time scheme – and that is what distinguishes narrative from simple *description* (which creates space in time), as well as from the *image* (which creates one space in another space).

The example of the cinematographic narrative easily illustrates these three possibilities: A motionless and isolated shot of a stretch of desert is an image (space-significate–space-signifier); several partial and successive shots of this desert waste make up a description (space-significate–time-signifier); several successive shots of a caravan moving across the desert constitute a narrative (time-significate–time-signifier).

This example was purposely simplified (in film, indeed, space is always present, even in the narrative, because the cinematic narrative is produced by images). But their simplification is of little importance here, and it was intended only to show that the narrative is, among other things, a system of temporal transformations. In any narrative, the narrative object is a more or less chronological sequence of events; in any narrative, the narrative instance takes the form of a sequence of signifiers that has a certain duration – for the literary narrative, the time it takes to read it; for the cinematographic narrative, the time it takes to see it, etc.

In still photography, by contrast, what is represented as a point in time that has been frozen; the viewer's intake is also supposed to be instantaneous; and, even when it is prolonged, it is not a reading of the signifiers in a single, controlled order of concatenations.

It is within the framework of this opposition between the narrative and the image that one can perhaps explain the awkward, hybrid position of description. We all assume that description differs from narration, and that is a classical distinction, but, on the other hand, a large number of narratives contain descriptions, and it is not even clear that descriptions exist other than as components of narratives. Thus, description appears simultaneously as the opposite of narration and as one of the great figures, or one of the important *moments*, of narration. This curious mixture of antinomy and kinship, which intuitively defines the relationship between narration and description, can be made a little clearer if one brings a third term into the system – the image. Narration and description are opposed in common to the image because their signifiers are temporalized, whereas the image's signifier is instantaneous; thus, the kinship. But within this 'narrative-descriptive' category, which is defined by a feature of the signifier, narration and description are contrasted by a feature of their significates, for in the narrative the signified is temporalized, whereas it is instantaneous in description; thus, the antinomy.

Within the narrative, the descriptive passage immediately reveals itself: it is the only one within which the temporal concatenation of the signifiers – though it is not interrupted – ceases to refer to the temporal relation (whether consecutive or not) among the corresponding significates, and the order it assigns to their signified elements is only one of spatial coexistence (that is to say, of relationships supposed to be constant whatever moment in time is chosen). From the narrative to the descriptive, we pass through a *change of intelligibility*, in the sense in which one speaks of a change of gears in automobiles.

III

A closed sequence, a temporal sequence: every narrative is, therefore, a discourse (the converse is not true; many discourses are not narratives – the lyric poem, the educational film, etc.).

What distinguishes a discourse from the rest of the world, and by the same token contrasts it with the 'real' world, is the fact that a discourse must necessarily be made by someone (for discourse is not language), whereas one of the characteristics of the world is that it is uttered by no one.

In Jakobsonian terms, one would say that a discourse, being a statement or sequence of statements, refers necessarily to a subject of the statement. But one should not hastily assume an author, for the notion of authorship is simply one of the forms, culturally bound and conditioned, of a far more universal process, which, for that reason, should be called the 'narrative process.' It is true that in certain highly elaborated narratives of modern Western society the subject of the statement is most often the author, but, aside from that, there are the myths, the folk tales, the many narrative films of everyday consumption, which are passed from hand to hand in the course of their industrial or 'craft' manufacturing, the many radio and television shows put together by teams (whether as an organized group or in gleeful disorder), etc. – in short, all the *authorless* narratives, at least in the sense 'author' has in the humanist tradition of 'high culture.'

Narratives without authors, but not without narrators. The impression that *someone is speaking* is bound not to the empirical presence of a definite, known, or knowable speaker but to the listener's spontaneous perception of the linguistic nature of the object to which he is listening; because it is speech, someone must be speaking.

Albert Laffay, in *Logique du cinéma*, has shown this to be true of film narrative. The spectator perceives images which have obviously been selected (they could have been other images) and arranged (their order could have been different). In a sense, he is leafing through an album of predetermined pictures, and it is not he who is turning the pages but some 'master of ceremonies,' some 'grand image-maker' ('*grand imagier*') who (before being recognized as the author, if it is an *auteur* film, or, if not, in the absence of an author) is first and foremost the film itself as a linguistic object (since the spectator always knows that what he is seeing is a film), or more precisely a sort of 'potential linguistic focus' ('*foyer linguistique virtuel*') situated somewhere behind the film, and representing the basis that makes the film possible. That is the filmic form of the narrative instance, which is necessarily present, and is necessarily perceived, in any narrative.

IV

A closed sequence, a temporal sequence, discourse – therefore, the perception of the narrative as real, that is, as being really a narrative, must result in rendering the recited object *unreal*.

I will not linger over deliberately imaginary narratives (fantastic tales, legends, etc.); far from being convincing examples of the process of *unrealization* (*irréalization*), which is at the heart of every narrative act, they would divert our attention toward a second level of unrealization, which is unnecessary and is very different from the first. Whether the narrated event follows nonhuman logic (a pumpkin metamorphosed into a carriage, etc.) or the ordinary logic of everyday life ('realistic' tales of various kinds), it has, because it is perceived as narrated, already been unrealized. Realism is not reality. No one expects to meet in the street the hero of some scrupulously realistic contemporary novel. Realism affects the organization of the contents, not narration as a status. On one level of perception, Emma Bovary is no less imaginary than Cinderella's fairy godmother.

We must, however, go one step further, for, along with realistic stories (which nobody believes have really occurred), there are also *real stories*: accounts of historical occurrences (the assassination of Marat), accounts of daily life (I tell a friend what I have done the evening before), accounts to oneself (my memories as I recall them), and the news accounts of film, radio, the press, etc. Now, these 'true' accounts are characterized, just as much as the imaginary accounts, by the form of unreality that we are examining here. The reader of a history book knows that Marat is not actually being assassinated now; the friend to whom I am talking understands that, although I am describing my activities, I am no longer living them (or, more precisely, that, because the narrative act is, in turn, another part of my life, that part of my life I am recounting to him ceases to be lived as it is being told); the viewer of television news does not consider himself a direct witness to the event the images bring to him.

Reality assumes *presence*, which has a privileged position along two parameters, space and time; only the *here* and *now* are completely real. By its very existence, the narrative suppresses the *now* (accounts of current life) or the *here* (live television coverage), and most frequently the two together (newsreels, historical accounts, etc.).

An account is perceived as such only as long as a margin, even an infinitesimal one, separates it from the fullness of *here* and *now*. Certain examples of minimum *unreality* are very enlightening: the paradoxical situation has occasionally been noted of participants in a political parade who, transistor radio in hand, were listening, while demonstrating, to the live coverage of their own demonstration. But, perhaps because the inordinate overvaluation of the specificity of the audiovisual media may occasionally blur more general truths, sufficient attention has not been given to the fact that, for the listening demonstrators, the radio report remained entirely an account; for, at the precise moment they were listening, they were no longer demonstrating (or at least it was not their listening self which was demonstrating), and the narrated parade they were hearing could only be confused with the demonstration they were taking part in from a positivistic point of view, introducing the notion of secondary information (whether or not the demonstrators had availed themselves of this intelligence). To be sure, between these two parades there is not the same difference as, say, between a parade held on May 15 and one held on May 16, but this order of difference is not the only possible one, and indeed one substantial parade can, as is the case here, correspond to two phenomenal parades. The first parade is the one the man with the radio knows he is participating in, and which he is experiencing instant after instant, at the precise point in the march where he finds himself each second – a parade that, like Fabrice at the battle of Waterloo, he will never dominate. The second is the one whose account he is listening to, and it is only the first parade made unreal – this unrealization being due to the presence of the newscaster, who is, however, notably absent from the first parade, as well as to a spatiotemporal displacement (reduced to a minimum in this example), which necessarily brings about the intrusion of the narrator. It is this second parade, and only this second parade, that the man with the radio can dominate, like the reader of Victor Hugo's 'Waterloo' (A.J. Greimas would say that the man with the radio is actually two actors: the demonstrating actor and the listening actor).

We are approaching a concept that has been developed frequently since Jean-Paul Sartre made his studies of the world of the imagination: reality does not tell stories, but memory, because it is an account, is entirely imaginative. Thus, an event must in some way have ended before its narration can begin. One might add that, in the case of the strictly simultaneous accounts that live television coverage offers, spatial displacement – that is, the fact of the image itself – can assume the sole of temporal displacement (which is the predominant feature of traditional narratives), thereby alone ensuring the correct functioning of narrative unrealization (otherwise how could one explain the remarkable absence of traumatism in the television-viewer?): the event described by live news coverage is real, but it occurs elsewhere. On the screen, it is unreal.

NOTE

1   It is morning. The hero, an architect, wakes up. He has had a bad night: always that same recurring dream. The telephone rings. It is a neighboring landowner who wishes to make some improvements on his property and invites the architect to spend the weekend at his manor. The hero accepts. Upon his arrival, he gradually recognizes the manor of his dream. The party takes place, and ends as the hero wakes up. He gets out of bed: so it was a dream after all. The same recurring dream. The telephone rings, etc. . . . .

ii THEORIES

Gérard Genette, 'Order in Narrative'*

See also:
Aristotle (1.i)
Barthes (2.iii)
Gibson (3.ii)
Lanser (5)
Diengott (5)
Derrida (6)
Miller (6)

NARRATIVE TIME?

> Narrative is a . . . doubly temporal sequence. . . . There is the time of the thing told and the time of the narrative (the time of the signified and the time of the signifier). This duality not only renders possible all the temporal distortions that are commonplace in narratives (three years of the hero's life summed up in two sentences of a novel or in a few shots of a 'frequentative' montage in film. etc.). More basically, it invites us to consider that one of the functions of narrative is to invent one time scheme in terms of another time scheme.[1]

The temporal duality so sharply emphasized here, and referred to by German theoreticians as the opposition between *erzählte Zeit* (story time) and *Erzählzeit* (narrative time),[2] is a typical characteristic not only of cinematic narrative but also of oral narrative, at all its levels of aesthetic elaboration, including the fully 'literary' level of epic recitation or dramatic narration (the narrative of Théramène,[3] for example). It is less relevant perhaps in other forms of narrative expression, such as the *roman-photo*[4] or the comic strip (or a pictorial strip, like the predella of Urbino, or an embroidered strip, like the 'tapestry' of Queen Matilda), which, while making up sequences of images and thus requiring a successive or diachronic reading, also lend themselves to, and even invite, a kind of global and synchronic look – or at least a look whose direction is no longer determined by the sequence of images. The status of written literary narrative in this respect is even more difficult to establish. Like the oral or cinematic narrative, it can only be 'consumed', and therefore actualized, in a *time* that is obviously reading time, and even if the sequentiality of its components can be undermined by a capricious, repetitive, or selective reading, that undermining nonetheless stops short of perfect analexia: one can run a film backwards, image by image, but one cannot read a text backwards, letter by letter, or even word by word, or even sentence by sentence, without its ceasing to be a text. Books are a little more constrained than people sometimes say they are by the celebrated *linearity* of the linguistic signifier, which is easier to deny in theory than eliminate in fact. However, there is no question here of identifying the status of written narrative (literary or not) with that of oral narrative. The temporality

---

* From *Narrative Discourse: An Essay in Method*, trans. J. E. Lewin (Cambridge: Cambridge University Press, 1997), pp. 142–50.

of written narrative is to some extent conditional or instrumental; produced in time, like everything else, written narrative exists in space and as space, and the time needed for 'consuming' it is the time needed for *crossing* or *traversing* it, like a road or a field. The narrative text, like every other text, has no other temporality than what it borrows, metonymically, from its own reading.

This state of affairs, we will see below, has certain consequences for our discussion, and at times we will have to correct, or try to correct, the effects of metonymic displacement; but we must first take that displacement for granted, since it forms part of the narrative game, and therefore accept literally the quasi-fiction of *Erzählzeit*, this false time standing in for a true time and to be treated – with the combination of reservation and acquiescence that this involves – as a *pseudo-time*.

Having taken these precautions, we will study relations between the time of the story and the (pseudo-) time of the narrative according to what seem to me to be three essential determinations: connections between the temporal *order* of succession of the events in the story and the pseudo-temporal order of their arrangement in the narrative, which will be the subject of the first chapter; connections between the variable *duration* of these events or story sections and the pseudo-duration (in fact, length of text) of their telling in the narrative – connections, thus, of *speed* – which will be the subject of the second chapter; finally, connections of *frequency*, that is (to limit myself to an approximate formulation), relations between the repetitive capacities of the story and those of the narrative, relations to which the third chapter will be devoted.

ANACHRONIES

To study the temporal order of a narrative is to compare the order in which events or temporal sections are arranged in the narrative discourse with the order of succession these same events or temporal segments have in the story, to the extent that story order is explicitly indicated by the narrative itself or inferable from one or another indirect clue. Obviously this reconstitution is not always possible, and it becomes useless for certain extreme cases like the novels of Robbe-Grillet, where temporal reference is deliberately sabotaged. It is just as obvious that in the classical narrative, on the other hand, reconstitution is most often not only possible, because in those texts narrative discourse never inverts the order of events without saying so, but also necessary, and precisely for the same reason: when a narrative segment begins with an indication like 'Three months earlier . . .' we must take into account both that this scene comes *after* in the narrative, and that it is supposed to have come *before* in the story: each of these, or rather the relationship between them (of contrast or of dissonance), is basic to the narrative text, and suppressing this relationship by eliminating one of its members is not only not sticking to the text, but is quite simply killing it.

Pinpointing and measuring these narrative *anachronies* (as I will call the various types of discordance between the two orderings of story and narrative) implicitly assume the existence of a kind of zero degree that would be a condition of perfect temporal correspondence between narrative and story. This point of reference is more hypothetical than real. Folklore narrative habitually conforms, at least in its major articulations, to chronological order, but our (Western) literary tradition, in contrast, was inaugurated by a characteristic effect of anachrony. In the eighth line of the *Iliad*, the narrator, having evoked the quarrel between Achilles and Agamemnon that he proclaims as the starting point of his narrative (*ex hou de ta prôta*), goes back about ten days to reveal the cause of the quarrel in some 140 retrospective lines (affront to Chryses – Apollo's anger – plague). We know that this beginning in *medias res*, followed by an expository return to an earlier period of time, will become one of the formal topoi of epic, and we also know how faithfully the style of novelistic narration follows in this respect the style of its remote ancestor, even in the heart of the 'realistic' nineteenth century. . . . We will thus not be so foolish as to claim that anachrony is either a rarity or a modern invention. On the contrary, it is one of the traditional resources of literary narration.

. . .

ANALEPSES

Every anachrony constitutes, with respect to the narrative into which it is inserted – onto which it is grafted – a narrative that is temporally second, subordinate to the first in a sort of narrative syntax that we met in the analysis we undertook above of a very short fragment from *Jean Santeuil*. We will henceforth call the temporal level of narrative with respect to which anachrony is defined as such, 'first narrative'. Of course – and this we have already verified – the embeddings can be more complex, and an anachrony can assume the role of first narrative with respect to another that it carries; and more generally, with respect to an anachrony the totality of the context can be taken as first narrative. . . .

This distinction is not as useless as it might seem at first sight. In effect, external analepses and internal analepses (or the internal part of mixed analepses) function for purposes of narrative analysis in totally different ways, at least on one point that seems to me essential. External analepses, by the very fact that they are external, never at any moment risk interfering with the first narrative, for their only function is to fill out the first narrative by enlightening the reader on one or another 'antecedent'. This is obviously the case with some of the examples already mentioned and it is also, and just as typically, the case with *Un amour de Swann* in the *Recherche du temps perdu*. The case is otherwise with internal analepses: since their temporal field is contained within the temporal field of the first narrative, they present an obvious risk of redundancy or collision. . . .

We have seen how the determination of *reach* allowed us to divide analepses into two classes, external and internal, depending on whether the point to which they reach is located outside or inside the temporal field of the first narrative. The mixed class – not, after all, much resorted to – is in fact determined by a characteristic of *extent*, since this class consists of external analepses prolonged to rejoin and pass beyond the starting point of the first narrative. . . .

[In Proust's *Recherche*] the boldest avoidance (even if the boldness is pure negligence) consists of forgetting the analeptic character of a section of narrative and prolonging that section more or less indefinitely on its own account, paying no attention to the point where it rejoins the first narrative. That is what happens in the episode – famous for other reasons – of the grandmother's death. It opens with an obviously analeptic beginning: 'I went upstairs, and found my grandmother not so well. For some time past, without knowing exactly what was wrong, she had been complaining of her health.' Then the narrative that has been opened in the retrospective mood continues uninterruptedly on up to the death, without ever acknowledging and signalling the moment (although indeed necessarily come to and passed beyond) when Marcel, returning from Mme de Villeparisis's, had found his grandmother 'not so well'. We can never, therefore, either locate the grandmother's death exactly in relation to the Villeparisis matinée, or decide where the analepsis ends and the first narrative resumes.[5] The case is obviously the same, but on a very much broader scale, with the analepsis opened in *Noms de pays: le pays*. We have already seen that this analepsis will continue to the last line of the *Recherche* without paying its respects in passing to the moment of the late insomnias, although these were its source in his memory and almost its narrative matrix: another retrospection that is more than complete, with an extent much greater than its reach, and which at an undetermined point in its career is covertly transformed into an anticipation. In his own way – without proclaiming it and probably even without perceiving it – Proust here unsettles the most basic norms of narration, and anticipates the most disconcerting proceedings of the modern novel.

PROLEPSES

Anticipation, or temporal prolepsis, is clearly much less frequent than the inverse figure, at least in the Western narrative tradition – although each of the three great early epics, the *Iliad*, the *Odyssey*, and the *Aeneid*, begins with a sort of anticipatory summary that to a certain extent justifies the formula Todorov applied to Homeric narrative: 'plot of predestination.'[6] The concern with narrative suspense that is characteristic of the 'classical' conception of the novel ('classical' in the broad sense, and whose center of gravity is, rather, in the nineteenth century) does not easily come to terms with such a practice. Neither, moreover, does the traditional fiction of a narrator who must appear more or less to discover the story at the same time that he tells it. Thus we will find very few prolepses in a Balzac, a Dickens, or a Tolstoy, even if the common practice, as we have already seen, of beginning *in medias res* (or yet, I may venture to say, *in ultimas res*), sometimes gives the illusion of it. It goes without saying that a certain load of 'predestination' hangs over the main part of the narrative in *Manon Lescaut* (where we know, even before Des Grieux opens his story, that it ends with a deportation), or a fortiori in *The Death of Ivan Ilych*, which begins with its epilogue.

The 'first-person' narrative lends itself better than any other to anticipation, by the very fact of its avowedly retrospective character, which authorizes the narrator to allude to the future and in particular to his present situation, for these to some extent form part of his role. Robinson Crusoe can tell us almost at the beginning that the lecture his father gave to turn him aside from nautical adventures was 'truly prophetic', even though at the time he had no idea of it, and Rousseau, with the episode of the combs, does not fail to vouch for not only his past innocence but also the vigor of his retrospective indignation: 'In writing this I feel my pulse quicken yet.'[7] Nonetheless, the *Recherche du temps perdu* uses prolepsis to an extent probably equaled in the whole history of narrative, even autobiographical narrative,[8] and is thus privileged territory for the study of this type of narrative anachrony. . . .

The importance of 'anachronic' narrative in the *Recherche du temps perdu* is obviously connected to the retrospectively synthetic character of Proustian narrative, which is totally present in the narrator's mind at every moment. Ever since the day when the narrator in a trance perceived the unifying significance of his story, he never ceases to hold all of its threads simultaneously, to apprehend simultaneously all of its places and all of its moments, to be capable of establishing a multitude of 'telescopic' relationships amongst them: a ubiquity that is spatial but also temporal, an 'omnitemporality'. . . .

But the very ideas of retrospection or anticipation, which ground the narrative categories of analepsis and prolepsis in 'psychology', take for granted a perfectly clear temporal consciousness and unambiguous relationships among present, past, and future. Only because the exposition required it, and at the cost of excessive schematization, have I until now postulated this to have always been so. In fact, the very frequency of interpolations and their reciprocal entanglement often embroil matters in such a way as to leave the 'simple' reader, and even the most determined analyst, sometimes with no way out. To conclude this chapter we shall examine some of these ambiguous structures which bring us to the threshold of *achrony* pure and simple. . . .

These proleptic analepses and analeptic prolepses are so many complex anachronies, and they somewhat disturb our reassuring ideas about retrospection and anticipation. Let us again recall the existence of open analepses (analepses whose conclusion cannot be localized), which therefore necessarily entails the existence of temporally indefinite narrative sections. But we also find in the *Recherche* some events not provided with any temporal reference whatsoever, events that we cannot place at all in relation to the events surrounding them. To be unplaceable they need only be attached not to some other event (which would require the narrative to define them as being earlier or later) but to the (atemporal) commentarial discourse that accompanies them – and we know what place that has in this work. . . . After the scene of the missed introduction to Albertine, in the *Jeunes filles en fleurs*, the narrator offers some reflections on the subjectivity of the feeling of love, then illustrates this theory with the example of a drawing master who had never known the color of the hair of a mistress he had passionately loved and who had left him a daughter ('I never saw her except with a hat on').[9] Here, no inference from the content can help the analyst define the status of an anachrony deprived of every temporal connection, which is an event we must ultimately take to be dateless and ageless: to be an achrony.

Now, it is not only such isolated events that express the narrative's capacity to disengage its arrangement from all dependence, even inverse dependence, on the chronological sequence of the story it tells. The *Recherche* presents, at least in two places, genuine *achronic structures*. . . . Only by naively confusing the narrative's syntagmatic order with the story's temporal order does one imagine, as hurried readers do, that the meeting with the Duchess or the episode of the steeples comes later than the scene at Montjouvain. The truth is that the narrator had the clearest of reasons for grouping together, in defiance of all chronology, events connected by spatial proximity, by climatic identity (the walks to Méséglise always take place in bad weather, those to Guermantes in good weather), or by thematic kinship (the Méséglise way represents the erotic-affective side of the world of childhood, that of Guermantes its aesthetic side); he thus made clear, more than anyone had done before him and better than they had, narrative's capacity for *temporal autonomy*.

NOTES

1   Christian Metz, *Film Language: A Semiotics of the Cinema*, trans. Michael Taylor (New York, 1974). p. 18. [Translator's note: I have altered this translation slightly so as to align its terms with the terms used throughout.]

2   See Gunther Müller, 'Erzählzeit und erzählte Zeit', *Festschrift für P. Kluckhohn und Hermann Schneider*, 1948; reprinted in *Morphologische Poetik* (Tübingen, 1968).

3   A character in Racine's *Phèdre*, proverbial for his narration of Hippolytus' death. [Translator]

4   Magazine with love stories told in photographs. [Translator]

5   Proust, *Recherche/Remembrance*, Random House edn, transl. Scott-Moncrieff/Mayor, 1934/1970.

6   Tzvetan Todorov, *The Poetics of Prose* (Ithaca, NY, and London, 1977), p. 65.

7   Rousseau, *Confessions*, Pléiade edn, p. 20.

8   The *Recherche* contains more than twenty proleptic sections of significant length, not counting simple allusions in the course of a sentence. The analepses of like definition are not more numerous, but it is true that they take up, by their extent, the quasi-totality of the text, and that it is atop that first retrospective layer that analepses and prolepses of the second degree are set.

9   *Recherche/Remembrance*, Random House edn, transl. Scott-Moncrieff/Mayor, 1934/1970, vol. I, p. 645.

Seymour Chatman, 'Point of View'*

See also
Booth (1.iii)
Prince (2.ii)
Lanser (5)
Diengott (5)
Iser (7)
Cohn (7)

Let us consider a rather straightforward literary example. *Dombey and Son* begins as follows:

> Dombey sat in the corner of the darkened room in the great armchair by the bedside, and son lay tucked up warm in a little basket bedstead, carefully disposed on a lew settee immediately in front of the fire and close to it, as if his constitution were analogous to that of a muffin, and it was essential to toast him brown while he was very new.

No reader, I take it, believes that the maker of the analogy between the baby and a toasted muffin is Mr Dombey, a man far too complacent about his first male offspring to entertain such a thought. So these are clearly the narrator's words (or, to be scrupulous, they are words assigned to the narrator by the implied author). It is traditional to say that the analogy represents the narrator's 'point of view,' which is here, as often in Dickens's

---

*   From *Coming to Terms: The Rhetoric of Narrative in Fiction and Film* (London: Cornell University Press, 1990), pp. 141–4.

novels, whimsical and gently ironic. But I would argue that the narrator is not to be imagined as literally *contemplating* the new baby and deciding, in that contemplation, that he resembles a muffin.

The convention has it, rather, that the narrator is performing his usual task of *reporting* this scene, and he introduces the muffin analogy the better to convey its unique flavor. The narrator, in this case omniscient and unidentified, is a reporter, not an 'observer' of the story world in the sense of literally witnessing it. It makes no sense to say that a story is told 'through' the narrator's perception since he/she/it is precisely *narrating*, which is not an act of perception but of presentation or representation, of transmitting story events and existents through words or images. It is naive, I think, to argue that this omniscient narrator 'got' this information by witnessing it. He is a component of the discourse: that is, of the mechanism by which the story world is rendered. No one wonders whether the narrator ever inhabited the story world of *Dombey and Son*. Though fictional, he is a different *kind* of fiction from Dombey or Dombey, Jr. He resides in an order of time and place different from that occupied by the characters; his is a different 'here-and-now.' And that's true for every narrator, no matter how minimal his/her/its distance from the 'here-and-now' of the story (as, for example, in the epistolary novel).

The narrator may have his own 'view of things,' of course. But we must lock 'view' with stern quotation marks to indicate the exact nature of the metaphor. Since it makes so little sense to say that the narrator literally sees Mr Dombey sitting there admiring his son, we might ask whether 'view' is not positively misleading as a term to describe the narrator's situation. It seems better to distinguish between narrator's and character's mental experiences in the story world as different *kinds* of experiences, but that is hard to do if we refer to both by the same term, whether 'point of view?' 'perspective,' or 'focalization.'

I am not asserting, of course, that only narrators have attitudes. Characters also have them (along with a whole range of other mental experiences), and they may differ sharply from those of the narrator. A particularly clear example occurs right after our introduction to Mr Dombey. Though others understand that Mrs Dombey was a 'lady with no heart to give him,' Mr Dombey

> would have reasoned: That a matrimonial alliance with himself *must*, in the nature of things, be gratifying and honourable to any woman of common sense. That the hope of giving birth to a new partner in such a house, could not fail to awaken a glorious and stirring ambition in the breast of the least ambitious of her sex. That Mrs. Dombey had entered on that social contract of matrimony: almost necessarily part of a genteel and wealthy station, even without reference to the perpetuation of family firms: with her eyes fully open to these advantages. That Mrs. Dombey had had daily practical knowledge of his position in society. That Mrs. Dombey had always sat at the head of his table, and done the honours of his house in a remarkable lady-like and becoming manner. That Mrs. Dombey must have been happy. That she couldn't help it.

Since it is the narrator who has just reported that there is reason to believe Mrs Dombey a 'lady with no heart to give,' he cannot lay claim to these sentiments or the language that expresses them. They are entirely Mr Dombey's attitude, his 'view' of things.

It is high time that we introduce a terminological distinction between these two loci of 'point of view': that of the narrator, and that of the character. I propose *slant* to name the narrator's attitudes and other mental nuances appropriate to the report function of discourse, and *filter* to name the much wider range of mental activity experienced by characters in the story world – perceptions, cognitions, attitudes, emotions, memories, fantasies, and the like.

'Slant' well captures, I think, the psychological, sociological, and ideological ramifications of the narrator's attitudes, which may range from neutral to highly charged. (I use the term in a totally nonpejorative sense. 'Angle' would work just as well.) The slant may be expressed implicitly or explicitly. When the narrator's slant is explicit – that is, put into so many words – we call it 'commentary,' particularly 'judgmental commentary.' Such commentary should not be confused with the characters' comments, anchored as they are to an observational post *within* the story world. Attitudes, of course, are rooted in ideology, and the narrator is as much a locus of ideology as anyone else, inside or outside the fiction. The ideology may or may not match that of any of the characters. And it may or may not match that of the implied or real author. It might be argued that in a sufficiently broad definition, attitudes are *all* that 'narrator's point of view' feasibly refers to.

Further, though it seems infelicitous to say that a narrator 'looks' at events and existents in the story world, that does not mean that he cannot look at events and existents in the *discourse* world that he occupies, to the extent that that world is fleshed out. The unnamed narrator of *Heart of Darkness* perceives sights and sounds, including Marlowe's voice, in that boat on the Thames. Mr Lockwood perceives, conceives, imagines, meditates about life at Wuthering Heights before Mrs Dean begins her story. But, I contend, it is in the nature of the case that neither can pierce the discourse membrane to experience the story world directly; they can experience it only vicariously, through the words of others. They *re-report* what others tell them. Marlowe and Mrs Dean did, of course, experience the original events, but they did so in their capacity as characters, not as narrators. 'Slant' delimits the mental activity on *this* side of the discourse–story barrier.

'Filter,' on the other hand, seems a good term for capturing something of the mediating function of a character's consciousness – perception, cognition, emotion, reverie – as events are experienced from a space within the story world. The effect has been well understood since Henry James. The story is narrated *as if* the narrator sat somewhere inside or just this side of a character's consciousness and strained all events through that character's sense of them. The very word 'inside' implies, logically, the discourse–story barrier discussed above. And the barrier, structurally, remains, whether the narrator continues to speak in his own voice or falls silent for long stretches or for the entire text. What I like about the term 'filter' is that it catches the nuance of the *choice* made by the implied author about which among the character's imaginable experiences would best enhance the narration – which areas of the story world the implied author wants to illuminate and which to keep obscure. This is a nuance missed by 'point of view,' 'focalization,' and other metaphors.

Gerald Prince, 'Introduction to the Study of the Narratee'*

See also:
Booth (1.iii)
Chatman (2.ii)
Prince (3.i)
Lanser (5)
Iser (7)
Cohn (7)

CLASSIFICATION OF NARRATEES

Thanks to the signals describing the narratee, we are able to characterize any narration according to the type of narratee to whom it is addressed. It would be useless, because too long, too complicated, and too imprecise, to distinguish different categories of narratees according to their temperament, their civil status, or their beliefs. On the other hand, it would be comparatively easy to classify narratees according to their narrative situation, to their position in reference to the narrator, the characters, and the narration.

Many narrations appear to be addressed to no one in particular: no character is regarded as playing the role of narratee and no narratee is mentioned by the narrator either directly ('Without a doubt, dear reader, you have never been confined in a glass bottle') or indirectly ('We could hardly do otherwise than pluck one of its flowers and present it to the reader'). Just as a detailed study of a novel such as *L'Education senti-mentale* or *Ulysses* reveals the presence of a narrator who tries to be invisible and to intervene as little as possible in the course of the events, so too a thorough examination of a narration that appears to have no narratee – the two works mentioned above as well as *Sanctuary*, *L'Etranger*, and *Un Coeur simple* – permits his discovery. The narrator of *Un Coeur simple*, for example, does not refer a single time to a narratee in an explicit manner. In his narrative, nonetheless, there are numerous passages indicating more or less clearly that he is addressing someone. It is thus that the narrator identifies the individuals whose proper names he mentions: 'Robelin, the farmer from Geoffosses . . . Liébard, the farmer from Touques . . . M. Bourais, a former lawyer.' It cannot be for himself that he identifies Robelin, Liébard, or M. Bourais; it must be for his narratee. Moreover, the narrator often resorts to comparisons in order to describe a character or situate an event, and each comparison defines more precisely the type of universe known to the narratee. Finally, the narrator sometimes refers to extra-textual experiences ('that confusion into which we are all thrown by the spectacle of extraordinary men'), which provide proof of the narratee's existence and information about his nature. Thus, even though the narratee may be invisible in a narration, he nonetheless exists and is never entirely forgotten.

In many other narrations, if the narratee is not represented by a character, he is at least mentioned explicitly by the narrator. The latter refers to him more or less frequently and his references can be quite direct (*Eugene Onegin*, *The Gold Pot*, *Tom Jones*) or quite indirect (*The Scarlet Letter*, *The Old Curiosity Shop*, *Les Faux-Monnayeurs*).

---

* In J. P. Tompkins (ed.), *Reader-Response Criticism* (Baltimore, MD: Johns Hopkins University Press, 1980), pp. 17–25.

Like the narratee of *Un Coeur simple*, these narratees are nameless and their role in the narrative is not always very important. Yet because of the passages that designate them in an explicit manner, it is easy to draw their portrait and to know what their narrator thinks of them. Sometimes, in *Tom Jones*, the narrator supplies so much information about his narratee, takes him aside so often, lavishes his advice upon him so frequently, that the latter becomes as clearly defined as any character.

Often instead of addressing – explicitly or implicitly – a narratee who is not a character, the narrator recounts his story to someone who is (*Heart of Darkness*, *Portnoy's Complaint*, *Les Infortunes de la vertu*). This character can be described in a more or less detailed manner. We know practically nothing about Doctor Spielvogel in *Portnoy's Complaint*, except that he is not lacking in perspicacity. On the other hand, in *Les Infortunes de la vertu*, we are informed about all of Juliette's life.

The narratee-character might play no other role in the narrative than that of narratee (*Heart of Darkness*). But he might also play other roles. It is not rare, for example, for him to be at the same time a narrator. In *L'Immoraliste*, one of the three individuals listening to Michel writes a long letter to his brother. In this letter, he repeats the story told to him by his friend, entreats his brother to shake Michel from his unhappiness, and records his own reactions to the narrative as well as the circumstances that led to his being present at its telling. Sometimes the narratee of a story can be at the same time its narrator. He doesn't intend the narration to be for anyone other than himself. In *La Nausée*, for example, as in most novels written in the form of a diary, Roquentin counts on being the only reader of his journal.

Then again, the narratee-character can be more or less affected, more or less influenced by the narrative addressed to him. In *Heart of Darkness*, the companions of Marlowe are not transformed by the story that he recounts to them. In *L'Immoraliste*, the three narratees, if they are not really different from what they were before Michel's account, are nonetheless 'overcome by a strange feeling of malaise.' And in *La Nausée*, as in many other works in which the narrator constitutes his own narratee, the latter is gradually and profoundly changed by the events he recounts for himself.

Finally, the narratee-character can represent for the narration someone more or less essential, more or less irreplaceable as a narratee. In *Heart of Darkness*, it's not necessary for Marlowe to have his comrades on the *Nellie* as narratees. He would be able to recount his story to any other group; perhaps he would be able to refrain from telling it at all. On the other hand, in *L'Immoraliste*, Michel wished to address his friends and for that reason gathered them around him. Their presence in Algeria holds out hope: they will certainly not condemn him, they will perhaps understand him, and they will certainly help him get over his current situation. And in *A Thousand and One Nights*, to have the caliph as narratee is the difference between life and death for Scheherazade. If he refuses to listen to her, she will be killed. He is thus the only narratee whom she can have.

Whether or not he assumes the role of character, whether or not he is irreplaceable, whether he plays several roles or just one, the narratee can be a listener (*L'Immoraliste*, *Les Infortunes de la vertu*, *A Thousand and One Nights*) or a reader (*Adam Bede*, *Le Père Goriot*, *Les Faux-Monnayeurs*). Obviously, a text may not necessarily say whether the narratee is a reader or a listener. In such cases, it could be said that the narratee is a reader when the narration is written (*Hérodias*) and a listener when the narration is oral (*La Chanson de Roland*).

... We could probably think of other distinctions or establish other categories, but in any case, we can see how much more precise and more refined the typology of narrative would be if it were based not only upon narrators but also upon narratees. The same type of narrator can address very different types of narratees. Thus, Louis (*Le Noeud de vipères*), Salavin (*Journal de Salavin*), and Roquentin (*La Nausée*) are three characters who all keep a journal and who are very conscious of writing. But Louis changes narratees several times before deciding to write for himself; Slavin does not regard himself as the sole reader of his journal; and Roquentin writes exclusively for himself. Then again, very different narrators can address narratees of the same type. The narrators of *Un Coeur simple* and *La Condition humaine* as well as Meursault in *L'Etranger* all address a narratee who is not a character, who doesn't know them and who is not familiar with the individuals presented in the text nor with the events recounted.

Nonetheless, it is not only for a typology of the narrative genre and for a history of novelistic techniques that the notion of the narratee is important. Indeed, this notion is more interesting, because it permits us to study better the way in which a narration functions. In all narrations, a dialogue is established between the narrator(s), the narratee(s), and the character(s).[1] This dialogue develops – and consequently the narration also – as a function of the distance separating them from each other. In distinguishing the different categories of narratees, we have already used this concept, but without dwelling upon it too much: it is clear that a narratee who has participated in the events recorded is, in one sense, much closer to the characters than a narratee who has never even heard of them. But the notion of distance should be generalized. Whatever the point of view adopted – moral, intellectual, emotional, physical – narrator(s), narratee(s), and character(s) can be more or less close to each other ranging from the most perfect identification to the most complete opposition.

... As there are often several narrators, several narratees, and several characters in a text, the complexity of the rapports and the variety of the distances that are established between them can be quite significant. In any case, these rapports and these distances determine to a great extent the way in which certain values are praised and others are rejected in the course of a narration and the way in which certain events are emphasized and others are nearly passed over in silence. They determine as well the tone and the very nature of the narration. In *Les Cloches de Bâle*, for example, the tone changes completely – and cannot but change – once the narrator decides to proclaim his friendship for the narratee and to speak to him more honestly and more directly than he had previously: abandoning romantic extravagance, he becomes quasi-documentary; leaving behind false detachment, he becomes brotherly. On the other hand, many ironic effects in narration depend upon the differences existing between two images of the narratee or between two (groups of) narratees (*Les Infortunes de la vertu*, *Werther*), upon the distance existing between narrator and narratee on the one hand and character on the other (*Un Amour de Swann*), or yet again upon the distance existing between narrator and narratee (*Tom Jones*). The complexity of a situation results sometimes from the instability of the distances existing between the narrator, the narratee, and the characters. If Michel's guilt – or innocence – is not clearly established, it is partly because several times he shows himself capable of overcoming the distance separating him from his friends, or, if one prefers, because his friends are unsure of how much distance to put between themselves and him. ...

THE NARRATEE'S FUNCTIONS

The type of narratee that we find in a given narrative, the relations that tie him to narrators, characters, and other narratees, the distances that separate him from ideal, virtual, or real readers partially determine the nature of this narrative. But the narratee exercises other functions that are more or less numerous and important and are more or less specific to him. It will be worth the effort to enumerate these functions and to study them in some detail.

The most obvious role of the narratee, a role that he always plays in a certain sense, is that of relay between the narrator and the reader(s), or rather between the author and the reader(s). Should certain values have to be defended or certain ambiguities clarified, this can easily be done by means of asides addressed to the narratee. Should the importance of a series of events be emphasized, should one reassure or make uneasy, justify certain actions or underscore their arbitrariness, this can always be done by addressing signals to the narratee. In *Tom Jones*, for example, the narrator explains to the narratee that prudence is necessary for the preservation of virtue, an explanation that allows us to judge better his hero, virtuous but imprudent: 'Prudence and circumspection are necessary even to the best men. . . . It is not enough that your designs, nay, that your actions, are intrinsically good, you must take care they shall appear so.' Likewise, we know that although Legrandin is a snob, he is not lying when he protests against snobbery because Marcel says quite clearly to his narratee: 'And indeed, that doesn't mean that Legrandin was not sincere when he inveighed against snobs.' Indeed, the mediation doesn't always operate that directly: thus, narrator–narratee relations are sometimes developed in the ironic mode and the reader cannot always interpret literally the statements of the former to the latter. There exist other conceivable relays than direct and explicit asides addressed to the narratee, other possibilities of mediation between authors and readers. Dialogues, metaphors, symbolic situations, allusions to a particular system of thought or to a certain work of art are some of the ways of manipulating the reader, guiding his judgments, and controlling his reactions. Moreover, those are the methods preferred by many modern novelists, if not the majority of them; perhaps because they accord or seem to accord more freedom to the reader, perhaps because they oblige him to participate more actively in the development of the narrative, or perhaps simply because they satisfy a certain concern for realism. The role of the narratee as mediator is rather reduced in these cases. Everything must still pass via the narratee since everything – metaphors, allusions, dialogues – is still addressed to him; but nothing is modified, nothing is clarified for the reader by this passage. Whatever the advantages may be of this type of mediator it should nonetheless be recognized that from a certain point of view, direct and explicit statements by the narrator to the narratee are the most economical and the most effective sort of mediation. A few sentences suffice to establish the true significance of an unexpected act or the true nature of a character; a few wards suffice to facilitate the interpretation of a complex situation. Although we can question indefinitely Stephen's esthetic maturity in *Portrait of the Artist as a Young Man* or the significance of a particular act in *A Farewell to Arms*, we always know exactly – or almost always – according to the text, what to think of Fabrice and la Sanseverina or of the intrigues of Mlle Michonneau.[2]

Besides the function of mediation, the narratee exercises in any narration a function of characterization. . . . In the case of narrator-characters, the function of characterization is important although it can be reduced to a minimum even here: because he is at a distance from everything and from himself, because his strangeness and solitude depend upon this distance, Meursault would not know how to engage in a true dialogue with his narratee and, thus, cannot be described by this dialogue. Nonetheless, the relations that a narrator-character establishes with his narratee reveal as much – if not more – about his character than any other element in the narrative. In *La Religeuse*, Sister Suzanne, because of her conception of the narratee and her asides addressed to him, emerges as much less naïve and much more calculating and coquettish than she would like to appear.

    . . . Moreover, the relations between the narrator and the narratee in a text may underscore one theme, illustrate another, or contradict yet another. Often the theme refers directly to the narrative situation and it is the narration as theme that these relations reveal. In *A Thousand and One Nights*, for instance, the theme of narration as life is emphasized by the attitude of Scheherazade toward the caliph and vice-versa: the heroine will die if her narratee decides not to listen to her any more, just as other characters in the narrative die because he will not listen to them: ultimately, any narrative is impossible without a narratee. But often, themes that do not concern the narrative situation – or perhaps concern it only indirectly – reveal the positions of the narrator and the narratee in relation to each other. In *Le Père Goriot*, the narrator maintains relations of power with his narratee. From the very beginning, the narrator tries to anticipate his narratee's objections, to dominate him, and to convince him. All means are used: the narrator coaxes, entreats, threatens, derides, and in the final analysis we suspect that he succeeds in getting the better of his narratee. In the last part of the novel, when Vautrin has been put in prison and Goriot is advancing more and more quickly toward death, the narrator rarely addresses his narratee. This is because the narrator has won the battle. He is now sure of his effects, of his domination, and he need no longer do anything but recount the story. This sort of war, this desire for power, can be found at the level of the characters. On the level of the events as well as on the level of narration, the same struggle takes place.

    If the narratee contributes to the thematic of a narrative, he is also always part of the narrative framework, often of a particularly concrete framework in which the narrator(s) and narratee(s) are all characters (*Heart of Darkness*, *L'Immoraliste*, *The Decameron*). The effect is to make the narrative seem more natural. The narratee like the narrator plays an undeniable *verisimilating* (*vraisemblabilisant*) role. Sometimes this concrete framework provides the model by which a work or narration develops. In *The Decameron* or in *L'Heptameron*, it is expected that each of the narratees will in turn become a narrator. More than a mere sign of realism or an index of verisimilitude, the narratee represents in these circumstances an indispensable element for the development of the narrative.

NOTES

1   We follow here in modifying the perspective, Wayne C. Booth, *The Rhetoric of Fiction* (Chicago, IL: University of Chicago Press, 1961), pp. 155 ff.

2   Ibid.

Jonathan Culler, 'Story and Discourse in the Analysis of Narrative'*

See also:
Aristotle (1.i)
Shlovsky (1.iii)
Tomashevsky (1.iii)
Todorov (2.iii)
Smith (3.ii)
Brooks (3.ii)
Derrida (6)
Miller (6)
Johnson (6)

To illustrate the issues involved, let us start with a familiar example, the story of Oedipus. The analysis of narrative would identify the sequence of events that constitutes the action of the story: Oedipus is abandoned on Mt Cithaeron; he is rescued by a shepherd; he grows up in Corinth; he kills Laius at the crossroads; he answers the Sphinx's riddle; he marries Jocasta; he seeks the murderer of Laius; he discovers his own guilt; he blinds himself and leaves his country. After identifying the *fabula*, one could describe the order and perspective in which these events are presented in the discourse of the play. Treating these events as the reality of the story, one then seeks to interpret the significance of the way in which they are portrayed. In the case of *Oedipus*, as in many other narratives, of which the detective story is only the most banal example, the discourse focuses on the bringing to light of a crucial event, identified as a reality which determines significance. Someone killed Laius and the problem is to discover what in fact happened at that fateful moment in the past.

One of millions of enthusiastic readers, Sigmund Freud, describes the play as follows:

> The action of the play consists of nothing other than the process of revealing, with cunning delays and ever-mounting excitement, that Oedipus himself is the murderer of Laius, but further, that he is the son of the murdered man and of Jocasta. Appalled at the abomination he has unwittingly perpetrated, Oedipus blinds himself and forsakes his home.

Freud emphasizes that the logic of signification here is one in which events, conceived as prior to and independent of their discursive representation, determine meanings: the play brings to light an awful deed which is so powerful that it imposes its meaning irrespective of any intention of the actor. The prior event has made Oedipus guilty, and when this is revealed he attains tragic dignity in accepting the meaning imposed by the revealed event.

This way of thinking about the play is essential, but there is a contrary perspective which is also essential to its force and which an apparently marginal element will help us to grasp. When Oedipus first asks whether anyone witnessed Laius's death he is told,

* *The Purist of Signs*, (London: Routledge & Kegan Paul, 1981) pp. 172–8, 86–7.

'All died save one, who fled in terror and could tell us only one clear fact. His story was that robbers, not one but many, fell in with the King's party and killed them.' And later when Oedipus begins to wonder whether he might not himself be the murderer he tells Jocasta that everything hangs on the testimony of this witness, whom they await. 'You say he spoke of robbers, that robbers killed him. If he still says robbers, it was not I. One is not the same as many. But if he speaks of one lone traveller, there is no escape, the finger points to me.' To which Jocasta answers, 'Oh, but I assure you, that was what he said. He cannot go back on it now; the whole town heard it, not only I.'

The only witness has publicly told a story that is incompatible with Oedipus's guilt. This possibility of innocence is never eliminated, for when the witness arrives Oedipus is interested in his relation to Laius and asks only about his birth, not about the murder. The witness is never asked whether the murderers were one or many.

I am not, of course, suggesting that Oedipus was really innocent and has been falsely accused for 2,400 years. I am interested in the significance of the fact that the possibility of innocence is never dispelled. The 'whole action of the play' is the revelation of this awful deed, but we are never given the proof, the testimony of the eye-witness. Oedipus himself and all his readers are convinced of his guilt but our conviction does not come from the revelation of the deed. Instead of the revelation of a prior deed determining meaning, we could say that it is meaning, the convergence of meaning in the narrative discourse, that leads us to posit this deed as its appropriate manifestation.

Once we are well into the play, we know that Oedipus must be found guilty, otherwise the play will not work at all; and the logic to which we are responding is not simply, an esthetic logic that affects readers of literary works. Oedipus, too, feels the force of this logic. It had been prophesied that Oedipus would kill his father; it had been prophesied that Laius would be killed by his son; Oedipus admits to having killed an old man at what may have been the relevant time and place; so when the shepherd reveals that Oedipus is in fact the son of Laius, Oedipus leaps to the conclusion, and every reader leaps with him, that he is in fact the murderer of Laius. His conclusion is based not on new evidence concerning a past deed but on the force of meaning, the interweaving of prophesies and the demands of narrative coherence. The convergence of discursive forces makes it essential that he become the murderer of Laius, and he yields to this force of meaning. Instead of saying, therefore, that there is a sequence of past events that are given and which the play reveals with certain detours, we can say that the crucial event is the product of demands of signification. Here meaning is not the effect of a prior event but its cause.

Oedipus becomes the murderer of his father not by a violent act that is brought to light but by bowing to the demands of narrative coherence and deeming the act to have taken place. Moreover, it is essential to the force of the play that Oedipus take this leap, that he accede to the demands of narrative coherence and deem himself guilty. If he were to resist the logic of signification, arguing that 'the fact that he's my father doesn't mean that I killed him,' demanding more evidence about the past event, Oedipus would not acquire the necessary tragic stature. In this respect the force of the narrative relies on the contrary logic, in which event is not a cause but an effect of theme. To describe this logic is not to quibble over details but to investigate tragic power.

Moreover, one might note that this contrary logic is in fact necessary to Freud's reading of the play, even though he himself stresses in his account the priority of event to meaning. If we were to follow this logic and say that the prior deed, committed without understanding, is what makes Oedipus guilty of patricide, then Oedipus can scarcely be said to have an Oedipus complex. But suppose we stress instead that as soon as Oedipus learns that Laius is his father he immediately declares what he has hitherto denied: if Laius is my father, he in effect says, then I must have killed him. If we emphasize this point, we can indeed identify an Oedipus complex: that is to say, a structure of signification – a desire to kill the father and a guilt for that desire – which does not result from an act but precedes it.

This logic by which event is a product of discursive forces rather than a given reported by discourse is essential to the force of the narrative, but in describing the play in this way we have certainly not replaced a deluded or incorrect model of narrative by a correct one. On the contrary, it is obvious that much of the play's power depends on the narratological assumption that Oedipus's guilt or innocence has already been determined by a past event that has not yet been revealed or reported. Yet the contrary logic in which Oedipus posits an act in response to demands of signification is essential to the tragic force of the ending. These two logics cannot be brought together in harmonious synthesis; each works by the exclusion of the other; each depends on a hierarchical relation between story and discourse which the other inverts. In so far as both these logics are necessary to the force of the play, they put in question the possibility of a coherent, noncontradictory account of narrative. They stage a confrontation of sorts between a semiotics that aspires to produce a grammar of narrative and deconstructive interpretations, which in showing the work's opposition to its own logic suggest the impossibility of such a grammar. If an analysis of the logic of signification shows that *Oedipus* requires a double reading, a reading according to incompatible principles, this would suggest both the importance of narratological analysis and the impossibility of attaining its goal.

If *Oedipus* seems a special case, in that the analysis turns on a possible uncertainty about the central event in the plot, let us consider an example from a very different period and genre, George Eliot's *Daniel Deronda*, as analyzed in a recent article by Cynthia Chase. Deronda, the adopted son of an English nobleman, is a talented, sensitive young man, moving in good society, who has been unable to decide on a profession. He happens to rescue a poor Jewish girl who was trying to drown herself, and later, in searching for her family, he meets her brother Mordecai, an ailing scholar with whom he begins to study Hebrew. He develops an intense interest in Jewish culture, falls in love with Mirah, the girl he has saved, and is accepted by Mordecai and others as a kindred spirit.

At this point, Deronda receives a summons from his mother, who, obeying her dead father's injunction, reveals to him the secret of his birth: he is a Jew. The novel emphasizes the causal force of this past event: because he was born a Jew he is a Jew. Origin, cause, and identity are linked in an implicit argument that is common to narrative. With the revelation of Deronda's parentage it is implied that his present character and involvement with things Jewish have been caused by his Jewish origin.

But on the other hand, as Chase notes,

> The sequence of events in the plot as a whole presents Deronda's revealed origins in a different perspective. The account of Deronda's situation has made it increasingly obvious to the reader that the progression of the hero's destiny – or,

that is to say, the progression of the story – positively requires a revelation that he is of Jewish birth. For Deronda's bildungsroman to proceed, his character must crystallize, and this must come about through a recognition of his destiny, which has remained obscure to him, according to the narrator's account, largely because of his ignorance of his origins. The suspenseful stress on Deronda's relationship with Mordecai and with Mirah orients his history in their direction, and Mordecai explicitly stresses his faith that Deronda is a Jew. Thus the reader comes upon Deronda's Jewish parentage as an inevitable inference to be drawn not simply from the presentation of Deronda's qualities and his empathy with the Jews but above all from the patent strategy and direction of the narrative. The revelation of Deronda's origins therefore appears as an effect of narrative requirements. The supposed cause of his character and vocation (according to the chapters recounting the disclosure), Deronda's origin presents itself (in the light of the rest of the text) rather as the effect of the account of his vocation: his origin is the effect of its effects.

By one logic Deronda's birth is a past cause of present effects; by another contrary logic, named by Deronda's friend Hans Meyrick in a flippant letter, one should speak rather of 'the present causes of past effects.' It is essential to stress here that, as in the case of Oedipus, there is no question of finding a compromise formulation that would do justice to both presentations of the event by avoiding extremes, for the power of the narrative depends precisely on the alternative use of extremes, the rigorous deployment of two logics, each of which works by excluding the other. It will not do to say, for example, that Deronda's involvement with Judaism is partly but not completely the result of his birth, and that the revelation of his birth is therefore in part an explanation and in part a narrative fulfillment. This sort of formulation is wrong because the power of Eliot's novel depends precisely on the fact that Deronda's commitment to Judaism and idealism, instead of to the frivolous society in which he has been raised, is presented as a free choice. To have exemplary moral value it must be presented as a choice, not as the ineluctable result of the hidden fact of parentage. It must also be presented as wholehearted, not as a dilettantish dabbling which would then be transformed into commitment by revelation of the fact of birth. The novel requires that Deronda's commitment to Judaism be independent of the revelation of his Jewishness – this is thematically and ethically essential – yet its account of Jewishness does not allow for the possibility of conversion and insists on the irreplaceability of origins: to be a Jew is to have been born a Jew. These two logics, one of which insists upon the causal efficacy of origins and the other of which denies their causal efficacy, are in contradiction but they are essential to the way in which the narrative functions. One logic assumes the primacy of events; the other treats the events as the products of meanings.

One could argue that every narrative operates according to this double logic, presenting its plot as a sequence of events which is prior to and independent of the given perspective on these events, and, at the same time, suggesting by its implicit claims to significance that these events are justified by their appropriateness to a thematic structure. As critics we adopt the first perspective when we debate the significance of a character's actions (taking those actions as given). We adopt the second perspective when we discuss the appropriateness or inappropriateness of an ending (when we debate whether these actions are appropriate expressions of the thematic structure which ought to determine them). Theorists of narrative have always, of course, recognized these two perspectives, but they have perhaps been too ready to assume that they can be held together, synthesized in some way without contradiction. Not only is there a contradiction, but it will characteristically manifest itself in narratives, as a moment that seems either superfluous – a loose end, as in *Oedipus Rex* or too neat, as in *Daniel Deronda*. Recent work on narrative has brought such moments to the fore, stressing their importance to the rhetorical force of narratives.

. . .

The analysis of narrative is an important branch of semiotics. We still do not appreciate as fully as we ought the importance of narrative schemes and models in all aspects of our lives. Analysis of narrative depends, as I have argued, on the distinction between story and discourse, and this distinction always involves a relation of dependency: either the discourse is seen as a representation of events which must be thought of as independent of that particular representation, or else the so-called events are thought of as the postulates or products of a discourse. Since the distinction between story and discourse can function only if there is a determination of one by the other, the analyst must always choose which will be treated as the given and which as the product. Yet either choice leads to a narratology that misses some of the curious complexity of narratives and fails to account for much of their impact. If one thinks of discourse as the presentation of story, one will find it difficult to account for the sorts of effects, discussed here, which depend upon the determination of story by discourse, a possibility often posed by the narrative itself. If, on the other hand, one were to adopt the view that what we call 'events' are nothing other than products of discourse, a series of predicates attached to agents in the text, then one would be even less able to account for the force of narrative. For even the most radical fictions depend for their effect on the assumption that their puzzling sequences of sentences are presentations of events (though we may not be able to tell what those events are), and that these events in principle have features not reported by the discourse, such that the selection operated by the discourse has meaning. Without that assumption, which makes the discourse a selection and even a suppression of possible information, texts would lack their intriguing and dislocatory power.

Neither perspective, then, is likely to offer a satisfactory narratology, nor can the two fit together in a harmonious synthesis; they stand in irreconcilable opposition, a conflict between two logics which puts in question the possibility of a coherent, noncontradictory 'science' of narrative. But this identification of a certain self-deconstructive force in narrative and the theory of narrative should not lead to rejection of the analytical enterprise that drives one to this discovery. In the absence of the possibility of synthesis, one must be willing to shift from one perspective to the other, from story to discourse and back again.

iii READINGS

Roland Barthes, 'Introduction to the Structural Analysis of Narratives'*

See also:
Aristotle (1.i)
Propp (1.iii)
Lévi-Strauss (2.i)
Metz (2.i)
Eco (2.iii)
Barthes (3.i)
Derrida (6)
Johnson (6)
Fish (7)

The narratives of the world are numberless. Narrative is first and foremost a prodigious variety of genres, themselves distributed amongst different substances – as though any material were fit to receive man's stories. Able to be carried by articulated language, spoken or written, fixed or moving images, gestures, and the ordered mixture of all these substances; narrative is present in myth, legend, fable, tale, novella, epic, history, tragedy, drama, comedy, mime, painting (think of Carpaccio's *Saint Ursula*), stained-glass windows, cinema, comics, news item, conversation. Moreover, under this almost infinite diversity of forms, narrative is present in every age, in every place, in every society; it begins with the very history of mankind and there nowhere is nor has been a people without narrative. All classes, all human groups, have their narratives, enjoyment of which is very often shared by men with different, even opposing,[1] cultural backgrounds. Caring nothing for the division between good and bad literature, narrative is international, transhistorical, transcultural: it is simply there, like life itself.

Must we conclude from this universality that narrative is insignificant? Is it so general that we can have nothing to say about it except for the modest description of a few highly individualized varieties, something literary history occasionally undertakes? But then how are we to master even these varieties, how are we to justify our right to differentiate and identify them? How is novel to be set against novella, tale against myth, drama against tragedy (as has been done a thousand times) without reference to a common model? Such a model is implied by every proposition relating to the most individual, the most historical, of narrative forms. It is thus legitimate that, far from the abandoning of any idea of dealing with narrative on the grounds of its universality, there should have been (from Aristotle on) a periodic interest in narrative form and it is normal that the newly developing structuralism should make this form one of its first concerns – is not structuralism's constant aim to master the infinity of utterances [*paroles*] by describing the 'language' ['*langue*'] of which they are the products and from which they can be generated. Faced with the infinity of narratives, the multiplicity of standpoints

---

* *Image – Music – Text*, (London: Fontana, 1977), trans. Stephen Heath, pp. 20–30.

– historical, psychological, sociological, ethnological, aesthetic, etc. – from which they can be studied, the analyst finds himself in more or less the same situation as Saussure confronted by the heterogeneity of language [*langage*] and seeking to extract a principle of classification and a central focus for description from the apparent confusion of the individual messages. Keeping simply to modern times, the Russian formalists, Propp, and Lévi-Strauss have taught us to recognize the following dilemma: either a narrative is merely a rambling collection of events, in which case nothing can be said about it other than by referring back to the storyteller's (the author's) art, talent, or genius – all mythical forms of chance[2] or else it shares with other narratives a common structure which is open to analysis, no matter how much patience its formulation requires. There is a world of difference between the most complex randomness and the most elementary combinatory scheme, and it is impossible to combine (to produce) a narrative without reference to an implicit system of units and rules.

Where then are we to look for the structures of narrative? Doubtless, in narratives themselves. *Each and every* narrative? Many commentators who accept the idea of a narrative structure are nevertheless unable to resign themselves to dissociating literary analysis from the example of the experimental sciences; nothing daunted, they ask that a purely inductive method be applied to narrative and that one start by studying all the narratives within a genre, a period, a society. This commonsense view is utopian. Linguistics itself, with only some three thousand languages to embrace, cannot manage such a program and has wisely turned deductive, a step which in fact marked its veritable constitution as a science and the beginning of its spectacular progress, it even succeeding in anticipating facts prior to their discovery.[3] So what of narrative analysis, faced as it is with millions of narratives? Of necessity, it is condemned to a deductive procedure, obliged first to devise a hypothetical model of description (what American linguists call a 'theory') and then gradually to work down from this model toward the different narrative species which at once conform to and depart from the model. It is only at the level of these conformities and departures that analysis will be able to come back to, but now equipped with a single descriptive tool, the plurality of narratives, to their historical, geographical and cultural diversity.[4]

Thus, in order to describe and classify the infinite number of narratives, a 'Theory' (in this pragmatic sense) is needed and the immediate task is that of finding it, of starting to define it. Its development can be greatly facilitated if one begins from a model able to provide it with its initial terms and principles. In the current state of research, it seems reasonable[5] that the structural analysis of narrative be given linguistics itself as founding model.

THE LANGUAGE OF NARRATIVE

1 Beyond the sentence

As we know, linguistics stops at the sentence, the last unit which it considers to fall within its scope. If the sentence, being an order and not a series, cannot be reduced to the sum of the words which compose it and constitutes thereby a specific unit, a piece of discourse, on the contrary, is no more than the succession of the sentences composing it. From the point of view of linguistics, there is nothing in discourse that is not to be found in the sentence: 'The sentence,' writes Martinet, 'is the smallest segment that is perfectly and wholly representative of discourse.'[6] Hence there can be no question of linguistics setting itself an object superior to the sentence, since beyond the sentence are only more sentences – having described the flower, the botanist is not to get involved in describing the bouquet.

And yet it is evident that discourse itself (as a set of sentences) is organized and that, through this organization, it can be seen as the message of another language, one operating at a higher level than the language of the linguists.[7] Discourse has its units, its rules, its 'grammar': beyond the sentence, and though consisting solely of sentences, it must naturally form the object of a second linguistics. For a long time indeed, such a linguistics of discourse bore a glorious name, that of Rhetoric. As a result of a complex historical movement, however, in which Rhetoric went over to belles-lettres and the latter was divorced from the study of language, it has recently become necessary to take up the problem afresh. The new linguistics of discourse has still to be developed, but at least it is being postulated, and by the linguists themselves.[8] This last fact is not without significance, for, although constituting autonomous object, discourse must be studied from the basis of linguistics. If a working hypothesis is needed for an analysis whose task is immense and whose materials infinite, then the most reasonable thing is to posit a homological relation between sentence and discourse insofar as it is likely that a similar formal organization orders all semiotic systems, whatever their substances and dimensions. A discourse is a long 'sentence' (the units of which are not necessarily sentences), just as a sentence, allowing for certain specifications, is a short 'discourse.' This hypothesis accords well with a number of propositions put forward in contemporary anthropology. Jakobson and Lévi-Strauss have pointed out that mankind can be defined by the ability to create secondary – 'self-multiplying' – systems (tools for the manufacture of other tools, double articulation of language, incest taboo permitting the fanning out of families) while the Soviet linguist Ianov supposes that artificial languages can only have been acquired after natural language: what is important for men is to have the use of several systems of meaning and natural language helps in the elaboration of artificial languages. It is therefore legitimate to posit a 'secondary' relation between sentence and discourse – a relation which will be referred to as homological, in order to respect the purely formal nature of the correspondences.

The general language [*langue*] of narrative is one (and clearly only one) of the idioms apt for consideration by the linguistics of discourse[9] and it accordingly comes under the homological hypothesis. Structurally, narrative shares the characteristics of the sentence without ever being reducible to the simple sum of its sentences: a narrative is a long sentence, just as every constative sentence is in a way the rough outline of a short narrative. Although there provided with different signifiers (often extremely complex), one does find in narrative, expanded and transformed proportionately, the principal verbal categories: tenses, aspects, moods, persons. Moreover the 'subjects' themselves, as opposed to the verbal predicates, readily yield to the sentence model; the actantial typology proposed by A.J. Greimas[10] discovers in the multitude of narrative characters the elementary functions of grammatical analysis. Nor does the homology suggested here have merely a heuristic value: it implies an identity between language and literature (inasmuch as the latter can be seen as a sort of privileged vehicle of narrative). It is hardly possible any longer to conceive of literature as an art that abandons all further relation with language the moment it has used it as an instrument to express ideas, passion, or beauty: language never ceases to accompany discourse, holding up to it the mirror of its own structure – does not literature, particularly today, make a language of the very conditions of language?[11]

2   *Levels of meaning*

From the outset, linguistics furnishes the structural analysis of narrative with a concept which is decisive in that, making explicit immediately what is essential in every system of meaning, namely its organization, it allows us both to show how a narrative is not a simple sum of propositions and to classify the enormous mass of elements which go to make up a narrative. This concept is that of *level of description*.[12]

A sentence can be described, linguistically, on several levels (phonetic, phonological, grammatical, contextual) and these levels are in a hierarchical relationship with one another, for, while all have their own units and correlations (whence the necessity for a separate description of each of them), no level on its own can produce meaning. A unit belonging to a particular level only takes on meaning if it can be integrated in a higher level; a phoneme, though perfectly describable, means nothing in itself: it participates in meaning only when integrated in a word, and the word itself must in turn be integrated in a sentence.[13] The theory of levels (as set out by Benveniste) gives two types of relations: distributional (if the relations are situated on the same level) and integrational (if they are grasped from one level to the next); consequently, distributional relations alone are not sufficient to account for meaning. In order to conduct a structural analysis, it is thus first of all necessary to distinguish several levels or instances of description and to place these instances within a hierarchical (integrationary) perspective.

The levels are operations.[14] It is therefore normal that, as it progresses, linguistics should tend to multiply them. Discourse analysis, however, is as yet only able to work on rudimentary levels. In its own way, rhetoric had assigned at least two planes of description to discourse: *dispositio* and *elocutio*.[15] Today, in his analysis of the structure of myth, Lévi-Strauss has already indicated that the constituent units of mythical discourse (mythemes) acquire meaning only because they are grouped in bundles and because these bundles themselves combine together.[16] As too, Tzvetan Todorov, reviving the distinction made by the Russian formalists, proposes working on two major levels, themselves subdivided: *story* (the argument), comprising a logic of actions and a 'syntax' of characters, and *discourse*, comprising the tenses, aspects, and modes of the narrative.[17] But however many levels are proposed and whatever definition they are given, there can be no doubt that narrative is a hierarchy of instances. To understand a narrative is not merely to follow the unfolding of the story, it is also to recognize its construction in 'stories,' to project the horizontal concatenations of the narrative 'thread' onto an implicitly vertical axis; to read (to listen to) a narrative is not merely to move from one word to the next, it is also to move from one level to the next. Perhaps I may be allowed to offer a kind of apologue in this connection. In 'The Purloined Letter,' Poe gives an acute analysis of the failure of the chief commissioner of the Paris police, powerless to find the letter. His investigations, says Poe, were perfect *'within the sphere of his speciality';*[18] he searched everywhere, saturated entirely the level of the 'police search,' but in order to find the letter, protected by its conspicuousness, it was necessary to shift to another level, to substitute the concealer's principle of relevance for that of the policeman. Similarly, the 'search' carried out over a horizontal set of narrative relations may well be as thorough as possible but must still, to be effective, also operate 'vertically': meaning is not 'at the end' of the narrative, it runs across it; just as conspicuous as the purloined letter, meaning eludes all unilateral investigation.

A great deal of tentative effort is still required before it will be possible to ascertain precisely the levels of narrative. Those that are suggested in what follows constitute a provisional profile whose merit remains almost exclusively didactic; they enable us to locate and group together the different problems, and this without, I think, being at variance with the few analyses so far.[19] It is proposed to distinguish three levels of description in the narrative work: the level of *'functions'* (in the sense this word has in Propp and Bremond), the level of *'actions'* (in the sense this word has in Greimas when he talks of characters as actants) and the level of *'narration'* (which is roughly the level of 'discourse' in Todorov). These three levels are bound together according to a mode of progressive integration: a function only has meaning insofar as it occupies a place in the general action of an actant, and this action in turn receives its final meaning from the fact that it is narrated, entrusted to a discourse which possesses its own code.

. . .

It may be that men ceaselessly reinject into narrative what they have known, what they have experienced; but if they do, at least it is in a form which has vanquished repetition and instituted the model of a process of becoming. Narrative does not show, does not imitate; the passion which may excite us in reading a novel is not that of a 'vision' (in actual fact, we do not 'see' anything). Rather, it is that of meaning, that of a higher order of relation which also has its emotions, its hopes, its dangers, its triumphs. 'What takes place' in a narrative is from the referential (reality) point of view literally *nothing*,[20] 'what happens' is language alone, the adventure of language, the unceasing celebration of its coming. Although we know scarcely more about the origins of narrative than we do about the origins of language, it can reasonably be suggested that narrative is contemporaneous with monologue, a creation seemingly posterior to that of dialogue. At all events, without wanting to strain the phylogenetic hypothesis, it may be significant that it is at the same moment (around the age of three) that the little human 'invents' at once sentence, narrative, and the Oedipus.

NOTES

1   It must be remembered that this is not the case with either poetry or the essay, both of which are dependent on the cultural level of their consumers.

2   There does, of course, exist an 'art' of the storyteller, which is the ability to generate narratives (messages) from the structure (the code). This art corresponds to the notion of *performance* in Chomsky and is far removed from the 'genius' of the author, romantically conceived as some barely explicable personal secret.

3   See the history of the Hittite *a*, postulated by Saussure and actually discovered fifty years later, as given in Emile Benveniste, *Problèmes de linguistique générale*.

4   Let us bear in mind the present conditions of linguistic description: '. . . linguistic "structure" is always relative not just to the data or corpus but also to the grammatical theory describing the data,' in E. Bach, *An Introduction to Transformational Grammars*; 'it has been

recognized that language must be described as a formal structure, but that the description first of all necessitates specification of adequate procedures and criteria and that, finally, the reality of the object is inseparable from the method given for its description,' Benveniste.

5   But not imperative: see Claude Bremond, 'La logique des possibles narratifs,' *Communications* 8 (1966), which is more logical than linguistic. (Bremond's various studies in this field have now been collected in a volume entitled, precisely, *Logique du récit*; his work consists in the analysis of narrative according to the pattern of possible alternatives, each narrative moment – or function – giving rise to a set of different possible resolutions, the actualization of any one of which in turn produces a new set of alternatives.)

6   André Martinet, 'Réflexions sur la phrase,' in *Language and Society*.

7   It goes without saying, as Jakobson has noted, that between the sentence and what lies beyond the sentence there are transitions; coordination, for instance, can work over the limit of the sentence.

8   See especially: Benveniste, op. cit., Chapter 10; Z.S. Harris, 'Discourse Analysis,' *Language* 28 (1952); N. Ruwet, 'Analyse structurale d'un poème français,' *Linguistics* 3 (1964).

9   One of the tasks of such a linguistics would be precisely that of establishing a typology of forms of discourse. Three broad types can be recognized provisionally: metonymic (narrative), metaphoric (lyric, poetry, sapiential discourse), enthymematic (intellectual discourse).

10 Greimas's own account can be found in *Sémantique structurale*.

11 Remember Mallarmé's insight at the time when he was contemplating a work of linguistics: 'Language appeared to him the instrument of fiction: he will follow the method of language (determine it). Languages self-reflecting. So fiction seems to him the very process of the human mind – it is this that sets in play all method, and man is reduced to will.' It will be recalled that for Mallarmé 'Fiction' and 'Poetry' are taken synonymously.

12 'Linguistic descriptions are not, so to speak, monovalent. A description is not simply "right" or "wrong" in itself . . . it is better thought of as more useful or less.' M.A.K. Halliday, 'General linguistics and its application to language teaching,' *Patterns of Language*.

13 The levels of integration were postulated by the Prague School (vid. J. Vachek, *A Prague School Reader in Linguistics*, Bloomington 1964, p. 468) and have been adopted since by many linguists. It is Benveniste who, in my opinion, has given the most illuminating analysis in this respect; op. cit., Chapter 10.

14 'In somewhat vague terms, a level may be considered as a system of symbols, rules, and so on, to be used for representing utterances,' Bach, op. cit.

15 The third part of rhetoric, *inventio*, did not concern language – it had to do with *res*, not with *verba*.

16 *Structural Anthropology*.

17 See T. Todorov, 'Les catégories du récit littéraire,' *Communications* 8 (1966) (Todorov's work on narrative is now most easily accessible in two books, *Littérature et signification; poétique de la prose*. For a short account in English, see "Structural analysis of narrative," *Novel* I, 3, (1969).)

18 This is in accordance with the Baudelaire version of the Poe story from which Barthes quotes; Poe's original reads: 'so far as his labors extended.'

19 I have been concerned in this introduction to impede research in progress as little as possible.

20 Mallarmé: 'A dramatic work displays the succession of exteriors of the act without any moment retaining reality and, in the end, anything happening.' *Crayonné au théâtre*.

Umberto Eco, 'Narrative Structure in Ian Fleming'*

See also
Shlovsky (1.iii)
Tomashevsky (1.iii)
Propp (1.iii)
Lévi-Strauss (2.i)
Barthes (2.iii)
Todorov (2.iii)
Barthes (3.i)
Mulvey (4)
Diengott (5)

6.1 THE OPPOSITION OF CHARACTERS AND OF VALUES

The novels of Fleming seem to be built on a series of oppositions which allow a limited number of permutations and interactions. These dichotomies constitute invariant features around which minor couples rotate as free variants. I have singled out fourteen couples, four of which are opposing characters, the others being opposing values, variously personified by the four basic characters:

1 Bond–M;
2 Bond–Villain;
3 Villain–Woman;
4 Woman–Bond;
5 Free World–Soviet Union;
6 Great Britain–Non-Anglo-Saxon Countries;
7 Duty–Sacrifice;
8 Cupidity–Ideals;
9 Love–Death;
10 Chance–Planning;
11 Luxury–Discomfort;
12 Excess–Moderation;
13 Perversion–Innocence;
14 Loyalty–Disloyalty.

These pairs do not represent 'vague' elements but 'simple' ones that are immediate and universal, and, if we consider the range of each pair, we see that the variants allowed in fact include all the narrative devices of Fleming.

6.2 PLAY SITUATIONS AND THE STORY AS A 'GAME'

The various pairs of oppositions (of which we have considered only a few possible variants) seem like the elements of an *ars combinatoria* with fairly elementary rules. It is clear that in the engagement of the two poles of each couple there are, in the course

---

* From *The Role of the Reader: Explorations in the Semiotics of Texts* (Bloomington: Indiana University Press, 1979), pp. 147–61.

of the novel, alternative solutions: the reader does not know at which point of the story the Villain defeats Bond or Bond defeats the Villain, and so on. But toward the end of the book the algebra has to follow a prearranged pattern: as in the Chinese game that 007 and Tanaka play at the beginning of *You Only Live Twice*, hand beats fist, fist beats two fingers, two fingers beat hand. M beats Bond, Bond beats the Villain, the Villain beats Woman, even if at first Bond beats Woman; the Free World beats the Soviet Union, England beats the Impure Countries, Death beats Love, Moderation beats Excess, and so on.

This interpretation of the story in terms of a game is not accidental. The books of Fleming are dominated by situations that we call 'play situations'. First are several archetypal situations such as the Journey and the Meal; the Journey may be by Machine (and here occurs a rich symbolism of the automobile, typical of our century), by Train (another archetype, this of obsolescent type), by Airplane, or by Ship. But a meal, a pursuit by machine, or a mad race by train always takes the form of a game. Bond decides the choice of foods as though they formed the pieces of a puzzle, prepares for the meal with the same scrupulous attention as that with which he prepares for a game of bridge (see the convergence, in a means–end connection, of the two elements in *Moonraker*), and he intends the meal as a play. Similarly, train and machine are the elements of a wager made against an adversary: before the journey is finished, one of the two has finished his moves and given checkmate.

At this point it is useless to record the occurrence of the play situations, in the true and proper sense of conventional games of chance, in each book. Bond always gambles and wins, against the Villain or some vicarious figure . . . here it must be said that, if these games occupy a prominent space, it is because they form a reduced and formalized model of the more general play situation that is the novel. The novel, given the rules of combination of oppositional couples, is fixed as a sequence of 'moves' inspired by the code and constituted according to a perfectly, prearranged scheme. The invariable scheme is the following:

A. M moves and gives a task to Bond;
B. Villain moves and appears to Bond (perhaps in vicarious forms);
C. Bond moves and gives a first check to Villain or Villain gives first check to Bond;
D. Woman moves and shows herself to Bond;
E. Bond takes Woman (possesses her or begins her seduction);
F. Villain captures Bond (with or without Woman, or at different moments);
G. Villain tortures Bond (with or without Woman);
H. Bond beats Villain (kills him, or kills his representative or helps at their killing);
I. Bond, convalescing, enjoys Woman, whom he then loses.

The scheme is invariable in the sense that all the elements are always present in every novel (so that it might be affirmed that the fundamental rule of the game is 'Bond moves and mates in eight moves'). That the moves always be in the same sequence is not imperative. A minute detailing of the ten novels under consideration would yield several examples of a set scheme we might call ABCDEFGHI (for example, *Dr No*), but often there are inversions and variations. Sometimes Bond meets the Villain at the beginning of the volume and gives him a first check, and only later receives his instructions from M. For example, *Goldfinger* presents a different scheme, BCDEACDFGDHEHI, where it is possible to notice repeated moves: two encounters and three games played with the Villain, two seductions and three encounters with women, a first flight of the Villain after his defeat and his ensuing death, and so on. In *From Russia, With Love*, the company of Villains increases – through the presence of the ambiguous representative Kerim, in conflict with a secondary Villain, Krilenku, and the two mortal duels of Bond with Red Grant and with Rosa Klebb, who was arrested only after having grievously wounded Bond – so that the scheme, highly complicated, is BBBBDA(BBC)EFGH (I). There is a long prologue in Russia with the parade of the Villain figures and the first connection between Tatiana and Rosa Klebb, the sending of Bond to Turkey, a long interlude in which Kerim and Krilenku appear and the latter is defeated, the seduction of Tatiana, the flight by train with the torture suffered by the murdered Kerim, the victory over Red Grant, the second round with Rosa Klebb, who, while being defeated, inflicts serious injury upon Bond. In the train and during his convalescence, Bond enjoys love interludes with Tatiana before the final separation.

Even the basic concept of torture undergoes variations, being sometimes a direct injustice, sometimes a kind of succession or course of horrors that Bond must undergo, either by the explicit will of the Villain (*Dr No*) or by accident during an escape from the Villain, but always as a consequence of the moves of the Villain (for example, a tragic escape in the snow, pursuit, avalanche, and hurried flight through the Swiss countryside in *On Her Majesty's Secret Service*).

Occurring alongside the sequence of fundamental moves are numerous side issues which enrich the narrative by unforeseen events, without, however, altering the basic scheme. For a graphic representation of this process, we may summarize the plot of one novel – *Diamonds Are Forever* – by placing on the left the sequence of the fundamental moves, on the right the multiplicity of side issues:

	Long curious prologue which introduces one to diamond smuggling in South Africa
Move A. M sends Bond to America as a sham smuggler	
Move B. Villains (the Spangs) appear indirectly in the description of them given to Bond	
Move D. Woman (Tiffany Case) meets Bond in the role of go-between	
	Detailed journey by air, in the background two vicarious Villains; play situations; imperceptible duel between hunters and prey
Move B. First appearance in the plane of vicarious Villain Winter (Blood Group F)	
Move B. Meeting with Jack Spang	

	Meeting with Felix Leiter, who brings Bond up to date about the Spangs
Move E. Bond begins the seduction of Tiffany	
	Long interval at Saratoga at the races; to help Leiter Bond in fact 'damages' the Spangs
Move C. Bond gives a first check to the Villain	
	Appearance of vicarious Villains in the mud bath and punishment of the treacherous jockey, anticipating symbolically the torturing of Bond; the whole Saratoga episode represents a play situation in miniature; Bond decides to go to Las Vegas; detailed description of the district
Move B. Appearance of Seraffimo Spang	
	Another long and detailed play situation; play with Tiffany as croupier gambling at table, indirect amorous skirmish with the woman, indirect gamble with Seraffimo; Bond wins money
Move C. Bond gives a second check to Villain	
	Next evening, long shooting match between cars; association of Bond and Ernie Cureo
Move F. Spang captures Bond	
	Long description of Spectre and the train-playing of Spang
Move G. Spang has Bond tortured	
	With the aid of Tiffany, Bond begins a fantastic flight by railway trolley through the desert followed by the locomotive-plaything driven by Seraffimo; play situation
Move H. Bond defeats Seraffimo, who crashes into the mountain on the locomotive	
	Rest with his friend Leiter, departure by ship, long amorous convalescence with Tiffany, exchanges of coded telegrams
Move E. Bond finally possesses Tiffany	

Move B.   Villain reappears in the form
          of Winter

Play situation on board ship; mortal
gamble played by infinitesimal moves
between the two killers and Bond; play
situation becomes symbolized on reduced
scale in the lottery on the course of the
ship; the two killers capture Tiffany;
acrobatic action by Bond to reach the
cabin and kill the killers

Move H.   Bond overcomes vicarious
          Villains finally

Meditations on death in the presence of
the two corpses; return home

Move I. Bond knows he can enjoy well-
        earned repose with Tiffany,
        and yet . . .

. . . deviations of the plot in South Africa,
where Bond destroys the last link of the
chain

Move H.   Bond defeats for the third time
          the Villain in the person of
          Jack Spang

For each of the ten novels it would be possible to trace a general plan. The collateral inventions are rich enough to form the muscles of the separate skeletons of narrative; they constitute one of the great attractions of Fleming's work, but they do not testify, at least not obviously; to his powers of invention. As we shall see later, it is easy to trace the collateral inventions to definite literary sources, and hence these act as familiar reference marks to romanesque situations acceptable to readers. The true and original story remains immutable, and suspense is stabilized curiously on the basis of a sequence of events that are entirely predetermined. The story of each book by Fleming, by and large, may be summarized as follows: Bond is sent to a given place to avert a 'science-fiction' plan by a monstrous individual of uncertain origin and definitely not English who, making use of his organizational or productive activity, not only earns money, but helps the cause of the enemies of the West. In facing this monstrous being, Bond meets a woman who is dominated by him and frees her from her past, establishing with her an erotic relationship interrupted by capture by the Villain and by torture. But Bond defeats the Villain, who dies horribly, and rests from his great efforts in the arms of the woman, though he is destined to lose her. One might wonder how, within such limits, it is possible for the inventive writer of fiction to function, since he must respond to a demand for the sensational and the unforeseeable. In fact, in every detective story and in every hard-boiled novel, there is no basic variation, but rather the repetition of a habitual scheme in which the reader can recognize something he has already seen and of which he has grown fond. Under the guise of a machine that produces information, the criminal novel produces redundancy; pretending to rouse the reader, it in fact reconfirms him in a sort of imaginative laziness and creates escape by narrating, not the Unknown, but the Already Known. In the pre-Fleming detective story, however, the immutable scheme is formed by the personality of the detective and of his colleagues, while within this scheme are unravelled unexpected events (and most unexpected of all is the figure of the culprit). On the contrary, in the novels of Fleming, the scheme even dominates the very chain of events. Moreover, the identity of the culprit, his characteristics, and his plans are always apparent from the beginning. The reader finds himself immersed in a game of which he knows the pieces and the rules – and perhaps the outcome – and draws pleasure simply from following the minimal variations by which the victor realizes his objective.

We might compare a novel by Fleming to a game of football in which we know beforehand the place, the numbers and personalities of the players, the rules of the game, and the fact that everything will take place within the area of the great pitch – except that in a game of football we do not know until the very end who will win. It would be more accurate to compare a novel by Fleming to a game of basketball played by the Harlem Globetrotters against a local team. We know with absolute confidence that the Globetrotters will win: the pleasure lies in watching the trained virtuosity with which they defer the final moment, with what ingenious deviations they reconfirm the foregone conclusion, with what trickeries they make rings round their opponents. The novels of Fleming exploit in exemplary measure that element of foregone play which is typical of the escape machine geared for the entertainment of the masses. Perfect in their mechanism, such machines represent the narrative structure which works upon a material which does not aspire to express any ideology. It is true that such structures inevitably entail ideological positions, but these do not derive so much from the structured contents as from the way of structuring them.

Tsvetan Todorov, 'The Typology of Detective Fiction'*

See also
Aristotle (1.i)
Propp (1.iii)
Shlovsky (1.iii)
Tomashevsky (1.iii)
Eco (2.iii)
Smith (3.ii)
Brooks (3.ii)
Le Guin (3.ii)
Bronfen (4)
Roof (5)

Detective fiction cannot be subdivided into kinds.
It merely offers historically different forms.
(Boileau and Narcejac, *Le Roman policier*, 1964)

If I use this observation as the epigraph to an article dealing precisely with 'kinds' of

---

* *The Poetics of Prose* (Oxford: Blackwell, 1978), pp. 70–8.

'detective fiction,' it is not to emphasize my disagreement 'with the authors in question, but because their attitude is very widespread; hence it is the first thing we must confront. Detective fiction has nothing to do with this question: for nearly two centuries, there has been a powerful reaction in literary studies against the very notion of genre. We write either about literature in general or about a single work, and it is a tacit convention that to classify several works in a genre is to devalue them. There is a good historical explanation for this attitude: literary reflection of the classical period, which concerned genres more than works, also manifested a penalizing tendency – a work was judged poor if it did not sufficiently obey the rules of its genre. Hence such criticism sought not only to describe genres but also to prescribe them; the grid of genre preeeded literary creation instead of following it.

The reaction was radical: the romantics and their present-day descendants have refused not only to conform to the rules of the genres (which was indeed their privilege) but also to recognize the very existence of such a notion. Hence the theory of genres has remained singularly undeveloped until very recently. Yet now there is a tendency to seek an intermediary between the too-general notion of literature and those individual objects which are works. The delay doubtless comes from the fact that typology is implied by the description of these individual works; yet this task of description is still far from having received satisfactory solutions. So long as we cannot describe the structure of works, we must be content to compare certain measurable elements, such as meter. Despite the immediate interest in an investigation of genres (as Albert Thibaudet remarked, such an investigation concerns the problem of universals), we cannot undertake it without first elaborating structural description: only the criticism of the classical period could permit itself to deduce genres from abstract logical schemas.

An additional difficulty besets the study of genres, one which has to do with the specific character of every esthetic norm. The major work creates, in a sense, a new genre and at the same time transgresses the previously valid rules of the genre. The genre of *The Charterhouse of Parma*, that is, the norm to which this novel refers, is not the French novel of the early nineteenth century; it is the genre 'Stendhalian novel' which is created by precisely this work and a few others. One might say that every great book establishes the existence of two genres, the reality of two norms: that of the genre it transgresses, which dominated the preceding literature, and that of the genre it creates.

Yet there is a happy realm where this dialectical contradiction between the work and its genre does not exist: that of popular literature. As a rule, the literary masterpiece does not enter any genre save perhaps its own; but the masterpiece of popular literature is precisely the book which best fits its genre. Detective fiction has its norms; to 'develop' them is also to disappoint them: to 'improve upon' detective fiction is to write 'literature,' not detective fiction. The whodunit par excellence is not the one which transgresses the rules of the genre, but the one which conforms to them: *No Orchids for Miss Blandish*[1] is an incarnation of its genre, not a transcendence. If we had properly described the genres of popular literature, there would no longer be an occasion to speak of its masterpieces. They are one and the same thing; the best novel will be the one about which there is nothing to say. This is a generally unnoticed phenomenon, whose consequences affect every esthetic category. We are today in the presence of a discrepancy between two essential manifestations; no longer is there one single esthetic norm in our society, but two; the same measurements do not apply to 'high' art and 'popular' art.

The articulation of genres within detective fiction therefore promises to be relatively easy. But we must begin with the description of 'kinds,' which also means with their delimitation. We shall take as our point of departure the classic detective fiction which reached its peak between the two world wars and is often called the whodunit. Several attempts have already been made to specify the rules of this genre (we shall return below to S. S. Van Dine's twenty rules); but the best general characterization I know is the one Butor gives in his own novel *Passing Time* (*L'Emploi du temps*). George Burton, the author of many murder mysteries, explains to the narrator that 'all detective fiction is based on two murders of which the first, committed by the murderer, is merely the occasion for the second, in which he is the victim of the pure and unpunishable murderer, the detective,' and that 'the narrative . . . superimposes two temporal series: the days of the investigation which begin with the crime, and the days of the drama which lead up to it.'

At the base of the whodunit we find a duality, and it is this duality which will guide our description. This novel contains not one but two stories: the story of the crime and the story of the investigation. In their purest form, these two stories have no point in common. Here are the first lines of a 'pure' whodunit:

a small green index-card on which is typed:

Odel, Margaret.

184 W. Seventy-first Street. Murder: Strangled about
11 P.M. Apartment robbed. Jewels stolen. Body found by
Amy Gibson, maid.
(S. S. Van Dine, The 'Canary' Murder Case)

The first story, that of the crime, ends before the second begins. But what happens in the second? Not much. The characters of this second story, the story of the investigation, do not act, they learn. Nothing can happen to them: a rule of the genre postulates the detective's immunity. We cannot imagine Hercule Poirot or Philo Vance[2] threatened by some danger, attacked, wounded, even killed. The hundred and fifty pages which separate the discovery of the crime from the revelation of the killer are devoted to a slow apprenticeship: we examine clue after clue, lead after lead. The whodunit thus tends toward a purely geometric architecture: Agatha Christie's *Murder on the Orient Express*, for example, offers twelve suspects; the book consists of twelve chapters, and again twelve interrogations, a prologue, and an epilogue (that is, the discovery of the crime and the discovery of the killer).

This second story, the story of the investigation, thereby enjoys a particular status. It is no accident that it is often told by a friend of the detective, who explicitly acknowledges that he is writing a book; the second story consists, in fact, in explaining how this very book came to be written. The first story ignores the book completely, that is, it never confesses its literary nature (no author of detective fiction can permit himself to indicate directly the imaginary character of the story, as it happens in 'literature'). On the other hand, the second story is not only supposed to take the reality of the book into account, but it is precisely the story of that very book.

We might further characterize these two stories by saying that the first – the story of the crime – tells 'what really happened,' whereas the second – the story of the investigation – explains 'how the reader (or the narrator) has come to know about it.' But these definitions concern not only the two stories in detective fiction, but also two aspects of every literary work which the Russian Formalists isolated forty years ago. They distinguished, in fact, the *fable* (story) from the *subject* (plot)[3] of a narrative: the story is what has happened in life, the plot is the way the author presents it to us. The first notion corresponds to the reality evoked, to events similar to those which take place in our lives; the second, to the book itself, to the narrative, to the literary devices the author employs. In the story, there is no inversion in time, actions follow their natural order; in the plot, the author can present results before their causes, the end before the beginning. These two notions do not characterize two parts of the story or two different works, but two aspects of one and the same work; they are two points of view about the same thing. How does it happen then that detective fiction manages to make both of them present, to put them side by side?

To explain this paradox, we must first recall the special status of the two stories. The first, that of the crime, is in fact the story of an absence: its most accurate characteristic is that it cannot be immediately present in the book. In other words, the narrator cannot transmit directly the conversations of the characters who are implicated, nor describe their actions: to do so, he must necessarily employ the intermediary of another (or the. same) character who will report, in the second story, the words heard or the actions observed. The status of the second story is, as we have seen, just as excessive; it is a story which has no importance in itself, which serves only as a mediator between the reader and the story of the crime. Theoreticians of detective fiction have always agreed that style, in this type of literature, must be perfectly transparent, imperceptible; the only requirement it obeys is to be simple, clear, direct. It has even been attempted – significantly – to suppress this second story altogether. One publisher put out real dossiers, consisting of police reports, interrogations, photographs, fingerprints, even locks of hair; these 'authentic' documents were to lead the reader to the discovery of the criminal (in case of failure, a sealed envelope, pasted on the last page, gave the answer to the puzzle: for example, the judge's verdict).

We are concerned then in the whodunit with two stories of which one is absent but real, the other present but insignificant. This presence and this absence explain the existence of the two in the continuity of the narrative. The first involves so many conventions and literary devices (which are in fact the 'plot' aspects of the narrative) that the author cannot leave them unexplained. These devices are, we may note, of essentially two types, temporal inversions and individual 'points of view': the tenor of each piece of information is determined by the person who transmits it, no observation exists without an observer; the author cannot, by definition, be omniscient as he was in the classical novel. The second story then appears as a place where all these devices are justified and 'naturalized': to give them a 'natural' quality, the author must explain that he is writing a book! And to keep this second story from becoming opaque, from casting a useless shadow on the first, the style is to be kept neutral and plain, to the point where it is rendered imperceptible.

Now let us examine another genre within detective fiction, the genre created in the United States just before and particularly after World War II, and which is published in France under the rubric '*série noire*' (the thriller); this kind of detective fiction fuses the two stories or in other words, suppresses the first and vitalizes the second. We are no longer told about a crime anterior to the moment of the narrative; the narrative coincides with the action. No thriller is presented in the form of memoirs: there is no point reached where the narrator comprehends all past events, we do not even know if he will reach the end of the story alive. Prospection takes the place of retrospection.

There is no story to be guessed; and there is no mystery, in the sense that it was present in the whodunit. But the reader's interest is not thereby diminished; we realize here that two entirely different forms of interest exist. The first can be called *curiositiy*; it proceeds from effect to cause: starting from a certain effect (a corpse and certain clues) we must find its cause (the culprit and his motive). The second form is *suspense*, and here the movement is from cause to effect: we are first shown the causes, the initial *données* (gangsters preparing a heist), and our interest is sustained by the expectation of what will happen, that is, certain effects (corpses, crimes, fights). This type of interest was inconceivable in the whodunit, for its chief characters (the detective and his friend the narrator) were, by definition, immunized: nothing could happen to them. The situation is reversed in the thriller: everything is possible, and the detective risks his health, if not his life.

I have presented the opposition between the whodunit and the thriller as an opposition between two stories and a single one; but this is a logical, not a historical classification. The thriller did not need to perform this specific transformation in order to appear on the scene. Unfortunately for logic, genres are not constituted in conformity with structural descriptions; a new genre is created around an element which was not obligatory in the old one: the two encode different elements. For this reason the poetics of classicism was wasting its time seeking a logical classification of genres. The contemporary thriller has been constituted not around a method of presentation but around the milieu represented, around specific characters and behavior; in other words, its constitutive character is in its themes. This is how it was described, in 1945, by Marcel Duhamel, its promoter in France: in it we find 'violence – in all its forms, and especially the most shameful – bearings, killings. . . . Immorality is as much at home here as noble feelings. . . . There is also love – preferably vile – violent passion, implacable hatred.' Indeed it is around these few constants that the thriller is constituted: violence, generally sordid crime, the amorality of the characters. Necessarily, too, the 'second story,' the one taking place in the present, occupies a central place. But the suppression of the first story is not an obligatory feature: the early authors of the thriller, Dashiell Hammett and Raymond Chandler, preserve the element of mystery; the important thing is that it now has a secondary function, subordinate and no longer central as in the whodunit.

This restriction in the milieu described also distinguishes the thriller from the adventure story, though this limit is not very distinct. We can see that the properties listed up to now – danger, pursuit, combat – are also to be found in an adventure story; yet the thriller keeps its autonomy. We must distinguish several reasons for this: the relative effacement of the adventure story and its replacement by the spy novel; then the thriller's tendency toward the marvelous and the exotic, which brings it closer on the one hand to the travel narrative, and on the other to contemporary science fiction; last, a tendency to description which remains entirely alien to the detective novel. The difference in the milieu and behavior described must be added to these other distinctions, and precisely this difference has permitted the thriller to be constituted as a genre.

One particularly dogmatic author of detective fiction, S. S. Van Dine, laid down, in 1928, twenty rules to which any self-respecting author of detective fiction must conform. These rules have been frequently reproduced since then (see for instance the book, already quoted from, by Boileau and Narcejac) and frequently contested. Since we are not concerned with prescribing procedures for the writer but with describing the genres of detective fiction, we may profitably consider these rules a moment. In their original form, they are quite prolix and may be readily summarized by the eight following points:

1   The novel must have at most one detective and one criminal, and at least one victim (a corpse).
2   The culprit must not be a professional criminal, must not be the detective, must kill for personal reasons.
3   Love has no place in detective fiction.
4   The culprit must have a certain importance:
    (a)   in life: not be a butler or a chambermaid.
    (b)   in the book: must be one of the main characters.
5   Everything must be explained rationally; the fantastic is not admitted.
6   There is no place for descriptions nor for psychological analyses.
7   With regard to information about the story, the following homology must be observed: 'author : reader = criminal : detective.'
8   Banal situations and solutions must be avoided (Van Dine lists ten).

If we compare this list with the description of the thriller, we will discover an interesting phenomenon. A portion of Van Dine's rules apparently refers to all detective fiction, another portion to the whodunit. This distribution coincides, curiously, with the field of application of the rules: those which concern the themes, the life represented (the 'first story'), are limited to the whodunit (rules 1–4a); those which refer to discourse, to the book (to the 'second story'), are equally valid for the thriller (rules 4b–7; rule 8 is of a much broader generality). Indeed in the thriller there is often more than one detective (Chester Himes's *For Love of Imabelle*) and more than one criminal (James Hadley Chase's *The Fast Buck*). The criminal is almost obliged to be a professional and does not kill for personal reasons ('the hired killer'); further, he is often a policeman. Love – 'preferably vile' – also has its place here. On the other hand, fantastic explanations, descriptions, and psychological analyses remain banished; the criminal must still be one of the main characters. As for rule 7, it has lost its pertinence with the disappearance of the double story. This proves that the development has chiefly affected the thematic part, and not the structure of the discourse itself (Van Dine does not note the necessity of mystery and consequently of the double story, doubtless considering this self-evident).

Certain apparently insignificant features can be codified in either type of detective fiction: a genre unites particularities located on different levels of generality. Hence the thriller, to which any accent on literary devices is alien, does not reserve its surprises for the last lines of the chapter; whereas the whodunit, which legalizes the literary convention by making it explicit in its 'second story,' will often terminate the chapter by a particular revelation ('You are the murderer,' Poirot says to the narrator of *The Murder of Roger Ackroyd*). Further, certain stylistic features in the thriller belong to it specifically. Descriptions are made without rhetoric, coldly, even if dreadful things are being described; one might say 'cynically' ('Joe was bleeding like a pig. Incredible that an old man could bleed so much.' Horace McCoy, *Kiss Tomorrow Goodbye*). The comparisons suggest a certain brutality (description of hands: 'I felt that if ever his hands got around my throat, they would make the blood gush out of my ears.' Chase, *You Never Know with Women*). It is enough to read such a passage to be sure one has a thriller in hand.

It is not surprising that between two such different forms there has developed a third, which combines their properties: the suspense novel. It keeps the mystery of the whodunit and also the two stories, that of the past and that of the present; but it refuses to reduce the second to a simple detection of the truth. As in the thriller, it is this second story which here occupies the central place. The reader is interested not only by what has happened but also by what will happen next; he wonders as much about the future as about the past. The two types of interest are thus united here – there is the curiosity to learn how past events are to be explained; and there is also the suspense: what will happen to the main characters? These characters enjoyed an immunity, it will be recalled, in the whodunit; here they constantly risk their lives. Mystery has a function different from the one it had in the whodunit: it is actually a point of departure, the main interest deriving from the second story, the one taking place in the present.

Historically, this form of detective fiction appeared at two moments: it served as transition between the whodunit and the thriller and it existed at the same time as the latter. To these two periods correspond two subtypes of the suspense novel. The first, which might be called 'the story of the vulnerable detective' is mainly illustrated by the novels of Hammett and Chandler. Its chief feature is that the detective loses his immunity, gets beaten up, badly hurt, constantly risks his life, in short, he is integrated into the universe of the other characters, instead of being an independent observer as the reader is (we recall Van Dine's detective-as-reader analogy). These novels are habitually classified as thrillers because of the milieu they describe, but we see that their composition brings them closer to suspense novels.

The second type of suspense novel has in fact sought to get rid of the conventional milieu of professional crime and to return to the personal crime of the whodunit, though conforming to the new structure. From it has resulted a novel we might call 'the story of the suspect-as-detective.' In this case, a crime is committed in the first pages and all the evidence in the hands of the police points to a certain person (who is the main character). In order to prove his innocence, this person must himself find the real culprit, even if he risks his life in doing so. We might say that, in this case, this character is at the same time the detective, the culprit (in the eyes of the police), and the victim (potential victim of the real murderers). Many novels by William Irish, Patrick Quentin, and Charles Williams are constructed on this model.

It is quite difficult to say whether the forms we have just described correspond to the stages of an evolution or else can exist simultaneously. The fact that we can encounter several types by the same author, such as Arthur Conan Doyle or Maurice Leblauc, preceding the great flowering of detective fiction, would make us tend to the second solution, particularly since these three forms coexist today. But it is remarkable that the evolution of detective fiction in its broad outlines has followed precisely the succession of these forms. We might say that at a certain point detective fiction experiences as an unjustified burden the constraints of this or that genre and gets rid of them in order to constitute a new code. The rule of the genre is perceived as a constraint once it becomes pure form and is no longer justified by the structure of the whole. Hence in novels by Hammett and Chandler, mystery had become a pure pretext, and the thriller which succeeded the whodunit got rid of it, in order to elaborate a new form of interest, suspense, and to concentrate on the description of a milieu. The suspense novel, which appeared after the great years of the thriller, experienced this milieu as a useless attribute, and retained only the suspense itself. But it has been necessary at the same time to reinforce the plot and to re-establish the former mystery. Novels which have tried to do without both mystery and the milieu proper to the thriller – for example, Francis Iles's *Premeditations* and Patricia Highsmith's *The Talented Mr Ripley* – are too few to be considered a separate genre.

Here we reach a final question: what is to be done with the novels which do not fit our classification? It is no accident, it seems to me, that the reader habitually considers novels such as those I have just mentioned marginal to the genre, an intermediary form between detective fiction and the novel itself. Yet if this form (or some other) becomes the germ of a new genre of detective fiction, this will not in itself constitute an argument against the classification proposed; as I have already said, the new genre is not necessarily constituted by the negation of the main feature of the old, but from a different complex of properties, not by necessity logically harmonious with the first form.

NOTES

1   Thriller by James Hadley Chase, first published in 1939. It is the subject of a famous essay by George Orwell, 'Raffles and Miss Blandish', (*Collected Essay, Journalism and Letters*, Vol 3).
2   Hercule Poirot is the detective in many of Agatha Christie's novels, and Philo Vance is the detective in many of S. S. Van Dine's novels.
3   This translation of the Russian formalists' terms, *fabula* and *sjuzet*, is not entirely satisfactory, since 'story' and 'plot' are used loosely and sometimes interchangeably in much criticism of prose fiction. 'Discourse' is perhaps a more satisfactory rendering of *sjuzet*.

3
Post-narratology

i REFLECTIONS

See also:
Metz (2.i)
Culler (2.ii)
Smith (3.ii)
Brooks (3.ii)
Gibson (3.ii)
Lanser (5)
Diengott (5)
Roof (5)
Derrida (6)
Johnson (6)
Kellner (8)

Gérard Genette, from *Narrative Discourse Revisited**

. . .

The term *narratology* (proposed by Tzvetan Todorov in 1969), together with the 'discipline' it designates, has in fact gained a little ground (very little) in France, where nourishment of a more aphrodisiac kind is often preferred. It has gained much more ground in other countries, including the United States, the Netherlands, and Israel.

To some people (including, at times, myself), the success the discipline has achieved is distressing. What irritates them is its 'soulless' and sometimes mindless technicalness and its pretension to the role of 'pilot science' in literary studies. One could easily counter the mistrust by arguing that, after all, the vast majority of literary (including poetic) texts are in the narrative mode and that it is therefore proper for narrativity to appropriate to itself the lion's share. But I am well aware that a narrative text can be viewed from other angles (for example, thematic, ideological, stylistic). The best, or the worst – in any case, the strongest – justification for the momentary hegemony of narratology seems to me to derive not so much from the importance of the object as from narratology's own degree of maturation and methodological elaboration. A famous scientist asserted in a flash of wit, at the beginning of this century, I believe: 'There is physics, then there is chemistry, which is a kind of physics, then there is stamp collecting.' No need to specify that Rutherford himself was a physicist, and a British subject. As we know, since then biology too has become a kind of chemistry, and even (if I have read Monod aright) a kind of mechanics. If (I say *if*) every form of knowledge is indeed situated somewhere between the two poles symbolized by rigorous mechanics and that blend of empiricism and speculation represented by philately, we can no doubt observe that literary studies

---

* Trans. J. E. Lewin (London: Cornell University Press, 1988), pp. 7–9.

today oscillate between the philately of interpretative criticism and the mechanics of narratology – a mechanics that, I think, has nothing of a general philosophy about it but that at its best is distinguished by *a respect for the mechanisms of the text*. Even so, I am not claiming that the 'progress' of poetics will consist of a gradual absorption of the entire field by its mechanical side. All I claim is that the respect in question deserves some respect itself, or some attention, even if only periodically.

Gerald Prince, 'On Narratology (Past, Present, Future)'*

. . .

Narratology has made it clear that, while narrative can have any number of functions (entertaining, informing, persuading, diverting attention, etc.), there are some functions that it excels at or is unique in fulfilling. Narrative always reports one or more changes of state but, as etymology suggests (the term *narrative* is related to the Latin *gnārus* – 'knowing,' 'expert,' 'acquainted with' – which itself derives from the Indo-European root *gnâ*, 'to know'), narrative is also a particular mode of knowledge. It does not merely reflect what happens; it discovers and invents what can happen. It does not simply record events; it constitutes and interprets them as meaningful parts of meaningful wholes, whether the latter are situations, practices, persons, or societies. As such, narrative can provide an explanation of individual fate as well as group destiny, the unity of a self as well as the nature of a collectivity. By showing that disparate situations and events compose one signifying structure (or vice versa) and, more specifically, by giving its own form of order and coherence to a possible reality, narrative supplies models for that reality's transformation or redescription and mediates between the law of what is and the human desire for what may be. Above all, perhaps, by instituting different moments in time and establishing links between them, by finding significant patterns in temporal sequences, by pointing to an end already partly contained in the beginning and to a beginning already partly containing the end, by exposing the meaning of time and imposing meaning on it, narrative reads time and teaches how to read it. In other words, narratology has helped to show how narrative is a structure and practice that illuminates temporality and human beings as temporal beings. Indeed, to speak most generally, narratology does have crucial implications for our self-understanding. To study the nature of narratives, to examine how and why it is that we can construct them, memorize them, paraphrase them, summarize and expand them, or organize them in terms of such categories as plot, narrator, narratee, and character is to study one of the fundamental ways – and a singularly human one at that – in which we *make* sense.

* *French Literature Series (Columbia)*, 17(1) (1990), pp. 1–2.

Roland Barthes, 'Textual analysis: Poe's "Valdemar" '*

See also:
Barthes (2.iii)
Johnson (6)

The structural analysis of narrative is at present in the course of full elaboration. All research in this area has a common scientific origin: semiology or the science of signification; but already (and this is a good thing) divergences within that research are appearing, according to the critical stance each piece of work takes with respect to the scientific status of semiology, or in other words, with respect to its own discourse. These divergences (which are constructive) can be brought together under two broad tendencies: in the first, faced with all the narratives in the world, the analysis seeks to establish a narrative model – which is evidently formal – a structure or grammar of narrative, on the basis of which (once this model, structure or grammar has been discovered) each particular narrative will be analysed in terms of divergences. In the second tendency, the narrative is immediately subsumed (at least when it lends itself to being subsumed) under the notion of 'text', space, process of meanings at work, in short, 'signifiance' (we shall come back to this word at the end), which is observed not as a finished, closed product, but as a production in progress, 'plugged in' to other texts, other codes (this is the intertextual), and thereby articulated with society and history in ways which are not determinist but citational. We have then to distinguish in a certain way structural analysis and textual analysis, without here wishing to declare them enemies: structural analysis, strictly speaking, is applied above all to oral narrative (to myth); textual analysis, which is what we shall be attempting to practise in the following pages, is applied exclusively to written narrative.[1]

Textual analysis does not try to describe the structure of a work; it is not a matter of recording a structure, but rather of producing a mobile structuration of the text (a structuration which is displaced from reader to reader throughout history), of staying in the signifying volume of the work, in its 'signifiance'. Textual analysis does not try to find out what it is that determines the text (gathers it together as the end-term of a causal sequence), but rather how the text explodes and disperses. We are then going to take a narrative text, and we're going to read it, as slowly as is necessary, stopping as often as we have to (being at ease is an essential dimension of our work), and try to locate and classify without rigour, not all the meanings of the text (which would be impossible because the text is open to infinity: no reader, no subject, no science can arrest the text) but the forms and codes according to which meanings are possible. We are going to locate the avenues of meaning. Our aim is not to find the meaning, nor even a meaning of the text, and our work is not akin to literary criticism of the hermeneutic type (which tries to interpret the text in terms of the truth believed to be hidden therein), as are Marxist or psychoanalytical criticism. Our aim is to manage to conceive, to imagine, to live the plurality of the text, the opening of its 'signifiance'. It is clear then that what is at stake in our work is not limited to the university treatment of the text (even if that

---

* In R. Young (ed.), *Untying the Text: A Post-structuralist Reader* (London: Routledge, 1981), pp. 172–94.

treatment were openly methodological), nor even to literature in general; rather it touches on a theory, a practice, a choice, which are caught up in the struggle of men and signs.

In order to carry out the textual analysis of a narrative, we shall follow a certain number of operating procedures (let us call them elementary rules of manipulation rather than methodological principles, which would be too ambitious a word and above all an ideologically questionable one, in so far as 'method' too often postulates a positivistic result). We shall reduce these procedures to four briefly laid out measures, preferring to let the theory run along in the analysis of the text itself. For the moment we shall say just what is necessary to begin as quickly as possible the analysis of the story we have chosen.

1   We shall cut up the text I am proposing for study into contiguous, and in general very short, segments (a sentence, part of a sentence, at most a group of three or four sentences); we shall number these fragments starting from 1 (in about ten pages of text there are 150 segments). These segments are units of reading, and this is why I have proposed to call them 'lexias'.[2] A lexia is obviously a textual signifier; but as our job here is not to observe signifiers (our work is not stylistic) but meanings, the cutting-up does not need to be theoretically founded (as we are in discourse, and not in 'langue',[3] we must not expect there to be an easily perceived homology between signifier and signified; we do not know how one corresponds to the other, and consequently we must be prepared to cut up the signifier without being guided by the underlying cutting-up of the signified). All in all the fragmenting of the narrative text into lexias is purely empirical, dictated by the concern of convenience: the lexia is an arbitrary product, it is simply a segment within which the distribution of meanings is observed; it is what surgeons would call an operating field: the useful lexia is one where only one, two or three meanings take place (superposed in the volume of the piece of text).

2   For each lexia, we shall observe the meanings to which that lexia gives rise. By meaning, it is clear that we do not mean the meanings of the words or groups of words which dictionary and grammar, in short a knowledge of the French language, would be sufficient to account for. We mean the connotations of the lexia, the secondary meanings. These connotation-meanings can be associations (for example, the physical description of a character, spread out over several sentences, may have only one connoted signified, the 'nervousness' of that character, even though the word does not figure at the level of denotation); they can also be relations, resulting from a linking of two points in the text, which are sometimes far apart (an action begun here can be completed, finished, much further on). Our lexias will be, if I can put it like this, the finest possible sieves, thanks to which we shall 'cream off' meanings, connotations.

3   Our analysis will be progressive: we shall cover the length of the text step by step, at least in theory, since for reasons of space we can only give two fragments of analysis here. This means that we shan't be aiming to pick out the large (rhetorical) blocks of the text; we shan't construct a plan of the text and we shan't be seeking its thematics; in short, we shan't be carrying out an explication of the text, unless we give the word 'explication' its etymological sense, in so far as we shall be unfolding the text, the foliation of the text. Our analysis will retain the procedure

of reading; only this reading will be, in some measure, filmed in slow-motion. This method of proceeding is theoretically important: it means that we are not aiming to reconstitute the structure of the text, but to follow its structuration, and that we consider the structuration of reading to be more important than that of composition (a rhetorical, classical notion).

4   Finally, we shan't get unduly worried if in our account we 'forget' some meanings. Forgetting meanings is in some sense part of reading: the important thing is to show departures of meaning, not arrivals (and is meaning basically anything other than a departure?). What founds the text is not an internal, closed, accountable structure, but the outlet of the text on to other texts, other signs; what makes the text is the intertextual. We are beginning to glimpse (through other sciences) the fact that research must little by little get used to the conjunction of two ideas which for a long time were thought incompatible: the idea of structure and the idea of combinational infinity; the conciliation of these two postulations is forced upon us now because language, which we are getting to know better, is at once infinite and structured.

I think that these remarks are sufficient for us to begin the analysis of the text (we must always give in to the impatience of the text, and never forget that whatever the imperatives of study, the pleasure of the text is our law). The text which has been chosen is a short narrative by Edgar Poe, in Baudelaire's translation: – The Facts in the Case of M. Valdemar –.[4] My choice – at least consciously, for in fact it might be my unconscious which made the choice – was dictated by two didactic considerations: I needed a very short text so as to be able to master entirely the signifying surface (the succession of lexias), and one which was symbolically very dense, so that the text analysed would touch us continuously, beyond all particularism: who could avoid being touched by a text whose declared 'subject' is death?

To be frank, I ought to add this: in analysing the 'signifiance' of a text, we shall abstain voluntarily from dealing with certain problems; we shall not speak of the author, Edgar Poe, nor of the literary history of which he is a part; we shall not take into account the fact that the analysis will be carried out on a translation: we shall take the text as it is, as we read it, without bothering about whether in a university it would belong to students of English rather than students of French or philosophers. This does not necessarily mean that these problems will not pass into our analysis; on the contrary, they will pass, in the proper sense of the term: the analysis is a crossing of the text; these problems can be located in terms of cultural quotations, of departures of codes, not of determinations.

A final word, which is perhaps one of conjuration, exorcism: the text we are going to analyse is neither lyrical nor political, it speaks neither of love nor society, it speaks of death. This means that we shall have to lift a particular censorship: that attached to the sinister. We shall do this, persuaded that any censorship stands for all others: speaking of death outside all religion lifts at once the religious interdict and the rationalist one.

ANALYSIS OF LEXIAS 1–17

(1) – The Facts in the Case of M. Valdemar –
(2) Of course I shall not pretend to consider it any matter for wonder, that the

extraordinary case of M. Valdemar has excited discussion. It would have been a miracle had it not – especially under the circumstances. (3) Through the desire of all parties concerned, to keep the affair from the public, at least for the present, or until we had further opportunities for investigation – through our endeavours to effect this – (4) a garbled or exaggerated account made its way into society, and became the source of many unpleasant misrepresentations, and, very naturally, of a great deal of disbelief.

(5) It is now rendered necessary that I give the *facts* – as far as I comprehend them myself.

(6) They are, succinctly, these:

(7) My attention, for the last three years, had been repeatedly drawn to the subject of Mesmerism; (8) and, about nine months ago, it occurred to me, quite suddenly, that in a series of experiments made hitherto, (9) there had been a very remarkable and most unaccountable omission: (10) – no person had as yet been mesmerised 'in articulo mortis'. (11) It remained to be seen, (12) first, whether, in such condition, there existed in the patient any susceptibility to the magnetic influence; (13) secondly, whether if any existed, it was impaired or increased by the condition; (14) thirdly, to what extent, or for how long a period, the encroachments of Death might be arrested by the process. (15) There were other points to be ascertained, (16) but these most excited my curiosity (17) – the last in especial, from the immensely important character of its consequences.

(1) – The Facts in the Case of M. Valdemar – [– La Vérité sur le cas de M. Valdemar –]

The function of the title has not been well studied, at least from a structural point of view. What can be said straight away is that for commercial reasons, society, needing to assimilate the text to a product, a commodity, has need of markers: the function of the title is to mark the beginning of the text, that is, to constitute the text as a commodity. Every title thus has several simultaneous meanings, including at least these two: (i) what it says linked to the contingency of what follows it; (ii) the announcement itself that a piece of literature (which means, in fact, a commodity) is going to follow; in other words, the title always has a double function; enunciating and deictic.

(a)   Announcing a truth involves the stipulation of an enigma. The posing of the enigma is a result (at the level of the signifiers): of the word 'truth' [in the French title]; of the word 'case' (that which is exceptional, therefore marked, therefore signifying, and consequently of which the meaning must be found); of the definite article 'the' [in the French title] (there is only one truth, all the work of the text will, then, be needed to pass through this narrow gate); of the cataphorical[5] form implied by the title: what follows will realise what is announced, the resolution of the enigma is already announced; we should note that the English says: – The Facts in the Case . . . –: the signified which Poe is aiming at is of an empirical order, that aimed at by the French translator (Baudelaire) is hermeneutic: the truth refers then to the exact facts, but also perhaps to their meaning. However this may be, we shall code this first sense of the lexia: 'enigma, position' (the enigma is the general name of a code, the position is only one term of it).

(b)   The truth could be spoken without being announced, without there being a
      reference to the word itself. If one speaks of what one is going to say, if language
      is thus doubled into two layers of which the first in some sense caps the second,
      then what one is doing is resorting to the use of a metalanguage. There is then
      here the presence of the metalinguistic code.

(c)   This metalinguistic announcement has an aperitive function: it is a question of
      whetting the reader's appetite (a procedure which is akin to 'suspense'). The
      narrative is a commodity the proposal of which is preceded by a 'patter'. This
      'patter', this 'appetiser' is a term of the narrative code (rhetoric of narration).

(d)   A proper name should always be carefully questioned, for the proper name is, if I
      can put it like this, the prince of signifiers; its connotations are rich, social and
      symbolic. In the name Valdemar, the following two connotations at least can be
      read: (i) presence of a socio-ethnic code: is the name German? Slavic? In any case,
      not Anglo-Saxon; this little enigma here implicitly formulated, will be resolved at
      number 19 (Valdemar is Polish); (ii) 'Valdemar' is 'the valley of the sea'; the oceanic
      abyss; the depths of the sea is a theme dear to Poe: the gulf refers to what is twice
      outside nature, under the waters and under the earth. From the point of view of
      the analysis there are, then, the traces of two codes: a socio-ethnic code and a (or
      the) symbolic code (we shall return to these codes a little later).

(e)   Saying 'M(onsieur) Valdemar' is not the same thing as saying 'Valdemar'. In a lot
      of stories Poe uses simple christian names (Ligeia, Eleonora, Morella). The presence
      of the 'Monsieur' brings with it an effect of social reality, of the historically real:
      the hero is socialised, he forms part of a definite society, in which he is supplied
      with a civil title. We must therefore note: social code.

METHODOLOGICAL CONCLUSIONS

The remarks which will serve as a conclusion to these fragments of analysis will not
necessarily be theoretical; theory is not abstract, speculative: the analysis itself, although
it was carried out on a contingent text, was already theoretical, in the sense that it
observed (that was its aim) a language in the process of formation. That is to say – or
to recall – that we have not carried out an explication of the text: we have simply tried
to grasp the narrative as it was in the process of self-construction (which implies at once
structure and movement, system and infinity). Our structuration does not go beyond
that spontaneously accomplished by reading. In concluding, then, it is not a question of
delivering the 'structure' of Poe's story, and even less that of all narratives, but simply
of returning more freely, and with less attachment to the progressive unfolding of the
text, to the principal codes which we have located.

       The word 'code' itself should not be taken here in the rigorous, scientific, sense of
the term. The codes are simply associative fields, a supra-textual organization of notations
which impose a certain idea of structure; the instance of the code is, for us, essentially
cultural: the codes are certain types of 'déjà-lu' [already read], of 'déjà-fait' [already
done]: the code is the form of this 'déjà', constitutive of all the writing in the world.

       Although all the codes are in fact cultural, there is yet one, among those we have
met with, which we shall privilege by calling it the *cultural code*: it is the code of
knowledge, or rather of human knowledges, of public opinions, of culture as it is

transmitted by the book, by education, and in a more general and diffuse form, by the whole of sociality. We met several of these cultural codes (or several sub-codes of the general cultural code): the scientific code, which (in our story) is supported at once by the principles of experimentation and by the principles of medical deontology; the rhetorical code, which gathers up all the social rules of what is said: coded forms of narrative, coded forms of discourse (the announcement, the résumé, etc.); metalinguistic enunciation (discourse talking about itself) forms part of this code; the chronological code: 'dating', which seems natural and objective to us today, is in fact a highly cultural practice – which is to be expected since it implies a certain ideology of time ('historical' time is not the same as 'mythical' time); the set of chronological reference-points thus constitute a strong cultural code (a historical way of cutting up time for purposes of dramatisation, of scientific appearance, of reality-effect); the socio-historical code allows the mobilisation in the enunciation, of all the inbred knowledge that we have about our time, our society, our country (the fact of saying 'M. Valdemar' and not 'Valdemar', it will be remembered, finds its place here). We must not be worried by the fact that we can constitute extremely banal notations into code: it is on the contrary their banality, their apparent insignificance that predisposes them to codification, given our definition of code: a corpus of rules that are so worn we take them to be marks of nature; but if the narrative departed from them, it would very rapidly become unreadable.

The code of communication could also be called the code of destination. Communication should be understood in a restricted sense; it does not cover the whole of the signification which is in a text and still less its 'signifiance'; it simply designates every relationship in the text which is stated as an address (this is the case of the 'phatic' code, charged with the accentuation of the relationship between narrator and reader), or as an exchange (the narrative is exchanged for truth, for life). In short, communication should here be understood in an economic sense (communication, circulation of goods).

The symbolic field (here 'field' is less inflexible than 'code') is, to be sure, enormous; the more so in that here we are taking the word 'symbol' in the most general possible sense, without being bothered by any of its usual connotations; the sense to which we are referring is close to that of psychoanalysis: the symbol is broadly that feature of language which displaces the body and allows a 'glimpse' of a scene other than that of the enunciation, such as we think we read it; the symbolic framework in Poe's story is evidently the transgression of the taboo of death, the disorder of classification, that Baudelaire has translated (very well) by the 'empiètement' ('encroachment') of life on death (and not, banally, of death on life); the subtlety of the story comes in part from the fact that the enunciation seems to come from an asymbolic narrator, who has taken on the role of the objective scientist, attached to the fact alone, a stranger to the symbol (which does not fail to come back in force in the story).

What we have called the code of actions supports the anecdotal framework of the narrative; the actions, or the enunciations which denote them, are organised in sequences; the sequence has an approximate identity (its contour cannot be determined rigorously, nor unchallengeably); it is justified in two ways: first because one is led spontaneously to give it a generic name (for example, a certain number of notations, ill-health, deterioration, agony, the mortification of the body, its liquefaction, group naturally under a stereotyped idea, that of 'medical death'); and, second, because the terms of the actional sequence are interlinked (from one to the next, since they follow one another throughout the narrative) by an apparent logic; we mean by that that the logic which institutes the actional sequence is very impure from a scientific point of view; it is only an apparent logic which comes not from the laws of formal reasoning, but from our habits of reasoning and observing: it is an endoxal, cultural logic (it seems 'logical' to us that a severe diagnosis should follow the observation of a poor state of health); and what is more this logic becomes confused with chronology: what comes 'after' seems to us to be 'caused by'. Although in narrative they are never pure, temporality and causality seem to us to found a sort of naturality, intelligibility, readability for the anecdote: for example, they allow us to resume it (what the ancients called the argument, a word which is at once logical and narrative).

One last code has traversed our story from its beginning: that of the enigma. We have not had the chance to see it at work, because we have only analysed a very small part of Poe's story. The code of the enigma gathers those terms through the stringing-together of which (like a narrative sentence) an enigma is posed, and which, after some 'delays', make up the piquancy of the narrative, the solution unveiled. The terms of the enigmatic (or hermeneutic) code are well differentiated: for example, we have to distinguish the positing of the enigma (every notation whose meaning is 'there is an enigma') from the formulation of the enigma (the question is exposed in its contingency); in our story, the enigma is posed in the [French] title itself (the 'truth' is announced, but we don't yet know about what question), formulated from the start (the scientific account of the problems linked to the planned experiment), and even, from the very start, delayed: obviously it is in the interests of every narrative to delay the solution of the enigma it poses, since that solution will toll its death-knell as a narrative: we have seen that the narrator uses a whole paragraph to delay the account of the case, under cover of scientific precautions. As for the solution of the enigma, it is not here of a mathematical order; it is in sum the whole narrative which replies to the question posed at the beginning, the question of the truth (this truth can however be condensed into two points: the proffering of 'I am dead', and the sudden liquefaction of the dead man when he awakes from hypnosis); the truth here is not the object of a revelation, but of a revulsion.

These are the codes which traverse the fragments we have analysed. We deliberately don't structure them further, nor do we try to distribute the terms within each code according to a logical or semiological schema; this is because for us the codes are only departures of 'déjà-lu', beginnings of intertextuality: the frayed nature of the codes does not contradict structure (as, it is thought, life, imagination, intuition, disorder, contradict system and rationality), but on the contrary (this is the fundamental affirmation of textual analysis) is an integral part of structuration. It is this 'fraying' of the text which distinguishes structure – the object of structural analysis, strictly speaking – from structuration – the object of the textual analysis we have attempted to practise here.

The textile metaphor we have just used is not fortuitous. Textual analysis indeed requires us to represent the text as a tissue (this is moreover the etymological sense), as a skein of different voices and multiple codes Which are at once interwoven and unfinished. A narrative is not a tabular space, a flat structure, it is a volume, a stereophony (Eisenstein placed great insistence on the counterpoint of his directions, thus initiating an identity of film and text): there is a field of listening for written narrative; the mode of presence of meaning (except perhaps for actional sequences) is not development, but 'explosion' [éclat]: call for contact, communication, the position of contracts, exchange, flashes [éclats] of references, glimmerings of knowledge, heavier, more penetrating blows, coming from the 'other scene', that of the symbolic, a discontinuity of actions which are attached to the same sequence but in a loose, ceaselessly interrupted way.

All this 'volume' is pulled forward (towards the end of the narrative), thus provoking the impatience of reading, under the effect of two structural dispositions: (a) distortion: the terms of a sequence or a code are separated, threaded with heterogeneous elements: a sequence seems to have been abandoned (for example, the degradation of Valdemar's health), but it is taken up again further on, sometimes much later; an expectation is created; we can now even define the sequence: it is the floating microstructure which constructs not a logical object, but an expectation and its resolution; (b) irreversibility: despite the floating character of structuration, in the classical, readable narrative (such as Poe's story), there are two codes which maintain a directional order; the actional code (based on a logico-temporal order) and the code of the enigma (the question is capped by its solution); and in this way an irreversibility of narrative is created. It is clearly on this point that modern subversion will operate: the avant-garde (to keep a convenient word) attempts to make the text thoroughly reversible, to expel the logico-temporal residue, to attack empiricism (the logic of behaviour, the actional code) and truth (the code of the enigma).

We must not, however, exaggerate the distance separating the modern text from the classical narrative. We have seen, in Poe's story, that one sentence very often refers to two codes simultaneously, without one's being able to choose which is the 'true' one (for example, the scientific code and the symbolic code): what is specific to the text, once it attains the quality of a text, is to constrain us to the undecidability of the codes. In the name of what could we decide? In the author's name? But the narrative gives us only an enunciator, a performer caught up in his own production. In the name of such and such a criticism? All are challengeable, carried off by history (which is not to say that they are useless: each one participates, but only as one voice, in the text's volume). Undecidability is not a weakness, but a structural condition of narration: there is no unequivocal determination of the enunciation: in an utterance, several codes and several voices are there, without priority. Writing is precisely this loss of origin, this loss of 'motives' to the profit of a volume of indeterminations or over-determinations: this volume is, precisely, 'signifiance'. Writing [écriture] comes along very precisely at the point where speech stops, that is from the moment one can no longer locate who is speaking and one simply notes that speaking has started.

NOTES

1   I have attempted the textual analysis of a whole narrative (which could not be the case here for reasons of space) in my book *S/Z*, Seuil, 1970 (trans. Richard Miller, London, Cape, 1975).

2   For a tighter analysis of the notion of the lexia, and moreover of the operating procedures to follow, I am obliged to refer to *S/Z* (pp. 13 ff.)

3   'Discourse' here corresponds to *parole* in Saussure's distinction between *langue* and *parole*.

4   *Histoires extraordinaires*, trans. Charles Baudelaire (Paris, NRF); Livre de poche, 1969, pp. 329–45 (*The Collected Works*, 3 vols, ed T. O. Mabbott (Cambridge, Harvard University Press, 1978), III, 1233–43. Translator's note: The fact that Barthes is working on the translation of a text originally in English evidently causes some extra problems of translation. Naturally I have used Poe's text; the quality of Baudelaire's translation is such that most of

Barthes's comments apply equally to the original. The notable exception to this is the title, and Barthes in fact explicitly comments on this, continuing, however, to use the word 'vérité' in the French title in support of his analysis. I have specified by notes in square brackets wherever this might lead to confusion.

5   There is no English equivalent to this word, by which Barthes seems to mean, 'answering or reflecting back on itself'.

ii RESPONSES

Barbara Hernstein Smith, 'Narrative Versions, Narrative Theories'*

See also
Plato (1.i)
Aristotle (1.i)
Culler (2.ii)
Todorov (2.iii)
Brooks (3.ii)
Derrida (6)
de Man (6)
Minh-Ha (9)

Contemporary narrative theory is, in many respects, a quite sophisticated area of study: it is international and interdisciplinary in its origins, scope, and pursuits and, in many of its achievements, both subtle and rigorous. It also appears to be afflicted, however, with a number of dualistic concepts and models, the continuous generation of which betrays a lingering strain of naive Platonism and the continued appeal to which is both logically dubious and methodologically distracting.

The sort of dualism to which I refer is discernible in several of the present essays and is conspicuous in the title of Seymour Chatman's recently published study, *Story and Discourse*. That doubling (that is, story *and* discourse) alludes specifically to a two-leveled model of narrative that seems to be both the central hypothesis and the central assumption of a number of narratological theories which Chatman offers to set forth and synthesize. The dualism recurs throughout his study in several other sets of doublet terms: 'deep structure' and 'surface manifestation,' 'content plane' and 'expression plane,' '*histoire*' and '*récit*,' '*fabula*' and and '*sjužet*,' and 'signified' and 'signifier' – all of which, according to Chatman, may be regarded as more or less equivalent distinctions: 'Structuralist theory argues that each narrative has two parts: a story (*histoire*) [that is,] the content . . . and a discourse (*discours*), that is, the expression, the means by which the content is communicated.'[1]

Chatman outlines various arguments that have been presented by various narrative theorists to support this model, one of which originates in the observation that the same story may exist in many different versions and, indeed, in many different modes and

---

* *Critical Inquiry*, 7 (1980), pp. 209–18.

media. Thus, in his essay, he notes that *Cinderella* may be manifested 'as verbal tale, as ballet, as opera, as film, as comic strip, as pantomime, and so on'[2] and, in *Story and Discourse*, elaborates Claude Bremond's claim that every narrative contains

> a layer of autonomous significance, endowed with a structure that can be isolated from the whole of the message. . . . [This basic and autonomous structure] may be transposed from one to another medium without losing its essential properties. . . . [Thus,] the subject of a story may serve as argument for a ballet, that of a novel can be transposed to stage or screen, one can recount in words a film to someone who has not seen it.[3]

'This transposability of the story,' remarks Chatman, 'is the strongest reason for arguing that narratives are indeed structures independent of any medium' (p. 20). Among the other related reasons are (1) that there is a difference between 'discourse-time' and 'story-time,' that is, between the length of time it takes to read (or hear) a narrative and the length of time occupied by the events referred to in it, and (2) that a set of events that occurred in one order can be narrated in another order or in what is called 'nonlinear sequence.' These facts and phenomena, it is claimed, require us to posit the existence of two independent levels of narrative structure: the first or basement level, underlying every narrative, is its 'deep structure' or 'basic story'; the second or upper level is the *narrative discourse* itself, where the basic story is 'actualized,' 'realized,' 'expressed,' or 'manifested' in some form – or in many different forms, modes, media, and, thus, *versions* (pp. 22–8).

There are many grounds, logical and empirical, on which one could take issue with this set of claims and arguments, and I shall not attempt to stake them all out here.[4] I shall attempt to demonstrate, however, that the set of narrative 'properties' or 'phenomena' frequently invoked by Chatman and other narratologists in connection with the two-leveled model of narrative structure neither requires nor supports that model but, on the contrary, reveals its major logical flaws and methodological limitations.

1   VERSIONS AND VARIANTS

There are a number of senses in which narratives are commonly said to *be* versions and, conversely, to *have* versions. To recall some of the most familiar: we speak of the King James version of Genesis, Shakespeare's version of Plutarch's *Life of Antony*, an abridged version of *Clarissa*, an expurgated version of *Lady Chatterley's Lover*, a movie version of *Barry Lyndon*, the star witness' version of the shooting, and my teenaged daughter's version of what happened in the girls' bathroom at school on Monday. Most of these versions seem to involve some sort of translated, transformed, or otherwise modified retelling of a particular prior narrative text; the last two seem to involve a narrative account from a particular perspective or from a perspective that is rather pointedly understood to be but one among many (actual or possible). These two major senses of narrative 'versions' – that is, as *retellings* of other narratives and as accounts told from a particular or partial *perspective* – will concern us throughout this discussion. I should like to turn now, however, to a specific example to which Chatman alludes, namely, *Cinderella*, and ask to what extent the existence of its many versions, in many modes and media, either supports or illustrates the two-leveled model of narrative.

We may consider, first, the claim that in any narrative the two levels are 'auto-nomous': that is, the repeated reference to a basic story that is independent of any of its versions, independent of any surface manifestation or expression in any material form, mode, or medium – and thus presumably also independent of any teller or occasion of telling and therefore of any human purposes, perceptions, actions, or interactions. As this description suggests, the narratologist's own versionless version of *Cinderella* – that is, its hypothetical basic story – bears an unmistakable resemblance to a Platonic ideal form: unembodied and unexpressed, unpictured, unwritten and untold, this altogether unsullied *Cinderella* appears to be a story that occupies a highly privileged ontological realm of pure Being within which it unfolds immutably and eternally. If this is what is meant by the basic story of *Cinderella* it is clearly unknowable – and, indeed, literally unimaginable – by any mortal being.

The narratologist might observe, at this point, that although the basic story of *Cinderella* is indeed 'an abstraction,' its features are not at all difficult to imagine, for it is simply the underlying plot of the fairy tale or what all the versions have in common. This basic story or deep-plot structure is revealed, he might say, whenever we construct a plot summary of any – or all – of the versions. Indeed, he might add, it is the fact that each of us would construct the *same* plot summary of *Cinderella* that demonstrates our intuitive apprehension of its basic story.

It will be instructive, however, to take note of the five hundred-page volume, published in 1893 by the British Folk-lore Society, entitled *Cinderella; three hundred and forty-five variants . . . abstracted and tabulated; with a discussion of mediaeval analogues and notes,* by Marian Roalfe Cox.[5] This volume does not include the cartoon version or the musical version, but it does include the familiar Grimm brothers' version, the earlier version by Charles Perrault, and abstracts of hundreds of other versions from all over Europe, North Africa, India, and the Middle East. In most of them, we find an initially ill-treated or otherwise unfortunate heroine, though sometimes her name is not Cinderella but Cencienta or Aschenputtel, Echenfettle, Fette-Mette or Tan Chan; and sometimes she isn't the youngest stepchild but the oldest daughter; and sometimes she is not a heroine but a hero; and usually the fairy godmother is a cat, a cow, or a tree; and the glass slipper is often a gold ring. Moreover, the turns of plot in many of these tales are likely to be disturbing or intriguing to someone who knows only one set of versions of the Grimm brothers' version. There is, for example, an Icelandic tale, collected in 1866, in which after Cinderella (who is named Mjadveig) marries the prince (who is the captain of a ship), the married couple invite the wicked stepmother to a feast on board the ship at which they serve her salted meat from twelve barrels which contain the remains of the ugly stepsisters, whom Mjadveig and her husband have previously murdered.[6]

I shall return to Cox and some other folklorists but, for the moment, I should like to draw a few morals from the 345 versions of *Cinderella*. The first, which I shall not belabor, is simply that all of us – critics, teachers and students of literature, and narra-tologists – tend to forget how relatively homogeneous a group we are, how relatively limited and similar are our experiences of verbal art, and how relatively confined and similar are the conditions under which we pursue the study of literature. It is likely that if each reader of this article were asked to give a plot summary of *Cinderella*, the individual summaries would indeed resemble each other fairly closely. The shape of the data is not in dispute; the question is how best to explain it, and I do not believe that we need invoke a two-leveled model to do it. For what the similarities would reveal, I think, is not the uniformity of the intuitively apprehended deep-plot structure of all the versions of *Cinderella* but rather (1) the similarity of our individual prior experiences of particular individual tellings designated *Cinderella*; (2) the similarity of the particular ways in which almost all of us have learned to talk about stories generally; and (3) the fact that all of us, in attempting to construct a plot summary in this particular context and in connection with these particular issues, would be responding to similar conditions and constraints. Because we are so accustomed to performing certain kinds of abstraction, abbreviation, and simplification in the name of 'giving plot summaries,' those operations come to seem natural, obvious, and nonarbitrary to us. The inclination and ability to perform precisely those operations are, however, by no means innate; they must be learned, and they may be learned differently – or not at all – and therefore performed differently, or not at all.

There is a second point here with even broader implications for narrative theory. Not only will different summaries of the same narrative be produced by people with different conventions, habits, and models of summarizing, but even given the *same* conventions, their summaries will be different if the motives and purposes of their summarizing are different. Thus, one would present a different plot summary of a given novel if one's motive were to advertise it to potential buyers or to deplore its sexism to a friend and still different if one were summarizing the novel in the course of presenting a new interpretation of it or of writing a critical biography of its author. Each of these summaries would simplify the narrative at a different level of abstraction, and each of them would preserve, omit, link, isolate, and foreground different features or sets of features in accord with the particular occasion and purposes of the summarizing. It is evident, moreover, that each of these summaries would, in effect, be another *version* of the novel: an abridged, and simplified version, to be sure, but, in that respect, like the one-volume version of *Clarissa* constructed for busy or impatient readers or like the abridged and simplified *Gulliver's Travels* constructed for the amusement of children. My point here is that what narratologists refer to as the basic stories or deep-plot structures of narratives are often not abstract, disembodied, or subsumed entities but quite manifest, material, and particular retellings – and thus versions – of those narratives, constructed, as *all* versions are, by someone in particular, on some occasion, for some purpose, and in accord with some relevant set of principles.

This point will be given further concreteness if we return to Cox's study of *Cinderella* and to its rather touching preface. Clearly the task of collecting, transcribing, classifying, and abstracting those 345 variants was an arduous one. Nevertheless, she wrote, she would 'in no wise begrudge the time which that labor has absorbed' if it helped to settle certain difficult questions, 'especially [the question] of the origins, independent or otherwise, of stories similar in their incident and wide spread in their distribution'[7]: that is, whether all the French, Spanish, German, and Italian Cinderellas, Aschenputtels, and Fette-Mettes were translations or transmissions, migrations or distortions, elaborations or degenerations of some single original story and, if so, whether that archetype or ur-story originated in Europe, or came from India by way of North Africa, or from Iceland by way of Norway, and so forth. Those questions were not, of course, settled by Cox's labors. Nor were they settled by the labors of her successor, Anna Birgitta Rooth, although the latter's study (*The Cinderella Cycle*, published in Lund in 1951) took into account several hundred additional variants and was conducted in accord with a considerably more sophisticated folkloristic methodology. Nor were the questions quite settled in 1974 by the Chinese folklorist Nai Tung-Ting who, after concluding from his examination of eighteen newly discovered Far Eastern variants that 'the earliest complete version of Cinderella on record seems to have arisen in North Vietnam,' nevertheless ends his book as follows:

> Finally, this writer is not maintaining that Cinderella *certainly* [emphasis added] originated in this region. He is merely pointing out that, with our limited knowledge, such a possibility cannot be ruled out. . . . This writer hopes that his humble study has added a little to our knowledge; he hopes as earnestly that he has also shown how much there is still to learn.[8]

In short, the origin of '*the* story of Cinderella' has not yet been determined. Moreover, in the view of most modern folklorists, it cannot be determined: not because the evidence is so meager – or so overwhelming – but rather because it becomes increasingly clear that to ask the question in that form is already to beg it.

By now, folklorists around the world have collected about a thousand variants of *Cinderella*. All of these stories are in some respects similar and in some respects dissimilar. The incidence, nature, and degrees of resemblance and disparity are so diverse, however, that they allow of just about every conceivable type of causal relation among the stories, including none at all. Cox left no record of her own more desperate speculations, but I think she began to suspect not only that the original version of the Cinderella story could not in the nature of things be tracked down but that the very concept of 'the story of Cinderella' might be an artifact of folkloristic assumptions and methodology. In any case, we might now say that the basic Cinderella who was sought by the early folklorists was neither before, behind, nor beneath the 345 variants but was, rather, *comprised* of them – and, more generally, that what *anyone* could mean by 'the story of Cinderella' would have to be some set of particular tellings that he or she determined (or agreed) were covariants of each other in accord with some particular, but arbitrary, set of relational criteria.

I emphasized a bit earlier that no narrative version can be independent of a particular teller and occasion of telling and, therefor that we may assume that every narrative version has been constructed in accord with some set of purposes or interests. The significance of this point for the concept of basic stories will be clearer if we recognize the potential range and variability of such purposes and interests. It will be useful, then, to take brief note of certain types of narratives which Cox did not include in her catalog of variants but which we would nevertheless have good reason to speak of as 'versions' of *Cinderella*.

There are, to begin with, such narratives as one might read in popular magazines about the careers of those movie stars and rock musicians who seem to rise recurrently from poverty and obscurity to exalted status in the glittering world of Hollywood or New York. One such magazine advertises on its cover: 'Read the Real-Life Cinderella-Story of Sylvester Stallone'; and it is clear that the story within *is* a version of *Cinderella* and that both are 'basically the same story' – rags-to-riches, as we sometimes put it, in a neat three-word plot summary (and version) of *Cinderella*.

There are also such retellings of the tale as the one that appears in Julius E. Heuscher's volume, *A Psychiatric Study of Myths and Fairy Tales: Their Origin, Meaning and Usefulness*. Heuscher offers a reading of *Cinderella* as basically a story of psycho-sexual development. The three visits to the prince's ball, he suggests, are occasions for erotic arousal from which the young girl flees, trying to evade sexual maturity. 'Eventually,' however, Heuscher tells us, 'Cinderella is able to confront her lover, and painlessly she lets the foot slip into the slipper.'[9] This reading is, of course, an 'interpretation' of *Cinderella*. It is also a retelling and thus a version of the tale; indeed, it also represents an attempt to identify the basic story of *Cinderella*, though it is certainly not the *same* basic story that might be identified by a folklorist or narratologist.

A supplementary catalog of *Cinderella*-variants might include other readings produced by other types of literary scholars – such as critics, biographers, and historians – who have had occasion to discover and/or construct versions of *Cinderella*. I recall, for example, a colleague who was able to demonstrate that all of Charles Dickens' novels are basically versions of *Cinderella*. Since this scholar did not claim that Dickens intended his novels as adaptations of or allusions to the fairy tale, it would be hard to say whether his own readings of *David Copperfield*, *Oliver Twist*, and *Great Expectations* as Cinderella-stories actually made those novels into versions of *Cinderella* or only discovered that they were versions. When we reconsider the work of Cox, Heuscher, and the magazine writer, we see that a troubling question arises here, namely, who is responsible for a version *being* a version? Can it be only someone who, like Rossini and Walt Disney, *designs and intends* a narrative as such? Or can it also be someone who, like Cox and the other folklorists, *identifies and classifies* it as such? And, in that case, can it not also, apparently, be someone who, like the Dickens scholar, *perceives and interprets* it as such?

Before attempting to solve that puzzle, I should mention a theological-minded friend who, when I revealed my interest in *Cinderella*, revealed to me in turn that the story is, basically, an allegory of Christian redemption: Cinderella is the soul, he said; her initial consignment to a place in the ashes represents the soul's initial confinement to the flesh; the fairy godmother is Grace, the transformation of the pumpkin is transubstantiation, and the prince. . . . I stopped him at that point, just as he was warming to the subject and beginning to explain how *Cinderella* is thus basically the same story as *The Divine Comedy*, *Pilgrim's Progress*, *King Lear*, and the *Aeneid*. I thought once more of Cox and the 345 variants, one of which is, in fact, what she called 'the King Lear branch' of the story.[10] I thought especially of her uneasy feeling, as she intimated it in the preface, that if she had continued her labors long enough, all stories would have turned out to be versions of *Cinderella* – and of my own increasing suspicion, as my friend spoke, that *Cinderella* would turn out to be basically all stories.

It has not been my intention here to display a chaos of paradoxes and infinite regresses. It has been, rather, to suggest how a consideration of the phenomenon of narrative versions leads repeatedly to certain conclusions that challenge either the validity or the necessity of the two-leveled model of narrative structure. I alluded earlier, in connection with the Platonic version of *Cinderella* projected by that model (disembodied, untold, unheard, and so forth), to the evident absence from that version of any tellers or occasions of telling and thus the absence of any human purposes, perceptions, actions, or interactions. I was not indulging there in the familiar humanistic pieties commonly directed against structuralist theories. My point was, rather, that *to the extent that contemporary narrative theory omits consideration of such variables, it drastically constricts its own explanatory resources*. I shall return to those variables in the second and third sections. Here, however, I should like to review and summarize the preceding general points:

1   For any particular narrative, there is no single *basically* basic story subsisting beneath it but, rather, an unlimited number of other narratives that can be *constructed in response* to it or *perceived as related* to it.

2   Among the narratives that can be constructed in response to a given narrative are not only those that we commonly refer to as 'versions' of it (for example, translations, adaptations, abridgements, and paraphrases) but also those retellings that we call 'plot summaries,' 'interpretations,' and, sometimes, 'basic stories.' None of these retellings, however, is more absolutely basic than any of the others.

3   For any given narrative, there are always *multiple* basic stories that can be constructed in response to it because basic-ness is always arrived at by the exercise of some set of operations, in accord with some set of principles, that reflect some set of interests, all of which are, by nature, variable and thus multiple. Whenever we start to cut back, peel off, strip away, lay bare, and so forth, we always do so in accord with certain assumptions and purposes which, in turn, create hierarchies of relevance and centrality; and it is in terms of these hierarchies that we will distinguish certain elements and relations as being central or peripheral, more important or less important, and more basic or less basic.

4   The form and features of any 'version' of a narrative will be a function of, among other things, the particular motives that elicited it and the particular interests and functions it was designed to serve. Some versions, such as translations and transcriptions, may be constructed in order to preserve and transmit a culturally valued verbal structure. Others, such as adaptations and abridgements, may be constructed in order to amuse or instruct a specific audience. And *some* versions, such as 'interpretations,' 'plot summaries,' and 'basic stories,' may be constructed in order to advance the objectives of a particular discipline, such as literary history, folklore, psychiatry – or, of course, narratology. None of these latter versions, however, is any less motivated or, accordingly, formally contingent than any of the other versions constructed to serve other interests or functions.

5   Among any array of narratives – tales or tellings – in the universe, there is an unlimited number of potentially perceptible *relations*. These relations may be of many different kinds and orders, including formal and thematic, synchronic and diachronic, and causal and non-causal. Whenever these potentially perceptible relations become actually perceived, it is by virtue of some set of interests on the part of the perceiver: thus different relations among narratives will be perceived by anthropologists and anthologists, theologians and folklorists, literary historians and narratologists. Since new sets of interests can emerge at any time and do emerge continuously, there can be no ultimately basic sets of relations among narratives, and thus also no 'natural' genres or 'essential' types, and thus also no limit to the number or nature of narratives that may sometime be seen as versions or variants of each other.

NOTES

1   Seymour Chatman, *Story and Discourse: Narrative Structure in Fiction and Film* (Ithaca, NY, and London, 1978), p. 19; all further references to this work will be included in the text.

2   Chatman, 'What Novels Can Do That Films Can't (and Vice Versa),' p. 118.

3   Claude Bremond, 'Le Message narratif,' *Communications* 4 (19640: 4; translated by Chatman and cited in *Story and Discourse*, p. 20.

4   I have taken issue with a number of them elsewhere; see 'Surfacing from the Deep,' *PTL: A Journal for Descriptive Poetics and Theory* 2 (1977): 151–82 (rpt. in *On the Margins of Discourse: The Relation of Literature to Language* (Chicago, 1978), pp. 157–201), for a general critique of the use of models and concepts drawn from transformational-generative linguistics in literary criticism and theory.

5   Cox, *Cinderella* (London, 1893).

6   Abstracted by Cox, pp. 144–5.

7   Cox, pp. lxxi–lxxii.

8   Nai Tung-Ting, *The Cinderella Cycle in China and Indo-China* (Helsinki, 1974), p. 40.

9   Julius E. Heuscher, *A Psychiatric Study of Myths and Fairy Tales* (Springfield, IL, 1974), p. 225.

10   Cox pp. lxvii *et passim*.

Peter Brooks, from *Reading for the Plot**

See also
Aristotle (1.i)
Shlovsky (1.iii)
Tomashevsky (1.iii)
Culler (2.ii)
Todorov (2.iii)
Barthes (3.i)
Smith (3.ii)
Gibson (3.ii)
de Lauretis (5)
de Man (6)

. . . Plot as it interests me is not a matter of typology or of fixed structures, but rather a structuring operation peculiar to those messages that are developed through temporal succession, the instrumental logic of a specific mode of human understanding. Plot, let us say in preliminary definition, is the logic and dynamic of narrative, and narrative itself a form of understanding and explanation.

Such a conception of plot seems to be at least compatible with Aristotle's understanding of *mythos*, the term from the *Poetics* that is normally translated as 'plot.' It is Aristotle's claim that plot (*mythos*) and action (*praxis*) are logically prior to the other parts of dramatic fictions, including character (*ethos*). *Mythos* is defined as 'the combination of the incidents, or things done in the story,' and Aristotle argues that of

---

*   *Reading for the Plot: Design and Intention in Narrative* (New York: Knopf Press, 1984), pp. 10–36.

all the parts of the story, this is the most important. It is worth quoting his claim once more:

> Tragedy is essentially an imitation not of persons but of action and life, of happiness and misery. All human happiness or misery takes the form of action; the end for which we live is a certain kind of activity, not a quality. Character gives us qualities, but it is in our actions – what we do – that we are happy or the reverse. In a play accordingly they do not act in order to portray the Characters; they include the Characters for the sake of the action. So that it is the action in it, i.e. its Fable or Plot, that is the end and purpose of the tragedy; and the end is everywhere the chief thing.

Later in the same paragraph he reiterates, using an analogy that may prove helpful to thinking about plot: 'We maintain, therefore, that the first essential, the life and soul, so to speak, of Tragedy is Plot; and that the Characters come second – compare the parallel in painting, where the most beautiful colours laid on without order will not give one the same pleasure as a simple black-and-white sketch of a portrait.' Plot, then, is conceived to be the outline or armature of the story, that which supports and organizes the rest. From such a view, Aristotle proceeds to derive three consequences. First, the action imitated by the tragedy must be complete in itself. This in turn means that it must have a beginning, a middle, and an end – a point wholly obvious but one that will prove to have interesting effects in its applications. Finally, just as in the visual arts a whole must be of a size that can be taken in by the eye, so a plot must be 'of a length to be taken in by the memory:' This is important, since memory – as much in reading a novel as in seeing a play – is the key faculty in the capacity to perceive relations of beginnings, middles, and ends through time, the shaping power of narrative.

But our English term 'plot' has its own semantic range, one that is interestingly broad and possibly instructive. The *Oxford English Dictionary* gives seven definitions, essentially, which the *American Heritage Dictionary* helpfully reduces to four categories:

1   (a) A small piece of ground, generally used for a specific purpose.
    (b) A measured area of land; lot.
2   A ground plan, as for a building; chart; diagram.
3   The series of events consisting of an outline of the action of a narrative or drama.
4   A secret plan to accomplish a hostile or illegal purpose; scheme.

There may be a subterranean logic connecting these heterogeneous meanings. Common to the original sense of the word is the idea of boundedness, demarcation, the drawing of lines to mark off and order. This easily extends to the chart or diagram of the demarcated area, which in turn modulates to the outline of the literary work. From the organized space, plot becomes the organizing line, demarcating and diagramming that which was previously undifferentiated. We might think here of the geometrical expression, plotting points, or curves, on a graph by means of coordinates, as a way of locating something, perhaps oneself. The fourth sense of the word, the scheme or conspiracy, seems to have come into English through the contaminating influence of the French *complot*, and became widely known at the time of the Gunpowder Plot. I would suggest that in modern literature this sense of plot nearly always attaches itself to the others: the organizing line of plot is more often than not some scheme or machination, a concerted plan for the accomplishment of some purpose which goes against the ostensible and dominant legalities of the fictional world, the realization of a blocked and resisted desire. Plots are not simply organizing structures, they are also intentional structures, goal-oriented and forward-moving.

Plot as we need and want the term is hence an embracing concept for the design and intention of narrative, a structure for those meanings that are developed through temporal succession, or perhaps better: a structuring operation elicited by, and made necessary by, those meanings that develop through succession and time. A further analysis of the question is suggested here by a distinction urged by the Russian Formalists, that between *fabula* and *sjužet*. *Fabula* is defined as the order of events referred to by the narrative, whereas *sjužet* is the order of events presented in the narrative discourse. The distinction is one that takes on evident analytic force when one is talking about a Conrad or a Faulkner, whose dislocations of normal chronology are radical and significant, but it is no less important in thinking about apparently more straightforward narratives, since any narrative presents a selection and an ordering of material. We must, however, recognize that the apparent priority of *fabula* to *sjužet* is in the nature of a mimetic illusion, in that the *fabula* – 'what really happened' – is in fact a mental construction that the reader derives from the *sjužet*, which is all that he ever directly knows. This differing status of the two terms by no means invalidates the distinction itself, which is central to our thinking about narrative and necessary to its analysis since it allows us to juxtapose two modes of order and in the juxtaposing to see how ordering takes place. In the wake of the Russian Formalists, French structural analysts of narrative proposed their own pairs of terms, predominantly *histoire* (corresponding to *fabula*) and *récit*, or else *discours* (corresponding to *sjužet*). English usage has been more unsettled. 'Story' and 'plot' would seem to be generally acceptable renderings in most circumstances, though a structural and semiotic analysis will find advantages in the less semantically charged formulation 'story' and 'discourse.'

'Plot' in fact seems to me to cut across the *fabula/sjužet* distinction in that to speak of plot is to consider both story elements and their ordering. Plot could be thought of as the interpretive activity elicited by the distinction between *sjužet* and *fabula*, the way we *use* the one against the other. To keep our terms straight without sacrificing the advantages of the semantic range of 'plot,' let us say that we can generally understand plot to be an aspect of *sjužet* in that it belongs to the narrative discourse, as its active shaping force, but that it makes sense (as indeed *sjužet* itself principally makes sense) as it is used to reflect on *fabula*, as our understanding of story. Plot is thus the dynamic shaping force of the narrative discourse.

III

I shall now bring this discussion of how we might talk about narrative plot to bear on two brief texts, the first of them located at the hermeneutic end of the spectrum – if we may use Barthes's two codes as 'poles' of narrative language for the moment – the other at the proairetic. The first is thus necessarily a detective story, Sir Arthur Conan Doyle's 'The Musgrave Ritual,' the history of one of Sherlock Holmes's early cases – prior to

Watson's arrival on the scene – which Holmes will recount to Watson to satisfy his curiosity concerning the contents of a small wooden box, to wit: 'a crumpled piece of paper, an old-fashioned brass key, a peg of wood with a ball of string attached to it, and three rusty old discs of metal.' The crumpled paper is a copy of the questions and answers of the ritual referred to in the title, the ritual recited by each male Musgrave at his coming of age. It has been the object of the indiscreet attention of Reginald Musgrave's butler, Brunton, who has been dismissed for his prying – then has disappeared, and shortly after him, the maid Rachel Howells, whom he loved and then jilted, whose footprints led to the edge of the lake, from which the county police recovered a linen bag containing 'a mass of old rusted and discolored metal and several dull-colored pieces of pebble or glass. Now all these separate enigmas must – as is ever the case in Holmes's working hypothesis – be related as part of the same 'chain of events.' Holmes needs, he says, 'to devise some common thread upon which they might all hang': precisely the interpretive thread of plot.

The key must lie in the ritual itself, which Musgrave considers 'rather an absurd business,' a text with no meaning other than its consecration as ritual, as rite of passage. Holmes believes otherwise, and he does so because the other curious outsider, Brunton, has done so. The solution of the case consists in taking the apparently meaningless metaphor of the ritual – seen by the Musgraves simply to stand for the antiquity of their house and the continuity of their line – and unpacking it as metonymy. The central part of the tale displays a problem in trigonometry in action, as Holmes interprets the indications of the ritual as directions for laying out a path on the ground, following the shadow of the elm when the sun is over the oak, pacing off measurements, and so forth: he literally plots out on the lawn the points to which the ritual, read as directions for plotting points, refers him, thus realizing the geometrical sense of plotting and the archaic sense of plot as a bounded area of ground. In the process, he repeats the plotting-out already accomplished by Brunton: when he thrusts a peg into the ground, he finds with 'exultation' that within two inches of it a depression marks where Brunton has set his peg. The work of detection in this story makes particularly clear a condition of all classic detective fiction, that the detective repeat, go over again, the ground that has been covered by his predecessor, the criminal. Tzvetan Todorov has noted that the work of detection that we witness in the detective story, which is *in praesentia* for the reader, exists to reveal, to realize the story of the crime, which is *in absentia* yet also the important narrative since it bears the meaning. Todorov identifies the two orders of story, inquest and crime, as *sjužet* and *fabula*. He thus makes the detective story the narrative of narratives, its classical structure a laying-bare of the structure of all narrative in that it dramatizes the role of *sjužet* and *fabula* and the nature of their relation. Plot, I would add, once more appears as the active process of *sjužet* working on *fabula*, the dynamic of its interpretive ordering.

Furthermore, in repeating the steps of the criminal-predecessor, Holmes is literalizing an act that all narrative claims to perform, since narrative ever, and inevitably – if only because of its use of the preterite – presents itself as a repetition and rehearsal (which the French language, of course, makes the same thing) of what has already happened. This need not mean that it did in fact happen – we are not concerned with verification – and one can perfectly well reverse the proposition to say that the claim to repeat in fact produces the event presented as prior: the story is after all a construction made by the reader, and the detective, from the implications of the narrative discourse, which is all he ever knows. What is important, whatever our decision about priority here, is the constructive, semiotic role of repetition: the function of plot as the active repetition and reworking of story in and by discourse.

Within the conventions of the detective story – and of many other narratives as well – repetition results in both detection and apprehension of the original plotmaker, the criminal: in this case Brunton, whom Holmes finally finds asphyxiated in a crypt in the cellar, into which he has descended for the treasure, and into which he has been sealed by the fiery Welsh maid Rachel Howells. Nonetheless, this solution, finding the *fabula* and its instigator, involves a considerable measure of hypothetical construction, since Brunton is dead and Rachel Howells has fled: verification of the *fabula* lies in its plausibility, its fitting the needs of explanation. And as soon as this level of the *fabula* – the story of the crime – has been constructed, it produces a further level, as Holmes and Musgrave re-examine the contents of the bag that Howells presumably threw into the lake, and Holmes identifies the dull pieces of metal and glass as the gold and jewels of the crown of the Stuarts. He thus at last designates the meaning of the ritual, which we had been content, for the duration of the inquest, to consider merely a trigonometric puzzle, a guide to plotting, and which at the last is restored to its meaning as rite of passage – but in a more nearly world- historical sense, since it was intended as a mnemonic aid to the Cavalier party, to enable the next Charles to recover the crown of his fathers once he had been restored to the throne. Watson says to Holmes at the start of the tale, 'These relics have a history, then?' And Holmes replies, 'So much so that they *are* history' (p. 445). Between 'having a history' and 'being history,' we move to a deeper level of *fabula*, and the spatio-temporal realization of the story witnessed as Holmes plots out his points on the lawn at the last opens up a vast temporal, historical recess, another story, the history of regicide and restoration, which is brought to light only because of the attempted usurpation of the servant Brunton. As Holmes says at the end, the ritual, the secret of its meaning lost, was passed down from father to son, 'until at last it came within reach of a man who tore its secret out of it and lost his life in the venture' (p. 458). Earlier we were told that Brunton was a 'schoolmaster out of place' when he entered service with the Musgraves, which may confirm our feeling that usurpation is the act of an intellectual alert to the explosive creative potential of stories. Usurpation is an infraction of order, an attempted change of place, preeminently what it takes to incite narrative into existence: to pull Holmes from his lethargy – described at the start of the tale, as he lies about with his violin and his books, 'hardly moving save from the sofa to the table' – and to begin the plotted life.

What I most wish to stress, in this reading of 'The Musgrave Ritual' as an allegory of plot, is how the incomprehensible metaphor of transmission must be unpacked as a metonymy, literally by plotting its cryptic indications out on the lawn. Narrative is this acting out of the implications of metaphor. In its unpacking, the original metaphor is enacted both spatially (the ground plan established by Holmes) and temporally (as we follow Holmes in his pacings and measurements). If the plotting of a solution leads to a place – the crypt with Brunton's body – this opens up temporal constructions – the drama played out between Brunton and Rachel Howells – which redirect attention to the object of Brunton's search, which then in turn opens up a new temporal recess, onto history. If we take metaphor as the paradigmatic axis that marks a synthetic grasp or presentation of a situation, the terminal points of the narrative offer a blinded metaphor of transmission (the ritual as 'absurd business') and an enlightened metaphor of transmission (the ritual as part of the history of English monarchy): beginning and end offer a good example of Todorov's 'narrative transformation,' where start and finish stand in the relation – itself metaphorical – of 'the same-but-different.' Todorov, however, says little about the dynamic processes of the transformation. What lies between the two related poles is the enactment of the first metaphor as metonymy – and then, a hypothetical and mental enactment of the results thus obtained – in order to establish the second, more fully semiotic metaphor. We start with an inactive, 'collapsed' metaphor and work through to a reactivated, transactive one, a metaphor with its difference restored through metonymic process. The structure is quite similar to that of 'All-Kinds-of-Fur,' where we had an initial collapse of the tension necessary to metaphor in the oversameness of threatened incest, followed by the compensatory overdifferentiation of the daughter become (disguised as) beast, resolved in the same-but-different of legitimate erotic union. In 'The Musgrave Ritual,' we are made to witness in much greater detail the concerted discourse of the transformation, which is no doubt necessary to the detective story, where what is at stake is a gain in knowledge, a self-conscious creation of meaning. But in every case of narrative, it seems fair to say, there must be enactment in order to produce transformation: the plotting-out of initial givens (the ritual, the impasse of misdirected desire) so that their uses may be transformed. Plot, once again, is the active interpretive work of discourse on story.

One could perhaps claim also that the result aimed at by plotting is in some large sense ever the same: the restoration of the possibility of transmission, a goal achieved by the successful transformations of both ('All-Kinds-of-Fur' and 'The Musgrave Ritual.' The nineteenth-century novel in particular will play out repeatedly and at length the problem of transmission, staging over and over again the relations of fathers to sons (and also daughters to mothers, aunts, madwomen, and others), asking where an inheritable wisdom is to be found and how its transmission is to be acted toward. If in Benjamin's thesis, to which I alluded earlier, 'Death is the sanction of everything that the storyteller can tell,' it is because it is at the moment of death that life becomes *transmissible*. The translations of narrative, its slidings-across in the transformatory process of its plot, its movements forward that recover markings from the past in the play of anticipation and retrospection, lead to a final situation where the claim to understanding is incorporate with the claim to transmissibility. One could find some of the most telling illustrations of this claim in the nineteenth century's frequent use of the framed tale which, dramatizing the relations of tellers and listeners, narrators and narratees, regularly enacts the problematic of transmission, looking for the sign of recognition and the promise to carry on, revealing, too, a deep anxiety about the possibility of transmission, as in Marlow's words to his auditors in *Heart of Darkness*: 'Do you see the story? Do you see anything?' Here again are questions that will demand fuller discussion later on.

One further lesson drawn from our reading of Sherlock Holmes's reading of the Musgrave ritual needs consideration here. In an essay called 'Story and Discourse in the Analysis of Narrative,' Jonathan Culler has argued that we need to recognize that narrative proceeds according to a 'double logic,' in that at certain problematic moments story events seem to be produced by the requirements of the narrative discourse, its needs of meaning, rather than vice-versa, as we normally assume. In other words, the apparently normal claim that *fabula* precedes *sjužet*, which is a reworking of the givens of *fabula*, must be reversed at problematic, challenging moments of narrative, to show that *fabula* is rather produced by the requirements of *sjužet*: that something must have happened because of the results that we know – that, as Cynthia Chase puts it about Daniel Deronda's Jewishness, 'his origin is the effect of its effects.' Culler cautions critics against the assumption that these two perspectives can be synthesized without contradiction. The 'contradiction' has, I think, been visible and a worry to some of the most perceptive analysts of narrative, and to novelists themselves, for some time: one can read a number of Henry James's discussions in the Prefaces as concerned with how the artificer hides, or glosses over, the contradiction; and Sartre's reflections on how the finalities of telling transform the told – eventually furnishing a basis for his rejection of the novel – touch on the same problem.

Yet I am not satisfied to see the 'contradiction' as a literary aporia triumphantly detected by criticism and left at that. The irreconcilability of the 'two logics' points to the peculiar work of understanding that narrative is called upon to perform, and to the paralogical status of its 'solutions.' Let me restate the problem in this way: prior events, causes, are so only retrospectively, in a reading back from the end. In this sense, the metaphoric work of eventual totalization determines the meaning and status of the metonymic work of sequence – though it must also be claimed that the metonymies of the middle produced, gave birth to, the final metaphor. The contradiction may be in the very nature of narrative, which not only uses but *is* a double logic. The detective story, as a kind of dime-store modern version of 'wisdom literature,' is useful in displaying the double logic most overtly, using the plot of the inquest to find, or construct, a story of the crime which will offer just those features necessary to the thematic coherence we call a solution, while claiming, of course, that the solution has been made necessary by the crime. To quote Holmes at the end of another of his cases, that of 'The Naval Treaty': 'The principal difficulty in your case . . . lay in the fact of there being too much evidence. What was vital was overlaid and hidden by what was irrelevant. Of all the facts which were presented to us we had to pick just those which we deemed to be essential, and then piece them together in their order so as to reconstruct this very remarkable chain of events.' Here we have a clear *ars poetica*, of the detective and of the novelist, and of the plotting of narrative as an example of the mental operation described by Wallace Stevens as 'The poem of the mind in the act of finding / What will suffice.'

It would be my further claim that narrative's nature as a contradictious double logic tells us something about why we have and need narrative, and how the need to plot meanings is itself productive of narrative.

. . .

If I emphasize plotting even more than plot, it is because the participle best suggests the dynamic aspect of narrative that most interests me: that which moves us forward as readers of the narrative text, that which makes us – like the heroes of the text often, and certainly like their authors – want and need plotting, seeking through the narrative text as it unfurls before us a precipitation of shape and meaning, some simulacrum of understanding of how meaning can be construed over and through time. I am convinced that the study of narrative needs to move beyond the various formalist criticisms that have predominated in our time: formalisms that have taught us much, but which ultimately – as the later work of Barthes recognized – cannot deal with the dynamics of texts as actualized in the reading process. My own interests . . . have more and more taken me to psychoanalysis and especially to the text of Freud: since psychoanalysis presents a dynamic model of psychic processes, it offers the hope of a model pertinent to the dynamics of texts. The validity of this approach can, of course, be tested only in the doing, in the readings for plots that will follow.

. . . We look to a convergence of psychoanalysis and literary criticism because we sense that there ought to be a correspondence between literary and psychic dynamics, since to an important degree we define and construct our sense of self through our fictions, within the constraints of a transindividual symbolic order. In the attempt to go beyond pure formalism – while never discarding its lessons – psychoanalysis promises, and requires, that in addition to such usual narratological preoccupations as function, sequence, and paradigm, we engage the dynamic of memory and the history of desire as they work to shape the recovery of meaning within time. Beyond formalism, Susan Sontag argued some years ago, we need an erotics of art.

Andrew Gibson, from *Towards a Postmodern Theory of Narrative**

See also:
Smith (3.ii)
Brooks (3.ii)
Lyotard (3.iii)
Lanser (5)
Roof (5)
Derrida (6)
Miller (6)
Jameson (8)
Weber (8)
Bhabha (9)

THE NARRATOLOGICAL IMAGINARY

In *The Psychoanalysis of Fire*, Bachelard sets out to study the psychological problem presented by our convictions about fire. He assumes that those convictions are charged with falsehoods inherited from the past. They therefore have only a superstitious force. In particular, Bachelard writes of endeavouring to study 'the efforts made by objective knowledge to explain the phenomena produced by fire, the pyromena'. This problem, he suggests,

> is not really one of scientific history, for the scientific part of the problem is falsified by the importation of the values whose action we have demonstrated in the previous chapters. As a result, we really have to deal only with the history of the confusions that have been accumulated in the field of science by intuitions about fire. These

* Edinburgh: Edinburgh University Press, 1996, pp. 1–8.

intuitions are epistemological obstacles which are all the more difficult to overcome since they are psychologically clearer.

(p. 59)

For Bachelard, the 'confusions' and 'epistemological obstacles' in question are 'intuitions' that are poetic in kind. Scientific thought claims to declare and authenticate itself in the break with or opposition to poetic knowledge. In fact, says Bachelard, science constantly resorts *to* the imagination and traffics in the world of images, in a discourse that is radically other to the discourse that it tells us is its own. And not only is there always a 'continuity' or interinvolvement of 'thought and reverie'. In 'this union of thought and dreams', says Bachelard, 'it is always the thought that is twisted and defeated' (ibid.). The precise purpose of his own psychoanalysis of the scientific mind is to prevent that defeat, to 'bind' the scientific mind 'to a discursive thought'. Far from continuing the reverie, this thought 'will halt it, break it down and prohibit it' (pp. 59–60).

There, is, then, a specifically Bachelardian conception of the imaginary as a complex of what he calls 'unconscious values' haunting the discourse of a given *savoir*. In the case of scientific discourse, Bachelard sees those values as unhelpful and a weakness. He wants to see them disempowered and dissolved. The Bachelardian idea of the imaginary has recently been noted and developed by the French feminist philosopher Michèle le Dœuff, most explicitly in *The Philosophical Imaginary*. Le Dœuff herself includes a Bachelardian essay on Galileo in that book. The essay draws out an iconography of error in the sciences. It shows the affective twists and turns, the imaginative or metaphorical connectives in what is supposed to be empirical discourse. Elsewhere, Le Dœuff carries this method over into philosophy itself. She suggests that philosophy is never pure of the literary, the poetic, narrative and descriptive. The 'allegedly complete rationality of theoretical work' is always compromised (ibid., p. 2). Indeed, philosophy has its own distinctive and traditional literary repertoire. That repertoire constitutes the 'philosophical imaginary'. In its resorts to the repertoire, we see how far philosophy repeatedly depends, not on logical argument alone, but on persuasion, rhetoric, seduction and fantasy. The philosophical imaginary constitutes 'the shameful face of philosophy' (p. 20). But the imaginary is not 'shameful' in its essence. It only appears shameful to philosophy – at least, as the latter has thus far defined itself. In fact, a poetic dimension is indispensable to philosophical discourse as a necessary supplement to the limits of logic. Philosophical discourse is therefore always a hybrid thing, and philosophers cannot escape its hybridity. They can only become more knowing and deliberate in their relation to the latter.

Bachelard and Le Dœuff clearly differ as to the most appropriate response to a given imaginary. I shall come back to that difference later. For the present, I just want to wonder whether, for all the subtleties of our various poststructuralisms, we have yet thought quite hard enough about the critical imaginary, particularly in the case of narratology. Predictably, however, the narratological imaginary has been very different to Bachelard's scientific or Le Dœuff's philosophical imaginary. Thought about narrative has traditionally concerned itself with two distinct kinds of space. The connection between them is profoundly ideological. On the one hand, there is the space of representation. This is understood as the space of the real, the homogenous space of the world. On the other hand, there is the space of the model or describable form. In this second dimension, the narratological imaginary has been haunted by something like the reverse of poetic intuition, by dreams of the geometric. Narratology is pervaded by a 'geometrics' as opposed to an 'energetics', in the sense in which Derrida uses the two terms in 'Force and Signification'. Derrida takes Rousset to task for granting 'an absolute privilege to spatial models, mathematical functions, lines and forms' (p. 16). For 'in the sphere of language and writing', Derrida goes on, quoting Leibniz's *Discourse on Metaphysics*, such models and forms 'are not so distinctive as is imagined, and . . . stand for something imaginary relative to our perceptions' (pp. 16–17). Narratology has turned away from the Leibnizian and Derridean caution. It has continued to grant Rousset's kind of 'absolute privilege' to geometrical description. It was precisely a geometrisation of textual space, for example, that underlay attempts to establish narrative grammars, like Todorov's grammar of the *Decameron*. 'The linguist', Greimas wrote, 'will not fail to take note that narrative structures present characteristics which are remarkably *recurrent*, and these recurrences allow for the recording of distinguishable *regularities*, and that they thus lead to the construction of a *narrative grammar*' (p. 794). Beneath this assertion and its terms – 'recurrence', 'regularity' – is a fantasy of a geometrical clarity, symmetry and proportion to narrative or the narrative text. The fantasy is also one of power. If it is evident in Todorov's grammar of the *Decameron*, it equally emerges in narratological descriptions of plot and narrative structure. Even an ostensibly non-geometrical narratological theme like 'focalisation' can lead to a geometrisation of the text. For example, when Mieke Bal provides her account of focalisation in *Arjuna's Penance* (a seventh-century Indian *bas relief*), she takes the 'logical relation' of 'successive events' in a 'causal' narrative 'chain' as her starting point (pp. 102–4). But she then supplements it with another dimension consisting of vertical 'layers', of which 'focalisation' is one. This kind of geometrisation of narrative was present in narratology from the start. Indeed, it virtually constituted one of the basic principles of narratology. According to Barthes, understanding narrative did not merely involve following 'the unfolding of the story'. The reader was also required to recognise the 'construction' of narrative 'in "storeys"' and project 'the horizontal concatenations of the narrative "thread" on to an implicitly vertical axis' (p. 87). In other words, any given narrative is a geometrically proportioned and 'storeyed' house of fiction, and the reader must reconstruct it as such. Barthes himself becomes such a reader in *S/Z* It has sometimes been suggested, most recently by Mieke Bal, that *S/Z* constituted a radical break with Barthes's earlier accounts of narrative and questioned their neat and orderly systematisations (pp. 299, 304). But as far as the geometrisation of the narrative text is concerned, *S/Z* merely offers a subtler version of the familiar procedure. This is perhaps most clearly evident in Barthes's diagrammatic account of *Sarrasine*. What purports to be a musical score is actually a grid. For Barthes, it functions as a concrete demonstration of his point that '*le texte classique est donc bien tabulaire*' (pp. 36–7). In fact, however, the 'tabulation' is the theorist's, and does no more than repeat a well-established gesture whereby the space of a given text is neatly segmented, symmetrically mapped, closed in and closed down by a geometrical system of thought or representation. This 'system' is evident everywhere in narratology: in its discussions of 'levels', 'frames', 'embedding' and 'Chinese box' narration; in Propp's conception of 'spheres of action', Iser's '*Gestalten*', Greimas's 'semiotic square' and Eco's 'intertextual frames'. It is implicit in narratological approaches to thematics, and responsible even for a spatialisation of narrative time. In the work of narratologists like

Seymour Chatman, character itself becomes a kind of geometrical construction, a paradigm of traits in which a 'vertical assemblage' intersects with 'the syntagmatic chain of events' (p. 127). The geometry of the text and its intelligibility become inseparable. This is hardly surprising. For narratology, geometry is a kind of universal law. The universal forms of narrative are taken to be geometric in nature. The earlier Barthes claimed that narrative is 'international, transhistorical, transcultural . . . simply there, like life itself' (p. 79). If this is the case, then the particular geometric manifestations of universal narrativity are merely instances of a larger geometry implicit in the human, narrative mind. This larger geometry is presumably what is gestured to in all the narratologists' diagrammatic representations of the narrative system as a whole, from F.K. Stanzel's typological circle to the various typological charts of the arch-geometrician of narrative, Genette. In *Palimpsestes*, Genette calls the repertoire of this larger geometry 'transtextuality', and refers to its categories, significantly, as not only general but transcendent (p. 7).

But narratology had its roots in structuralism. It has largely shared the latter's strengths and weaknesses. The weaknesses include an overly geometric schematisation of texts; a drive to universalise and essentialise the structural phenomena supposedly uncovered; and a tendency to conceive of 'universal' or 'essential' forms in geometric terms. In these and other respects, however, recent narratology has not so much broken with venerable traditions of thought about narrative and the novel as fulfilled them, brought them to a kind of completion, made explicit a kind of imagining that has long been latent within them. In other words, narratology constitutes a kind of delayed paradigm. In narratology, an aspect of the critical imaginary is finally brought to conscious light. Of course, not all thought whatsoever about narrative form has resorted to implicitly geometrical assumptions. But the geometrical theme has surely been a general if irregular dominant in narrative theory. This is evident in the reception of Genette's work in England and America. English and American critics have been noticeably positive in their responses to Genette. But this comes as no surprise. Genette's work has looked like a culmination or *non plus ultra* of a narratological geometry or technology of narrative that has clearly long been present in Anglo-American criticism. Some of Genette's typological charting, for example, is anticipated by and arguably a fulfilment of Wayne Booth's much earlier account of the distinctions between 'types of narration', or, as Booth himself puts it, his 'tabulation of the forms the author's voice can take' (p. 150). Genette's skilful geometrisation of narrative 'duration' owes much to Gunther Müller's work on *Erzählzeit* and *erzählte Zeit*. But it is also the culmination of a line of work that can be traced back to Percy Lubbock's account of the distinction between summary and scene, which Lubbock presents as reducible to measurable structural elements. We can go further back than Booth and Lubbock. The geometrical theme is repeatedly evident in Henry James's theory and criticism, the source of so much modern thinking about narrative. The theme is perhaps most clearly enunciated in the Preface to *Roderick Hudson*:

> Really, universally, relations stop nowhere, and the exquisite problem of the artist is eternally but to draw, by a geometry of his own, the circle within which they shall happily *appear* to do so.
>
> (p. 1041)

James's Prefaces return repeatedly to the idea of this 'geometry'. In particular, they return to it as a means of circumscribing or controlling what the Preface to *The Portrait Of a Lady* calls 'the lurking forces of expansion' in 'the fabulist's art . . . these necessities of upspringing in the seed, these beautiful determinations, on the part of the idea entertained, to grow as tall as possible, to push into the light and the air and thickly flower there' (p. 1072). In the Preface to *Roderick Hudson*, the important geometrical figure is the circle. In the Preface to *The Awkward Age*, on the other hand, more generally, the concern is with artistic 'measurements' resulting ('after much anguish') in 'decent symmetries' (p. 1122). In James's account of 'In the Cage', it is more a question of setting a 'scenic system' into 'play', with its 'massing of elements' in terms of regular recurrences and 'intervals' (p. 1171). The geometric theme is often intertwined with either the theme of pictorialism or that of narrative architectonics. In the Preface to *The Portrait of a Lady*, geometrics emerge in the concept of a 'careful and proportioned pile of bricks' that 'arches over' the novel's basic plot of ground, 'constructionally speaking' (p. 1080). In the Preface to *The Awkward Age*, on the other hand, Jamesian geometrics produce the image of the text as 'small square canvas' (p. 1121). We can even go further back than James. 'Geometrics' appear in Fielding's adherence to rules connected with the Unities and the doctrine of 'epic regularity', a doctrine which still had its weight for Scott, Dickens, Trollope, Hardy and Ford Madox Ford. Geometrics are evident in Fielding's praise of Charlotte Lennox's *The Female Quixote* as having a 'regularity' to its 'connections' that is missing in *Don Quixote* itself, with its 'loose, unconnected adventures'. Thus the order of the former's parts cannot be 'transversed' without 'injury to the whole'. For Fielding, Charlotte Lennox institutes the novel as an organised, spatial system whose elements are so interlinked that they constitute a stable geometry. Fielding's contemporaries saw Fielding himself as doing the same, praising *Tom Jones* for 'the grace and symmetry' of its plot. The words, here, are Richard Cumberland's, and Cumberland thought of Fielding as achieving a kind of eighteenth-century equivalent of Jamesian geometry, curbing unruly 'excrescences', keeping 'monsters, and prodigies and every species of unnatural composition' at bay (pp. 215–16).

Narrative theory, then, as repeatedly constructed the space of the text as a unitary, homogenous space, determined by and organised within a given set of constants. Narratological space has seldom been disturbed by blurrings, troubling ambivalences or multiplications. In it, boundaries are clearly defined and categories clearly distinguished. Proportions and regularities establish and maintain certain harmonious and orderly relations. The most recent developments in narratology have hardly disturbed those relations at all. The 1980s saw the growth of what I shall call a revisionist narratology as exemplified in the work of Peter Brooks, Ross Chambers, Karl Kroeber, James Phelan and others. In one way or another, such theorists both drew on and sought to move beyond the rigidities of narratological structuralism. But they also returned to and promoted concepts and concerns – plot, storytelling, theme – that narratology was seen as having sought to discredit or reduce in significance. What remain unchanged in the various revisionist models – have partly been consolidated by them – are the dimensions of narratological space. The latest developments in American narratology have only further reconfirmed narratological geometrics. Such developments stem from modal logic, philosophy of science and artificial intelligence, and are associated with the work of Marie-Laure Ryan, Katherine Hayles, Paisley Livingston *et al*. In Chapter

7 of her recent book on narrative theory, for instance, Ryan not only reinstates plot as the most general feature of narrative and sets it before us in terms of a state-transition diagram. She also sketches a system of automatic story generation according to the assumption that there are basic, cognitive elements to all narratives. We are back with emphasis to the early narratologists' assumption of a unity and homogeneity to mental and cognitive behaviour; in other words, to the supposed purity, clarity, uniformity and universality of narrative space.

iii BEYOND

Jean-François Lyotard, from *The Postmodern Condition**

See also:
Lévi-Strauss (2.i)
Barthes (2.iii)
Derrida (6)
Jameson (8)
Weber (8)
Kellner (8)
Bhabha (9)

THE PRAGMATICS OF NARRATIVE KNOWLEDGE

. . . . Knowledge is not the same as science, especially in its contemporary form; and science, far from successfully obscuring the problem of its legitimacy, cannot avoid raising it with all of its implications, which are no less sociopolitical than epistemological. Let us begin with an analysis of the nature of 'narrative' knowledge; by providing a point of comparison, our examination will clarify at least some of the characteristics of the form assumed by scientific knowledge in contemporary society. In addition, it will aid us in understanding how the question of legitimacy is raised or fails to be raised today.

Knowledge [*savoir*] in general cannot be reduced to science, nor even to learning [*connaissance*]. Learning is the set of statements which, to the exclusion of all other statements, denote or describe objects and may be declared true or false. Science is a subset of learning. It is also composed of denotative statements, but imposes two supplementary conditions on their acceptability: the objects to which they refer must be available for repeated access, in other words, they must be accessible in explicit conditions of observation; and it must be possible to decide whether or not a given statement pertains to the language judged relevant by the experts.

But what is meant by the term *knowledge* is not only a set of denotative statements, far from it. It also includes notions of 'knowhow,' 'knowing how to live,' 'how to listen'

* Trans. G. Bennington and B. Massumi (Manchester: Manchester University Press, 1984), pp. 18–23.

[*savoir-faire, savoir-vivre, savoir-écouter*], etc. Knowledge, then, is a question of competence that goes beyond the simple determination and application of the criterion of truth, extending to the determination and application of criteria of efficiency (technical qualification), of justice and/or happiness (ethical wisdom), of the beauty of a sound or color (auditory and visual sensibility), etc. Understood in this way, knowledge is what makes someone capable of forming 'good' denotative utterances, but also 'good' prescriptive and 'good' evaluative utterances. . . . It is not a competence relative to a particular class of statements (for example, cognitive ones) to the exclusion of all others. On the contrary, it makes 'good' performances in relation to a variety of objects of discourse possible: objects to be known, decided on, evaluated, transformed. . . . From this derives one of the principal features of knowledge: it coincides with an extensive array of competence-building measures and is the only form embodied in a subject constituted by the various areas of competence composing it.

Another characteristic meriting special attention is the relation between this kind of knowledge and custom. What is a 'good' prescriptive or evaluative utterance, a 'good' performance in denotative or technical matters? They are all judged to be 'good' because they conform to the relevant criteria (of justice, beauty, truth, and efficiency respectively) accepted in the social circle of the 'knower's' interlocutors. The early philosophers called this mode of legitimating statements opinion. The consensus that permits such knowledge to be circumscribed and makes it possible to distinguish one who knows from one who doesn't (the foreigner, the child) is what constitutes the culture of a people.

This brief reminder of what knowledge can be in the way of training and culture draws on ethnological description for its justification. But anthropological studies and literature that take rapidly developing societies as their object can attest to the survival of this type of knowledge within them, at least in some of their sectors. The very idea of development presupposes a horizon of nondevelopment where, it is assumed, the various areas of competence remain enveloped in the unity of a tradition and are not differentiated according to separate qualifications subject to specific innovations, debates, and inquiries. This opposition does not necessarily imply a difference in nature between 'primitive' and 'civilized' man, but is compatible with the premise of a formal identity between 'the savage mind' and scientific thought; it is even compatible with the (apparently contrary) premise of the superiority of customary knowledge over the contemporary dispersion of competence.

It is fair to say that there is one point on which all of the investigations agree, regardless of which scenario they propose to dramatize and understand the distance separating the customary state of knowledge from its state in the scientific age: the preeminence of the narrative form in the formulation of traditional knowledge. Some study this form for its own sake; others see it as the diachronic costume of the structural operators that according to them, properly constitute the knowledge in question; still others bring to it an 'economic' interpretation in the Freudian sense of the term. All that is important here is the fact that its form is narrative. Narration is the quintessential form of customary knowledge, in more ways than one.

First, the popular stories themselves recount what could be called positive or negative apprenticeships (*Bildungen*): in other words, the successes or failures greeting the hero's undertakings. These successes or failures either bestow legitimacy upon social institutions (the function of myths), or represent positive or negative models (the successful or unsuccessful hero) of integration into established institutions (legends and tales). Thus the narratives allow the society in which they are told, on the one hand, to define its criteria of competence and, on the other, to evaluate according to those criteria what is performed or can be performed within it.

Second, the narrative form, unlike the developed forms of the discourse of knowledge, lends itself to a great variety of language games. Denotative statements concerning, for example, the state of the sky and the flora and fauna easily slip in; so do deontic statements prescribing what should be done with respect to these same referents, or with respect to kinship, the difference between the sexes, children, neighbors, foreigners, etc. Interrogative statements are implied, for example, in episodes involving challenges (respond to a question, choose one from a number of things); evaluative statements also enter in, etc. The areas of competence whose criteria the narrative supplies or applies are thus tightly woven together in the web it forms, ordered by the unified viewpoint characteristic of this kind of knowledge.

We shall examine in somewhat more detail a third property, which relates to the transmission of narratives. Their narration usually obeys rules that define the pragmatics of their transmission. I do not mean to say that a given society institutionally assigns the role of narrator to certain categories on the basis of age, sex, or family or professional group. What I am getting at is a pragmatics of popular narratives that is, so to speak, intrinsic to them. For example, a Cashinahua storyteller always begins his narration with a fixed formula: 'Here is the story of – , as I've always heard it told. I will tell it to you in my turn. Listen.' And he brings it to a close with another, also invariable, formula: 'Here ends the story of –. The man who has told it to you is – (Cashinahua name), or to the Whites – (Spanish or Portuguese name).'

A quick analysis of this double pragmatic instruction reveals the following: the narrator's only claim to competence for telling the story is the fact that he has heard it himself. The current narratee gains potential access to the same authority simply by listening. It is claimed that the narrative is a faithful transmission (even if the narrative performance is highly inventive) and that it has been told 'forever': therefore the hero, a Cashinahuan, was himself once a narratee, and perhaps a narrator, of the very same story. This similarity of condition allows for the possibility that the current narrator could be the hero of a narrative, just as the Ancestor was. In fact, he is necessarily such a hero because he bears a name, declined at the end of his narration, and that name was given to him inconformity with the canonic narrative legitimating the assignment of patronyms among the Cashinahua.

The pragmatic rule illustrated by this example cannot, of course, be universalized. But it gives insight into what is a generally recognized property of traditional knowledge. The narrative 'posts' (sender, addressee, hero) are so organized that the right to occupy the post of sender receives the following double grounding: it is based upon the fact of having occupied the post of addressee, and of having been recounted oneself, by virtue of the name one bears, by a previous narrative – in other words, having been positioned as the diegetic reference of other narrative events. The knowledge transmitted by these narrations is in no way limited to the functions of enunciation; it determines in a single stroke what one must say in order to be heard, what one must listen to in order to speak, and what role one must play (on the scene of diegetic reality) to be the object of a narrative.

Thus the speech acts relevant to this form of knowledge are performed not only by the speaker, but also by the listener, as well as by the third party referred to. The knowledge arising from such an apparatus may seem 'condensed' in comparison with what I call 'developed' knowledge. Our example clearly illustrates that a narrative tradition is also the tradition of the criteria defining a threefold competence – 'know-how,' 'knowing how to speak,' and 'knowing how to hear' [savoir-faire, savoir-dire, savoir-entendre] – through which the community's relationship to itself and its environment is played out. What is transmitted through these narratives is the set of pragmatic rules that constitutes the social bond.

A fourth aspect of narrative knowledge meriting careful examination is its effect on time. Narrative form follows a rhythm; it is the synthesis of a meter beating time in regular periods and of accent modifying the length or amplitude of certain of those periods. This vibratory, musical property of narrative is clearly revealed in the ritual performance of certain Cashinahua tales: they are handed down in initiation ceremonies, in absolutely fixed form, in a language whose meaning is obscured by lexical and syntactic anomalies, and they are sung as interminable, monotonous chants. It is a strange brand of knowledge, you may say, that does not even make itself understood to the young men to whom it is addressed!

And yet this kind of knowledge is quite common; nursery rhymes are of this type, and repetitive forms of contemporary music have tried to recapture or at least approximate it. It exhibits a surprising feature: as meter takes precedence over accent in the production of sound (spoken or not), time ceases to be a support for memory to become an immemorial beating that, in the absence of a noticeable separation between periods, prevents their being numbered and consigns them to oblivion. Consider the form of popular sayings, proverbs, and maxims: they are like little splinters of potential narratives, or molds of old ones, which have continued to circulate on certain levels of the contemporary social edifice. In their prosody can be recognized the mark of that strange temporalization that jars the golden rule of our knowledge: 'never forget.'

Now there must be a congruence between this lethal function of narrative knowledge and the functions, cited earlier, of criteria formation, the unification of areas of competence, and social regulation. By way of a simplifying fiction, we can hypothesize that, against all expectations, a collectivity that takes narrative as its key form of competence has no need to remember its past. It finds the raw material for its social bond not only in the meaning of the narratives it recounts, but also in the act of reciting them. The narratives? reference may seem to belong to the past, but in reality it is always contemporaneous with the act of recitation. It is the present act that on each of its occurrences marshals in the ephemeral temporality inhabiting the space between the 'I have heard' and the 'you will hear.'

The important thing about the pragmatic protocol of this kind of narration is that it betokens a theoretical identity between each of the narrative's occurrences. This may not in fact be the case, and often is not, and we should not blind ourselves to the element of humor or anxiety noticeable in the respect this etiquette inspires. The fact remains that what is emphasized is the metrical beat of the narrative occurrences, not each performance's differences in accent. It is in this sense that this mode of temporality can be said to be simultaneously evanescent and immemorial.

Finally, a culture that gives precedence to the narrative form doubtless has no more of a need for special procedures to authorize its narratives than it has to remember its past. It is hard to imagine such a culture first isolating the post of narrator from the others in order to give it a privileged status in narrative pragmatics, then inquiring into what right the narrator (who is thus disconnected from the narratee and diegesis) might have to recount what he recounts, and finally undertaking the analysis or anamnesis of its own legitimacy. It is even harder to imagine it handing over the authority for its narratives to some incomprehensible subject of narration. The narratives themselves have this authority. In a sense, the people are only that which actualizes the narratives: once again, they do this not only by recounting them, but also by listening to them and recounting themselves through them; in other words, by putting them into 'play' in their institutions – thus by assigning themselves the posts of narratee and diegesis as well as the post of narrator.

There is, then, an incommensurability between popular narrative pragmatics, which provides immediate legitimation, and the language game known to the West as the question of legitimacy – or rather, legitimacy as a referent in the game of inquiry. Narratives, as we have seen, determine criteria of competence and/or illustrate how they are to be applied. They thus define what has the right to be said and done in the culture in question, and since they are themselves a part of that culture, they are legitimated by the simple fact that they do what they do.

Donald N. McCloskey, 'Storytelling in Economics'*

See also:
Plato (1.i)
Benjamin (1.iii)
Lévi-Strauss (2.i)
Metz (2.i)
Le Guin (3.ii)
Lyotard (3.iii)
Borsch-Jakobsen (4)
Bennington (6)
Felman (8)
Gates (9)

. . . . A story answers a model.

But likewise a model answers a story. If the biologist gives the evolutionary story first, and the listener then asks, 'But why?', the biologist will answer with a metaphor: 'The reason why the crabs will die off is that poorly located glands would serve poorly in the emergencies of crabby life. . . .' The glands would not be located according to the metaphor of maximizing: that's why.

Among what speakers of English call the sciences, metaphors dominate physics and stories dominate biology. Of course, the modes can mix. That we humans regard metaphors and stories as antiphonal guarantees they will. Mendel's thinking about

---

* C. Nash (ed.), *Narratives in Culture: The Uses of Storytelling in the Sciences, Philosophy and Literature* (London and New York: Routledge, 1990), pp. 6–7.

genetics is a rare case in biology of pure modelling, answered after a long while by the more usual storytelling. In 1902 W.S. Sutton observed homologous pairs of grasshopper chromosomes. He answered the question put to a metaphor – '*Why* does the Mendelian model of genes work?' – with a story: 'Because, to begin with, the genes are arranged along pairs of chromosomes, which I have seen, one half from each parent.'

The modes of explanation are more closely balanced in economics. An economist explains the success of cotton farming in the antebellum American South indifferently with static, modelling arguments (the South in 1860 had a comparative advantage in cotton) or with dynamic, storytelling arguments (the situation in 1860 was an evolution from earlier successes). The best economics, indeed, combines the two. Ludwig von Mises' famous paper of 1920 on the impossibility of economic calculation under socialism was both a story of the failures of central planning during the recently concluded war and a model of why any replacement for the market would fail.

The metaphors are best adapted to making predictions of tides in the sea or of shortages in markets, simulating out into a counterfactual world. (One could use here either an evolutionary story from the history of science or a maximizing model from the sociology or philosophy of science.) Seventeenth-century physics abandoned stories in favour of models, giving up the claim to tell in a narrative sense how gravity reached up and pulled things down; it just did, according to such-and-such an equation – let me show you the model. Similarly a price control on apartments will yield shortages; don't ask how it will in sequence; it just will, according to such-and-such an equation – let me show you the model.

On the other hand the storytelling is best adapted to explaining something that has already happened, like the evolution of crabs or the development of the modern corporation. The Darwinian story was notably lacking in models, and in predictions. Mendel's model, which offered to explain the descent of man by a metaphor rather than by a story, was neglected for thirty-four years, all the while that evolutionary stories were being told.

The contrast carries over to the failures of the two modes. When a metaphor is used too boldly in narrating a history it becomes ensnared in logical contradictions, such as those surrounding counterfactuals. If a model of an economy is to be used to imagine what would have happened to Britain in the absence of the industrial revolution then the contradiction is that an economy of the British sort did in fact experience an industrial revolution. A world in which the Britain of 1780 did not yield up an industrial revolution would have been a very different one, before and after 1780. The model wants to eat the cake and have all the ingredients, too. It contradicts the story. Likewise, when a story attempts to predict something, by extrapolating the story into the future, it contradicts some persuasive model. The story of business cycles can organize the past, showing capitalist economies bobbing up and down. But it contradicts itself when it is offered as a prediction of the future. If the models of business cycles could predict the future there would be no surprises, and consequently no business cycles.

The point is that economists are like other human beings in that they both use metaphors and tell stories. They are concerned both to explain and to understand, *erklären* and *verstehen*.

Bernard S. Jackson, 'Narrative Theories and Legal Discourse'[*]

NARRATIVE IN THE JUSTIFICATION OF LEGAL DECISIONS

Both judges and academic writers internalize (some, of course, more successfully than others) narrative rules as to those types of justificatory strategy which are most likely to prove acceptable according to the conventions of the audience concerned. Here, we do indeed move away from the social construction of ordinary, common-sense knowledge, into the sphere of the construction of the knowledge of a particular sub-group. However, the processes are essentially the same, even if the 'semiotic group' and the 'codes' they use are different. Knowledge of rhetorical strategy, of the kinds of arguments which are likely to persuade, and the modes of presenting those arguments, are far from adequately represented in doctrinal textbooks. They depend upon internalization of observed behaviour – in particular, through observation of those forms of behaviour which are 'sanctioned' (recognized) with approval by the sub-group concerned and those which provoke a hostile reaction. In this way, narrative typifications of successful persuasion are built up, generating what Karl Llewellyn termed the 'trained intuition of the lawyer'.

Such rules are internalized not simply as strategies of persuasion, but as truth-creating procedures, so that certain types of argument do genuinely appear to be more persuasive than others. This may well come about by conversion of the practical effect of the argument into a quality of the argument perceived to be inherent in it. But of course, the plausibility of justificatory discourse is not a purely semantic matter. There is no one best answer in terms of the argument (in the abstract) most likely to succeed. For the narrative rules concerned specify typifications not only of arguments but of enunciations of arguments: who proposes the argument (the authority of the enunciator), how it is proposed (the rhetoric of its presentation), when and where it is proposed (the context of the enunciation). Through everyday interaction, and sometimes in highly institutionalized forms (such as dining together at the Inns of Court in England), narrative typifications of the pragmatics of courtroom interaction are built up. These apply to doctrinal justification as much as to courtroom tactics. The point is worth stressing in relation to doctrinal justification, in the light particularly of the 'narrative' theories of Ronald Dworkin.

Dworkin has suggested that the reasoning of judges in 'hard cases' presents significant parallels with the practices of a different group of professional interpreters, the literary critics. Legal argument employs a form of coherence which is not a purely legal construct. Legal reasoning is a 'holistic' form of meaning, which depends upon semiotic processes similar to those found in literature. At the same time, Dworkin does not claim that the semiotic processes are identical in the two forms of discourse: his 'Hercules' is not interchangeable with Northrop Frye, Frank Kermode, or Umberto Eco. Because of the particular democratic values underlying the legal system – the values which Dworkin seeks to affirm and promote through his analysis of legal reasoning – the discretion of the judge is limited in particular ways. There exist, for example, two

---

[*] C. Nash (ed.), *Narratives in Culture: The Uses of Storytelling in the Sciences, Philosophy and Literature* (London and New York: Routledge, 1990), pp. 42–5.

different types of legal sign, which the judge must distinguish: 'principles' and 'policies'. In my opinion, Dworkin (like Bennett and Feldman) makes a significant contribution to the study of legal signification, by pointing to a level of analysis which may be regarded as between the 'deep level' of Greimasian analysis and the 'surface level' which we find in socio-linguistics. However, he commits an error very comparable to that here attributed to Bennett and Feldman. He reduces to a single semantic level an activity whose pragmatics equally call for narrativization.

At different times, Dworkin has used two different models of literary activity, which he appears to regard as interchangeable, but which are better regarded as distinct. The first is the activity of the literary critic, looking back on a completed text, and asking questions about it. He invites us to imagine, for example, a meeting of literary critics discussing Dickens' novel *David Copperfield*. One asks: Did David have a homosexual relationship with Steerforth? There is nothing in the novel which explicitly says that he did, or did not; nor is there anything in the novel (he assumes) from which either a positive or a negative answer to that question can necessarily be inferred. Nevertheless Dworkin argues, the literary critics could intelligibly debate this question, on the basis of what hypothesis as to the nature of David's relationship with Steerforth best coheres with the facts actually stated in the novel. For this notion, Dworkin proposes the name 'facts of narrative consistency'. The discovery of law in difficult cases is, he claims, like that. The law is to be regarded as a literary whole, but one consisting of norms rather than facts.

Elsewhere, Dworkin uses the model of a 'chain novel'. One author writes the first chapter of a novel, and gives it to a second author, who must write the second chapter. The latter passes the 'story so far' (chapters 1–2) to a third author, and s/he adds the third chapter. The construction of the novel proceeds in this way, until it is completed (whatever that means). At each point of the chain, Dworkin suggests, the freedom of action of the author becomes more limited, as the amount of data with which the new chapter must 'fit' increases. Each successive author is thus progressively more constrained. Increasingly, s/he discovers what is implicit in what goes before, rather than creates something entirely new.

There is, of course, a significant difference between these two models. In the first, the text is completed before the literary critics set to work; in the second, the literati are engaged in the construction of the text. Dworkin might object that each author in the chain novel already has no less finite a text (from which to derive criteria of 'fit') than do the literary critics in surveying *David Copperfield*. Nevertheless, I suggest that Dworkin here reveals what at worst is the ambiguity, and at best the complexity, of the nature of judicial activity itself. The judge *is* at one and the same time both author and critic. At one and the same time the judge is addressing a variety of different audiences. But each of these audiences constitutes a semiotic group with its own narrativized conventions. In rendering judgment on contested legal issues, the judge addresses doctrinal audiences (who will indeed view the decision in terms of its 'fit' with a pre-existing body of doctrine), judicial audiences (fellow-judges, whose criteria of a good decision may be somewhat different), and most particularly the audience of that particular litigation, for whom s/he has to make a specific decision, and to whom the nature of that decision is far more important than the legal grounds on which it is given. There is no doubt, in this latter respect, that the activity of the judge is creative: when the decision is given, an entirely new legal speech-act is performed, which creates a new state of affairs for the parties to the litigation. In short, the judge takes part in several different stories, of fact discovery, of law discovery, and of the (theoretically separable) activity of adjudication, whereby legal rules are 'applied' to facts. In those stories, s/he performs a multitude of different actantial roles. Dworkin's failure to recognize the difference between such stories as discussion amongst critics on the one hand and participation in a chain novel on the other reflects his neglect of the pragmatic level. Criteria of plausible justification are as much a function of success or failure in playing a particular role in the narratives of successful criticism or successful adjudication as of the inherent reasonableness of what is said in the justificatory discourse.

Rom Harré, 'Some Narrative Conventions of Scientific Discourse'*

SCIENTIFIC WRITING AND SPEAKING AS NARRATIVE

. . . . If trust and faith are the operative principles, so to speak, then the wherewithal for displays of character must be an important part of a scientist's repertoire. I mean 'character' in the moral sense. An upright character must be readable in the accounts. Nothing shifty or perverse, self-serving or self-deceiving must leak through the solid wall of integrity. If 'I know . . .' is to be read as 'Trust me that . . .', character becomes an epistemological variable, for on the assessment of character hangs one's readiness to give that trust, to have that faith. But in normal circumstances it comes without asking, so to speak, for it is created just by the presumption that the author of the performative utterances we call a scientific discourse is a bona fide member of the scientific community. Taken this way, that community reveals something of the character of religious orders, such as the Benedictines. The discourse must display the narrative contentions typical of the productions of members of the Order.

For the material of this section I am greatly indebted to a paper by K. Wales. In scientific lecturing and more informal talk the pronoun 'we' is very prominent, to the virtual exclusion of 'I', even when the context makes it clear that the speaker could only be referring to his or her own individual activities or thoughts. Exophoric pronouns are those which are disambiguated for reference only if the hearer is fully apprised of the context of use, for instance by being present on the occasion of utterance. All indexical pronouns are exophoric. Third-person pronouns are examples of endophora since their sense can be grasped from the text alone. Wales distinguishes between specific exophora, in which the immediate context is relevant, and generalized exophora, in which a graph of what she calls the 'context of culture' is all that is required. So for example when a speaker uses 'we' to refer to the scientific community it is the context of culture rather than the specific context of that very utterance that is germane to a grasp of its referential force. In short it does not mean [+ ego, +voc], that is, speaker plus addressee.

Wales offers an analysis of the peculiar use of pronouns in scientific discourse based on the principle that there is a tendency for *all* pronouns in English to acquire an

---

* C. Nash (ed.), *Narrative in Culture: The Uses of Storytelling in the Sciences, Philosophy and Literature* (London and New York, Routledge, 1990), pp. 84–5.

egocentric force in both specific and generalized exophoric uses. The choice of 'we' rather than 'I' is a narrative convention which has the effect of a rhetorical distancing of the speaker from an overt self-reference to make the egocentricity of advice or knowledge or whatever it may be more palatable. . . . The editorial 'we', still to be found in journalism, excludes the addressee as a referent, that is it is not the 'nudge nudge' and cosy 'we' of complicity, but implies that ego is a member of and spokesman for a larger corporation.

The academic 'we' might seem at first glance to be just a version of the editorial 'we'. Like the latter it is mutedly egocentric but it is not mainly used to imply teamwork. Rather, it is used to draw the listener into complicity, to participate as something more than an audience. Wales cites the prevalence of this pronoun with verbs of saying, showing, thinking, anticipating, postponement, and return. The implication is that the audience is not only passively following what is going on but actively participating in the process of thought – and thereby committed to the results and conclusions of that process. A narrative structure is created within which the interlocutor is trapped, since the ephemeral special relationship created by the discourse prevents that addressee taking up a hostile or rejecting stance to what has been said. Trust in the other is induced through the device of combining it with trust in oneself. The force of the pluralizing of reference is even more marked with the alternative 'Let's. . . .' Thus as Wales put it,

> the surface meaning of joint activity [+ ego, +voc] frequently disguises only thinly the true agentive 'I' or (its target) 'you', and that, more generally, the authoritative persuasive voice of the ego will 'contaminate' the illusion of modesty. 'We' can acquire the very connotations its use has sought to avoid.
>
> (p. 33)

At this point I can make good the claim that in the innocent use of 'we' a narrative convention rather than a purely rhetorical device is at work. One way of looking at the foregoing is as a sketch of a story line in which the plot of a human drama culminating in a scientific discovery is unfolded.

Susan McClary, 'The Impromptu That Trod on a Loaf: or How Music Tells Stories'*

For the last ten years or so, musicologists have hotly debated the question of whether or not music can be said to engage in narrative processes, and several significantly different positions have emerged within the field. No one questions that music often supports *sung* narratives (e.g. in epics or ballads). Yet the music in such instances usually serves as a vehicle, its own structure confined to strophic repetitions to keep it from competing with the verbal act of narration.

But can music itself tell stories? Or do we, rather, as Carolyn Abbate suggests, mistake our own narrations of what we perceive in music's temporal unfolding for music

---

* *Narrative*, 5 (1) (1997), pp. 20–4.

itself narrating? Abbate's skepticism is compounded by her criteria that narratives employ the past tense and that they have an actual narrating voice – neither of which ordinarily obtains within music that operates independently of some verbal apparatus. And indeed if we were to restrict the word to its narrower definitions, then much of what I and others want to call 'narrative' in music would not qualify. Our phenomenon seems closer to the direct presentation of plots in plays or films, in which we rarely have a mediating narrator but in which we experience the dramatic sequence of events as they occur. Yet certain narratologists, such as Paul Ricoeur, extend their theories to plays, films, and many other cultural media, and the kinds of musical procedures I associate with narrative would also count under such circumstances.

Musicologists turn to the narrative theories that have emerged within literary studies for a variety of reasons. Some of these – for instance, Anthony Newcomb and Patrick McCreless – are attracted by the structuralist dimension of narratology: it offers new ways of dealing with formal relationships as they are manifested over time, yet it need not violate the sense of autonomous, self-contained structure still central to music aesthetics.

Only a few of us in musicology (notably Lawrence Kramer, Rose Rosengard Subotnik, and myself) have wanted to read pieces of instrumental music as cultural texts, observing not only their formal properties, but also their *content*. And because discussions of content often lead to critical commentary on that content, our work has been rather more controversial within our discipline. Not satisfied with delivering the loaf as a still-intact structure, we often tread on it as a steppingstone to somewhere else – to critiques of Enlightenment Reason, of Orientalism, of gender ideologies. And if we are not thereby condemned to sink into an Andersonian morass, we are nevertheless regularly pelted with accusations of literalism, ventriloquism, or even (the cruelest cut of all) simple ignorance of the self-sufficiency of musical form.

Consequently, I am pleased to have the occasion to articulate my own position yet again. I have not turned to narrative models simply to find ways of dealing with music's temporality. For although all music unfolds over time, most repertories in the history of the planet – and even most kinds of music in the Eurocentric West – do not do anything I would classify as narrative within the music itself. To be sure, a sixteenth-century madrigal often traces a sequence of events in its poetic text, and the music may inflect and heighten the effects of the narrative offered in the lyrics. But even the most sophisticated Renaissance-music critic would be hard-pressed to reconstitute that story in the absence of the words: the structure of the piece, albeit designed to correspond allegorically to the poetry, does not aspire to independent narrative coherence. And this is true of European music in general before around 1700.

Similarly, more recent music does not usually resemble narrative. In fact, beginning with Debussy, Stravinsky, and Schoenberg and extending to the experiments of John Cage, the avant-garde music of the twentieth century has been self-consciously ANTI-narrative. The radical compositional devices associated with primitivism, expressionism, and chance emerged as attempts at breaking the hegemony of narrativizing musical processes, so engrained by 1900 that extreme solutions such as these seemed the only recourse. In our own moment at the end of this tumultuous century, we have settled into a way of experiencing time that involves the repetition of tiny units: despite the obvious differences between Philip Glass's opera *Akhnaten* and Snoop Doggy Dog's gangsta raps, they share a cyclic mode of parsing out time – a mode informed variously by non-Western musics such as Indian ragas or Balinese gamalan, by the blues procedures that have dominated the mainstream of Western musical practice for nearly a hundred years, by postdisco dance styles, and (or so Fredric Jameson and Jean Baudrillard would contend in their critiques of postmodern culture) by habits instilled in us by late capitalism. Whatever the sources of this increasingly pervasive process, it assiduously resists narrative structuring, even when its lyrics tell stories.

The music that narrates by itself is that very repertory celebrated for having transcended signification: the instrumental music, stretching roughly from Vivaldi through Mahler, that relies on what we call 'purely musical' procedures for coherence – in other words, the European canon from 1700 to 1900. I am not referring merely to program music, which makes its intended content explicit through a title or appended storyline, nor am I suggesting that all these pieces have 'hidden programs' waiting to be ferreted out. My claim is that even the most austere, apparently self-contained of the pieces produced within this repertory attain their coherence and effectiveness as cultural artifacts through processes aligned with narrative.

Let me explain what I mean. The tonality that undergirds this music relies on a number of important principles. First, it produces a teleological model of time organized in terms of beginning, middle, and end. These function, respectively, to introduce the particular issues (themes, affects, dilemmas, dichotomies) to be dealt with over the course of the piece; then to depart from home base and explore various potentialities latent within the opening materials; and finally to restore certainty in a dénouement that secures (*almost* inevitably) the key of the opening, thus resolving the tensions that have kept the piece in motion.

Second, within this overall linear framework, a whole range of events may occur: obstacles, reversals, conflicts, surprises, anticipations, delays, defeats and triumphs – both temporary and final. The degree to which the certainty of the outcome appears in jeopardy will affect our tendency to hear the piece as a quest, as a cliff-hanger, as a performed reconciliation between contrasting states, or as just the abstract unfolding of rational processes. Yet the tonal framework – our knowledge in advance that pieces are supposed to conclude in the opening key, regardless of what happens in the interim – enables these feints and dodges while always assuring the acculturated listener that reason will prevail in the end.

Moreover the security of the tonal background makes possible the staged confrontation and negotiation between many kinds of cultural dichotomies, which vary according to time and place. Whatever the oppositions that arise in the course of a tonal process, their ultimate compatibility is all but assured by the conciliatory framework they inhabit. Vivaldi's concertos, for instance, perform the tensions and mutual interdependence between a stable social unit and virtuosic individualism. The sonata procedure that dominates the later eighteenth century focuses on the constitution of subjectivity out of dynamic processes of 'becoming' and an unchanging, authentic interiority. And in Domenico Scarlatti's mid-eighteenth-century single-movement sonatas, exotic Spanish elements may disrupt the unmarked discourse of mainstream Europe, then retreat to affirm the normative status of the unmarked materials, which return along with the principal key to articulate formal closure.

As confidence in musical expostulation developed among composers in the late eighteenth century, other elements usually associated more strongly with literary practices began to appear in symphonies, sonatas, and quartets. The opening theme, for instance, increasingly takes on the attributes of a protagonist or central agent whose actions, passions, and travails the listener is invited to follow. Moreover, apparently innocuous details start to stamp their consequences 'organically' on the unfolding of pieces, producing plots that sometimes threaten to overwhelm the certainty promised in advance by the tonal contract.

We do not teach students in music schools about tonality in this way. Rather, music theorists have emphasized the mechanics of the system: how to know when the piece is in a particular key and when it has moved to another, how to explain the logic linking one moment to the next. To be sure, composers and performers require such technical skills if they are to produce a particular impression of coherence. But pedagogical methodology has sometimes been mistaken for the entire burden of the music – a confusion only too happily perpetuated in the aesthetics we inherited from post-1848 Germany, when an increasingly radical version of formal autonomy became fetishized as a means of warding off unpleasant or inconvenient aspects of content.

So why drag issues of narrative into the discussion of this music at this late. date? Frankly, if narratology only offered me another (even if trendier) vocabulary for dealing with formal relationships, I would not bother with it. Musicology has enough abstruse structuralist models all of its own devising; we don't really need Greimasian squares to complicate matters.

I began my own interrogation of music and narrative long before I had read any literary theory, back in the mid-1960s when I worked as a chamber-music coach. When I played the piano by myself, I intuited certain ways of 'making sense' in music, and it was only when I encountered others whose performances sounded inert that I started devising verbal strategies for explaining scores. I was repeatedly flabbergasted when good technical musicians failed to notice struggle or miraculous arrivals or anything other than just . . . notes on the page, and I understood my job as pointing up these events and explicating the contexts (formal, expressive, historical, cultural) within which they became significant.

As scholars from all disciplines have become increasingly concerned with narrative, many very different models for considering narrativity and technical vocabularies for designating various elements have emerged. These have assisted me in so far as they have broadened the notion of 'narrative' beyond strictly literary practices, thus making such principles available to me as a musicologist. But although the theoretical issues involved interest me to some degree, my work is far more concerned with examining the kinds of stories told through music at particular moments in history. As a scholar who is actually more invested in musical repertories both before and after this narra-tivizing phase, I want to understand why music – most particularly *instrumental* music – assumed this mode of organization in the eighteenth and nineteenth centuries.

It is important to recall that during the nineteenth century virtually all cultural enterprises in Europe aspired to the condition of narrative, whether historiography, philosophy, biology, political science, painting, or psychoanalysis. As theorists such as Ricoeur and Hayden White explain, narrative allows for the introduction, interaction, and eventual resolution of apparently incompatible elements within a unified process, and practitioners within all these enterprises found such a dynamic, though ultimately stable, pattern extremely satisfying. Not surprisingly, this totalizing habit of cultural thought – which may be more evident to us in retrospect than those in its thrall – also informed musical procedures.

But we can be even more specific. The era between around 1700 and 1900 represents that period in European cultural history most focused on notions of the centered Self: how it is constituted from heterogeneous elements, how it relates to others, how it achieves autonomous coherence, and so on. In short, I would contend that this repertory of instrumental music (which is free of what that age regarded as the corrupting, trivializing influence of language) traces narratives of subjective becoming or *Bildung*. This is its principal cultural work, and this is also why its procedures seemed so significant that they were not supposed to be sullied by verbal explanation.

As I mentioned above in my brief descriptions of Vivaldi, Scarlatti, and so on, cultural work of this sort takes place even in the most conventional of examples. Indeed, pieces that proceed without a hitch through the process of exposition, development, and reconciliation may perform this task most powerfully, for they affirm this structure of experience as entirely normative and without viable alternative. The string quartet movement that wafts by our tables as high-tone Muzak in class-conscious restaurants asks not to be attended to, but merely to fit in with the décor and other accoutrements as part of an unshakable world of cultural certainty.

But it is easier to perceive this ideology when our expectations are frustrated – when, in other words, a piece fails or refuses to work as the contract guarantees. Not only does it tread on a loaf and suffer the consequences, but its descent into hell gives us a perspective form which to interrogate the everyday world of generic musical norms.

John Berger, 'Stories'*

See also:
Mulvey (4)
Heath (4)

If photographs quote from appearance and if expressiveness is achieved by what we have termed the long quotation, then the possibility suggests itself of composing with numerous quotations, of communicating not with single photographs but with groups or sequences. But how should these sequences be constructed? Can one think in terms of a truly photographic narrative form?

There is already an established photographic practice which uses pictures in sequence: the reportage photo-story. These certainly narrate, but they narrate descriptively from the outsider's point of view. A magazine sends photographer X to city Y to bring back pictures. Many of the finest photographs taken belong to this category. But the story told is finally about what the photographer saw at Y. It is not directly about the experience of those living the event in Y. To speak of their experience with images

---

* John Berger and Jean Mohr, *Another Way of Telling*, (London: Writers' and Readers' Publishing Co-Operative Society, 1982), pp. 279–89.

it would be necessary to introduce pictures of other events and other places, because subjective experience always connects. Yet to introduce such pictures would be to break the journalistic convention.

Reportage photo-stories remain eye-witness accounts rather than stories, and this is why they have to depend on words in order to overcome the inevitable ambiguity of the images. In reports ambiguities are unacceptable; in stories they are inevitable.

If there is a narrative form unique to photography, will it not resemble that of the cinema? Surprisingly, photographs are the opposite of films. Photographs are retro-spective and are received as such: films are anticipatory. Before a photograph you search for *what was there*. In a cinema you wait for what is to come next. All film narratives are, in this sense, *adventures*: they advance, they arrive. The term *flashback* is an admission of the inexorable impatience of the film to move forward.

By contrast, if there is a narrative form intrinsic to still photography, it will search for what happened, as memories or reflections do. Memory itself is not made up of flashbacks, each one forever moving inexorably forward. Memory is a field where different times coexist. The field is continuous in terms of the subjectivity which creates and extends it, but temporally it is discontinuous.

Amongst the ancient Greeks, Memory was the mother of all the Muses, and was perhaps most closely associated with the practice of poetry. Poetry at that time, as well as being a form of story-telling, was also an inventory of the visible world; metaphor after metaphor was given to poetry by way of visual correspondences.

Cicero, discussing the poet Simonides who was credited with the invention of the art of memory, wrote: 'It has been sagaciously discerned by Simonides or else discovered by some other person, that the most complete pictures are formed in our minds of the things that have been conveyed to them and imprinted on them by the senses, but that the keenest of all our senses is the sense of sight, and that consequently perceptions received by the ears or by reflection can be most easily retained if they are also conveyed to our minds by the mediation of the eyes.'

A photograph is simpler than most memories, its range more limited. Yet with the invention of photography we acquired a new means of expression more closely associated with memory than any other. The Muse of photography is not one of Memory's daughters, but Memory herself. Both the photograph and the remembered depend upon and equally oppose the passing of time. Both preserve moments, and propose their own form of simultaneity, in which all their images can coexist. Both stimulate, and are stimulated by, the inter-connectedness of events. Both seek instants of revelation, for it is only such instants which give full reason to their own capacity to withstand the flow of time.

Photographs can relate the particular to the general. This happens, as I have shown, even within a single picture. When it happens across a number of pictures, the nexus of relative affinities, contrasts and comparisons can be that much wider and more complex.

. . .

Let me first return to the traditional story.

The dog came out of the forest is a simple statement. When that sentence is followed by *The man left the door open*, the possibility of a narrative has begun. If the tense of the second sentence is changed into *The man had left the door open*, the possibility becomes almost a promise. Every narrative proposes an agreement about the unstated but assumed connections existing between events.

One can lie on the ground and look up at the almost infinite number of stars in the night sky, but in order to tell stories about those stars they need to be seen as constellations, the invisible lines which can connect them need to be assumed.

No story is like a wheeled vehicle whose contact with the road is continuous. Stories walk, like animals or men. And their steps are not only between narrated events but between each sentence, sometimes each word. Every step is a stride over something not said.

The suspense story is a modern invention (Poe, 1809–1849) and consequently today one may tend to overestimate the role of suspense, the waiting-for-the-end, in story-telling. The essential tension in a story lies elsewhere. Not so much in the mystery of its destination as in the mystery of the spaces between its steps towards that destination.

All stories are discontinuous and are based on a tacit agreement about what is not said, about what connects the discontinuities. The question then arises: Who makes this agreement with whom? One is tempted to reply: The teller and the listener. Yet neither teller nor listener is at the centre of the story: they are at its periphery. Those whom the story is about are at the centre. It is between their actions and attributes and reactions that the unstated connections are being made.

One can ask the same question in another way. When the tacit agreement is acceptable to the listener, when a story makes sense of its discontinuities, it acquires authority as a story. But where is this authority? In whom is it invested? In one sense, it is invested in nobody and it is nowhere. Rather, the story invests with authority its characters, its listener's past experience and its teller's words. And it is the authority of all these together that makes the action of the story – what happens in it – worthy of the action of its being told, and vice versa.

The discontinuities of the story and the tacit agreement underlying them fuse teller, listener and protagonists into an amalgam. An amalgam which I would call the story's *reflecting subject*. The story narrates on behalf of this subject, appeals to it and speaks in its voice.

If this sounds unnecessarily complicated, it is worth remembering for a moment the childhood experience of being told a story. Were not the excitement and assurance of that experience precisely the result of the mystery of such a fusion? You were listening. You were in the story. You were in the words of the story-teller. You were no longer your single self; you were, thanks to the story, *everyone it concerned*.

The essence of that childhood experience remains in the power and appeal of any story which has authority. A story is not simply an exercise in empathy. Nor is it merely a meeting-place for the protagonists, the listener and the teller. A story being told is a unique process which fuses these three categories into one. And ultimately what fuses them, within the process, are the discontinuities, the silent connections, agreed upon in common.

Supposing one tries to narrate with photography. The technique of the *photo-roman* offers no solution, for there photography is only a means of reproducing a story constructed according to the conventions of the cinema or theatre. The characters are actors, the world is a decor. Supposing one tries to arrange a number of photographs, chosen from the billions which exist, so that the arrangement speaks of experience. Experience as contained within a life or lives. If this works, it may suggest a narrative form specific to photography.

The discontinuities within the arrangement will be far more evident than those in a verbal story. Each single image will be more or less discontinuous with the next. Continuities of time, place or action may occur, but will be rare. On the face of it there will be no story. And yet in story-telling, as I have tried to show above, it is precisely an agreement about discontinuities which allows the listener to 'enter the narration' and become part of its reflecting subject. The essential relation between teller, listener (spectator) and protagonist(s) may still be possible with an arrangement of photographs. It is, I believe, only their roles, relative to one another, which are modified, not their essential relationship.

The spectator (listener) becomes more active because the assumptions behind the discontinuities (the unspoken which bridges them) are more far-reaching. The teller becomes less present, less insistent, for he no longer employs words of his own; he speaks only through quotations, through his choice and placing of the photographs. The protagonist (at least in our story) becomes omnipresent and therefore invisible; she is manifest in each connection made. One might say that she is defined by *the way she wears the world*, the world about which the photographs supply information. Before she wears it, it is her experience which sews it together.

If, despite these changes of role, there is still the fusion, the amalgam of the *reflecting subject*, one can still talk of a narrative form. Every kind of narrative situates its reflecting subject differently. The epic form placed it before fate, before destiny. The nineteenth-century novel placed it before the individual choices to be made in the area where public and private life overlap. (The novel could not narrate the lives of those who virtually had no choice.) The photographic narrative form places it before the task of memory: the task of continually *resuming* a life being lived in the world. Such a form is not concerned with events as facts – such as is always claimed for photography; it is concerned with their assimilation, their gathering and their transformation into experience.

The precise nature of this as yet experimental narrative form may become still clearer if I very briefly discuss its use of montage. If it does narrate, it does so through its montage.

Eisenstein once spoke of 'a montage of attractions'. By this he meant that what precedes the film-cut should attract what follows it, and vice versa. The energy of this attraction could take the form of a contrast, an equivalence, a conflict, a recurrence. In each case, the cut becomes eloquent and functions like the hinge of a metaphor. The energy of such a montage of attractions could be shown like this:

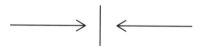

Yet there was in fact an intrinsic difficulty in applying this idea to film. In a film, with its thirty-two frames per second, there is always a third energy in play: that of the reel, that of the film's running through time. And so the two attractions in a film montage are never equal. They are like this:

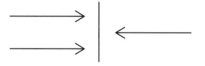

In a sequence of still photographs, however, the energy of attraction, either side of a cut, does remain equal, two-way and *mutual*. Such an energy then closely resembles the stimulus by which one memory triggers another, irrespective of any hierarchy, chronology or duration.

In fact, the energy of the montage of attractions in a sequence of still photographs destroys the very notion of *sequences* – the word which, up to now, I have been using for the sake of convenience. The sequence has become a field of coexistence like the field of memory.

Photographs so placed are restored to a living context: not of course to the original temporal context from which they were taken – that is impossible – but to a context of experience. And there, *their ambiguity at last becomes true*. It allows what they show to be appropriated by reflection. The world they reveal, frozen, becomes tractable. The information they contain becomes permeated by feeling. Appearances become the language of a lived life.

II

diaspora

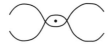

(Jacques Derrida)

4
Psychoanalysis

Laura Mulvey, 'Visual Pleasure and Narrative Cinema'[*]

See also:[†]
Metz (2.i)
Berger (3.iii)
Lanser (5)
Homans (5)
de Lauretis (5)
Roof (5)
Derrida (6)
Johnson (6)
Minh-Ha (9)

PLEASURE IN LOOKING/FASCINATION WITH THE HUMAN FORM

A   The cinema offers a number of possible pleasures. One is scopophilia (pleasure in looking). There are circumstances in which looking itself is a source of pleasure, just as, in the reverse formation, there is pleasure in being looked at. Originally, in his *Three Essays on Sexuality*, Freud isolated scopophilia as one of the component instincts of sexuality which exist as drives quite independently of the erotogenic zones. At this point he associated scopophilia with taking other people as objects, subjecting them to a controlling and curious gaze. His particular examples centre on the voyeuristic activities of children, their desire to see and make sure of the private and forbidden (curiosity about other people's genital and bodily functions, about the presence or absence of the penis and retrospectively, about the primal scene). In this analysis scopophilia is essentially active. (Later, in 'Instincts and Their Vicissitudes', Freud developed his theory of scopophilia further, attaching it initially to pre-genital auto-eroticism, after which, by analogy, the pleasure of the look is transferred to others. There is a close working here of the relationship between the active instinct and its further development in a narcissistic form.) Although the instinct is modified by other factors, in particular the constitution of the ego, it continues to exist as the erotic basis for pleasure in looking at another person as object. At the extreme, it can become fixated into a perversion, producing obsessive voyeurs and Peeping Toms whose only sexual satisfaction can come from watching, in an active controlling sense, an objectified other.

   At first glance, the cinema would seem to be remote from the undercover world of the surreptitious observation of an unknowing and unwilling victim. What is seen on

---

[*] *Screen*, 16(3) (1975), reprinted in A. Easthope (ed.), *Contemporary Film Theory* (London and New York: Longman, 1996), pp. 113–19.
[†] Part II is divided into thematic sections in which each text is relevant to every other text in the section. Therefore, the cross-referencing in Part II does not list texts in the same section as the referencing appears.

the screen is so manifestly shown. But the mass of mainstream film, and the conventions within which it has consciously evolved, portray a hermetically sealed world which unwinds magically, indifferent to the presence of the audience, producing for them a sense of separation and playing on their voyeuristic fantasy. Moreover the extreme contrast between the darkness in the auditorium (which also isolates the spectators from one to another) and the brilliance of the shifting patterns of light and shade on the screen helps to promote the illusion of voyeuristic separation. Although the film is really being shown, is there to be seen, conditions of screening and narrative conventions give the spectator an illusion of looking in on a private world. Among other things, the position of the spectators in the cinema is blatantly one of repression of their exhibitionism and projection of the repressed desire onto the performer.

B   The cinema satisfies a primordial wish for pleasurable looking, but it also goes further, developing scopophilia in its narcissistic aspect. The conventions of mainstream film focus on the human form. Scale, space, stories are all anthropomorphic. Here, curiosity and the wish to look intermingle with a fascination with likeness and recognition: the human face, the human body, the relationship between the human form and its surroundings, the visible presence of the person in the world. Jacques Lacan has described how the moment when a child recognises its own image in the mirror is crucial for the constitution of the ego. Several aspects of this analysis are relevant here. The mirror phase occurs at a time when children's physical ambitions outstrip their motor capacity, with the result that their recognition of themselves is joyous in that they imagine their mirror image to be more complete, more perfect than they experience in their own body. Recognition is thus overlaid with misrecognition: the image recognised is conceived as the reflected body of the self, but its misrecognition as superior projects this body outside itself as an ideal ego, the alienated subject which, reintrojected as an ego ideal, prepares the way for identification with others in the future. This mirror moment predates language for the child.

Important for this article is the fact that it is an image that constitutes the matrix of the imaginary, of recognition/misrecognition and identification, and hence of the first articulation of the I, of subjectivity. This is a moment when an older fascination with looking (at the mother's face, for an obvious example) collides with the initial inklings of self-awareness. Hence it is the birth of the long love affair/despair between image and self-image which has found such intensity of expression in film and such joyous recognition in the cinema audience. Quite apart from the extraneous similarities between screen and mirror (the framing of the human form in its surroundings, for instance), the cinema has structures of fascination strong enough to allow temporary loss of ego while simultaneously reinforcing it. The sense of forgetting the world as the ego has come to perceive it (I forgot who I am and where I was) is nostalgically reminiscent of that pre-subjective moment of image recognition. While at the same time, the cinema has distinguished itself in the production of ego ideals, through the star system for instance. Stars provide a focus or centre both to screen space and screen story where they act out a complex process of likeness and difference (the glamorous impersonates the ordinary).

C   Sections A and B have set out two contradictory aspects of the pleasurable structures of looking in the conventional cinematic situation. The first, scopophilic, arises from pleasure in using another person as an object of sexual stimulation through sight. The second, developed through narcissism and the constitution of the ego, comes from identification with the image seen. Thus, in film terms, one implies a separation of the erotic identity of the subject from the object on the screen (active scopophilia), the other demands identification of the ego with the object on the screen through the spectator's fascination with and recognition of his like. The first is a function of the sexual instincts, the second of ego libido. This dichotomy was crucial for Freud. Although he saw the two as interacting and overlaying each other, the tension between instinctual drives and self-preservation polarises in terms of pleasure. But both are formative structures, mechanisms without intrinsic meaning. In themselves they have no signification, unless attached to an idealisation. Both pursue aims in indifference to perceptual reality, and motivate eroticised phantasmagoria that affect the subject's perception of the world to make a mockery of empirical objectivity.

During its history, the cinema seems to have evolved a particular illusion of reality in which this contradiction between libido and ego has found a beautifully complementary fantasy world. In *reality* the fantasy world of the screen is subject to the law which produces it. Sexual instincts and identification processes have a meaning within, the symbolic order which articulates desire. Desire, born with language, allows the possibility of transcending the instinctual and the imaginary, but its point of reference continually returns to the traumatic moment of its birth: the castration complex. Hence the look, pleasurable in form, can be threatening in content, and it is woman as representation/image that crystallises this paradox.

WOMAN AS IMAGE, MAN AS BEARER OF THE LOOK

A In a world ordered by sexual imbalance, pleasure in looking has been split between active/male and passive/female. The determining male gaze projects its fantasy on to the female figure, which is styled accordingly. In their traditional exhibitionist role women are simultaneously looked at and displayed, with their appearance coded for strong visual and erotic impact so that they can be said to connote *to-be-looked-at-ness*. Woman displayed as sexual object is the *leitmotif* of erotic spectacle: from pin-ups to strip-tease, from Ziegfeld to Busby Berkeley, she holds the look, and plays to and signifies male desire. Mainstream film neatly combines spectacle and narrative. (Note, however, how in the musical song-and-dance numbers interrupt the flow of the diegesis.) The presence of woman is an indispensable element of spectacle in normal narrative film, yet her visual presence tends to work against the development of a story-line, to freeze the flow of action in moments of erotic contemplation. This alien presence then has to be integrated into cohesion with the narrative. As Budd Boetticher has put it:

> What counts is what the heroine provokes, or rather what she represents. She is the one, or rather the love or fear she inspires in the hero, or else the concern he feels for her, who makes him act the way he does. In herself the woman has not the slightest importance.

(A recent tendency in narrative film has been to dispense with this problem altogether; hence the development of what Molly Haskell has called the 'buddy movie', in which the active homosexual eroticism of the central male figures can carry the story without distraction.) Traditionally, the woman displayed has functioned on two levels: as erotic object for the characters within the screen story, and as erotic object for the spectator within the auditorium, with a shifting tension between the looks on either side of the screen. For instance, the device of the show-girl allows the two looks to be unified technically without any apparent break in the diegesis. A woman performs within the narrative; the gaze of the spectator and that of the male characters in the film are neatly combined without breaking narrative verisimilitude. For a moment the sexual impact of the performing woman takes the film into a no man's land outside its own time and space. Thus Marilyn Monroe's first appearance in *The River of No Return* and Lauren Bacall's songs in *To Have and Have Not*. Similarly, conventional close-ups of leg (Dietrich, for instance) or a face (Garbo) integrate into the narrative a different mode of eroticism. One part of a fragmented body destroys the Renaissance space, the illusion of depth demanded by the narrative; it gives flatness, the quality of cut-out or icon, rather than verisimilitude, to the screen.

B   An active/passive heterosexual division of labour has similarly controlled narrative structure. According to the principles of the ruling ideology and the psychical structures that back it up, the male figure cannot bear the burden of sexual objectification. Man is reluctant to gaze at his exhibitionist like. Hence the split between spectacle and narrative supports the man's role as the active one of advancing the story, making things happen. The man controls the film fantasy and also emerges as the representative of power in a further sense: as the bearer of the look of the spectator, transferring it behind the screen to neutralise the extra-diegetic tendencies represented by woman as spectacle. This is made possible through the processes set in motion by structuring the film around a main controlling figure with whom the spectator can identify. As the spectator identifies with the main male protagonist, he projects his look on to that of his like, his screen surrogate, so that the power of the male protagonist as he controls events coincides with the active power of the erotic look, both giving a satisfying sense of omnipotence. A male movie star's glamorous characteristics are thus not those of the erotic object of the gaze, but those of the more perfect, more complete, more powerful ideal ego conceived in the original moment of recognition in front of the mirror. The character in the story can make things happen and control events better than the subject/spectator, just as the image in the mirror was more in control of motor co-ordination.

In contrast to woman as icon, the active male figure (the ego ideal of the iden-tification process) demands a three-dimensional space corresponding to that of the mirror recognition, in which the alienated subject internalised his own representation of his imaginary existence. He is a figure in a landscape. Here the function of film is to reproduce as accurately as possible the so-called natural conditions of human perception. Camera technology (as exemplified by deep focus in particular) and camera movements (determined by the action of the protagonist), combined with invisible editing (demanded by realism), all tend to blur the limits of screen space. The male protagonist is free to command the stage, a stage of spatial illusion in which he articulates the look and creates the action. (There are films with a woman as main protagonist, of course. To analyse this phenomenon seriously here would take me too far afield. Pam Cook and Claire Johnston's study of *The Revolt of Mamie Stover* in Phil Hardy (ed.), *Raoul Walsh*

(Edinburgh, 1974), shows in a striking case how the strength of this female protagonist is more apparent than real.)

C   Sections IIIA and B have set out a tension between a mode of representation of woman in film and conventions surrounding the diegesis. Each is associated with a look: that of the spectator in direct scopophilic contact with the female form displayed for his enjoyment (connoting male fantasy) and that of the spectator fascinated with the image of his like set in an illusion of natural space, and through him gaining control and possession of the woman within the diegesis. (This tension and the shift from one pole to the other can structure a single text. Thus both in *Only Angels Have Wings* and *To Have and Have Not*, the film opens with the woman as object of the combined gaze of spectator and all the male protagonists in the film. She is isolated, glamorous, on display, sexualised. But as the narrative progresses she falls in love with the main male protagonist and becomes his property, losing her outward glamorous characteristics, her generalised sexuality, her show-girl connotations; her eroticism is subjected to the male star alone. By means of identification with him, through participation in his power, the spectator can indirectly possess her too.)

But in psychoanalytic terms, the female figure poses a deeper problem. She also connotes something that the look continually circles around but disavows: her lack of a penis, implying a threat of castration and hence unpleasure. Ultimately, the meaning of woman is sexual difference, the visually ascertainable absence of the penis, the material evidence on which is based the castration complex essential for the organisation of entrance to the symbolic order and the law of the father. Thus the woman as icon, displayed for the gaze and enjoyment of men, the active controllers of the look, always threatens to evoke the anxiety it originally signified. The male unconscious has two avenues of escape from this castration anxiety: preoccupation with the re-enactment of the original trauma (investigating the woman, demystifying her mystery), counter-balanced by the devaluation, punishment or saving of the guilty object (an avenue typified by the concerns of the *film noir*); or else complete disavowal of castration by the substitution of a fetish object or turning the represented figure itself into a fetish so that it becomes reassuring rather than dangerous (hence overvaluation, the cult of the female star).

This second avenue, fetishistic scopophilia, builds up the physical beauty of the object, transforming it into something satisfying in itself. The first avenue, voyeurism, on the contrary, has associations with sadism: pleasure lies in ascertaining guilt (immediately associated with castration), asserting control and subjugating the guilty person through punishment or forgiveness. This sadistic side fits in well with narrative. Sadism demands a story, depends on making something happen, forcing a change in another person, a battle of will and strength, victory/defeat, all occurring in a linear time with a beginning and an end. Fetishistic scopophilia, on the other hand, can exist outside linear time as the erotic instinct is focused on the look alone. These contradictions and ambiguities can be illustrated more simply by using works by Hitchcock and Sternberg, both of whom take the look almost as the content or subject matter of many of their films. Hitchcock is the more complex, as he uses both mechanisms. Steinberg's work, on the other hand, provides many pure examples of fetishistic scopophilia.

Laura Mulvey, 'Afterthoughts on "Visual Pleasure and Narrative Cinema" Inspired by *Duel in the Sun*'*

NARRATIVE GRAMMAR AND TRANS-SEX IDENTIFICATION

The 'convention' cited by Freud (active/masculine) structures most popular narratives, whether film, folk-tale or myth (as I argued in 'Visual Pleasure'), where his metaphoric usage is acted out literally in the story. Andromeda stays tied to the rock, a victim, in danger, until Perseus slays the monster and saves her. It is not my aim, here, to debate the rights and wrongs of this narrative division of labour or to demand positive heroines, but rather to point out that the 'grammar' of the story places the reader, listener or spectator *with* the hero. The woman spectator in the cinema can make use of an age-old cultural tradition adapting her to this convention, which eases a transition out of her own sex into another. In 'Visual Pleasure' my argument took as its axis a desire to identify a pleasure that was specific to cinema, that is the eroticism and cultural conventions surrounding the look. Now, on the contrary, I would rather emphasise the way that popular cinema inherited traditions of story-telling that are common to other forms of folk and mass culture, with attendant fascinations other than those of the look.

Freud points out that 'masculinity' is, at one stage, ego-syntonic for a woman. Leaving aside, for the moment, problems posed by his use of words, his general remarks on stories and day-dreams provide another angle of approach, this time giving a cultural rather than psychoanalytic insight into the dilemma. He emphasises the relationship between the ego and the narrative concept of the hero:

> It is the true heroic feeling, which one of our best writers has expressed in the inimitable phrase, 'Nothing can happen to me!' It seems, however, that through this revealing characteristic of invulnerability we can immediately recognise His Majesty the Ego, the hero of every day-dream and every story.

Although a boy might know quite well that it is most *unlikely* that he will go out into the world, make his fortune through prowess or the assistance of helpers, and marry a princess, the stories describe the male fantasy of ambition, reflecting something of an experience and expectation of dominance (the active). For a girl, on the other hand, the cultural and social overlap is more confusing. Freud's argument that a young girl's day-dreams concentrate on the erotic ignores his own position on her early masculinity and the active day-dreams necessarily associated with this phase. In fact, all too often, the erotic function of the woman is represented by the passive, the waiting (Andromeda again), acting above all as a formal closure to the narrative structure. Three elements can thus be drawn together: Freud's concept of 'masculinity' in women, the identification triggered by the logic of a narrative grammar, and the ego's desire to fantasise itself in a certain, active, manner. All three suggest that, as desire is given cultural materiality in a text, for women (from childhood onwards) trans-sex identification is a *habit* that very

---

* *Framework* 15/16/17 (1981), pp. 12–15. Reprinted in A. Easthope (ed.), *Contemporary Film Theory* (London and New York: Longman, 1996), pp. 128–30.

easily becomes *second nature*. However, this Nature does not sit easily and shifts restlessly in its borrowed transvestite clothes.

THE WESTERN AND OEDIPAL PERSONIFICATIONS

Using a concept of character function based on V. Propp's *Morphology of the Folk-tale*, I want to argue for a chain of links and shifts in narrative pattern, showing up the changing function of 'woman'. The Western (allowing, of course, for as many deviations as one cares to enumerate) bears a residual imprint of the primitive narrative structure analysed by Vladimir Propp in folk-tales. Also, in the hero's traditional invulnerability, the Western ties in closely with Freud's remarks on day-dreaming. (As I am interested primarily in character function and narrative pattern, not in genre definition, many issues about the Western as such are being summarily side-stepped.) For present purposes, the Western genre provides a crucial node in a series of transformations that *comment* on the function of 'women' (as opposed to 'man') as a narrative signifier and sexual difference as personification of 'active' or 'passive' elements in a story.

In the Proppian tale, an important aspect of narrative closure is 'marriage', a function characterised by 'princess' or equivalent. This is the only function that is sex-specific, and thus essentially relates to the sex of the hero and his manageability. This function is very commonly reproduced in the Western, where, once again, 'marriage' makes a crucial contribution to narrative closure. However, in the Western the function's presence has also come to allow a complication in the form of its opposite, 'not marriage'. Thus, while the social integration represented by marriage is an essential aspect of the folk-tale, in the Western it can be accepted . . . or not. A hero can gain in stature by refusing the princess and remaining alone (Randolph Scott in the Ranown series of movies). As the resolution of the Proppian tale can be seen to represent the resolution of the Oedipus complex (integration into the symbolic), the rejection of marriage personifies a nostalgic celebration of phallic, narcissistic omnipotence. Just as Freud's comments on the 'phallic' phase in girls seemed to belong in limbo, without a place in the chronology of sexual development, so, too, does this male phenomenon seem to belong to a phase of play and fantasy difficult to integrate exactly into the Oedipal trajectory.

The tension between two points of attraction, the symbolic (social integration and marriage) and nostalgic narcissism, generates a common splitting of the Western hero into two, something unknown in the Proppian tale. Here two functions emerge, one celebrating integration into society through marriage, the other celebrating resistance to social demands and responsibilities, above all those of marriage and the family, the sphere represented by woman. A story such as *The Man Who Shot Liberty Valance* juxtaposes these two points of attraction, and spectator fantasy can have its cake and eat it too. This particular tension between the double hero also brings out the underlying significance of the drama, its relation to the symbolic, with unusual clarity. A folk-tale story revolves around conflict between hero and villain. The flashback narration in *Liberty Valance* seems to follow these lines at first. The narrative is generated by an act of villainy (Liberty rampages, dragon-like, around the countryside). However the development of the story acquires a complication. The issue at stake is no longer how the villain will be defeated, but how the villain's defeat will be inscribed into history, whether the *upholder* of law as a symbolic system (Ranse) will be seen to be victorious or the *personification* of law in a more primitive manifestation (Tom), closer to the good or the right. *Liberty Valance*, as it uses a flashback structure, also brings out the poignancy of this tension. The 'present-tense' story is precipitated by a funeral, so that the story is shot through with nostalgia and sense of loss. Ranse Stoddart mourns Tom Doniphon.

This narrative structure is based on an opposition between two irreconcilables. The two paths cannot cross. On one side there is an encapsulation of power, and phallic attributes, in an individual who has to bow himself out of the way of history; on the other, an individual impotence rewarded by political and financial power, which, *in the long run*, in fact becomes history. Here the function 'marriage' is as crucial as it is in the folk-tale. It plays the same part in creating narrative resolution, but is even more important in that 'marriage' is an integral attribute of the upholder of the law. In this sense Hallie's choice between the two men is predetermined. Hallie equals princess equals Oedipal resolution rewarded, equals repression of narcissistic sexuality in marriage.

Stephen Heath, 'Narrative Space'*

See also:
Plato (1.i)
Bakhtin (1.iii)
Metz (2.i)
Chatman (2.ii)
Gibson (3.ii)
Berger (3.iii)
Cohn (7)
Ricoeur (7)
Jameson (8)

. . .

Those terms, as they have been described here, are the terms of a constant welding together: screen and frame, ground and background, surface and depth, the whole setting of movements and transitions, the implication of space and spectator in the taking place of film as narrative. The classical *economy* of film is its organization thus as organic unity and the *form* of that economy is narrative, the *narrativization* of film. Narrative, as it were, determines the film which is contained in its process in that determination, this 'bind' being itself a process – precisely the narrativization. The narration is to be held on the narrated, the enunciation on the enounced; filmic procedures are to be held as narrative instances (very much as 'cues'), exhaustively, without gap or contradiction. What is sometimes vaguely referred to as 'transparency' has its meaning in this narrativization: the proposal of a discourse that disavows its operations and positions in the name of a signified that it proposes as its pre-existent justification. 'Transparency', moreover, is entirely misleading in so far as it implies that narrativization has necessarily to do with some simple 'invisibility' (anyway impossible – no one has yet seen a signified

* *Screen*, 17(3), (Autumn 1976), pp. 68–112. Reprinted in A. Easthope (ed.), *Contemporary Film Theory* (London and New York: Longman, 1996), pp. 81–94.

without a signifier). The narration may well be given as visible in its filmic procedures; what is crucial is that it be given as visible *for the narrated* and that the spectator be caught up in the play of *that* process, that the *address* of the film be clear (does anyone who has watched, say, *The Big Sleep* seriously believe that a central part of Hollywood films, differently defined from genre to genre, was not the address of a process with a movement of play and that that was not a central part of their pleasure?).

Within this narrativization of film, the role of the character-look has been fundamental for the welding of a spatial unity of narrative implication. In so many senses, every film is a veritable drama of vision and this drama has thematically and symptomatically 'returned' in film since the very beginning: from the fascination of the magnifying glass in *Grandma's Reading Glass* to Lina's short-sightedness in *Suspicion* to the windscreen and rear-view mirror of *Taxi Driver*, from the keyhole of *A Search for Evidence* to the images that flicker reflected over Brody's glasses in *Jaws* as he turns the pages of the book on sharks, finding the images of the film to come and which he will close as he closes the book; not to mention the extended dramatizations such as *Rear Window* or *Peeping Tom*. How to make sense in film if not through vision, film with its founding ideology of vision as truth? The drama of vision in the film returns the drama of vision of the film: the spectator will be bound to the film as spectacle as the world of the film is itself revealed as spectacle on the basis of a narrative organization of look and point of view that moves space into place through the image-flow; the character, figure of the look, is a kind of perspective within the perspective system, regulating the world, orientating space, providing directions – and for the spectator.

Film works at a loss, the loss of the divisions, the discontinuities, the absences that structure it – as, for example, the 'outside' of the frame, off-screen space, the *hors-champ*. Such absence is the final tragedy of a Bazin, who wants to believe in cinema as a global consciousness of reality, an illimitation of picture frame and theatre scene –

> The screen is not a frame like that of a picture, but a mask which allows us to see a part of the event only. When a person leaves the field of the camera, we recognize that he or she is out of the field of vision, though continuing to exist identically in another part of the scene which is hidden from us. The screen has no wings . . .[1]

– but who can only inspect the damage of 'camera angles or prejudices',[2] acknowledge none the less the frame, the scene, the mask, the hidden, the absent. The sequence-shot-with-deep-focus long take functions as a utopia in this context – the ideal of a kind of 'full angle', without prejudices, but hence too without cinema; the ideal recognized in *Bicycle Thieves*, 'plus de cinéma'.[3]

Burch writes that 'off-screen space has only an intermittent or, rather, *fluctuating* existence during any film, and structuring this fluctuation can become a powerful tool in a film-maker's hands'.[4] The term 'fluctuation' is excellent, yet it must be seen that the work of classical continuity is not to hide or ignore off-screen space but, on the contrary, to contain it, to regularize its fluctuation in a constant movement of reappropriation. It is this movement that defines the rules of continuity and the fiction of space they serve to construct, the whole functioning according to a kind of metonymic lock in which off-screen space becomes on-screen space and is replaced in turn by the space it holds off, each joining over the next. The join is conventional and ruthlessly selective (it generally leaves out of account, for example, the space that might be supposed to be masked at the top and bottom of the frame, concentrating much more on the space at the sides of the frame or on that 'in front', 'behind the camera', as in variations of field/reverse field), and demands that the off-screen space recaptured must be 'called for', must be 'logically consequential', must arrive as 'answer', 'fulfilment of promise' or whatever (and not as difference or contradiction) – must be narrativized. Classical continuity, in other words, is an order of the pregnancy of space in frame; one of the narrative acts of a film is the creation of space[5] but what gives the moving space its coherence in time, decides the metonymy as a 'taking place', is here 'the narrative itself', and above all as it crystallizes round character as look and point of view. The fundamental role of these is exactly their pivotal use as a mode of organization and organicization, the joining of a film's constructions, the stitching together of the overlaying metonymies.

'If in the left of the frame an actor in close-up is looking off right, he has an empty space in front of him; if the following shot shows an empty space to the left and an object situated to the right, then the actor's look appears to cross an orientated, rectilinear, thus logical space: it seems to bear with precision on the object. One has an eye-line match.'[6] The look, that is, joins form of expression – the composition of the images and their disposition in relation to one another – and form of content – the definition of the action of the film in the movement of looks, exchanges, objects seen, and so on. Point of view develops on the basis of this joining operation of the look, the camera taking the position of a character in order to show the spectator what he or she sees.[7] Playing on the assumption of point of view, a film has an evident means of placing its space, of giving it immediate and holding significance; Burch talks of the establishment of an organization founded on the 'traditional dichotomy between the "subjective camera" (which "places the spectator in the position of a character") and the "objective camera" (which makes the spectator the ideal, immaterial "voyeur" of a pro-filmic pseudo-reality)'.[8]

This account, however, requires clarification. The point-of-view shot is 'subjective' in that it assumes the position of a subject-character but to refer to that assumption in terms of 'subjective camera' or 'subjective image' can lead to misunderstanding with regard to the functioning of point of view. Subjective images can be many things; Mitry, for example, classifies them into five major categories:

> the purely mental image (more or less impracticable in the cinema); the truly subjective or analytical image (i.e. what is looked at without the person looking), which is practicable in small doses; the semi-subjective or associated image (i.e. the person looking + what is looked at, which is in fact looked at from the view-point of the person looking), the most generalizable formula; the complete sequence given over to the imaginary, which does not raise special problems; and finally the memory image, which is in principle simply a variety of the mental image but, when presented in the form of a flash-back with commentary, allows for a specific filmic treatment which is far more successful than in the case of other mental images.[9]

The point-of-view shot includes 'the semi-subjective or associated image' (its general mode) and 'the truly subjective or analytical image (its pure mode, as it were) in that classification but not necessarily any of the other categories (a memory sequence, for instance, need not contain any point-of-view shots); what is 'subjective' in the point-of-view shot is its spatial positioning (its place), not the image or the camera.

To stress this is to stress a crucial factor in the exploitation of the film image and its relation to point-of-view organization. Within the terms of that organization, a true subjective image would effectively need to mark its subjectivity *in the image itself*. Examples are common: the blurred image of Gutman in *The Maltese Falcon* is the subjective image of the drugged Spade; the blurring of focus marks the subjectivity of the image, exclusively Spade's, and the spectator is set not simply *with* Spade but *as* Spade. They are also limited, since they depend exactly on some recognizable – marking – distortion of the 'normal' image, a narratively motivated aberration of vision of some kind or another (the character is drugged, intoxicated, short-sighted, terrified . . . down to he or she running, with hand-held effects of the image 'jogging', or even walking, with regular speed of camera movement forward matched on a shot that effectively establishes the character as in the process of walking; the latter represents the lowest limit on the, scale since the camera movement is there a weak subjective marking of the image which itself remains more or less 'normal' – except, of course, and hence this limit position of the banal action of walking, that the normal image is precisely static, that movement in a central perspective system can quickly become a problem of vision). The implication of this, of course, is then the strength of the unmarked image as a constant third person – the vision of picture and scene, the Quattrocento view, Burch's 'voyeur' position – *which is generally continued within point-of-view shots themselves*; the point-of-view shot is marked as subjective in its emplacement but the resulting image is still finally (or rather firstly) objective, the objective sight of what is seen from the subject position assumed. Indicatively enough, the general mode of the point-of-view shot is the shot which shows both what is looked at and the person looking. Instances of the pure shot, showing what is looked at without the person looking, however, are equally conclusive. Take the shot in *Suspicion* of the telegram that Lina receives from Johnnie to tell her of his intention to attend the Hunt Ball: the telegram is clearly shown from Lina's reading position and the end of the shot – the end of the reading – is marked by her putting down her glasses on to the telegram lying on a table, the glasses thus coming down into frame; the position of the shot is marked as subjective with Lina but the image nevertheless continues to be objective. 'the real case' for the narrative.[10]

Point of view, that is, depends on an overlaying of first and third person modes. There is no radical dichotomy between subjective point-of-view shots and objective non-point-of-view shots; the latter mode is the continual basis over which the former can run in its particular organization of space, its disposition of the images. The structure of the photographic image – with its vision, its scene, its distance, its normality – is to the film somewhat as language is to the novel: the grounds of its representations, which representations can include the creation of an acknowledged movement of point of view. This is the sense of the spectator identification with the camera that is so often remarked upon (Benjamin: 'the audience's identification with the actor is really an identification with the camera'; Metz: 'the spectator can do no other than identify with the camera').[11] The spectator must *see* and this structuring vision is the condition of the possibility of the disposition of the images via the relay of character look and viewpoint which pulls together vision and narrative. Emphasis was laid earlier on the structures of the structuring vision that founds cinema; what is emphasized now is the dependence of our very notion of point of view on those structures; dependence at once in so far as the whole Quattrocento system is built on the establishment of point of view, the central position of the eye, and in so far as the mode of representation thus defined brings with it fixity and movement in a systematic complicity of interaction – brings with it, that is, the 'objective' and the 'subjective', the 'third person' and the 'first person', the view and its partial points, and finds this drama of vision as the resolving action of its narratives.

Identification with the camera, seeing, the 'ideal picture' of the scene: 'the usual scene in a classical film is narrated as if from the point of view of an observer capable of moving about the room.'[12] Such movement may be given in editing or by camera movement within a shot, and the importance accruing to some master view that will define the space of the mobility has been noted. Movement, in fact, will be treated as a supplement to produce precisely the 'ideal *picture*' (going to the movies is going to the pictures): on the basis of the vision of the photographic image, that is, it will provide the 'total' point of view of an observer capable of moving about the room without changing anything of the terms of that vision, the scene laid out for the central observer (and spectator); every shot or refraining adds a difference, but that difference is always the same image, with the organization – the continuity, the rules, the matches, the pyramid structures – constantly doing the sum of the *scene*.

That said, it remains no less true, as has again been noted and as will become important later on, that movement represents a potentially radical disturbance of the smooth stability of the scenographic vision (hence the need for a systematic organization to contain it). Such a disturbance, however, is not as simple as is sometimes suggested and it is necessary briefly to consider at this stage two instances of disturbance as they are conventionally described; both bear on the mobility of the camera.

The first is that of what Branigan characterizes as the impossible place: 'To the extent that the camera is located in an "impossible" place, the narration questions its own origin, that is, suggests a shift in narration.'[13] 'Impossible', of course, is here decided in respect of the 'possible' positions of the observer moving about, the disturbance involved seen as a disjunction of the unity of narration and narrated, enunciation and enounced. Thus defined, impossible places are certainly utilized in classical narrative cinema, with examples ranging from the relatively weak to the relatively strong. At one end of the range, the weak examples would be any high or low angles that are not motivated as the point of view of a character; or, indeed, any high or low angles that, while so motivated, are nevertheless sufficiently divergent from the assumed normal upright observing position as to be experienced as in some sense 'impossible' in their peculiarity (the most celebrated – and complex – example is the dead-man-in-the-coffin point of view in *Vampyr*).[14] At the other end, the strong examples – those intended by Branigan – can be illustrated by a description of two shots from *Killer's Kiss*: (1) as Davey, the boxer-hero, is seen stooping to feed his goldfish, there is a cut to a shot through the bowl, from the other side, of his face peering in as the feed drops down; since the bowl is on a table against a wall, the place taken by the camera is not possible; (2) Rappello, the dance-hall owner, furious at being left by the heroine, is drinking in a back-room, its walls covered with posters and prints; a close-up of a print showing two men leering from a window is followed by a shot of Rappello who throws his drink at the camera ('at the screen'!); a crack appears as the drink runs down a plate of glass; impossibly, the shot was from 'in' the print. The second – and related – instance of disturbance is that of the development of camera movement as a kind of autonomous figure; what Burch calls 'the camera designated as an "omnipotent and omniscient" (i.e. manipulative and pre-cognitive) presence'.[15] This presence too is utilized in classical narrative cinema and weak and strong examples can once more be indicated. In *Taxi Driver*, Travis Bickle is seen phoning Betsy after the porno-film fiasco; as he stands talking into the pay-phone, fixed on a wall inside a building, the camera tracks right and stops to frame a long empty corridor leading out to the street; when Travis finishes his call, he walks into frame and exits via the corridor. The tracking movement designates the camera with a certain autonomy – there is an effect of a casual decision to go somewhere else, off to the side of the narrative – but the example is ultimately weak: the corridor is eventually brought into the action with Travis's exit and, more importantly, it has its rhyming and thematic resonances – the corridors in the rooming-house used by Iris, the marked existential atmosphere of isolation, nothingness, etc. Stronger examples are provided in the work of an Ophuls or a Welles – the spectacular tracking shot at the start of *Touch of Evil* or the intense mobility in many of the shots at the end of that same film.

These two instances of disturbance have been characterized here in their existence in established cinema simply to make one or two points directly in the context of the present account. Thus, the examples given of autonomy of camera movement are all clearly operating in terms of 'style' (Welles, Ophuls, the tics of a new American commercial cinema that has learnt a consciousness of style). The crucial factor is not the valuation of camera movement, be it autonomous, but the point at which a certain work on the camera in movement produces the normality of the third person objective basis as itself a construction, gives it as role or fiction and breaks the balance of the point-of-view system. Similarly, the examples of the impossible place from *Killer's Kiss*, which also have their reality as stylistic marking in the film, are without critically disruptive extension in themselves, are simply *tricks* (in the sense of spatial prestidigitations): the impossible place is entirely possible if held within a system that defines it *as such*, that it confirms in its signified exceptionality. The felt element of trick, moreover, raises the general point of the realization of film as process. It is too readily assumed that the operation – the determination, the effect, the pleasure of – classical cinema lies in the attempt at an invisibility of process, the intended transparency of a kind of absolute 'realism' from which all signs of production have been *effaced*. The actual case is much more complex and subtle, and much more telling. Classical cinema does not efface the signs of production, it *contains* them, according to the narrativization described above. It is that process that is the action of the film for the spectator – what counts is as much the representation as the represented, is as much the production as the product. Nor is there anything surprising in this: film is not a static and isolated object but a series of relations with the spectator it imagines, plays and sets as subject in its movement. The process of film is then perfectly available to certain terms of excess – those of that movement in its subject openings, its energetic controls. 'Style' is one area of such controlled excess, as, again, more powerfully, are genres in their specific version of process. The musical is an obvious and extreme example with its systematic 'freedom' of space – crane choreography – and its shifting balances of narrative and spectacle; but an example that should not be allowed to mask the fundamental importance of the experience of process in other genres and in the basic order of classical cinema on which the various genres are grounded. Which is to say, finally, that radical disturbance is not to be linked to the mere autonomization of a formal element such as camera movement; on the contrary, it can only be effectively grasped as a work that operates at the expense of the classical suppositions of 'form' and 'content' in cinema, posing not autonomies but contradictions in the process of film and its narrative-subject binding.

The construction of space as a term of that binding in classical cinema is its implication for the spectator in the taking place of film as narrative; implication-process of constant refinding – space regulated, orientated, continued, reconstituted. The use of look and point-of-view structures – exemplarily, the field/reverse field figure (not necessarily dependent, of course, on point-of-view shots)[16] – is fundamental to this process that has been described in terms of suture, a stitching or tying as in the surgical joining of the lips of a wound.[17] In its movement, its framings, its cuts, its intermittences, the film ceaselessly poses an absence, a lack, which is ceaselessly recaptured for – one needs to be able to say 'forin' – the film, that process binding the spectator as subject in the realization of the film's space.

   In psychoanalysis, 'suture' refers to the relation of the individual as subject to the chain of its discourse where it figures missing in the guise of a stand-in; the subject is an effect of the signifier in which it is represented, stood in for, taken place (the signifier is the narration of the subject).[18] Ideological representation turns on – supports itself from – this 'initial' production of the subject in the symbolic order (hence the crucial role of psychoanalysis, as potential science of the construction of the subject, with historical materialism), directs it as a set of images and fixed positions, metonymy stopped into fictions of coherence. What must be emphasized, however, is that stopping – the functioning of suture in image, frame, narrative, etc. – is exactly a process: it counters a productivity, an excess, that it states and restates in the very moment of containing in the interests of coherence – thus the film frame, for example, exceeded from within by the outside it delimits and poses and has ceaselessly to recapture (with post-Quattrocento painting itself, images are multiplied and the conditions are laid for a certain mechanical reproduction that the photograph will fulfil, the multiplication now massive, with image machines a normal appendage of the subject). The process never ends, is always *going on*; the construction-reconstruction has always to be renewed; machines, cinema included, are there for that – and their ideological operation is not only in the images but in the suture.

   The film poses an image, not immediate or neutral,[19] but posed, framed and centred. Perspective-system images bind the spectator in place, the suturing central position that is the sense of the image, that sets its scene (in place, the spectator *completes* the image as its subject). Film too, but it also moves in all sort of ways and directions, flows with energies, is potentially a veritable festival of affects. Placed, that movement is all the value of film in its development and exploitation: reproduction of life and the engagement of the spectator in the process of that reproduction as articulation of coherence. What moves in film, finally, is the spectator, immobile in front of the screen. Film is the regulation of that movement, the individual as subject held in a shifting and placing of desire, energy, contradiction, in a perpetual retotalization of the imaginary (the set scene of image and subject). This is the investment of film in narrativization; and crucially for a coherent space, the unity of place for vision.

   Once again, however, the investment is in the process. Space comes in place through procedures such as look and point-of-view structures, and the spectator with it as subject in its realization. A reverse shot folds over the shot it joins and is joined in turn by the reverse it positions; a shot of a person looking is succeeded by a shot of the object looked at which is succeeded in turn by a shot of the person looking to confirm the object as seen; and so on, in a number of multiple imbrications. *Fields* are made, *moving* fields, and the process includes not just the completions but the definitions of absence for completion. The suturing operation is in the process, the give and take of absence and presence, the play of negativity and negation, flow and bind. Narrativization, with its continuity, closes, and is that movement of closure that shifts the spectator as subject in its terms: the spectator is the *point* of the film's spatial relations – the turn, say, of shot to reverse shot their subject-passage (point-of-view organization, moreover, doubles over that passage in its third/first person layerings). Narrativization is scene and movement, movement and scene, the reconstruction of the subject in the pleasure of that balance (with genres as specific instances of equilibrium) – *for* homogeneity, containment. What is foreclosed in the process is not its production – often signified as such, from genre instances down to this or that 'impossible' shot – but the terms of the unity of that production (narration on narrated, enunciation on enounced), the other scene of its vision of the subject, the outside – heterogeneity, contradiction, history – of its coherent address.

NOTES

1 André Bazin, *Qu'est-ce que le cinéma?*, vol. II (Paris: Cerf, 1959), p. 100.

2 Bazin, *Qu'est-ce que le cinéma?*, vol. IV, p. 57.

3 Ibid., p. 59. For discussion of Bazin on neo-realism, see Christopher Williams's article of that title in *Screen*, 14, 4 (Winter 1973/74): 61–8.

4 Noël Burch, *Theory of Film Practice* (London: Secker & Warburg, 1973), p. 21.

5 Edward Branigan, 'The Space of *Equinox Flower*', *Screen*, 17, 2 (Summer 1976): 103.

6 *Apprendre le cinéma*, special issue of *Image et son*, 194 (May 1966): 148.

7 For a detailed analysis of the point-of-view shot, see Branigan, 'Formal Permutations of the Point-of-View Shot', *Screen*, 16, 3 (Autumn 1975): 54–64.

8 Noël Burch and Jorge Dana, 'Propositions', *Afterimage*, 5 (Spring 1974): 45.

9 As summarized by Metz in his 'Current Problems in Film Theory', *Screen*, **14**, 1/2 (Spring/Summer 1973): 49.

10 In fact, and not surprisingly, the less narratively 'metonymical' and the more 'metaphorical' is what is looked at in the pure point-of-view shot (without the marking of image distortion), the nearer such a shot will come to subjectivizing the image. Released from prison at the beginning of *High Sierra*, Roy Earle is shown walking through a park, breathing the air of freedom; shots of him looking up are followed by shots of tree tops against the sky, with a certain effect of subjectivization in so far as the tree tops against the sky are outside the immediate scope of the movement of the narrative and, objectively useless (unlike Lina's telegram in *Suspicion*), belong only for Roy's character (he was born of a modest farming family and is not the hardened criminal his reputation would have him be).

11 Walter Benjamin, *Illuminations* (London: Fontana, 1970), p. 230; C. Metz, 'Le signifiant imaginaire', *Communications*, 23 (1975): 35; translation, 'The Imaginary Signifier', *Screen*, 16, 2 (Summer 1975): 52.

12 Edward Branigan, 'Narration and Subjectivity in Cinema', mimeo (Madison: University of Wisconsin, 1975), p. 24.

13   Ibid.

14   Discussed by R. Barthes, 'Diderot, Brecht, Eisenstein', *Screen*, 15, 2 (Summer 1974): 38; Branigan, 'Formal Permutations', p. 57; and M. Nash,' *Vampyr* and the Fantastic', *Screen*, 17, 3 (Autumn 1976): 32–3, 54–60.

15   Burch and Dana, op. cit., p. 45.

16   Salt distinguishes three varieties of field/reverse field and assigns an order and approximate dates for their respective appearances: 'It is necessary to distinguish between different varieties of angle – reverse-angle cuts; the cut from a watcher to his point of view was the first to appear; the cut from one long shot of a scene to another more or less oppositely angled long shot, which must have happened somewhat later – the first example that can be quoted is in *Røoverens Brud* (Viggo Larsen, 1907); and the cut between just-off-the-eye-line angle – reverse-angle shots of two people interacting – the earliest example that can be quoted occurs in *The Loafer* (Essanay, 1911).' Barry Salt, 'The Early Development of Film Form', *Film Forum*, 1 (Spring 1976): 98.

17   For details of the introduction and various accounts of suture, see Stephen Heath, 'On Suture', in *Questions of Cinema* (London: Macmillan, 1981), pp. 86–101.

18   Cf. J-A. Miller, 'La suture', *Cahiers pour l'analyse*, 1 (1966): 37–49; translation, 'Suture,' *Screen*, 18, 4 (Winter 1977/78): 24–34.

19   'Another characteristic of the film image is its neutrality.' *Encylopaedia Britannica* (Macropaedia), vol. 12 (Chicago, etc., 1974), p. 498.

Elizabeth Bronfen, 'Spectral Stories'*

See also:
Benjamin (1.iii)
Brooks (3.ii)
Lanser (5)
de Lauretis (5)
Miller (6)
Johnson (6)
Minh-Ha (9)

Storytellers are Death's secretaries. It is Death who hands them the file. The file is full of sheets of uniformly black paper but they have eyes for reading them and from this file they construct a story for the living.

(John Berger)

Set against mortality and oblivion, narrators also consume death. Absent from the world and therefore 'dead' as a social person, feeding off previous 'inanimate' texts, producing fictions that in turn are alive in the realm of the imaginary but immaterial in respect to social reality, storytellers are positioned in an intermediary site between life and death. Their power of imagination is like a vampire, feeding off this exchange, for they rely on a preservation and production of 'dead' figures – the teller's and the listener's temporary social death and the uncanny presence as absence that fictions embody. Or, to reverse

* *Over Her Dead Body: Death, Femininity and the Aesthetic* (Manchester: Manchester University Press, 1992), pp. 349–55.

the analogy, storytellers are like revenants in that the liminal realm between life and death inspires and produces fictions. Blanchot suggests that when we tell stories we are resting on an unclosed grave and the emptiness of the grave is what makes language true even as this void is also a reality which lets death come into being.

Dickens's *Great Expectations* (1861)[1] can be read as a novel about the way the art of storytelling conjoins representation with the revenant and with the intermediary. In so doing it reveals that the rhetoric of death is like a sword that cuts both ways. Fictions are shown to feed off the teller's and the listener's proximity to death even as real death breaks into the realm where fancies and fictions are born and nourished to disrupt the illusions that these macabre representations produced. Linking femininity, death and the emergence of fiction over the body of a revenant bride, this novel centres on Miss Havisham, a woman who remains beyond her social death to provoke a mystery and inspire a tale. From within her self-made tomb, she moulds a surrogate daughter Estella (as the instrument of revenge) and mothers the fanciful expectations of a surrogate son Pip (as the privileged object of destruction). Disempowered in life, she gains demonic power by speaking from the position of an empty grave. In this transitional site, fiction is more 'real' than social or natural reality, precisely owing to its proximity to death. As a world without substance, it stands in double opposition to the reality of the living. Furthermore, commenting self-reflexively on the scenario it enacts, Dickens's novel also shows that the act of storytelling involves listeners and speakers that are absent from the world, doubles of their social selves, at the same time that, located in such a liminal realm, fiction also produces tales about doubles, about figures and plots emerging out of absence.

André Green argues that the work of reading and writing occurs in a private space. Though the writer and the reader are absent to each other they are mutually positioned in the site of a transnarcissistic communication, where the writer's and the reader's doubles communicate through the fictional text. Since the figure of the double signifies death and since absence implies potential death the pleasures fictions offer, he concludes, draw their power from death. Dickens's novel represents precisely such a scene of death-inspired transnarcissistic communication, where the absence as doubling of speaker and addressee in a liminal realm occurs. Strictly speaking, of course, no written but rather oral texts are produced and fictions are heard and acted out. Reformulating Green's scenario one can say that the speaker Miss Havisham and the listeners Estella and Pip are present to each other and their fictions are materialised at their bodies. These narratives, mark a turn back to a literal form of signification even as the actors are also caught in a figural absence and self-doubling.

Imaginary activity, symbolisation and the creation of fictions serve to negate reality, to repair or mitigate one's own destructive impulses and patch up wounds to one's narcissism. In that it presupposes loss, storytelling involves the work of mourning, with the engendered text transforming a narcissistic wound into a fictitious positivity. The site of fiction is transitional because it is posed between the inner and the outer, with the speaker, the addressee and the unfolding plot uncannily present-in-absence, absent-in-presence. In that it suspends rules of reality and plausibility, it is the realm of endless potentiality and in that it comprises both an aspect of doubling and of absence, it shows the fascination for and the power of the split even as it articulates this power over a void, a lack. In Green's terms, the storyteller or producer of fictions is, therefore, significantly 'caught between the double and the absent', and it is precisely this dual figure I wish to trace in my discussion of *Great Expectations*. Here the tellers and listeners of fictional stories are doubles because each produces or receives another image of her or himself and exists in another world. And each is absent, because they emerge from an absence of social reality and return to a void; the nullification of romantic illusions in the case of the two children and the silence death induces in the spectral bride.

Miss Havisham, an 'immensely rich and grim lady', leads a 'life of seclusion' in a dismal barricaded house (81). Though she is not the only character in the novel who makes art out of life, the duplicitous plot she enacts by paying Pip to 'go and play' in her presence for her 'diversion' interlaces the great romantic with the great economic expectations of Dickens's protagonist in such a monstrous fashion that its disclosure deconstructs the folly underlying both. Significantly, the realm where Pip's self-fashioning (by which he creates an image of himself that transcends his social position) is born and thrives, is her artificial crypt. And the woman who authors these fanciful expectations, these 'poor dreams', who awakens Pip's creative even if deluded poetic faculties, is repeatedly described as a revenant.

When Pip sees her for the first time, he recalls a 'ghastly waxwork' of a personage lying in state, which he had seen at a fair, as well as 'a skeleton in the ashes of a rich dress' that had been dug out of a vault. This first sight is supremely uncanny, because at Miss Havisham's body the inanimate comes to life again – 'Now, waxwork and skeleton seemed to have dark eyes that moved and looked at me' (87). She is not only the material embodiment of a living dead, but more importantly, a living sign of the bride as a dead woman. She is dressed in the rich white materials, the satin laces, silks and jewels of her bridal gown, a long white veil and bridal flowers in her hair. She is 'not quite finished dressing', the room in which she receives Pip is scattered with half-packed trunks. Furthermore both bride and dresses are withered, her hair white, her eyes sunken, her body shrunk to skin and bone, and all the objects that were once white are now yellow; unused or ragged, paled, decayed objects. In this strange, melancholy, candlelit realm she has buried herself alive.

All clocks have stopped at twenty minutes to nine, all objects have remained unchanged, while her own gestures and appearance endlessly repeat that fatal moment. After more than a decade, her bridal dress looks 'like grave-clothes', her longveil 'like a shroud', and inmidst 'this arrest of everything', she herself sits 'corpse-like'. Yet this is a double arrestation of death – the representation of a sudden cessation of life and a seizure that puts death under erasure. Even as time, change, and that is to say the facticity of natural mortal existence, have artificially been put to a stop 'a long time ago', Miss Havisham and her surroundings have become a superlative sign for mutability and decay, the enactment of death inmidst life. When the narrating Pip recalls this scene long after it has occurred, he evokes 'bodies buried in ancient times, which fall to powder in the moment of being distinctly seen'. He further implicitly refers to the vampire myth by suggesting that she looked as if 'the admission of the natural light of day would have struck her to dust' (90).

As Pip learns later on from one of her relatives, she was a rich, proud and spoilt heiress, who fell passionately in love with an impostor. A conspiracy between the groom and the bride's disinherited half-brother turned the wedding day into an event of 'cruel mortification'. Instead of the groom, a letter breaking off the engagement arrived, and

Miss Havisham, once she had recovered from the 'bad illness' that this announcement engendered, took the hysteric's dissimulation of her non-existence to a superlative degree, simultaneously affirming and denying her wounded narcissism. Refusing ever again to look 'upon the light of day', she lays her entire house to waste so as to turn it into a museum that preserves and exhibits precisely the moment of this 'cruel mortification'. The unaltered wedding clothes, trousseau and wedding banquet table mark for ever the moment of excessive expectation and excessive loss (205). In this case the masculine gaze which ironically preserves her against any breakdown of her self-sustaining hysteric discourse is that of the absent groom Compeyson.

In her dissimulation of the waiting bride, Miss Havisham is indeed caught between the double and the absent. She is absent, because socially dead, addressing the outside world with missives written from within the silence of her barricaded, wasted mansion. People who wish for any exchange with her must enter this intermediary realm between life and death. In part her hysterical discourse discloses that the jilted bride is socially dead in any case. At the same time she explicitly uses this self-fashioning to demonstrate that with the loss of her loved object, with her heart broken, any further existence is merely a mechanical continuation of the body. Indeed she takes the metaphor literally. Since the organ that sustains life by pumping blood and inspiring love has been broken, she becomes bloodless and withers away, even as her transactions with others become heartless.

Against real suicide she opts for what could almost be seen as a parody of the dead bride theme – the staging of her process of waiting for a bridegroom as waiting for death. She is not merely absent but also double, in part because she remains, in the figure of a double of her former self, beyond her social death. The lawyer Jaggers also compares her to the nocturnal vampire when he says that she will not eat in the presence of others, but rather 'wanders about in the night, and then lays hands on such food as she takes' (263). Pip himself observers her one night wandering through her empty, mildewed realm, 'in a ghostly manner, making a low cry' and carrying a 'bare candle in her hand' (325). In addition, Pip articulates the notion that she, as a figure of death, expresses death's desire not only for herself but for him as well, when in 'fancy' he sees a body with Miss Havisham's face hang by the neck from the wooden beam on the side of her house, all in yellow white, her movement as though 'she were trying to call me' (94). Significantly this 'childish association' is revived many years later just before her actual death. Finally, her half-brother Arthur also evokes this image of the dead bride calling her survivors to death in the nightmare vision preceeding his own demise. In this dream representation he sees the sister whom he helped destroy 'awful mad', dressed like Ophelia, all in white, with white flowers in her hair and 'where her heart's broke . . . there's drops of blood'. In his fancy this harbinger of death shakes the shroud ever her arm at him (363).

Above all, however, Miss Havisham is a double in the sense that she incessantly re-enacts the moment of supreme loss, using a materialised form of fiction, namely her body dressed in the guise of the eternal bride, to transform a narcissistic wound into positivity. In the hysteric repetition as representation of her bridal preparations, staged for her own benefit and for her relatives who visit her annually on her birthday, she not only inextricably conflates dead girl and bride. Rather she also doubles herself by staging a self-representation which preserves the moment of loss, ensures perpetual mourning even as, by virtue of the re-enactment, she also stages a triumph over loss and 'castration'. Yet Miss Havisham does not only use this potential transitional realm to represent her process of dying, to make the effect of her broken heart a continual spectacle for others. She also uses this liminality to mould her peers into two plots – one economic, one romantic – of which Pip serves as the interstice.

The first plot involves those who patiently observe her dying because they are speculating on an inheritance. Once again she takes a metaphor literally when, with Pip's help, she evokes a macabre rendition of such cannibalism for the eyes of these 'self-seeking relatives'. In the room where the table, now covered with dust and mould, had been set for her wedding feast, her rotten bride-cake hidden by cobwebs and the habitat of mice and beetles, she dictates the procedure of her wake. 'When the ruin is complete,' she explains, she wishes that 'they lay me dead, in my bride's dress on the bride's table' (117). In this sketch, her body thus placed serves as a fully materialised sign, signifies superlatively her tragic romance and is meant to be 'the finished curse upon him' who transformed her from bride to living corpse. In the same testamentary gesture she also designates the place where, in respect to her dead, laid out body, each relative is meant to sit during the wake, so as visually to invoke their wish to feast on this wealthy relative. Once again the rhetoric of the double inhabiting such a premature rehearsal of one's death is observed by Pip. He has some 'vague misgivings that she might get upon the table then and there and die at once, the complete realization of the ghastly waxwork at the Fair' (113); and he shudders at the uncanny possibility that this fiction may become real. He also has the impression that, as Miss Havisham describes her wake, she is 'looking at the table as if she stood looking at her own figure lying there' (117).

From the moment Pip is introduced into her mansion, she encourages his fancy that she 'would do something' for him. Once he has acquired 'a handsome property' from a secret unnamed source, she can, however, use this 'coincidence' to add another dimension to her inheritance plot. She leads Pip on in his mistaken conviction that she is his benefactress, his 'fairy godmother', and in so doing fosters both her relatives and his delusion that he has superseded them as heir in her will. While for the relatives this plot is merely a sign of her proud nature, Pip connects his economic speculation – that he has mysteriously been given money so as to be removed from his present sphere of life and raised as a gentleman in London – to the second plot Miss Havisham concocts from within her crypt. This second fiction, originally implanted by her in his imagination, concerns his love for her adoptive daughter Estella. From the beginning he realises that the 'diversion' Miss Havisham sought by calling him was not the vicarious pleasure of watching children play but rather the tie she wished to establish between these two adoptive children. Only later does he learn, however, that far from being the privileged heir, he has been chosen as the first victim to test the effectiveness of the monster which Miss Havisham, not unlike Frankenstein, has moulded inmidst her mansion of decay. Though it is not his death she seeks, her aim is to inflict a similar mortal wound to his narcissism, to break his heart in repetition of her own castration. For she has raised Estella into a beautiful but hard, haughty and capricious girl, 'stole her heart away and put ice in its place' (412) so as 'to wreak revenge on the male sex' (200).

From the start, the girl's condescending attitude toward him inspires a sense of humiliation at the same time that it turns her into an idealised love object to be desired from afar. The disruption her acquaintance causes to his previous existence significantly produces fictions in more than one sense. Because he, as a child, can neither adequately describe the strangeness he encounters in the Havisham crypt, nor is willing to confess the humiliation he experiences there, he invents 'marvels', and relates 'pretended experiences' to his sister (97). The events in this transitional space – the card game with a beautiful girl, played 'by candle light in the room with the stopped clocks' (157) before the eyes of a living wax figure – spur on Pip's imagination and let him produce wild fictions. The lies he tells are, however, also experiments in fashioning himself in images more appealing than reality and it is precisely such acts of artificial self-fashioning which Miss Havisham fosters, though in another sense, when she repeatedly asks Pip whether Estella grows 'prettier and prettier'. By soliciting his comment on her beauty she implies that her beauty is in some sense contingent on his gaze, something developed for him. Owing to the double of himself she fosters, the image of him as a potential suitor for Estella, Pip becomes dissatisfied with his social position and wants to fashion himself so as 'to be a gentleman on her account' (156). In retrospect he recalls that the influence of the mysterious 'dull old house', where daylight never entered, where time had stopped, 'bewildered' him and each time after his annual visit, he hated his trade and was ashamed of his home (152). When he suddenly discovers his great economic and educational expectations, he believes Miss Havisham not only means to 'make my fortune when my time is out' (160) but that she will do so because 'she intended me for Estella' (174).

In this potential space between social life and death, Miss Havisham is a vampire in another sense. She uses the lives of others to feed her desire for revenge on the man who misused her, by recreating her adoptive daughter into her artificial double who embodies what she lacks. In this beautiful and brilliant woman, in whose looks and gestures Pip finds 'that tinge of resemblance to Miss Havisham which may often be noticed to have been acquired by children' (259), her surrogate mother has produced a monstrous woman without a heart, without memory, to assuage her broken heart, her incurable 'steady memory', which can't forget her wounded pride. At the same time that she seems to keep her dying body alive by sucking the energy from this daughter by adoption, invigorating herself at the thought that Estella will do to Pip and other men after him what was done to her, she also inspires or feeds the imagination of this first victim. Like Dracula, who transforms the women he bites into revenants, she gives Pip some of her spectral blood in the sense that she engenders in his mind other, potential images of the self. For Pip also turns into a double of himself in this transitional realm, when he imagines himself as the rich young lover of Estella whom he could not and will not become in social reality. Pip serves in part as the audience for Miss Havisham's own staging of death, in part as the privileged victim of her lethal creation. Yet in the process, he also emerges as her other double, as a living image of her own broken heart and thus diametrically opposed to the perfect image of a non-woundable self which she has materialised at Estella's body.

NOTE

1   All numbers in brackets are page references in *Great Expectations*.

5
Sexual Difference

Susan S. Lanser, 'Toward a Feminist Narratology'*

See also:
Barthes (3.i)
Brooks (3.ii)
Gibson (3.ii)
Mulvey (4)
Bronfen (4)
Johnson (6)
Minh-Ha (9)

. . .

Given a literary climate at best indifferent to narratology, my desire to explore the compatibility of feminism and narratology is also a way to think about what narratology can and cannot do, what place it might have in the contemporary critical environment of American departments of literature, and how it might enrich the hermeneutical enterprise for critics who are not themselves theorists of narrative. My immediate task, however, will be more circumscribed: to ask whether feminist criticism, and particularly the study of narratives by women, might benefit from the methods and insights of narratology and whether narratology, in turn, might be altered by the understandings of feminist criticism and the experience of women's texts. It is in the frank desire to say yes to both these questions that this essay has been conceived. It is in the supposition that the readers of this journal are more involved with narratology than with feminism that my emphasis will be on the second question rather than the first.

There are compelling reasons why feminism (or any explicitly political criticism) and narratology (or any largely formal poetics) might seem incompatible. The technical, often neologistic, vocabulary of narratology has alienated critics of many persuasions and may seem particularly counterproductive to critics with political concerns. Feminists also tend to be distrustful of categories and oppositions, of 'a conceptual universe organized into the neat paradigms of binary logic' – a distrust which explains part of the attraction of feminist theory to Derridean deconstruction. But there are (at least) three more crucial issues about which feminism and narratology might differ: the role of gender in the construction of narrative theory, the status of narrative as mimesis or semiosis, and the importance of context for determining meaning in narrative.

The most obvious question feminism would ask of narratology is simply this: upon what body of texts, upon what understandings of the narrative and referential universe, have the insights of narratology been based? It is readily apparent that virtually no work in the field of narratology has taken gender into account, either in designating a canon or in formulating questions and hypotheses. This means, first of all, that the

* *Style*, 20 (3) (1986), pp. 342–6.

narratives which have provided the foundation for narratology have been either men's texts or texts treated as men's texts. Genette's formulation of a 'Discours du récit' on the basis of Proust's *A la recherche du temps perdu*, Propp's androcentric morphology of a certain kind of folktale, Greimas on Maupassant, Iser on male novelists from Bunyan to Beckett, Barthes on Balzac, Todorov on the *Decameron* – these are but evident examples of the ways in which the masculine text stands for the universal text. In the structuralist quest for 'invariant elements among superficial differences', for (so-called) universals rather than particulars, narratology has avoided questions of gender almost entirely. This is particularly problematic for those feminist critics – in this country, the majority – whose main interest is the 'difference or specificity of women's writing'. The recognition of this specificity has led not only to the rereading of individual texts but to the rewriting of literary history; I am suggesting that it also lead to a rewriting of narratology that takes into account the contributions of women as both producers and interpreters of texts.

This challenge does not deny the enormous value of a body of brilliant narrative theory for the study of women's works; indeed, it has been applied to such writers as Colette (Bal, 'The Narrating and the Focalizing') and Eliot (Costello) and is crucial to my own studies of narrative voice in women's texts. It does mean that until women's writings, questions of gender, and feminist points of view are considered, it will be impossible even to know the deficiencies of narratology. It seems to me likely that the most abstract and grammatical concepts (say, theories of time) will prove to be adequate. On the other hand, as I will argue later in this essay, theories of plot and story may need to change substantially. And I would predict that the major impact of feminism on narratology will be to raise new questions, to add to the narratological distinctions that already exists. . . .

A narratology for feminist criticism would also have to reconcile the primarily semiotic approach of narratology with the primarily mimetic orientation of most (Anglo-American) feminist thinking about narrative. This difference reminds us that 'literature is at the juncture of two systems'; one can speak about it as

> a representation of life
> an account of reality
> a mimetic document

and as

> a non-referential linguistic system
> an enunciation supposing a narrator and a listener
> primarily a linguistic construct.

Traditionally, structuralist narratology has suppressed the representational aspects of fiction and emphasized the semiotic, while feminist criticism has done the opposite. Feminist critics tend to be more concerned with characters than with any other aspect of narrative and to speak of characters largely as if they were persons. Most narratologists, in contrast, treat characters, if at all, as 'patterns of recurrence, motifs which are continually recontextualized in other motifs'; as such, they 'lose their privilege, their central status, and their definition'. This conception could seem to threaten one of feminist criticism's deepest premises: that narrative texts, and particularly texts in the novelistic tradition, are profoundly (if never simply) referential – and influential – in their representations of gender relations. The challenge to both feminism and narratology is to recognize the dual nature of narrative, to find categories and terms that are abstract and semiotic enough to be useful, but concrete and mimetic enough to seem relevant for critics whose theories root literature in 'the real conditions of our lives'.

The tendency to pure semiosis is both cause and effect of a more general tendency in narratology to isolate texts from the contexts of their production and reception and hence from what 'political' critics think of as literature's ground of being – the 'real world.' This is partly a result of narratology's desire for a precise, scientific description of discourse, for many of the questions concerning the relationship of literature to the 'real world' – questions of why, so what, to what effect – are admittedly speculative. Thus 'when narratology does attempt to account for the contextual, it does so in terms of narrative conventions and codes. Yet their capacity to account for social, historical or contextual differences always remains limited by the original formalist closure within which such codes and conventions are defined'. This is why early in the history of formalism, critics like Medvedev and Bakhtin called for a 'sociological poetics' that would be dialectically theoretical and historical: 'Poetics provides literary history with direction in the specification of the research material and the basic definitions of its forms and types. Literary history amends the definitions of poetics, making them more flexible, dynamic, and adequate to the diversity of the historical material'. My insistence on writing women's texts into the historical canon of narratology has precisely this aim of making it more adequate to the diversity of narrative.

Finally, feminist criticism would argue that narratology itself is ideological, indeed in an important sense fictional. One need not agree wholeheartedly with Stanley Fish that 'formal units are always a function of the interpretive model one brings to bear (they are not "in the text")', to recognize that no interpretive system is definitive or inevitable. But as Fish also reminds us, every theory must believe itself the best theory possible. Formalist-structuralist narratology may 'know' that its categories are not immanent, but it proceeds as if there were 'a stable and immediately knowable text, directly available to classificatory operations that are themselves neutral and innocent of interpretive bias'. Feminist criticism has simply not had this luxury: in its critique of masculine bias, it has of necessity taken the view that theory sometimes says more about the reader than about the text.

A narratology for feminist criticism would begin, then, with the recognition that revision of a theory's premises and practices is legitimate and desirable. It would probably be cautious in its construction of systems and favor flexible categories over fixed sets. It would scrutinize its norms to be sure of what they are normative. It would be willing to look afresh at the question of gender and to re-form its theories on the basis of women's texts, as Robyn Warhol's essay on the 'engaging narrator' (in *PMLA*) begins to do. In both its concepts and its terminology, it would reflect the mimetic as well as the semiotic experience that is the reading of literature, and it would study narrative in relation to a referential context that is simultaneously linguistic, literary, historical, biographical, social, and political. Granted, narratology might have to be willing to cede some precision and simplicity for the sake of relevance and accessibility, to develop terminology less confusing, say, than a series like analepsis, prolepsis, paralepsis, and metalepsis. The valuable and impressive work that has been done in the field would be opened to a critique and supplement in which feminist questions were understood to contribute to a richer, more useful, and more complete narratology For as I have been trying to suggest, a narratology that cannot adequately account for women's narratives is an inadequate narratology for men's texts as well.

A re-formed narratology should be of particular interest to feminist critics because fiction is the dominant genre in the study of women and literature. The necessarily semiotic nature of even a revised narratology will help to balance feminist criticism's necessarily mimetic commitments. The comprehensiveness and care with which narratology makes distinctions can provide invaluable methods for textual analysis. As Mieke Bal argues, 'The use of formally adequate and precise tools is not interesting in itself, but it can clarify other, very relevant issues and provide insights which otherwise remain vague'. Narratology and feminist criticism might profitably join forces, for example, to explore the teleological aspects of narrative, which have concerned narratologists like Ann Jefferson and Marianna Torgovnick and feminist critics like Rachel Blau DuPlessis. I can imagine a rich dialogue between Armine Mortimer Kotin's and Nancy K. Miller's analyses of the plot of *La Princesse de Clèves*. And a major benefit of narratology is that it offers a relatively independent (pre-textual) framework for studying groups of texts. It could, for example, provide a particularly valuable foundation for exploring one of the most complex and troubling questions for feminist criticism: whether there is indeed a 'woman's writing' and/or a female tradition, whether men and women do write differently. For given the volatile nature of the question, the precision and abstraction of narratological systems offers the safety for investigation that more impressionistic theories of difference do not. This kind of research would demonstrate the particular responsiveness of narratology to certain problems for which other theories have not been adequate and hence illustrate value for feminist scholarship.

Nilli Diengott, 'Narratology and Feminism*

See also:
Bal (2.i)
Genette (2.ii)
Prince (2.ii)
Barthes (2.iii)
McClary (3.iii)
Johnson (6)

. . .

I will now take up Lanser's comments one by one. She says her task is to examine how 'the study of narratives by women might benefit from the methods and insights of narratology and whether narratology, in turn, might be altered by the understandings of feminist criticism and the *experience* of women's texts' (342; my emphasis).

Narratology, which Lanser recognizes as a formal poetics (343), focuses on an object of inquiry defined by the science itself and is concerned with taxonomies,

* *Style*, 22 (1) (1988), pp. 44–50

categorization, distinctions, all for the purpose of describing the system behind literary narratives. Therefore, it could not possibly be altered by the *experience* of women's texts, which belongs either to the actual 'life of literature' in the sense defined above – that is, to criticism or to interpretation, depending on how experience is understood.

Lanser's main concern, however, is with three issues on which feminism and narratology differ: 'the role of gender in the construction of narrative theory, the status of narrative as mimesis and semiosis, and the importance of context for determining meaning in narrative' (343).

To take the last issue first, since it is the easiest to refute. Determining meaning in narrative is what interpretation, not theoretical poetics, is all about.

As to the role of gender in the construction of theory, I do not even understand how it is an issue. The structuralist-inspired narrative poetics with which I am familiar and which constitute Lanser's frame of reference as well as the main body of narrative theory – those of Genette, Prince, Chatman, Bal, Rimmon-Kenan, to mention the most famous ones – are indeed gender indifferent. Their tables of contents display such titles as time (order, duration, frequency), focalization, the focalized, narration, or characterization. Lanser herself admits that the 'most abstract and grammatical concepts (say, theories of time) will prove to be adequate for a feminist narratology but that theories of plot and story may need to change substantially' (344). I will deal with plot and story later, but my question now is why are focalization or narration or any of the other categories or taxonomies less abstract than time? Why are they inadequate to describe the system underlying narratives written by female or male writers? The whole point of the above mentioned different narratalogical enterprises is that they are focused on the most general and abstract concepts for the purposes of describing the system. Focalization, for example, describes 'who sees' and the object seen, as distinguished from a separate but no less significant question for systematic inquiry as well as for the narrative system of 'who tells,' or narration. These are highly abstract categories just like time, and they are totally indifferent to gender. They focus on examining the position of the seer or teller *vis-à-vis* the events, and the only answers possible are that the focalizer and/or the narrator are external or internal. Whether the focalizer or narrator is female or male is entirely insignificant. Gender can be of great significance, however, in interpretation, where questions such as, 'Is the specific text focalized externally from within by a woman or a man?' *are* pertinent. But interpretation is *not* narratology, *not* theoretical poetics.

As for the meaning of Lanser's second point, that feminist criticism is mimetic whereas narratology is semiotic, it is not very clear. She says that feminist critics 'tend to be more *concerned with characters* than with any other aspect of narrative and to speak of characters largely as if they were persons' while narratologists, if they discuss characters, see them merely as patterns or motifs, a treatment that threatens one of feminism's deepest premises 'that narrative texts . . . are profoundly (if never simply) referential – and influential – in their representations of gender relations' (344; my emphases). What I have emphasized suggests to me that she is describing interpretations of texts where one, indeed, discusses characters. But narratology is a theoretical activity. It is not concerned with characters but with methods of characterization. Insofar as it takes up the question of character (the abstract notion) – and not all narrative poetics do (for instance, Genette) – it is concerned with its construction or with the question of what character is.

According to Lanser, the emphasis on semiosis in narratology results in decontextualization. Again this is precisely what theoretical poetics, as opposed to criticism or to literary history, is based on: constructing the synchronically. Context has significance for the canon. Lanser claims, therefore that 'writing women's texts into the historical canon of narratology' (345) is designed to make it more adequate. There is nothing wrong with widening the canon, but that is the task with which literary history or perhaps historical poetics may be concerned. For theoretical poetics, canonicity never even presents a problem. For its specific exemplifications of the taxonomies or categories, theoretical poetics is indifferent to both gender and value: Barbara Cartland and Proust can serve equally for exemplifying types of narration or prolepses.

It appears then that what Lanser has to say about the issues on which narratology and feminist criticism differ is inherent to the object and methods of inquiry that narratology as a theoretical poetics is focused on. Her analysis is based on a confusion of theoretical poetics with other fields within the study of literature, such as interpretation, historical poetics, or criticism.

Having analyzed the points of divergence, Lanser suggests a general program for reconciling the two. She says that feminist narratology 'must be willing to cede some precision and simplicity for the sake of relevance and accessibility' (345). First, exactly how much does ceding 'some' precision and simplicity involve? But more importantly, as a theoretical enterprise trying to describe a system, narratology is *not* relevant to anything but the questions it poses. And any theory that does *not* strive for precision and simplicity is working in opposition to what theory is all about. Relevance and accessibility are just pleasant-sounding slogans designed to allay the fears of those suspicious of theory.

Lanser is not satisfied with outlining the general program for the reconciliation of feminism and narratology, but cites a specific example indicating a beginning of such a reconciliation: Warhol's article. I find Warhol's essay, however, hardly convincing for Lanser's project. Warhol indeed discusses a certain type of narrator in women's texts (by the way, not exactly noncanonical writers). What is of significance is that what Lanser thinks is a refinement of current typologies of narrators or narratees under the label 'engaging narrator' can be found in current narratological typologies under the more abstract category of 'degree of perceptibility'. Specifically, 'perceptibility' covers comments, judgments, generalizations, and other types of appeals by narrators. Thus, an 'engaging narrator' is merely one type of such commentary. But a systematic theoretical study strives for the most comprehensive categories, not for the most specific. It therefore seems to me that Warhol's category is best placed under a descriptive poetics dealing with a rhetorical device typical of female writers in the nineteenth century as can be inferred from Warhol's concluding remarks (817). Furthermore, how is a more 'complete narratology' (Lanser 345) attained by this subcategory as opposed, for instance, to Genette's landmark distinction, for theoretical poetics, between focalization and narration? This distinction indeed makes for a more complete, because more precise and comprehensive, narrative poetics than 'point of view' theories.

In light of my comments so far, I must agree with Lanser that feminist critics could benefit 'from the comprehensiveness and care with which narratology makes distinctions' (346), and this is precisely what my response aims to show: that feminist critics, even of the best kind, as I think Lanser is, are not always clear in their own minds about defining their object of inquiry.

. . .

CONCLUSION

To sum up, I have tried to argue that there is no need, indeed, no possibility of reconciling feminism with narratology. Whereas narratology is quite clear about its premises and methods, feminist critics seem not to be very clear about their object of inquiry. Furthermore, if I may take Lanser as exemplifying an attitude of some feminists, it seems that they feel compelled to appropriate fields of study which rely on totally different premises and questions to their own enterprise. I am not claiming that Lanser is not discussing important issues in her analysis. What she does has its value and legitimacy, but it has nothing to do with narratology.

Perhaps feminist critics should be reminded of Crane's fine statement made quite some time ago (when New Criticism was showing similar 'imperialistic" tendencies) that critical controversies often stem from the fact that critics appear to disagree when, in fact, they are not giving 'answers to the same question about the same object' and that it is perfectly beneficial and legitimate to have 'a pluralism of questions', providing critics *are aware* that they *are* asking different questions.

Teresa de Lauretis, 'Desire in Narrative'*

See also:
Propp (1.iii)
Lévi-Strauss (2.i)
Barthes (2.iii)
Barthes (3.i)
Brooks (3.ii)
Mulvey (4)
Bronfen (4)
Johnson (6)
Bhabha (9)
Minh-Ha (9)

THE QUESTION OF DESIRE

'Sadism demands a story,' writes Laura Mulvey in the essay already cited on several occasions ['Visual Pleasure and Narrative Cinema', in this volume]. The proposition, with its insidious suggestion of reversibility, is vaguely threatening. (Is a story, are all stories, to be claimed by sadism?) The full statement reads: 'Sadism demands a story, depends on making something happen, forcing a change in another person, a battle of will and strength, victory/defeat, all occurring in a linear time with a beginning and an end.[1] This sounds like a common definition of narrative, yet is offered as a description of sadism. Are we to infer that sadism is the causal agent, the deep structure, the generative force of narrative? Or at least coextensive with it? We would prefer to think the proposition is biased or at best particular, pertinent to some narrative genres like the

* *Alice Doesn't: Feminism, Semiotics, Cinema* (London: Macmillan, 1988), pp. 103–12.

thriller (after all, she is speaking of Hitchcock's films), but surely not applicable to all narratives, not universally valid. For, as Roland Barthes once stated, narrative is universal, is present in every society, age, and culture:

> Carried by articulated language, spoken or written, fixed or moving images, gestures, and the ordered mixture of all these substances; narrative is present in myth, legend, fable, tale, novella, epic, history, tragedy, drama, comedy, mime, painting (think of Carpaccio's *Saint Ursula*), stained glass windows, cinema, comics, news item, conversation. . . . Caring nothing for the division between good and bad literature, narrative is international, transhistorical, transcultural: it is simply there, like life itself.[2]

Barthes's famous essay served as introduction to the 1966 issue of *Communications*, devoted to the structural analysis of narrative, a seminal work in what has become known as narratology and undoubtedly a cornerstone in narrative theory. The volume and the work of its contributors owed much to a variety of sources, from structural linguistics to Russian Formalism and Prague School poetics, as did all semiological research in its early stages; but its coming to existence at that particular time must be traced directly to the publication, in 1958, of Lévi-Strauss's *Anthropologie structurale* and the English translation of Propp's *Morphology of the Folktale*.[3] The early structural studies were concerned with the logic of narrative possibilities, of actions and their patterned arrangement, be it the logic of a diachronic unfolding of the actions performed by the characters (Propp's 'functions' and '*dramatis personae*'); or the logic of a paradigmatic distribution of semantic macrounits (Lévi-Strauss's 'mythemes') and the relations among them; or, in Barthes's own more finely articulated model, the logic of a vertical ('hierarchical') integration of narrative instances and levels of description.

Not surprisingly, none of these models would support or even admit of a connection between sadism and narrative that may presuppose the agency of desire. Or more exactly, none would admit of a *structural* connection between sadism and narrative; that is to say, one by which the agency of desire might be seen somehow at work in that logic, that 'higher order of relation,' that 'passion of meaning' which narrative, Barthes says, excites in us. The structural models would consider sadism or desire as types of thematic investment, to he located on the level of content, and thus preempt the possibility of an integral relationship, a mutual structural implication of narrative with desire and *a fortiori* sadism. Curiously, however, Barthes ends his essay with this statement: 'It may be significant that it is at the same moment (around the age of three) the little human "invents" at once sentence, narrative, and the Oedipus' (p. 124). He will of course pursue the relation between narrative and Oedipal structuration, as it is mediated by language, in later works from *S/Z* to *The Pleasure of the Text*. But in so doing – this too may be significant – Barthes drifts further and further away from his own semiological model, and, far from seeking to establish an analytic structural framework, his writing will become increasingly fragmented and fragmentary, personal a subject's discourse. Nevertheless, once suggested, the connection between narrative and the Oedipus, desire and narrative, not only appears to be incontestable but, divesting itself from Barthes's singular critical *iter*, urges a reconsideration of narrative structure – or better, narrativity.

Since the early structural analyses, semiotics has developed a dynamic, processual view of signification as a work(ing) of the codes, a production of meaning which involves a subject in a social field. The object of narrative theory, redefined accordingly, is not therefore narrative but narrativity; not so much the structure of narrative (its component units and their relations) as its work and effects. Today narrative theory is no longer or not primarily intent on establishing a logic, a grammar, or a formal rhetoric of narrative; what it seeks to understand is the nature of the structuring and destructuring, even destructive, processes at work in textual and semiotic production. It was again Barthes who, in his notion of the text, sketched out a new direction and a useful critical approach to the question of narrativity: 'The work can be held in the hand, the text is held in language, only exists in the movement of a discourse . . . or again, *the Text is experienced only in an activity of production*' (p. 157).

To ask in what ways and by what means desire works along with narrativity, within the movement of its discourse, requires attention to two distinct but interrelated line inquiry. First, the re-examination of the relations of narrative to genres on the one hand, and to epistemological frameworks on the other; thus, the understanding of the various conditions of presence of narrative in forms of representation that go from myth and folktale to drama, fiction, cinema, and further, historical narration, the case history, up to what Turner calls 'social dramas.' Narrative has been the focus of much recent critical debate. A comparison of the 1980 special issue of *Critical Inquiry* on narrative, for example, with the 1966 *Communications* mentioned earlier indicates a shift in emphasis. The 'transhistorical,' narratological view of narrative structures seems to have given way to an attempt to historicize the notion of narrative by relating it to the subject and to its implication in, or dependence on the social order, the law of meaning; or to the transformative effects produced in processes of reading and practices of writing. More often than not, however, those efforts all but reaffirm an integrative and ultimately traditional view of narrativity. Paradoxically, in spite of the methodological shift away from the notion of structure and toward a notion of process, they end up de-historicizing the subject and thus universalizing the narrative process as such. The problem, I believe, is that many of the current formulations of narrative process fail to see that subjectivity is engaged in the cogs of narrative and indeed constituted in the relation of narrative, meaning, and desire; so that the very work of narrativity is the engagement of the subject in certain positionalities of meaning and desire. Or else they fail to locate the relation of narrative and desire where it takes place, where that relation is materially inscribed – in a field of textual practices. Thus, finally, they fail to envisage a materially, historically, and experientially constituted subject, a subject engendered, we might say, precisely by the process of its engagement in the narrative genres.

Second, then, the relation of narrative and desire must be sought within the specificity of a textual practice, where it is materially inscribed. This is especially obvious when one considers narrativity in cinema, where the issue of material specificity (not simply of 'techniques') is unavoidable and in fact has long been a central question of film theory – whence the value, the relevance of cinema for any general theory of narrative. But within film theory, too, a certain shifting of emphasis has occurred with regard to narrative. While narrative film has always been the primary area of reference for critical and theoretical discourses on cinema, narrative structuration has received on the whole much less attention than have the technical, economic, ideological, or aesthetic aspects of filmmaking and film viewing.[4] Moreover, the issue of narrative has served as a bone of contention, as well as a rigid criterion of discrimination, between dominant, mainstream cinema and avant-garde or independent practices. The distinction is not unlike that often made between mainstream fiction and metafiction or antinarrative; except that in cinema that distinction is articulated and defined in political terms.

Because of the material specificity of cinema – its near-total and unmediated dependence on the socioeconomic and the technological – film theory and film practice stand in a close-knit relationship, bound by strict ties of historical proximity. Thus it is not by pure coincidence that the return to narrative on the part of theory, its increasing concern with narrativity, corresponds to a return of narrative in alternative and avant-garde film practices. That does not mean that the emergence of narrative would mark an apolitical or reactionary turn. On the contrary, as Claire Johnston first noted back in 1974, narrative is a major issue in women's cinema; a feminist strategy should combine, rather than oppose, the notions of film as a political tool and film as entertainment. The political, analytical work of women's cinema is to bring home the fact that 'cinema involves the production of signs,' and 'the sign is always a product'; that what the camera grasps is not reality as such but 'the "natural" [naturalized] world of the dominant ideology. . . . The "truth" of our oppression cannot be "captured" on celluloid with the "innocence" of the camera: it has to be constructed, manufactured.' Thus, she insisted, the project of feminist film criticism was to build up a systematic body of knowledge about film and to develop the means to interrogate male bourgeois cinema; but that knowledge must then feed back into filmmaking practices, where what is at stake is 'the working through,' the question, of desire. 'In order to counter our objectification in the cinema, our collective fantasies must be released: women's cinema must embody the working through of desire: such an objective demands the use of the entertainment films.'[5] Very much out of this same concern, in a recent essay on sexual identity in melodrama, Laura Mulvey addresses the question of pleasure for the female spectator and turns to consider the positionalities of identification available to her in narrative cinema, which are 'triggered by the logic of narrative grammar.'[6]

For feminist theory in particular, the interest in narrativity amounts to a *theoretical return* to narrative and the posing of questions that have been either preempted or displaced by semiotic studies. That return amounts, as is often the case with any radical critique, to a rereading of the sacred texts against the passionate urging of a different question, a different practice, and a different desire. For if Metz's work on *la grande syntagmatique* left little room for a consideration of the working of desire in narrative structuration, Barthes's discourse on the pleasure of the text at once erotic and epistemological, also develops from his prior hunch that a connection exists between language, narrative, and the Oedipus. Pleasure and meaning move along the triple track he first outlined, and the tracking is from the point of view of Oedipus, so to speak, its movement is that of a masculine desire.

> The pleasure of the text is . . . an Oedipal pleasure (to denude, to know, to learn the origin and the end), if it is true that every narrative (every unveiling of the truth) is a staging of the (absent, hidden, or hypostatized) father – which would explain the solidarity of narrative forms, of family structures, and of prohibitions of nudity.[7]

The analogy that Robert Scholes proposes between narrative and sexual intercourse again affirms, in the manner of a *reductio ad absurdum*, what seems to be the inherent maleness of all narrative movement:

> The archetype of all fiction is the sexual act. In saying this I do not mean merely to remind the reader of the connection between all art and the erotic in human nature. Nor do I intend simply to suggest an analogy between fiction and sex. For what connects fiction – and music – with sex is the fundamental orgasmic rhythm of tumescence and detumescence, of tension and resolution, of intensification to the point of climax and consummation. In the sophisticated forms of fiction, as in the sophisticated practice of sex, much of the art consists of delaying climax within the framework of desire in order to prolong the pleasurable act itself. When we look at fiction with respect to its form alone, we see a pattern of events designed to move toward climax and resolution, balanced by a counter-pattern of events designed to delay this very climax and resolution.[8]

Lightly gliding over a further parallelism linking the content of the fictional work with the 'possible procreative content' and the 'necessary emotional content' of the sexual act, Scholes proceeds to look closely at what he calls 'the meaning of the fictional act.' The analogy still holds. In both cases, fiction and sex, the act 'is a reciprocal relationship. It takes two.' Unless the writer writes or the reader reads 'for his own amusement,' pursuing solitary pleasures ('but these are acts of mental masturbation,' observes the critic, determined to run his metaphor into the ground), 'in the full fictional act [they] share a relationship of mutual dependency. The meaning of the fictional act itself is something like love.' And in the end, 'when writer and reader make a "marriage of true minds," the act of fiction is perfect and complete.'

Those of us who know no art of delaying climax or, reading, feel no incipient tumescence, may well be barred from the pleasure of this 'full fictional act'; nor may we profit from the rhythm method by which it is attained. But knowing, as one does, how rare a thing a marriage of true minds can be, and then how rarely it lasts beyond the first few chapters; and knowing, furthermore, how the story usually goes, one might be brought to wonder: is Mulvey perhaps not wrong, after all, in seeing a connection between sadism and narrative? And the suggestion that the connection is one of mutual implication all already appears much less far-fetched, and all the more outrageous. In the following pages I shall seek to explore further the nature of that connection which, I suspect, is constitutive of narrative and of the very work of narrativity.

Suppose we were to ask the question: What became of the Sphinx after the encounter with Oedipus on his way to Thebes? Or, how did Medusa feel seeing herself in Perseus' mirror just before being slain? To be sure, an answer could be found by perusing a good textbook of classical mythology; but the point is, no one knows offhand and, what is more, it seldom occurs to anyone to ask. Our culture, history, and science do not provide an answer; but neither do the modern mythologies, the fictions of our social imagination, the stories and the images produced by what may be called the psychotechnologies of our everyday life. Medusa and the Sphinx, like the other ancient monsters, have survived inscribed in hero narratives, in someone else's story, not their own; so they are figures or markers of positions – places and topoi – through which the hero and his story move so their destination and to accomplish meaning.

Classical mythology of course was populated with monsters, beings awesome to behold, whose power to capture vision, to lure the gaze, is conveyed in the very etymon of the word 'monster.' But only a few have survived past the dark ages into Renaissance epos, and beyond the age of reason into the imaginary of modernism; and perhaps not by chance the few that have survived are narratively inscribed within stories of heroes and semantically associated with boundary. What these monsters stand for, to us, is the symbolic transposition of the place where they stand, the literary topos being literally, in this case, a topographical projection; the *limen*, frontier between the desert and the city, threshold to the inner recesses of the cave or maze, metaphorizes the symbolic boundary between nature and culture, the limit and the test imposed on man.

The ancient monsters had a sex, as did the gods, in a mythology whose painstakingly rich articulation of sexual difference was to be boiled down to the stark Platonic opposition man/non-man. And again in the modern mythologies, the gender of monsters, unlike the sex of angels, is a carefully worked out representation. The Minotaur, for example, imprisoned at the center of the labyrinth in Crete, exacts his toll in human lives indiscriminately (seven girls, seven boys) as would a natural plague; more beast than man, he represents the bestial, animal side of man that must be sought out and conquered. The issue of Pasifae's unnatural union with a bull, he is described as 'half bull and half man' but referred to as 'the Cretan Bull' or even, with unwitting irony, by the patronymic 'Minos' bull.'[9] In *Fellini's Satyricon* he is represented with a man's body and the head of a bull. Medusa and the Sphinx, on the contrary, are more human than animal, and definitely female: the latter has the body of a winged lion but a woman's head; Medusa is female and beautiful, although she too is connected with bestiality (she was Poseidon's lover and pregnant with his offspring when Perseus killed her, and from her body, as her head was severed, sprang forth the winged horse Pegasus). Medusas power to cast the spell which in many cultures is actually called 'the evil eye,' is directly represented in her horribly 'staring eyes,' which are a constant feature of her figurative and literary representations; while the serpents in their hair or 'girdles' are a variable attribute of all three Gorgons, together with other monstrous features such as wings, 'a lolling tongue,' or 'grinning heads.'[10]

Medusa's power, her evil look, is more explicit than the Sphinx's but both achieve analogous long-term effects: they not only kill or devour, but blind as well. The legends of Perseus and Oedipus in which they are inscribed, make it clear that their threat is to man's vision, and their power consists in their enigma and 'to-be-looked-at-ness' (in Mulvey's word), their luring of man's gaze into the 'dark continent,' as Freud put it, the enigma of femininity. They are obstacles man encounters on the path of life, on his way to manhood, wisdom, and power; they must be slain or defeated so that he can go forward to fulfill his destiny – and his story. Thus we don't know, his story doesn't tell, what became of the Sphinx after the encounter with Oedipus, though some may claim to have caught a glimpse of her again in the smile of Mona Lisa, and others, like mythologist H. J. Rose, simply state that she 'killed herself in disgust,' after Oedipus solved her riddle – and married Jocasta.[11] Medusa, of course, was slain, though she too is still laughing, according to Hélène Cixous.[12] The questions we might ask are obvious. Why did the Sphinx kill herself (like Jocasta), and why the disgust? Why did Medusa not wake up her own slaying, or did she perhaps *have* to be asleep? Let us ask our questions, then – if we can.

In an essay entitled 'Rereading Femininity' Shoshana Felman points out how Freud's own interrogation of the 'riddle' of femininity, his very asking of the question 'woman' ('What does a woman want?'), paradoxically excludes women from the question, bars them from asking it themselves. She quotes Freud's words:

> Throughout history people have knocked their heads against the riddle of the nature of femininity. . . . Nor will *you* have escaped worrying over this problem – those of you who are men; to those of you who are women this will not apply – you are yourselves the problem.

And she comments:

> A question, Freud thus implies, is always a question of desire; it springs out of a desire which is also the desire for a question. Women, however, are considered merely as the *objects* of desire, and as the *objects* of the question. To the extent that women '*are* the question,' they cannot *enunciate* the question; they cannot be the speaking *subjects* of the knowledge or the science which the question seeks.[13]

What Freud's question really asks, therefore, is 'What is femininity – for men?' In this sense it is a question of desire: it is prompted by men's desire for woman, and by men's desire to know. Let me now elaborate this point a little further. Freud's is a question addressed to men both in the sense that the question is not asked of women ('to those of you who are women, this will not apply') and that its answer is *for* men, reverts to men. The similarity between this 'riddle' and the riddle of the Sphinx is striking, for in the latter, also, the term of address is man. Oedipus is addressed, he solves the riddle, and his answer, the very meaning or content of the riddle, is – man, universal man, Oedipus therefore. However, the apparent syntactical parallelism of the two expressions, 'the riddle of the Sphinx' and 'the riddle of femininity,' disguises one important difference, the source of enunciation: *who* asks the question? While Oedipus is he who answers the riddle posed by the Sphinx, Freud stands in both places at once, for he first formulates – defines – the question and then answers it. And we shall see that his question, what is femininity, acts precisely as the impulse, the desire that will generate a narrative, the story of femininity, or how a (female) child with a bisexual disposition becomes a little girl and then a woman.

What must be stressed in this respect, however obvious it may seem, is that Freud's evocation of the myth of Oedipus is mediated by the text of Sophocles. The Oedipus of psychoanalysis is the *Oedipus Rex*, where the myth is already textually inscribed, cast in dramatic literary form, and thus sharply focused on the hero as mover of the narrative, the center and term of reference of consciousness and desire. And indeed in the drama it is Oedipus who asks the question and presses for an answer that will come back to him with a vengeance, as it were. 'Not Creon, you are your own worse enemy,' foretells Tiresias. As for the Sphinx, she is long gone and little more than a legend in the world of the tragedy, the plague-ridden city of Thebes. She only served to test Oedipus and qualify him as hero. Having fulfilled her narrative function (the function of the Donor, in Propp's terms), her question is now subsumed in his; her power, his; her fateful gift of knowledge, soon to be his. Oedipus's question then, like Freud's, generates a narrative, turns into a quest. Thus not only is a question, as Felman says, always a question of desire; a story too is always a question of desire.

But whose desire is it that speaks, and whom does that desire address? The received interpretations of the Oedipus story, Freud's among others, leave no doubt. The desire is Oedipus's, and though its object may be woman (or Truth or knowledge or power), its term of reference and address is man: man as social being and mythical subject, founder of the social order, and source of mimetic violence; hence the institution of the incest prohibition, its maintenance in Sophocles's Oedipus as in Hamlet's revenge of his father, its costs and benefits, again, for man. However, we need not limit our understanding of the inscription of desire in narrative to the Oedipus story proper, which is in fact paradigmatic of all narratives. According to Greimas, for instance, the semantic structure of all narrative is the movement of an actant-subject toward an actant-object. In this light, it is not accidental that the central Bororo myth in Lévi-Strauss's study of over eight hundred North and South American myths is an autochthonous variant of the Greek myth of Oedipus; or that the circus act of the lion tamer, analyzed by Paul Bouissac, is semiotically constructed along a narrative and clearly Oedipal trajectory.

NOTES

1 Laura Mulvey, 'Visual Pleasure and Narrative Cinema,' *Screen* 16, no. 3 (Autumn 1975): 14.

2 Roland Barthes, 'Introduction to the Structural Analysis of Narratives') in *Image-Music-Text*, trans. Stephen Heath (New York: Hill and Wang, 1977), p. 79. All further references to this volume will be cited in the text.

3 Contributors to the volume included Claude Bremond, A.-J. Greimas, and Tzvetan Todorov (on whose work Barthes draws heavily for his model); plus Umberto Eco and Christian Metz, whose paper 'La grande syntagmatique du film narratif' virtually opened up the area of structural-semiotic analysis of cinema.

4 Metz's work on narrative structuration in classical cinema – *Film Language: A Semiotics of the Cinema*, trans. Michael Taylor (New York: Oxford University Press, 1974), and *Language and Cinema* (The Hague and Paris: Mouton, l974) – had a great impact on the development of film theory (see, for example, Stephen Heath, 'The Work of Christian Metz' in *Screen Reader 2* (London: SEFT, 1981), pp. 138–61); but was soon overshadowed by Metz's own subsequent work, *The Imaginary Signifier*, trans. Ben Brewster *et al.* (Bloomington: Indiana University Press, 1981), which shifted attention in the direction of psychoanalysis and questions of spectatorship.

5 Claire Johnston, 'Women's Cinema as Counter-Cinema,' in Claire Johnston, ed., *Notes on Women's Cinema* (London: SEFT, 1974), pp. 28 and 31.

6 'In *Visual Pleasure* my argument was axed around a desire to identify a pleasure that was specific to cinema, that is the eroticism and cultural conventions surrounding the look. Now, on the contrary, I would rather emphasise the way that popular cinema inherited traditions of story telling that are common to other forms of folk and mass culture, with attendant fascinations other than those of the look.' Laura Mulvey, 'Afterthoughts on "Visual Pleasure and Narrative Cinema" inspired by *Duel in the Sun* (King Vidor, 1946),' *Framework*, no. 15/16/17 (1981): 13.

7   Roland Barthes, *The Pleasure of the Text*, trans. Richard Miller (New York: Hill and Wang, 1975), p. 10.

8   Robert Scholes, *Fabulation and Metafiction* (Urbana: University of Illinois Press, 1979), p. 26. The following quotes are from p. 27.

9   H. J. Rose, *The Handbook of Greek Mythology* (New York: Dutton, 1959), p. 183. On the representation of difference in ancient Greek society, and the shift it underwent in the transition from literary-mythic to philosophical discourse between the fifth and the fourth centuries BC, see Page du Bois, *Centaurs and Amazons: Women and the Pre-History of the Great Chain of Being* (Ann Arbor: The University of Michigan Press, 1982).

10   Rose, p. 30.

11   Ibid, p. 188.

12   Hélène Cixous, 'The Laugh of the Medusa,' trans. Keith Cohen and Paula Cohen, in *New French Feminisms*, ed. Elaine Marks and Isabelle de Courtivron (Amherst: The University of Massachusetts Press, 1980), pp. 245–64. All further references to this work will be cited in the text.

13   Shoshana Felman, 'Rereading Feminity,' *Yale French Studies*, no. 62 (1981), pp. 19 and 21. The text she quotes from is Freud, 'Femininity,' in *New Introductory Lectures on Psychoanalysis*, trans. James Strachey (New York: Norton, 1965), p. 112. In his biography of Freud, Ernest Jones states: 'There is little doubt that Freud found the psychology of women more enigmatic than that of men. He said once to Marie Bonaparte: "The great question that has never been answered and which I have not yet been able to answer, despite my thirty years of research into the feminine soul, is 'What does a woman want?'"' (*Sigmund Freud: Life and Work*, vol. 2, London, 1955, p. 468).

Judith Roof, from *Come As You Are: Sexuality and Narrative**

See also:
Forster (1.ii)
Barthes (2.iii)
Todorov (2.iii)
Barthes (3.i)
Mulvey (4)
Bronfen (4)
Derrida (6)
Johnson (6)

COMING TO

I have never begun a novel with such misgiving. If I call it a novel it is only because I don't know what else to call it. I have a little story to tell and I end neither with a death nor a marriage. Death ends all things and so is the comprehensive conclusion of a story, but marriage finishes it very properly too and the sophisticated are ill-advised to sneer at what is by convention termed a happy ending. It is a sound instinct of the common people which persuades them that with this all that needs to be said is said. When male

* New York: Columbia University Press, 1996, pp. xiii–xxvi

and female, after whatever vicissitudes you like, are at last brought together they have fulfilled their biological function and interest passes to the generation that is to come.

W. Somerset Maugham, *The Razor's Edge*, p. 1)

. . .

THE NARRATIVE OF NARRATIVE

'To raise the question of the nature of narrative,' Hayden White observes, 'is to invite reflection on the very nature of culture and, possibly, even on the nature of humanity itself.' Linking narrative to culture and humanity, White sketches narrative's pivotal operation not as the mere proliferation of stories but rather as a complete and definitive engagement with our concepts of culture. Declaring narrative's total omnipresence, Roland Barthes asserts that 'narrative is international, transhistorical, transcultural: it is simply there, like life itself.' Of course, narrative is not 'simply there'; its shapes, assumptions, and operations manifest a complex, naturalized process of organization, relation, and connection. Narrative is so subtly and ubiquitously operative that I cannot even define it except through narrative – a narrative of narrative where parts come together to make a sensible whole. And you would not be able to comprehend my observations about narrative unless I cast them in a narrative form.

Narrative constantly reproduces the phantom of a whole, articulated system, where even the concept of a system is a product of narrative, where the idea that there are such things as parts and wholes is already an effect of a narrative organizing. As a pervasive sense of the necessary shape of events and their perception and as the process by which characters, causes, and effects combine into patterns recognized as sensical, narrative is the informing logic by which individuality, identity, and ideology merge into a cooperative and apparently unified vision of the truths of existence. As a set of ordering presumptions by which we make sense of perceptions, events, cause/effect relations (and even the idea that sense can be produced by a notion of cause/effect), and life, narrative permeates and orders any representation we make to ourselves or to others. As a cultural, psychological, ideological dynamic, narrative aligns disparate forces and elements into productive configurations of difference and opposition. These configurations produce the perpetual opportunity for synthesis, for totalizing, cathartic gestures linked to insight, knowledge, reproduction, and temporary stability.

Narrative's pervasiveness makes it difficult to locate. One discourse among many, narrative appears to organize our understandings of discourse and its divisions. Its omnipresence, ranging from the local and idiosyncratic to the cultural and philosophical, makes narrative seem both artifact and organizing principle, text and the embodiment of ideology itself. This sense of narrative ubiquity is further bolstered by the fact that narrative does not exist or operate separately from other modes – identity, ideology, subjectivity, and sexuality – by which we organize existence and experience. The significant categories of life are already narrative both in our apprehension of them as significant and in our understanding of that significance. While narrative's organizing function seems to situate it as a powerful ur-force, its ubiquity is probably more an effect of its representational capabilities. Narrative's intersection of language, psychology, and ideology makes it an appropriate and compelling construct for the negotiation and containment of the contradictions and anxieties that inevitably attend the focal and delusively stable organizations of existence.

Its myriad loci suggest that narrative both operates like ideology and is shaped by ideology. Generally speaking, 'ideology is the system of ideas and representations which dominate the mind of a man [*sic*] or a social group.' While this is Louis Althusser's reading of Marx's concept of ideology in a context quite different from any analysis of narrative, it has the virtue of proposing ideology as a system that operates in some relation to representations. For Althusser, ideology operates as a part of dominant apparatus, representing 'the imaginary relationship of individuals to their real conditions of existence'. The material conditions of production comprise the context for this rendering of ideology; ideology is one way the relations of production are reproduced. While narrative undoubtedly participates in constructing, managing, and reproducing this 'imaginary relationship,' narrative's far-reaching and diverse operation suggests that a less focused framework might better capture narrative's aegis.

Roland Barthes' rendering of ideology is probably more descriptive of an ideology coextensive with narrative's broad context. In his examination of the cultural operation of myth, Barthes sees bourgeois ideology as a particular confusion of nature and history, where the historical is rendered natural. While this confusion explains specific ways the bourgeoisie has rendered its interests universal, the model of an ideology that works through 'signs which pass themselves off as natural, which offer themselves as the only conceivable way of viewing the world,' which 'convert culture into nature,' which '"naturalize" social reality' and 'make it seem as innocent and unchangeable as Nature itself,' resonates with both narrative's ubiquity and its seemingly mimetic logic.

Narrative appears, thus, to reproduce natural experience, but the logic of its representation recalls Althusser's concern about how the relations of production are reproduced. While the 'natural' events that seem to account for narrative's shape – the events Maugham so nicely summarizes – appear to be natural, they are in fact not only reproductions of the quintessentially naturalized 'biological function' of human reproduction, they are also metaphors of capitalist relations of production. The connection between reproduction and production occurs in their common appeal to a productive joinder. Where in human reproduction male and female come together to produce offspring, in capitalist production capital and labor come together to generate products. Reiterating a similar dynamic – the same dynamic Maugham identifies as the model of a good novel – reproduction, production, and the ways that we understand and represent them are the very processes and institutions naturalized in and by ideology. The connection between human heterosexual reproduction and capitalist production provides an irresistible merger of family and state, life and livelihood, heterosexual order and profit whose formative presence and naturalized reiterations govern the conceptions, forms, logic, and operation of narrative. As ideology, this pattern of joinder to product also accounts for the countless analogies to child/product – knowledge, mastery, victory, another narrative, identity, and even death – that occupy the satisfying end of the story.

Narrative's apparent rendition of life experience, then, is already an ideological version of (re)production produced by the figurative cooperation of a naturalized capitalism and heterosexuality. Narrative's dynamic enacts ideology and narrative's constant production proliferates that ideology continually and naturally, as if it were simply a fact of life and sense itself.

Like trying to define narrative without narrative, how can we determine narrative's ideologies without somehow reiterating them? Looking for ideology as a defining characteristic means already acquiescing to an understanding of narrative that assumes that narrative has an ideology, that such an ideology might be discerned through reading narratives or theories of narrative, and that discovering such an ideology, like discovering an origin, would account for narrative's complex dynamic. But even the search for narrative's origin – for some primitive narrative that provides the pattern for all narratives – assumes narrative's conventional logic and assumptions. Refinding these assumptions in the place of an originary but fictive protonarrative means defining narrative and its ideology through narrative and its ideology. In other words, if positing an originary narrative risks an unwilling tautology – defining the conclusion by projecting it into the premises – such tautology is inevitable. The only way to combat it is to be aware of it, as long as that awareness is not itself already a narrative convention.

Since deducing an ideology cannot be accomplished except through ideology, perhaps I should look to those places where narrative asserts its own ideology 'with a vengeance,' as Teresa de Lauretis might characterize such excess, in those narratives openly about narrative. At least these cases offer the illusion that narrative speaks openly about itself. Privileging self-conscious narrative, however, still reflects the operation of an ideology (that consciousness and recognition of one's ideology exempts one from its operations), though self-reflectivity implies a more conscious, hence supposedly less self-interested site of analysis. The tendency to tautology is further deferred when several apparently self-reflective processes intersect; where, for example, self-conscious processes of narrative coalesce with the self-reflective analysis of human development as sometimes happens in Sigmund Freud's writings. Here the circular paradox of narrative ideology becomes visible at least on one level, since the coexistence and comparison of narrative's narrative and narratives of development bring their premises and interrelation into starker relief. This is not, however, to recommend a genre such as autobiography as an ideal specimen text, since what is crucial is not the self-reflectivity of the process of narrating 'self' but rather the sense that there is no subject, no 'self' to narrate, that self, like narration, cannot exist except through narrative. And even this connection does not escape the furtive cast of some preexistent narrative of narrative, some notion of the story's ending and how we get there.

THE NARRATIVE OF SEXUALITY

In the concluding 'Summary' to his 1905 'Three Essays on the Theory of Sexuality,' Sigmund Freud simultaneously narrates a brief history of human sexual development and his theory of it. It is not surprising that history and theory are entangled, since Freud's theory of sexuality in 1905 is already narrative, performing a politic of sexualities in narrative terms and a narrative dynamic in sexual terms. Freud's pervasive liquid metaphors of sexuality simultaneously serve as the fluid figures of narrative progress. Characterizing libido as a current of water whose physical demand is simply to flow freely to its destined end, Freud envisions both story and sexuality as a single strong stream gushing gleefully into the wide sea of human generation. This oceanic finale exalts both healthy heterosexuality and *the* satisfying story. Any impediments to an unobstructed flow force the current away from its appointed end into tiny, doomed side streams, their deviance spawning a degenerate or perverted story in place of the felicitous convergence of river and sea.

Freud begins his exposition of sexuality with an essay on the 'Sexual Aberrations.'
He begins this way not only because such aberrations contrast with the mechanisms
of normative sexuality but also because the sheer ubiquity of aberrations represents an
all-important rebuttal to what Freud summarizes as the existing mainstream, but incorrect
narrative of sexuality:

> Popular opinion has quite definite ideas about the nature and characteristics of
> this sexual instinct. It is generally understood to be absent in childhood, to set in
> at the time of puberty in connection to the process of coming to maturity and to
> be revealed in the manifestations of an irresistible attraction exercised by one sex
> upon the other; while its aim is presumed to be sexual union, or at all events actions
> leading in that direction.

Outlining a linear chronological trajectory from absence to presence, Freud characterizes
this narrative as a 'false picture' containing 'a number of errors, inaccuracies and hasty
conclusions'. One hasty conclusion is the narrative's conclusion, hasty because there
have not been enough impediments in the way of its realization. One inaccuracy is
infantile sexuality's absence from the beginning. But the real problem with the story is
that it is a completely unsatisfying narrative, going from nothing to something without
threat, risk, conflict, impediment, or motive. Without the possibility that something might
go wrong, the saving force of heterosexual attraction means nothing.

Freud's own narrative of sexuality begins with the aberrations that provide the
damming stuff against which the hero of normative heterosexuality must struggle. It is
as if Freud takes the narrative of sexuality apart, initially enacting aberrations' deviance
to prove that they are necessary to the story, highlighting their presence to underline his
understanding of the sexual narrative as complex, ambivalent, and suspenseful. Tracing
aberrations in the first essay and infantile sexuality in the second, Freud connects the
two in the third as necessary parts of the sexuality's narrative:

> We were thus led to regard any established aberration from normal sexuality as
> an instance of developmental inhibition and infantilism. Though it was necessary
> to place in the foreground the importance of the variations in the original dis-
> position, a cooperative and not an opposing relation was to be assumed as existing
> between them and the influences of actual life. It appeared, on the other hand,
> that since the original disposition is necessarily a complex one, the sexual instinct
> itself must be something put together from various factors, and that in the
> perversions it falls apart, as it were, into its components. The perversions were thus
> seen to be on the one hand inhibitions, and on the other hand dissociations, of
> normal development. Both these aspects were brought together in the supposition
> that the sexual instinct of adults arises from a combination of a number of impulses
> of childhood into a unity, an impulsion with a single aim.

Detailing a chronological narrative that proceeds from risky multiplicity to productive
singularity, Freud's story features a struggle and victory instead of the erroneous
account's inevitable and unmotivated line of least resistance. In his narrative, Freud
situates the perversions as the spot where the story falls apart, a spot that is also a part

of the story, serving its function as inhibition or dissociation only in relation to the narrative's ultimate end, 'the discharge of the sexual substances'. While 'the final outcome of sexual development lies in what is known as the normal sexual life of the adult, in which the pursuit of pleasure comes under the sway of the reproductive function and in which the component instincts, under the primacy of a single erotogenic zone, form a firm organization directed towards a sexual aim attached to some extraneous sexual object', perversions, chronologically and analogically linked to infancy and foreplay, threaten to substitute themselves for this normal end pleasure. 'The motive for proceeding further with the sexual process then disappears, for the whole path is cut short, and the preparatory act in question takes the place of the normal sexual aim'.

Supplanting the proper conclusion, perversions cut the story short, in a sense preventing a story at all by tarrying in its preparations. But this premature abridgment only has significance in relation to the 'normal'; we only know the story is cut short because we know what length the story is supposed to be. Perversion, then, acquires its meaning as perversion precisely from its threat to truncate the story; it distorts the narrative, preventing the desirable confluence of sexual aim and object and male and female, precluding the discharge of sexual substances, and hindering reproduction. And yet the aberrations are the foreplay necessary to ever getting to the end at all. Comprised of perversions, foreplay leads to the proper play of confluence and discharge; without perverse foreplay, no discharge would occur. An integral threat, the perversions are absolutely indispensable to the story; their possibility and presence complicate the narrative of sexuality, making Freud's story the right story – right because it is a narrative instead of the simplistic developmental trajectory commonly held to be the truth of sex, right because his narrative of sexuality reenacts sexuality's narrative configuration.

Freud, however, may be far more right about the story and its ideological imperatives than he is about the nature of sexuality. In his account the final leap from perversion to normalcy is accomplished without motive as the effect of an inherent, automatic, naturalized heterosexual desire. 'No doubt the strongest force working against a permanent inversion of the sexual object is the attraction which the opposing sexual characters exercise upon one another,' he speculates. And even if homosexuality, at least between men, might also result in the good end Freud assigns to the story – the desirable discharge of sexual substances – the underlying, satisfying requisite for the real story is not just discharge but discharge in the correct venue, naturally derived from the inevitable attraction between the sexes and leading to reproduction, the only function that can disqualify all but heterosexuality from the main stream.

In Freud's story, the naturalized primacy of heterosexuality constitutes a 'normal' that appears without motive, one that is so ideological as to be completely natural. The reproductive demand of the end of the story produces this normalcy rather than reproduction being the logical end to an inevitable – and irresistible – heterosexuality. Reproduction produces heterosexuality instead of heterosexuality necessarily leading to reproduction. This governing reproductive ideology is not any literal command to go forth and multiply; rather, it is the expression of an ideology of value and meaning that resides in the pattern of joiner to product where products parallel such other metaphorically reproductive yields as children, knowledge, and victory. The reproductive imperatives of the story produce heterosexuality as the magical, motiveless mechanism that turns everything right, while homosexuality and other perversions – also necessary elements – make all fail to cohere, exposing the story's parts in a meaningless, short-circuited, truncated, narrative gratification that heterosexuality seals up again. The sexual players have their metaphorical parts and the narrative has its reproductive engine.

THE SEXUALITY OF NARRATIVE

> Two women (instead of a woman and a man) overcoming parental opposition, surviving the wilderness, enjoying domestic bliss together, achieving orgasm with a finger instead of a penis is only Romeo and Juliet again with two differences: happy endings – of both kinds.
>
> (Bertha Harris, 'What We Mean to Say,' p. 6)

While Freud complicates and to some extent reverses the polarities of the commonly held account of sexual development, his understanding of sexuality is already heavily influenced by narrative, not as the specific shape of a specific story but as a way of organizing cause/effect relations. His narrative is already governed by a heterosexual ideology, or heteroideology, reflected both in the story of the development of literal heterosexuality and in the ways narrative functions to distribute sexualities in meta-phorical positions in a narrative dynamic that proceeds from parts to a whole, from little tributaries to the big stream that was there all along. Narrative's sexuality is, thus, not so much the literal heterosexual content of a story as D. A. Miller claims: 'the couple is in full and open possession of a story, a story, moreover, that one hardly exaggerates in our culture to call *the* story. Outside the heterosexual themes of marriage and oedipalized family (the former linked to the latter as its means of transmission), the plots of bourgeois life . . . would all be pretty much unthinkable.' Rather, our very understanding of narrative as a primary means to sense and satisfaction depends upon a metaphorically heterosexual dynamic within a reproductive aegis.

Its reproductive impetus and metaphorically sexualized positions of hetero versus homo do not, however, entirely define the sexuality of narrative. While for the most part Freud's story of sexuality explains rather than captures or expresses the sexualities it describes, when it brings diverse positions together in a coherent and meaningful whole coincident with the appearance of heterosexuality, it enacts heterosexuality through narrative's dynamic. In like fashion, the perverse, as in Freud's theory of sexuality, plays within and against structure. This perverse, as Roland Barthes elaborates it in *The Pleasure of the Text*, performs through the text of pleasure and the text of bliss, both fugitives from narrative, the former produced as the comfort yielded by going with 'the text that comes from culture and does not break with it,' and the latter generated by the narrative's edges, seductive appearances, in the 'seam' between 'culture and its destruction.'

For Barthes, a text's eroticism is only indirectly linked to a sexuality he locates as an appurtenance of the father. Defining sexuality as an 'Oedipal pleasure (to denude, to know, to learn the origin and the end)', the Oedipal pattern Barthes delineates is the same as the narrative dynamic I have just described as enacted by Freud's own narrative assumptions. Narrative and sexuality join at the Oedipal; therefore neither Barthes' text of pleasure nor bliss has a sexuality insofar as each exists apart from or in playful relation to that Oedipal. Instead they are erotic, gaining a sexual cast only when either the bliss of reading or the blissful text directly engages the Oedipal that imports the heterosexual, familial, masterful tropes of knowledge, identity, gender, and sexuality. Pleasure comes when the 'body pursues its own ideas', protected from Oedipal sexuality 'by perversion which shields bliss from the finality of reproduction'. Eroticism comes from a dynamic produced by a concatenation of edges, gaps, loss, and desire, but is structurally unfixed except as it coexists with and is produced and enjoyed despite cultural imperative.

Structurally, the counterreproductive perverse seems to occupy the space between sexuality and eroticism, between narrative and the body, between structure and an almost unimaginable lack of structure – that site structurally fixed at death or origins as the two loci where structure provides the illusion of the perverse's disappearance. While Freud categorizes homosexualities as perverse, as examples of something gone wrong at the beginning or end of the sexual story, the perverse in turn jeopardizes the sexual system itself, threatening no structure and no narrative in a system dependent upon both. It is tempting to locate Barthes' perverse bliss as a gay text, but to do so is to reinscribe bliss as a discrete category within a still governing narrative heteroideology. Defining the perverse as homosexual threatens to import the entire narrative heterodynamic, arresting textual play in favor of a fixed narrative impetus labeled homosexual.

Thus, one can only enjoy bliss without a structural fix. Its dynamic, vaguely parasitic on the memory of narrative, is textual rather than narrative, that is, is produced by properties of the text as text (language, image, rhetoric) as they play through and around narrative. To have sexuality is to have narrative; to have narrative is to have sexuality. As circular as this relation might seem, what is important is the distinction it suggests between structure as represented both by the desires of narrative and of sexuality and by a different desire, produced by the dynamic intersection of text and reading, narrative and not, and both at the same time.

6
Deconstruction

Jacques Derrida, 'The Law of Genre'*

See also:
Plato (1.i)
Aristotle (1.i)
Propp (1.iii)
Shlovsky (1.iii)
Lévi-Strauss (2.i)
Genette (2.ii)
Culler (2.ii)
Barthes (2.iii)
Todorov (2.iii)
Barthes (3.i)
Smith (3.ii)
Gibson (3.ii)
Lyotard (3.iii)
Mulvey (4)
Lanser (5)
Ricoeur (7)
Weber (8)
Bhabha (9)

What I shall try to convey to you now will not be called by its generic or modal name. I shall not say this drama, this epic, this novel, this novella or this *récit* – certainly not this *récit*. All of these generic or modal names would be equally valid or equally invalid for something which is not even quite a book, but which was published in 1973 in the editorial form of a small volume of thirty-two pages. It bears the title *La Folie du jour* [approximately: The Madness of the Day]. The author's name: Maurice Blanchot. In order to speak about it, I shall call this thing La Folie du jour, its given name which it bears legally and which gives us the right, as of its publication date, to identify and classify it in our copyright records at the Bibliothèque Nationale. One could fashion a non-finite number of readings from *La Folie du jour*. I have attempted a few myself, and shall do so again elsewhere, from another point of view. The *topos* of view, sight, blindness, *point of view* is, moreover, inscribed and traversed in *La Folie du jour* according to a sort of permanent revolution that engenders and virtually brings to the light of day points of view, twists, versions, and reversions of which the sum remains necessarily uncountable and the account, impossible. The deductions, rationalizations, and warnings that I must inevitably propose will arise, then, from an act of unjustifiable violence. A brutal and mercilessly depleting selectivity will obtrude upon me, upon us, in the name of a law that *La Folie du jour* has, in its turn, already reviewed, and with the foresight that a certain kind of police brutality is perhaps an inevitable accomplice to our concern for professional competence.

* *Critical Inquiry*, 7 (1980), pp. 62–70.

What will I ask of *La Folie du jour*? To answer, to testify, to say what it has to say with respect to the law of mode or the law of genre and, more precisely, with respect to the law of the *récit*, which, as we have just been reminded, is a mode and not a genre.

On the cover, below the title, we find no mention of genre. In this most peculiar place that belongs neither to the title nor to the subtitle, nor even simply to the corpus of the work, the author did not affix, although he has often done so elsewhere, the designation '*récit*' or 'novel,' maybe (but only maybe) by erroneously subsuming both of them, Genette would say, under the unique category of the genre. About this designation which figures elsewhere and which appears to be absent here, I shall say only two things:

1   On the one hand it commits one to nothing. Neither reader nor critic nor author are bound to believe that the text preceded by this designation conforms readily to the strict, normal, normed, or normative definition of the genre, to the law of the genre or of the mode. Confusion, irony, the shift in conventions toward a new definition (in what name should it be prohibited?), the search for a supplementary effect, any of these things could prompt one to entitle as *novel* or *récit* what in truth or according to yesterday's truth would be neither one nor the other. All the more so if the words '*récit*,' 'novel,' '*ciné-roman*,' 'complete dramatic works' or, for all I know, 'literature' are no longer in the place which conventionally mentions genre but, as has happened and will happen again (shortly), they are found to be holding the position and function of the title itself, of the work's given name.

2   Blanchot has often had occasion to modify the genre-designation from one version of his work to the next or from one edition to the next. Since I am unable to cover the entire spectrum of this problem, I shall simply cite the example of the '*récit-*' designation effaced between one version and the next of *Death Sentence* (trans. Lydia Davis (Barrytown, NY, 1978)) at the same time as a certain epilogue is removed from the end of a double *récit* which, in a manner of speaking, constitutes this book. This effacement of '*récit*,' leaving a trace that, inscribed and filed away, remains as an effect of supplementary relief which is not easily accounted for in all of its facets. I cannot arrest the course of my lecture here, no more than I can pause to consider the very scrupulous and minutely differentiated distribution of the designations '*récit*' and 'novel' from one narrative work to the next, no more than I can question whether Blanchot distinguished the genre and mode designations, no more than I can discuss Blanchot's entire discourse on the difference between the narratorial voice and the narrative voice which is, to be sure, something other than a mode. I would point out only one thing; at the very moment the first version of *Death Sentence* appears, bearing mention as it does of '*récit*,' the first version of *La Folie du jour* is published with another title about which I shall momentarily speak.

La Folie du jour, then, makes no mention of genre or mode. But the word '*récit*' appears at least four times in the last two pages in order to name the theme of *La Folie du jour*, its sense or its story, its content or part of its content – in any case, its decisive proceedings and stakes. It is a *récit* without a theme and without a cause entering from the outside; yet it is without interiority. It is the *récit* of an impossible *récit* whose 'production' occasions what happens or, rather, what remains, but which does not relate it, nor relate to it as to an outside reference, even if everything remains foreign to it and out of bounds. It is even less feasible for me to relate to you the story of *La Folie du jour* which is staked precisely on the possibility and the impossibility of relating a story. Nonetheless, in order to create the greatest possible clarity, in the name of daylight itself, that is to say (as will become clear), in the name of the law, I shall take the calculated risk of flattening out the unfolding or coiling up of this text, its permanent revolution whose rounds are made to recoil from any kind of flattening. And this is why the one who says 'I,' and the one after all who speaks to us, who 'recites' for us, this one who says 'I' tells his inquisitors that he cannot manage to constitute himself as narrator (in the sense of the term that is not necessarily literary) and tells them that he cannot manage to identify with himself sufficiently or to remember himself well enough to gather the story and *récit* that are demanded of him – which the representatives of society and the law require of him. The one who says 'I' (who does not manage to say 'I') seems to relate what has happened to him or, rather, what has nearly happened to him after presenting himself in a mode that defies all norms of self-presentation: he nearly lost his sight (his facility for *viewing*) following a traumatic event – probably an assault. I say 'probably' because *La Folie du jour* wholly upsets, in a discrete but terribly efficient manner, all the certainties upon which so much of discourse is constructed: the value of an event, first of all, of reality, of fiction, of appearance and so on, all this being carried away by the disseminal and mad polysemny of 'day,' of the word 'day,' which, once again, I cannot dwell upon here. Having nearly lost his sight (*vue*), having been taken in by a kind of medico-social institution, he now resides under the watchful eye of doctors, handed over to the authority of these specialists who are representatives of the law as well, legist doctors who demand that he testify – and in his own interest, or so it seems at first – about what happened to him so that remedial justice may be dispensed. His faithful *récit* – (but let me borrow for the sake of simplicity, and because it conforms fairly well to this context, the English word 'account') – hence, his faithful account of events should render justice unto the law. The law demands a narrative account.

   Pronounced four times in the last three pages of *La Folie du jour*, the word 'account' does not seem to designate a literary genre but rather a certain type or mode of discourse. That is, in effect, the appearance of it. Everything seems to happen as if the account – the question of or rather the demand for the account, the response, and the nonresponse to the demand – found itself staged and figured as one of the themes, objects, stakes in a more bountiful text, *La Folie du jour* whose genre would be of another order and would in any case overstep the boundaries of the account with all its generality and all its genericity. The account itself would of course not cover this generic generality of the literary corpus named *La Folie du jour*. Now we might already feel inclined to consider this appearance suspect, and we might be jolted from our certainties by an allusion that 'I' will make: the one who says 'I,' who is not by force of necessity a narrator, nor necessarily always the same, notes that the representatives of the law, those who demand of him an account in the name of the law, consider and treat him, in his personal and civil identity, not only as an 'educated' man – and an educated man, they often tell him, ought to be able to speak and recount; as a competent subject, he ought to be able to know how to piece together a story by saying 'I' and 'exactly' how things happened to him – they regard him not only as an 'educated' man, but also as a writer. He is writer and reader, a creature of 'libraries,' *the* reader of this account. This is not sufficient cause, but it is, in any case, a first clue and one whose impact incites us to think that the required account does not simply remain in a relationship that is extraneous to literature or even to a literary genre. Lest we not be content with this suspicion, let us weigh the possibility of the inclusion of a modal structure within a vaster, more general corpus, whether literary or not and whether or not related to the genre. Such an inclusion raises questions concerning edge, borderline, boundary, and abounding which do not arise without a fold.

What sort of a fold? According to which fold and which figure of enfoldment?

Here are the three final paragraphs; they are of unequal length, with the last of these comprising approximately one line:

They demanded: Tell us 'exactly' how things happened. – An account? I began: I am neither learned nor ignorant. I have known some joy. This is saying too little. I related the story in its entirety, to which they listened, it seems, with great interest – at least initially. But the end was a surprise for them all. 'After that beginning,' they said, 'you should proceed to the facts.' How so? The account was over.

I should have realized that I was incapable of composing an account of these events. I had lost the sense of the story; this happens in a good many illnesses. But this explanation only made them more demanding. Then I noticed, for the first time, that they were two and that this infringement on their traditional method – even though it can be explained away by the fact that one of them was an eye doctor, the other a specialist in mental illnesses – increasingly gave our conversation the character of an authoritarian interrogation, overseen and controlled by a strict set of rules. To be sure, neither of them was the chief of police. But being two, due to that, they were three, and this third one remained firmly convinced, I am sure, that a writer, a man who speaks and reasons with distinction, is always capable of recounting the facts which he remembers.

An account? No, no account, nevermore.

In the first of the three paragraphs that I have just cited, he claims that something is to begin after the word 'account' punctuated by a question mark (An account? – herein implied: they want an account, is it then an account that they want? 'I began . . .'). This something is nothing other than the first line on the first page of *La Folie du jour*. These are the same words, in the same order, but this is not a citation in the strict sense for, stripped of quotation marks, these words commence or recommence a quasi-account that will engender anew the entire sequence comprising this new point of departure. In this way, the first words ('I am neither learned nor ignorant . . .') that come after the word 'account' and its question mark, that broach the beginning of the account extorted by the law's representatives – these first words mark a collapse that is unthinkable, irrepresentable, unsituable within a linear order of succession, within a spatial or temporal sequentiality, within an objectifiable topology or chronology. One sees, without seeing, one reads the crumbling of an upper boundary or of the initial edge in *La Folie du jour*, uncoiled according to the 'normal' order, the one regulated by common law, editorial convention, positive law, the regime of competency in our logo-alphabetical culture, etc. Suddenly, this upper or initial boundary, which is commonly called the first line of a book, is forming a pocket inside the corpus. It is taking the form of an *invagination* through which the trait of the first line, the borderline, splits while remaining the same and traverses yet also bounds the corpus. The 'account' which he claims is beginning at the end and, by legal requisition, is none other than the one that has begun from the beginning of *La Folie du jour* and in which, therefore, he gets around to saying that he begins, etc. And it is without beginning or end, without content and without edge. There is only content without edge – without boundary or frame – and there is only edge without content. The inclusion (or occlusion, inocclusive invagination) is interminable: it is an analysis of the account that can only turn in circles in an unarrestable, inenarrable, and insatiably recurring manner – but one terrible for those who, in the name of the law, require that order reign in the account, for those who want to know, with all the required competence, 'exactly' how this happens. For if 'I' or 'he' continued to tell what he has told, he would end up endlessly returning to this point and beginning again to begin, that is to say, to begin with an end that precedes the beginning. And from the viewpoint of objective space and time, the point at which he stops is absolutely unascertainable ('I have told them the entire story . . .'), for there is no 'entire' story except for the one that interrupts itself in this way.

A lower edge of invagination will, if one can say so, respond to this 'first' invagination of the upper edge by intersecting it. The 'final line' resumes the question posed *before* the 'I began' (An account?) and bespeaks a resolution or promises it, tells of the commitment made no longer to give an account. As if he had already given one! And yet, yes (yes and no), an account has taken place. Hence the last word: 'An account? No, no account, nevermore.' It has been impossible to decide whether the recounted event and the event of the account itself ever took place. Impossible to decide whether there was an account, for the one who barely manages to say 'I' and to constitute himself as narrator recounts that he has not been able to recount – but what, exactly? Well, everything, including the demand for an account. And if an assured and guaranteed decision is impossible, this is because there is nothing more to be done than to commit oneself, to perform, to wager, to allow chance its chance – to make a decision that is essentially edgeless, bordering perhaps only on madness.

Yet another impossible decision follows, one which involves the promise 'No, no account, nevermore': Is this promise a part of or apart from the account? Legally speaking, it is party to *La Folie du jour*, but not necessarily to the account or to the simulacrum of the account. Its trait splits again into an internal and external edge. It repeats – without citing – the question apparently posed above (an account?) of which it can be said that, in this permanent revolution of order, it follows, doubles, or reiterates it in advance. Thus another lip or invaginating loop takes shape here. This time the lower edge creates a pocket in order to come back into the corpus and to rise again on this side of the upper or initial line's line of invagination. This would form a double chiasmatic invagination of edges:

A   'I am neither learned nor ignorant . . .'
B   'An account? I began:'
A'   'I am neither learned nor ignorant . . .'
B'   'An account? No, no account, nevermore . . .'

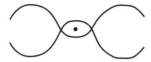

'I began . . .'

It is thus impossible to decide whether an event, account, account of event, or event of accounting took place. Impossible to settle upon the simple borderlines of this corpus, of this ellipse unremittingly repealing itself within its own expansion. When we fall back on the poetic consequences enfolded within this dilemma, we find that it becomes difficult indeed to speak here with conviction about an account as a determined mode included within a more general corpus or one simply related, in its determination, to other modes or, quite simply, to something other than itself. All is narrative account and nothing is; the account's outgate remains within the account in a non-inclusive mode, and this structure is itself related so remotely to a dialectical structure that it even inscribes dialectics in the account's ellipse. All is account, nothing is: and we shall not know whether the relationship between these two propositions – the strange conjunction of the account and the accountless – belongs to the account itself. What indeed happens when the edge pronounces a sentence?

Faced with this type of difficulty – the consequences or implications of which cannot be deployed here – one might be tempted to take recourse in the law or the rights which govern published texts. One might be tempted to argue as follows: all these insoluble problems of delimitation are raised 'on the inside' of a book classified as a work of literature or literary fiction. Pursuant to these juridical norms, this book has a beginning and an end that leave no opening for indecision. This book has a determinable beginning and end, a title, an author, a publisher, its distinctive denomination is *La Folie du jour*. At this place, where I am pointing, on this page, right here, you can see its first word; here, its final period, perfectly situable in objective space. And all the sophisticated transgressions, all the infinitesimal subversions that may captivate you are not possible except within this enclosure for which these transgressions and subversions moreover maintain an essential need in order to take place. Furthermore, on the inside of this normed space, the word 'account' does not name a literary operation or genre, but a current mode of discourse, and it does so regardless of the formidable problems of structure, edge, set theory, the part and whole, etc., that it raises in this 'literary' corpus.

That is all well and good. But in its very relevance, this objection cannot be sustained – for example, it cannot save the modal determination of the account – except by referring to extra-literary and even extra-linguistic juridical norms. The objection makes an appeal to the law and calls to mind the fact that the subversion of La Folie du jour needs the law in order to take place. Whereby the objection reproduces and accomplishes its staging within *La Folie du jour*: the account, mandated and prescribed by law but also, as we shall see, commanding, requiring, and producing law in turn. In short, the whole critical scene of competence in which we are engaged is *party to and* part of *La Folie du jour* in whole and in part, the whole is a part.

The whole does nothing but begin. I could have begun with what resembles the absolute beginning, with the juridico-historical order of this publication. What has been lightly termed the first version of *La Folie du jour* was not a book. Published in the journal *Empédocle* (2 May 1949), it bore another title – indeed, several other titles. On the journal's cover, here it is, one reads:

> Maurice Blanchot
> *Un récit?*
> [*An Account?*]

Later, the question mark disappears twice. First, when the title is reproduced within the journal in the table of contents:

> Maurice Blanchot
> *Un récit*
> [*An Account*],

then below the first line:

Un récit	[*An Account*
par	by
Maurice Blanchot	M. B.]

Could you tell whether these titles, written earlier and filed away in the archives, make up a single title, titles of the same text, titles of the account (which of course figures as an impracticable mode in the book), or the title of a genre? Even if the latter were to cause some confusion, it would be of the sort that releases questions already implemented and enacted by *La Folie du jour*. This enactment enables in turn the denaturalization and deconstitution of the oppositions nature/history and mode/genre.

Now let us turn to some of these questions. First, to what could the words 'An Account' refer in their manifold occurrences and diverse punctuations? And precisely how does reference function here? In one case, the question mark can *also* serve as a supplementary remark indicating the necessity of all these questions as the insolvent character or indecision: Is this an account? Is it an account that I entitle? asks the title in entitling. Is it an account that they want? What entitles them? Is it an account as discursive mode or as literary operation, or perhaps even as literary genre whose theme would be mode or genre? Likewise, the title could excerpt, as does a metonymy, a fragment of the account without an account (to wit, the words 'an account' with and without a question mark), but such an iterative excepting is not citational. For the title, guaranteed and protected by law but also making law, retains a referential structure which differs radically from the one underlying other occurrences of the 'same' words in the text. Whatever the issue – title, reference, or mode and genre – the case before us always involves the law and, in particular, the relations formed around and to law. All the questions which we have just addressed can be traced to an enormous matrix that generates the non-thematizable thematic power of a simulated account: it is this inexhaustible writing which recounts without telling, and which speaks without recounting.

Account of an accountless account, an account without edge or boundary, account all of whose visible space is but some border of itself without 'self,' consisting of the framing edge without content, without modal or generic boundaries – such is the law of this textual event, of this text that also speaks the law, its own and that of the other as reader of this text which, speaking the law, also imposes itself as a law text, as the text of the law. What, then, is the law of the genre of this singular text? It is law, it is the figure of the law which will also be the invisible center, the themeless theme of *La Folie du jour* or, as I am now entitled to say, of 'An account?'

Paul de Man, 'Reading (Proust)'*

See also
Booth (1.iii)
Culler (2.ii)
Barthes (3.i)
Smith (3.ii)
Brooks (3.ii)
Lyotard (3.iii)
Ricoeur (7)
Felman (8)
Said (9)
Bhabha (9)

The central text on reading [standard French edition of Proust (Paris: Bibliotheque de la Pleiade)] (p. 83, 1. 38 to p. 88, 1. 16) develops in the wake of this initial complication. It has all the appearances of a set piece, so firmly constructed that it constantly attracts attention to its own system and invites representation by means of synoptic diagrams. The text follows 'from inside to outside the layers simultaneously juxtaposed in [the] consciousness . . .' of the reader (p. 87, 1. 22). It extends the complexity of a single moment in time upon an axis oriented from maximum intimacy to the external world. This construct is not temporal, for it involves no duration. The diachrony of the passage, as the narrative moves from a center towards a periphery, is the spatial representation of a differential but complementary articulation within one single moment. For a novel that claims to be the narrative extension of one single moment of recollection, the passage undoubtedly has paradigmatic significance. The transposition of the present moment into a consecutive sequence would correspond to the act of fiction-writing as the narration of the moment. This act would then be coextensive with the act of self-reading by means of which the narrator and the writer, now united in one, fully understand their present situation (including all its negative aspects) by means of the retrospective recapitulation of its genesis. Nor would it differ from the response available to the reader of *A la recherche du temps perdu* who, mediated by Proust's novel, understands the narrative voice as the dispenser of a true knowledge that also includes him.[1] The 'moment' and the 'narration' would be complementary and symmetrical, specular reflections of each other that could be substituted without distortion. By an act of memory or of anticipation,

---

* *Allegories of Reading: Figural Language in Rousseau, Nietzsche, Rilke and Proust* (New Haven, CT: Yale University Press, 1979), pp. 67–72.

the narrative can retrieve the full experience of the moment. We are back in the totalizing world of the metaphor. Narrative is the metaphor of the moment, as reading is the metaphor of writing.

The passage is indeed ordered around a central, unifying metaphor, the 'single and unbending projection of all the forces of my life' ('même et infléchissable jaillissement de toutes les forces de ma vie') within which the various levels of reading are said to constitute 'sections at the different levels of an iridescent fountain that appeared to be motionless'[2] (p. 87, II. 18–19). The figure aims at the most demanding of reconciliations, that of motion and stasis, a synthesis that is also at stake in the model of narrative as the diachronic version of a single moment. The continuous flow ('jaillissement') of the narrative represents an identity that is beyond the senses and beyond time as something accessible to sight and sensation and therefore comprehensible and articulated, just as the unique and timeless[3] fascination of reading can be divided into consecutive layers shaped like the concentric rings of a tree trunk. Within a closed system of part and whole, the complementarity of the vertical juxtaposition and the horizontal succession is firmly established. With regard to the narrative, the proof of this complementarity will be the absence of interruptions, the lack of jagged edges which allows for the characterization of the novel's narrative texture as a play of fragmentation and reunification that can be called 'fondu,' (i.e. smooth (Gérard Genette)) or 'soudé' (i.e. welded (Proust)).[4] The continuity is not only apparent in the fluency of the transitions or in the numberless symmetries of the composition, but also in the strict coherence between meaning and structure. The passage is a persuasive case in point: to the stated assertion that reading is grounded in a firm relationship between inside and outside corresponds a text that is structured in a particularly rigorous and systematic way. But if the complementarity were to be an illusion, a very different story would ensue, more like the loss of entropy that occurs as one moves from Françoise's hot coffee to the kitchen maid's tepid shaving water.

The persuasive value of the passage depends on one's reading of the fountain as an entity which is both immobile and iridescent. The iridescence is prefigured a few pages earlier in the description of consciousness as a 'shimmering screen' ('un écran diapré') (p. 84, 1. 13). The miraculous interference of water and light in the refracted rainbow of the color spectrum makes its appearance throughout the novel, infallibly associated with the thematics of metaphor as totalization.[5] It is the perfect analogon for the figure of complementarity, the differences that make up the parts absorbed in the unity of the whole as the colors of the spectrum are absorbed in the original white light. The solar myth of *A la recherche du temps perdu* would then be condensed in the scarf of Iris, as when the flower metaphors associated with girls and women are said to 'appear at once on their two sides, like complementary colors' (p. 86, 1. 20). The 'necessary link' between the imagined figure and its sensory qualities make it more seductive than the empirical, 'real' landscape of Combray. Unlike this real landscape, the symbolic one is 'a true part of Nature itself, worthy of study and meditation' (p. 86, 1. 34).

The superiority of the 'symbolic' metaphor over the 'literal,' prosaic, metonymy is reasserted in terms of chance and necessity. Within the confines of the fiction, the relationship between the figures is indeed governed by the complementarity of the literal and the figural meaning of the metaphor. Yet the passage seems oddly unable to remain sheltered within this intra-textual closure. The complementarity is first asserted with reference to the narrator's relationship to the landscape he inhabits, but it soon extends towards another binary set of themes, those of 'love' and 'voyage': 'Therefore, if I always imagined, surrounding the woman I loved, the landscape I most keenly wished to see at that moment . . . it was not because a mere association of ideas existed between them. No, it is because my dreams of love and of travel were only moments – which I now artificially disentangle . . . – in the single and unbending projection of all the forces of my life' (p. 87, II. 11–21). But what is here called 'love' and 'travel' are not, like the narrator and his natural setting, two intra-textual moments in a fiction, but rather the irresistible motion that forces any text beyond its limits and projects it towards an exterior referent. The movement coincides with the need for a meaning. Yet at the beginning of the passage Marcel has stated the impossibility for any consciousness to get outside itself, suggesting this very ideality, paradoxically enough, by means of an analogy derived from a physical phenomenon: 'When I saw something external, my awareness of the fact that I was seeing it remained between the object and myself, bordering it as with a thin spiritual layer that prevented me from touching it directly; the object would evaporate, so to speak, before I could come into contact with it, just as a red-hot body that approaches a wet object is unable to touch its humidity, since it is always preceded by a zone of vapor' (p. 84, II. 5–13). Three pages further on, it seems that the language of consciousness is unable to remain thus ensconced and that, like so many objects and so many moments in Proust's novel, it has to turn itself out and become the outer enveloping surface.[6] For if we have the impression of being constantly surrounded by our consciousness [âme], it is not as by an unmovable prison; much rather, we feel carried by it in a perpetual impulse to move beyond itself and to reach outside . . .' (p. 86, 11. 39–42). The epistemological significance of this impulse is clearly stated when, a few paragraphs earlier, we heard of a 'central belief . . . that made ceaseless motions from inside outward, toward the discovery of truth' (p. 84, II. 36–7). Like Albertine, consciousness refuses to be captive and has to take flight and move abroad. This reversal by which the intra-textual complementarity chooses to submit itself to the test of truth is caused by 'the projection of all the forces of life.'

Proust's novel leaves no doubt that this test must fail; numberless versions of this failure appear throughout the pages of the *Recherche*. In this section, it is stated without ambiguity: 'We try to find again, in things that have thus become dear to us, the reflection that our consciousness [âme] has projected upon them; we are disappointed in discovering that, in their natural state, they lack the seduction that, in our imagination, they owed to the proximity of certain ideas . . .' (p. 87, 11. 2–7). Banal when taken by itself, the observation acquires considerable negative power in context, when one notices that it occurs at the center of a passage whose thematic and rhetorical strategy it reduces to naught. For if the 'proximity' between the thing and the idea of the thing fails to pass the test of truth, then it fails to acquire the complementary and totalizing power of metaphor and remains reduced to 'the chance of a mere association of ideas.' The co-presence of intra- and extra-textual movements never reaches a synthesis. The relationship between the literal and the figural senses of a metaphor is always, in this sense, metonymic, though motivated by a constitutive tendency to pretend the opposite.

The image of the iridescent fountain is a clear case in point. Everything orients the trope towards the seduction of metaphor: the sensory attractiveness, the context, the affective connotations, all cooperate to this aim. As soon however as one follows Proust's

own injunction to submit the reading to the polarity of truth and error (a gesture that
can be repressed but never prevented), statements or strategies that tended to remain
unnoticed become apparent and undo what the figure seemed to have accomplished. The
shimmering of the fountain then becomes a much more disturbing movement, a vibration
between truth and error that keeps the two readings from converging. The disjunction
between the aesthetically responsive and the rhetorically aware reading, both equally
compelling, undoes the pseudo-synthesis of inside and outside, time and space, container
and content, part and whole, motion and stasis, self and understanding, writer and reader,
metaphor and metonymy, that the text has constructed. It functions like an oxymoron,
but since it signals a logical rather than a representational incompatibility, it is in fact
an aporia. It designates the irrevocable occurrence of at least two mutually exclusive
readings and asserts the impossibility of a true understanding. on the level of the figuration
as well as of the themes.

The question remains whether by thus allowing the text to deconstruct its own metaphors
one recaptures the actual movement of the novel and comes closer to the negative
epistemology that would reveal its hidden meaning. Is this novel the allegorical narrative
of its own deconstruction? Some of its most perceptive recent interpreters seem to think
so when they assert, like Gilles Deleuze, the 'powerful unity' of the *Recherche* despite
its inherent fragmentation or, like Genette, stress the 'solidity of the text' despite the
perilous shuttle between metaphor and metonymy.

What is at stake is the possibility of including the contradictions of reading in a
narrative that would be able to contain them. Such a narrative would have the universal
significance of an allegory of reading. As the report of the contradictory interference of
truth and error in the process of understanding, the allegory would no longer be subject
to the destructive power of this complication. To the extent that it is not itself demon-
strably false, the allegory of the play of truth and falsehood would ground the stability
of the text.

NOTES

1   'In truth, each reader is, when he reads, the actual [*propre*] reader of himself' (3:911).
2   In a famous passage of *The Prelude*, Wordsworth speaks of 'The stationary blast of
        waterfalls' (VI, 1. 626). A more literal and less benevolent version of this same waterspout
        appears in *Sodome et Gomorrhe*: the fountain designed by Hubert Robert that splashes
        Mme d'Arpajon to the great merriment of the grand duke Wladimir (2:657).
3   '. . . the concentration of my reading, like the magic of a deep sleep . . . had erased the ringing
        of the golden church bells on the sky-blue surface of silence' (1:88, II. 2–5).
4   For example, in a passage referring to Vinteuil's septuor: '. . . two entirely different modes
        of questioning, the one breaking up a pure and continuous line into brief requests, the
        other welding [*soudant*] stray fragments into one single, sturdy frame' (3:255). Gérard
        Genette ('Métonymie chez Proust,' p. 60) mentions a passage from Proust's correspondence
        (*Correspondence* [Paris, 1970], 2:86) which uses the expression 'espèce de fondu.'
5   Some examples among many others: Elstir's workshop is compared to a 'block of rock-
        crystal, of which one of the facets, already cut and polished, shines like an iridescent mirror'
        (1:835); Françoise's famous asparagus 'reveal in their nascent colors of early dawn, in their

suggestions of rainbows . . . [their] costly essence' (1:121); 'if I could have analyzed the prism [of the duchess de Guermante's eyes] . . . the essence of the unknown life that appeared in them might have been revealed to me' (2:53); 'the art of Vinteuil, like that of Elstir, reveals [the ineffable character of individuality] by expressing into the colors of the spectrum the intimate being of the worlds we call individuals . . .' (3:258); 'just as the spectrum represents for us the composition of light, the harmony of a Wagner or the color of an Elstir allows us to know the qualitative essence of another individual's sensations . . .' (3:159).

6   The metonymy by which the covered-up entity becomes its own cover [*enveloppé* becoming *enveloppant*] is much in evidence in the concluding section of this passage, where 'the afternoons have gradually surrounded and enclosed' the hours: the spatial container becomes the temporally contained, and vice versa. The famous passage on the 'carafes de in Vivonne' (1:168) is the *locus classicus* of this figure. Gérard Genette quotes it, and it has since been much commented upon, without however exhausting the connotations of its context and of its tropological significance. Walter Benjamin well perceived the importance of this metonymy when he compared Proust's figures to a rolled-up sock which is its own outside and which, when unrolled, like the Möbius strip, is also its own inside ('Zum Rude Proust,' *Illuminationen* (Frankfurt am Main, 1955), p. 308).

J. Hillis Miller, 'Line'*

See also:
Aristotle (1.i)
Genette (2.ii)
Culler (2.ii)
Barthes (3.i)
Brooks (3.ii)
Heath (4)
Bronfen (4)
Ricoeur (7)
Kellner (8)
Bhabha (9)

How should the critic thread her or his way into the labyrinthine problems of narrative form, and in particular into the problem of repetition in fiction? The line of the line itself? The motif, image, concept, or formal model of the line, however, far from being a 'clue' to the labyrinth, turns out . . . to be itself the labyrinth. To follow the motif of the line will not be to simplify the knotted problems of narrative form but to retrace the whole tangle from the starting place of a certain point of entry.

    . . .

To begin at the beginning with the physical aspects of the book, the novel as book, its conditions of production and use. The linearity of the written or printed book is a puissant support of logocentrism. The writer, Walter Pater or Elizabeth Gaskell, George Eliot or Charles Dickens, sits at a desk and spins out on the page a long thread or filament of ink. Word follows word from the beginning to the end. The manuscript is set for printing in the same way, whether letter by letter, by linotype, or from tape by computer. The

---

* *Ariadne's Thread: Storylines* (New Haven, CT: Yale University Press, 1992), pp. 1–25.

reader follows, or is supposed to follow, the text in the same way, reading word by word and line by line from the beginning to the end. This linearity is broken, in the Victorian novel for example, only by the engravings that juxtapose 'illustrations' in another medium to the continuous flow of printed words, or by anything in the words on the page which in one way or another says, see page so and so. An example of this is the repetition from one place to another of the same word, phrase, or image. The physical, social, and economic conditions of the printing and distribution of Victorian books, that is, the breaking of the text into numbered or titled parts, books, or chapters, and publication in parts either separately or with other material in a periodical, interrupts this linearity but does not transform it into something else. The text of a Victorian novel, to remain with that as prime example for the moment, with its divisions into chapters and parts, is like bits of string laid end to end in series. Its publication in parts over a period of time that, in the case of Dickens's big novels, was almost two years in length, only emphasizes this linearity. Publication in parts gives that linearity an explicitly temporal dimension, a dimension already present in the time it takes to follow a novel word by word, line by line, page by page. Victorian readers had to read one part of *Bleak House* and then, after an interval, the next part, and so on. The spurious instantaneous unity or simultaneity of the single volume held in one's hand was further broken by the fact that Victorian novels, even when their scattered parts were gathered in volume form, were often printed in two, three, or even four volumes. The linearity of a novel is always temporal. It is an image of time as a line. Martin Heidegger, in *Sein und Zeit* and elsewhere, has shown how all the language of temporality is contaminated by spatial terms. From Aristotle on, according to Heidegger, this spatializing of time has reinforced the systematic assumptions of logocentric metaphysics. More recently, Paul Ricoeur, in *Temps et récit*, has explored the relation between notions of time in Aristotle and St Augustine and forms of narrative coherence in our tradition.[1] One must distinguish sharply, however, between effects of discontinuity, spaces or hiatuses between segments of a narrative line, and true disturbances of the line that make it curve back on itself, recross itself, tie itself in knots. Those spaces may have a powerful effect, in one way or another, on the meaning, but they are not in themselves forms of repetition breaking linearity.

. . .

The image of the line, it is easy to see, cannot be detached from the problem of repetition. Repetition might be defined as anything that happens to the line to trouble its straightforward linearity: returnings, knottings, recrossings, crinklings to and fro, suspensions, interruptions. As Ruskin says in *Fors Clavigera*, the Daedalian labyrinth, made from a single thread or path curved and recurved, may serve as a model for everything 'linear and complex' since. The phrase is an oxymoron. It names a line that is not simply linear, not a straightforward movement from beginning to middle to end. In what follows, I shall explore the way linear terminology and linear form used to discuss realistic fiction subverts itself by becoming 'complex' – knotted, repetitive, doubled, broken, phantasmal.

To put down first, pell-mell, like the twisted bits of string in the pockets of the narrator of *Cranford*, some line images as they are associated with narrative form or with the everyday terminology of storytelling: narrative line, lifeline, byline, main line, drop me

a line, 'break up their lines to weep,' linotype, what's my line?, genealogical line, genetic
strain, affiliation, defile, thread of the story, ficelle, lineaments, crossroads, impasse,
dénouement, cornered, loose thread, marginal, trope, chiasmus, hyperbole, crisis, double
bind, tie that binds, circulation, recoup, engraving, beyond the pale, trespass, crossing
the bar, missing link, marriage tie, couple, coupling, copulation, plot, double plot, subplot, spin a yarn, get an angle on, the end of the line.

It may be possible gradually to untwist these hanks, to lay them end to end in a
neat series, to make an orderly chain of them, knot added to knot in macramé, or to
crochet them into a fabric making a visible figure, a figure in the carpet. Initially to be
emphasized is how rich and complex is the family of terms involving the line image
– figures of speech, idioms, slang, conceptual words, or narrative motifs like Hercules
at the crossroads. Dozens of examples spring to mind in proliferating abundance, like
a tangled skein of yarn bits. This is especially the case if the line is extended slightly to
include the adjacent figures of cutting, weaving, and setting limits, drawing boundary
lines. How can one find the law of this tangled multitude or set limits to it? The notions
of legislation (imposed from without or found within) and of boundary are themselves
already images of the line. (*Lex* is from the root *lege*, to collect. It is the same root as
that for *logic* and coil.) The thing to be defined enters into and contaminates the definer,
according to a recurrent aporia.

One can see that the line image, in whatever region of narrative terms it is used,
tends to be logocentric, monological. The model of the line is a powerful part of the
traditional metaphysical terminology. It cannot easily be detached from these implications
or from the functions it has within that system. Narrative event follows narrative event
in a purely metonymic line, but the series tends to organize itself or to be organized into
a causal chain. The chase has a beast in view. The end of the story is the retrospective
revelation of the law of the whole. That law is an underlying 'truth' that ties all together
in an inevitable sequence revealing a hitherto hidden figure in the carpet. The image of
the line tends always to imply the norm of a single continuous unified structure determined by one external organizing principle. This principle holds the whole line together,
gives it its law, controls its progressive extension, curving or straight, with some *arché*,
telos, or ground. Origin, goal, or base: all three come together in the gathering movement of logos. *Logos* in Greek meant transcendent word, speech, reason, proportion,
substance, or ground. The word comes from *legein*, to gather, as in English collect,
legislate, legend, or coil.

What is the status of these etymologies? Identification of the true meaning of the
word? Some original presence rooted in the ground of immediate experience, physical
or metaphysical? By no means. They serve rather to indicate the lack of enclosure of a
given word. Each word inheres in a labyrinth of branching interverbal relationships going
back not to a referential source but to something already, at the beginning, a figurative
transfer, according to the Rousseauistic or Condillacian law that all words were originally
metaphors. The searcher through the labyrinth of words, moreover, often encounters
for a given word not a single root, but rather forks in the etymological line leading to
bifurcated or trifurcated roots or to that philologist's confession of archeological
ignorance: 'Origin unknown.' No reason (that I can see) prevents there being bends
or absolute breaks in the etymological line. The realm of words is a free country. Or is
it? No reason (that I can see) forbids deploying a given sound or sign to uses entirely

without affiliation to its figurative roots. Or is this impossible? What coercion does the word itself, as a material base, exert over the range of meanings one can give it? Can one bend, but not break, the etymological line? In any case, the effect of etymological retracing is not to ground the word solidly but to render it unstable, equivocal, wavering, groundless. All etymology is false etymology, in the sense that some bend or discontinuity always breaks up the etymological line. If the line suggests always the gatherings of the word, at the same time, in all the places of its use, the line contains the possibility of turning back on itself. In this turning it subverts its own linearity and becomes repetition. Without the line there is no repetition, but repetition is what disturbs, suspends, or destroys the line's linearity, like a soft wintry aurora playing behind its straightforward logic.

Linear terminology describing narrative tends to organize itself into links, chains, strands, figures, configurations, each covering one of the topographical regions I have identified as basic to the problematic of realist fiction: time, character, the narrator, and so on. To identify line terminology used for stories, bit of string by bit of string, will be to cover the whole ground, according to the paradox of Ariadne's thread. That thread maps the whole labyrinth, rather than providing a single track to its centre and back out. The thread is the labyrinth and at the same time it is a repetition of the labyrinth.

The bits of string I have gathered may be organized in nine areas of linear terminology.

First come the physical aspects of writing or of printed books: letters, signs, hieroglyphs, folds, bindings, and margins, as well as letters in the sense indicated in the phrase 'drop me a line.'

A second region of linear terminology involves all the words for narrative line or diegesis: dénouement, curve of the action, turn of events, broken or dropped thread, line of argument, story line, figure in the carpet – all the terms, in short, assuming that narration is the retracing of a story that has already happened. Note that these lines are all figurative. They do not describe the actual physical linearity of lines of type or of writing. Nor do most of them even describe the sequence of chapters or episodes in a novel. Most name rather the imagined sequence of the events narrated.

A third topic is the use of linear terms to describe character, as in the phrases 'life line,' or 'what's my line?' Physiognomy is the reading of character from facial lineaments. The word *character* itself is a figure meaning the outward signs in the lines on a person s face of his inward nature. A character is a sign, as in the phrase 'Chinese written character.'

A fourth place is all the terminology of interpersonal relations: filiation, affiliation, marriage tie, liaison, genetic or ancestral line, and so on. One cannot talk about relations among persons without using the line images.

Another region is that of economic terminology. The language of interpersonal relations borrows heavily from economic words, as in 'expense of spirit in a waste of shame,' or when one says 'pay him back' or 'repay him with interest' or speaks of someone as 'out of circulation.' Many, if not all, economic terms involve linear imagery: circulation, binding promise or contract, recoup, coupon, margin, cutback, line your pockets, on the line (which means ready for immediate expenditure), currency, current, and pass current.

Another area of narrative terminology involves topography: roads, cross-roads, paths, frontiers, gates, windows, doors, turnings, journeys, narrative motifs like Oedipus murdering Laius at the place where three roads cross or Hercules at the crossroads.

Another topic for investigation is illustrations for novels. Most nineteenth-century novels were of course illustrated by etchings or engravings, that is, by pictures printed from plates incised with lines. Ruskin in *Ariadne Florentina* (1873–75) has investigated this use of the line to make a repeatable design.[2]

Another region for investigation is figurative language in the text of a novel. The terminology for figures of speech is strongly linear, as when one speaks of tropes, of topoi, of chiasmus, of ellipsis, of hyperbole, and so on.

A final topos in the criticism of fiction is the question of realistic representation. Mimesis in a 'realistic' novel is a detour from the real world that mirrors that world and in one way or another, in the cultural or psychic economy of production and consumption, leads the reader back to it.

Each of these topological areas invites separate discussion. The image, figure, or concept of the line threads its way through all the traditional terms for storywriting or storytelling. Line images make the dominant figure in this particular carpet. The peculiarity of all these regions of criticism is that there are no terms but figurative ones to speak of any of them. The term *narrative line*, for example, is a catachresis. It is the violent, forced, or abusive importation of a term from another realm to name something which has no proper name. The relationship of meaning among all these areas of terminology is not from sign to thing but a displacement from one sign to another sign that in its turn draws its meaning from another figurative sign, in a constant displacement. The name for this displacement is allegory. Storytelling, usually thought of as the putting into language of someone's experience of life, is in its writing or reading a hiatus in that experience. Narrative is the allegorizing along a temporal line of this perpetual displacement from immediacy. Allegory in this sense, however, expresses the impossibility of expressing unequivocally, and so dominating, what is meant by experience or by writing. My exploration of the labyrinth of narrative terms is in its turn to be defined as a perhaps impossible search for the center of the maze, the Minotaur or spider that has created and so commands it all.

The reasons for this impossibility may be variously formulated. Perhaps it might be better to say, since what is in question here is the failure of reason, that the inability of the mind to reach the center of narrative's maze and so dominate it may be encountered from various directions. One way is in the blind alley reached when any term or family of terms is followed as far as it will go as a means of talking about objective aspects of specific novels. No one thread (character, realism, interpersonal relation, or whatever) can be followed to a central point where it provides a means of overseeing, controlling, and understanding the whole. Instead it reaches, sooner or later, a crossroad, a blunt fork, where either path leads manifestly to a blank wall. This double blind is at once the failure to reach the center of the labyrinth and at the same time the reaching of a false center, everywhere and nowhere, attainable by any thread or path. These empty corridors are vacant of any presiding Minotaur. The Minotaur, as Ruskin saw, is a spider, Arachne-arachnid who devours her mate, weaver of a web that is herself. This ubiquitous figure both hides and reveals an absence, an abyss.

The impasse in the exploration of a given novel or a given term in narrative criticism occurs differently in each case, yet in each case it is experienced as something irrational, alogical. The critic suffers a breakdown of distinctions – for example, that between figurative and literal language, or between the text and that extratextual reality the text mirrors, or between the notion that the novel copies something and the notion that it makes something happen. The critic may be unable to decide, of two repeating elements, which is the original of which, which the 'illustration' of the other, or whether in fact they repeat or are rather heterogeneous, inassimilable to a single pattern, whether they are centered, double-centered, or acentric. The critic may be unable to tell whether a given textual knot is 'purely verbal' or has to do with 'life.' The reader may experience the impossibility of deciding, in a given passage, who is speaking, the author, the narrator, or the character, where or when, and to whom. Such a passage in its undecidability bears the indelible traces of being a written document, not something that could ever be spoken by a single voice and so returned to a single *logos*. Always, in such passages, something is left over or missing, something is too much or too little. This forbids imputing the language back to a single mind, imagined or real. In one way or another the monological becomes dialogical, the unitary thread of language something like a Möbius strip, with two sides and yet only one side. An alternative metaphor would be that of a complex knot of many crossings. Such a knot may be in one region untied, made unperplexed, but only at the expense of making a tangle of knotted crossings at some other point on the loop. The number of crossings remains stubbornly the same.

The critic, in a further frustration, may experience the impossibility of detaching a part of narrative form from the whole knot of problems and so understanding that. He cannot separate one piece and explore it in isolation. The part/whole, inside/outside division breaks down. The part turns out to be indistinguishable from the whole. The outside is already inside. Character in the novel, for example, may not be defined without talking about interpersonal relations, about time, about figures of speech, about mimesis, and so on.

The critic may also experience the impossibility of getting outside the maze and seeing it from without, giving it its law or finding its law, as opposed to trying to reach a commanding center by exploration from within. Any terminology of explication is already folded into the text the critic is attempting to see from without. This is related to the impossibility of distinguishing analytical terminology, the terms the critic needs to interpret novels, from terminology used inside the novels themselves. Any novel already interprets itself. It uses within itself the same kind of language, encounters the same impasses, as are used and encountered by the critic. The critic may fancy himself safely and rationally outside the contradictory language of the text, but he is already entangled in its web. Similar blind forks or double binds are encountered in the attempt to develop a general 'theoretical' terminology for reading prose fiction and, on the other hand, in the attempt to eschew theory, to go to the text itself and, without theoretical presuppositions, to explicate its meaning.

Criticism of a given novel or body of novels should therefore be the following of one or another track until it reaches, in the text, one or another of these double blinds, rather than the attempt to find a presupposed unity. Such a unity always turns out to be spurious, imposed rather than intrinsic. This can be experienced, however, only through the patient work of following some thread as far, deep into the labyrinth of the text, as it will go. Such an effort to read is not the 'deconstruction' of a given novel. It is rather a discovery of the way the novel deconstructs itself in the process of constructing its web of storytelling. These blind alleys in the analysis of narrative may not by any means be avoided. They may only be veiled by some credulity making a standing place where there is an abyss – for example, in taking consciousness as a solid ground. The thinly veiled chasm may be avoided only by stopping short, by taking something for granted in the terminology one is using rather than interrogating it, or by not pushing the analysis of the text in question far enough so that the impossibility of a single definitive reading emerges.

The impasse of narrative analysis is a genuine double blind alley. It results first from the fact that there is in no region of narrative or of its analysis a literal ground – in history, consciousness, society, the physical world, or whatever – for which the other regions are figures. The terminology of narrative is therefore universally catachresis. Each is a trope breaking down the reassuring distinction between figure and ground, base of so much theoretical seeing.

The other fork of this double blind is the fact that the terminology of narrative may by no effort be compartmentalized, divided into hanks of different colored thread. The same terms must be used in all regions. All the topoi overlap. Neither the critic nor the novelist can, for example, talk about sexual relations without at the same time using economic terminology (getting, spending, and so on), or without talking about mimetic representations (reproduction), or about topography (crossings), and in fact about all the other topics of narrative. The language of narrative is always displaced, borrowed. Therefore any single thread leads everywhere, like a labyrinth made of a single line or corridor crinkled to and fro.

Take, as an example of this, the letter X. It is a letter, a sign, but a sign for signs generally and for a multitude of relations involving ultimately interchanges among all nine of my places. X is a crossroads, the figure of speech called chiasmus, a kiss, a fish, Christ, the cross of the crucifixion, an unknown in mathematics, the proofreader's sign for a broken letter, a place marked on a map (X marks the spot), an illustration (as when we say, 'See figure X'), the signature of an illiterate person, the sign of an error or erasure ('crossed out'), the indication of degrees of fineness (as in the X's on a sack of flour or sugar), the place of encounters, reversals, and exchanges, the region of both/ and or either/or ('She is my ex-wife'), the place of a gap, gape, or yawning chasm, the undecidable, the foyer of genealogical crossings, the sign of crossing oneself, of the X chromosome, of crisis, of the double cross, of star-crossed lovers, of cross-examination, or cross-stitching, of cross-purposes, of the witch's cross, of the crisscross (originally Christ-cross), and of the cross child. X is, finally, the sign of death, as in the skull and crossbones, or the crossed-out eyes of the cartoon figure who is baffled, unconscious, or dead: XX. In all these uses, the 'ex' means out of, beside itself, displaced. The real and visible rises, exhales, from the unreal, or does the unreal always appear as the intervening veil or substitute for the absent real, as, in stanza 18 of Wallace Stevens's 'Man with the Blue Guitar,' daylight comes 'Like light in a mirroring of cliffs,/Rising upward from a sea of ex.'[3]

Daylight, the visible and nameable, is always doubly derived, secondary. It rises from the sea and then is further displaced by its mirroring from the cliffs in a wandering like that of all those terms I have been examining. This movement makes the source itself unreal, a sea of ex. Stevens speaks, in section 13 of 'An Ordinary Evening in New Haven,' of the approach of night, from which the light comes and to which it returns, as 'the big X of the returning primitive.'[4] The real and the unreal, the metaphorical and the literal, the figure and the ground, constantly change places, in oscillating chiasmus, for 'ex'ample in Stevens's contradictory explanation of 'sea of ex' in his letters. To Renato Poggioli he wrote: 'A sea of ex means a purely negative sea. The realm of has-been without interest or provocativeness.' To Hy Simons: 'Sea of Ex. The imagination takes us out of (Ex) reality into a pure irreality. One has this sense of irreality often in the presence of morning light on cliffs which then rise from a sea that has ceased to be real and is therefore a sea of Ex.'[5] Which is unreal, which real, the sea or the light? It cannot be decided. Whatever one sees is unreal and creates as its ground a phantasmal real, which becomes unreal in its turn when one turns to it.

NOTES

1   See Paul Ricoeur, *Temps et récit, vol. 1* (Paris: Editions du Seuil, 1983), pp. 19–84; Ricoeur, *Time and Narrative, vol. 1*, trans. Kathleen McLaughlin and David Pellauer (Chicago: University of Chicago Press, 1984), pp. 5–51.

2   I investigate this region of narrative criticism in a book entitled *Illustration* (Cambridge University Press, 1992).

3   Wallace Stevens, 'The Man with the Blue Guitar,' in *The Collected Poems of Wallace Stevens* (New York: Alfred A. Knopf, 1954), p. 175.

4   Stevens, 'An Ordinary Evening in New Haven,' in *Collected Poems*, p. 274.

5   *The Letters of Wallace Stevens*, ed. Holly Stevens (New York: Alfred A. Knopf, 1966), pp. 783, 360.

Barbara Johnson, 'The Critical Difference: BartheS/BalZac'*

See also:
Barthes (2.iii)
Barthes (3.i)
Brooks (3.ii)
Mulvey (4)
Bronfen (4)
Lanser (5)
De Lauretis (5)
Roof (5)
Bhabha (9)
Minh-Ha (9)

Literary criticism as such can perhaps be called the art of rereading. I would therefore like to begin by quoting the remarks about rereading made by Roland Barthes in *S/Z*:

* *The Critical Difference: Essays in the Contemporary Rhetoric of Reading* (London: Johns Hopkins University Press, 1980), pp. 3–8.

Rereading, an operation contrary to the commercial and ideological habits of our society, which would have us 'throw away' the story once it has been consumed ('devoured'), so that we can then move on to another story, buy another book, and which is tolerated only in certain marginal categories of readers (children, old people, and professors), rereading is here suggested at the outset, for it alone saves the text from repetition (*those who fail to reread are obliged to read the same story everywhere*).[1]

(My emphasis)

What does this paradoxical statement imply? First, it implies that a single reading is composed of the already-read, that what we can see in a text the first time is already in us, not in it; in us insofar as we ourselves are a stereotype, an already-read text; and in the text only to the extent that the already-read is that aspect of a text that it must have in common with its reader in order for it to be readable at all. When we read a text once, in other words, we can see in it only what we have already learned to see before.

Secondly, the statement that those who do not reread must read the same story everywhere involves a reversal of the usual properties of the words *same* and *different*. Here, it is the consuming of different stories that is equated with the repetition of the same, while it is the rereading of the same that engenders what Barthes calls the 'text's difference.' This critical concept of difference, which has been valorized both by Saussurian linguistics and by the Nietzschean tradition in philosophy – particularly the work of Jacques Derrida – is crucial to the practice of what is called deconstructive criticism. I would therefore like to examine here some of its implications and functions.

In a sense, it could be said that to make a critical difference is the object of all criticism as such. The very word *criticism* comes from the Greek verb *krinein*, 'to separate or choose,' that is, to differentiate. The critic not only seeks to establish standards for evaluating the differences between texts but also tries to perceive something uniquely different within each text he reads and in so doing to establish his own individual difference from other critics. But this is not quite what Barthes means when he speaks of the text's difference. On the first page of *S/Z*, he writes:

> This difference is not, obviously, some complete, irreducible quality (according to a mythic view of literary creation), it is not what designates the individuality of each text, what names, signs, finishes off each work with a flourish; on the contrary, it is a difference which does not stop and which is articulated upon the infinity of texts, of languages, of systems: a difference of which each text is the return.
>
> (p. 3)

In other words, a text's difference is not its uniqueness, its special identity. It is the text's way of differing from itself. And this difference is perceived only in the act of rereading. It is the way in which the text's signifying energy becomes unbound, to use Freud's term, through the process of repetition, which is the return not of sameness but of difference. Difference, in other words, is not what distinguishes one identity from another. It is not a difference between (or at least not between independent units), but a difference within. Far from constituting the text's unique identity, it is that which subverts the very idea of identity, infinitely deferring the possibility of adding up the sum of a text's parts or meanings and reaching a totalized, integrated whole.

Let me illustrate this idea further by turning for a moment to Rousseau's *Confessions*. Rousseau's opening statement about himself is precisely an affirmation of difference: 'I am unlike anyone I have ever met; I will even venture to say that I am like no one in the whole world. I may be no better, but at least I am different' (Penguin edition, 1954, p. 17). Now, this can be read as an unequivocal assertion of uniqueness, of difference between Rousseau and the whole rest of the world. This is the boast on which the book is based. But in what does the uniqueness of this self consist? It is not long before we find out: 'There are times when I am so unlike myself that I might be taken for someone else of an entirely opposite character' (p. 126). 'In me are united two almost irreconcilable characteristics, though in what way I cannot imagine' (p. 112). In other words, this story of the self's difference from others inevitably becomes the story of its own unbridgeable difference from itself. Difference is not engendered in the space between identities; it is what makes all totalization of the identity of a self or the meaning of a text impossible.

It is this type of textual difference that informs the process of deconstructive criticism. *Deconstruction* is not synonymous with *destruction*, however. It is in fact much closer to the original meaning of the word *analysis*, which etymologically means 'to undo' – a virtual synonym for 'to de-construct.' The de-construction of a text does not proceed by random doubt or arbitrary subversion, but by the careful teasing out of warring forces of signification within the text itself. If anything is destroyed in a deconstructive reading, it is not the text, but the claim to unequivocal domination of one mode of signifying over another. A deconstructive reading is a reading that analyzes the specificity of a text's critical difference from itself.

I have chosen to approach this question of critical difference by way of Barthes's *S/Z* for three reasons:

1   Barthes sets up a critical value system explicitly based on the paradigm of difference, and in the process works out one of the earliest, most influential, and most lucid and forceful syntheses of contemporary French theoretical thought;

2   The Balzac story that Barthes chooses to analyze in *S/Z* is itself in a way a study of difference – a subversive and unsettling formulation of the question of sexual difference;

3   The confrontation between Barthes and Balzac may have something to say about the critical differences between theory and practice, on the one hand, and between literature and criticism, on the other.

I shall begin by recalling the manner in which Barthes outlines his value system:

Our evaluation can be linked only to a practice, and this practice is that of writing. On the one hand, there is what it is possible to write, and on the other, what it is no longer possible to write. . . . What evaluation finds is precisely this value: what can be written (rewritten) today: the *writerly* [*le scriptible*]. Why is the writerly our value? Because the goal of literary work (of literature as work) is to make the reader no longer a consumer, but a producer of the text. . . . Opposite the writerly text is its countervalue, its negative, reactive value: what can be read, but not written: the *readerly* [*le lisible*]. We call any readerly text a classic text.

(p. 4)

Here, then, is the major polarity that Barthes sets up as a tool for evaluating texts: the readerly versus the writerly. The readerly is defined as a product consumed by the reader; the writerly is a process of production in which the reader becomes a producer: it is 'ourselves writing.' The readerly is constrained by considerations of representation: it is irreversible, 'natural,' decidable, continuous, totalizable, and unified into a coherent whole based on the signified. The writerly is infinitely plural and open to the free play of signifiers and of difference, unconstrained by representative considerations, and transgressive of any desire for decidable, unified, totalized meaning.

With this value system, one would naturally expect to find Barthes going on to extoll the play of infinite plurality in some Joycean or Mallarméan piece of writerly obscurity, but no; he turns to Balzac, one of the most readerly of readerly writers, as Barthes himself insists. Why then does Barthes choose to talk about Balzac? Barthes skillfully avoids confronting this question. But perhaps it is precisely the way in which Barthes's choice of Balzac does not follow logically from his value system – that is, the way in which Barthes somehow differs from himself – which opens up the critical difference we must analyze here.

Although Balzac's text apparently represents for Barthes the negative, readerly end of the hierarchy, Barthes's treatment of it does seem to illustrate all the characteristics of the positive, writerly end. In the first place, one cannot help but be struck by the plurality of Barthes's text, with its numerous sizes of print, its 'systematic use of digression,' and its successive superposable versions of the same but different story, from the initial reproduction of Girodet's *Endymion* to the four appendixes, which repeat the book's contents in different forms. The reading technique proper also obeys the demand for fragmentation and pluralization, and consists of 'manhandling' the text:

> What we seek is to sketch the stereographic space of writing (which will here be a classic, readerly writing). The commentary, based on the affirmation of the plural, cannot work with 'respect' to the text; the tutor text will ceaselessly be broken, interrupted without any regard for its natural divisions . . . the work of the commentary, once it is separated from any ideology of totality, consists precisely in *manhandling* the text, *interrupting* it [lui couper la parole]. What is thereby denied is not the *quality* of the text (here incomparable) but its 'naturalness.'
>
> (p. 15)

Barthes goes on to divide the story diachronically into 561 fragments called *lexias* and synchronically into five so-called voices or codes, thus transforming the text into a 'complex network' with 'multiple entrances and exits.'

The purpose of these cuts and codes is to pluralize the reader's intake, to effect a resistance to the reader's desire to restructure the text into large, ordered masses of meaning: 'If we want to remain attentive to the plural of a text . . . we must renounce structuring this text in large masses, as was done by classical rhetoric and by secondary-school explication: no construction of the text' (pp. 11–12). In leaving the text as heterogeneous and discontinuous as possible, in attempting to avoid the repressiveness of the attempt to dominate the message and force the text into a single ultimate meaning, Barthes thus works a maximum of disintegrative violence and a minimum of integrative violence. The question to ask is whether this 'anti-constructionist' (as opposed to 'de-constructionist' fidelity to the fragmented signifier succeeds in laying bare the functional plurality of Balzac's text, or whether in the final analysis a certain systematic level of textual difference is not also lost and flattened by Barthes's refusal to reorder or reconstruct the text.

Let us now turn to Balzac's *Sarrasine* itself. The story is divided into two parts: the story of the telling and the telling of the story. In the first part, the narrator attempts to seduce a beautiful Marquise by telling her the second part; that is, he wants to exchange narrative knowledge for carnal knowledge. The lady wants to know the secret of the mysterious old man at the party, and the narrator wants to know the lady. Story-telling, as Barthes points out, is thus not an innocent, neutral activity, but rather part of a bargain, an act of seduction. But here the bargain is not kept; the deal backfires. The knowledge the lady has acquired, far from bringing about her surrender, prevents it. In fact, the last thing she says is: 'No one will have *known* me.'

It is obvious that the key to this failure of the bargain lies in the content of the story used to fulfill it. That story is about the passion of the sculptor Sarrasine for the opera singer La Zanibinella, and is based not on knowledge but on ignorance: the sculptor's ignorance of the Italian custom of using castrated men instead of women to play the soprano parts on the operatic stage. The sculptor, who had seen in La Zambinella the perfect female body for the first time realized in one person, a veritable Pygmalion's statue come to life, finds out that this image of feminine perfection literally has been carved by a knife, not in stone but in the flesh itself. He who had proclaimed his willingness to die for his love ends up doing just that, killed by La Zambinella's protector.

How is it that the telling of this sordid little tale ends up subverting the very bargain it was intended to fulfill? Barthes's answer to this is clear: 'castration is contagious' – 'contaminated by the castration she has just been told about, [the Marquise] impels the narrator into it' (p. 36).

What is interesting about this story of seduction and castration is the way in which it unexpectedly reflects upon Barthes's own critical value system. For in announcing that 'the tutor text will ceaselessly be broken, interrupted without any regard for its natural divisions,' is Barthes not implicitly privileging something like castration over what he calls the 'ideology of totality'? 'If the text is subject to some form,' he writes, 'this form is not unitary . . . finite; it is the fragment, the slice, the cut up or erased network' (p. 20; translation modified). Indeed, might it not be possible to read Balzac's opposition between the ideal woman and the castrato as metaphorically assimilable to Barthes's opposition between the readerly and the writerly? Like the readerly text, Sarrasine's deluded image of La Zambinella is a glorification of perfect unity and wholeness:

> At that instant he marveled at the ideal beauty he had hitherto sought in life, seeking in one often unworthy model the roundness of a perfect leg; in another, the curve of a breast; in another, white shoulders; finally taking some girl's neck, some woman's hands, and some child's smooth knees, without ever having encountered

under the cold Parisian sky the rich, sweet creations of ancient Greece. La Zambinella displayed to him, *united*, living, and delicate, those exquisite female forms he so ardently desired.

(pp. 237–8; emphasis added)

But like the writerly text, Zambinella is actually fragmented, unnatural, and sexually undecidable. Like the readerly, the soprano is a product to be 'devoured' ('With his eyes, Sarrasine devoured Pygmalion's statue, come down from its pedestal' (p. 238)), while, like the writerly, castration is a process of production, an active and violent indetermination. The soprano's appearance seems to embody the very essence of 'woman' as a *signified* ('This was woman herself . . .' (p. 248)), while the castrato's reality, like the writerly text, is a mere play of signifiers, emptied of any ultimate signified, robbed of what the text calls a 'heart': 'I have no heart,' says Zambinella, 'the stage where you saw me . . . is my life, I have no other' (p. 247).

Here, then, is the first answer to the question of why Barthes might have chosen this text; it explicitly thematizes the opposition between unity and fragmentation, between the idealized signified and the discontinuous empty play of signifiers, which underlies his opposition between the readerly and the writerly. The traditional value system that Barthes is attempting to reverse is thus already mapped out within the text he analyzes. Three questions, however, immediately present themselves: (1) Does Balzac's story really uphold the unambiguousness of the readerly values to which Barthes relegates it? (2) Does Balzac simply regard ideal beauty as a lost paradise and castration as a horrible tragedy? (3) If Barthes is really attempting to demystify the ideology of totality, and if his critical strategy implicitly gives a positive value to castration, why does his analysis of Balzac's text still seem to take castration at face value as an unmitigated and catastrophic horror?

NOTE

1   Numbers in brackets refer to R. Barthes (1974) *S/Z*, trans. R. Howard (New York: Hill and Wang).

7
Phenomenology

Wolfgang Iser, 'A Conversation with Wayne Booth'*

See also:
Booth (1.iii)
Metz (2.i)
Chatman (2.ii)
Prince (2.ii)
Derrida (6)
de Man (6)

Wayne Booth   Rather than pursue any of those questions that would be extrinsic to your enterprise, I'd like to try out two related questions that might be prefaced with some such query as: 'Do you see the possibility for a further chapter on . . . ?'

(1) What I would miss most, if I took your book as an effort to describe everything important that happens to me when I read a fictional text, is an account of my irresistible impulse to deal with the text as a person, or, if you prefer, as the act of a person, the implied author. You do, of course, talk occasionally about the implied author, but you consistently avoid personifying *the text* as implied author, or as a reader and author dramatized in a joint action together.

In most of my reading of fiction and poetry, and in much of my reading and viewing of drama, I find prominent in both thought and emotion not only the interest of the reconstructive steps you describe but also my sense of a person addressing me as his prospective friend, crony, co-conspirator, fellow victim, prospective convert, or what not, and I thus find that my responses are often best put not in your terms of seeking a *meaning* or becoming 'entangled in the text', but rather in the terms of love or hate, admiration or detestation, good or bad fellowship, domination or seduction, and so on.

Here, then, is my first question: Do you see any use, building from what you have done, in exploring the ways in which authors imply and often achieve such personal, powerfully dramatic bondings? Would a consideration, say, of Kenneth Burke's 'dramatic' vocabulary, describing texts not only as interesting bodies of meaning but as dramatic personal encounters accomplishing many different ends, be a possible addition to what you have done? Burke is fond of making wonderful long lists of the great miscellany of literary purposes that contrast sharply with our usual reductions to one grand purpose, or at most two: mimetic/didactic; pleasure/instruction; dulce/utile. In 'Literature as Equipment for Living,' for example, he describes literary works as helping us to select enemies and allies, to socialize our losses, to ward off the evil eye, to purify or desanctify our worlds, to propitiate our gods; as consoling and admonishing and exhorting us; as foretelling, instructing, charting, and praying.

* *Prospecting: From Reader Response to Literary Anthropology* (Baltimore, MD: Johns Hopkins University Press, 1993), pp. 57–66.

Could one add such talk to what you have done? Or do you see it as in conflict because it is so obviously not 'aesthetic'? In short, is your relatively emotion-free account of encounters with *texts* in conflict with Burke's (or any other) language of dramatic encounter with authors, or could it serve as a basis for extending into such matters?

In thinking about this question I have found myself wondering why you were in general so chary of affective responses to the text. You seldom talk about the text arousing any desire except for our interest in its 'meaning.' The 'tenterhooks of suspense,' for example, that Virginia Woolf mentions in her reading of Austen play no significant role in your own analysis; the stimulation of 'desires,' described in your quotation from W. D. Harding (p. 158), is also not given much attention – except, of course, the desire to discover a meaning. I don't want to suggest that you never touch on such matters, only that they play no strong functional role in an analysis that quite rightly insists on talking about functions.

One might view my trouble here as simply a variant of the first question: Is what I see as a neglect of matters like laughter, tears, fear, horror, disgust, joy, and celebration inherent to your analysis or simply something that requires a supplemental account, 'another chapter'?

(2) I am not at all sure that I have figured out what you mean by the 'implied reader.' At times you talk as if you would restrict the term to something like 'the totality of tasks of interpretation *required* by a given text.' At other times you seem to extend it to include 'the totality of inferences *allowed* by a given text.' Sometimes the implied reader spreads over the whole of what is allowed and at other times he becomes sharply distinguished from either the 'fictitious reader' dramatized in the text, or the flesh-and-blood reader who exists independently of the text, or the ideal reader.

Perhaps a re-reading of your book will clear this up for me, but meanwhile I hope that the following question can be answered within the scope allowed for your reply here:

Would your conception of the implied reader be underlined, or destroyed, or enriched, by saying that the reader-in-the-text, at least when the text is what we call fictional, is *always* a double figure? He is *both* a credulous or 'pretending' person, and a doubter. The first could be said to accept all the moves required including fantastic steps, like turning young men into beetles, and incredible beliefs, such as 'people can live happily forever after.' The second is a more sophisticated ambassador from the 'real world,' one who is able to permit or even encourage the credulous activity of his twin but who knows all the while that some parts of what is embraced during the reading do not accord with his beliefs back in the 'real world.'

I have slowly discovered that my own discussion of the implied author in *The Rhetoric of Fiction* was too simple in this respect, as you suggest in Chapter 2. It seemed at times to say that the author we find implied in the text has cut all of his moorings with the 'real world,' and it thus led some readers into awkward ways of talking about how we in fact do make valid inferences from implied authors to real authors. But both the author and the reader in the text are not simple, single, credulous folk who believe in all the norms of the work, including beetle-metamorphoses: they are complex folk who can pretend to believe and yet remember that they are pretending. They are thus like those sophisticated spectators Samuel Johnson talks about when he refutes the importance of unity of place; they are never troubled by being transported from Egypt to Rome between scenes, because they had never fully believed themselves anywhere but in the theater. Like those spectators, the implied reader must be able to carry out both demands simultaneously; if he misplays either role, the fiction will be destroyed. And both roles are implied in the text.

You often imply this inescapable double effect, but when you *talk* about it, you seem to see the *implied* reader as only the credulous reader in the text, while the resisting, criticizing, modifying, remembering of the real world is all done somehow by the 'real reader' as *not* implied in the text. Do I misread you? If not, would you see any way to deal with what seems to me inescapable, that the text does absolutely imply, indeed demand, a reader who can perform both of the described roles? Surely it could not succeed, as fiction, if it did not.

Another way of putting this question would be to ask what moves, taken by the 'real reader' after the reading experience, would distress the implied author of a given work. (You see how I sneak in my language of personification! Does it seem unreasonable to talk of an implied author being distressed? It does not to me, since I carry with me a picture of the author after the reading is over – that is, I go on 'reading' a work, in a sense, long after I have put down the physical object, and I can surely distress or please the implied author – whom I have after all made for myself in reconstructing the text – by violating his beliefs and desires.) It seems to me self-evident that the implied author of any *didactic* work, at least, whether we define such works as simple and blatant, like Aesop's fables, or subtle and complex, like Milton's epics, would be distressed if, after I put down the work, I said to myself, 'Well, now I can go back to my previous beliefs about overweening pride or about how the ways of God are to be justified.' But is it not equally true that some of the norms of even the most fully purified *non-didactic* works are clearly seen by the implied author as not simply taken up for the duration and then dropped (for me the question of what the real writer felt about them is entirely separate, though not beyond speculation).

In short, some beliefs and norms are for the implied author fixed, and some are not; he implies that some not only can be applied in the real world but should be (e.g. in *Ulysses*, sensitivity to delicate distinctions of verbal tone is important, and that sensitivity is not to be shucked off when we stop reading); and some are merely provisional for the duration (e.g. again in *Ulysses*, Stephen Dedalus is a real person with a theory about *Hamlet* – a belief that *is* to be shucked off after reading).

I've chosen here extreme and easy examples to illustrate the double nature of the persons implied, but obviously the chief interest to criticism, and particularly to evaluative criticism (which of course is not your immediate concern) would lie in the range of discriminations such doubling would allow in our descriptions of the implied readers we are to become. Such interest will be greatest precisely at those points at which the discrimination between fixed and unfixed norms is hardest to make. A whole new kind of 'ethical criticism' might become possible if we learned how to distinguish books that invite us to embrace fixed norms that are not, on cool reflection after the reading experience, supportable, from those whose implied authors survive intact, in all their complexity, after our most rigorous criticism.

If this does not seem to you a promising direction for some kind of criticism of ethical effects on real readers, effects that result from the implied readers they have joined (or become), what is *your* way of dealing with the fact – and surely it is a fact – that who we are in 'real life' is in large part a result of the friendships we have made with various implied authors?

Wolfgang Iser It may well be, as Professor Booth has suggested, that my exposition of the dialogue between text and reader gives rise to a host of charges along the lines of the old questions and old answers that have beset and plagued literary criticism in our time. Up to a point I may even have asked for it by leveling criticism at entrenched positions. However, I could not agree more with Professor Booth in that 'continuations of ancient debates about the primacy of author, text and reader . . . are pointless,' and that the various unhelpful responses that have sprung to his mind might in the final analysis be extrinsic to what I had intended to do.

The event that takes place between text and reader is a peculiarly difficult region to chart. Literary criticism has so far been very hesitant in coming to grips with the intangible processes operative between text and reader. This may be one reason why it lags behind the social sciences, which have devised different frameworks to encompass these seemingly ungraspable operations of dyadic interaction. Devising a framework for literary communication would imply exploring the basic asymmetry between a literary text and its potential reader; one would have to describe this asymmetry in terms of why and how it triggers, stimulates, and even controls the developing communication between text and reader. Focusing on this area implies rearranging the traditional set of questions and answers in literary criticism, and a rearrangement of this kind will – as Professor Booth has suggested – invite all kinds of critical reservations from those who not only have well-established opinions on what text, author, reader, subjectivism, and objectivism are, but who also know for sure that what they know is true. If text-processing is a covered process, then an explanation of how literature communicates requires a heuristic model in order to spotlight the basic features of this transaction.

This brings me to Professor Booth's first question. Basically I would admit that there is 'the possibility of a further chapter on. . . . ' As to the one that Professor Booth proposes, I should like to emphasize a distinction that I consider to be important. If a reader's reading gives prominence to 'dramatic bondings' with the author, who may emerge as 'friend, crony, co-conspirator, fellow-victim, prospective convert,' such a relationship can only arise from an operation carried out by the reader. The image of the author gradually gaining shape in the mind's eye of the reader presupposes consistency-building, without which no image, even of an author, could be entertained in one's imagination. Consistency-building in turn is governed, of course, by the reader's preferences, predilections, codes, and also his unconscious disposition. Consequently this very process is bound to be selective, and its outcome indicates both the implications of the text and the preferences of the reader. The reader's relationship with the author therefore results from a sequence of imaginings, in the course of which he ideates the author as crony or as prospective friend, and he can only experience such a 'bonding' because he has been caught up in the very ideas that the text has stimulated him into producing. Thus the encounter with the author may be all the more powerful as we have not encountered him in person but in a text-guided, though self-produced, image; the subsequent affective reaction to something we have produced ourselves may then account for the laughter, tears, fear, horror, and so forth that Professor Booth has mentioned.

Now if there were a further chapter to my book on readers' reactions to 'dramatic bondings' with an author, I would show that these indicate certain preferences in the reader concerned – preferences that manifest themselves in the very selections the reader has made within the network of possible connections between textual segments.

Furthermore, I do not – as Professor Booth quite rightly assumes – consider these 'products' as aesthetic; I would, however, maintain that they issue forth from an aesthetic effect indicated, developed, and carried out in text-processing. It may be in the nature of an aesthetic effect that it eventually results in something non-aesthetic, that is, practical, and in this respect I would subscribe to all those suggestions that Professor Booth has quoted from Kenneth Burke's 'Literature as Equipment for Living.' I would even go so far as to say that the very importance of these practical or (as Professor Booth suggests toward the end of his statement) ethical results necessitates a much more detailed inspection of the processes that enable an aesthetic effect to arise and transmute itself into something non-aesthetic. I have focused on these hidden processes, and have tried to devise a framework in order to come to grips with them; such a framework may enable us not only to spotlight the transmutation, but also to assess the results at which each individual reader may arrive, thereby revealing his governing codes and habitual orientations.

If I had to tack on another chapter to my book concerning the reader's particular image of the implied author, I would continue to follow my initial line and emphasize not so much the personification of the text, but the particular type of 'conversation' to which the implied author invites his potential reader. There is always a game going on between author and reader, and I am not sure to what extent one could separate the image of an implied author from the part that each plays in that game. The two are clearly tied together, and so the image of the implied author appears less a self-sufficient entity than a function of seducing, tempting, exasperating, affirming, and pleasing the reader – thereby indicating that the very image is a constitutive feature for the cooperative enterprise that is a basic condition of the literary text.

As to the second question regarding my concept of the 'implied reader,' I also meant to stress the double figure of the reader-in-the-text, although perhaps not exactly along the lines Professor Booth has developed. We are in agreement that the implied reader designates the reader's role and is not identical with the dramatized fictitious reader (which I consider to be a textual strategy and thus an integral *feature* of the reader's role). As a rule we readers slip into the role mapped out by the text. The split that then occurs, and that is responsible for the double figure, is due to the fact that on the one hand we are prepared to assume the role, and yet on the other we cannot completely cut ourselves off from what we are – not least as we have to understand what we are given to perform. Thus, the double figure – at least to my mind – is not inscribed into the reader-in-the-text, but comes about whenever we perform the role assigned to us by placing ourselves at the disposal of someone else's thoughts, thereby relegating our own beliefs, norms, and values to the background. This also holds true in the instances Professor Booth has enumerated, when the reader's role itself becomes more complicated. I would not deny that in certain texts this role is itself marked by a split, in the sense that the reader is cast both as a credulous person and as a doubter of his own credulity; Joyce may be a case in point. Nevertheless, a role marked by this dichotomy is still related to the disposition of the real reader, as its function is to draw him into the text and thus separate him, at least temporarily, from his habitual orientation. So there may be a double figure inscribed into the very role the reader is given to perform, but this does not affect the basic split that always occurs between role and habitual orientation.

Now, this situation gives rise to two consequences. There is definitely a graded range of relationships between the real reader and his role. Even if he is absorbed in the role, his preferences, dispositions, and attitudes will still govern his relationship to what the role offers him. Scott's *Waverley Novels* are a striking example in this respect. The role provided by them has been differently actualized by nineteenth-century readers, children, and twentieth-century readers. Obviously the role itself is not only subject to selective realizations, but will also be differently actualized according to prevailing codes. Still I would maintain that in all instances the basic split between the role assumed and the habitual orientation of the reader is bound to occur.

This ties in with the second consequence to be drawn. Whenever the split occurs – I have suggested that it results in a 'contrapuntally structured personality' in reading – the resultant tension calls for resolution. The resolution, however, cannot come about simply by restoring habitual orientation to the self which had been temporarily relegated to the background. Playing the role involves incorporating the new experience. Consequently, the reader is affected by the very role he has been given to play, and his being affected does not reinvoke his habitual orientation but mobilizes the spontaneity of the self. The type of mobilized spontaneity will depend, though, on the nature of the text to which we have made ourselves present in playing the role. It will cast the released spontaneity into a certain shape and thus begin to mold what it has called forth. As the nature and the extent of released spontaneity are governed by the individuality of the text, a layer of the reader's personality is brought to light which had hitherto remained hidden in the shadows. In this sense something is formulated in the reader under conditions that are not set by himself and that thus enable the experience to penetrate into his consciousness. This marks the point where the split between habitual orientation and role may result in what Professor Booth calls 'criticism of ethical effects on real readers.' I attach as much importance to this as does Professor Booth, and it was my endeavor to give a phenomenologically oriented account of the way in which a literary text begins to claw its way into us. The reader-in-the-text, or what I have called the implied reader, is meant as a heuristic concept that will help us to focus on the split and thus establish a framework for assessing the variegated types of realization that occur whenever we read.

There are two minor points to which I should like to address myself briefly. If I have given the impression that I seem obsessed by 'seeking a meaning' this is due to the fact that I should like to move the discussion of meaning on to a different plane: not what the meaning is, but how it is produced. This seems to me to require investigation in view of the fact that we take something for granted of which we have so little knowledge. My basic concern, however, is not with meaning-assembly as such but with what I have termed the aesthetic object, which has to be created in the act of reading by following the instructions given in the text. Analysis of production is important for two closely related reasons: (1) the aesthetic object the reader is given to build involves him in an experience that he himself has to bring about, and (2) as the aesthetic object emerges from the aspects and schemata given in the text, it provides a vantage point for assessing and evaluating these very aspects or schemata, which in themselves represent extratextual realities. Thus, the aesthetic object – text-guided though reader-produced – makes the reader react to the world represented in the text. In this respect it has both an experiential and a cognitive consequence, and as these are virtually inseparable, their impact is all the more powerful. This impact is important for exactly those reasons with which Professor Booth concludes his argument, and so I would maintain that the production of the aesthetic object requires the closest possible analysis.

The second point relates to 'the discrimination between fixed and unfixed norms' in texts set up by the implied author. I agree with Professor Booth that this discrimination is very hard to make, and I am basically skeptical whether we ever shall arrive at a clear-cut decision as to which is which. My skepticism is nourished by the history of interpretation, which indicates clearly that what one generation used to regard as fixed norms in an author have been either downgraded or made taboo by the next, in consequence of which the qualification of fixed and unfixed has been shifted. Still, there seems to be a hermeneutic process discernible in that history. Late nineteenth-century Shakespearean criticism, for instance, focused on organic unity of character, whereas early in the twentieth century, the historically and sociologically oriented school considered the very breaks in Shakespearean characters to be the fixed norms, as they provide the audience with information necessary for its understanding of what the character is meant to convey. This complete reversal from organic unity to discrepancy as the fixed norms in Shakespeare's character-building testifies to an important hermeneutic relationship in the history of interpretation. What had been emphasized by the Bradley 'school' now became a closed door for the Stoll and Schücking 'school', which nevertheless was conditioned, though negatively, by what had been the seemingly unshakable findings of the previous generation of Shakespearean scholars. Consequently, the findings of one generation imprint themselves on those of the next by blocking certain roads and thereby conditioning the opening up of opposed, deviating, and contrasting lines of thought.

If we want to assess fixed or unfixed norms in an author, we must not only reflect on our own position, but also on the kind of reshuffling which has taken place in the history of interpretation. This means that we must take into account far more factors than have hitherto been considered when norms have been declared fixed or unfixed. Any such declarations must be accompanied by a reflective reason that, in turn, will also say something about ourselves. This again ties in with the kind of ethical criticism for which Professor Booth makes such a strong plea and to which I too would be prepared to subscribe, for the study of literature may not only result in ethical consequences but, through these very consequences, should reveal something of the specific makeup of ourselves and our faculties, which are activated and acted upon by literature.

Dorrit Cohn, from *Transparent Minds: Narrative Modes for Presenting Consciousness in Fiction**

See also:
Benjamin (1.iii)
Chatman (2.ii)

* Princeton, NJ: Princeton University Press, 1978, pp. 9–17.

Prince (2.ii)
Mulvey (4)
Heath (4)
Diengott (5)
de Lauretis (5)
Johnson (6)
Jameson (8)

This view of the historical continuity underlies my typological approach to the presentation of consciousness in fiction. Despite the theoretical and historical importance of the subject, previous studies of its formal implications have been disappointingly rapid and incomplete. They fall into two basic categories:

1   Studies (mostly published in the United States) that focus on the stream-of-consciousness novel, and especially on *Ulysses*, generally treating the subject as though consciousness had appeared in fiction only on Bloomsday. This limited orientation oversimplifies the formal problem by reducing all techniques to a single and vague 'stream-of-consciousness technique,' and at the same time over-complicates it by association with broad psychological and aesthetic issues. Leon Edel's influential historical study, *The Modern Psychological Novel*, for example, yields no clarity at all concerning formal devices. Robert Humphrey's brief chapter on basic techniques in *Stream of Consciousness in the Modern Novel* is the most differentiated discussion that has come out of this approach, but it suffers from characteristic limitations and confusions.

2   Studies (mostly published abroad) that apply to the techniques for presenting consciousness the model of the techniques for quoting spoken discourse. They have generally applied simple correspondences between direct discourse and interior monologue, between indirect discourse and narrative analysis, and between the intermediary 'free indirect' forms of both spoken and silent discourse (*style indirect libre* in French, *erlebte Rede* in German). This approach, which has a long and venerable history in French and German stylistics, has been updated by stylistic linguists in the last decade and applied in the context of modern fictional modes. An article by Derek Bickerton is of special interest in this regard, since it forges a bridge between literary and linguistic approaches to the subject: he translates the techniques Humphrey identified empirically in the stream-of-consciousness novel into the basic grammatical categories of quotation. The same basic method is applied by the French literary structuralists, notably by Gérard Genette in his influential 'Discours du récit.' Under the heading 'récit de paroles,' Genette pairs spoken and silent discourse according to degrees of 'narrative distance,' arriving at a threefold division between the poles of pure narration (diegesis) and pure imitation (mimesis).

This linguistically based approach has the great advantage of supplying precise grammatical and lexical criteria, rather than relying on vague psychological and stylistic ones. But it oversimplifies the literary problems by carrying too far the correspondence between spoken discourse and silent thought. Speech is, by definition, always verbal. Whether thought is always verbal is to this day a matter of definition and dispute among psychologists. Most people, including most novelists, certainly conceive of consciousness as including 'other mind stuff' (as William James called it), in addition to language. This 'stuff' cannot be quoted – directly or indirectly; it can only be narrated. One of the drawbacks of this linguistic approach is therefore that it tends to leave out of account the entire nonverbal realm of consciousness, as well as the entire problematic relationship between thought and speech.

Though my own discussion of the modes for rendering consciousness will be more literary than linguistic in its attention to stylistic, contextual, and psychological aspects, I take simple linguistic criteria for my starting-point in naming and defining three basic techniques.

1   *Psycho-narration.* The most indirect technique has no fixed name; the terms 'omniscient description' and 'internal analysis' have been applied, but neither is satisfactory. 'Omniscient description' is too general: anything, not only the psyche, can be described 'omnisciently.' 'Internal analysis' is misleading: 'internal' implies a process occurring *in*, rather than *applied to*, a mind (cf. internal bleeding); 'analysis' does not allow for the plainly reportorial, or the highly imagistic ways a narrator may adopt in narrating consciousness.

My neologism 'psycho-narration' identifies both the subject-matter and the activity it denotes (on the analogy to psychology, psychoanalysis). At the same time it is frankly distinctive, in order to focus attention on the most neglected of the basic techniques. Stream-of-consciousness critics have acknowledged its existence only grudgingly, since all fictional psyches since *Ulysses* supposedly come at the reader directly, without the aid of a narrator; Robert Humphrey even declares that it is 'something of a shock' to find writers like Dorothy Richardson 'using conventional description by an omniscient author – without any attempt on the part of the author to disguise the fact.' And linguistic-structuralist critics, by reducing the technique to an unvoiced indirect discourse, disregard the ironic or lyric, reductive or expansive, sub- or super-verbal functions that psycho-narration can perform, precisely because it is not primarily a method for presenting mental language.

2   *Quoted monologue.* The tendency to polarize techniques historically has even more lastingly confused the technique that, from a purely grammatical point of view, is simplest to define. According to the post-Joycean canon interior monologue was supposed not to have existed before *Ulysses* (with the notable exception of Dujardin's novel *Les Lauriers sont coupés*). But what was to be done with direct thought-quotations in novels like *Le Rouge et le noir* or *Crime and Punishment*? Most critics accepted the thesis developed by Dujardin in his book *Le monologue intérieur*, where he draws a sharply divisive line between quotations of the mind found in stream-of-consciousness novels and those found in more traditional novels. Insisting that the term 'interior monologue' should be reserved for the modern 'flowing' variety of thought-quotations, they have suggested such terms as 'traditional monologue' or 'silent soliloquy' for thought-quotations found in pre-Joycean novels. The tendency has been to distinguish between them on both psychological and stylistic grounds: the interior monologue is described as associative, illogical, spontaneous; the soliloquy as rhetorical, rational, deliberate.

Staccato rhythms, ellipses, profuse imagery are attributed to the interior monologue; more ordinary discursive language patterns to the soliloquy.

Even though this division has a certain historical validity, it is impossible to decide on the basis of such nuances whether a text is, or is not, an interior monologue: many quotations of fictional minds (in both pre- and post-Joycean novels) contain both logical *and* associative patterns, so that their degree of 'fluidity' may vary from moment to moment (and from interpreter to interpreter). The interior monologue–soliloquy distinction, moreover, makes one lose track of the twin denominators common to all thought-quotations, regardless of their content and style: the reference to the thinking self in the first person, and to the narrated moment (which is also the moment of locution) in the present tense. This overarching grammatical structure clearly differentiates the most direct technique from the other techniques for rendering consciousness in a third-person context. As for the term 'interior monologue': since the interiority (silence) of self-address is generally assumed in modern narrative, 'interior' is a near-redundant modifier, and should, on strictly logical grounds, be replaced by 'quoted.' But the term 'interior monologue' is so solidly entrenched (and has such a long and colorful history in the modern tradition) that more would be lost than gained in discarding it completely. I will therefore use the combined term 'quoted interior monologue,' reserving the option to drop the second adjective at will, and the first whenever the context permits.

3   *Narrated monologue.* The final basic technique in the third-person context is the least well-known in English criticism. Even such sophisticated genre critics as Scholes and Kellogg discern only 'two principal devices for presenting the inner life': narrative analysis and interior monologue. This dual division leaves a wide empty middle for the technique that probably renders the largest number of figural thoughts in the fiction of the last hundred years, but bears no standard English name. The French and German terms (*style indirect libre* and *erlebte Rede*) are sometimes used, as well as 'free indirect speech,' 'indirect interior monologue,' 'reported speech,' etc. I have previously tagged this technique 'narrated monologue,' a name that suggests its position astride narration and quotation. Linguistically it is the most complex of the three techniques: like psycho-narration it maintains the third-person reference and the tense of narration, but like the quoted monologue it reproduces verbatim the character's own mental language.

In sum, three types of presentation of consciousness can be identified in the context of third-person narration, to each of which I devote a chapter in the first part of my study. In capsule formulation: 1) psycho-narration: the narrator's discourse about a character's consciousness; 2) quoted monologue: a character's mental discourse; 3) narrated monologue: a character's mental discourse in the guise of the narrator's discourse.

Strangely, the study of techniques for rendering consciousness has focused almost exclusively on third-person narrative texts (with the notable exception of texts cast entirely in interior monologue form). The fact that autobiographical narrators also have inner lives (their own past inner lives) to communicate has passed almost unnoticed. But *retro*spection into a consciousness, though less 'magical,' is no less important a component of first-person novels than *in*spection of a consciousness is in third-person novels. The same basic types of presentation appear, the same basic terms can apply, modified by prefixes to signal the modified relationship of the narrator to the subject of his narration: psycho-narration becomes self-narration (on the analogy with self-analysis), and monologues can now be either self-quoted, or self-narrated.

If it were merely a matter of surveying an analogous territory in which 'he thought' is replaced by 'I thought' the bipartite division of my study into third- and first-person narrative forms would lead to nothing but redundancies. But the parallelism between them stops as soon as one goes beyond the definition of the basic techniques. There is, for one thing, a profound change in narrative climate as one moves between the two territories – a change that has been underrated in recent structuralist approaches. It stems from the altered relationship between the narrator and his protagonist when that protagonist is his own past self. The narration of inner events is far more strongly affected by this change of person than the narration of outer events; past thought must now be presented as *remembered* by the self, as well as expressed by the self (i.e. subject to what David Goldknopf calls the 'confessional increment'). All this substantially alters the function of the three basic techniques in autobiographical narration.

But there is another and far more important reason for the division by person: where the most direct method for the presentation of consciousness is concerned, a radical dissymmetry appears between third- and first-person forms. In third-person context the direct expression of a character's thought (in first-person form) will always be a quotation, a quoted monologue: But this direct expression of thought can be presented outside a narrative context as well, and can shape an independent first-person form of its own: the type of text also normally referred to as 'interior monologue' (*Les Lauriers sont coupés*, 'Penelope'). At this point it becomes clear that the term 'interior monologue' has been designating two very different phenomena, without anyone's ever stopping to note the ambiguity: 1) a narrative technique for presenting a character's consciousness by direct quotation of his thoughts in a surrounding narrative context; and 2) a narrative *genre* constituted in its entirety by the silent self-communion of a fictional mind. Though the technique and the genre share some psychological implications and stylistic features, their narrative presentations are entirely different: the first is mediated (quoted explicitly or implicitly) by a narrating voice that refers to the monologist by third-person pronoun in the surrounding text; the second, unmediated, and apparently self-generated, constitutes an autonomous first-person form, which it would be best to regard as a variant – or better, a limit-case – of first-person narration.

This terminological ambiguity too originated with Dujardin, who had a special reason to conflate the two meanings: his claim that *Les Lauriers sont coupés* was the sole ancestor of *Ulysses* would have been weakened if he had drawn attention to the basic structural difference between the two works: the absence of a narrative context in his own novels and its presence in Joyce's. But it is obvious on the face of it that *Ulysses* is not an interior-monologue novel in the same sense as *Les Lauriers* is. Joyce's awareness of this difference is apparent in his own description of Dujardin's novel, as reported by Valéry Larbaud: 'In that book the reader finds himself established, from the first lines, in the thoughts of the principal personage, and the uninterrupted unrolling of that thought, replacing the usual form of narrative, conveys to us what this personage is doing and what is happening to him.' He could scarcely have meant this description to apply to *Ulysses*, since (with the notable exception of the final 'Penelope' section) interior monologue is everywhere embedded in a third–person narrative medium. The 'first lines' of most of its sections (including of course the first lines of the entire work), far from establishing the reader 'in the thoughts of the principal personage,' are clearly told in 'the usual form of narrative.' Wherever the monologue technique appears in *Ulysses*, it alternates with narration, and these narratorial incursions, no matter how brief, permeate the self-locution with a discontinuous element, even as they relieve it of certain notorious difficulties of the autonomous form (e.g. the description of the monologist's own gestures and surroundings). No matter how untraditional their Joycean modulations, such sections as 'Proteus' or 'Hades' are therefore *structurally* analogous to the quoted monologues in the novels of Stendhal or Dostoevsky rather than to the autonomous form of Dujardin's novel.

It is probably no coincidence that Joyce's comment on *Les Lauriers* dates precisely from the time when he was writing 'Penelope,' the only section of *Ulysses* that does have a structure analogous to that of Dujardin's novel. The comment itself still stands today as the most accurate capsule description we have of the interior monologue as a separate fictional form: a first-person genre that, for the sake of clarity, I will call '*autonomous* interior monologue,' a term that accurately reflects its same-different relationship to the quoted interior monologue. For this autonomous form also, we can again safely drop the second adjective in most instances. An alternate term I will sometimes use is 'interior monologue text' (or 'novel').

Despite its notoriety, the autonomous interior monologue in its pure form is a very rare species, even if we count in (as we must) the separate sections from larger texts that take this form ('Penelope,' or Mann's Goethe monologue). Yet it is a genre that is entwined with other first-person genres in far more intricate ways than has generally been understood. Both typologically and historically there are multiple intermediate stages between autobiographical and monologic texts, and the two categories can be separated only by closely examining these transitional variations. In this region, the study of techniques for rendering consciousness therefore necessarily spills over into the larger problem of narrative genres (and *the* narrative genre), with the autonomous monologue acting as an essential touchstone for defining what the 'usual form of narrative' is – by what it isn't.

Paul Ricoeur, 'Narrative Time'*

See also:
Plato (1.i)
Aristotle (1.i)
Bakhtin (1.iii)
Lévi-Strauss (2.i)
Genette (2.ii)
Lyotard (3.iii)
Heath (4)
Derrida (6)
de Man (6)
Miller (6)
Kellner (8)
Bhabha (9)

* *Critical Inquiry*, 7 (1980), pp. 169–76.

1   PRESUPPOSITIONS

My first working hypothesis is that narrativity and temporality are closely related – as closely as, in Wittgenstein's terms, a language game and a form of life. Indeed, I take temporality to be that structure of existence that reaches language in narrativity and narrativity to be the language structure that has temporality as its ultimate referent. Their relationship is therefore reciprocal.

This structural reciprocity of temporality and narrativity is usually overlooked because, on the one hand, the epistemology of history and the literary criticism of fictional narratives take for granted that every narratives takes place within an uncriticized temporal framework, within a time that corresponds to the ordinary representation of time as a linear succession of instants. Philosophers writing on time, too, usually over-look the contribution of narrative to a critique of the concept of time. They either look to cosmology and physics to supply the meaning of time or they try to specify the inner experience of time without any reference to narrative activity. Narrative function and the human experience of time thus remain strangers. In order to show the reciprocity between narrativity and temporality, I shalt conduct this study as an analysis with two foci: for each feature of narrative brought out by reflection on either history or fictional narrative, I shall attempt to find a corresponding feature of temporality brought out by an existential analysis of time.

A second working hypothesis intervenes here: starting from the pole of temporality, there are different degrees of temporal organization. While this idea stems from division II of Heidegger's *Being and Time*,[1] one will not find here a blind submission to Heidegger's analyses. Quite the contrary; on the essential points, important and even fundamental corrections in the Heideggerian conception of time will result from applying a Heideggerian framework to the question of narrativity along with some recourse to other great philosophers of temporality and historicality, from Aristotle and Augustine to Gadamer. From the outset however, I agree with Heidegger that the ordinary representation of time as a linear series of 'nows' hides the true constitution of time, which, if we follow the inverse order of that presented in *Being and Time*, is divided into at least three levels.

At the level closest to that of the ordinary representation of time, the first temporal structure is that of time as that 'in' which events take place. It is precisely this temporal structure that is leveled off by the ordinary representation of time. An analysis of narrative will help to show in what way this 'within-time-ness' already differs from linear time, even though it tends toward linearity due to its datable, public, an measurable nature and as a result of its dependence on points of reference in the world.

At a deeper level, time is more properly 'historicality.' This term does not coincide with the within-time-ness of which I have just spoken, nor with 'temporality' as such, which refers to the deepest level. Let us restrict ourselves here to characterizing histori-cality in terms of the emphasis placed on the weight of the past and, even more, in terms of the power of recovering the 'extension' between birth and death in the work of 'repetition.' This final trait is so decisive that, according to Heidegger, it alone permits objective history to be grounded in historicality. Finally, Heidegger invites us to move beyond historicality itself to the point at which temporality springs forth in the plural unity of future, past, and present. It is here that the analysis of time is rooted in that of 'care,' particularly as care reflecting on itself as mortal.

Joining this second working hypothesis to the first, I shall try to check the successive stages of the analysis of temporality itself against an analysis of narrativity, which is itself composed of several levels.

My third working hypothesis concerns the role of narrativity. The narrative structure that I have chosen as the most relevant for an investigation of the temporal implications of narrativity is that of the 'plot.' By plot I mean the intelligible whole that governs a succession of events in any story. This provisory definition immediately shows the plot's connecting function between an event or events and the story. A story is *made out of* events to the extent that plot *makes* events *into* a story. The plot, therefore, places us at the crossing point of temporality and narrativity: to be historical, an event must he more than a singular occurrence, a unique happening. It receives its definition from its contribution to the development of a plot. Still, the temporal implications of the plot, on which my whole paper focuses, are precisely those overlooked by anti-narrativist writers in the field of historiography and by structuralists in the field of literary criticism. In both fields, the emphasis on nomological models and paradigmatic codes results in a trend that reduces the narrative component to the anecdotic surface of the story. Thus both the theory of history and the theory of fictional narratives seem to take it for granted that whenever there is time, it is always a time laid out chronologically, a linear time, defined by a succession of instants.

My suspicion is that both anti-narrativist epistemologists and structuralist literary critics have overlooked the temporal complexity of the narrative matrix constituted by the plot. Because most historians have a poor concept of 'event' – and even of 'narrative' – they consider history to be an explanatory endeavor that has severed its ties with storytelling. And the emphasis on the surface grammar in literary narration leads literary critics to what seems to me to be a false dichotomy: either remaining caught in the labyrinthine chronology of the told story or moving radically to an a-chronological model. This dismissal of narrative as such implies a similar lack of concern in both camps for the properly *temporal* aspects of narrative and therefore for the contribution that the theory of narrative could offer to a phenomenology of time experience. To put it bluntly, this contribution has been almost null because *time* has disappeared from the horizon of the theories of history and of narrative. Theoreticians of these two broad fields seem even to be moved by a strange resentment toward time, the kind of resentment that Nietzsche expressed in his *Zarathustra*.

2   WHAT OCCURS HAPPENS 'IN' TIME

I will now fashion together a theory of narrative and a theory of time and, by moving back and forth between them, attempt to correlate the stages of the analysis of narrative with the different depths in the analysis of time. If, in this effort at comparison, the analysis of time most often performs the role of guide, the analysis of narrative, in its turn, serves as a critical and decisive corrective to it.

At the first level of our inquiry, the relation to time expressed by the preposition 'in' – to happen 'in' time – serves as our guide. What is at stake in an existential analysis – such as Heidegger's – is the possibility of discerning those characteristics by which within-time-ness differs from the ordinary representation of time, even though it is easily leveled off into this representation. I shall compare this existential analysis of time with the analysis of what may seem most superficial in narrativity, that is, the *development* of a plot and its correlate, the ability *to follow* a story.

First, a brief review of the main features of the Heideggerian analysis of within-time-ness: this level is defined by one of the basic characteristics of care – our thrownness among things – which makes the description of our temporality dependent on the description of the things of our concern. Heidegger calls these things of our concern *das Vorhandene* ('subsisting things which our concern counts on') and *das Zuhandene* ('utensils offered to our manipulation'). Heidegger calls this trait of concern 'preoccupation' or 'circumspection.' As we shall see later, concern has other traits that are more deeply hidden, and because of these hidden, deep traits, it has fundamental temporal modes. But however inauthentic our relationship to things, to ourselves, and to time may be, preoccupation, the everyday mode of concern, nevertheless already includes characteristics that take it out of the external domain of the objects of our concern, referring it instead to our concern in its existential constitution. It is remarkable that in order to point out these properly existential characteristics, Heidegger readily turns to what we say and do with regard to time. This method is, not surprisingly, very close to that found in ordinary language philosophy: the plane on which we are placing ourselves in this initial phase of investigation is precisely the one on which ordinary language truly is what J. L. Austin and others have said it is, namely, a treasure-house of expressions appropriate to what is specifically human in experience. It is therefore language, with its storehouse of meanings, that keeps the description of concern, in the modality of preoccupation or circumspection, from slipping back into the description of the things of our concern and from remaining tied to the sphere of *vorhanden* and *zuhanden*.

Within-time-ness, then, possesses its own specific features which are not reducible to the representation of linear time, a neutral series of abstract instants. Being in time is already something quite different from measuring intervals between limiting instants; it is first of all *to reckon with* time and so to calculate. It is because we do reckon with time and make calculations that we have the need to measure, not the other way around. It should therefore be possible to give an existential description of this reckoning before the measuring it calls for. It is here that expressions such as 'having time to,' 'taking time to,' 'wasting time,' and so on, are most revealing. The same is true of the grammatical network of verbal tenses, and likewise of the far-ranging network of adverbs of time: then, after, later, earlier, since, till, while, until, whenever, now that, and so forth. All these extremely subtle and finely differentiated expressions point out the datable and public character of the time of preoccupation.

It is our preoccupation, not the things of our concern, that determines the sense of time. It is because there is a *time to do* this, a right time and a wrong time, that we can reckon *with* time. If within-time-ness is so easily interpreted in terms of the ordinary representation of time, this is because the first measurements of the time of our preoccupation are borrowed from the natural environment – first of all from the play of light and of the seasons. In this respect, a day is the most natural of measures. 'Dasein,' Heidegger says, 'historizes *from day to day* (p. 466). But a day is not an abstract measure; it is a magnitude which corresponds to our concern and to the world into which we are thrown. The time it measures is that in which it is *time to* do something (*Zeit zu*), where 'now' means 'now that'; it is the time of labors and days. It is therefore important to see the shift in meaning that distinguishes the 'now' belonging to this time of preoccupation from 'now' in the sense of an abstract instant, which as part of a series defines the line of ordinary time. The existential now is determined by the present of preoccupation, which is a 'making-present,' inseparable from awaiting and retaining. It is because, in preoccupation, concern tends to contract itself into this making-present and to obliterate its dependency with regard to awaiting and retaining that the now isolated in this way can fall prey to the representation of the now as an isolated abstract instant. In order to preserve the meaning of now from this reduction to an abstraction, it is important to attend to the way in which we 'say now' (*Jetz-sagen*) in everyday acting and suffering. 'Saying "now,"' says Heidegger, 'is the discursive Articulation of a *making-present* which temporalizes itself in a unity with a retentive awaiting' (p. 469). And again, 'The making-present which interprets itself – in other words, that which has been interpreted and is addressed in the "now" – is what we call "time"' (p. 460). So we see how, as a result of certain practical circumstances, this interpretation is bent in the direction of the representation of linear time. Saying 'now' becomes for us synonymous with reading the hour on the face of a clock. As long as the hour and the clock are still perceived as derivations of the day that links concern with the light of the world, saying 'now' retains its existential significance; but when the machines used to measure time are cut off from this primary reference to natural measures, saying 'now' is turned into a form of the abstract representation of time.

Turning to narrative activity, I shall now attempt to show that the time of the simplest story also escapes the ordinary notion of time conceived of as a series of instants succeeding one another along an abstract line oriented in a single direction. The phenomenology of the act of following a story may serve as our point of departure.[2] Let us say that story describes a series of actions and experiences made by a number of characters, whether real or imaginary. These characters are represented either in situations that change or as they relate to changes to which they then react. These changes, in turn, reveal hidden aspects of the situation and of the characters and engender a new predicament that calls for thinking, action, or both. The answer to this predicament advances the story to its conclusion.

Following a story, correlatively, is understanding the successive actions, thoughts, and feelings in question insofar as they present a certain directedness. By this I mean that we are pushed ahead by this development and that we reply to its impetus with expectations concerning the outcome and the completion of the entire process. In this sense, the story's conclusion is the pole of attraction of the entire development. But a narrative conclusion can be neither deduced nor predicted. There is no story if our attention is not moved along by a thousand contingencies. This is why a story has to be followed to its conclusion. So rather than being predictable, a conclusion must be acceptable. Looking back from the conclusion to the episodes leading up to it, we have to be able to say that this ending required these sorts of events and this chain of actions. But this backward look is made possible by the teleological movement directed by our expectations when we follow the story. This is the paradox of contingency, judged 'acceptable after all,' that characterizes the comprehension of any story told.

If we now compare this brief analysis of the development of a plot to the Heideggerian concept of within-time-ness, we can say that the narrative structure confirms the existential analysis. To begin, it is clear that the art of storytelling places the narrative 'in' time. The art of storytelling is not so much a way of reflecting on time as a way of taking it for granted. We can apply to storytelling Heidegger's remark that 'factical Dasein takes time into its reckoning, without any existential understanding of temporality' (p. 456). And it is indeed to factical *Dasein* that the art of storytelling belongs, even when the narrative is fictional. It is this art that makes all the adverbs enumerated above directly significant – then, next, now, and so on. When someone, whether storyteller or historian, starts recounting, everything is already spread out in time. In this sense, narrative activity, taken without further reflection, participates in the dissimulation both of historicality and, even more so, of the deeper levels of temporality. But at the same time, it implicitly states the truth of within-time-ness insofar as it possesses its own authenticity, the authenticity of its inauthenticity, if one may so put it, and it therefore presents an existential structure quite as original as the other two existential categories of time that frame it.

To take an example, the heroes of stories reckon *with* time. They have or do not have time *for* this or that. Their time can be gained or lost. It is true to say that we measure this time of the story because we count it and that we count it because we reckon with it. The time of the story retains this reckoning at the threshold of measurement, at the point where it reveals our thrownness, by which we are abandoned to the changing of day into night. This time is already reckoned time on which dating operates; but it is not yet time in which the natural measure of 'days' is replaced by artificial measures, that is, measures taken from physics and based on an instrumentation that follows the progress of the investigation of nature. In a narrative, the measuring of time is not yet released from time reckoning because this reckoning is still visibly rooted in preoccupation. It is as true to say of narrative as of preoccupation that the 'day' is the natural measure and that 'Dasein historizes *from day to day.*'

For these reasons, the time of a narrative is public time, but not in the sense of ordinary time, indifferent to human beings, to their acting and their suffering. Narrative time is public time in the same sense that within-time-ness is, before it is leveled off by ordinary time. Moreover, the art of storytelling retains this public character of time while keeping it from falling into anonymity. It does so, first, as time common to the actors, as time woven in common by their interaction. On the level of the narrative, of course, 'others' exist: the hero has antagonists and helpers: the object of the quest is someone else or something else that another can give or withhold. The narrative confirms that 'in the "most intimate" Being-with-one-another of several people, they can say "*now*" and say it "*together.*" . . . The "now" which anyone expresses is always said in the publicness of Being-in-the-world with one another' (p. 463).

This first side of public time is, in some sense, internal to the interaction. But the narrative has a second relationship to public time: external public time or, we might say, the time of the public. Now a story's public is its audience. Through its recitation, a story is incorporated into a community which it gathers together. It is only through the written text that the story is open to a public that, to borrow Gadamer's expression, amounts to anyone who can read. The published work is the measure of this public. But even so, this public is not just anyone at all, it is not 'they'; instead, it is they lifted out of anonymity in order to make up an invisible audience, those whom Nietzsche called 'my own.' This public does not fall back into they – in the sense in which a work is said to fall into the public domain – except through a leveling off similar to that by which within-time-ness is reduced to ordinary time, knowing neither day nor hour, recognizing no 'right' time because no one feels concerned by it.

A final trait of within-time-ness is illustrated by the time of the narrative. It concerns the primacy of the present in preoccupation. We saw that for Heidegger, saying 'now' is interpreting the making-present which is accorded a certain preference by pre-occupation, at the expense of awaiting and retaining. But it is when within-time-ness is leveled of that saying 'now' slips into the mathematical representation of the instant characteristic of ordinary time. Saying 'now' must therefore continually be carried back to making present if this abstract representation is to be avoided.

Now narratives invite a similar, yet quite original, reinterpretation of this saying 'now.' For a whole category of narratives, in fact (those which according to Robert Scholes and Robert Kellogg stem from the epic matrix[3] and those which Vladimir Propp and Algirdas Greimas place under the title of the quest), narrative activity is the privileged discursive expression of preoccupation and its making-present. It is privileged because these narratives exhibit a feature that the Heideggerian analysis of saying 'present' – an analysis that is too brief and too centered around 'reading the hour' – does not encounter, namely, the phenomenon of 'intervention' (which, by way of contrast, at the center of Henrik von Wright's analyses in action theory). These narratives, in fact, represent a person acting, who orients him- or herself in circumstances he or she has not created, and who produces consequences he or she has not intended. This is indeed the time of the 'now that . . . ,' wherein a person is both abandoned and responsible at the same time.

NOTES

1   Martin Heidegger, *Being and Time*, trans. John Macquarrie and Edward Robinson (New York, 1962); all further references to this work will be included in the text.
2   Here I am borrowing from W. B. Gallie's *Philosophy and the Historical Understanding* (New York, 1964).
3   See Robert Scholes and Robert Kellogg's *The Nature of Narrative* (New York, 1966).

8
History

Shoshana Felman, from *Testimony: Crises of Witnessing in Literature, Psychoanalyis and History**

See also
Benjamin (1.iii)
Lyotard (3.iii)
Bronfen (4)
Ricoeur (7)
Said (9)
Bhabha (9)

CAMUS' *THE PLAGUE*, OR A MONUMENT TO WITNESSING

What we call history we usually conceive of as a discipline of inquiry and as a mode of knowledge. What we call narrative we usually conceive of as a mode of discourse and as a literary genre. The relationship between narrative and history has been posited, time and again, both in theories of narrative and in theories of history. I will define here narrative, along with Barbara Herrnstein Smith, as 'verbal acts consisting of *someone telling someone else that something happened*.'[1] That 'something happened' in itself is history; that 'someone is telling someone else that something happened' is narrative. If narrative is basically a verbal act that functions as a historiographical report, history is, parallelly but conversely, the establishment of the facts of the past through their narrativization.

Between narrative and history

'The term history,' writes Hegel in his *Lectures on the Philosophy of History*, 'unites the objective and the subjective side, and denotes . . . not less what *happened* than the *narration*[2] of what happened. This union of the two meanings we must regard as of a higher order than mere outward accident; we must suppose historical narrations to have appeared contemporaneously with historical deeds and events.'[3] Although this classical philosophy of history, which claimed to unravel history, on the one hand, as the manifestation of a definite principle of progress and, on the other, as the materialization of a universal, overarching meaning, was, as one historian puts it, 'consumed in the holocaust of two world wars,'[4] contemporary theorists of history still by and large subscribe, on different grounds, to the view of the necessity of historical narrativization and of the inherent relationship between history and narrative. 'Historians,' writes Louis Mink, 'generally claim that they can give at least partial explanations of past events.' But historical explanation requires a certain perspective. 'The insistence on historical

* London and New York: Routledge, 1992, pp. 93–111

perspective seems to be more than a mere recommendation of the attitude of objectivity. . . . It is at least in part a claim that for the historical understanding of an event one must know its consequences as well as its antecedents; that the historians must look before *and* after . . . ; that in *some* sense we may understand a particular event by locating it correctly in a narrative sequence.'[5] History is thus contingent on interpretive narrativization. 'And it is these [*interpretive* hypotheses] which historians generally believe in some way distinguish history as *interpretive narrative* from chronology on the one hand and "science" on the other' (p. 36). 'The major point of difficulty in attempting to transform history into a cumulative science,' argues Mink, 'is not one of the *logic of evidence* but one of the *meaning of conclusions*' (p. 39). Detachable conclusions are possible in science, but not in history: 'despite the fact that an historian may "summarize" conclusions in the final chapter, it seems clear that these are seldom or never detachable conclusions; not merely their validity but their meaning refers back to the ordering of evidence in the total argument. The significant conclusions, one might say, are ingredient in the argument itself, . . . in the sense that they are *represented by the narrative order itself*' (p. 39).

The question I would like to address in the present essay is the following: If narrative is defined by a claim to establish a certain history, and if history is defined by a claim to explain events through their narrativization, is the mode of operation of these mutual claims (from history to narrative and from narrative to history) itself subject to history? Has contemporary history – with its cataclysm of the Second World War and the Holocaust – left intact the traditional shuttle movement between narrative and history? If not, what is the impact of the Holocaust on the mutual claims of history and narrative and the manner in which they are implicated in each other? Can contemporary narrative historically bear witness, not simply to the impact of the Holocaust but to the way in which the impact of *history as holocaust* has modified, affected, shifted the very modes of the relationship between narrative and history?

Under Western eyes, or the contemporary witness

As an initial textual approach, I will attempt to search for answers to these questions in the postwar narrative writings of Albert Camus.

Why Camus?

Because Camus, I would maintain, exemplifies the way in which traditional relationships of narrative to history *have changed* through the historical necessity of involving literature in action, of creating a new form of *narrative as testimony* not merely to record, but to rethink and, in the act of its rethinking, in effect *transform history* by bearing literary witness to the Holocaust. I will argue that Camus does indeed exemplify this literary witness to the Holocaust and this new, transformational relationship between narrative and history,[5-bis] even though it is by no means clear or obvious that his texts in any way refer to, or claim to deal with, the Holocaust as such.

'There is no such thing as a literature of the Holocaust, nor can be,' writes Elie Wiesel.[6] The fact that the author of this statement is himself the best-known writer of the Holocaust adds sharpness to the paradox of its pronouncement. I would like, however, to take this statement of impossibility seriously, and to explore the implications of its paradox in a different sense. What if we did not know what a literature of the Holocaust is, or might be? What if we did not know what the Holocaust is, or might be? What if, by reading, we could only try to find out, leaving the space of such a question open?

Granting that it might well be that 'there is no such thing as a literature of the Holocaust, nor can there be,' I propose to test the impact of the Holocaust on narrative (on the relationship of narrative to history) precisely in a writer who *does not* present himself, and *is not officially identified as*, a writer of (about) the Holocaust.

I wish, moreover, to explore the meaning of the Holocaust for a specifically *non-Jewish* European writer, one who, in his fate as Frenchman, was nonetheless immediately implicated in the cataclysm of the Second World War.

. . .

Testimony as a crisis

> 'That's not it,' Rambert rejoined. 'Until now I always felt a stranger in this town, and that I'd no concern with you people. *But now that I have seen what I have seen, I know that I'm from here* [je sais que je suis d'ici], whether I want it or not. This business is everybody's business [cette histoire nous concerne tous]. [p. 174, TM]

Bearing witness to the way in which 'this history concerns us all,' *The Plague* partakes of an *apprenticeship in history* through an apprenticeship in witnessing. The relationship of narrative to history is not, however, as unproblematic as the opening chapter seemed to indicate, since the witness – or the witnessing – which joins the two is *not a given*. The historical apprenticeship takes place only through a *crisis in*, and a consequent *transformation of*, the witness. And it is only through the medium of that crisis that the event can speak, and that the narrative can lend its voice to history. If the narrative is truly *claimed* by history, it is by virtue of that radical discontinuity, that radical change the witness has undergone:

> If only he could put the clock back and be once more the man who, at the outbreak of the epidemic, had had only one thought and one desire: to escape and return to the woman he loved! But that, he knew, was out of the question now; he had changed too greatly. The plague had forced on him a detachment which, try as he might, he couldn't think away, and which like a formless fear haunted his mind. Almost he thought the plague had ended too abruptly, he hadn't had time to pull himself together. Happiness was bearing down on him full speed, the event outrunning expectation.
>
> (pp. 273–4)

'Almost he thought the event had ended too abruptly, he hadn't had time to pull himself together.' The event outrunning expectation, history outruns the narrative, as though the narrative did not quite have the time to catch its breath and to catch up with history, to catch up with the full significance as well as the abruptness, the overwhelming aspect of the crisis and of the change that history has meant.

Knowledge and memories

Nevertheless, the narrative is testimony to an apprenticeship of history and to an apprenticeship of witnessing insofar as this historical crisis of the witness brings about a certain form of *cognition*. 'Now that I have seen what I have seen,' said Rambert, '*I know* that I'm from here.' However anguishing and ground shaking, seeing leads to knowing, a knowing that, in some ill-understood way, might be ground breaking. Rieux, in turn, in his double role as a doctor (involved witness) and as a narrator (a 'historian,' witness of the other witnesses), *learns something* from the witnessing and from the telling, and his testimony takes stock of this knowledge:

> Tarrou had 'lost the match,' as he put it. But what had he, Rieux, won? No more than the experience of *having known* plague and remembering it, of *having known* friendship and remembering of, of *knowing* affection and being destined one day to remember it. So all a man could win in the conflict between plague and life was *knowledge* and memories . . . .
>
> Knowing meant that: a living warmth, and a picture of death [Une chaleur de vie et une image de mort, c'était cela la connaissance].
>
> (pp. 270–1)

The task of the testimony is to impart that knowledge: a firsthand, carnal knowledge of victimization, of what it means to be 'from here' (from quarantine), wherever one is from; a firsthand knowledge of a historical passage through death, and of the way life will forever be inhabited by that passage and by that death; knowledge of the way in which 'this history concerns us all,' in which 'this business' of the Plague 'is everybody's business'; knowledge of the way in which history is the body's business knowledge of a 'total condemnation.'

NOTES

1   'Narrative Versions, Narrative Theories', in *On Narrative*, ed. N. J. T. Mitchell, Chicago and London: University of Chicago Press, 1980, 1981, p. 228.
2   In the quoted passages, italics are mine unless otherwise indicated.
3   G. W. F. Hegel, *The Philosophy of History*, trans. J. Sibree, New York: 1956, p. 60.
4   Louis Mink, 'The Autonomy of Historical Understanding', in *History and Theory*, vol. V, no. 1, Middletown, CT, Wesleyan University Press, 1966, p. 24.
5   *Ibid.*, p. 33. Hereafter, page references to this article will be given in parenthesis in the text.
5-bis See also Chapter 1, III, 'Narrative and Testimony: Albert Camus.'
6   In *Confronting the Holocaust*, ed. Alvin Rosenfeld and Irving Greenberg, Bloomington and London: Indiana University Press, p. 4.

Fredric Jameson, from *The Political Unconscious: Narrative as a Socially Symbolic Act**

See also:
Plato (1.i)
Bakhtin (1.iii)
Lévi-Strauss (2.i)
Gibson (3.ii)
Lyotard (3.iii)
Heath (4)
Cohn (7)
Said (9)
Gates (9)

The Marxian vision of history . . . has sometimes, as we have observed, been described as a 'comic' archetype or a 'romance' paradigm.[1] What is meant thereby is the salvational or redemptive perspective of some secure future, from which, with William Morris' Time Traveller, we can have our 'fill of the pleasure of the eyes without any of that sense of incongruity, that dread of approaching ruin, which had always beset me hitherto when I had been among the beautiful works of art of the past.'[2] In such a future, indeed, or from its perspective, our own cultural tradition – the monuments of power societies (for Goethe, the *Iliad* was a glimpse into hell) as well as the stories of fierce market competition and the expressions of commodity lust and of the triumph of the commodity form – will be read as children's books, recapitulating the barely comprehensible memory of ancient dangers.

Even from the standpoint of an ideal of realism (traditionally in one form or another the central model of Marxist aesthetics as a narrative discourse which unites the experience of daily life with a properly cognitive, mapping, or wellnigh 'scientific' perspective[3]) this apparently contradictory valorization of romance has much to be said for it. Let Scott, Balzac, and Dreiser serve as the non-chronological markers of the emergence of realism in its modem form; these first great realisms are characterized by a fundamental and exhilarating heterogeneity in their raw materials and by a corresponding versatility in their narrative apparatus. In such moments, a generic confinement to the existent has a paradoxically liberating effect on the registers of the text, and releases a set of heterogeneous historical perspectives – the past for Scott, the future for Balzac, the process of commodification for Dreiser – normally felt to be inconsistent with a focus on the historical present. Indeed, this multiple temporality tends to be sealed off and recontained again in 'high' realism and naturalism, where a perfected narrative apparatus (in particular the threefold imperatives of authorial depersonalization, unity of point of view, and restriction to scenic representation) begins to confer on the 'realistic' option the appearance of an asphyxiating, self-imposed penance. It is in the context of the gradual reification of realism in late capitalism that romance once again comes to be felt as the place of narrative heterogeneity and of freedom from that reality principle to which a now oppressive realistic representation is the hostage. Romance now again seems to offer the possibility of sensing other historical rhythms,

---

* London: Methuen Press, pp. 103–7

and of demonic or Utopian transformations of a real now unshakably set in place; and Frye is surely not wrong to assimilate the salvational perspective of romance to a re-expression of Utopian longings, a renewed meditation on the Utopian community, a re-conquest (but at what price?) of some feeling for a salvational future.

The association of Marxism and romance therefore does not discredit the former so much as it explains the persistence and vitality of the latter, which Frye takes to be the ultimate source and paradigm of all storytelling.[4] On this view, the oral tales of tribal society, the fairy tales that are the irrepressible voice and expression of the underclasses of the great systems of domination, adventure stories and melodrama, and the popular or mass culture of our own time are all syllables and broken fragments of some single immense story.

Yet Frye's identification of narrative in general with the particular narrative genre of romance raises the apparently unrelated issue of genre criticism, which, though thoroughly discredited by modern literary theory and practice, has in fact always entertained a privileged relationship with historical materialism. The first extended exercise in Marxist literary criticism – the letters of Marx and Engels to Lassalle about the latter's verse tragedy, *Franz von Sickingen*[5] – was indeed essentially generic; while the most developed corpus of Marxist literary analysis in our own time, the work of Georg Lukács, spanning some sixty years, is dominated by concepts of genre from beginning to end. I take it, indeed, as one of the moments of 'high seriousness' in the history of recent Marxist thought that when the aging Lukács felt the urgency of supporting Solzhenitsyn's denunciation of Stalinism but also of responding to the religious and antisocialist propaganda to which the latter lent his talent and the authority of his personal suffering, he did so by sitting down at his desk and producing a piece of genre criticism. The strategic value of generic concepts for Marxism clearly lies in the mediatory function of the notion of a genre, which allows the coordination of immanent formal analysis of the individual text with the twin diachronic perspective of the history of forms and the evolution of social life.

Meanwhile, in the other traditions of contemporary literary criticism, generic perspectives live something like a 'return of the repressed.' Frye's own work, so resolutely organized around narrative, owed its widespread influence to the New Critical context in which it first appeared, and in which the fundamental object of literary study had been only too narrowly construed as the lyric, or poetic language. Contemporary structural and semiotic methods also, with their rigorous self-imposed restriction to discrete individual texts, have known the re-emergence of a meditation on hitherto marginalized types of discourse: legal language, the fragment, the anecdote, autobiography, Utopian discourse, the fantastic, novelistic description (or *ekphrasis*), the preface, the scientific treatise, which are increasingly conceived as so many distinct generic modes.

What literary criticism seems unable to do without completely, however, literary production has in modern times ceaselessly and systematically undermined. The emancipation of the 'realistic novel' from its generic restrictions (in the tale, the letter, the framed *récit*), the emergence, first of modernism, with its Joycean or Malarmean ideal of a single Book of the world, then of the postmodernist aesthetic of the text or of *écriture*, of 'textual productivity' or schizophrenic writing – all seem rigorously to exclude traditional notions of the literary kinds, or of systems of the fine arts, as much by their practice as by their theory.

Nor is it difficult to see why this has been so. Genres are essentially literary *institutions*, or social contracts between a writer and a specific public, whose function is to specify the proper use of a particular cultural artifact. The speech acts of daily life are themselves marked with indications and signals (intonation, gesturality contextual deictics and pragmatics) which ensure their appropriate reception. In the mediated situations of a more complicated social life – and the emergence of writing has often been taken as paradigmatic of such situations – perceptual signals must be replaced by conventions if the text in question is not to be abandoned to a drifting multiplicity of uses (as *meanings* must, according to Wittgenstein, be described). Still, as texts free themselves more and more from an immediate performance situation, it becomes ever more difficult to enforce a given generic rule on their readers. No small part of the art of writing, indeed, is absorbed by this (impossible) attempt to devise a foolproof mechanism for the automatic exclusion of undesirable responses to a given literary utterance.

It is not merely the performance situation, but the generic contract and institution itself, which, along with so many other institutions and traditional practices, falls casualty to the gradual penetration of a market system and a money economy. With the elimination of an institutionalized social status for the cultural producer and the opening of the work of art itself to commodification, the older generic specifications are transformed into a brand-name system against which any authentic artistic expression must necessarily struggle. The older generic categories do not, for all that, die out, but persist in the half-life of the subliterary genres of mass culture, transformed into the drugstore and airport paperback lines of gothics, mysteries, romances, bestsellers, and popular biographies, where they await the resurrection of their immemorial, archetypal resonance at the hands of a Frye or a Bloch. Meanwhile, it would seem necessary to invent a new, historically reflexive, way of using categories, such as those of genre, which are so clearly implicated in the literary history and the formal production they we traditionally supposed to classify and neutrally to describe.

NOTES

1   Hayden White *Metahistory* (Baltimore: Johns Hopkins University Press, 1973); pp. 281–2: 'Hegel's Comic conception of history was based ultimately on his belief in the right of life over death; "life" guaranteed to Hegel the possibility of an ever more adequate form of social life throughout the historical future. Marx carried this Comic conception even further; he envisioned nothing less than the dissolution of that "society" in which the contradiction between consciousness and being had to be entertained as a fatality for all men in all times. It would not, then, be unjust to characterize the final vision of history which inspired Marx in his historical and social theorizing as a Romantic one. But his conception did not envisage humanity's redemption as a deliverance from time itself. Rather, his redemption took the form of a reconciliation of man with a nature denuded of its fantastic and terrifying powers, submitted to the rule of technics, and turned to the creation of a genuine community.'

2   William Morris, *News from Nowhere*, ch. xx (London: Longmans, Green, 1903), p. 188.

3   The canonical statements are those of Georg Lukács; see in particular, *Studies in European Realism* (New York: Grosset & Dunlap, 1964), and *Realism in Our Time*, trans. J. and N. Mander (New York: Harper, 1964). See also my 'Reflections in Conclusion' to the collection

of materials on the so-called Brecht-Lukács debate, *Aesthetics and Politics* (London: New Left Books, 1977), pp. 196–213.

4   Notthrop Frye, *The Secular Scripture* (Cambridge, MA: Harvard University Press, 1976), pp. 28–31.

5   Karl Marx and Friedrich Engels, *Über Kunst und Literatur* (Berlin: 1953), pp. 129–67.

Samuel Weber, 'Capitalizing History: Thoughts on *The Political Unconscious*'*

See also:
Gibson (3.ii)
Lyotard (3.iii)
Derrida (6)
De Man (6)
Miller (6)
Bennington (6)
Fish (7)
Ricoeur (7)
Said (9)
Bhabha (9)

The deal is tempting, no doubt. And all the more so, since it comes cushioned in a most attractive, self-critical, gift-wrapping: The ideological critique (of Marxism) does not depend on some dogmatic or 'positive' conception of (itself) as a system. Rather, it is simply the place of an imperative to totalize, an imperative, Jameson adds, that can also be directed at Marxism itself, in its various forms, in order to reveal 'their own local ideological limits or strategies of containment' (p. 53). As ideological criticism, then, Marxism is 'simply' the place of the imperative to totalize, nothing more, nothing less. But can that place be so simple to find, especially if its name can often be distorted or disguised by forms of Marxism which themselves must be subjected to 'the imperative to totalize'? If Marxism can transcend such deficiencies, if it can be criticized in *its own name*, it is only because its own 'place' is coextensive with another space which bears *another* name, that of History. Writ large. And it is with this gesture, capitalizing History, that Jameson takes up the challenge of 'post-structuralist' thought, which, as is clear throughout *The Political Unconscious*, is both the most immediate adversary and the (more or less) silent partner.

The 'post-structuralist' challenge to History, as I have already suggested, entails its persistent suspicion of the teleological perspective of totalization in which historical 'development' has traditionally been conceived. This suspicion goes back at least to Nietzsche who, in *The Genealogy of Morals* for instance, argued that the 'assigning' of 'purposes' as the 'meaning' of a phenomenon is nothing but a mode of interpretation that seeks to impose itself by masking its particular, partisan character in the guise of the thing itself. A process which is not merely 'performative,' but agonistically and violently so, dislodging the previously dominant interpretive scheme in order to take its

* *Diacritics* (1983), pp. 20–5

place. Such a process can present itself as the mere 'constatation' of a teleological, or entelechical movement of its object, of which it is the simple *porte-parole*. History, then, whether as ethnocentrism (Lévi-Strauss), phallogocentrism (Derrida), the genetic/developmental stages of object-development (Lacan), or as a strategy of power operating by the exclusion of discontinuity (Foucault), has been subjected to a re-examination that has tended both to question the qualities of self-identity, universality and objective necessity hitherto attributed to it, and to redefine that attribution itself as part of a strategy that seeks to impose itself precisely by denying its own strategic, partisan character.

It is evident that such a move bears certain resemblances to the conception of thought as ideology developed by Marxism. The difference, of course, is that whereas Marxism retains the oppositions of 'science' and 'ideology,' of true and false consciousness, as well as the notion of historical objectivity as their indispensable and constitutive dividing-line, most of the thinkers mentioned either explicitly or implicitly include all of these categories in the agonistic process itself.

Jameson's response to this challenge is to perform precisely the gesture that he seeks to exclude by attributing it to 'ideology': that of attempting to 'contain' the adversary. This 'strategy of containment,' which the ideology-critique of Marxism, Jameson asserts, seeks to expose through its 'imperative to totalize' (but is not such an imperative itself already the mirror-image of what it seeks to contain?), consists of two gestures: acknowledgment and incorporation.

Acknowledgment:

> *The Political Unconscious* accordingly turns on the dynamics of the act of interpretation and presupposes, as its organizational fiction, that we never really confront a text immediately, in all its freshness as a thing-in-itself. Rather, texts come before us as the always-already-read; we apprehend them through sedimented layers of previous interpretations, or – if the text is brand-new – through the sedimented reading habits and categories developed by those inherited interpretive traditions. . . . [Hence,] our object of study is less the text itself than the interpretations *through* which we attempt to confront and to appropriate it.
>
> (pp. 9–10, my emphasis)

After this, one might have expected a study of the procedures, mechanisms and approaches of interpretation in terms of their strategic, agonistic operation on 'the academic marketplace.' But such a discussion, presumably, would not simply 'cancel and preserve' all competing critical positions, it would not simply assign them their proper place – it would displace them in a space that could no longer be safely contained by the 'discipline' of literary studies, as we know it today. The analysis of the literary text, not as a self-identical *object*, but as an element in a highly conflictual, ambivalent power-struggle, would have consequences for the organization and practice of the discipline of literary studies, as it is institutionally established, of which not the least disruptive would be the redefinition of its 'borders,' its relation to other disciplines and above all, to other modes, of thought, whether these have been disciplined already or not. What would ultimately be raised is the issue of the existing definition and delimitation of knowledge, as well as the conditions of its practice: in short, the discipline and the university.

But the acknowledgment of the dependency of texts upon their interpretation remains just that: an *isolated* act without any further consequence.[1] Perhaps this is because the informing intention is not to disrupt 'the academic marketplace today,' but rather to stake out the claims of Marxism 'within' it. In any case, the terms in which the relation of texts to interpretation, and hence, to the 'Homeric battlefield' *within* which the latter is said to take place, already announces what is to come: if texts are only given to us 'through' sedimented layers of previous interpretations, 'through' sedimented reading habits, then they still remain what they are, in and of themselves, even after passing through those layers of sedimentation. The text may be *mediated* by its interpretations, but its meaning is not structurally constituted by these readings; rather, it is *contained* in the text, just as the text itself is contained within the space of History.

And it is here that the second gesture, *incorporation*, emerges. History in *The Political Unconscious* names that space which contains and comprehends everything else, including first and foremost, the 'text.' Hence, Jameson's insistence on the fact that History and text are inseparable, but also non-identical:

> History is *not* a text, not a narrative, master or otherwise, but . . . an absent cause [which] is inaccesible to us except in textual form. . . . Our approach to it and to the Real necessarily passes through its prior textualization, its narrativization in the political unconscious.
>
> (p. 35, author's emphasis)

The text, then, is something that we must necessarily pass *through*, on our way somewhere else, to something as 'prior' to the text as the latter is prior to our 'approach to it': History, as 'absent cause.'

Viewed from a formal perspective – which is not necessarily the same as a formalist one – Jameson's defense of Marxism is caught in a double bind: it criticizes its competitors for being ideological in the sense of practicing 'strategies of containment,' that is, of drawing lines and practicing exclusions that ultimately reflect the particularities – the partiality and partisanship – of special interests seeking to present themselves as the whole. But at the same time its own claim to offer an alternative to such ideological containment is itself based on a strategy of containment, only upon one which seeks to identify itself with a whole more comprehensive than that of its rivals.

If there is a difference, then, between 'Marxism' and 'ideology,' it cannot be determined purely at the level of *form*, since both seek to contain and to comprehend their competitors in the name of a certain objectivity. The difference, rather, must reside in the kind of objectivity appealed to. Which is why, towards the end of the long, introductory theoretical chapter, Jameson finally, after telling us what History is *not* (a text, a narrative), attempts to tell us what it *is*:

> History is therefore the experience of Necessity, and it is this alone which can forestall its thematization or reification as a mere object of representation or as one master code among many others. Necessity is not in that sense a type of content, but rather the inexorable form of events; it is therefore a narrative category . . . a retextualization of History.
>
> (p. 102)

If the Marxist comprehension of History is distinct from ideological strategies of containment, it is not, strangely enough, because of the *contents* of that History, but because of its *form*. Marxism, it turns out, *is* form after all, or rather, a certain kind of form. Not that of narrative as such, but that of a particular type of narrative, that which tells us 'why what happened . . . had to happen the way it did' (p. 101). Necessity, then, the, experience of which defines History, is that form of narrative which is ultimately, and in principle, self-identical; the story it tells could not be told otherwise, could not be changed, altered or modified, without being falsified and losing its necessity. If History is thus the 'absent cause,' Necessity is the equally 'absent story', the Idea (in the Kantian sense) of a Story, of a Text, of a Narration that could not be told otherwise than it is – and hence, which 'is' not, which is absent, functioning only as a kind of regulative idea. But this idea is no mere fiction since through its putative absence it can be *invoked* to produce or to justify very real effects and practices: for instance, the legitimacy of judging actual, mundane narratives in terms of a text that is identical-to-itself, but whose identity is never immediately present-as-such. As an 'absent cause,' such identity – whether it is called 'History', 'Literature,' 'Work,' 'Author' or whatever – always requires an intermediary, a *critical* spokesman in order to be *heard*. It cannot speak for itself, but must be spoken for. And yet, it must also provide the basis for distinguishing between true and false spokesmen, for is this not the essence, and justification, of the critical project and its practices?

And yet, if this is so, then the most dramatic of Jameson's attempts to provide a positive definition of History – 'History is what hurts . . . what refuses desire and sets inexorable limits to individual as well as collective praxis' [p. 102] – raises the question: hurts *whom*? The readers of *The Political Unconscious*? Its author? The brokers in the academic marketplace? Their customers? But what if all of these were searching precisely for some instance that might set 'inexorable limits' to their 'praxis,' which, for want of authorized limits, was in the process of losing its sense of self-legitimacy? What, in short, if critics *desired* to be 'hurt' in this way, as a lesser evil, rather than to court the risks of being left beside themselves, 'beside the point,' by desires they no longer controlled? Would 'History', Jameson's History, still simply 'hurt,' or simply 'refuse desire'? The desire, for instance, to capitalize (on) History?

It seems likely, on the contrary, that a good many of those whose existence is tied to the academic marketplace would be neither hurt nor frustrated by a History which can be described as follows:

> This is indeed the ultimate sense in which History as ground and untranscendable horizon needs no particular theoretical justification: we may be sure that its alienating necessities will not forget us, however much we might prefer to ignore them.
>
> (p. 102)

Not to be forgotten, even by 'alienating necessities,' may yet be preferable to the current uncertainties traversing the profession in regard to its social status and its institutional future. To hear that 'History as ground and untranscendable horizon needs no particular theoretical justification' is doubtless music to the ears of many scholars and critics for whom recent theoretical discussion has rendered the ground upon which the discipline has been based less than solid, and its horizons anything but clear or 'untranscendable.'

Like Fish's 'institution' or 'interpretive community,' then, Jameson's History' recommends itself as the best means of Saving the Text (and those who live by it):

> It is in detecting the traces of that uninterrupted narrative, in restoring to the surface of the text the repressed and buried reality of this fundamental history, that the doctrine of a political unconscious finds its function and its necessity.
>
> (p. 20)

And, we might add, it is here that it also 'finds' much of its appeal; like Fish, Jameson could assure his readers (if he so chose), that the Marxism of *The Political Unconscious* will not be an engine of exproportion, but of appropriation: that it will help them in their efforts to appropriate the text, to enrich themselves by enriching the texts, that we will 'have everything that we always had,' only more, better and safer than before. It is no accident that Jameson recommends Marxism in terms of its superior 'semantic richness,' which in turn is directly related to its conception of History. The methadology outlined in *The Political Unconscious* capitalizes directly upon this notion of History:

> Such semantic enrichment and enlargement of the inert givens and materials of a particular text must take place within three concentric frameworks, which mark a widening out of the sense of the social ground of a text.
>
> (p. 75)

These three 'frameworks' – the 'symbolic' or 'political' (in the narrower sense of events); the 'social,' and the 'historical' – can be described as 'concentric' only because their center is identified with the 'inert givens and materials of a particular text' – a text, in short, whose particularity coincides with its *inertia*, the fact that it is, once and for all, in its proper place *within* History, that is within a story waiting to be told, once and for all, in the one and only way. Like the movement of Capital itself, this story is never finished, but its end is always in sight. It is, Jameson suggests, a 'single, great collective story' with 'a single, fundamental theme . . . the collective struggle to wrest a realm of Freedom from a realm of Necessity.' This great struggle produces 'vital episodes in a single, vast unfinished plot' (pp. 19–20). It is this plot, then, that *The Political Unconscious* suggests it is the critic's business to discover, it is a plot that promises to keep critics in business indefinitely – on the condition that its unity, singularity and self-identity are not themselves seen as an effect of interpretation, of narration, of 'textualization' but rather as their center and frame, their ground and horizon.

But this plot, with its lure of limitless enrichment, contrasts strangely with the story it tells, and *The Political Unconscious* constantly returns to it like a criminal to the scene of the crime. The reader is thus led to reflect upon the tension that pervades *The Political Unconscious*, between the 'struggle' that is said to constitute the ultimate subject-matter of texts and of their interpretations, on the one hand, and on the other, an essentially 'constative' or 'contemplative' conception of the process of interpretation itself. For notwithstanding the early remark about its agonistic, conflictual character, interpretation is described as a more or less faithful reconstruction, reproduction or resuscitation of the 'buried reality' – or treasures – of the text. Conflict is thus confined to the thematic element of literature, leaving its hermeneutical discovery to pursue its mission of 'semantic enrichment' without any of the trials and tribulations associated with primitive accumulation as described by Marx.

The reason for this, of course, is that the problems faced by *The Political Unconscious* are determined not by the needs of primitive accumulation, but by the crisis of over-accumulation. Translated into the particular area of literary criticism, this is manifest in the fact that the problems of the discipline arise not from a scarcity of interpretive productivity, but from its excess. The problem is not so much how to interpret, but how to valorize interpretation, at a time when it is in danger of asphyxiation from its uncontrolled proliferation. And it is here, in its response to this problem, that *The Political Unconscious* is most revealing, of its own strategies and of the 'battlefield' *within* which they are designed to operate.

In order to judge and evaluate individual interpretations, however, there must be standards available that are themselves more than purely individual in character. Thus, the problem of arbitration leads inevitably to one of the major concerns of *The Political Unconscious*, the necessity of rethinking the relation between *individual* and *collective*. 'One of the most urgent tasks for Marxist theory today,' remarks Jameson, towards the end of the book, 'is (to construct) a whole new logic of collectively dynamics, with categories that escape the taint of some mere application of terms drawn from individual experience' (p. 294). It is from this standpoint that Jameson interprets the structuralist and post-structuralist critique of subjectivity; however, he does not seem to realize that the *rapprochement* could work the other way as well: that the problem of 'individualism' might well be reinterpreted in terms of the aporias of constitutive subjectivity, a move that has been attempted by Derrida, Lacan, Foucault, but also, before them (albeit in a more Hegelian vein), by Adorno and Horkheimer. In this perspective, what could be more individualist than the notion of History as a 'single, vast unfinished plot' ready to appropriate everything – all otherness – as a part of itself? What could be more individualist than the notion of Historical Necessity as a story that cannot be told otherwise (and yet which, necessarily, always is)?

NOTE

1   In *Inhibition, Symptom and Anxiety*, Freud describes 'isolating' as one of the 'techniques' that the ego can substitute for repression, to attain similar results. Instead of the objectionable idea being simply excluded from consciousness, 'its associative connections are suppressed or interrupted.' Freud emphasizes that such a tendency is to be found in normal thoughts as well, where 'concentration provides a pretext' – or an occasion – 'to keep away not only what is irrelevant or unimportant, but, above all, what is unsuitable because it is contradictory.' Contradiction, here, excludes dialectical synthesis (S. Freud, *Inhibition, Symptom and Anxiety*, Norton Library edition, New York, 1959, pp. 46–7). I have discussed the more general implications of 'isolating' in my *Legend of Freud* (University of Minnesota Press, Minneapolis, 1982), Part I.

Hans Kellner, 'Narrativity in History: Post-structuralism and Since'*

See also:
Benjamin (1.iii)
Bakhtin (1.iii)
Lyotard (3.iii)
Derrida (6)
Ricoeur (7)
Said (9)
Bhabha (9)

POST-STRUCTURALISM, HISTORY, NARRATIVE

Recent debates among historians on narrative often suggest that what is at issue is a simple decision: Should the historian tell a story (that is, narrate his material in a chronological, cause-effect way), or not? To choose not to tell a story is to be more 'modern,' following the social and economic sciences in presenting synchronic, and quantitative if possible, models of past affairs. New historical methods and recently explored kinds of documentation often deal with the general and the mass, rather than the particular and the individual; modelled on computers and lacking in 'events,' this 'new' history, which flourished in the 1960s and 1970s, established the basis for a non-narrative history that challenged the traditional core of historical knowledge. Even the turn to storytelling by certain prominent non-narrative historians only served to mark the distinction; tales of personal life in heretical medieval villages, or of returning husbands with uncertain identities, were distinctly *different* from the earlier work of these historians. The stories seemed to be luxury articles, earned as indulgences after the drudgery of economic, social, climatological, family, and demographic history. Indeed, the stories were often by-products of such research.

During the same period of time, roughly the twenty years from 1965 to 1985, another movement of thought emerged, which looked at forms of knowledge from quite an opposite perspective. While historians were confidently processing larger and larger quantities of information, producing broader comparisons and conclusions, and in general extending the historical domain toward a goal of a 'total history,' the counter-movement sought, like Penelope, to unravel the weaving of texts and to question wherever possible both the meaning and the tactics and conditions which made meaning possible in written texts of all sorts. History was for some of them a special target; they considered it both dependent upon and reinforcing the oppressive and inescapable atmosphere of 'humanism.'

Both movements, at first, found their theoretical inspiration in France; both found essential, practical support in the large and varied world of American academia. The post-war *Annales* 'school' of historians has by now seen three generations, each with its own style and interests. The movements once marked as 'structuralist' have similarly changed and developed to such an extent that the term 'post-structuralist' is conventionally used in the United States at least to designate the idiosyncratic and difficult

* *History and Theory*, 26 (1987), pp. 1–9.

thinkers who have challenged the primacy and security of meaning, of history, of narrative, and of the idea of 'man' which is constructed by these practices.

To study the writings of the 'unravelers,' the opponents of the extensive and totalizing forms of reading which information technology has made into the tacit current model of knowledge, is to suspect that the debate over narrative history is a good deal more complex than the recent debates among historians might suggest. My purpose here is to present an image of post-structuralist thinking on narrative and its intricate relationship with history and to sketch the work of three writers on historical narrativity. I am looking for common threads which might serve as guides for those studies of historical writing which desire neither to dissolve history into the area of pure textuality in which it will have little or no identity, nor to accept the representationality of historical writing on its own traditional terms of 'getting the story straight.'

At the risk of bringing down on my head the objection that 'argument by selective example is philosophically unpersuasive, a rhetorical device not a scientific proof,'[1] I shall sketch an image of post-structural thought about narrative and history by discussing briefly a few quotation from prominent figures. These figures might reject the term post-structuralist, which is a term current primarily in the United States; even the small group of writers sampled here differs in more ways than they might agree. A properly post-structuralist reading might well find important ways in which each passage differs from itself, offering a play of contending voices repressed by readings that stress their meaning and their essence. This said, I can only add that a survey of post-structuralist thought is a project that runs against the grain of post-structuralism. What follows is meant, therefore, as a point of departure, not a conclusion.

> (182) *He reaped the fruits of his genius by winning the sculpture prize.* * ACT.
> 'Career': 4: to win a prize.
> (183) *established by the Marquis de Marigny, the brother of Mme Pompadour, who did so much for the arts.* * REF. History (Mme de Pompadour).
> (184) *Diderot hailed the statue by Bouchardon's pupil as a masterpiece.* * ACT.
> 'Career': 5. to be praised by a great critic. * REF. History of literature (Diderot as art critic).
> (Roland Barthes, *S/Z*, trans. R. Miller (New York, 1974), p. 101)

So much of Roland Barthes' work has dealt with history and historical texts that it seems absurd to enter this corpus by way of a quotation from *S/Z*, Barthes' unique and meticulous decoding of a story by Balzac. The quotation itself requires decoding: the parenthetical numbers refer to the numbered segments (quoted in italics) into which Barthes has divided Balzac's text; the abbreviations marked by an asterisk (for example, 'REF', 'ACT,' and so on) designate the five codes which Barthes traces through the tale in his search for the conditions which give rise to the creation of meaning in this text. In *S/Z*, as we can see, 'History' figures within a single code, the Referential, among the five which constitute this version of narrative poetics. What makes this instance important for a consideration of post-structuralist explorations of history and narrative is that it signalled a change in Barthes' way of approaching narrative.

In his work of the 1960s, heavily influenced by the formalism of early structuralism, which he had done much to articulate, Barthes presents narrative as 'international, transhistorical, transcultural; it is simply there, like life itself.'[2] Naturally, the model Barthes used to describe narrative was that of language; it follows that, for him, mimesis, or realistic representation, is a matter of codes that are largely conventional. At about the same time, Barthes wrote related essays on 'Historical Discourse' and 'The Reality Effect' that spelled out in the structuralist terms of the mid-1960s how the illusions of reality are achieved in the realistic texts of both history and fiction. Certainly, narrative and the narrative competence of readers were essential parts of the referential and rational illusion. 'In fully constituted "flowing" discourse the facts function irresistibly either as indexes or as links in an indexical sequence; even an anarchic presentation of the facts will at least convey the meaning "anarchy" and suggest a particular philosophy of history of a negative kind.'[3] This flowing narrative discourse carries its own message independent of its subject matter: the gist of this message has to do with the meaningful relatedness of the facts in the discourse. Even meaninglessness or anarchy is meaningful in this view. Narrative is irresistible.

Returning to the quotation from *S/Z* cited above, we see that history serves there merely as one of the systems of reference which generate the 'effect of reality' in narrative, just as, in a different way, it is narrative that creates the possibility of historical discourse. Both history and narrative have for Barthes a mythic dimension, in the sense of myth developed in his work of the 1950s. The essence of this myth is the conversion of history into nature, and the essence of the myths of our own day is the process by which the dominant cultural forces transform the reality of the world into images of that world.[4] Myth is a meta-language, an allegory in that it gives structure to a gap between its surface and its content, and history is mythologized by its subservience to 'irresistible' narrativity.[5]

> What can a science of writing begin to signify, if it is granted . . . that historicity itself is tied to the possibility of writing; to the possibility of writing in general, beyond those particular forms of writing in the name of which we have long spoken of peoples without writing and without history. Before being the object of history – of an historical science – writing opens the field of history – of historical becoming. And the former (*Historie* in German) presupposes the latter (*Geschichte*).
>
> The science of writing should therefore look for its object at the roots of scientificity. The history of writing should turn back toward the origin of historicity. A science of the possibility of science? A science of science which would no longer have the form of *logic* but that of grammatics? A history of the possibility of history which would no longer be an archaeology, a philosophy of history or a history of philosophy?
>
> (Jacques Derrida, *Of Grammatology*, trans. G. C. Spivak
> (Baltimore and London, 1976), pp. 27–8)

The characteristic prose of Jacques Derrida, with its personified substantives, its inquisitory nominatives ('A science of the possibility of science?'), semantic conundrums ('a science of science'), passive modalities ('if it is granted'), implied assertions ('which would no longer have the form of'), mixed concretes and abstractions ('the roots of scientificity'), ambiguous relationships ('in the name of which'), and so on, is easier to identify and even describe than to penetrate. But this is not because Derrida does not write well – his prose is clearly an inextricable part of his thought, like Milton's no less difficult prose – but because, like Lacan and other modern writers, he takes great pains to perform the rigors of his thinking in his work. Derrida's project is a science of sciences that will delve the roots of the generalized writing which he takes to be the unacknowledged and repressed counterpart of the privileged voice of centered and locatable meaning that has dominated the 'history of metaphysics.'

Those who follow this project find that reading even the rational, commonsense world of historical writing is fraught with dangers and pitfalls.[6] The contradictory voices brought forth by deconstructive readers are generated by the fact that writing for them is constituted by a system of negative 'traces' which mark an absence; the negative hermeneutics of Derridean analysis arrives at a dispersed, even chaotic, field of signifiers posed against the meaning-oriented, false coherence always sought (and always found, even in paradox and error) by the 'logocentric' reading of the tradition. That this tradition supports itself as a discourse of morality and a discourse of power by means of its image of itself, its history, is clear. The 'origin of historicity' referred to above is not, or is not only, the origin of history-writing as the histories of historiography locate it; it is the origin of the possibility of historicity, of being in history, which is a vital part of the creation of 'humanity' as our culture represents it. Thus, Derrida is usually taken to be one of the radically anti-historical inheritor-critics of the structural linguist Ferdinand de Saussure.

The fundamental concepts which make history possible, that is to say, orderly, are undermined by Derrida, and dispersed by a discourse that confesses it must make use of these concepts at every turn (hence, the importance of Derrida's style, which calls attention to its inevitable implication in language by what has been called 'sawing off the branch on which you are seated'). This process of reading, well described as the 'careful teasing out of warring forces of signification within the text itself,' strives to leave no essential concepts unexamined, while welcoming the paradoxes, problems, and intricacies that are routinely overlooked by less rigorous readings.[7] The material assumptions of totality, identity, self-agreement, and so forth yield before this analysis; all of the logocentric human sciences of Western metaphysics come under scrutiny - history most of all, perhaps.[8] Cause, in particular, which can be seen as merely the product of narrative structures once the world is considered as a text, is a trap, always to be questioned.[9]

> As to the problem of fiction, it seems to me to be a very important one; I am well aware that I have never written anything but fictions. I do not mean to say, however, that truth is therefore absent. It seems to me that the possibility exists for fiction to function in truth, for a fictional discourse to induce effects of truth, and for bringing it about that a true discourse engenders or 'manufactures' something that does not yet exist, that is, 'fictions' it. One 'fictions' history on the basis of a political reality that makes it true, one 'fictions' a politics not yet in existence on the basis of a historical truth.
>
> (Michel Foucault, 'The History of Sexuality' (an interview), in *Power/Knowledge Selected Interviews and Other Writings, 1972–1977*, ed. C. Gordon, trans. C. Gordon, L. Marshall, J. Mepham, and K. Soper (New York, 1980), p. 193)

Michel Foucault's importance for historical theory scarcely needs mention; it was his 'revolutionization of history' which led many to the desire to 'forget' him.[10] Although his earlier work, especially *Madness and Civilization* and *The Order of Things*, put forth a highly rationalized image of modern Western history implicitly based upon the sequentiality of the ordering principles found in rhetorical tropes; the work of the 1970s (reflected in the theory of historical 'fictions' above) extends his scope in such a way as to call these very presuppositions into question as constructs towards a goal.[11]

When Foucault asserts that our enlightening, demystifying liberators actually repress us with their scientific authority, based on surveys, experimentation, and research, the open-endedness inherent in the critique expressed in the quotation above becomes manifest. In beginning his *History of Sexuality*, for instance, he posits as a problem, not the repression of sexual practices, but rather the discourse surrounding the discovery and attack on such alleged repressions. 'The question I would like to pose is not, Why are we repressed? but rather, Why do we say, with so much passion and so much resentment against our most recent past, against our present, and against ourselves, that we are repressed?'[12] Foucault's emphasis on the *discourse* about repression rather than the alleged repression itself is characteristic of his work. He repeatedly examines authoritative 'discourses,' particularly the meliorist and value-free discourses of enlightened modern social improvers (medicine, psychiatry, penology, and so on) in such a way as to unearth, 'genealogically,' the will to power embodied by *all* appeals to authority. For this reason, I stress the emphasis on 'fictionality' and 'truth' in his own work expressed above.

'Truth' and 'reality' are, of course, the primary authoritarian weapons of our time, an era characterized by nothing more than the debate over what is true of reality. Despite the obviously constructed nature of these twin concepts, which Foucault like other post-structuralists points up again and again, he will not dispense with them, but rather examines the way in which discourse creates reality, as reality creates discourse. His own fictions, therefore, are true because they are based upon a certain reality; this reality is real, in part, because it has been figured by his fictions. Insofar as Foucault is the opponent of what is 'natural' and 'common sensical,' insofar as he unmasks these as merely the *doxa*, the dominant opinion of our time, he links himself with Barthes as a radical historicist, who surveys the past 'under the sign of the Other,' confronting (that is, creating) a stark sense of repressed differences in history.[13]

> If it were to come out in a new day that the logocentric project had always been, undeniably, to *found* (fund) phallocentrism, to insure for masculine order rationale equal to history itself?
>
> Then all stories would have to be told differently, the future would be incalculable, the historical forces would, will, change hands, bodies; another thinking as yet not thinkable will transform the functioning of all society.
>
> (Hélène Cixous, 'Sorties,' *New French Feminisms*, ed. E. Marks and
> I. de Courtivron (Amherst, 1980), p. 93)

The de-naturalizing that seems so much a part of post-structuralist practice appears most complex, contradictory, and provocative among feminists, who are concerned with the dilemmas of entering a discourse which, by its very structure as rational, sequential thought, they assert, excludes a certain notion of *woman*, as body, freedom, Other. Among these modes of masculine, phallocentric writing, history is particularly indicted because it is not only the substance of a story which has, to a large extent, excluded women from its scope, but far more important from a post-structuralist perspective, because its alliance with narrative has indentured it to hidden forms of authority which are far more repressive to *woman* than being nameless in histories. 'Nearly the entire history of writing is confounded with the history of reason, of which it is at once the effect, the support, and one of the privileged alibis' (Cixous, 'Sorties,' p. 249).

The problem confronted for Cixous is how to speak, to find a voice within a discourse of reason and representation which has not only failed generally to speak of woman, but has more generally repressed the possibility of speaking as a woman from our very imaginations. Only an occasional poet, the foe of representationalism, has managed briefly to open a crack in which for a moment, woman might appear. 'Woman un-thinks the unifying, regulating history that homogenizes and channels forces, herding contradictions into a single battlefield' (Cixous, 'Sorties,' p. 252). Logocentrism, the term which denotes Derrida's concept of the word-centered, conceptual history of Western metaphysics, is equated with phallocentrism, the need to claim authority by defining, clarifying, making sequential points, leading to conclusions.[14] The danger is the theoretical, the authority of the signified, of essentialized meaning and definitions themselves. All of these traps are encased in a form of writing that leads through text-time to a goal, like histories, and which we may call narrative.[15]

If the attentions of structuralism and its aftermath to history have a coherent direction – that is, if we choose to make plausible historic sense out of them – then it seems to me that this direction must lead toward a thoroughgoing examination of the process of reading. It is reading that is the key, that has been redefined by post-structuralist practice, and revealed as a process far more elusive and problematic than before. In a sense, reading has been re-invented.

While formalist structural narratology seems to have reached a state of near technical perfection, offering an array of useful tools for foregrounding and examining aspects of texts, or of any phenomena that may be treated as though they were written texts, its treatment of the essential concept of the reader has, in general, been limited to matters of competence and how readers are constituted by texts. Post-structuralism has produced a practice of reading which has enacted the difficulty, even the impossibility, of trusting readings based on a simple, communicative model.[16]

The post-structuralist trajectory continues Roland Barthes' project of demythologizing; the myth is the conversion of history (the contingent, the force of the letter, human discourse) into nature (what is absolute, common-sense, beyond doubt, universally granted). As more and more of the accepted and inevitable components of human life are revealed as construction, no particular perspective can claim to be a privileged, secure basis. Although the post-structuralist thinker might point to a term, a scheme, a tactic, as a master viewpoint at any given moment, it is more than likely the next work will discard that term or scheme and erect an entirely new one. Their creation of jargons and specialized, neologistic vocabularies is authorized precisely by subsequent rejection and replacement by other jargons and vocabularies; the perils of language require that it be treated as scaffolding, always waiting to be taken down. One might say, with Hélène

Cixous, that the chaos of reality occasionally peeps through a crack, a poetic moment; but narrative and history; for the post-structuralist, are guilty until proven innocent.

NOTES

1   This observation is made by Lawrence Stone, 'The Revival of Narrative: Reflections on a New Old History,' *Past and Present* 85 (1979), discussed below.

2   Roland Barthes, 'Introduction to the Structural Analysis of Narrative (1996),' in *Image–Music–Text*, trans. S. Heath (New York, l977), p. 79.

3   Barthes, 'Historical Discourse,' in *Introduction to Structuralism*, ed. M. Lane (New York, 1970), p. 153.

4   Barthes, *Mythologies* (Paris, 1957), pp. 215, 229. Yet these political writings of the 1950s (which maintained that, yes, the left also made myths, but that these myths were 'inessential'), which would have seemed to herald a career trajectory of historical demystification, led in fact to Barthes' great battle with the establishment of literary history in France over his book *On Racing*. At the beginning of the last chapter of this book, he cited a 'naive and touching' program on French radio which sought to suggest to its listeners that art and history are interconnected by introducing musical selection – '1789: Convocation of the Estates General, recall of Necker, concerto for strings #4 in c minor, by B. Galuppi.'

    In his *Sade, Fourier, Loyola* (Paris, 1971), Barthes would produce a reply to chronological history by treating three figures from disparate areas of endeavor and different centuries, organizing his discussion without regard for chronology (going so far as to divide his discussion of Sade into two sections separated by Loyola and Fourier, thus repeating in his text the 'mania for cutting up' which he describes in his subjects). The final section, a dozen pages long in the English translation, is called 'Lives' and presents a series of unconnected statements ('biographemes') about Sade and Fourier (but not Loyola). These fragments are not only unconnected, but pointedly lack any consistency of narrative voice: some are bare statements of fact ('4. Fourier hated old cities: Rouen.'); some pointedly imitate the stupidities of Flaubert's 'received ideas': ('2. Fourier was contemporary with the two greatest events of Modern History: the Revolution and the Empire. Yet in this social philosopher's work, no trace of these two cataclysms.'); some suggest the histories that might be made from such fragments ('7. Inter-Text. Claude de Saint-Martin, Senancour, Restif de la Bretonne, Diderot, Rousseau, Kepler, Newton.'); the last, which ends the book, notes '12. Fourier had read Sade.' – a fact of no more importance for Barthes than the fact that Loyola had not read Sade.

5   Barthes: *Mythologies*, p. 200, and Louis-Jean Calvet, *Roland Barthes: un regard politique sur le signe* (Paris, 1973), pp. 39–44.

6   Among many examples of post structuralist readings of historical discourse, see Linda Orr's *Jules Michelet: Nature, History, Language* (Ithaca, 1977); 'Tocqueville et l'histoire incompréhensible,' *Poétique* 49 (1982), pp. 51–70; 'L'Autorité "populaire" de l'historiographie romantique,' *Romanic Review* 73 (1982), pp. 463–72. See also Dominick LaCapra's readings of Allan Janik and Stephen Toulmin's *Wittgenstein's Vienna* in LaCapra's *Rethinking Intellectual History: Texts, Contexts, Language* (Ithaca, 1983), and of Carlo Ginzburg's *The Cheese and the Worms* in LaCapra's *History and Criticism* (Ithaca, 1985).

7   Barbara Johnson, *The Critical Difference* (Baltimore and London, l980), p. 5.

8   An interesting survey of these issues is found in 'Text and History: Epilogue, 1984,' an

essay added to the Expanded Edition of Robert Weimann's *Structure and Society in Literary History*. Weimann takes issue with the contention in Michael Ryan's *Marxism and Deconstruction* that there is 'a radical concept of history in Derrida' (Weimann, *Structure and Society in Literary History* (Baltimore and London, 1984), p. 277, citing Ryan, *Marxism and Deconstruction* (Baltimore and London, 1982), p. 57.) He grants, however, that Derridean philosophy offers a 'certain mode of textual analysis which, by analogy, can prove potentially helpful in dismantling any monistic, mechanical, or idealist approaches to historical data, events, and gestures' (p. 278). I take this to mean that deconstruction is appropriate to everything except dialectical materialism.

9   Examples of the sort of assumptions questioned by Derrida are easy to find; the assumptions seem perfectly 'natural.' For example, in a review of Lynn Hunt's *Politics, Culture, and Class in the French Revolution*, Robert Darnton writes: 'Split by incompatible arguments, the book pulls the reader in opposite directions – toward sociology on one side and hermeneutics on the other' (*New York Review of Books*, 31 Jan 1985, p.). That arguments should be compatible, that readers should be pulled in only one direction, that the author is in charge of the reader's performance, and that sociology and hermeneutics (or any forces in a text) should be 'connected' somehow at the end of a responsible work, are all epistemological and (primarily) aesthetic assumptions built into the discourses analyzed by Derrida.

10   For example, Paul Veyne's 'Foucault revolutionne l'histoire,' in *Comment on écrit l'histoire* (Paris, 1978). 'Is Foucault still a historian? There is no true or false answer to this question, since history itself is one of those false natural objects: it is what we have made of it, it has not ceased to change, it does not survey an eternal horizon.' (p. 242) See also Allan Megill's 'The Reception of Foucault by Historians,' in *Journal of the History of Ideas* 48 (1987), pp. 117–41.

11   On the tropology in Foucault, see Hayen White, 'Foucault Decoded: Notes from Underground,' *History and Theory* 12 (1973), pp. 23–54.

12   Foucault, *The History of Sexuality*, trans. R. Hurley (New York, 1978), pp. 1, 9.

13   Paul Ricoeur, *The Reality of the Historical Past* (Milwaukee, 1984), ch. 2.

14   The notion of the phallus referred to here is central to an understanding of Jacques Lacan. It is not a human organ of any sort, but rather a reference to the ancient processions in which a veiled phallus was carried about. For Loran, the phallus is a signifier which creates desire for the unveiling of a signified, of meaning and truth; since this is always deferred by the nature of desire, it is desire of the phallus which is the basic motor of the inter-subjective economy because of the universality of castration. Jacques Lacan, 'The Signification of the Phallus,' in *Ecrits: A Selection*, trans. A. Sheridan (New York, 1977), pp. 281–91.

15   Post-structuralist consideration of narrative from a feminist perspective tends to conflate the weight of history and the ends-oriented exchange value of narrative. Maria Minich Brewer writes: 'We [interpreters of twentieth-century texts] read and describe with relative ease texts of fiction that contain a multiplicity of narrative voices, dissolution of characters, and perturbations in the logic of events and temporal developments. The challenge to narrative constraints in modern texts may seem to stem from a discontinuity created between essential terms: process without assigned Finality; multiple textual effects without an identifiable Cause; Writing that possesses neither a simple Origin nor End; signifiers without immediate access to a privileged Signified.' 'A Loosening of Tongues: From Narrative Economy to Women Writing,' in *MLN* 99 (1984), p. 1141.

16   The narratological literature is already vast. Useful introductions in English are Shlomith

Rimmon-Kenan, *Narrative Fiction: Contemporary Poetics* (London and New York, 1983); Gérard Genette, *Narrative Discourse: An Essay in Method*, trans. J. E. Lewin (Ithaca, 1980); and Wallace Martin, *Recent Theories of Narrative* (Ithaca, 1986). The classic statement of a communications model of poetics, which was a starting-point for structuralists and a system to be dismantled by post-structuralists, is Roman Jakobson's 'Linguistics and Poetics,' in *The Structuralists From Marx to Lévi-Strauss*, ed. R. and F. DeGeorge (Garden City, 1972), pp. 84–124.

In stressing the importance of reading as a category of research for historians, I am not referring primarily to the 'history of reception,' as the Germans and Swiss have pursued it, nor the 'sociology of literature,' as the French have pursued it, nor to histories of publishing and printing à la Robert Darnton and Elizabeth Eisenstein, nor to attempts to discover whether more Renaissance readers were reading Plutarch or Polybius. These unquestionably respectable pursuits all deal with an essentiaiized view of the book, of context, and of society, and with the partial exception of *Rezeptions-geschichte* have little sense of reading as process, nor of the reciprocal construction of text and reader, nor of conflicting voices within the text, nor of codes which make reading possible, nor of narratological categories.

That such a pursuit of signs, codes, and the like need not be a formalist exercise conducted in an 'historical vacuum' – such exercises, to be sure, are often of great value – is demonstrated by Hayden White's essay on Droysen, and on how his *Historik* functions to construct a particular kind of bourgeois reader. 'Droysen's *Historik*: Historical Writing as a Bourgeois Science,' in *The Content of the Form: Narrative Discourse and Historical Representation* (Baltimore, 1987), pp. 83–103.

9
Race

Edward Said, from *Culture and Imperialism**

See also
Benjamin (1.iii)
Lévi-Strauss (2.i)
Lyotard (3.iii)
McCloskey (3.ii)
de Man (6)
Felman (8)
Jameson (8)
Weber (8)

We called ourselves 'Intrusive' as a band; for we meant to break into the accepted halls of English foreign policy, and build a new people in the East, despite the rails laid down for us by our ancestors.

(T. E. Lawrence, *The Seven Pillars of Wisdom*)

NARRATIVE AND SOCIAL SPACE

Nearly everywhere in nineteenth- and early twentieth-century British and French culture we find allusions to the facts of empire, but perhaps nowhere with more regularity and frequency than in the British novel. Taken together, these allusions constitute what I have called a structure of attitude and reference. In *Mansfield Park*, which within Jane Austen's work carefully defines the moral and social values informing her other novels, references to Sir Thomas Bertram's overseas possessions are threaded through; they give him his wealth, occasion his absences, fix his social status at home and abroad, and make possible his values, to which Fanny Price (and Austen herself) finally subscribes. If this is a novel about 'ordination', as Austen says, the right to colonial possessions helps directly to establish social order and moral priorities at home. Or again, Bertha Mason, Rochester's deranged wife in *Jane Eyre*, is a West Indian, and also a threatening presence, confined to an attic room. Thackeray's Joseph Sedley in *Vanity Fair* is an Indian nabob whose rambunctious behaviour and excessive (perhaps undeserved) wealth is counterpointed with Becky's finally unacceptable deviousness, which in turn is contrasted with Amelia's propriety, suitably rewarded in the end; Joseph Dobbin is seen at the end of the novel engaged serenely in writing a history of the Punjab. The good ship *Rose* in Charles Kingsley's *Westward Ho!* wanders through the Caribbean and South America. In Dickens's *Great Expectations*, Abel Magwitch is the convict transported to Australia whose wealth – conveniently removed from Pip's triumphs as a provincial lad flourishing in London in the guise of a gentleman–ironically makes possible the great expectations Pip entertains. In many other Dickens novels businessmen have connections with the

* London: Chatto and Windus, 1993, pp. 73–81.

empire, Dombey and Quilp being two noteworthy examples. For Disraeli's *Tancred* and Eliot's *Daniel Deronda*, the East is partly a habitat for native peoples (or immigrant European populations), but also partly incorporated under the sway of empire. Henry James's Ralph Touchett in *Portrait of a Lady* travels in Algeria and Egypt. And when we come to Kipling, Conrad, Arthur Conan Doyle, Rider Haggard, R. L. Stevenson, George Orwell, Joyce Cary, E. M. Forster, and T. E. Lawrence, the empire is everywhere a crucial setting.

The situation in France was different, in so far as the French imperial vocation during the early nineteenth century was different from England's, buttressed as it was by the continuity and stability of the English polity itself. The reverses of policy, losses of colonies, insecurity of possession, and shifts in philosophy that France suffered during the Revolution and the Napoleonic era meant that its empire had a less secure identity and presence in French culture. In Chateaubriand and Lamartine one hears the rhetoric of imperial grandeur; and in painting, in historical and philological writing, in music and theatre one has an often vivid apprehension of France's outlying possessions. But in the culture at large – until after the middle of the century – there is rarely that weighty, almost philosophical sense of imperial mission that one finds in Britain.

There is also a dense body of American writing, contemporary with this British and French work, which shows a peculiarly acute imperial cast, even though paradoxically its ferocious and colonialism, directed at the Old World, is central to it. One thinks, for example, of the Puritan 'errand into the wilderness' and, later, of that extraordinarily obsessive concern in Cooper, Twain, Melville, and others with United States expansion westward, along with the wholesale colonization and destruction of native American life (as memorably studied by Richard Slotkin, Patricia Limerick, and Michael Paul Rogin); an imperial motif emerges to rival the European one. . . .

As a reference, as a point of definition, as an easily assumed place of travel, wealth, and service, the empire functions for much of the European nineteenth century as a codified, if only marginally visible, presence in fiction, very much like the servants in grand households and in novels, whose work is taken for granted but scarcely ever more than named, rarely studied (though Bruce Robbins has recently written on them), or given density. To cite another intriguing analogue, imperial possessions are as usefully *there*, anonymous and collective, as the outcast populations (analysed by Gareth Stedman Jones) of transient workers, part-time employees, seasonal artisans; their existence always counts, though their names and identities do not, they are profitable without being fully there. This is a literary equivalent, in Eric Wolf's somewhat self-congratulatory words, of 'people without History',[4] people on whom the economy and polity sustained by empire depend, but whose reality has not historically or culturally required attention.

In all of these instances the facts of empire are associated with sustained possession, with far-flung and sometimes unknown spaces, with eccentric or unacceptable human beings, with fortune-enhancing or fantasized activities like emigration, money-making, and sexual adventure. Disgraced younger sons are sent off to the colonies, shabby older relatives go there to try to recoup lost fortunes (as in Balzac's *La Cousine Bette*), enterprising young travellers go there to sow wild oats and to collect exotica. The colonial territories are realms of possibility, and they have always been associated with the realistic novel. Robinson Crusoe is virtually unthinkable without the colonizing mission that permits him to create a new world of his own in the distant reaches of the African, Pacific, and Atlantic wilderness. But most of the great nineteenth-century realistic novelists are less assertive about colonial rule and possessions than either Defoe or late writers like Conrad and Kipling, during whose time great electoral reform and mass participation in politics meant that imperial competition became a more intrusive domestic topic. In the closing year of the nineteenth century, with the scramble for Africa, the consolidation of the French imperial Union, the American annexation of the Philippines, and British rule in the Indian subcontinent at its height, empire was a universal concern.

. . .

To regard imperial concerns as constitutively significant to the culture of the modern West is, I have suggested, to consider that culture from the perspective provided by anti-imperialist resistance as well as pro-imperialist apology. What does this mean? It means remembering that Western writers until the middle of the twentieth century, whether Dickens and Austen, Flaubert or Camus, wrote with an exclusively Western audience in mind, even when they wrote of characters, places, or situations that referred to, made use of, overseas territories held by Europeans. But just because Austen referred to Antigua in *Mansfield Park* or to realms visited by the British navy in *Persuasion* without any thought of possible responses by the Caribbean or Indian natives resident there is no reason for us to do the same. We now know that these non-European peoples did not accept with indifference the authority projected over them, or the general silence on which their presence in variously attenuated forms is predicated. We must therefore read the great canonical texts, and perhaps also the entire archive of modern and pre-modern European and American culture, with an effort to draw out, extend, give emphasis and voice to what is silent or marginally present or ideologically represented (I have in mind Kipling's Indian characters) in such works.

In practical terms, 'contrapuntal reading' as I have called it means reading a text with an understanding of what is involved when an author shows, for instance, that a colonial sugar plantation is seen as important to the process of maintaining a particular style of life in England. Moreover, like all literary texts, these are not bounded by their formal historic beginnings and endings. References to Australia in *David Copperfield* or India in *Jane Eyre* are made because they *can be*, because British power (and not just the novelist's fancy) made passing references to these massive appropriations possible; but the further lessons are no less true: that these colonies were subsequently liberated from direct and indirect rule, a process that began and unfolded while the British (or French, Portuguese, Germans, etc.) were still there, although as part of the effort at suppressing native nationalism only occasional note was taken of it. The point is that contrapuntal reading must take account of both processes, that of imperialism and that of resistance to it, which can be done by extending our reading of the texts to include what was once forcibly excluded – in *L'Etranger*, for example, the whole previous history of France's colonialism and its destruction of the Algerian state, and the later emergence of an independent Algeria (which Camus opposed).

Each text has its own particular genius, as does each geographical region of the world, with its own overlapping experiences and interdependent histories of conflict. As far as the cultural work is concerned, a distinction between particularity and sovereignty (or hermetic exclusiveness) can usefully be made. Obviously no reading should try to generalize so much as to efface the identity of a particular text, author, or movement. By the same token it should allow that what was, or appeared to be, certain for a given work or author may have become subject to disputation. Kipling's India in *Kim* has a quality of permanence and inevitability that belongs not just to that wonderful novel but to British India, its history, administrators, and apologists and, no less important, to the India fought for by Indian nationalists as their country to be won back. By giving an account of this series of pressures and counter-pressures in Kipling's India, we understand the process of imperialism itself as the great work of art engages them, and of later anti-imperialist resistance. In reading a text, one must open it out both to what went into it and to what its author excluded. Each cultural work is a vision of a moment, and we must juxtapose that vision with the various revisions it later provoked – in this case, the nationalist experiences of post-independence India.

In addition, one must connect the structures of a narrative to the ideas, concepts, experiences from which it draws support. Conrad's Africans, for example, come from a huge library of *Africanism*, so to speak, as well as from Conrad's personal experiences. There is no such thing as a *direct* experience, or reflection, of the world in the language of a text. Conrad's impressions of Africa were inevitably influenced by lore and writing about Africa, which he alludes to in *A Personal Record*; what he supplies in *Heart of Darkness* is the result of his impressions of those texts interacting creatively, together with the requirements and conventions of narrative and his own special genius and history. To say of this extraordinarily rich mix that it 'reflects' Africa, or even that it reflects an experience of Africa, is somewhat pusillanimous and surely misleading. What we have in *Heart of Darkness* – a work of immense influence, having provoked many readings and images – is a politicized, ideologically saturated Africa which to some intents and purposes was the imperialized place, with those many interests and ideas furiously at work in it, not just a photographic literary 'reflection' of it.

This is, perhaps, to overstate the matter, but I want to make the point that far from *Heart of Darkness* and its image of Africa being 'only' literature, the work is extraordinarily caught up in, is indeed an organic part of, the 'scramble for Africa' that was contemporary with Conrad's composition. True, Conrad's audience was small; and, true also, he was very critical of Belgian colonialism. But to most Europeans, reading a rather rarefied text like *Heart of Darkness* was often as close as they came to Africa, and in that limited sense it was part of the European effort to hold on to, think about, plan for Africa. To represent Africa is to enter the battle over Africa, inevitably connected to later resistance, decolonization, and so forth.

Works of literature, particularly those whose manifest subject is empire, have an inherently untidy, even unwieldy aspect in so fraught, so densely charged a political setting. Yet despite their formidable complexity, literary works like *Heart of Darkness* are distillations, or simplifications, or a set of choices made by an author that are far less messy and mixed up than the reality. It would not be fair to think of them as abstractions, although fictions such as *Heart of Darkness* are so elaborately fashioned by authors and so worried over by readers as to suit the necessities of narrative which, as a result, we must add, makes a highly specialized entry into the struggle over Africa.

So hybrid, impure, and complex a text requires especially vigilant attention as it is interpreted. Modern imperialism was so global and all-encompassing that virtually nothing escaped it; besides, as I have said, the nineteenth-century contest over empire is still continuing today. Whether or not to look at the connections between cultural texts and imperialism is therefore to take a position *in fact taken* – either to study the connection in order to criticize it and think of alternatives for it, or not to study it in order to let it stand, unexamined and, presumably, unchanged. One of my reasons for writing this book is to show how far the quest for, concern about, and consciousness of overseas dominion extended – not just in Conrad but in figures we practically never think of in that connection, like Thackeray and Austen – and how enriching and important for the critic is attention to this material, not only for the obvious political reasons but also because, as I have been arguing, this particular kind of attention allows the reader to interpret canonical nineteenth- and twentieth-century works with a newly engaged interest.

Henry Louis Gates, Jr., 'Thirteen Ways of Looking at a Black Man'*

See also:
Lévi-Strauss (2.i)
Lyotard (3.iii)
McCloskey (3.iii)
Jackson (3.iii)
de Lauretis (5)
de Man (6)
Miller (6)
Jameson (8)
Weber (8)

Every day, in every way, we are getting meta and meta,' the philosopher John Wisdom used to say, venturing a cultural counterpart to Émile Coué's famous mantra of self-improvement. So it makes sense that in the aftermath of the Simpson trial the focus of attention has been swiftly displaced from the verdict to the reaction to the verdict, and then to the reaction to the reaction to the verdict, and, finally, to the reaction to the reaction to the reaction to the verdict – which is to say, black indignation at white anger at black jubilation at Simpson's acquittal. It's a spiral made possible by the relay circuit of race. Only in America.

   An American historian I know registers a widespread sense of bathos when he says, 'Who would have imagined that the Simpson trial would be like the Kennedy assassination – that you'd remember where you were when the verdict was announced?' But everyone does, of course. The eminent sociologist William Julius Wilson was in the red-carpet lounge of a United Airlines terminal, the only black in a crowd of white travellers, and found himself as stunned and disturbed as they were. Wynton Marsalis, on tour with his band in California, recalls that 'everybody was acting like they were above watching it, but then when it got to be ten o'clock – zoom, we said, "Put the verdict on!"' Spike Lee was with Jackie Robinson's widow, Rachel, rummaging through a trunk filled with her husband's belongings, in preparation for a bio-pic he's making on the athlete. Jamaica Kincaid was sitting in her car in the parking lot of her local grocery store in Vermont, listening to the proceedings on National Public Radio, and she didn't pull

* *New Yorker*, 23 October 1995, pp. 56–8.

out until after they were over. I was teaching a literature seminar at Harvard from twelve to two, and watched the verdict with the class on a television set in the seminar room. That's where I first saw the sort of racialized response that itself would fill television screens for the next few days: the white students looked aghast, and the black students cheered. 'Maybe you should remind the students that this is a case about two people who were brutally slain, and not an occasion to celebrate,' my teaching assistant, a white woman, whispered to me.

The two weeks spanning the O. J. Simpson verdict and Louis Farrakhan's Million Man March on Washington were a good time for connoisseurs of racial paranoia. As blacks exulted at Simpson's acquittal, horrified whites had a fleeting sense that this race thing was knottier than they'd ever supposed – that, when all the pieties were cleared away, blacks really *were* strangers in their midst. (The unspoken sentiment: *And I thought I knew these people.*) There was the faintest tincture of the Southern slave-owner's disquiet in the aftermath of the bloody slave revolt led by Nat Turner – when the gentleman farmer was left to wonder which of his smiling, servile retainers would have slit *his* throat if the rebellion had spread as was intended, like fire on parched thatch. In the day or so following the verdict, young urban professionals took note of a slight *froideur* between themselves and their nannies and babysitters – the awkwardness of an unbroached subject. Rita Dove, who recently completed a term as the United States Poet Laureate, and who believes that Simpson was guilty, found it 'appalling that white people were so outraged – more appalling than the decision as to whether he was guilty or not.' Of course, it's possible to overstate the tensions. Marsalis invokes the example of team sports, saying, 'You want your side to win, whatever the side is going to be. And the thing is, we're still at a point in our national history where we look at each other as sides.'

The matter of side-taking cuts deep. An old cartoon depicts a woman who has taken her errant daughter to see a child psychiatrist. 'And when we were watching "The Wizard of Oz"' the distraught mother is explaining, 'she was rooting for the wicked witch!' What many whites experienced was the bewildering sense that an entire population had been rooting for the wrong side. 'This case is a classic example of what I call interstitial spaces,' says Judge A. Leon Higginsbotham, who recently retired from the federal Court of Appeals, and who last month received the Presidential Medal of Freedom. 'The jury system is predicated on the idea that different people can view the same evidence and reach diametrically opposed conclusions.' But the observation brings little solace. If we disagree about something so basic, how can we find agreement about far thornier matters? For white observers, what's even scarier than the idea of that black Americans were plumping for the villain, which is a misprision of value, is the idea that black Americans didn't recognize him *as* the villain, which is a misprision of fact. How can conversation begin when we disagree about reality? To put it at its harshest, for many whites a sincere belief in Simpson's innocence looks less like the culture of protest than like the culture of psychosis.

Perhaps you didn't know that Liz Claiborne appeared on 'Oprah' not long ago and said she didn't design her clothes for black women – that their hips were too wide. Perhaps you didn't know that the soft drink Tropical Fantasy is manufactured by the Ku Klux Klan and contains a special ingredient designed to sterilize black men. (A warning flyer distributed in Harlem a few years ago claimed that these findings were vouchsafed on the television program '20/20.') Perhaps you didn't know that the Ku Klux Klan has a similar arrangement with Church's Fried Chicken – or is it Popeye's?

Perhaps you didn't know these things, but a good many black Americans think they do, and will discuss them with the same intentness they bring to speculations about the 'shadowy figure' in a Brentwood driveway. Never mind that Liz Claiborne has never appeared on 'Oprah,' that the beleaguered Brooklyn company that makes Tropical Fantasy has gone as far as to make available an FDA assay of its ingredients, and that those fried-chicken franchises pose a threat mainly to black folks' arteries. The folklorist Patricia A. Turner, who has collected dozens of such tales in an invaluable 1993 study of rumor in African-American culture, 'I Heard It Through the Grapevine,' points out the patterns to be found here: that these stories encode regnant anxieties, that they take root under particular conditions and play particular social roles, that the currency of rumor flourishes where 'official' news has proved untrustworthy.

Certainly the Fuhrman tapes might have been scripted to confirm the old saw that paranoids, too, have enemies. If you wonder why blacks seem particularly susceptible to rumors and conspiracy theories, you might look at a history in which the official story was a poor guide to anything that mattered much, and in which rumor sometimes verged on the truth. Heard the one about the LA cop who hated interracial couples, fantasized about making a bonfire of black bodies, and boasted of planting evidence? How about the one about the federal government's forty-year study of how untreated syphilis affects black men? For that matter, have you ever read through some of the FBIs COINTELPRO files? ('There is but one way out for you,' an FBI scribe wrote to Martin Luther King, Jr., in 1964, thoughtfully urging on him the advantages of suicide. 'You better take it before your filthy, abnormal, fraudulent self is bared to the nation.')

People arrive at an understanding of themselves and the world through narratives – narratives purveyed by schoolteachers, newscasters, 'authorities,' and all the other authors of our common sense. Counternarratives are, in turn, the means by which groups contest that dominant reality and the fretwork of assumptions that supports it. Sometimes delusion lies that way; sometimes not. There's a sense in which much of black history is simply counternarrative that has been documented and legitimatized, by slow, hard-won scholarship. The 'shadowy figures' of American history have long been our own ancestors, both free and enslaved. In any case, fealty to counternarratives is an index to alienation, not to skin color: witness Representative Helen Chenoweth, of Idaho, and her devoted constituents. With all the appositeness of allegory, the copies of 'The Protocols of the Elders of Zion' sold by black venders in New York – who are supplied with them by Lushena Books, a black-nationalist book wholesaler – were published by the white supremacist Angriff Press, in Hollywood. Paranoia knows no color or coast.

Finally, though, it's misleading to view counternarrative as another pathology of disenfranchisement. If the MIA myth, say, is rooted among a largely working-class constituency, there are many myths – one of them known as Reagaism – that hold considerable appeal among the privileged classes. 'So many white brothers and sisters are living in a state of denial in terms of how deep white supremacy is seated in their culture and society,' the scholar and social critic Cornel West says. 'Now we recognize that in a fundamental sense we really do live in different worlds.' In that respect, the reaction to the Simpson verdict has been something of an education. The novelist Ishmael

Reed talks of 'wealthy white male commentators who live in a world where the police don't lie, don't plant evidence – and drug dealers give you unlimited credit.' He adds, 'Nicole, you know, also dated Mafia hit men.'

'I think he's innocent, I really do,' West says. 'I do think it was linked to some drug subculture of violence. It looks as if both O.J. and Nicole had some connection to drug activity. And the killings themselves were classic examples of that drug culture of violence. It could have to do with money owed – it could have to do with a number of things. And I think that O. J. was quite aware of and fearful of this.' On this theory, Simpson may have appeared at the crime scene as a witness. 'I think that he had a sense that it was coming down, both on him and on her, and Brother Ron Goldman just happened to be there,' West conjectures. 'But there's a possibility also that O. J. could have been there, gone over and tried to see what was going on, saw that he couldn't help, split, and just ran away. He might have said, "I can't stop this thing, and they are coming at me to do the same thing." He may have actually run for his life.'

To believe that Simpson is innocent is to believe that a terrible injustice has been averted, and this is precisely what many black Americans, including many prominent ones, do believe. Thus the soprano Jessye Norman is angry over what she sees as the decision of the media to prejudge Simpson rather than 'educate the public as to how we could possibly look at things a bit differently.' She says she wishes that the real culprit 'would stand up and say, "I did this and I am sorry I caused so much trouble."' And while she is sensitive to the issue of spousal abuse, she is skeptical about the way it was enlisted by the prosecution: 'You have to stop getting into how they were at home, because there are not a lot of relationships that could be put on television that we would think, OK, that's a good one. I mean, just stop pretending that this is the case.' Then, too, she asks, 'Isn't it interesting to you that this Faye Resnick person was staying with Nicole Brown Simpson and that she happened to have left on the eighth of June? Does that tell you that maybe there's some awful coincidence here?' The widespread theory about murderous drug dealers Norman finds 'perfectly plausible, knowing what drugs do,' and she adds, 'People are punished for being bad.'

There's a sense in which all such accounts can be considered counternarratives, or fragments of them – subaltern knowledge, if you like. They dispute the tenets of official culture; they do not receive the imprimatur of editorialists or of network broadcasters; they are not seriously entertained on 'MacNeil/Lehrer.' And when they do surface they are given consideration primarily for their ethnographic value. An official culture treats their claims as it does those of millenarian cultists in Texas, or Marxist deconstructionists in the academy: as things to be diagnosed, deciphered, given meaning – that is, *another* meaning. Black folk say they believe Simpson is innocent, and then the white gatekeepers of a media culture cajolingly explain what black folk really mean when they say it, offering the explanation from the highest of motives: because the alternative is a population that, by their lights, is not merely counternormative but crazy. Black folk may mean anything at all; just not what they say they mean.

Homi K. Bhabha, 'DissemiNation: Time, Narrative and the Margins of the Modern Nation'*

See also:
Bakhtin (1.iii)
Lévi-Strauss (2.i)
Culler (2.ii)
Gibson (3.ii)
Lyotard (3.iii)
Derrida (6)
de Man (6)
Miller (6)
Ricoeur (7)
Weber (8)

THE TIME OF THE NATION

The title of this chapter – DissemiNation – owes something to the wit and wisdom of Jacques Derrida, but something more to my own experience of migration. I have lived that moment of the scattering of the people that in other times and other places, in the nations of others, becomes a time of gathering. Gatherings of exiles and *émigrés* and refugees; gathering on the edge of 'foreign' cultures; gathering at the frontiers; gatherings in the ghettos or cafés of city centres; gathering in the half-life, half-light of foreign tongues, or in the uncanny fluency of another's language; gathering the signs of approval and acceptance, degrees, discourses, disciplines; gathering the memories of under-development, of other worlds lived retroactively; gathering the past in a ritual of revival; gathering the present. Also the gathering of people in the diaspora: indentured, migrant, interned; the gathering of incriminatory statistics, educational performances legal statutes, immigration status – the genealogy of that lonely figure that John Berger named the seventh man. The gathering of clouds from which the Palestinian poet Mahmoud Darwish asks 'Where should the birds fly after the last sky?'

In the midst of these lonely gatherings of the scattered people, their myths and fantasies and experiences, there emerges a historical fact of singular importance. More deliberately than any other general historian, Eric Hobsbawm writes the history of the modern Western nation from the perspective of the nation's margin and the migrants' exile. The emergence of the later phase of the modern nation, from the mid-nineteenth century is also one of the most sustained periods of mass migration within the West, and colonial expansion in the East. The nation fills the void left in the uprooting of communities and kin, and turns that loss into the language of metaphor. Metaphor, as the etymology of the word suggests, transfers the meaning of home and belonging, across the 'middle passage', or the central European steppes, across those distances, and cultural differences, that span the imagined community of the nation-people.

The discourse of national*ism* is not my main concern. In some ways it is the historical certainty and settled nature of that term against which I am attempting to write of the Western nation as an obscure and ubiquitous form of living the *locality* of culture.

---

* In *The Location of Culture* (London and New York: Routledge, 1994), pp. 139–46.

This locality is more *around* temporality than *about* historicity: a form of living that is more complex than 'community'; more symbolic than 'society'; more connotative than 'country'; less patriotic than *patrie*; more rhetorical than the reason of State; more mythological than ideology; less homogeneous than hegemony; less centred than the citizen; more collective than 'the subject'; more psychic than civility; more hybrid in the articulation of cultural differences and identifications than can be represented in any hierarchical or binary structuring of social antagonism.

In proposing this cultural construction of nationness as a form of social and textual affiliation, I do not wish to deny these categories their specific histories and particular meanings within different political languages. What I am attempting to formulate in this chapter are the complex strategies of cultural identification and discursive address that function in the name of 'the people' or 'the nation' and make them the immanent subjects of a range of social and literary narratives. My emphasis on the temporal dimension in the inscription of these political entities – that are also potent symbolic and affective sources of cultural identity – serves to displace the historicism that has dominated discussions of the nation as a cultural force. The linear equivalence of event and idea that historicism proposes, most commonly signifies a people, a nation, or a national culture as an empirical sociological category or a holistic cultural entity. However, the narrative and psychological force that nationness brings to bear on cultural production and political projection is the effect of the ambivalence of the 'nation' as a narrative strategy. As an apparatus of symbolic power, it produces a continual slippage of categories, like sexuality, class affiliation, territorial paranoia, or 'cultural difference' in the act of writing the nation. What is displayed in this displacement and repetition of terms is the nation as the measure of the liminality of cultural modernity.

Edward Said aspires to such secular interpretation in his concept of 'wordliness' where 'sensuous particularity as well as historical contingency . . . exist *at the same level of surface particularity* as the textual object itself' (my emphasis). Fredric Jameson invokes something similar in his notion of 'situational consciousness' or national allegory, 'where the telling of the individual story and the individual experience, cannot but ultimately involve the whole laborious telling of the collectivity itself.' And Julia Kristeva speaks perhaps too hastily of the pleasure of exile – 'How can one avoid sinking into the mire of common sense, if not by becoming a stranger to one's own country, language, sex and identity?' – without realizing how fully the shadow of the nation falls on the condition of exile – which may partly explain her own later, labile identifications with the images of *other* nations: 'China', 'America'. The entitlement of the nation is its metaphor: *Amor Patria*; *Fatherland*; *Pig Earth*; *Mothertongue*; *Matigari*; *Middlemarch*; *Midnight's Children*; *One Hundred Years of Solitude*; *War and Peace*; *I Promessi Sposi*; *Kanthapura*; *Moby-Dirk*; *The Magic Mountain*; *Things Fall Apart*.

There must be a tribe of interpreters of such metaphors – the translators of the dissemination of texts and discourses across cultures – who can perform what Said describes as the act of secular interpretation.

> To take account of this horizontal, secular apace of the crowded spectacle of the modern nation . . . implies that no single explanation sending one back immediately to a single origin is adequate. And just as there are no simple dynastic answers, there are no simple discrete formations or social processes.

If, in our travelling theory, we are alive to the *metaphoricity* of the peoples of imagined communities – migrant or metropolitan – then we shall find that the space of the modern nation-people is never simply horizontal. Their metaphoric movement requires a kind of 'doubleness' in writing a temporality of representation that moves between cultural formations and social processes without a centred causal logic. And such cultural movements disperse the homogeneous, visual time of the horizontal society. The secular language of interpretation needs to go beyond the horizontal critical gaze if we are to give 'the nonsequential energy of lived historical memory and subjectivity' its appropriate narrative authority. We need another time of *writing* that will be able to inscribe the ambivalent and chiasmatic intersections of time and place that constitute the problematic 'modern' experience of the Western nation.

How does one write the nation's modernity as the event of the everyday and the advent of the epochal? The language of national belonging comes laden with atavistic apologues, which has led Benedict Anderson to ask: 'But why do nations celebrate their hoariness, not their astonishing youth?' The nation's claim to modernity, as an autonomous or sovereign form of political rationality, is particularly questionable if, with Partha Chatterjee, we adopt the postcolonial perspective:

> Nationalism . . . seeks to represent itself in the image of the Englightenment and fails to do so. For Enlightenment itself, to assert its sovereignty as the universal ideal, needs its Other; if it could ever actualise itself in the real world as the truly universal, it would in fact destroy itself.

Such ideological ambivalence nicely supports Gellner's paradoxical point that the historical necessity of the idea of the nation conflicts with the contingent and arbitrary signs and symbols that signify the affective life of the national culture. The nation may exemplify modern social cohesion but

> Nationalism is not what it seems, and *above all not what it seems to itself*. . . . The cultural shreds and patches used by nationalism are often arbitrary historical inventions. Any old shred would have served as well. But in no way does it follow that the principle of nationalism . . . is itself in the least contingent and accidental.
>
> (My emphasis)

The problematic boundaries of modernity are enacted in these ambivalent temporalities of the nation-space. The language of culture and community is poised on the fissures of the present becoming the rhetorical figures of a national past. Historians transfixed on the event and origins of the nation never ask, and political theorists possessed of the 'modern' totalities of the nation – 'homogeneity, literacy and anonymity are the key traits' – never pose, the essential question of the representation of the nation as a temporal process.

It is indeed only in the disjunctive time of the nation's modernity – as a knowledge caught between political rationality and its impasse, between the shreds and patches of cultural signification and the certainties of a nationalist pedagogy – that questions of nation as narration come to be posed. How do we plot the narrative of the nation that must mediate between the teleology of progress tipping over into the 'timeless' discourse of irrationality? How do we understand that 'homogeneity' of modernity – the people – which, if pushed too far, may assume something resembling the archaic body of the despotic or totalitarian mass? In the midst of progress and modernity, the language of ambivalence reveals a politics 'without duration', as Althusser once provocatively wrote: 'Space without places, time without duration.' To write the story of the nation demands that we articulate that archaic ambivalence that informs the *time* of modernity. We may begin by questioning that progressive metaphor of modern social cohesion – *the many as one* – shared by organic theories of the holism of culture and community, and by theorists who treat gender, class or race as social totalities that are expressive of unitary collective experiences.

Out of many one: nowhere has this founding dictum of the political society of the modern nation – its spatial expression of a unitary people – found a more intriguing *image* of itself than in those diverse languages of literary criticism that seek to portray the great power of the idea of the nation in the disclosures of its everyday life; in the telling details that emerge as metaphors for national life. I am reminded of Bakhtin's wonderful description of a national *vision of emergence* in Goethe's *Italian Journey*, which represents the triumph of the Realistic component over the Romantic. Goethe's realist narrative produces a national-historical time that makes visible a specifically Italian day in the detail of its passing time: 'The bells ring, the rosary is said, the maid enters the room with a lighted lamp and says: *Felicissima notte!* . . . *If one were to force a German clockhand on them, they would be at a loss.*' For Bakhtin, it is Goethe's vision of the microscopic, elementary, perhaps random, tolling of everyday life in Italy that reveals the profound history of its locality (*Lokalität*), the spatialization of historical time, 'a creative humanization of this locality, which transforms a part of terrestrial space into a place of historical life for people'.

The recurrent metaphor of landscape as the inscape of national identity emphasizes the quality of light, the question of social visibility, the power of the eye to naturalize the rhetoric of national affiliation and its forms of collective expression. There is, however, always the distracting presence of another temporality that disturbs the contemporaneity of the national present, as we saw in the national discourses with which I began. Despite Bakhtin's emphasis on the realist vision in the emergence of the nation in Goethe's work, he acknowledges that the origin of the nation's visual *presence* is the effect of a narrative struggle. From the beginning, Bakhtin writes, the Realist and Romantic conceptions of time coexist in Goethe's work, but the ghostly (*Gespenstermässiges*), the terrifying (*Unerfreuliches*), and the unaccountable (*Unzuberechnendes*) are consistently surmounted by the structuring process of the visualization of time: 'the necessity of the past and the necessity of its place in a line of continuous development . . . finally the aspect of the past being linked to the necessary future.' National time becomes concrete and visible in the chronotype of the local, particular, graphic, from beginning to end. The narrative structure of this *historical* surmounting of the 'ghostly' or the 'double' is seen in the intensification of narrative synchrony as a graphically visible position in space: 'to grasp the most elusive course of pure historical time and fix it through unmediated contemplation.' But what kind of 'present' is this if it is a consistent process of surmounting the ghostly time of repetition? Can this national time-space be as fixed or as immediately visible as Bakhtin claims?

If in Bakhtin's 'surmounting' we hear the echo of another use of that word by Freud in his essay on 'The "uncanny"', then we begin to get a sense of the complex time of the national narrative. Freud associates *surmounting* with the repressions of a 'cultural' unconscious; a liminal, uncertain state of cultural belief when the archaic emerges in the midst of margins of modernity as a result of some psychic ambivalence or intellectual uncertainty. The 'double' is the figure most frequently associated with this uncanny process of 'the doubling, dividing and interchanging of the self'. Such 'double-time' cannot be so simply represented as visible or flexible in 'unmediated contemplation'; nor can we accept Bakhtin's repeated attempt to read the national space as achieved only in the *fullness of time*. Such an apprehension of the 'double and split' time of nations representation, as I am proposing, leads us to question the homogeneous and horizontal view associated with the nation's imagined community. We are led to ask whether the *emergence* of a national perspective – of an élite or subaltern nature – within a culture of social contestation, can ever articulate its 'representative' authority in that fullness of narrative time and visual synchrony of the sign that Bakhtin proposes.

Two accounts of the emergence of national narratives seem to support my suggestion. They represent the diametically opposed world views of master and slave which, between them, account for the major historical and philosophical dialectic of modem times. I am thinking of John Barrell's splendid analysis of the rhetorical and perspectival status of the 'English gentleman' within the social diversity of the eighteenth-century novel; and of Houston Baker's innovative reading of the 'new *national* modes of sounding, interpreting and speaking the Negro in the Harlem Renaissance'.

In his concluding essay Barrell demonstrates how the demand for a holistic, representative vision of society could only be represented in a discourse that was *at the same time* obsessively fixed upon, and uncertain of, the boundaries of society, and the margins of the text. For instance, the hypostatized 'common language' which was the language of the gentleman whether he be Observer, Spectator, Rambler, 'Common to all by virtue of the fact that it manifested the peculiarities of none' – was primarily defined through a process of negation – of regionalism, occupation, faculty – so that this centred vision of 'the gentleman' is so to speak 'a condition of empty potential, one who is imagined as being able to comprehend everything, and yet who may give no evidence of having comprehended anything.'

A different note of liminality is struck in Baker's description of the 'radical maroonage' that structured the emergence of an insurgent Afro-American expressive culture in its expansive, 'national' phase. Baker's sense that the 'discursive project' of the Harlem Renaissance is modernist is based less on a strictly literary understanding of the term, and more on the agonistic enunciative conditions within which the Harlem Renaissance shaped its cultural practice. The transgressive, invasive structure of the black 'national' text, which thrives on rhetorical strategies of hybridity, deformation, masking, and inversion, is developed through an extended analogy with the guerilla warfare that became a way of life for the maroon communities of runaway slaves and fugitives who lived dangerously, and insubordinately, 'on the frontiers or margins of *all* American promise, profit and modes of production'. From this liminal, minority position where, as Foucault would say, the relations of discourse are of the nature of warfare, the force of the people of an Afro-American nation emerge in the extended metaphor of maroonage. For 'warriors' read writers or even 'signs':

these highly adaptable and mobile warriors took maximum advantage of local environments, striking and withdrawing with great rapidity, making extensive use of bushes to catch their adversaries in cross-fire, fighting only when and where they chose, depending on reliable intelligence networks among non-maroons (both slave and white settlers) and often communicating by horns.

Both gentleman and slave, with different cultural means and to very different historical ends, demonstrate that forces of social authority and subversion or subalternity may emerge in displaced, even decentred strategies of signification. This does not prevent these positions from being effective in a political sense, although it does suggest that positions of authority may themselves be part of a process of ambivalent identification. Indeed the exercise of power may be both politically effective and psychically *affective* because the discursive liminality through which it is signified may provide greater scope for strategic manoeuvre and negotiation.

It is precisely in reading between these borderlines of the nation-space that we can see how the concept of the 'people' emerges within a range of discourses as a double narrative movement. The people are not simply historical events or parts of a patriotic body politic. They are also a complex rhetorical strategy of social reference: their claim to be representative provokes a crisis within the process of signification and discursive address. We then have a contested conceptual territory where the nation's people must be thought in double-time; the people are the historical 'objects' of a nationalist pedagogy, giving the discourse an authority that is based on the pre-given or constituted historical origin *in the past*; the people are also the 'subjects' of a process of signification that must erase any prior or originary presence of the nation-people to demonstrate the prodigious, living principles of the people as contemporaneity as that sign of the *present* through which national life is redeemed and iterated as a reproductive process.

The scraps, patches and rags of daily life must be repeatedly turned into the signs of a coherent national culture, while the very act of the narrative performance interpellates a growing circle of national subjects. In the production of the nation as narration there is a split between the continuist, accumulative temporality of the pedagogical, and the repetitious, recursive strategy of the performative. It is through this process of splitting that the conceptual ambivalence of modern society becomes the site of *writing the nation*.

Trin Minh-Ha, 'Grandma's Story'*

See also
Benjamin (1.iii)
Chatman (2.ii)
Smith (3.ii)
Berger (3.iii)
Lanser (5)
Derrida (6)

* In *Women, Native, Other: Writing, Postcoloniality and Feminism* (Bloomington and Indianapolis: Indiana University Press, 1994), pp. 119–51.

Cohn (7)
Felman (8)

See all things howsoever they flourish
Return to the root from which they grew
This return to the root is called Quietness

(Lao Tzu, *Tao-te-ching*, 16 (trans. A. Waley))

TRUTH AND FACT: STORY AND HISTORY

Let me tell you a story. For all I have is a story. Story passed on from generation to generation, named Joy. Told for the joy it gives the storyteller and the listener. Joy inherent in the process of storytelling. Whoever understands it also understands that a story, as distressing as it can be in its joy, never takes anything away from anybody. Its name, remember, is Joy. Its double, Woe Morrow Show.

> Let the one who is diseuse, one who is mother who waits nine days and nine nights be found. Restore memory. Let the one who is diseuse, one who is daughter restore spring with her each appearance from beneath the earth. The ink spills thickest before it runs dry before it stops writing at all.
>
> (Theresa Hak Kyung Cha)

Something must be said. Must be said that has not been *and* has been said before. 'It will take a long time, but the story must be told. There must not be any lies' (Leslie Marmon Silko). It will take a long time for living cannot be told, not merely told: living is not livable. Understanding, however, is creating, and living, such an immense gift that thousands of people benefit from each past or present life being lived. The story depends upon every one of us to come into being. It needs us all, needs our remembering, understanding, and creating what we have heard together to keep on coming into being. The story of a people. Of us, peoples. Story, history, literature (or religion, philosophy, natural science, ethics) – all in one. They call it the tool of primitive man, the simplest vehicle of truth. When history separated itself from story, it started indulging in accumulation and facts. Or it thought it could. It thought it could build up to History because the Past, unrelated to the Present and the Future, is lying there in its entirety, waiting to be revealed and related. The act of revealing bears in itself a magical (not factual) quality – inherited undoubtedly from 'primitive' storytelling – for the Past perceived as such is a well-organized past whose organization is already given. Managing to identify with History, history (with a small letter h) thus manages to oppose the factual to the fictional (turning a blind eye to the 'magicality' of its claims); the story-writer – the historian – to the storyteller. As long as the transformation, manipulations, or redistributions inherent in the collecting of events are overlooked, the division continues its course, as sure of its itinerary as it certainly dreams to be. Story-writing becomes history-writing, and history quickly sets itself apart, consigning story to the realm of tale, legend, myth, fiction, literature. Then, since fictional and factual have come to a point where they mutually exclude each other, fiction, not infrequently, means lies, and fact, truth. DID IT REALLY HAPPEN? IS IT A TRUE STORY?

I don't want to listen to any more of your stories [Maxine Hong Kingston screamed at her champion-story-talker mother]; they have no logic. They scramble me up. You lie with stories. You won't tell me a story and then say, 'This is a true story,' or 'This is just a story.' I can't tell the difference. I don't even know what your real names are. I can't tell what's real and what you made up.

Which truth? the question unavoidably arises. The story has been defined as 'a free narration, not necessarily factual but truthful in character . . . [It] gives us human nature in its bold outlines; history, in its individual details.' Truth. Not one but two: truth and fact, just like in the old times when queens were born and kings were made in Egypt. (Queens and princesses were then 'Royal Mothers' from birth, whereas the king wore the crown of high priest and did not receive the Horus-name until his coronation.) Poetry, Aristotle said, is truer than history. Storytelling as literature (narrative poetry) must then be truer than history. If we rely on history to tell us what happened at a specific time and place, we can rely on the story to tell us not only what might have happened, but also what is happening at an unspecified time and place. No wonder that in old tales storytellers are very often women, witches, and prophets. The African griot and griotte are well known for being poet, storyteller, historian, musician, and magician – all at once. But why truth at all? Why this battle for truth and on behalf of truth? I do not remember having asked grandmother once whether the story she was telling was true or not. Neither do I recall her asking me whether the story I was reading to her was true or not. We knew we could make each other cry, laugh, or fear, but we never thought of saying to each other, 'This is just a story.' A story is a story. There was no need for clarification – a need many adults considered 'natural' or imperative among children – for there was no such thing as 'a blind acceptance of the story as literally true.' Perhaps the story has become *just* a story when I have become adept at consuming truth as fact. Imagination is thus equated with falsification, and I am made to believe that if, accordingly, I am not told or do not establish in so many words what is true and what is false, I or the listener may no longer be able to differentiate fancy from fact (*sic*). Literature and history once were/still are stories: this does not necessarily mean that the space they form is undifferentiated, but that this space can articulate on a different set of principles, one which may be said to stand outside the hierarchical realm of facts. On the one hand, each society has its own politics of truth; on the other hand, being truthful is being in the in-between of all regimes of truth. Outside specific time, outside specialized space: 'Truth embraces with it all other abstentions other than itself' (T. Hak Kyung Cha).

KEEPERS AND TRANSMITTERS

Truth is when it is itself no longer. Diseuse, Thought-Woman, Spider-Woman, griotte, story-teller, fortune-teller, witch. If you have the patience to listen, she will take delight in relating it to you. An entire history, an entire vision of the world, a lifetime story. Mother always has a mother. And Great Mothers are recalled as the goddesses of all waters, the sources of diseases and of healing, the protectresses of women and of child-bearing. To listen carefully is to preserve. But to preserve is to burn, for understanding means creating.

Let the one who is diseuse, Diseuse de bonne aventure. Let her call forth.
Let her break open the spell cast upon time upon time again and again.
(T. Hak Kyung Cha)

The world's earliest archives or libraries were the memories of women. Patiently transmitted from mouth to ear, body to body, hand to hand. In the process of storytelling, speaking and listening refer to realities that do not involve just the imagination. The speech is seen, heard, smelled, tasted, and touched. It destroys, brings into life, nurtures. Every woman partakes in the chain of guardianship and of transmission. In Africa it is said that every griotte who dies is a whole library that burns down (a 'library in which the archives are not classified but are completely inventoried' [A. Hampate Ba]). Phrases like 'I sucked it at my mother's breast' or 'I have it from Our Mother' to express what has been passed down by the elders are common in this part of the world. Tell me and let me tell my hearers what I have heard from you who heard it from your mother and your grandmother, so that what is said may be guarded and unfailingly transmitted to the women of tomorrow, who will be our children and the children of our children. These are the opening lines she used to chant before embarking on a story. I owe that to you, her and her, who owe it to her, her and her. I memorize, recognize, and name my source(s), not to validate my voice through the voice of an authority (for we, women, have little authority in the History of Literature, and wise women never draw their powers from authority), but to evoke her and sing. The bond between women and word. Among women themselves. To produce their full effect, words must, indeed, be chanted rhythmically, in cadences, off cadences.

> My great-grandmama told my grandmama the part she lived through that my grandmama didn't live through and my grandmama told my mama what they both lived through and my mama told me what they all lived through and we were supposed to pass it down like that from generation to generation so we'd never forget. Even though they'd burned everything to play like it didn't ever happen.
> (Gayl Jones)

In this chain and continuum, I am but one link. The story is me, neither me nor mine. It does not really belong to me, and while I feel greatly responsible for it, I also enjoy the irresponsibility of the pleasure obtained through the process of transferring. Pleasure in the copy, pleasure in the reproduction. No repetition can ever be identical, but my story carries with it their stories, their history, and our story repeats itself endlessly despite our persistence in denying it. *I don't believe it. That story could not happen today.* Then someday our children will speak about us here present, about those days when things like that could happen:

> It was like I didn't know how much was me and Mutt and how much was Great Gram and Corregidora – like Mama when she had started talking like Great Gram. But was what Corregidora had done to *her*, to *them*, any worse than what Mutt had done to me, than what we had done to each other, than what Mama had done to Daddy, or what he had done to her in return. . . .
> (Gayl Jones)

Upon seeing her you know how it was for her. You know how it might have been.
You recline, you lapse, you fall, you see before you what you have seen before.
Repeated, without your even knowing it. It is you standing there. It is you waiting
outside in the summer day.

(T. Hak Kyung Cha)

Every gesture, every word involves our past, present, and future. The body never stops
accumulating, and years and years have gone by mine without my being able to stop
them, stop it. My sympathies and grudges appear at the same time familiar and unfamiliar
to me; I dwell in them, they dwell in me, and we dwell in each other, more as guest than
as owner. My story, no doubt, is me, but it is also, no doubt, older than me. Younger
than me, older than the humanized. Unmeasurable, uncontainable, so immense that
it exceeds all attempts at humanizing. But humanizing we do, and also overdo, for the
vision of a story that has no end – no end, no middle, no beginning; no start, no stop,
no progression; neither backward nor forward, only a stream that flows into another
stream, an open sea – is, the vision of a madwoman. 'The unleashed tides of muteness,'
as Clarice Lispector puts it. We fear heights, we fear the headless, the bottomless, the
boundless. And we are in terror of letting ourselves be engulfed by the depths of muteness.
This is why we keep on doing violence to words: to tame and cook the wild-raw, to adopt
the vertiginously infinite. Truth does not make sense; it exceeds meaning and exceeds
measure. It exceeds all regimes of truth. So, when we insist on telling over and over again,
we insist on repetition in re-creation (and vice versa). On distributing the story into
smaller proportions that will correspond to the capacity of absorption of our mouths,
the capacity of vision of our eyes, and the capacity of bearing of our bodies. Each story
is at once a fragment and a whole; a whole within a whole. And the same story has always
been changing, for things which do not shift and grow cannot continue to circulate.
Dead. Dead times, dead words, dead tongues. Not to repeat in oblivion.

Sediment. Turned stone. Let the one who is diseuse dust breathe away the distance
of the well. Let the one who is diseuse again sit upon the stone nine days and nine
nights. thus. Making stand again, Eleusis.

(T. Hak Kyung Cha)

STORYTELLING IN THE 'CIVILIZED' CONTEXT

The simplest vehicle of truth, the story is also said to be 'a phase of communication,'
'the natural form for revealing life.' Its fascination may be explained by its power both
to give a vividly felt insight into the life of other people and to revive or keep alive the
forgotten, dead-ended, turned-into-stone parts of ourselves. To the wo/man of the West
who spends time recording and arranging the 'data' concerning storytelling as well as
'the many rules and taboos connected with it,' this tool of primitive wo/man has provided
primitive peoples with opportunities 'to train their speech, formulate opinions, and
express themselves' (Anna Birgitta Rooth). It gives 'a sympathetic understanding of
their limitations in knowledge, and an appreciation of our privileges in civilization, due
largely to the struggles of the past' (Clark W. Hetherington). It informs of the explanations
they invented for 'the things [they] did not understand,' and represents their religion, 'a

religion growing out of fear of the unknown' (Katherine Dunlap Cather). In summary, the story is either a mere practice of the art of rhetoric or 'a repository of obsolete customs' (A. Skinner). It is mainly valued for its artistic potential and for the 'religious beliefs' or 'primitive-mind'-revealing superstitions mirrored by its content. (Like the supernatural, is the superstitious another product of the Western mind? For to accept even temporarily Cather's view on primitive religion, one is bound to ask: which [institutionalized] religion does not grow out of fear of the unknown?) Associated with backwardness, ignorance, and illiteracy, storytelling in the more 'civilized' context is therefore relegated to the realm of children. 'The fact that the story is the product of primitive man,' wrote Herman H. Home, 'explains in part why the children hunger so for the story.' 'Wherever there is no written language, wherever the people are too unlettered to read what is written,' Cather equally remarked, 'they still believe the legends. They love to hear them told and retold . . . As it is with unlettered peasants today, as it was with tribesmen in primitive times and with the great in medieval castle halls, it still is with the child.' Primitive means elementary, therefore infantile. No wonder then that in the West storytelling is treasured above all for its educational force in the kindergarten and primary school. The mission of the storyteller, we thus hear, is to 'teach children the tales their *fathers* knew,' to mold ideals, and to 'illuminate facts.' For children to gain 'right feelings' and to 'think true,' the story as a pedagogical tool must inform so as to keep their opinion 'abreast of the scientific truth of the time, instead of dragging along in the superstitions of the past.' But for the story to be well-told information, it must be related 'in as fascinating a form as [in] the old myths and fables.' Patch up the content of the new and the form of the old, or impose one on the other. The dis-ease lingers on. With (traditional but non-superstitious?) formulas like 'once upon a time' and 'long, long ago,' the storyteller can be reasonably sure of 'making a good beginning.' For many people truth has the connotation of uniformity and prescription. Thinking true means thinking in conformity with a certain scientific (read 'scientistic') discourse produced by certain institutions. Not only has the 'civilized' mind classified many of the realities *it does not understand* in the categories of the untrue and the superstitious, it has also turned the story – as total event of a community, a people – into a *fatherly* lesson for children of a certain age. Indeed, in the 'civilized' context, only children are allowed to indulge in the so-called fantastic or the fantastic-true. They are perceived as belonging to a world apart, one which adults (compassionately) control and populate with toys – that is to say, with false human beings (dolls), false animals, false objects (imitative, diminutive versions of the 'real'). 'Civilized' adults fabricate, structure, and segregate the children's world; they invent toys for the latter to *play* with and stories of a specially adapted, more digestive kind to absorb, yet they insist on molding this world according to the scientifically true – the real, obviously not in its full scale, but in a reduced scale: that which is supposed to be the (God-like-) child's scale. Stories, especially 'primitive-why stories' or fairy tales, must be carefully sorted and graded, for children should neither be 'deceived' nor 'duped' and 'there should never be any doubt in [their] mind as to what is make-believe and what is real.' In other words, the difference 'civilized' adults recognize in the little people's world is a mere matter of scale. The forms of constraint that rule these bigger people's world and allow them to distinguish with certainty the false from the true must, unquestionably, be exactly the same as the ones that regulate the smaller people's world. The apartheid type of difference continues to operate in all spheres of 'civilized' life. There does not seem to be any possibility either as to the existence of such things as, for example, two (or more) different realms of make-believe or two (or more) different realms of truth. The 'civilized' mind is an indisputably clear-cut mind. If once upon a time people believed in the story and thought it was true, then why should it be false today? If true and false keep on changing with the times, then isn't it true that what is 'crooked thinking' today may be 'right thinking' tomorrow? What kind of people, we then wonder, walk around asking obstinately: 'Is there not danger of making liars of children by feeding them on these [fairy] stories?' What kind of people set out for northern Alaska to study storytelling among the Indians and come round to writing: 'What especially impressed me was their eagerness to make me understand. To me this eagerness became a proof of the high value they set on their stories and what they represented'? What kind of people, indeed, other than the very kind for whom the story is *just* a story'?

A REGENERATING FORCE

An oracle and a bringer of joy, the storyteller is the living memory of her time, her people. She composes on life but does not lie, for composing is not imagining, fancying, or inventing. When asked, 'What is oral tradition?' an African 'traditionalist' (a term African scholars consider more accurate than the French term 'griot' or 'griotte,' which tends to confuse traditionalists with mere public entertainers) would most likely be nonplussed. As A. Hampate Ba remarks, '[s/he] might reply, after a lengthy silence. 'It is total knowledge,' and say no more.' She might or might not reply so, for what is called here 'total knowledge' is not really nameable. At least it cannot be named (so) without incurring the risk of sliding right back into one of the many slots the 'civilized' discourse of knowledge readily provides it with. The question 'What is oral tradition?' is a question-answer that needs no answer at all. Let the one who is civilized, the one who invents 'oral tradition,' let him define it for himself. For 'oral' and 'written' or 'written' versus 'oral' are notions that have been as heavily invested as the notions of 'true' and 'false' have always been. (If writing, as mentioned earlier, does not express language but encompasses it, then where does the written stop? The line distinguishing societies with writing from those without writing seems most ill-defined and leaves much to be desired . . .) Living is neither oral nor written – how can the living and the lived be contained in the merely oral? Furthermore, when she composes on life she not only gives information, entertains, develops, or expands the imagination. Not only educates. Only practices a craft. 'Mind breathes mind,' a civilized man wrote, 'power feels power, and absorbs it, as it were. The telling of stories refreshes the mind as a bath refreshes the body; it gives exercise to the intellect and its powers; it tests the judgment and the feelings.' Man's view is always reduced to man's mind. For this is the part of himself he values most. THE MIND. The intellect and its powers. Storytelling allows the 'civilized' narrator above all to renew his mind and exercise power through his intellect. Even though the motto reads 'Think, act, and feel,' his task, he believes, is to ease the passage of the story *from mind to mind*. She, however, who sets out to revive the forgotten, to survive and supersede it ('From stone. Layers. Of stone upon stone between the layers, dormant. No more' [T. Hak Kyung Cha].), she never speaks of and cannot be content with mere matters of the mind – such as mind transmission. The storyteller has long been known as a personage of power. True, she partakes in this living heritage of power. But her powers do more than illuminate or refresh the mind. They extinguish as quickly as they set fire. They wound as easily as they soothe. And not necessarily the mind. Abraham Lincoln accurately observed that the sharpness of a refusal, or the edge of a rebuke, may be blunted by an appropriate story, so as to save wounded feeling and yet serve the purpose . . . story-telling as an emollient saves me much friction and distress.' Yet this is but one more among the countless functions of storytelling. Humidity, receptivity, fecundity. Again, her speech is seen, heard, smelled, tasted, and touched. Great Mother is the goddess of all waters, the protectress of women, and of childbearing, the unweary sentient hearer, the healer and also the bringer of diseases. She who gives always accepts, she who wishes to preserve never fails to refresh. Regenerate.

> She was already in her mid-sixties
> when I discovered that she would listen to me
> to all my questions and speculations.
> I was only seven or eight years old then.
>   (Leslie Marmon Silko)

Salivate, secrete the words. No water, no birth, no death, no life. No speech, no song, no story, no force, no power. The entire being is engaged in the act of speaking-listening-weaving-procreating. If she does not cry she will turn into stone. Utter, weep, wet, let it flow so as to break through (it). Layers of stone amidst layers of stone. Break with her own words. The interrelation of woman, water, and word pervades African cosmogonies. Among the Dogon, for example, the process of regeneration which the eight ancestors of the Dogon people had to undergo was carried out in the waters of the womb of the female Nummo (the Nummo spirits form a male and female Pair whose essence is divine) *while she spoke* to herself and to her own sex, accompanied by the male Nummo's voice. 'The spoken Word entered into her and wound itself round her womb in a spiral of eight turns . . . the spiral of the Word gave to the womb its regenerative movement.' Of the fertilizing power of words and their transmissions through women, it is further said that:

> the first Word had been pronounced [read 'scanned'] in front of the genitalia of a woman . . . The Word finally came from the ant-hill, that is, from the mouth of the seventh Nummo [the seventh ancestor and master of speech], which is to say from a woman's genitalia.
>   The Second Word, contained in the craft of weaving, emerged from a mouth, which was also the primordial sex organ, in which the first childbirths took place.

Thus, as a wise Dogon elder (Ogotemmêli) pointed out, 'issuing from a woman's sexual part, the Word enters another sexual part, namely the ear.' (The ear is considered to be bisexual, the auricle being male and the auditory aperture, female.) From the ear, it will, continuing the cycle, go to the sexual part where it encircles the womb. African traditions conceive of speech as a gift of God/dess and a force of creation. In Fulfulde, the word for 'speech' (*haala*) has the connotation of 'giving strength,' and by extension of 'making material.' Speech is the materialization, externalization, and internalization of the vibrations of forces. That is why, A. Hampate Ba noted, 'every manifestation of a force in any form whatever is to be regarded as its speech . . . everything in the universe speaks . . . If speech is strength, that is because it creates a *bond of coming-and-going* which generates *movement and rhythm* and therefore *life and action* [my italics]. This movement to and fro is symbolized by the weaver's feet going up and down . . . (the symbolism of the loom is entirely based on creative speech in action).' Making material: spinning and weaving is a euphonious heritage of wo/mankind handed on from generation to generation of weavers within the clapping of the shuttle and the creaking of the block – which the Dogon call 'the creaking of the Word.' 'The cloth was the Word'; the same term, *soy*, is used among the Dogon to signify both the woven material and the spoken word. Life is a perpetual to and fro, a dis/continuous releasing and absorbing of the self. Let her weave her story within their stories, her life amidst their lives. And while she weaves, let her whip, spur, and set them on fire. Thus making them sing again. Very softly a-new a-gain.

. . .

'TELL IT THE WAY THEY TELL IT'

It is a commonplace for those who consider the story to be just a story to believe that, in order to appropriate the 'traditional' storytellers' powers and to produce the same effects as theirs, it suffices to 'look for the structure of their narratives.' *See them as they see each other*, so goes the (anthropological) creed. 'Tell it the way *they* tell it instead of imposing *our* structure,' they repeat with the best of intentions and a conscience so clear that they pride themselves on it. Disease breeds disease. Those who function best within definite structures and spend their time structuring their own or their peers' existences must obviously 'look for' that which, according to their 'findings' and analyses, is supposed to be 'the structure of their [the storytellers'] narratives.' What we 'look for' is un/fortunately what we shall find. The anthropologist, as we already know, does not find things; s/he *makes* them. And makes them up. The structure is therefore not something given, entirely external to the person who structures, but a projection of that person's way of handling realities, here narratives. It is perhaps difficult for an analytical or analytically trained mind to admit that recording, gathering, sorting, deciphering, analyzing and synthesizing, dissecting and articulating are already 'imposing our [/a] structure,' a structural activity, a structuring of the mind, a whole mentality. (Can one 'look for a structure' without structuring?) But it is particularly difficult for a dualistic or dualistically trained mind to recognize that 'looking for the structure of their narratives' already involves the separation of the structure from the narratives, of the structure from that which is structured, of the narrative from the narrated, and so on. It is, once more, as if form and content stand apart; as if the structure can remain fixed, immutable, independent of and unaffected by the changes the narratives undergo; as if a structure can only function as a standard mold within the old determinist schema of cause and product. Listen, for example, to what a man of the West had to say on the form of the story:

> Independent of the content which the story carries, and which may vary from history to nonsense, is the form of the story which is practically the same in all stories. The content is varied and particular, the form is the same and universal.

> Now there are four main elements in the form of each story, viz. the beginning, the development, the climax, and the end.

Just like the Western drama with its four or five acts. A drama whose naïve claim to universality would not fail to make this man of the West our laughingstock. 'A good story,' another man of the West asserted, 'must have a beginning that rouses interest, a succession of events that is orderly and complete, a climax that forms the story's point, and an end that leaves the mind at rest.' No criteria other than those quoted here show a more thorough investment of the Western mind. Get *them* – children, story-believers – *at the start*; *make your point* by ordering events to a definite *climax*; then *round out to completion*; descend to a rapid close – not one, for example, that puzzles or keeps them puzzling over the story, but one that *leaves the mind at rest*. In other words, to be 'good' a story must be built in conformity with the ready-made idea some people – Western adults – have of reality, that is to say, a set of prefabricated schemata (prefabricated by whom?) they value out of habit, conservatism, and ignorance (of other ways of telling and listening to stories). If these criteria are to be adopted, then countless non-Western stories will fall straight into the category of 'bad' stories. Unless one makes it up or invents a reason for its absence, one of these four elements required always seems to be missing. The stories in question either have no development, no climax that forms the story's point, or no end that leaves the mind at rest. (One can say of the majority of these stories that their endings precisely refute such generalization and rationale for they offer no security of this kind. An example among endless others is the moving story of 'The Laguna People' passed on by Marmon Silko, which ends with a little girl, her sister, and the people turning into stone while they sat on top of a mesa, after they had escaped the flood in their home village below. Because of the disquieting nature of the resolution here, the storytellers (Marmon Silko and her aunt) then add, as a compromise to the fact-oriented mind of today's audience: 'The story ends there. / Some of the stories / Aunt Susi told / have this kind of ending. / There are no explanations.' There is no point (to be) made either.) 'Looking for the structure of *their* narratives' so as to 'tell it the way *they* tell it' is an attempt at remedying this ignorance of other ways of telling and listening (and, obviously, at re-validating the nativist discourse). In doing so, however, rare are those who realize that what they come up with is not 'structure of *their* narratives' but a reconstruction of the story that, at best, makes a number of its functions appear. Rare are those who acknowledge the unavoidable transfer of values in the 'search' and admit that 'the attempt will remain largely illusory: we shall never know if the other, into whom we cannot, after all, dissolve, fashions from the elements of [her/]his social existence a synthesis exactly superimposable on that which we have worked out.' The attempt will remain illusory as long as the controlled succession of certain mental operations which constitutes the structural activity is not made explicit and dealt with – not just mentioned. Life is not a (Western) drama of four or five acts. Sometimes it just drifts along; it may go on year after year without development, without climax, without definite beginnings or endings. Or it may accumulate climax upon climax, and if one chooses to mark it with beginnings and endings, then everything has a beginning and an ending. There are, in this sense, no good or bad stories. In life, we usually don't know when an event is occurring; we think it is starting when it is already ending; and we don't see its in/significance. The present, which saturates the total field of our environment, is often invisible to us. The structural activity that does not carry on the cleavage between form and content but emphasizes the interrelation of the material and the intelligible is an activity in which structure should remain an unending question: one that speaks him/her as s/he speaks it, brings it to intelligibility.

'THE STORY MUST BE TOLD. THERE MUST NOT BE ANY LIES'

'Looking for the structure of their narratives' is like looking for the pear shape in Erik Satie's musical composition *Trois Pièces en Forme de Poire* (Three Pieces in a Pear Shape). (The composition was written after Satie met with Claude Debussy, who criticized his music for 'lacking of form.') If structure, as a man (R. Barthes) pertinently defines it, is 'the residual deposit of duration,' then again, rare are those who can handle it by letting it come, instead of hunting for it or hunting it down, filling it with their own marks and markings so as to consign it to the meaningful and lay claim to it. '*They see no life / When they look / they see only objects.*' The ready-made idea they have of reality prevents their perceiving the story as a living thing, an organic process, a way of life. What is taken for stories, only stories, are fragments of/in life, fragments that never stop interacting while being complete in themselves. A story in Africa may last three months. The storyteller relates it night after night, continually, or s/he starts it one night and takes it up again from that point three months later. Meanwhile, as the occasion arises, s/he may start on yet another story. Such is life . . . :

> The gussucks [the Whites] did not understand the story; they could not see the way it must be told, year after year as the old man had done, without lapse or silence. . . .
>   It began a long time ago,' she intoned steadily . . . she did not pause or hesitate; she went on with the story, and she never stopped. . . .

'Storyteller,' from which these lines are excerpted, is another story, another gift of life passed on by Marmon Silko. It presents an example of multiple storytelling in which story and life merge, the story being as complex as life and life being as simple as a story. The story of 'Storyteller' is the layered making of four storytellers: Marmon Silko, the woman in the story, her grandmother, and the person, referred to as 'the old man.' Except for Marmon Silko who plays here the role of the coordinator, each of these three storytellers has her/his own story to live and live with. Despite the differences in characters or in subject matter, their stories closely interact and constantly overlap. The woman makes of her story a continuation of her grandmother's, which was left with no ending – the grandmother being thereby compelled to bear it (the story) until her death, her knees and knuckles swollen grotesquely, 'swollen with anger' as she explained it. She bore it, knowing that her granddaughter will have to bear it too: 'It will take a long time,' she said 'but the story must be told. There must not be any lies.' Sometime after her death, exactly when does not matter, when the time comes, the granddaughter picks up the story where her grandmother left it and carries it to its end accordingly, the way 'it must be told.' She carries it to a certain completion by bringing in death where she intends to have it in her story: the white storeman who lied in her grandma's story and was the author of her parents' death would have to pay for his lies, but his death would also have to be of his own making. The listener/reader does not (have to) know whether the storeman in the granddaughter's story is the same as the one who, according to the grandmother, 'left right after that [after he lied and killed]' (hence making it apparently impossible for the old woman to finish her story). A storeman becomes *the* storeman, the man in the store, the man in the story. (The truthfulness of the story, as we already know, does not limit itself to the realm of facts.) Which story? The story. What grandma began, granddaughter completes and passes on to be further completed. As a storyteller, the woman (the granddaughter) does not, directly kill; she decides when and where that storeman will find death, but she does not carry out a hand-to-hand fight and her murder of him is no murder in the common, factual sense of the term: all she needs to do is set in motion the necessary forces and let them act on their own.

> They asked her again, what happened to the man from the Northern Commercial Store. 'He lied to them. He told them it was safe to drink. But I will not lie. . . . I killed him,' she said, 'but I don't lie.'

When she is in jail, the Gussuck attorney advises her to tell the court the truth which is that it was an accident, that the storeman ran after her in the cold and fell through the ice. That's all what she has to say – then 'they will let [her] go home. Back to [her] village.'

> She shook her head. 'I will not change the story, not even to escape this place and go home. I intended that he die. The story must be told as it is.' The attorney exhaled loudly; his eyes looked tired. 'Tell her that she could not have killed him that way. He was a white man. He ran after her without a parka or mittens. She could not have planned that.'

When the helpful, conscientious (full-of-the-white-man's-complex-of-superiority) attorney concludes that he will do 'all [he] can for her' and will explain to the judge that 'her mind is confused,' she laughs out loud and finally decides to tell him the story anew: '*It began a long time ago . . .* ' (my italics). He says she could not have killed that white man because, again, for him the story is just a story. But Thought-Woman, Spider-Woman is a fairy and a witch who protects her people and tells stories to effect cures. As she names Death, Death appears. The spell is cast. Only death gives an ending to the stories in 'Storyteller.' (The old man's story of the giant bear overlaps with the granddaughter's story and ends the moment the old man – the storyteller – dies.) Marmon Silko as a storyteller never loses sight of the difference between truth and fact. Her naming retains the accuracy and magic of our grandmothers' storytelling without ever confining itself to the realm of factual naming. It is accurate because it is at once extremely flexible and rigid, not because it wishes to stick to certain rules of correctness for reasons of mere conservatism (scholars studying traditional storytelling are often impressed by the storyteller's 'necessity of telling the stories correctly,' as they put it). It is accurate because it partakes in the setting into motion of forces that lie dormant in us. Because, as African storytellers sing, 'the tongue that falsifies the word / taints the blood of [her/]him that lies.' Because she who bears it in her belly cannot cut herself off from herself. Off from the bond of coming-and-going. Off from her great mothers.

III
taxonomies

A book that could be exhaustively indexed would already be its own index.

(Geoffrey Bennington)

A chronology of narrative theory in the twentieth century

1900–1910

Modernism foregrounds the importance of narrative in the experience of the external world, while producing experimental writing which recognises the structural and contingent nature of narrative: critical work by Joseph Conrad, Henry James, Virginia Woolf. The new science of psychoanalysis is based on the recuperation of a narrative of trauma and cure with a narrator (analysand) and narratee (analyst).

W. E. B. Du Bois, *The Souls of Black Folk* (1903).
Sigmund Freud, 'Creative Writers and Daydreaming' (1908).

1910–1920

High point of Russian Formalist approach to narrative between the Bolshevik Revolution and the Stalinist repression. *Opoyaz* (Society for the Study of Poetic Language) founded in St Petersburg in 1914. Roman Jakobson leaves Russia for Czechoslovakia in 1920 and helps introduce formalist techniques to Central and Western Europe. Ferdinand de Saussure gives *Course in General Linguistics* in Geneva during the war years.

Victor Shlovsky, 'Art as Technique' (1917).
T. S. Eliot, 'Tradition and the Individual Talent' (1919).
Sigmund Freud, *Beyond the Pleasure Principle* (1920).

1920–1930

Formalists attacked in 1923 by Trotsky, then by the Soviet Commissar for Education in 1924. Some attempts to reconcile formalism and Marxism follow. Group officially disciplined by 1930 and exponents chose to follow Soviet orthodoxy. Jakobson recognised as an important figure in the Prague Linguistic Circle by 1926.

Percy Lubbock, *The Craft of Fiction* (1921).
Edward Sapir, *Language* (1921).
E. M. Forster, *Aspects of the Novel* (1926).
Vladimir Propp, *Morphology of the Folktale* (1928).
Mikhail Bakhtin, *The Formal Method in Literary Scholarship* (1928).

1930–1940

The work of formalism is complemented by a focused consideration of narrative and history, partly as a 'corrective' to unorthodox thinking and partly in response to the ideological contests of the day. Benjamin's great essay stands out from this time. Important work by Georges Bataille and Antonin Artaud.

William Empson, *Seven Types of Ambiguity* (1930).
Walter Benjamin, 'The Storyteller' (1936).

1940–1950

Formation of phenomenological and linguistic circles in Europe (particularly in Geneva) which provide many of the future structuralists. A postwar generation of literary critics in Europe begin to move away from formalist and (literary) historical concerns into an engagement with European philosophy, especially Heidegger: work by Jean-Paul Sartre and Maurice Blanchot. New Criticism becomes the dominant strand in Anglo-American considerations of narrative.

Vladimir Propp, 'Oedipus in the Light of Folklore' (1944).
Eric Auberach, *Mimesis* (1946).
Cleanth Brooks, *The Well Wrought Urn* (1947).

Rene Wellek and Austin Warren, *Theory of Literature* (1949).

1950–1960

Beginnings of structuralist narratology. Work appears in French but little known in the English-speaking academy. However, the question of language makes inroads into Anglo-American thinking as well with important work by Chomsky and Austin.

Roland Barthes, *Writing Degee Zero* (1953).
Roland Barthes, *Mythologies* (1957).
Noam Chomsky, *Syntactic Structures* (1957).
Northrop Frye, *Anatomy of Criticism* (1957).
Ian Watt, *The Rise of the Novel* (1957).
Claude Lévi-Strauss, *Structural Anthropology* (1958).
Cleanth Brooks and Robert Penn Warren, *Understanding Fiction* (1959).

1960–1970

High point of structuralist narratology, which by the time it has been translated to the English-speaking world is all but over as an intellectual force. However, New Criticism begins to develop its own tradition of the formal analysis of narrative (see Wayne Booth). A growing interest in certain French thinkers (Barthes, Derrida, Lacan) emerges within the Anglo-American academy, and a brand of American structuralism (Scholes, Kellog, Chatman) begins to develop. The decade ends with a call to move away from the restrictions of formalism (see Geoffrey Hartman).

Wayne Booth, *The Rhetoric of Fiction* (1961).
John L. Austin, *How to Do Things With Words* (1962).
Arthur C. Danto, *Analytical Philosophy of History* (1965).
L. T. Lemon and R. J. Rees (eds) *Russian Formalist Criticism: Four Essays* (1965).
Roland Barthes, *Introduction a l'analyse structurale des récits* (1966).
Gérard Genette, *Figures I* (1966).

A. J. Greimas, *Semantique Structurale* (1966).
Robert Scholes and Robert Kellog, *The Nature of Narrative* (1966).
Frank Kermode, *The Sense of an Ending* (1967).
Gérard Genette, *Figures II* (1969).
Roland Barthes, *S/Z* (1970).
G. Hartman, *Beyond Formalism* (1970).

1970–1980

An acceleration in the Anglo-American reception of recent French thought, combined with the availability of new reader-response theories. The British film journal *Screen* publishes Barthes, Lacan *et al.* in English: proves a productive space for the engagement of psychoanalysis with narrative. Narratology is well established as an interest in the English-speaking world by the end of the decade – deconstruction is on its way.

J. Hillis Miller (ed.), *Aspects of Narrative* (1971).
Wolfgang Iser, 'The Reading Process: A Phenomenological Approach', (1971).
Gérard Genette, *Figures III* (1972).
Hayden White, *Metahistory* (1973).
Roland Barthes, *The Pleasure of the Text* (1975).
Laura Mulvey, 'Visual Pleasure and Narrative Cinema' (1975).
Stephen Heath, 'Narrative Space' (1976).
Leo Bersani, *A Future for Astyanax* (1976).
Seymour Chatman, *Story and Discourse* (1978).
Dorrit Cohn, *Transparent Minds* (1978).
Edward Said, *Orientalism* (1978).
Paul de Man, *Allegories of Reading* (1979).
Umberto Eco, *The Role of the Reader* (1979).
Frank Kermode, *The Genesis of Secrecy: On the Interpretation of Narrative* (1979).

1980–1990

Widespread dissemination of narrative theories as 'critical theory' becomes the mainstream of the Anglo-American academy. Active structuralism has all but died out, especially in France. Early 1980s produce a series of important works which combine psychoanalysis and gender to discuss 'narrative desire'. Availability of student textbooks on narrative. After English-language translation of Lyotard, narrative becomes a focus for the discussion of postmodernism. Narrative is subject to a rigorous consideration by both post-structuralist analysis and philosophy. The decade ends with narrative showing its resilience and centrality in two important collections (see Homi K. Bhabha and James Phelan).

Fredric Jameson, *The Political Unconscious* (1981).

W. J. T. Mitchell (ed.), *On Narrative* (1981).

Wayne Booth, *The Rhetoric of Fiction, 2nd Edition* (1983).

Robert Conn Davis (ed.), *Lacan and Narration* (1983).

Shlimmoth Rimmon-Kenan, *Narrative Fiction: Contemporary Poetics* (1983).

Peter Brooks, *Reading for the Plot* (1984).

Teresa de Lauretis, 'Desire in Narrative' (1984).

Linda Hutcheon, *Narcissistic Narrative* (1984).

Jean-François Lyotard, *The Postmodern Condition* (1984).

Paul Ricoeur, *Time and Narrative* (vols, 1, 2, 3:1984, 1985, 1988).

Mieke Bal, *Narratology* (1985).

Jacques Derrida, *Parages* (1986).

Henry Louis Gates, Jr., *The Signifying Monkey* (1988).

Gérard Genette, *Narrative Discourse Revisited* (1988).

Homi K. Bhabha (ed.), *Nation and Narration* (1989).

James Phelan (ed.), *Reading Narrative: Form, Ethics, Ideology* (1989).

Seymour Chatman, *Coming to Terms* (1990).

1990–2000

The post-structuralist narrative diaspora is well established, with narrative analysis enjoying a life not limited to the confines of literary studies. Many recognised 'narratologists' now carry their inquiries into interdisciplinary and 'post-narratological' spaces. Questions of race and sexuality have proved to be particularly interesting sites for narrative theory. However, a range of specialist narrative journals regularly carry articles on narrative and ethics, the law, history, visual culture, information technology, science, the Holocaust, space, the body, film, and so on.

Christopher Nash (ed.), *Narrative in Culture* (1990).

Mieke Bal, *Remembering Rembrandt* (1991).

Jean Bebin-Masi (ed.), *Narrative in Nice, Style* (1992).

J. Hillis Miller, *Ariadne's Thread: Storylines* (1992)

Keith Jenkins (ed.), *The Postmodern History Reader* (1992).

Paul Gilroy, *The Black Atlantic* (1993).

Edward Said, *Culture and Imperialism* (1993).

Trin Minh-Ha, *Woman, Native, Other* (1994).

Judith Roof, *Come As You Are: Sexuality and Narrative* (1996).

Susan McClary, *De-Tonations: Narrative and Signification in Absolute Music* (1998).

Herman Beavers (ed.), *Narrative*, special edition, 'Narrative and Multiculturalism' (1999).

Martin McQuillan (ed.), *The Narrative Reader* (2000).

A glossary of narrative terms

The following short glossary is intended to supplement the specific selection of this volume. For more comprehensive glossaries see A. J. Gremias (1982), Gerald Prince (1989) and Onega and Landa (1997).

Achrony: A narrative event without any temporal connection to other events. Genette (1985), Bal (1985).

Act: A narrated event which brings about a state of change by an agent. For example, 'the girl released the bear' is an act but 'it rained last week' is not. Chatman (1978), Greimas and Courtes (1982).

Actant: Greimas' term corresponding to Propp's 'dramatis persona'. According to Greimas there are six actants: Subject, Object, Sender, Receiver, Helper and Opponent. The equivalent terms in Propp are: Hero, Sought-For-Person, Dispatcher, Helper, Donor and Vilain/False-Hero. An actant, such as the Subject/Hero, occupies actantial roles determined by the narrative trajectory. Actants are different from characters in that several characters can fulfil the role of a single actant (e.g. the Magnificent Seven correspond to the role of Subject/Hero). Actants operate at the level of a narrative's deep structure unlike characters. Actants operate within an actantial model by which a narrative is structured according to the relations between actants. Greimas (1970), Greimas and Courtes (1982), Scholes (1974), Culler (1975).

Action: A series of connected events showing unity and purpose and, according to Aristotle, exhibiting a beginning, a middle and an end. A syntagmatic organisation of acts. Barthes defines action as a group of functions operating under the same actants. Aristotle, Barthes (1975), Chatman (1978), Greimas and Courtes (1982).

Addressee: One of the constitutive parts of a communicative act. The addressee receives a message from the addresser. Jakobson (1960).

Agent: One who acts and influences the course of events. In Bremond's terminology an agent is distinct from a 'patient', the latter being affected by processes rather than actively influencing them. Bremond (1973), Scholes (1974), Todorov (1981).

Algebrisation: The converse of Shklovsky's defamiliarisation in which techniques are used to render perception over-familiar in order to ensure the least expenditure of perceptual effort. Lemon and Reis (1965).

Allegory: (Gk. Other speaking) A narrative which (through rhetorical figures such as metaphor, allusion, symbolism etc.) can be read as saying something quite different from its ostensible story. De Man suggests that allegory is the general condition of narrative since all language can always be read as saying something other than intended by the speaker. De Man (1979), Derrida (1989a).

Anachrony: A discontinuity between the order in which events happen and the order in which they are (re)told in a narrative. For example, *The Usual Suspects* begins *in medias res* and returns to recount previous events. Anachrony can move backwards in time (retrospection, analepsis, flashback), or forward in time (anticipation, prolepsis, flashforward). Genette (1985), Chatman (1978), Bal (1985).

Analepsis: An anachrony which moves backwards in time (a flashback). For example: 'She paused as she held the flower, just as they had done last summer when it was picked, before putting it in her book'. Genette (1985), Rimmon (1976).

Anterior Narration: A narration of events which takes place before those events happen, e.g. in instances of fortune-telling. Prince (1982).

Antinarrative: A text which seems to adopt the conventions of narrative but systematically works to question, subvert or undermine those conventions (e.g. Beckett's *Molloy* or Robbe-Grillet's *Jealousy*). It can be argued that the inversions and complications characteristic of such texts only serve to reinforce rather than dissolve a narrative logic. At the least, such subversion depends upon that which it subverts. Chatman (1978).

Aporia: A rhetorical figure of doubt in which the conditions of possibility of an event or concept are, paradoxically, its own conditions of impossibility resulting in an interpretive impasse or moment of undecideability. Given such a contradiction, an impossible resolution can be reached by working the aporia through in the textual apparatus of a narrative. Derrida (1993), Jameson (1981).

Author: The real author as a producer of a narrative is not to be confused with the 'implied author' or a 'narrator'. Unlike a narrator or an implied author the real author does not exist within, and cannot be deduced from, the narrative itself. Booth (1983), Chatman (1978).

Autodiegetic narrative: A first-person narrative in which the narrator is also the principal character or hero (e.g. *Great Expectations* or *The Opposite of Sex*). Genette (1985).

Beginning: The initial incident in a plot or action. All action follows from this beginning, and so the beginning provides narrative with its forward-moving temporality. Aristotle, Said (1975), Prince (1982), Brooks (1984), Martin (1986).

Cardinal function: In Barthes' taxonomy, that part of a narrative which cannot be removed from the narrative action in order for versions of the narrative to be characterised as such. That which is logically essential to the narrative action (e.g. Cinderella's poverty). Barthes (1975).

Causality: A relation of cause and effect between events or actions. In Barthes (1975) the readerly confusion between chronology and causality (consecutiveness rather than consequence) is one of the principal motivations of narrativity. The operation of narrative depends upon the confusion of the *post hoc ergo propter hoc* fallacy whereby what-comes-after-X is interpreted as what-is-caused-by-X. Aristotle, Barthes (1975), Chatman (1978), Prince (1982), Todorov (1981).

Character: (1) Noun. An anthropomorphic actor or existent. (2) Adjective. In Aristotle one of the qualities (along with thought) that an agent has. Aristotle, Forster (1963), Frye (1957), Scholes and Kellogg (1966), Bremond (1973), Barthes (1974), Chatman (1978), Cixous (1974), Docherty (1983).

Chronotope: Lit. time-space. Bakhtin's formulation for explaining the interrelation between temporal and spatial categories in artistic representation. For example, the motif of the road in, say Bunyan, Kerouac or *Thelma and Louise* designates both a sense of place and the temporal attribute of locomotion. Bakhtin (1981).

Code: (1) In Barthes a model of cultural or linguistic knowledge from which a narrative is woven. A narrative will be a combination or interweaving of codes and a single unit within a narrative can signify in terms of one or more codes (paroairetic, hermeneutic, referential, semic, symbolic). (2) Part of the deep structure of language from which acts of communication are produced. The sender and receiver of a communication will, in part, share a set of codes (a system of norms, rules and assumptions) from which surface structure communication is produced. Here code is analogous to Saussure's *langue*, and the message analogous to *parole*. Barthes (1974, 1981), Culler (1975), Jakobson (1960), Prince (1982), Martin (1986).

Complex story: A story combing at least two minimal narratives through linking, embedding or alternation: (e.g. Bill Clinton was in trouble and Newt Gingrich had a large majority in the Senate; then Bill did better than expected in mid-term elections and saved his presidency; then Newt, despite his majority, was forced to resign. This complex story arises from embedding 'Bill was in trouble; then Bill did better than expected' into 'Newt had a majority; then Newt resigned'). Prince (1973).

Conative function: A communicative act which focuses on the addressee. Similarly, a piece of narrative which focuses on the narratee (e.g. 'Can you imagine what I did then dear reader?'). Jakobson (1960), Prince (1982).

Constative: A speech act which reports events or states circumstances and therefore has the property of being either true or false (e.g. 'Edinburgh is the capital of Scotland' or 'Crocodiles live in the sewers of New York'). In Austin (1990) constatives are used to say something rather than to perform an act (performatives). However, Austin goes on to argue that all constatives are also performatives. For example, in so far as a narrative could be said to be constative it could also be said to perform the act of reporting. Austin (1990), Pratt (1977).

Counterplot: A sequence of actions set against the intended result of the main plot (e.g. if the main plot is 'Bond rescues girl and saves the world', then the counterplot would be the actions of the villain to oppose this: 'Villain kidnaps the girl and intends world domination'). Souvage (1965).

Covert narrator: An undramatised or non-intrusive narrator who presents the story with a minimum of narratorial mediation (e.g. James Joyce's 'The Dead'). Covert narration is the mode of positivistic historiography. Chatman (1978).

Cultural code: One of Barthes' codes (sometimes called the referential code) in which already known cultural knowledge determines the production of a narrative. Barthes (1974, 1981).

Deep structure: In Chomsky (1965), deep structure is the underlying set of rules and paradigms in language from which surface structure is generated by a set of operations and transformations. The deep–surface distinction is analogous to Saussure's *langue* and *parole*. Often applied to an understanding of so-called 'narrative grammars' (e.g. in Greimas, while actants and actantial relations are the abstract deep structure of a narrative, they generate the actors and actorial relations of the surface structure). Chomsky (1965).

Defamiliarisation: An artistic technique which makes the familiar seem strange by jolting the reader/viewer out of habitual perception. For Shklovsky, defamiliarisation is the *raison d'être* of art. Shklovsky, in Lemon and Rees (1965).

Deitic: A term within an utterance which designates the context of the utterance: 'here', 'there', 'now', 'then', 'I', 'you', 'her', 'yesterday', 'tomorrow' (e.g. 'Will *you* be *here* with *me* *tomorrow*?', where 'you' is the addressee, 'me' the addresser, 'tomorrow' the time, 'here' the place). Benveniste (1971), Hamburger (1973).

Denouement: The end of a story, more specifically the unravelling of the complication in a plot, or its resolution.

Diachronic analysis: The study of change within a system (e.g. linguistic or narrative) across a period of time. Saussure (1966).

Dialogic narrative: A polyphonic narrative composed of the interaction of several voices none of which is superior to, or priviliged above, any other. Unlike a monologic narrative, the voice of the narrator is not taken as the single point of authority in the narrative but as one contribution to knowledge among others. Initially, Bakhtin identified the dialogic as a property of Dostoevsky's narratives but later extended the description as a general phenomenon. Bakhtin (1981, 1984), Pascal (1977).

Diegesis: (1) The space (or fictional world) in which narrated events occur (Fr. *diegese*). (2) Telling, recounting or narrating as opposed to showing or enacting as in drama (Fr. *diegesis*). Plato, Aristotle, Genette (1985, 1988).

Diegetic level: The level at which an event or existent is related to a given diegesis (*diegese*) (e.g. intradiegetic, extradiegetic, homodiegetic, etc.). Genette (1985, 1988).

Discourse: (1) In narratology a distinction is made between discourse (equivalent terms *récit*, *sjuzet*) and story (*histoire*, *fabula*). Discourse is the set of narrated events and situations as they are presented to the reader or listener; story is the sequence of events and situations as they would appear in chronological order; discourse is the plot as opposed to the basic story. (2) The narrating of a story rather than the narrated. Discourse consists of both the medium (written,

oral, cinematic) and the form (the order of presentation, the point of view, the narrator, etc.). Culler (1975), Benveniste (1971), Genette (1976, 1985, 1988), Chatman (1978).

Donor: According to Propp, one of the seven fundamental roles a character may adopt in a fairy-tale (also actant, anti-donor, dramatis personae, sphere of action). Analogous to Greimas' 'helper', the donor provides the hero with an agent (often magical) which eventually enables the story's resolution. Propp (1968).

Double bind: An experience of impossible contradiction which one cannot help but respond to, for example, the sentence 'the sentence is not true' or 'do not read this sentence' places the reader in an impossible position which has to be experienced. *See* **aporia.** Derrida (1980, 1993), Culler (1981), Miller (1986, 1995), Johnson (1980).

Double logic of narrative: The twin and contradictory gesture of narrative production whereby a narrative will simultaneously present the primacy of the story (*histoire*, *fabula*) over discourse (*récit*, *sjuzet*) as well as stressing the importance of discourse over story. In the first gesture, event is the origin of meaning; in the second, event is the effect of the production of meaning within particular narrative circumstances. This aporia constitutes the driving force of narrativity. Culler (1981), Brooks (1984).

Duration: The set of circumstances and phenomena which relate story time to discourse time. Story time can be greater than, equal to, or smaller than discourse time (e.g. 'He sat there for days and years. Twenty years later he was older and wiser'; here the story spans over twenty years but takes moments to tell). Metz (1974a), Chatman (1978), Genette (1985), Prince (1982).

Ellipsis: An implicit or explicit temporal break in narrative sequence as a way of moving a story along (e.g. (explicit) 'The week passed without incident so we shall say no more about it', (implicit) 'The next morning we got up for breakfast' (here the insignificant events of the night are skipped over rather than narrated)). Chatman (1978), Genette (1985), Prince (1982).

End: The last incident in a plot or sequence of actions. No more action follows an end and therefore the end brings the story to a conclusion, although not necessarily a satisfactory one. In this way the end provides a focus and organising principle for meaning in a narrative. According to Barthes, and others, narrative production (readerly or writerly) is a desire to reach the end, and the end is the motivating principle of narrative production. Aristotle, Benjamin (1992), Barthes (1975), Kermode (1967), Brooks (1984), Ricoeur (Vol. 2, 1985).

Event: A happening, action, or change of state revealed in discourse. Along with existents, events are the fundamental constituents of the story. Chatman (1978).

Existent: An actor or important object within a story (e.g. '*Batman* drives the *batmobile*'). Along with events, existents are the fundamental constituents of the story. Chatman (1978).

Extradiegetic: External to any diegesis (*diegese*). An extradiegetic narrator is one who is neither involved in the story related nor any subsequent framing narrative Genette (1985, 1988), Rimmon (1976), Lanser (1981).

Fabula: In Russian formalism, the basic story events in chronological order. *See* **discourse**. Erlich (1965), Chatman (1978), Brooks (1984).

Fiction: A narrative in which some or all events and existents retain a suspended relation between reference and meaning (e.g. *Casablanca* is fiction, *The Word at War* is non-fiction). Derrida (1992).

First-person narrative: A narrative in which the narrator is a character in the action recounted and is designated by an 'I' (e.g. *Great Expectations*). Prince (1982).

Focalisation: The perspective from which events are narrated. Focalisation can be internal (the story told through the perspective of characters), fixed (only one perspective), variable (different perspectives adopted in turn to comment on different events), multiple (different perspectives adopted to comment on the same event), external (presentation is limited to a character's words and actions but no thoughts or feelings), or zero (when there is no locatable focalisation). Bal (1981a, 1983, 1985), Genette (1985, 1988), Rimmon-Kenan (1983).

Foreshadowing: A technique whereby a significant event in the future is hinted at in advance (e.g. Anikan Skywalker's fear as a child will lead him to the dark-side of the Force as Darth Vader). Brooks and Warren (1959), Chatman (1978).

Formalism: A critical method which concentrates on the formal dimensions of a literary text (such as word choice, syntax, rhyme scheme or narrative structure) to the exclusion of content or meaning (such as historical or social dimensions). The most severe critiques of narratology tend to view it as an extreme formalism. American New Criticism is also characterised as formalist although the critical attitudes of such 'close reading' are quite different from structuralism. Again, so-called Russian formalism is distinct from either new criticism or structuralism. In fact, Russian formalism, while being interested in form, is at pains to subordinate literary form to general political and revolutionary concerns. Lemon and Rees (1965), Hartman (1970), Brooks (1984).

Frame narrative: A narrative which provides a frame (setting, explanation, occasion) to another narrative embedded within (e.g. the editor's narrative in *Confession and Memoirs of a Justified Sinner*, or the contemporary salvage sequences in *Titanic*).

Free direct discourse: A mode of representation in which a character's thoughts or utterances are presented as they occur to the character without narratorial mediation or tag or punctuation (e.g. 'She stood at the door. I'm out of here, this sucks'). Chatman (1978), Genette (1985, 1988), Lanser (1981), Todorov (1981).

Free indirect discourse: Sometimes called *style indirect libre*. A mode of presentation in which a character's thoughts and utterances are offered without narratorial mediation or tag but in the manner of indirect speech or representation (e.g. 'He was outraged. How could they think that people like him should pay taxes'). Bakhtin (1981), Bal (1985), Chatman (1978), Cohn (1978), Todorov (1981).

Frequency: The relationship between the number of times an event occurs and the number of times it is recounted (e.g. the same event can be retold several times by different characters). Genette (1985), Rimmon-Kenan (1983).

Function: (1) For Propp, function constitutes the fundamental deep structuring principle of actions within a narrative. He lists thirty-one functions from which actions in the Russian fairy-tale are generated. The same act can mean different things in different narratives depending on which function it is related to (e.g. 'Bill killed the bear' can be a heroic act which saves the day in one story, and an act of villainy in another story). (2) In Barthes, a distinction is made between function and index. A function is a narrative unit metonymically related to other units in the same sequence by chronology or consequence. An index is a unit metaphorically related to other units by means other than chronology or consequence (e.g. themat-

ically). Barthes identifies cardinal functions (units logically necessary to the narrative) and catalysts (minor events in a narrative, the elimination of which would not disrupt the narrative's chronological and causal coherence. Propp (1968), Bremond (1973), Greimas (1970, 1983), Scholes (1974), Barthes (1975), Culler (1975).

Genre: (1) A kind; a literary type or style. Narrative genres include epic, romance, espionage, detective, war stories, etc. (2) Fr. genre, gender. Derrida makes some play on the correspondence in French of the word for gender (genre) and literary genres. He provides a critique of narratology's taxonomies by showing that genre (gender and literary) is always mixed. Therefore, while rigorous boundaries between types are always necessary in the construction of narrative theory we should remember that such boundaries are always contested by real narratives. Derrida (1980).

Gnarus: Etymological root of narrative, narrating, narration, narrator, etc. Latin from the Indo-European root *gna* ('to know'). So, literally, the narrator is the one who knows, narration is a form of knowledge and so on. Miller (1981), Lyotard (1991).

Hermeneutic code: A code through which a narrative is produced by positing a question or enigma and working along a path to resolution or revelation. For example, detective narratives are strongly associated with this code. Barthes (1974), Culler (1975), Prince (1982).

Heterodiegetic narrative: A narrative in which the narrator is not part of the events recounted (e.g. Scheherazade in *Arabian Nights* is a heterodiegetic narrator but is not an extradiegetic one). Genette (1985, 1988), Lanser (1981).

Histoire: *See* story.

Homodiegetic narrative: A narrative in which the narrator is a character in the events recounted (e.g. *The Great Gatsby*). Genette (1985, 1988), Lanser (1981).

Hypodiegetic narrative: A narrative embedded within another narrative, sometimes called a meta-diegetic narrative or pseudo-diegetic narrative (whenever its embedded status is forgotten as such) (e.g. the monster's account in *Frankenstein*). Bal (1985), Rimmon-Kenan (1983).

Illocutionary act: A speech act which performs a deed while saying something (e.g. 'I promise to be there'). The accomplishment of an illocutionary act depends upon what Austin calls felicitous conditions (e.g. 'When I promise to come I am not lying or speaking to someone or about something else'). Austin (1962), Searle (1969), Pratt (1977), Chatman (1978).

Implied author: The author's mask or persona as reconstructed from the text. Unlike the real author, the implied author is immanent within the text and can be inferred from the entire text. The implied author is said to be responsible for the design, norms and values a text adheres to. Unlike the narrator, the implied author is not inscribed in the narrative as a teller but is taken to be accountable for the selection and combination of events (e.g. a real author can provide two distinct implied authors of two different narratives. It is often difficult to discern the implied author in the case of absent or covert narrators but often very clear, as in the case of homodiegetic narratives such as *The Great Gatsby* or *Great Expectations*). Iser (1974, 1978), Chatman (1978), Bal (1981b), Booth (1983), Genette (1988).

Implied reader: The audience presupposed by a text or the persona of a reader imposed by the norms and values of a narrative. A text has one implied reader but can have more than one real reader able to read in opposition to the values assumed by the text. The implied reader is the audience for the implied author and so is distinct from the narratee who is the audience of the narrator. As with the implied author, some narratives make it easier than others to identify and distinguish the implied reader. Iser (1974, 1978), Booth (1983), Genette (1988).

In medias res: A technique in which the telling of a narrative begins with an important event rather than the first chronological event of the story. Now used as an ordering principle to allow the narrator to return to an earlier period of time later in the narrative. However, originally used in the epic as a principle of selection in which the narrator begins his or her telling at a point pertinent to the account without recounting previous events because the audience was already familiar with those events (e.g. The Illiad begins *in medias res* rather than *ab ovo* with, for instance, an account of Helen's birth). Horace (1974).

Intertext: (1) A text (or texts) cited or rewritten by another text and upon which the meaning of the latter text depends (e.g. Joyce's *Ulysses* and Homer's *Odyssey* (2) Two texts joined by a relation of intertextuality. Barthes (1981).

Intertextuality: In a restricted sense, a relation between texts in which one cites, rewrites or transforms the other (e.g. *Hamlet* and *The Lion King*). In a general sense, relations between texts through which the infinite differential network of traces, knowledges and signifying practices produce meaning. This latter sense is derived by Kristeva from Bakhtin. Kristeva (1980), Barthes (1981), Culler (1981), Genette (1982).

Intradiegetic: To be part of the diegesis (*diegese*) of a (primary) narrative (e.g. Pip is an intradiegetic narrator in *Great Expectations*). However, an intradiegetic narrator is not the same as a homodiegetic narrator (e.g. Walton in *Frankenstein* does not tell his own story but remains implicated within the diegesis set up by his framing narrative). Rimmon (1976), Genette (1985, 1988), Lanser (1981).

Isochrony: (1) A steadiness in narrative temporality (e.g. 'I worked for an hour, ate for an hour, read for an hour'). (2) Equality between story time and discourse time. Genette (1985). Bal (1985).

Isodiegetic: To be part of the same diegesis (*diegese*) (e.g. Marlow and his mates on the Nellie in *Heart of Darkness* are isodiegetic while the mates and Kurtz are not). Genette (1985).

Kernel: In Barthes, kernels are logically necessary to a narrative. *See* **cardinal function.** Barthes (1975), Chatman (1978).

Langue: The grammar or system of codes governing the production of meaningful utterances within a system of communication. *Langue* is analogous of Chomsky's deep structure, while *parole* is analogous to surface structure. For Saussure, *langue* is the proper object of study for linguistics, and equivalently narrative grammars, rather than individual narratives, are the proper object of study for narratology. However, Saussure makes explicitly clear the impossibility of separating *langue* from *parole* in actual linguistic events, and that the distinction is purely a conceptual one for the ease of analysis. This important point is not always adhered to in some narrative theory. Saussure (1966).

Lexia: A unit of text or meaning, variable in length, allowing for the best or richest possibilities of analysis. Barthes (1974).

Locutionary act: A speech act, which says something by producing a statement in accordance with grammatical rules (e.g. 'Edinburgh is the capital of Scotland'). Austin (1990), Searle (1969).

Logos: (1) The subject matter, topic or thought in a narrative. According to Aristotle, the logos provides the material for the mythos (or plot) of a narrative. This distinction between logos and mythos is suggestive of that between story and discourse or *fabula* and *sjuzet*. (2) In phenomenology and deconstruction the order of logos (Gk. 'word', more generally 'meaning' or 'sense') constitutes the conceptual order of Western discourse which systematically privileges the presence of speech over writing, univocal meaning over polyvocal meaning. While the limiting operations of logos are to be resisted or 'deconstructed', Derrida makes it clear that it is impossible in principle to escape from the logos. Narrative might be said to be of the order of logos as it constructs identity against difference. Aristotle, Chatman (1978), Derrida (1980).

Metadiegetic: *See* **hypodiegetic narrative.**

Metalepsis: The intrusion into a diegetic level by a being from another level (e.g. when the extradiegetic narrator of *The French Lieutenant's Woman* sits next to Charles, the main character, on a train). Genette (1985, 1988).

Metanarrative: A narrative which makes the production of narrative its topic. A self-reflexive narrative which calls attention to its own status as narrative through reference to its own terms of production (e.g. *The Hour of the Star*, or *Aunt Julia and the Script-Writer*). Hutcheon (1984).

Metaphor: A figure of speech in which a thing, concept or notion is compared to, identified with or substituted for another (e.g. 'Men are animals'). Jakobson suggests that the metaphoric and metonymic processes represent two important poles of linguistic activity. The metaphoric function of language combines units of discourse through relations of similarity and substitution. The metonymic function combines units through contiguity. Narrative has been identified as primarily metonymic, working through relations of contiguity or as a syntagmatic (rather than a paradigmatic/metaphoric) chain. However, metaphoric substitution is also an important means of producing narrative (e.g. all detective narratives are related through their shared similarities). Jakobson (1956), Culler (1981), Brooks (1984).

Metonymy: A figure of speech in which a thing, concept or notion stands in for another (e.g. 'The crown of England will perish', where 'crown' stands for the royal family and related establishment). *See* **metaphor.**

Middle: The actions in a narrative which come between the end and the beginning. The middle is that which, paradoxically, leads the reader towards the end and also delays the end. Judith Roof suggests that the idea of the middle, as an in-between space, provides queer narrative with a point of resistance to the hetero-patriarchal normativity of the 'birth' of the beginning and the 'marriage' of the end. Aristotle, Brooks (1984), Roof (1996).

Mimesis: Plato distinguishes between mimesis (imitation of actions, when a poet adopts a persona to deliver a speech) and diegesis (recounting, when a poet speaks in their own voice). Mimesis therefore involves no narratorial mediation, while mediation defines diegesis. For Aristotle, all art is imitation (mimetic) and verbal narrative is merely the imitation of an action via linguistic means. In his reading of Aristotle, Paul Ricoeur offers a threefold model of mimesis in which plot (the narrative process which helps us configure the experience of human time) mediates between the practical field of human activity and time as it is experienced in works of narrative. Plato, Aristotle, Frye (1957), Auberach (1957), Genette (1985), Ricoeur (Vol. 1, 1984, Vol. 2, 1985).

Minimal narrative: A narrative relating a single event (e.g. 'He sat down'). Genette (1988).

Mise en abyme: A replica of a text or narrative embedded within that text or narrative (e.g. Caroline Rose writing a book called *The Comforters* in the novel *The Comforters*).

Montage: A technique whereby the meaning of a given narrative sequence comes from the juxtaposition of units rather than their contiguity (e.g. the use of 'newsreels' in John Dos Passos' *U.S.A*). More often associated with filmic narrative. Metz (1974a).

Myth: (1) A traditional narrative of a religious or ritualistic kind, which justifies or represents an exemplary truth. According to Lévi-Strauss, the structure of myth can be represented by a four-square homology A:B:C:D where A is to B as C is to D. Here an irreconcilable contradiction is 'resolved' through its representation in terms of another, more familiar paradox. For example, the Oedipus myth describes the non-autochtonous origin of man in terms of the over- and underestimation of kinship ties. (2) In Barthes, the semiotic or narrative operation in capitalist society which presents bourgeois ideology as natural or common-sense. Frye (1957), Lévi-Strauss (1968) (1965–71), Scholes and Kellog (1966), Greimas (1987), Barthes (1982).

Mytheme: A miminal constituent of myth. Lévi-Strauss (1968).

Mythos: A plot or arrangement of incidents. *see* **logos** (1). Aristotle, Chatman (1978).

Narratee: One who is narrated to as inscribed in the text. The narratee exists on the same diegetic level as the narrator. Distinct from the reader or implied reader. Genette (1985), Prince (1980, 1982).

Narration: (1) The production of a narrative. Narration can be posterior (coming after the narrated events), anterior (preceding the events in time), simultaneous (occurring at the same time as the events), or intercalated (situated between two moments of action as in epistolary novels). (2) Another term for discourse. Todorov (1966, 1981), Prince (1982), Genette (1985).

Narrative: The difficulty in defining this term might identify 'narrative' as what Geoffrey Bennington would call 'transcendental contraband', the very term which narrative theory wishes us to understand but which it cannot explain. In Judith Roof's phrase, narrative is the logic which can never be explained but always narrated. As the introduction to this volume showed, the definition of the term 'narrative' is unstable and still 'up for grabs'. The meanings listed below indicate the elasticity of this term: (1a) A recounting (process and product, verb and noun) of one or more real or fictional events by one or more narrators to one or more narratees. Such a definition relies on the idea of an event as a past action, and so rules out drama as 'narrative' because drama reveals actions in the present tense. However, according to this definition, mere descriptions like 'The cat sat on the mat' are narratives because it communicates an event. (1b) So, narratologists such as Prince (1982) and Rimmon-Kenan (1983) suggest that a narrative must compose at least two events, neither of which entails or logically presupposes the other. Todorov (1966, 1978, 1981) and Greimas (1987) further argue that to distinguish it from random listing, a narrative must be a coherent whole with a continuant subject. Hence, 'The cat sat on the mat, then the dog sat on the mat'. (2) Following the double-layered model of structralism, a narrative consists of two parts: story and discourse. Story is a temporal sequence of events. Discourse is the mode of representation of that story. Narrative is the interrelation of the two as an articulation. (3) Further, narrative is the production of surface units of meaning from a set of deep structure functions. Propp

(1968), Chomsky (1957, 1965). Greimas (1983) goes on to read narrative as a set of transformations related to a limited number of specific orientations (goals, contracts, receiving, etc.). Greimas' definition tends to work best with the canonical narratives he analyses. (4) In later Barthes (1981), a context-bound exchange is produced by the desire of one (or more) of the interlocuters. (5) While the same story can be retold, each narrative is unique. Smith (1980). Each narrative is irreducible to any other narrative because the retelling of stories only results in their reinscription in the form of another narrative, and there is no basically basic or Ur narrative. This leads Smith to conclude that as every narrative utterance is unique, there is no set of grammatical relations by which any narrative can be derived from or related to any other narrative. Therefore, it is impossible to distinguish narrative from most forms of everyday discourse. She notes, 'it is questionable if we can draw any logically rigorous distinction between . . . narrative discourse and any other form of verbal behaviour.' (6) Derrida (1980) demonstrates the impossibility of what he calls 'the law of genre', i.e. the impossibility of the rigorous purity of taxonomies and typologies required to uphold the structuralist model of narrative, and the simultaneous necessity of such boundaries and borders in order to allow narrative to be conceptualised. In this sense narrative is an aporia. (7) For Lyotard (1984, 1992) narrative is a mode of knowledge, from the Latin root 'gnarus', to know. Knowledge is articulated and communicated in society in the form of narratives. Therefore, narratives define the possibilities of knowledge and, hence, action in any given society. Thus, narratives are legitimised by the very fact that they exist. A knowledge of the narratives of a community or society distinguishes an indigenous person from an outsider. (8) In both Ricoeur (vols 1–3, 1984, 1985, 1988) and Derrida (1992b, 1993), narrative is the necessary form for the expression of human temporality.

Human beings understand the construction of an idea of the present, past and future through their use of narrative. Therefore, narrative is a fundamental expression of the question of being as a moment of presence (narratives help humans to imagine themselves existing in a 'now' because narratives claim to relate in the present a 'past-now' recovered through the narrator's telling). Narrative is both the process and the consequence of this temporal structuration.

Narrative closure: A conclusion which brings the sequence of narrative action to an end, providing it with a sense of unity, completion, resolution and finality. All narratives end but not all provide closure (e.g. the ambiguous ending *of Heart of Darkness*). Kermode (1967), Smith (1968), Miller (1981).

Narrative code: The fluid system of rules, norms, values and assumptions through which a narrative produces meaning. The codes within the system (hermeneutic, proairetic, symbolic, etc.) interweave with one another to produce complex signifying units. Barthes (1974, 1981), Prince (1977, 1982).

Narrative competence: The ability to understand and produce narrative. Lyotard suggests that competence in relation to a particular set of narratives defines a member of a particular community because narratives make knowable what is possible within a community. Prince (1981), Lyotard (1984).

Narrative contract: The agreement between a narrator and narratee which predicates the telling of a tale (e.g. If you listen I will tell you the truth; if you are interesting I will listen). The contract is perhaps one of the important ways in which the question of narrative is related to the law and to the problems of economy (exchange). Barthes (1974), Brooks (1984), Chambers (1984).

Narrative grammar: A set of rules and formula which determine or account for the production of narrative structures. Narrative grammars either attempt to account for a finite number of narratives (e.g. the Russian fairy-tale) or all, and only, narratives. Sometimes called 'narrative syntax', such formula seek to identify a finite number of rules from which narrative can be generated. This is the basic task of narratology. Todorov (1969), Prince (1973, 1980, 1982), Pavel (1976).

Narrative sentence: In the analytic philosophy of historiography, a sentence which refers to at least two events separated in time but describing only the earlier one (e.g. 'Prime Minister Blair went to school in the 1970s' refers both to the 1970s and a period of time beginning in 1997, but describes only the former). According to Danto, narrative sentences are signs of the ways in which narrative is teleologically determined. Danto (1965).

Narrativity: (1) The orientation of a narrative which makes that narrative possible *qua* narrative (e.g. desire for closure, the double logic of narrative, etc.). (2) The group of properties characteristic of narrative which distinguishes it from non-narrative. A narrative's 'narrative-ness'. (3) As a term within narrative theory, 'narrativity' gained a greater currency as a consequence of post-structuralist critiques of formalism and structuralism. Consequently, narrativity is commonly associated with the fluidity of structuration rather than structure. Greimas (1970), Prince (1982), Brooks (1984).

Narratology: (1) The structuralist-led theory of narrative which seeks to identify what all, and only, narratives have in common. Narratology examines the nature, form and function of narrative across genre and media. By proposing narrative as a object of rigorous scientific inquiry ('ology') narratology seeks to produce a comprehensive and universal narrative grammar. Term first proposed by Todorov

(1969). (2) More loosely, a generic term for narrative theory. Todorov (1969), Bal (1977, 1985), Prince (1981–82), Genette (1988), Pavel (1985), Onega and Landa (1997).

Narrator: The one who narrates as inscribed in a text. A narrator exists on the same diegetic level as its corresponding narratee. Distinct from the author or implied author. Scholes and Kellog (1966), Bal (1981), Booth (1983), Prince (1982).

Nucleus: In Barthes, a nucleus (like kernels) is logically essential to a narrative. *See* **cardinal function.** Barthes (1975), Chatman (1978).

Omnipresent narrator: A ubiquitous narrator who has the ability to be in several places and time zones simultaneously (e.g. the narrator of *Anna Karenin*). Omnipresent narrators are indicative of narrative historiography and are not necessarily omniscient. Chatman (1978).

Omniscient narrator: A narrator who knows (or seems to know) everything that is going on in a narrative (e.g. the narrator of *Madam Bovary*). Nicholas Royle (1990) identifies omniscient narration with a form of telepathy. Genette (1985), Booth (1983), Cohn (1978).

Order: The set of relations which determine the difference or correspondence between the order in which events are recounted and the order in which they are said to have happened. These relations can include chronological order, anachrony (retrospection/anticipation, analepses/ prolepses, flashback/flashforward), achrony, or syllepsis (non-chronological order). Chatman (1978), Genette (1985), Prince (1982).

Paradigm: (1) A basic model of narrative from which other narratives can be generated using a fixed set of transformations (e.g. the Oedipus story is said to be paradigmatic of desire in narrative). (2) In Jakobson, the paradigmatic

axis of language works (as the principle of selection) in conjunction with the syntagmatic axis (the principle of contiguity) to produce linguistic meaning. *See* **metaphor** and **metonymy.** Jakobson (1956), Saussure (1966), Brooks (1984).

Parole: *See langue*

Performative: A speech act which performs (does something) rather than stating a case (saying something) (e.g. 'I promise to come' performs the act of, or makes, a promise). A narrator can be said to perform a story by making a contract with the narratee. *See* **constative.** Austin (1990), Pratt (1977).

Perlocutionary act: A speech act which performs but is discernible in terms of the effect it has on the addressee (e.g. 'I promise to be there' may convince the listener that I am sincere in my intentions). Similarly, a narrator's speech acts may produce effects on the narratee. Austin (1990), Pratt (1977).

Plot: (1) The main events of a narrative, briefly summed up to provide a condensed account of the narrative. (2) In Aristotle (mythos) taken to be a synonym for discourse or *sjuzet*. (3) Forster distinguishes between story, 'the King died, and then the Queen died', and plot, 'The King died, and then the Queen died of grief'. Where story is determined by chronology and plot is determined by consequence or causality. (4) Following Brooks (1984), the desiring dynamic in narrative which moves the reader and story towards the end, while simultaneously delaying that end, of a narrative. Aristotle, Frye (1957), Brooks and Warren (1959), Scholes and Kellogg (1966), Shlovsky (1965), Chatman (1978), Brooks (1984), Ricoeur (vol. 1, 1984).

Point of view: (1) The perceptual position from which narrated events are presented (e.g. ominiscient, internal (focused on a character), variable (moving from character to character), or multiple (the same event narrated more than once by different characters)). (2) After Genette, the question of who sees rather than who speaks? *See also* **focalisation.** Henry James, Lubbock, Brooks and Warren (1959), Bal (1983, 1985), Chatman (1978), Cohn (1981), Lanser (1981), Todorov (1981), Rimmon-Kenan (1983), Genette (1985, 1988).

***Post hoc ergo propter hoc* fallacy:** According to Barthes (reading Aristotle), narrativity is sustained by the confusion between what-comes-after-X and what-is-caused-by-X (e.g. 'The family left Glasgow and Jane became sad' in which Jane's sadness is assumed to derive from the family leaving Glasgow). Scholasticism identifies such confusion between chronology and consequence with the Latin term '*post hoc ergo propter hoc*' [after thing therefore because of thing]. Aristotle, Barthes (1975).

Proairetic code: In Barthes, the code which governs the production of plot by weaving units of action into greater sequences. Barthes (1974, 1981), Culler (1975).

Prolepsis: An anachrony which presents future events before they chronologically occur in the story, a flashforward. Genette (1985).

Psychonarration: A narrative which presents the thoughts rather than the words of a narrator. Dorrit Cohn offers a typology of psychonarration, including narratted monologue, quoted monologue, free direct style, etc. Cohn (1966, 1978).

Reader: The interpreter, decoder or producer of meaning within a written or oral narrative. Unlike the implied reader or narratee, the real reader is not immanent or discernible within the text. Chatman (1978), Eco (1979), Booth (1983).

Readerly text (*texte lisible*): A closed text which

only offers a moderate amount of ploysemy. A text which imposes itself within fixed reading strategies and well-defined hermeneutic approaches. A narrative in which the reader is the passive consumer of meaning imposed by the text. Barthes distinguishes between readerly texts and writerly texts (texts generous in their plurality); he reads 'Sarasine' and 'Valdemar' as readerly texts while managing to demonstrated their rich potential. Barthes (1974).

Reality effect: A name, place or event presented in the course of a narrative to make the story appear real (e.g. setting the action of the fictional *Madame Bovary* in a real French town, Rouen). Barthes (1982a).

Referential code: In Barthes, the code whereby a narrative is woven by reference to a given cultural background (literary, scientific, historical knowledges, shared prejudices and stereotypes or cultural phenomena). The referential code is important in producing realist narratives. Barthes (1974, 1981).

Reliable narrator: (1) A narrator who provides an accurate account of narrated events. (2) More technically, a narrator who behaves in accordance with the implied author's norms (e.g. the gospel narrators). Booth (1983).

Satellite: A minor plot event not logically essential to the narrative action, as opposed to kernels. Satellites fill in the narrative space between crucial events. Barthes (1975), Chatman (1978).

Second-person narrative: A narrative in which the narratee is the protagonist and is told their own story (e.g. Butor's *A Change of Heart*). Morrissette (1965), Genette (1988).

Seme: (1) A minimal unit of meaning. A basic or elementary semantic feature. 2. A unit of the semic code. *See* **semic code.** Barthes (1974), Culler (1975), Chatman (1978), Greimas (1983).

Semic code: The code through which narrative produces character and setting (e.g. 'He was a respected schoolmaster, the member of several committees on public morality, a determined golfer, angry letter writer, conservative party activist, Freemason, and secret rubber fetishist', where the public duties are semes of the character's bourgeois status and the private habits semes of contradiction or hypocrisy. Barthes (1974, 1981).

Semiotic square: A structuralist-inspired model for the visual representation of a semantic logic which describes a narrative's elementary structure of signification, e.g.

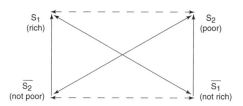

Where

◄─────► : relation of contradiction
◄--- ► : relation of contrariety
─────► : relation of complementarity

For example: 'Monica loved Bill but Bill was married to Hilary. All of Bill's time was taken up by Kenneth who wanted to expose Bill and Hilary. Hilary did not know about Monica but would not be pleased if she found out. Kenneth wanted Monica to tell him all about Bill,' can be represented by:

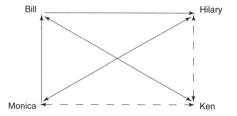

Lévi-Strauss, Greimas (1970, 1983), Bremond (1973).

Sign: Saussure proposes the sign as the basic unit of language which links a signifier (a sound image such as 'tree') to a signified (the concept or thing named by 'tree'). Neither signified nor signifier can in effect by separated from each other, the difference posited here is purely conceptual. The relation between signifier and signified is arbitrary (there is no existential link between the concept and sound, e.g. in French the same concept 'tree' has the signifier 'arbor') and conventional (users of the same language agree to use the signifier 'tree' or 'arbor'). A sign system (the network of interrelated signs) is a system of negative differences (a signifier refers to a particular signified because it does not refer to other signifieds, e.g. the sound 'tree' does not refer to the concepts dog, cat, love, Germany, instantity, etc.) with no positive terms (no one term is privileged above any other). Structuralism builds on Saussure's model of the sign system to analysis other systems such as narrative.

Sjuzet: Russian formalist synonym for discourse, as opposed to *fabula* (story). Erlich (1965), Chatman (1978), Brooks (1984).

Speech act: An utterance considered as a goal-directed act. Speech acts are classified in Austin (1990) as either constative (saying something) or performative (doing something). For a reading and rethinking of Austin's philosophy of speech acts see Derrida. Searle (1969), Pratt (1977), Chatman (1978), Lanser (1981), Derrida (1988), Austin (1990).

Story: (1) A synonym for *histoire* or *fabula*, as used by Culler (1975). The what happens of a narrative rather than how it is presented. (2) Forster distinguishes between story, 'The King died, and then the Queen died', and plot, 'The King died, and then the Queen died of grief'. Where story is determined by chronology and plot is determined by consequence or causality. (3) Capitalised, 'Story', signifying the abstract concept of narrativity (e.g. 'Story is everywhere' and so in more loose usage a synonym). (4) While all stories are narratives (a recounting of events) not all narratives are stories (*see* Introduction). Forster (1963), Lemon and Rees (1965), Benveniste (1971), Culler (1975), Chatman (1978), Genette (1985).

Stream of consciousness: A form of psycho-narration which represents a character's consciousness as a random and illogical flow of thought (e.g. Molly Bloom's monologue in *Ulysses*). Different from interior monologue which respects the grammatical conventions of standard writing. Scholes and Kellogg (1966), Chatman (1978), Cohn (1978).

Structure: The overall network of relations between units within a narrative. Structure accounts for the relations between parts and each other as well as parts and the whole. As the name suggests, structuralism makes structure its primary object of inquiry. Barthes (1975), Chatman (1978).

Subplot: A unified sequence of actions within a narrative which are subordinate (or complimentary) to the main plot (e.g. if the love interests of Charles constitute the main plot of *The French Lieutenant's Woman*, the love interest of Sam (Charles' servant) is a subplot).

Surface structure: The means by which meaning is presented in individual narratives, transforming deep structure into a realised narrative (e.g. in Greimas' model specific surface structure actors are generated from a finite number of deep structure actantial roles or paradigms). Chomsky (1965).

Symbolic code: In Barthes, the code whereby a narrative produces symbolic meaning. For example, a unit can become symbolic if it takes on the nature of an image, metaphor, leitmotif, etc. Barthes (1974, 1981).

Synchronic analysis: The study of a sign system as it appears at one particular moment while ignoring the historical evolution of that system. Saussure (1966).

Syntagm: (1) A relation of contiguity between two or more units. Narrative works through syntagmation, joining units together in consecutive and consequential relations (e.g. John got up, then Jane got up and ate her breakfast). (2) Greimas identifies three types of syntagms: performative (relating to struggles and tests), contractual (the establishing and revoking of contracts) and disjunctional (involving movement and displacement). (3) In Jakobson, the syntagmatic axis (the principle of connection) combines with paradigmatic axis (the principle of selection) to produce linguistic meaning. Jakobson (1956), Saussure (1966), Greimas (1970).

Teleology: Lit. the study of the end. Narrative is said to be teleological insofar as it compels the reader towards the end of the story, the end giving shape and coherence to the preceding narrative. Teleological assumptions in a non-fictional discourse (such as Marxism or Christianity) are a way of identifying its status as narrative. Kermode (1979), Miller (1992).

Third-person narrative: A narrative in which the narrator is not a character in the action and refers to the actors in the third person (he, she, they) (e.g. *The Trial*). Prince (1982), Genette (1983).

Time: Ricoeur proposes that narrative is the central means whereby humans come to understand temporality. It is, simultaneously, through the experience of narratives (fiction and historical) that we learn how to organise time, and through the experience of time that we come to develop narrative competence. Since humans cannot exist outside of an experience of time, humans might be said to be narrative animals '*homo fabulans*'. However, Ricoeur stresses the primacy of being over narrative. Ricoeur (vol. 1, 1984).

Undecidability: The experience of being unable to come to a decision when faced with two or more contradictory meanings or interpretations. Not the same as 'indeterminacy' which suggests that a decision has been made, and that decision is that a decision cannot be reached. In contrast, undecidability stresses the active and interminable challenge of being unable to decide. Derrida (1992, 1993), Miller (1992), Bhabha (1994).

Unreliable narrator: (1) A narrator whose trustworthiness is undermined by events as deduced from the narrative (e.g. Humbert Humbert in *Lolita*). (2) More technically, a narrator whose actions are not in accordance with the implied author's norms and values. Chatman (1978), Booth (1983).

Verisimilitude: A textual characteristic in which the text bears a close resemblance to a truth or reality which precedes the text (e.g. Dickens' urban settings are (more or less) an accurate portrait of nineteenth-century London). Genette (1968), Culler (1975), Todorov (1981).

Voice: (1) Who speaks in the narrative. (2) That which determines the narrator and the narrating moment, governing the relations between narrating and narrated. (3) An important focus for feminist and postcolonial analysis of narrative in which the question of who speaks is suggestive of the power relations at work in a narrative (e.g. colonised persons telling their own story in their own language rather than having a colonising or mediating voice speaking on their behalf (compare *Jane Eyre* to *Wide Sargasso Sea*)). Genette (1980), Brewer (1984), Lonon (1990).

Writerly text (*texte scriptible*): A text which resists established or determining codes and conventions of reading. A text which opens itself to a generous/infinite polysemy; one which is to be 'written' by the reader as a producer of meaning rather than constrained within a reading imposed by the text (as in a readerly text). Barthes (1974).

Zero focalisation: A variety of focalisation or point of view in which the narrated events are presented without a locatable perceptual position, e.g. *Vanity Fair*. Genette (1985).

A checklist of narrative theories

NOTE

Given all that this book will have had to say on the question of classification and taxonomy, it would now seem inappropriate to attempt a complete codification of the expansive and expanding field of narrative theory. Such a select bibliography can never be anything other than 'select'; should it be more than that it would cease to be a bibliography as such. Therefore the partial account which follows is designed merely to complement the sections of this volume. Accordingly, and unfortunately, the listings below only make reference to texts available in English-language translations, except where the text in question is either little known or specifically augments the reader's understanding of a theorist's output (such is the arbitrary nature of the transgression which mixes categorical boundaries). For fuller bibliographies of non-English language texts see Hawkes (1983), Rimmon-Kenan (1983), Martin (1986), and Prince (1989).

The full title of the journal listed below as *Narrative* is *Narrative: The Journal of the Society for the Study of Narrative Literature*, ed. James Phelan (Ohio: Ohio State University Press). Amid the narratological diaspora of the 1990s it provides a focus for sustained writing on topics in narrative theory, and every issue will be of interest to devotees of narrative. It is of course impossible to list here every article published in this journal. Other recent journals of interest include *The Journal of Narrative Technique*, *Narrative Inquiry* (previously *Journal of Narrative and Life History*), and *Narrative and Memory*.

Part I Openings

1 FORM AND DISCOURSE

i Classical analysis

Dorsch, T. S. (ed. and trans.), *Classic Literary Criticism: Aristotle, Horace, Longinus* (Harmondsworth: Penguin, 1965).

Horace, *The Art of Poetry*, trans. B. Raffel (Albany: SUNY Press, 1974).

Plato, *The Republic*, trans. F. M. Cornford (Oxford: Oxford University Press, 1941).

ii Twentieth-century analysis

Auberach, E., *Mimesis: The Representation of Reality in Western Literature* (Garden City, NY: Doubleday, 1957. First published 1946).

Austin, J. L., *How to Do Things with Words* (Oxford: Oxford University Press, 1990).

Bakhtin, M. (V. N. Volochinov), 'Discours inderict libre en francais, en allemend, et en russe', in *Le Marxisme et la Philosophie du langage* (Paris: Minuit, 1979. First published 1929).

Bakhtin, M., *The Dialogic Imagination: Four Essays*, ed. M. Holquist, trans. C. Emerson and M. Holquist (Austin: University of Texas Press, 1981).

Bakhtin, M., *Problems of Dostoevsky's Poetics*, ed. and trans. C. Emerson (Manchester: Manchester University Press, 1984).

Bakhtin, M., *Speech Genres and Other Late Essays*, ed. C. Emerson and M. Holquist trans. V. W. McGhee (Austin: University of Texas Press, 1986).

Bakhtin, M., *Art and Answerability: Early Philosophical Essays*, ed. M. Holquist and V. Liapunov trans. V. Liapunov (Austin: University of Texas Press, 1990).

Bakhtin, M. and Medvedev, P. *The Formal Method in Literary Scholarship: A Critical Introduction to Sociological Poetics*, trans.

A. Wehrle (London: Johns Hopkins University Press, 1978).

Beardsley, M., *Aesthetics: Problems in the Philosophy of Criticism* (New York: Harcourt Brace, 1958).

Benjamin, W., 'The Storyteller', in *Illuminations*, ed. H. Arendt, trans. H. Zohn (London: HarperCollins, 1992).

Blanchot, M., 'The Narrative Voice (the 'he', the neuter)', in *The Gaze of Orpheus and Other Literary Essays*, trans. L. Davis (New York: Station Hill, 1981).

Blanchot, M., *The Work of Fire*, trans. C. Mandell (Stanford, CA: Stanford University Press, 1995).

Booth, W. C., *The Rhetoric of Fiction* (Chicago: The University of Chicago Press, 1961).

Booth, W. C., *A Rhetoric of Irony* (Chicago: University of Chicago Press, 1974).

Booth, W. C., *The Rhetoric of Fiction, 2nd Edition* (Chicago: University of Chicago Press, 1983).

Brooks, C., *The Well Wrought Urn* (New York: Harcourt, Brace and World, 1947).

Brooks, C. and Warren, R. P., *Understanding Fiction* (New York: Appleton-Century-Crofts, 1959).

Erlich, V., *Russian Formalism: History-Doctrine* (The Hague: Mouton, 1955, revised edn 1965).

Forster, E. M., *Aspects of the Novel* (Harmondsworth: Penguin, 1963).

Frye, N., *Anatomy of Criticism* (Princeton, NJ: Princeton University Press, 1957).

Garvin, P. L. (ed. and trans.), *A Prague School Reader on Aesthetics, Literary Structure and Style* (Washington, DC: Georgetown University Press, 1964).

Kermode, F., *The Sense of an Ending* (New York: Oxford University Press, 1967).

Kermode, F., *The Genesis of Secrecy: On the Interpretation of Narrative* (Cambridge, MA: Harvard University Press, 1979).

Kermode, F., 'Secrets and Narrative Sequence', *Critical Inquiry*, 7, 1980.

Kermode, F., *The Art of Telling: Essays on Fiction* (Cambridge, MA: Harvard University Press, 1983).

Labov, W., *Language in the Inner City* (Philadelphia: University of Pennsylvania Press, 1972a).

Labov, W., 'The Transformation of Experience in Narrative Syntax', in *The Social Stratification of English in New York City* (London: Routledge & Kegan Paul, 1972b).

Labov, W. and Waletzky, J., 'Narrative Analysis: Oral Versions of Personal Experience', in J. Helm (ed.), *Essays on the Verbal and Visual Arts: Proceedings of the 1966 Annual Spring Meeting* (Seattle: University of Washington Press, 1967).

Lemon, L. T. and Rees, R. J. (eds), *Russian Formalist Criticism: Four Essays* (Lincoln: University of Nebraska Press, 1965).

Lubbock, P., *The Craft of Fiction* (New York: Viking Press, 1963. First published 1921).

Matejka, L. and Pomorska, K. (eds), *Readings in Russian Poetics: Formalist and Structuralist Views* (Cambridge, MA: MIT Press, 1971).

Mukarovsky, J., 'Standard Language and Poetic Language', in *Linguistics and Literary Style*, ed. Donald C. Freeman (New York and London: Holt Rinehart and Winston, 1970).

Pratt, M. L., *Toward a Speech Act Theory of Literary Discourse* (Bloomington: Indiana University Press, 1977).

Propp, V., 'Edip v svete fol'klora' ('Oedipus in the Light of Folklore'), *Serija filologiceskich nauk*, 9 (72) (1944), pp. 138–75.

Propp, V., *Morphology of the Folktale*, trans. L. Scott (Austin: University of Texas Press, 1968).

Propp, V., *Theory and History of Folklore*, ed. A. Liberman trans. A. Y. Martin and R. P. Martin (Minneapolis: University of Minnesota Press, 1984).

Searle, J., *Speech Acts* (Cambridge: Cambridge University Press, 1969).

Searle, J., 'A Classification of Illocutionary Acts', *Language in Society*, 5 (1976), pp. 1–23.

Scholes, R. (ed.), *Approaches to the Novel* (San Francisco: Chandler, 1961).

Scholes, R., *The Fabulators* (New York: Oxford University Press, 1967).

Scholes, R., *Fabulation and Metafiction* (Urbana: University of Illinois Press, 1979).

Scholes, R. and Kellog, R., *The Nature of Narrative* (New York: Oxford University Press, 1966).

Shklovsky, V., 'On the Connection between Devices of *Syuzhet* Construction and General Stylistic Devices', in *Russian Formalism*, ed. S. Bann and J. E. Bowlt (New York: Barnes and Noble, 1973).

Watt, I., *The Rise of the Novel* (Berkeley: University of California Press, 1957).

Wellek, R. and Warren, A., *Theory of Literature* (New York: Harcourt Brace, 1949).

Savage, J., *An Introduction to the Study of the Novel* (Ghent: Story-Scientia, PVBA, 1965).

2 STRUCTURALISM

i Definitions

Bal, M., *Narratology: Introduction to the Theory of Narrative*, trans. C. van Boheemen (London: University of Toronto Press, 1985).

Benveniste, E., *Problems in General Linguistics* (Miami: University of Miami Press, 1971).

Bremond, C., *Logique du récit* (Paris: Sueil, 1973).

Chatman, S. (ed.), *Literary Style: A Symposium* (London: Oxord University Press, 1971).

Chatman, S. (ed.), *Approaches to Poetics* (New York and London: Columbia University Press, 1973).

Culler, J., *Structuralist Poetics: Structuralism, Linguistics and the Study of Literature* (London: Routledge, 1975).

Genette, G., 'Raisemblance et Motivation', *Communiçations*, 11 (1968), pp. 5–21.

Girard, R., 'French Theories of Fiction: 1947–1974', *Bucknell Review*, 22 (1) (1976), pp. 117–26.

Greimas, A. J., 'Elements of a Narrative Grammar', *Diacritics*, 7 (1977), pp. 23–40.

Greimas, A. J., *Semiotics and Language: An Analytical Dictionary*, trans. Larry Crist *et al.* (Bloomington: Indiana University Press, 1982).

Hawkes, T., *Structuralism and Semiotics* (London: Methuen, 1977, revised edn 1983).

Heath, S., McCabe, C. and Prendergast, C. (eds), *Signs of the Times* (Cambridge: Granta Press, 1971).

Hrushovski, B. and Ben-Porat, Z., *Structuralist Poetics in Israel* (Tel-Aviv: The Porter Institute for Poetics and Semiotics, 1974).

Lévi-Strauss, C., *The Savage Mind* (Chicago: Chicago University Press, 1966).

Lévi-Strauss, C., *The Scope of Anthropology*, trans. S. O. Paul and R. A Paul (London: Cape, 1967).

Lévi-Strauss, C., *Structural Anthropology*, trans. C. Jacobson and B. G. Schoepf (London: Allen Lane, 1968).

Lévi-Strauss, C., *Totenism*, trans. R. Needham, (Hammondsworth: Penguin, 1969).

Lévi-Strauss, C., *The Raw and the Cooked*, trans. J. Weightman and D. Weightman (London: Cape, 1970).

Lévi-Strauss, C., *Triste Tropiques*, trans. J. Weightman and D. Weightman (London: Cape, 1973a).

Lévi-Strauss, C., *From Honey to Ashes*, trans. J. Weightman and D. Weightman (London: Cape, 1973b).

Lothe, J., *Narrative in Fiction and Film: An Introduction* (Oxford: Oxford University Press, 2000).

Macksey, R. and Donato, E. (eds), *The Structuralist Controversy: The Languages of Criticism and the Sciences of Man* (Baltimore, MD: Johns Hopkins University Press, 1970).

Martin, W., *Recent Theories of Narrative* (Ithaca: Cornell University Press, 1986).

Metz, C., *Film Language* (London: Oxford University Press, 1974a).

Metz, C., *Language and Cinema* (The Hague: Mouton, 1974b).

Prince, G., 'Remarques Sur les Signes Métanarratifs', *Degrés*, 11–12 (1977), pp. 1–10.

Prince, G., 'Narrative Analysis and Narratology', *New Literary History*, 13 (1981/2), pp. 179–88.

Prince, G., *Narratology: The Form and Functioning of Narrative* (Berlin: Mouton, 1982).

Prince, G., *A Dictionary of Narratology* (Lincoln: University of Nebraska Press, 1989).

Sapir, E., *Language* (New York: Harcourt Brace, 1921).

Sapir, E., *Selected Writings in Language Culture and Personality*, ed. David G Mandelbaum, (Berkeley: University of California Press, 1949).

Scholes, R., *Structuralism in Literature: An Introduction* (New Haven, CT, and London: Yale University Press, 1974).

Scholes, R., *Semiotics and Interpretation* (New Haven, CT: Yale University Press, 1982).

Sebok, T. A. (ed.), *Style in Language* (Cambridge, MA: MIT Press, 1960).

Sebok, T. A. (ed.), *The Tell-Tale Sign: A Survey of Semiotics* (Netherlands: Lisse, 1975).

Rimmon-Kenan, S., *Narrative Fiction: Contemporary Poetics* (London: Methuen, 1983).

Saussure, F. de, *Course in General Linguistics*, trans. W. Baskin (New York: McGraw-Hill, 1966).

Todorov, T., 'Les catégories du récit littéraire', *Communiçations*, 8 (1966), pp. 125–51.

Todorov, T., *Introduction to Poetics*, trans. R. Howard (Minneapolis: University of Minnesota Press, 1981).

Whorf, B. L., *Language, Thought and Reality*, ed. John B. Carroll, (Cambridge, MA: MIT Press, 1956).

ii Theories

Bal, M., 'Notes on Narrative Embedding', *Poetics Today*, 2 (1981a), pp. 41–59.

Bal, M., 'The Laughing of Mice, or: On Focalization', *Poetics Today*, 2 (1981b), pp. 202–10.

Bal, M., 'The Narrating and the Focalising: A Theory of Agents in Narrative', *Style*, 17 (1983), pp. 234–69.

Bremond, C., 'Morphology of the French folktale', *Semiotica*, 2 (1970), pp. 247–76.

Bremond, C., 'The Logic of Narrative Possibilities', *New Literary History*, 11 (1980), pp. 387–411.

Chatman, S., *Story and Discourse* (London: Cornell University Press, 1978).

Chomsky, N., *Syntactic Structures* (The Hague: Mouton, 1957).

Chomsky, N., *Aspects of the Theory of Syntax* (Cambridge, MA: MIT Press, 1965).

Cixous, H., 'The Character of Character', *New Literary History*, 5 (1974), pp. 383–402.

Culler, J., *The Pursuit of Signs* (London: Routledge & Kegan Paul, 1981).

Genette, G., *Figures I* (Paris: Seuil, 1966), *Figures II* (1969), *Figures III* (1972).

Genette, G., 'Boundaries of Narrative', *New Literary History*, 8 (1976), pp. 1–15.

Genette, G., *Palimpsestes: La Littérature au Second Degrée* (Paris: Editions du Seuil, 1982).

Genette, G., *Narrative Discourse: An Essay in Method*, trans. J. E. Lewin (Ithaca: Cornell University Press, 1985).

Genette, G., *Fiction and Diction*, trans. C. Porter (Ithaca: Cornell University Press, 1993).

Genette, G., *Paratexts: Thresholds of Interpretation*, trans. J. E., Lewin (Cambridge: Cambridge University Press, 1997).

Genette, G., *Palimpsestes*, trans. C. Newman (Lincoln: University of Nebraska Press, 1999).

Greimas, A. J., 'Narrative Grammar: Units and Levels', *Modern Language Notes*, 86 (1971), pp. 793–806.

Greimas, A. J., *Structural Semantics: An Attempt at Method*, trans. D. McDowell, R. Schlefier and A. Velie (Lincoln: University of Nebraska Press, 1983).

Greimas, A. J., *On Meaning: Selected Writings in Semiotic Theory*, trans. P. J Perron and F. H. Collins (Minneapolis: University of Minneapolis Press, 1987).

Greimas, A. J. and Courtes, J., 'The Cognitive Dimension of Narrative Discourse', *New Literary History*, 7 (1976), pp. 433–47.

Greimas, A. J. and Courtes, J., *Semiotics and Language: An Analytic Dictionary*, trans. L. Crist *et al.* (Bloomington: Indiana University Press, 1982).

Jakobson, R., 'Two Aspects of Language and Two Types of Aphasic Disturbances', in Roman Jakobson and Morris Halle, *Fundamentals of Language* (The Hague: Mouton, 1956).

Jakobson, R., 'Closing Statement: Linguistics and Poetics', in T. Sebeok (ed.), *Style in Language* (Cambridge, MA: MIT Press, 1960).

Jakobson, R., *Jakobson on Language*, ed. L. R Waugh *et al.* (London: Harvard University Press, 1990).

Metz, C., 'Story/Discourse (A Note on Two Kinds of Voyeurism)', in *The Imaginary Signifier*, trans. C. Britton (Bloomimgton: Indiana University Press, 1981).

Pavel, T. G., *La Syntaxe Narrative des Tragédies de Corneille* (Paris: Klinchsrech, 1976).

Pavel, T. G., 'Remarks on Narrative Grammars', *Poetics*, 8 (1973), pp. 5–30.

Prince, G., *A Grammar of Stories* (The Hague: Mouton, 1973).

Prince, G., 'Introduction to the Study of the Narratee', in J. P. Tompkins (ed.), *Reader-Response Criticism* (Baltimore, MD: Johns Hopkins University Press, 1980a).

Prince, G., 'Aspects of a Grammar of Narrative', *Poetics Today*, 1 (3) (1980b), pp. 49–63.

Prince, G., 'Narrative Pragmatics, Message, and Point', *Poetics*, 12 (1983), pp. 527–36.

Rimmon, S., 'A Comprehensive Theory of Narrative: Génette's *Figures III* and the Structuralist Study of Fiction', *PTL*, 1 (1976), pp. 33–62.

iii Readings

Barthes, R., 'Introduction a l'analyse structurale des récits', in *Communiçations*, 8 (1966).

Barthes, R., *Elements of Semiology*, trans. A. Lavers and C. Smith (London: Cape, 1967).

Barthes, R., 'Introduction to the Structural Analysis of Narrative', in S. Heath (ed.), *Image-Music-Text* (London: Fontana, 1977a).

Barthes, R., *Roland Barthes by Roland Barthes*, trans. R. Howard (London: Macmillan, 1977b).

Barthes, R., *Mythologies*, ed. and trans. A. Lavers (London: Granada, 1982a).

Barthes, R., *Selected Writings*, ed. S. Sontag (London: Collins, 1982b).

Barthes, R., *The Rustle of Language*, trans. R. Howard, (London: Blackwell, 1986).

Barthes, R., *Criticism and Truth*, ed. and trans. K. P. Keunema (London: Athlone, 1987).

Barthes, R., *The Responsibility of Forms: Critical Essays on Music, Art, and Representation*, (Oxford: Blackwell, 1995).

Chambers, R., *Story and Situation: Narrative Seduction and the Power of Fiction* (Minneapolis: University of Minnesota Press, 1984).

Chatman, S., *Coming to Terms: The Rhetoric of Narrative in Fiction and Film* (London: Cornell University Press, 1990).

Crosman, I., *Metaphoric Narration* (Chapel Hill: University of North Carolina Press, 1978).

Eco, U., *A Theory of Semiotics* (Bloomington and London: Indiana University Press, 1976).

Eco, U., *The Role of the Reader: Explorations in the Semiotics of Texts* (Bloomington: Indiana University Press, 1979).

Eco, U. and Del Buono, E., *The Bond Affair* (London: Macdonald, 1966).

Genette, G. 'On the First-Person Novel', *New Literary History*, 9 (1) (Fall 1977).

Genette, G., Barthes, R. and Todorov, T. (eds), *Recherches des Proust* (Paris: Editions du Seil, 1980).

Genette, G., Debray-Genette, R. and Todorov, T. (eds), *Travail de Flaubert* (Paris: Editions du Seuil, 1983).

Genette, G., Benichou, P. and Todorov, T., *Pensee de Rousseau* (Paris: Editions du Seuil, 1984).

Greimas, A. J. (ed.), *Sign, Language, Culture* (The Hague: Mouton, 1970).

Pascal, R., *Design and Truth in Autobiography* (Cambridge, MA: Harvard University Press, 1960).

Pascal, R., *The Dual Voice: Free Indirect Speech and Its Functioning in the Nineteenth-Century European Novel* (Manchester: Manchester University Press, 1977).

Todorov, T., *Grammaire du Décaméron* (The Hague: Mouton, 1969).

Todorov, T., *The Poetics of Prose* (Oxford: Blackwell, 1978).

3 POST-NARRATOLOGY

i Reflections

Bal, M., 'Narratology and the Rhetoric of Trashing', *Comparative Literature*, 44 (3) (Summer 1992), pp. 293–306.

Barthes, R., *S/Z*, trans. R. Howard (New York: Hill and Wang, 1974).

Barthes, R., *The Pleasure of the Text*, trans. R. Miller (New York: Hill and Wang, 1975).

Barthes, R., 'Textual Analysis: Poe's "Valdemer"', in R. Young (ed.), *Untying the Text: A Post-structuralist Reader* (London: Routledge, 1981).

Barthes, R., *Sollers Writer*, trans. P. Thody (Minneapolis: University of Minnesota Press, 1987).

Bebin-Masi, J. (ed.), *Narrative in Nice, Style*, 26 (3) (1992).

Booth, W. C., 'Rhetorical Critics Old and New: The Case of Gerard Genette', in *Reconstructing Literature*, ed. L. Terner (Totawa: Barnes & Noble, 1983).

Booth, W. C., 'Where is the Authorial Audience in Biblical Narrative – and in other "Authorative" Texts?', *Narrative*, 4 (3) (1996).

Chambers, R., *Room for Maneuver: Reading Oppositional Narrative* (Chicago, IL: University of Chicago Press, 1991).

Chambers, R., 'Reading, Mourning, and the Death of the Author', *Narrative*, 5 (1) (1997).

Chatman, S., 'Narratological Empowerment', *Narrative*, 1 (1) (1993).

Chatman, S., 'How Loose Can Narrators Get? (And How Vulnerable Can Narratees Be?)' *Narrative*, 3 (3) (1995).

Cohn, D. and Genette, G., 'Nouveaux nouveaux discours du recit', *Poetique*, 2 (2) (1985), pp. 101–9.

Cortazzi, M., *Narrative Analysis* (London: Falmer Press, 1993).

Genette, G., *Narrative Discourse Revisited*, trans. J.E Lewin (London: Cornell University Press, 1988).

Hopkins, M. F., 'Some Sites and Sightings of Narrative Theory in the Eighties', *Text and Performance Quarterly*, 9 (1) (1989), pp. 89–95.

Onega, S. and Landa, J. (ed.), *Narratology* (London and New York: Longman, 1997).

Pavel, T., *The Poetics of Plot: The Case of English Renaissance Drama* (Minneapolis: University of Minnesota Press, 1985).

Prince, G., 'On Narratology (Past, Present, Future)', *French Literature Series (Columbia)*, 17 (1) (1990), pp. 1–14.

Prince, G., 'On Narratology: Criteria, Corpus, Context', *Narrative* 3 (1) (1995).

Riessman, C. K., *Narrative Analysis* (London: Sage Publications, 1993).

Scholes, R., *Textual Power* (New Haven, CT: Yale University Press, 1985).

Scholes, R. and Comely, N. R., 'Responsible Extravagance: Reading after Post-structuralism', *Narrative*, 1 (1) (1993).

ii Responses

Banfield, A., *Unspeakable Sentences: Narration and Representation in the Language of Fiction* (Boston, MA, and London: Routledge & Kegan Paul, 1982).

Bordwell, D., *Narration in the Fiction Film* (Madison: University of Wisconsin Press, 1985).

Brooke-Rose, C., *Stories, Theories & Things* (Cambridge: Cambridge University Press, 1991).

Brooke-Rose, C., 'Splilitcrit', *Narrative*, 4 (1) (1996).

Brooks, P., *Reading for the Plot: Design and Intention in Narrative* (New York: Knopf Press, 1984).

Cohan, S. and Shires, L. M., *Telling Stories: A Theoretical Analysis of Narrative Fiction* (London and New York: Routledge, 1988).

Cornis-Pope, M., 'Post-structuralist Narratology and Critical Writing: A Figure in the Carpet Textshop', *Journal of Narrative Techniques* 20 (2) (1990), pp. 245–65.

Cornis-Pope, M., *Hermeneutic Desire and Critical Rewriting: Narrative Interpretation in the Wake of Poststructuralism* (London: Macmillan, 1992).

Currie, M., *Postmodern Narrative Theory* (London: Macmillan, 1998).

Dipple, E., *The Unresolvable Plot: Reading Contemporary Fiction* (London and New York: Routledge, 1988).

Docherty, T., *Reading (Absent) Character: Towards a Theory of Characterization in Fiction* (Oxford: Clarendon Press, 1983).

Fehn, A., Hoesterey, I. And Tatar, M., *Neverending Stories: Toward a Critical Narratology* (Princeton, NJ: Princeton University Press, 1992).

Friedman, S. S., 'Spatialization: A Strategy for Reading Narrative', *Narrative*, 1 (1) (1993).

Gibson, A., *Reading Narrative Discourse: Studies in the Novel from Cervantes to Beckett* (London: Macmillan, 1990).

Gibson, A., *Towards a Postmodern Theory of Narrative* (Edinburgh: Edinburgh University Press, 1996).

Hawthorn, J. (ed.), *Narrative: From Malory to Motion Pictures* (London: Arnold, 1985).

Heath, S., *The Nouveau Roman: A Study in the Practice of Writing* (London: Elek, 1972).

Kristeva, J., *Desire in Language: A Semiotic Approach to Literature and Art*, ed. L. S. Roudiez (Oxford: Blackwell, 1980).

Kristeva, J., *Revolution in Poetic Language*, trans. M. Waller (New York: Columbia University Press, 1984).

Kroeber, K., *Retelling/Rereading: The Fate of Storytelling in Modern Times* (New Brunswick: Rutgers University Press, 1990).

Le Guin, U. K., 'It was a dark and stormy night, or, why are we huddling around this camp fire?, *Critical Inquiry*, 7 (1980), pp. 187–95.

Lokke, V. L., 'Narratology, Obsolescent Paradigms, and "Scientific" Poetics; or, Whatever Happened to *PTL?*', *Modern Fiction Studies*, 33 (3) (1987), pp. 545–59.

Malouzynski, M. P., 'Mikhail Bakhtin and Contemporary Narrative Theory', *University of Ottowa Quarterly*, 53 (1) (1983), pp. 51–65.

Miller, D. A., *Narrative and Its Discontents: Problems of Closure in the Traditional Novel* (Princeton, NJ: Princeton University Press, 1981).

Mitchell, W. J. T. (ed.), *On Narrative* (Chicago, IL: Chicago University Press, 1981).

Morrissette, B., 'Narrative "You" in Contemporary Literature', *Comparative Literature Studies*, 2 (1965), pp. 1–24.

Morrissette, B., *Novel and Film: Essays in Two Genres*, (Chicago University Press, 1985).

Nelson, R. J., *Causality and Narrative in French Fiction from Zola to Robbe-Grillet* (Columbus: Ohio University Press, 1990).

O'Neill, P., *Fictions of Discourse: Reading Narrative Theory* (London: University of Toronto Press, 1994).

Phelan, J., *Reading People, Reading Plots: Character, Progression and the Interpretation of Narrative* (Chicago: University of Chicago Press, 1989a).

Phelan, J. (ed.), *Reading Narrative: Form, Ethics, Ideology* (Ohio: Ohio State University Press, 1989b).

Rabinowitz, P. J., '"Betraying the Sender": The Rhetoric and Ethics of Fragile Texts', *Narrative*, 2 (3) (1994).

Rabinowitz, P. J., 'Zoning Out of Literary Studies', *Narrative*, 3 (3) (1995).

Raval, S., 'Recent Books on Narrative Theory: an Essay Review', *Modern Fiction Studies*, 33 (3) (1987), pp. 559–70.

Reid, I., *Narrative Exchanges* (London: Routledge, 1992).

Ryan, M-L., 'The Models of Narrativity and Their Visual Metaphors', *Style*, 26 (3) (1992), pp. 368–87.

Singer, A., 'The Methods of Form: On Narrativity and Social Consciousness', *Sub-Stance*, 41 (1983), pp. 64–77.

Smith, B. H., 'Narrative Versions, Narrative Theories', *Critical Inquiry*, 7 (1980).

Smith, B. H., *Poetic Closure: A Study of How Poems End* (Chicago: Chicago University Press, 1968).

Smith, B.H., *On the Margin of Discourse: The Relation of Literature to Language* (Chicago: University of Chicago Press, 1979).

Smith, B. H., *Contingencies of Value: Alternative Perspectives for Critical Theory* (Cambridge, MA: Harvard University Press, 1988).

Sturgess, P. J. M., *Narrativity: Theory and Practice* (Oxford: Clarendon Press, 1992).

Suvin, D., 'On Metaphoricity and Narrativity in Fiction: The Chronotope as the *Differentia Generica*', *Sub-Stance*, 48 (1986), pp. 51–67.

iii Beyond

Beer, G., *Darwin's Plots: Evolutionary Narrative in Darwin, George Eliot and Nineteenth-century Fiction* (London: Routledge, 1983).

Berger, J., *Ways of Seeing* (London: Penguin, 1988).

Berger, J. and Mohr, J., *Another Way of Telling* (London: Writers and Readers Publishing Co-operative Society, 1982).

Currie, M. (ed.), *Metafiction* (London and New York: Longman, 1995).

Deleuze, G. and Guattari, F., *Anti-Oedipus: Capitalism and Schizophrenia*, trans. R. Hurley *et al.* (London: Athlone Press, 1984).

Deleuze, G. and Guattari, F., *Mille Plateaux: Capitalism and Schizophrenia Volume 2*, trans. B Massumi (London: Athlone Press, 1988).

Goffman, E., *Frame Analysis: An Essay on the Organization of Experience* (New York: Harper, 1974).

Goffman, E., *The Presentation of Self in Everyday Life* (London: Penguin, 1980).

Harvey, D., *The Condition of Postmodernity* (Oxford: Blackwell, 1992).

Hutcheon, L., *Narcissistic Narrative: The Metafictional Paradox* (London: Methuen, 1984).

Hutcheon, L., *A Theory of Parody: The Teachings of Twentieth-century Art Forms* (London: Methuen, 1985).

Hutcheon, L., *A Poetics of Postmodernism: History, Theory, Fiction* (New York: Routledge, 1988).

Hutcheon, L., *The Politics of Postmodernism* (London and New York: Routledge, 1989).

Lyotard, J-F., 'Petite economie libidinale d'un dispositif narratif', *Des dispositifs pulsionnels*, Union Generale d'Editions, 10/18 (1973).

Lyotard, J-F., *The Postmodern Condition*, trans. G. Bennington and B. Massumi (Manchester: Manchester University Press, 1984).

Lyotard, J-F., *The Differend: Phrases in Dispute*, trans. G. Van den Abbeele (Manchester: Manchester University Press, 1988).

Lyotard, J-F., *The Inhuman: Reflections on Time*, trans. G. Bennington and R. Bowlby, (Cambridge: Polity Press, 1991).

Lyotard, J-F., *The Postmodern Explained to Children: Correspondence 1982–85* (London: Turnaround, 1992).

McClary, S., 'The Impromtu that Trod on a Loaf: or How Music Tells Stories', *Narrative*, 5 (1) (1997).

McClary, S., *De-Tonations: Narrative and Signification in Absolute Music* (London: Wesleyan University Press, 1998).

McCloskey, D. N., *The Rhetoric of Economics* (Madison: University of Wisconsin Press, 1985).

Nash, C. (ed.), *Narrative in Culture: The Uses of Storytelling in the Sciences, Philosophy and Literature* (London and New York: Routledge, 1990).

Pfeil, F., *Another Tale to Tell: Politics and Narrative in Postmodern Culture* (London: Verso, 1990).

Ryan, M-L., *Possible Worlds, Artificial Intelligence and Narrative Theory* (Bloomington: Indiana University Press, 1991).

Waugh, P., *Metafiction: The Theory and Practice of Self-conscious Fiction* (London and New York: Methuen, 1984).

Part II DIASPORA

4 PSYCHOANALYSIS

Bersani, L., *A Future for Astyanax: Character and Desire in Literature* (London: Little Brown, 1976).

Bersani, L. and Dutoit, U., *The Forms of Violence: Narrative in Assyrian Art and Modern Culture* (New York: Little Brown, 1985).

Borch-Jakobsen, M., 'Is Psychoanalysis a Scientific Fairy Tale?', *Narrative*, 7 (1) (1999), pp. 56–71.

Borch-Jakobsen, M., 'Much Ado About Nothing: A Reply to Claudia Brodsky's Reply', *Narrative* 7 (1) (1999), pp. 120–3.

Brooks, P., 'Narrative Desire', *Style*, 18 (3) (1984), pp. 312–27.

Brooks, P., 'Psychoanalytic Constructions and Narrative Meaning', *Paragraph*, 7 (1986), pp. 55–76.

Brooks, P., 'The Tale Versus the Novel', in M. Spilka and C. McCracken-Flesher (eds), *Why the Novel Matters: A Postmodern Perplex* (Bloomington: Indiana University Press, 1990).

Brooks, P., *Body Work: Objects of Desire in Modern Narrative* (Cambridge, MA: Harvard University Press, 1993).

Brooks, P., *Psychoanalysis and Storytelling* (Oxford: Blackwell, 1994).

Chase, C., 'Oedipal Textuality: Reading Freud'sReading of Oedipus', *Diacritics*, 9 (1979), pp. 54–68.

Clayton, J., 'Narrative and Theories of Desire', *Critical Inquiry*, 16 (1) (Autumn 1989), pp. 35–53.

Davis, R. C. (ed.), *Lacan and Narration: The Psychoanalytic Difference in Narrative Theory* (Baltimore, MD: Johns Hopkins University Press, 1983).

De Lauretis, T., 'Gaudy Rose: Eco and Narcissism', *Substance*, 47 (1985), pp. 13–29.

Freud, S., *Beyond the Pleasure Principle*, in J. Strachey (ed.), *The Standard Edition of the Complete Psychological Works* (London: Hogarth Press, 1953), Vol.18, pp. 1–64.

Freud, S., 'Creative Writers and Daydreaming' (1908), in J. Strachey (ed.), *The Standard Edition of the Complete Psychological Works of Sigmund Freud* (London: Hogarth Press, 1953), Vol. 9, pp. 143–53.

Girard, R., *Deceit, Desire, and the Novel: Self and Other in Literary Structure* (Baltimore, MD: Johns Hopkins University Press, 1961).

Heath, S., 'Narrative Space', *Screen*, 17 (3) (Autumn 1976), pp. 68–112.

Heath. S., *Questions of Cinema* (London: Macmillan, 1981).

Mulvey, L., 'Visual Pleasure and Narrative Cinema', *Screen*, 16 (3) (Autumn 1975), pp. 6–18.

Mulvey, L., 'Afterthoughts on "Visual Pleasure and Narrative Cinema" Inspired by *Duel in the Sun*', *Framework*, 15/16/17 (1981), pp. 12–15. Both articles reprinted in A. Easthope (ed.), *Contemporary Film Theory* (London and New York: Longman, 1996).

Rashkin, E., *Family Secrets and the Psychoanalysis of Narrative* (Princeton, NJ: Princeton University Press, 1992).

Rimmon-Kenan, S. (ed.), *Discourse in Psychoanalysis and Literature* (London and New York: Methuen, 1987).

Schafer, R., *Narrative Actions in Psychoanalysis* (Worcester, MA: Clark University Press, 1981).

Žižek, S., *Looking Awry: An Introduction to Jacques Lacan through Popular Culture* (London: MIT Press, 1992a).

Žižek, S. (ed.), *Everything You Always Wanted to Know about Lacan (but Were Afraid to Ask Hitchcock)* (London: Verso, 1992b).

5 SEXUAL DIFFERENCE

Armstrong, N., *Desire and Domestic Fiction: A Political History of the Novel* (New York: Oxford University Press, 1987).

Bal, M., *Remembering Rembrandt: Beyond the Word–Image Opposition* (Cambridge: Cambridge University Press, 1991).

Brewer, M. M., 'A Loosening of Tongues: from Narrative Economy to Women Writing', *Modern Language Notes*, 99 (5) (1984), pp. 1141–61.

Brewer, M. M., 'Surviving Fictions: Gender and Difference in Postmodern and Postnuclear Narrative', *Discourse*, 9 (1987), pp. 37–52.

Bronfen, E., *Over Her Dead Body: Death, Femininity, and the Aesthetic* (Manchester: Manchester University Press, 1992).

Curti, L., *Female Stories, Female Bodies: Narrative, Identity and Representation* (London: Macmillan, 1998).

De Lauretis, T., *Alice Doesn't: Feminism, Semiotics, Cinema* (London: Macmillan, 1984).

De Lauretis, T., *Technologies of Gender* (Bloomington: Indiana University Press, 1987).

De Lauretis, T., *The Practice of Love: Lesbian Sexuality and Perverse Desire* (Bloomington: Indiana University Press, 1996).

Diengott, N., 'Narratology and Feminism', *Style*, 22 (1) (1988), pp. 42–60.

Doane, M. A., *The Desire to Desire: The Woman's Film of the 1940's* (London: Macmillan, 1988).

Farwell, M., 'Heterosexual Plots and Lesbian Subtexts: Toward a Theory of Lesbian Narrative Space', in K. Jay and J. Glasgow (eds), *Lesbian Texts and Contexts: Radical Revisions* (New York: New York University Press, 1990).

Foucault, M., *The History of Sexuality: Volume 1, An Introduction*, trans. R. Hurley (London: Penguin, 1990).

Foucault, M., *The History of Sexuality: Volume 2, The Use of Pleasure*, trans. R. Hurley, (London: Viking, 1986a).

Foucault, M., *The History of Sexuality: Volume 3, The Care of the Self*, trans. R. Hurley (London: Viking, 1986b).

Hite, M., *The Other Side of the Story: Structures and Strategies of Contemporary Feminist Narrative* (Cornell: Cornell University Press, 1989).

Hollinger, K., '"The Look," Narrativity, and the Female Spectator in *Vertigo*', *Journal of Film and Video*, 39 (4) (1987), pp. 18–27.

Homans, M., 'Feminist Fictions and Feminist Theories of Narrative', *Narrative*, 2 (1) (1994), pp. 3–16.

Lanser, S. S., *The Narrative Act: Point of View* (Princeton, NJ: Princeton University Press, 1981).

Lanser, S. S., 'Toward a Feminist Narratology', *Style*, 20 (3) (1986), pp. 341–63.

Lanser, S. S., *Fictions of Authority: Women Writers and the Narrative Voice* (Cornell: Cornell University Press, 1992).

Lanser, S. S., 'Sexing the Narrative: Property, Desire, and the Engendering of Narratology', *Narrative*, 3 (1) (1995).

Lovell, T., *Consuming Fiction* (London: Verso, 1987).

Roof, J., *Come As You Are: Sexuality and Narrative* (New York: Columbia University Press, 1996).

Sedgewick, E. K., *Between Men: English Literature and Male Homosocial Desire* (New York: Columbia University Press, 1985).

Sedgewick, E. K., *Epistemology of the Closet* (Hemel Hempstead: Harvester Wheatsheaf, 1991).

Sedgewick, E. K., *Tendencies* (London: Routledge, 1994).

Showalter, E., 'On Hysterical Narrative', *Narrative*, 1 (1) (1993), pp. 24–35.

Warhol, R., *Gendered Interventions: Narrative Discourse in the Victorian Novel* (New Brunswick, NJ: Rutgers University Press, 1989).

6 DECONSTRUCTION

Bennington, G., *Lyotard: Writing the Event* (Manchester: Manchester University Press, 1988).

Bennington, G., 'Postal Politics and the Institution of the Nation', in *Legislations: the Politics of Deconstruction* (London: Verso, 1994).

Brooks, P., Felman, S. and Miller, J. H. (eds), *The Lesson of Paul de Man* (New Haven, CT: Yale University Press, 1986). Originally a special edition of *Yale French Studies*, 69 (1985).

Culler, J., *On Deconstruction: Theory and Criticism after Structuralism* (London: Routledge, 1983).

Culler, J., *Framing the Sign* (Oxford: Blackwell, 1988).

De Man, P., *Blindness and Insight: Essays in the Rhetoric of Contemporary Fiction* (New York: Oxford University Press, 1971).

De Man, P., *Allegories of Reading: Figural Language in Rousseau, Nietzsche, Rilke and Proust* (New Haven, CT: Yale University Press, 1979).

Derrida, J., *Of Grammatology*, trans. G.C. Spivak (Chicago: Chicago University Press, 1976).

Derrida, J., 'Living On: Border Lines', trans. J. Hulbert, in H. Bloom *et al.* (eds), *Deconstruction and Criticism* (London: Routledge, 1979).

Derrida, J., 'The Law of Genre', *Critical Inquiry*, 7 (1980).

Derrida, J., 'Title: To be Specified', *Sub-Stance*, 31 (1981), pp. 5–22.

Derrida, J., *Margins of Philosophy*, trans. A. Bass (Brighton: Harvester Press, 1982).

Derrida, J., *Parages* (Paris: Galilée, 1986).

Derrida, J., *Limited Inc [.] a,b,c*, ed. G. Graff (Evanston, IL: Northwestern University Press, 1988a).

Derrida, J., 'The Deaths of Roland Barthes', trans. P-A. Brault and M. Nass, in H. J. Silverman (ed.), *Philosophy and Non-Philosophy since Merleu-Ponty* (London: Routledge, 1988).

Derrida, J., *Memoires for Paul de Man (Revised Edition)*, ed. E. Cadava and A. Ronell (New York: Columbia University Press, 1989a).

Derrida, J., 'Biodegradables: Seven Diary Fragments', trans. P. Kamuf, *Critical Inquiry*, 15 (4) (1989b), pp. 812–74.

Derrida, J., *Between the Blinds: A Derrida Reader*, ed. P. Kamuf (London: Harvester Wheatsheaf 1991).

Derrida, J., *Acts of Literature*, ed. D. Attridge (London: Routledge, 1992a).

Derrida, J., *Given Time: 1. Counterfeit Money*, trans. P. Kamuf (London: University of Chicago Press, 1992b).

Derrida, J., *Aporias*, trans. T. Dutoit (Stanford, CA: Stanford University Press 1993).

Derrida, J., 'The Retrait of Metaphor', in J. Wolfreys (ed.), *Writing Performances: A Derrida Reader* (Edinburgh: Edinburgh University Press, 1998).

Derrida, J. and Bennington, G., *Jacques Derrida: Derridabase/Circumfession*, trans. G. Bennington (London: University of Chicago Press, 1993).

Hartman, G., *Beyond Formalism* (New Haven, CT, and London: Yale University Press, 1970).

Jacobs, C., *Telling Time* (London: Johns Hopkins University Press, 1993).

Johnson, B., *The Critical Difference: Essays in the Contemporary Rhetoric of Reading* (London: Johns Hopkins University Press, 1980).

Johnson, B., *A World of Difference* (Baltimore, MD: Johns Hopkins University Press, 1987).

Miller, J. H. (ed.), *Aspects of Narrative* (New York: Columbia University Press, 1971).

Miller, J. H., 'Narrative and History', *ELH*, 41 (1974), pp. 455–73.

Miller, J. H., 'The Problematic Ending in Narrative', *Nineteenth Century Fiction*, 33 (1978), pp. 3–7.

Miller, J. H., 'The Figure in the Carpet', *Poetics Today*, 1 (3) (1980), pp. 107–18.

Miller, J. H., 'A Guest in the House: Reply to Shlomith Rimmon-Kenan's Reply', *Poetics Today*, 2 (1b) (1980/1), pp. 189–91.

Miller, J. H., 'From Joyce to Narrative Theory and from Narrative Theory to Joyce', in B. Benstock (ed.), *The Seventh of Joyce* (Bloomington and London: Indiana University Press, 1982a).

Miller, J. H., *Fiction and Repetition: Seven English Novels* (Cambridge, MA: Harvard University Press, 1982b).

Miller, J. H., *The Ethics of Reading* (New York: Columbia University Press, 1986).

Miller, J. H., 'But are things as we think they are? (A Review of Paul Ricoeur's *Time and Narrative*)', *Times Literary Supplement*, 9–15 October 1987, No. 4410, pp. 1104–5.

Miller, J. H., 'Heart of Darkness Revisited', in *Heart of Darkness: A Case Study in Contemporary Criticism*, ed. R. Murflin (New York: St Martin's Press, 1989).

Miller, J. H., 'Narrative', in *Critical Terms for Literary Study*, ed. F. Lentricchia and T. McLaughlin (Chicago: University of Chicago Press, 1990).

Miller, J. H., *Ariadne's Thread: Storylines* (New Haven, CT: Yale University Press, 1992).

Miller, J. H., *Topographies* (Stanford, CA: Stanford University Press, 1995).

Rimmon-Kenan, S., 'Deconstructive Reflections on Deconstruction: In Reply to J. Hillis Miller', *Poetics Today*, 2 (1b) (1980/1), pp. 185–8.

Royle, N., *Telepathy and Literature: Essays on the Reading Mind* (Oxford: Blackwell, 1990).

7 PHENOMENOLOGY

Cohn, D., 'Narrated Monologues: Definition of Fictional Style', *Comparative Literature*, 18 (1966), pp. 97–112.

Cohn, D., *Transparent Minds: Narrative Modes for Presenting Consciousness in Fiction* (Princeton, NJ: Princeton University Press, 1978).

Cohn, D., 'The Encirclement of Narrative: On Franz Stanzel's *Theorie des Erzahlens*', *Poetics Today*, 2 (1981), pp. 157–82.

Coste, D., *Narrative as Communication* (Minneapolis: University of Minnesota Pess, 1989).

Fish, S., 'Literature in the Reader: Effective Stylistics', *New Literary History* 5 (1970), pp. 245–68.

Fish, S., *Is There a Text In This Class? The Authority of Interpretive Communities* (Cambridge, MA: Harvard University Press, 1980).

Hamburger, K., *The Logic of Literature* (Bloomington: Indiana University Press, 1973).

Iser, W., 'The Reading Process: A Phenomenological Approach', *New Literary History*, 3 (1971), pp. 279–99.

Iser, W., *The Implied Reader* (Baltimore, MD: Johns Hopkins University Press, 1974).

Iser, W., *The Act of Reading: A Theory of Aesthetic Response* (Baltimore, MD: Johns Hopkins University Press, 1978).

Iser, W., *Prospecting: From Reader Response to Literary Anthropology* (Baltimore, MD: Johns Hopkins University Press, 1989).

Iser, W., *The Fictive and the Imaginary: Charting Literary Anthropology*

(Baltimore, MD, and London: Johns Hopkins University Press, 1993).

Jauss, H. R., *Toward an Aesthetic of Reception* (Minneapolis: University of Minnesota Press, 1982).

Miller, J. H., *Charles Dickens: the World of his Novels* (London: Indiana University Press, 1969).

Ricoeur, P., *History and Truth*, ed. and trans. C. Kelbey (Evanston, IL: Northwest University Press, 1965).

Ricoeur, P., *Freud and Philosophy: An Essay on Interpretation*, trans. D. Savage (London: Yale University Press, 1970).

Ricoeur, P., *Interpretation Theory: Discourse and Surplus in Meaning* (Fort Worth: Texas Christian University Press, 1976).

Ricoeur, P., *The Rule of Metaphor: Multi-disciplinary Studies of the Creation of Meaning in Language*, trans. R. Czerny *et al.* (London: Routledge, 1978).

Ricoeur, P., 'Narrative Time', *Critical Inquiry*, 7 (Autumn 1980).

Ricoeur, P. *et al.* (eds), *La Narrativité* (Paris: Editions du Centre National de Recherche Scientifique, 1980).

Ricoeur, P., *Hermeneutics and the Human Sciences: Essays on Language, Action and Interpretation*, ed. and trans. J. Thompson (Cambridge: Cambridge University Press, 1981).

Ricoeur, P., *Time and Narrative* (vols. 1, 2, 3), trans. K. McLaughlin and D. Pellauer (London: University of Chicago Press, 1984; 1985; 1988).

Stanzel, F. K., *A Theory of Narrative* (Cambridge: Cambridge University Press, 1984).

8 HISTORY

Anchor, R., 'Narrativity and the Transformation of Historical Consciousness', *Clio: A Journal of Literature, History and the Philosophy of History*, 16 (2) (1987), pp. 121–37.

Armstrong, N. and Tennenhouse, L.,

'History, Poststructuralism and the Question of Narrative', *Narrative*, 1 (1) (1993).

Callinicos, A., *Theories and Narratives: Reflections on the Philosophy of History* (Cambridge: Polity Press, 1995).

Danto, A. C., *Analytical Philosophy of History* (Cambridge, MA: Harvard University Press, 1965).

Eagleton, T. *Water Benjamin, Or, Towards a Revolutionary Criticism* (London: Verso, 1978).

Eagleton, T. and Milne, D. (eds), *Marxist Literary Theory: A Reader* (Oxford: Blackwell, 1996).

Felman, S. and Laub, D., *Testimony: Crises of Witnessing in Literature, Psychoanalyis and History* (London and New York: Routledge, 1992).

Foucault, M., *The Order of Things: An Archaeology of the Human Sciences*, trans. from the French (London: Tavistock Publications, 1970).

Foucault, M., *The Archaeology of Knowledge*, trans. A Sheridan (London: Tavistock, 1972).

Jameson, F., *Marxism and Form* (Princeton, NJ, and London: Princeton University Press, 1971).

Jameson, F., *The Prison-House of Language: A Critical Account of Structuralism and Russian Formalism* (Princeton, NJ, and London: Princeton University Press, 1972).

Jameson, F., *The Political Unconscious: Narrative as a Socially Symbolic Act* (Ithaca: Cornell University Press, 1981).

Jameson, F., *Postmodernism, or the Cultural Logic of Late Capitalism* (London: Verso, 1991).

Jenkins, K. (ed.), *The Postmodern History Reader* (London: Routledge, 1992).

Kellner, H., 'Narrativity in History: Post-structuralism and Since', *History and Theory*, 26 (1987), pp. 1–29.

Kellner, H., '"As Real as it Gets . . ." Ricoeur and Narrativity', *Philosophy Today*, 34 (3) (1990), pp. 229–42.

Lenin, V. I., *Lenin On Literature and Art*, ed. T. Borodulina (Moscow: Progress Publishers, 1967).

Lukács, G., 'Narrate or Describe?', in *Writer and Critic, and Other Essays* (New York: Grosset & Dunlap, 1971).

Lukács, G., *The Theory of the Novel*, trans. A. Bostock (London: Merlin, 1978).

Lukács, G., *The Meaning of Contemporary Realism*, trans. J. Maunder and N. Maunder (London: Merlin, 1979).

Mink, L. O., 'History and Fiction as Modes of Comprehension', *New Literary History*, 1, 1969–70, pp. 541–58.

Mink, L. O., 'Narrative Form as a Cognitive Instrument', in R. H. Canary and H. Kozicki (eds), *The Writing of History: Literary Form and Historical Understanding* (Madison: University of Wisconsin Press, 1978).

Weber, S., 'Capitalizing History: Thoughts on *The Political Unconscious*', *Diacritics* (summer 1983).

White, H., *Metahistory: The Historical Imagination in Nineteenth-Century Europe* (Baltimore, MD: Johns Hopkins University Press, 1973).

White, H., *Tropics of Discourse: Essays in Cultural Criticism* (Baltimore, MD: Johns Hopkins University Press, 1978).

White, H., 'The Value of Narrativity in the Representation of Reality', *Critical Inquiry*, 7 (1980), pp. 5–27.

White, H., 'The Question of Narrativity in Contemporary Historical Theory', *History and Theory*, 23 (1984), pp. 1–33.

White, H., *The Content of Form: Narrative Discourse and Historical Representation* (Baltimore, MD: Johns Hopkins University Press, 1987).

9 RACE

Anderson, B., *Imagined Communities* (London: Verso, 1983).

Andrews, A. L., *To Tell a Free Story* (Urbana and Chicago: University of Illinois Press, 1986).

Ashcroft, B., Griffiths, G. and Tiffin, H. (eds), *The Empire Writes Back: Theory and Practice in Post-Colonial Literatures* (London: Routledge, 1989).

Baker, H. A. Jr., *Singers of Daybreak: Studies in Black American Literature* (Washington, DC: Howard University Press, 1974).

Baker, H. A. Jr., *Modernism and the Harlem Renaissance* (Chicago: University of Chicago Press, 1987).

Beavers, H. (ed.), *Narrative*, 7 (2) (1999), special edition, 'Narrative and Multiculturalism'.

Bhabha, H. K. (ed.), *Nation and Narration* (London and New York: Routledge, 1989).

Bhabha, H. K., *The Location of Culture* (London and New York: Routledge, 1994).

Davies, C. T. and Gates, H. L. (eds), *The Slave's Narrative* (New York: Oxford University Press, 1985).

Du Bois, W. E. B., *The Souls of Black Folk: Essays and Sketches* (New York, 1961. First published 1903).

Gates, H. L. Jr., (ed.), *Black Literature and Literary Theory* (London: Methuen, 1984).

Gates, H. L. Jr., (ed.), *'Race', Writing, and Difference* (Chicago: Chicago University Press, 1986).

Gates, H. L. Jr., Introduction, *The Classic Slave Narratives* (New York: Mentor, 1987).

Gates, H. L. Jr., *The Signifying Monkey: A Theory of Afro-American Literary Criticism* (Oxford: Oxford University Press, 1988).

Gates, H. L. Jr., 'Thirteen Ways of Looking at a Black Man', *New Yorker*, 23 October 1995.

Gilroy, P., *There Ain't No Black in the Union Jack* (London: Unwin Hyman, 1989).

Gilroy, P., *The Black Atlantic: Modernity and Double Consciousness* (London: Verso, 1993).

Gooding-Williams, R. (ed.), *Reading Rodney King: Reading Urban Uprising* (New York: Routledge, 1993).

Hulme, P., *Colonial Encounters: Europe and the Native Carribbean 1492–1797* (London: Routledge, 1992).

Hutcheon, L. and Hutcheon, M., 'Otherhood Issues: Post-National Operatic Narratives', *Narrative*, 3 (1) (1995).

Jackson, B., *'Get Your Ass in the Water and Swim Like Me': Narrative Poetry from the Black Oral Tradition* (Cambridge, MA: Harvard University Press, 1974).

Lonon, B., *The Appropriated Voice* (Ann Arbour: University of Michigan Press, 1990).

Loomba, A., 'Dead Women Tell No Tales: Issues of Female Subjectivity, Subaltern Agency and Tradition in Colonial and Post-Colonial Writings on Widow Immolation in India', *History Workshop Journal*, 36 (1993).

McLintock, A., '"The Very House of Difference": Race, Gender, and the Politics of South African Women's Narrative in *Poppie Nongena*', in D. LaCapra (ed.), *The Bounds of Race: Perspectives on Hegemony and Resistance* (Ithaca, NY and London: Cornell University Press, 1991).

McLintock, A., *Imperial Leather: Race, Gender and Sexuality in the Colonial Contest* (London: Routledge, 1995).

Moore-Gilbert, B., *Post-Colonial Theory: Contexts, Practices, Politics* (London: Verso, 1997).

Pratt, M. L., *Imperial Eyes: Studies in Travel Writing and Transculturation* (London: Routledge, 1992).

Rimmon-Kenan, S., 'Narration, Doubt, Retrieval: Toni Morrison's *Beloved*', *Narrative*, 4 (2) (1996).

Robertson, G., Mash, M., Tickner, L., Bird, J., Curtis, B. and Putnam, T. (eds), *Travellers' Tales: Narratives of Home and Displacement* (London and New York: 1992).

Said, E., *Beginnings: Intention and Method* (New York: Basic Books, 1975).

Said, E., *Orientalism* (London: Penguin, 1991).

Said, E., *The World, the Text and the Critic* (Cambridge, MA: Harvard University Press, 1983).

Said, E., *Culture and Imperialism* (London: Chattos and Windus, 1993).

Sekora, J. and Turner, D. (eds), *The Art of the Slave Narrative: Original Essays in Criticism and Theory* (Macomb: Western Illinios University Press, 1982).

Smith, V., 'Reading the Intersection of Race and Gender in Narratives of Passing', *Diacritics*, 24 (2–3) (summer-fall, 1994), pp. 43–57.

Spivak, G. C., *In Other Worlds* (London: Routledge, 1988).

Spivak, G. C., *The Post-Colonial Critic: Interviews, Strategies, Dialogues* (London: 1990).

Spivak, G. C., *Outside in the Teaching Machine* (London: Routledge, 1993).

Spivak, G. C., *A Critique of Post-Colonial Reason: Toward a History of the Vanishing Present* (London: Routledge, 1999).

Stepto, R. B., *From Behind the Veil: A Study of Afro-American Narrative* (Urbana: University of Illinois Press, 1979).

Trin Minh-Ha, *Woman, Native, Other: Writing, Postcoloniality and Feminism* (Bloomington and Indianapolis: Indiana University Press, 1994).

Young, R., *White Mythologies: Writing, History and the West* (London: Routledge, 1990).

Young, R., *Colonial Desire: Hybridity in Theory, Culture and Race* (London: Routledge, 1995).

Ware, V., *Beyond the Pale; White Women, Racism, and History* (London: Verso, 1992)

Wiegman, R., *American Anatomies: Theorizing Race and Gender* (Durham and London: Duke University Press, 1995).

Index

actant 211
action 43
actors 83
Adam Bede 100
aesthetics 206, 248, 266
agents 83
Althusser, Louis 18, 213, 295
The Ambassadors 69, 70
anachrony 92, 93
analepses 93, 200
Andrew of Crete 60, 62
anthropology 1, 75–81, 85, 144, 208
aporia 1, 12, 13, 14, 15, 16, 18, 19, 25, 27,
    28, 29
architecture 56
Aristotle xi, xii, 39–44, 72, 146, 232, 253
art 54, 109, 111, 167, 260
artificial intelligence 156
Atwood, Margaret 11, 16, 21, 22, 29n, 32n
Austen, Jane 245, 284, 286, 289
Austin, John 258
author 73, 88, 110, 141, 247, 272
autobiography 94, 253–4

Bachelard, Gaston 152
Bakhtin, Mikhail xi, 9, 31n, 53–8, 200,
    295, 296
Bal, Mieke 81–6, 154, 199, 201
Balzac, Honoré de 9, 56, 94, 199, 240–3,
    262, 285
Barchester Towers 72
Barry Lyndon 139
Barthes, Roland xii, 2, 7, 9, 10, 25, 109–15,
    130–8, 152, 154, 155, 199, 207, 213,
    214, 219, 238, 239–43, 276, 277, 279,
    280, 281n, 307
Baudelaire, Charles 132, 133, 135
Baudrillard, Jean 167
Beckett, Samuel 199
being 15, 19, 140, 258, 260

Bellow, Saul 72
Benjamin, Walter xi, 8, 20, 23, 46–53, 150,
    187, 199
Bennet, Andrew 2, 3, 8
Berger, John 170–5, 192, 292
Berkley, Busby 179
Bhabha, Homi K. 292–7
Bibliothèque Nationale (Paris) 220
The Big Sleep (film) 185
Bildungsroman 48
biography 57
biology 161, 167
Blanchot, Maurice 9, 22, 193, 220–30
Bleak House 232
Bond, James 115–19
Booth, Wayne 69–75, 155, 245–7
Brave New World 70
Bremond, Claude 5, 84, 113, 139
Bronfen, Elizabeth 192–8
Brooks, Peter 5, 7, 9, 16, 145–52, 156
Brothers Grimm 150
buddy movies 179
Burke, Kenneth 243, 245, 248
Butor, Michel 73n

Cage, John 167
Camus, Albert 73, 101, 262–5, 286
Cartland, Barbara 201
Cashinahua 159–60
castration complex 179, 181, 196, 242
catachresis 235
The Catcher in the Rye 72
causality 45, 68, 107, 144, 154, 213
Cervantes, Miguel de 69
Chambers, Ross 156
Chandler, Raymond 124, 127
character 40, 73, 129, 145–6, 236
Chase, Cynthia 106, 151
Chatman, Seymour 5,6, 8, 96–9, 137, 139,
    155, 202

Chomsky, Noam　4, 113n
Christie, Agatha　122, 126
chronology　68, 183, 220, 257, 262, 274
chronotope　53–8
Cinderella　6, 9, 139–43
Cixous, Hélène　209, 280, 281
Clarrisa　139, 141
class　167
closure　xii, 20, 22, 27, 183
codes　116, 132, 163, 200
Cohn, Dorrit　250–5
Colette (Sidonie Gabrielle)　199
comic strips　82, 109, 139
competence　160
Compton-Burnett, Ivy　72
computers　231
conclusion　259
Condillac, E. B. de　233
Conrad, Joseph　9, 285, 286, 287, 288
context　10–14
contrapuntality　22–7, 286–8
cosmology　75
counternarrative　22–7, 290
Cranford　232
Crime and Punishment　252
Culler, Jonathan　104–9, 150
culture　158

Daniel Deronda　106–8, 151
Darwin, Charles　162
Dead of Night (film)　87
death　19, 27, 49–51, 136, 150, 192, 308
Debussy, Claude　167, 307
The Decameron　103, 154, 199
deconstruction　xii, 10, 106, 278, 290
déjà lu　134, 136
De Lauretis, Teresa　3, 7, 16, 18, 20, 22,
　　204–12, 215
Deleuze, Gilles　230
De Man, Paul　227–31
dénouement　233
Derrida, Jacques　9, 12, 13, 14, 20, 28, 29,
　　220–7, 154, 198, 233, 270, 274, 277,
　　278, 292
desire　16–20, 152, 178, 206
detective fiction　120–7

Dickens, Charles　94, 96, 143, 156, 165,
　　193, 231, 284, 285, 286
diegesis　159, 161, 179–81
Diengott, Nilli　201–4
difference　237, 240
discourse　4, 5, 108, 137
Disney, Walt　143
The Divine Comedy　143
Dombey and Son　96
donor　210
Don Quixote　46, 55, 156
Dostoevsky, Feodor　9, 253
double logic　108, 150
Doyle, Arthur Conan　126, 147, 285
dramatised narration　71
dramatis personae　208
Dr Faustus　71, 73
Dryden, Jon　69
dualism　4, 5, 6, 143
Duel in the Sun　182–4
Dworkin, Ronald　163, 165

economy　14–16, 135, 136, 184, 206, 272
Eco, Umberto　115–20, 154, 163
Egypt　246, 285, 299
Einstein, Albert　53, 172
Eliot, George　106–8, 231, 285, 293
Eliot. T. S.　85, 86
ellipsis　235, 253
embedding　154
end　46
enlightenment　52, 167, 294
epic　46, 166, 172
ethics　246, 249, 298
etymology　234
Eugene Onegin　67, 99
event　83, 84
exchange　14–16, 17, 18, 21
extra-diegetic　181
extra-textual　249

Les Faux Monnayes　99, 100
fabula　4, 5, 83–5, 104, 137, 147
fairy tales　46, 52, 82, 143, 302
Farrakan, Louis　289
Faulkner, William　71, 147

Fellini, Frederico 209
Felman, Shoshana 210–11, 262–6
femininity 210
feminism 3, 153, 179, 198, 200
fetishism 181
figuration 230, 234, 235
film noir 181
Fish, Stanley 200, 273
flashback 167
Flaubert, Gustav 70, 99
Fleming, Ian 115
film 1, 3, 9, 11, 88–90, 172, 178–191
filter 98
first-person narration 69, 70, 94, 253, 254
focalization 97, 98, 202
folklore 58–62, 140
foreplay 217
formalism 4, 9, 11, 110, 112, 122, 147, 151, 167, 200
Forster, E.M. xi, 44–6, 285
Foucault, Michel 25–7, 32n, 270, 274, 278, 279
Frankenstein 195
Freud, Sigmund 59, 78–9, 104, 105, 152, 158, 177, 179, 181, 209, 210, 211, 237, 270, 274n, 295
frequency 92
Frye, Northrop 163, 268
functions 208
futurism 63

Gadamar, Hans-Georg 256, 260
Gaskill, Elizabeth 231
Gates, Henry Louis 22–3, 288–92
gaze 177
gender 167
Genette, Gerard 35n, 91–6, 128–9, 155, 199, 201, 203, 228, 251
geometry 154
ghosts 195–7, 232 238, 295
Gibson, Andrew 152–7
gift relation 14, 15
Glass, Philip 167
gnārus 2, 129
God 246, 302
Goethe, J. W. 255, 266, 295

Gogol, Nicolay 55
The Golden Ass 55
gothic 56, 268
grammar 8, 9, 65, 112, 181, 202, 257
The Great Gatsby 72
Greimas, A. J. 84, 86, 90, 111, 113n, 154, 165, 167, 199, 211, 261
Gulliver's Travels 70, 141

Hamlet 70, 211, 246
Hammett, Dashiell 124, 127
Harlem Globetrotters 120
Harré, Rom 165–6
Heart of Darkness 71, 72, 98, 100, 103, 150
Heath, Stephen 184–92
Hegel, G.W.F. 262, 274
Heidegger, Martin 232, 256–62
Hemingway, Ernest 70, 102
hermeneutics 9
heterosexuality 180, 215
Highsmith, Patricia 127
histoire 4, 5, 137
historiography 11, 50, 262
history xii, 42, 53, 89, 137, 226, 256, 260
Hitchcock, Alfred 181, 208
Holmes, Sherlock 148
holocaust 262
homosexuality 180, 216
horror 245
Huckleberry Finn 72, 73
Hugo, Victor 90
hysteria 18

identity 239, 293
ideology 9, 10, 19, 28, 98, 128, 181, 185, 242, 294
imperialism 24
implied author 70, 96, 98, 246, 248
implied reader 245, 246
incest taboo 111
interior monolgue 253, 254
interminability 16–20
inter-subjectivity 7, 8, 10, 11, 12, 13, 14, 16, 17, 18, 19, 20, 21, 23, 24, 25, 26, 28
invagination 224

Iser, Wolfgang 154, 199, 244–50
iteration 10–14, 17

Jakobson, Roman 8, 9, 10, 30n, 88, 111, 114n
Jakson, Bernard 163–5
James, Henry 9, 71, 98, 151, 155–6, 285
James, William 252
Jameson, Fredric 8, 20, 27, 32n, 168, 266–9, 293
Jaws (film) 185
Job 71
Johnson, Barbara 238–44
Joyce, James 71, 99, 102, 241, 246, 248, 251, 252, 254, 255, 267
Judas 60

Kant, Immanuel 57n, 272
Kellner, Hans 275–84
Kellogg, Robert 253, 261
Kermode, Frank 163
Kincaid, Jamaica 288
Kipling, Rudyard 52, 285, 286, 287
Klu Klux Klan 290
knowledge 157–8

labyrinth 231, 235
Lacan, Jacques 14, 15, 16, 17, 24, 31 n, 32 n, 171, 270, 278, 282 n
Lady Chatterley's Lover 139
language 7, 8, 13, 14
Lanser, Susan 198–201
law 155, 222–30
Lawrence, D. H. 139
Lee, Spike 288
legitimation 157
Le Guin, Ursula K. 18–19, 21
Le Rouge et le Noir 252
Leskov, Nikolai 46
levels 154
Lévi-Strauss, Claude 75–81, 86, 110, 111, 112, 270
Lewis, C. S. 84
Lewis, Monk 56
lexias 131–7, 241
lietmotif 179

limits 14, 21, 27, 42, 223
L'Imoraliste 100, 103
line 231–7
linguistics 110
Lispector, Clarice 301
literature xii, 7, 10, 12, 22, 28–9, 33n, 44, 53, 54, 82, 146, 198, 223, 247, 250
logocentrism 231, 233, 270, 278
Lubbock, Percy 155
Lyotard, Jean-François 2, 32n, 157–61

McClary, Susan 166–70
McCloskey, Donald 161–3
Madam Bovary 89
madness 224–7
Mahler, Gustav 168
Mallarmé, Stéphane 241, 267
The Maltese Falcon 187
The Man Who Shot Liberty Valence 182–3
Marat 89
margins 233
Monroe, Marilyn 180
Marsalis, Wynton 288
Marx, Karl 214, 266, 268, 290
masculinity 181, 199, 207, 280
Maugham, Somerset 214
Mauppasant, Guy de 199
Mauss, Marcel 14
Medusa 208
melodrama 207
memory 50, 152, 167
metafiction 19, 207
metalepses 200
metaphor 228, 230
metaphysics 15, 20, 278
metonymy 8, 12, 15, 92, 229, 230
Metz, Christain 86–91, 95n, 187, 207
Middlemarch 69
Miller, D. A. 219
Miller, J. Hillis 231–8
Miller, Nancy K. 201
Milton, John 246, 278
mimesis 244, 251
Minh-Ha, Trin 297–309
Mobius strip 231n, 236
Moll Flanders 72

Mona Lisa 209
monologue 252
montage 87, 172
motif 68, 202, 231
Mulvey, Laura 177–84, 204, 207, 208
music 165
muzak 167
myth 75–81, 86, 143, 158

narcissism 183, 184, 193, 195
narratees 99, 129, 150, 161
narrativity 7, 8, 11, 13, 14,16, 18, 22, 27,
  205–6, 276
narratology xi, 3, 4, 13, 16, 21, 81–137,
  201, 280
narrators 69–74, 99, 129, 135, 150, 192,
  203
New Criticism 204, 267
Nietzsche, Friedrich 257, 260, 269
novel 9, 11, 13, 44, 46, 50, 54, 57, 63, 65,
  82, 94, 235

Oedipus 18, 58–62, 75–81, 104–8, 113,
  183–4, 205, 207, 219, 235
Oedipus at Colonus 60
Oedipus Rex 60, 108, 210
The Old Curiosity Shop 99
omniscient narration 69, 97, 252
One Thousand and One Nights 45, 50, 60,
  100, 103
ontology 20
opera 67, 242
orality 1, 46, 88, 90, 100, 300–8
orientalism 167
otherness 16, 20, 21, 23, 25, 279, 280

paradigmatic axis 8, 10, 11, 12
paralepses 200
Pater, Walter 231
Peeping Tom 185
Phelan, James 156
phenomenology xii
philosophy xii, 43, 57n, 129, 167, 256, 298
photography 87, 167, 170–5, 188, 190
photo-stories 171
physics 162

Picasso, Pablo 64
Pilgrim's Progress 143
Plato xi, 5, 37–9, 138, 140
plot 39–46, 53n, 58, 63, 66–8, 122, 199,
  233
Poe, Edgar Alan 52, 72, 112, 132–7, 172
poetry 42, 85, 88, 171
point of view 96, 186, 190, 191, 203
Poirot, Hercule 122, 126
popular literature 120
Portnoy's Complaint 100
post-colonialism 23
post-narratology xii, 7, 129
post-structuralism xi, 153
power 26
Prince, Gerald 99–104, 129–30
prolepses 200
Propp, Vladimir xi, 58–63, 110, 112, 183,
  199, 208, 261
Proust, Marcel 9, 93, 94, 95, 101, 199, 203,
  227–31
psychoanalysis xii, 16, 135, 152, 167
psycho-narration 252
Pushkin, Alexander 68
Pygmalion 241–3

quattrocento view 187, 190
quest 260

race xii
readers 223, 230
readerly text 241
realism 89
Rear Window 185
récit 5, 138
Remembrance of Things Past 71, 72 93
representation 37–9
reproduction 217
revolution 222
rhetoric 111, 241, 252
Richardson, Dorothy 252
Ricoeur, Paul xi, 4, 7, 8, 9, 15, 21, 28, 167,
  255–62
Rimmon-Kenan, Shlimoth 202
Robbe-Grillet, Alain 9, 92
Robinson Crusoe 94

Rome 246
Roof, Judith xii, 3, 13, 212–20
Rousseau, Jean-Jacques 94, 233, 240
Royle, Nicholas 2, 3, 8
Rushdie, Salman 25
Ruskin, John 232, 235, 293

sadism 181, 204
Said, Edward 23–5, 284–8, 293
St Augustine 232, 256
St Gregory 60, 62
Sartre, Jean-Paul 72, 100, 151
Saussure, Ferdinand de 28, 29–30n, 113n, 239, 278
The Scarlet Letter 99
Schoenberg, Arnold 167
Scholes, Robert 208, 253, 261
science 128, 130, 152, 157, 162
scopophilia 177
Scott, Randolph 183
Scott, Walter 56, 156, 249, 262
semiotics 7, 106, 130, 163, 200
sexual difference xii, 183
sexuality 181
Shakespeare, William 143, 249
Shelley, Mary 195
Shlovsky, Victor xi, 63–7
silence 18, 19, 27, 172
Simpson, O.J. 288
simulacra 13, 151
Singer, Alan 8
sjužet 4, 5, 137, 147
slant 98
Smith, Barbara Hernstein 5–7, 9, 11, 12, 138–45, 262
Snoop Doggy Dog 167
socialism 162
social science 247
Sons and Lovers 72
Sophocles 60, 210
space 53–8, 73, 130, 183, 295
spectatorship 173, 181, 185–6, 188, 190
speech acts 8
speed 92
sphinx 52, 60, 77, 80–1, 104, 208
Stallone, Sylvester 142

Stanislavaskij's audition 9
Stanzel, F. K. 155
Stendhal 56, 57, 121, 253
Stevens, Wallace 151, 237
Stevenson, Robert Louis 53, 285
story 1, 4, 8, 44, 45, 66–8, 83, 85, 92, 108, 122, 137
storytelling 49–53
Stravinsky, I. F. 167
string 234
structuralism 6, 7, 8, 9, 11, 73–156
structuration 7, 130
style indirect libre 251
Suspicion 185, 187
symbolic 137, 228
syntagmatic axis 8, 10–13, 16–18, 20–22, 27

tapestry 90
Taxi Driver 185, 188
technology 80, 181
teleology 20–2
television 1, 89, 90
text 83, 130, 136, 244
textuality 11
theology 144
theory 110
third-person narration 69, 70, 71, 73, 253, 254
Thomashevsky, Boris 67–69
time xii, 7, 14, 15, 20, 53–8, 67, 73, 87, 253, 256
titles 226
Todorov, Tsvetan xii, 9, 112, 113, 120–8, 148, 150, 153, 199
To Have and Have Not (film) 180, 181
Tolstoy, Leo 94, 293
Tom Jones 70, 72, 101, 102, 156
Tom Thumb 83, 84, 99, 100
Totalisation 20–2
Tragedy 40, 109, 146
Tristram Shandy 21, 63, 69, 70, 71
Troilus and Criseyde 72

Vampyr 188
Van Dine, S. S. 125

Vanity Fair 70, 284
verisimilitude 103, 181
Victoria, Queen 232
villain 119
Vivaldi, Antonio 167
voyeurism 186

Walpole, Horace 56
Warhol, Robyn 200
Weber, Samuel 269–75
Welles, Orson 188
White, Hayden 167, 214, 268n

Winfray, Oprah 289
Winterson, Jeanette 31n
Wittgenstein, Ludwig 7, 8, 17, 25, 256, 268
Woolf, Virginia 245
World War I 46
World War II 120, 242
writerly text 240
Wuthering Heights 98

X 237–9

zero degree 92